Preface

Welcome to the revised and enlarged edition of *Childhood Education in the Church!* The book was published originally in 1975 and was reprinted ten times. Since its first publication, the book has been distributed widely nationally and internationally. It has been used as a textbook in Christian college classrooms by professional staff members in Christian education and by local church children's workers in Christian education.

In the ten years the book has been in print, new areas of content, issues, concerns, and bibliographical resources have emerged in reaching and teaching children. These new areas are reflected in this revision. As editors, we want the book to continue to serve as a comprehensive, current textbook and resource for those who are ministering to children.

In the revised edition some areas of the text have been restructured, and the sections of the book have been given new unit titles. Several of the units have been rearranged, as well as chapters within the units. The seven units of the book are these: *Reaching and Teaching Children: An Overview; Understanding the Developmental Stages of Children; Meeting Special Education Needs; Organizing, Administering, and Supervising Children's Ministries; Helping Children Develop Spiritually; Utilizing Methods and Materials; Ministering to Children Beyond the Church.*

All the chapters within the units have been revised, either slightly or moderately. Several new chapters have been added: "How Children Think and Learn," "Understanding Third and Fourth Graders," "Teaching Exceptional Children," "Supervising Children's Ministries," "Managing the Classroom Effectively," "Methods and Materials for Children," "Using Computers with Children," and "The Role of Home Schooling." All bibliographies have been updated. A few areas have been expanded more than others simply because more writing has been done in those areas since the book was first published.

Several of the writers who contributed to the original edition have revised demands of their jobs and then to fulfill civic and social obligations."[1]

In the churches, we may hope that we have done better, but since we all are caught, whether we like it or not, under the magnetic spell of our culture and its social dynamics, the matter deserves our scrutiny. Where, really, do children stand in our churches? Are they at the center of our concern or only at the focal point of our extravagant display?

CHILDREN NUMBER ONE?

Americans may idolize their children and imitate their teenagers, but evidently they do not place them first in their affections. History stands witness to the fact that no tribe or nation survives for long when it neglects to pass along its values—that store of treasured beliefs and practices which it holds dearer than life. And the long history of humanity is chiefly the account of families, tribes, and nations who have patiently and persistently loved and protected their young. Contrary to popular opinion, this is the construction placed on human history even by some "survival of the fittest" anthropologists. Loren Eisley noted that human history is not one which is dominated by tooth and claw, that humans have "not really survived by toughness in a major sense . . . [but by their] tenderness." Eisley notes particularly the long childhood in the human species, the lengthy helplessness and dependence of children, and the survival based on affection and care.[2]

If there is wide agreement that children need our central attention, it is not so easily demonstrated that they are getting our best. We may spend ludicrous sums of money to feed, clothe, and entertain them, but these expenditures hardly make them human. And it is this humanizing energy they need most, for children derive their genuine character as human beings chiefly through learning rather than through heredity. The frightening effects produced by isolation and sense starvation, found in deserted and abused children, remind us of their need for tenderness, intimacy with adults, and teaching.

But Dr. Bronfenbrenner reminds us that modern technological society has conspired to cut children off from adults—their reasonable source for learning the store of treasured beliefs and ways of living. First, we isolate children from the tribe by moving out of clans and into suburbia. Then, we cut them off from ourselves by stratifying the lonely, nuclear family—each member living virtually to himself and associating only with his peers.[3]

The net result is that children know increasingly fewer adults. Children are

1. Urie Bronfenbrenner et al., "And the Last Shall Be First," Report of Forum 15: Children and Parents Together in the World, White House committee document, p. 1.
2. Loren Eisley, "An Evolutionist Speaks His Mind," in *Adventures of the Mind,* ed. Richard Thruelsen and John Kobler (New York: Random, Vintage Books, 1958), 1:6.
3. See Urie Bronfenbrenner, "The Unmaking of the American Child," in *Two Worlds of Childhood* (New York: Russell Sage, 1970), pp. 95-119.

transported from the front door to schools where they mill around in ever larger buildings with literally mobs of peers. After school, they study, club, or roam in packs of peers as they wait for parents to provide dinner and to hand over the keys to an automobile so they can continue the narrow age-level segregation into the night. It would be easy to suggest that our children have invented this kind of life-style. But the fact is, we did it. We invented baby-sitters and the thousand things that conspire to keep our children out of our lives. They have accurately read our arms-length-and-no-more relationships as indifference and neglect. Today's climate in North America is such that children have few alternatives but to cling to the available sources of attention and security: their age mates and television. Neither is a particularly helpful source of values nor a suitable model from which to conclude what is human about humans. Peers have only their own impoverished experience to share. Television, easily a powerful influence, is a suspicious custodian of the nursery, with dubious morals and lack of principles.

So the generations, having sensed their own neglect, quickly gather their isolation about themselves and set their feet against all others. It is as if a malignant nodule had exploded in our society to set every horizontal age group against every other. The college student confesses that he cannot communicate with his younger brother. The high school student looks with contempt on the fourth grader, and the junior high youngster would not bother with a preschool child—except for baby-sitting money. To put it plainly, affection across the generations has gone out of our lives; we live as strangers under the same roof with our own children.[4]

GOD'S DESIGN FOR CHILDHOOD

Jean Piaget, that remarkable Swiss psychologist who spent most of his very long life observing children and studying their ways of thinking, was confronted often with what he called "the American question." The question goes like this: "If there are stages that children reach at given norms of ages, can we accelerate these stages?" To such efforts to speed up everything, Piaget answered by pointing out that it takes, for example, from nine to twelve months before a human baby develops the sense that an object is still there when you place a blind between the baby and the object. Kittens go through the same stages as children, but they do it in three months. "Is this an advantage or isn't it?" Piaget asked. Then he answered: "We can certainly see our answer in one sense. The kitten is not going to go much further. The child has taken longer, but he is capable of going further, so it seems to me that the nine months

---

4. See also Bronfenbrenner's more elaborate version of the above as "The Split Level American Family." *Saturday Review* 50, no. 37 (7 October, 1967): 60-66.

probably were not for nothing."[5] This attitude of Piaget seems appropriate in any study of ourselves, and especially so when we seek to unravel a theory of humanity based upon what we can observe from Holy Scripture and from history.

The opening chapters of Genesis suggest that our first parents came from the hand of God fully grown. Created in the "image of God," they were fully formed spiritually, emotionally, and physically. The account is plainly set down to illustrate their intimate fellowship with God, their acceptance of themselves and of each other in maturity and poise, and their obvious physical capability. These priceless endowments, which all other human beings would derive from heredity and environment, were God's direct gift to the original man and the original woman.[6]

All other humans, however, have been the product of another sort of formation process—that of "parenting." Only a tiny fraction of the human race ever has had a course in child psychology or in "marriage and the family," yet the race has survived. The quality of family relationships is probably more related to faithfulness to a handful of unchanging principles that may be observed in a biblical view of humanity and family than in much of today's theorizing.

The book of Genesis underscores the importance of both male and female in the creative process of producing children and in the home environment where children grow. Intimacy and interdependence in the household made both parents equally available to the child, a clue that speaks to today's concern over the learning of sex-appropriate behavior and resolving the frustrations of young males who are deprived of male models, many for most of their waking hours and some for their entire childhood.

Learning to "have dominion" and to honor the living God are learned undoubtedly most efficiently by walking in the shadow of parents who live out their teaching. If one had to choose between formal schooling and informal learning from parents, even in the total effects on today's parent-starved children, the schools would lose. The most difficult learning task in all of life, the learning of one's native language, is accomplished chiefly during the preschool years, by use of informal and indirect methods, and under the tutelage of parents. The best language laboratories and intensive instruction can never match what parents do without tapes, films, or earphones.

We get only glimpses of childhood training and teaching patterns through the Old Testament. The affirmation of faith in the Shema recorded in Deuteronomy 6:4-5 is followed by directions calling for believers to keep God's com-

5. Jean Piaget, quoted in Frank Jennings, "Jean Piaget: Notes on Learning," *Saturday Review* 50 (20 May 1967):82.
6. See Donald M. Joy, *Bonding: Relationships in the Image of God* (Waco, Tex.: Word, 1985) for chapters dealing specifically with the doctrine of creation and inferences from the "image of God."

mandments in their own hearts and to repeat them to their children. The instruction was to be in the form of speaking both indoors and outdoors, visual reminders bound to foreheads and wrists, and written text on the doorposts of the houses and on the gates. Such education was comprehensive in scope and made virtually all of life a school. It acknowledged that children are immersed in a total curriculum of experience, and it detailed fundamental teaching-learning modes as contemporary as Jerome Bruner's "action, image, and language" forms of representation.[7]

The Hebrew pattern for transmitting values and beliefs consisted especially of handing on the treasured store from father to son. It has been suggested by modern observers that the male conscience develops differently from that of the female. The male is both more ruggedly committed to his father's values and more rigidly and inflexibly formed in those values than the female, thus making the male particularly well suited for transgenerational transmission of values and for applying them in the tough situations of marketplace and government.[8] It is almost universally observed that in clashes of ideologies and values, males more violently defend their own, battling to death in wars of varying dimensions. Women and children have been spared and taken captive from time immemorial, but men seem always to have been more fiercely welded to their values, hopeless of reformation or reindoctrination, hence better conservators of value systems.

This transgenerational communications system is clearly displayed in Psalm 78:5-6 (NASB):

> For He established a testimony in Jacob,
> And appointed a law in Israel,
> Which He commanded our fathers,
> That they should teach them to their children;
> That the generation to come might know,
> even the children yet to be born.

A similar pattern, clearly set within family life, shows up in Proverbs 4:1-4 (NASB):

> Hear, O sons, the instruction of a father,
> And give attention that you may gain understanding,
> For I give you sound teaching;
> Do not abandon my instruction.
> When I was a son to my father,
> Tender and the only son in the sight of my mother,

---

7. See Jerome S. Bruner's discussion of "modes of representation" in *Toward a Theory of Instruction* (Cambridge: Harvard U., 1966), pp. 44-46, passim.
8. See, for example, R. S. Lee, *Your Growing Child and Religion* (New York: Macmillan, 1963), pp. 67-68, 97, 203.

Then he taught me and said to me,
"Let your heart hold fast my words;
Keep my commandments and live."

"Father" and "son" were labels somewhat larger than strict usage in North America today would allow. They had tribal overtones, and one saw his own actual offspring as the "sons" of his own father and grandfather also. As the tribal tasks were divided, formal instruction was arranged in the synagogue school, but the sense of urgency remained high for transmitting community values—beliefs of the larger family.

"No nation has ever set the child in the midst more deliberately than the Jews did," writes William Barclay.[9] He cites both Scripture and early Hebrew writings to illustrate his point. The Midrash commentary on Exodus 25:34 interprets "blossoms" as referring to children: "And in the lampstand [there shall be] four cups shaped like almond blossoms" (NASB). The Jews were sure, says Barclay, that of all people, the child was dearest to God. "Touch not mine anointed, and do my prophets no harm" of 1 Chronicles 16:22 was regarded as referring to children, the "anointed," and to their teachers, "my prophets." Extreme writings suggested that these schools were more important even than worship: "Perish the sanctuary, but let the children go to school."[10] Josephus, too, underscores childhood instruction: "Our chief ambition is for the education of our children. . . . We take most pains of all with the instruction of children, and esteem the observations of the laws, and the piety corresponding with them, the most important affair of our whole life."[11]

Such education and such concern persists into New Testament times, and Jesus' comments about children and their importance seem in harmony with this long-term Jewish attitude toward childhood. Lest we should too quickly identify that concern and those schools with our own, let it be noted that such training (*a*) sought no commitment to God, but assumed it, (*b*) was exclusively education in holiness, (*c*) consisted of rote mastery of Jewish Scriptures and writings, and (*d*) was for boys only.

JESUS AND THE CHILD

The gospels, written by and for adults, reflect the fact that children were allowed to be children in Jesus' day. There was no preoccupation with them as objects of prophetic or salvation utterances. A certain aloofness seemed to emerge easily from a society that completely committed itself to the processes of family and synagogue education for transmitting its treasured beliefs and life-styles. So the New Testament has little to say about children. There exist

9. William Barclay, *Educational Ideals in the Ancient World* (formerly *Train Up a Child*) (Grand Rapids: Baker, 1974), p. 11.
10. *Babylonian Shabbat* 119 *b*, cited in Barclay, p. 12.
11. Josephus, *Against Apion* 1. 12, cited in Barclay, p. 12.

occasional allusions to them, however, suggesting that they were present and that they sometimes came playing and running into the presence of Jesus and the apostles.

Jesus was apparently never too busy for children, and we have no record of His becoming impatient with them. He took them in His arms (Mark 10:16). He set a child in the midst of a crowd to draw a lesson for the adults (Mark 9:36-37), and He at least once cited children's games as an analogy of His own unheeded ministry with adults (Matt. 11:16-17). Among His sternest warnings are those against causing a little child to stumble or go astray (Matt. 18:5-6). Jesus knew what we often forget—that parents, even earthly and evil ones, love their children and want to give them the best gifts (Luke 11:13).

When His disciples bickered and pushed for selfish status, Jesus called a child and set the youngster in front of them (Mark 9:33-37). He proceeded to illustrate with the child that (*a*) entering the kingdom of God requires a humility like that of a child; (*b*) children are somehow numbered among those who believe in Christ; and (*c*) their guardian angels in heaven enjoy a privileged place, looking directly into the face of the Father. Looked at as a whole instead of fragments (Matt. 18:1-10), Jesus' allusions to childhood in this passage instruct us in some troubling ways: (*a*) He seems to have offered no direct instruction or summons to children; (*b*) He placed no evangelistic claim on children calling them to belief or to repentance; (*c*) He made no effort to draw them into His following as disciples.[12]

This attitude toward children which emerges in the gospels continues through the entire New Testament. Virtually nothing is said about what or how to teach children. They are to obey their parents (Eph. 6:1). Their fathers are to bring them up in the "nurture and admonition of the Lord" (Eph. 6:4). Bishops, deacons, and elders are to be faithful and successful in the rearing of their own children (1 Tim. 3:1-4; Titus 1:6). Fathers are to be careful not to deal so harshly with their children that they become discouraged (Col. 3:21).

With this scant list, we see the entire scope of New Testament teachings about childhood education. There is no prescribed curriculum. What religious education did exist in Jewish synagogues is not alluded to, and there is not so much as a hint that Christians made any arrangements for the religious instruction of their children outside of the home.

CHILDREN IN CHURCH HISTORY

In the early centuries of the church, no provision was made for the education of children, either in basic literacy or in Christian faith. Classes were formed in the first and second centuries for new converts, and, presumably,

---

12. We might dismiss these observations by concluding that Jesus merely reflected the attitudes of His own culture toward children. But we dare not indulge in the unbiblical practice of reading our own children's programs back into the passage and making it support what we have come to think is proper with children.

older children found themselves in these converts' classes, called "catechumenal schools." The classes were "graded," or grouped, according to the level appropriate to the individual person's commitment. "Hearers" were allowed to listen to the reading of Scripture and to sermons. "Kneelers" were allowed to remain afterward for prayers and for more instruction; they were examined as to daily Christian discipline and habits of life. "The chosen" were given intensive theological instruction and were prepared for baptism. The catechumenal schools continued for several centuries, but they deteriorated after about the fifth century.[13]

Catechetical schools appeared late in the second century and were for the training of ministers and Christian scholars. These were established throughout the Christian world, and a pattern formed by which a cluster of congregations would jointly sponsor an "episcopal" or "cathedral" school. Even so, they were not for all children or even for all boys. They admitted only those who were in preparation for the priesthood of the church.

Not until the decades following the Reformation did Christian concern focus upon basic literacy education for children in general or upon the usefulness of Bible study in the education of the young. Martin Luther was committed to a broad education of children. But it was John Amos Comenius, late in the sixteenth century, who urged a thoroughly Christian education for all children. Comenius, Philip Spener, and August Hermann Francke were the moving forces who introduced Bible study to Christian education in any large sense. The early centuries had employed a certain amount of Scripture in the rote teaching of catechumens, but the printing press now made possible the wider use of Scripture. It was to become for several centuries the chief means of teaching reading.

Robert Raikes's early Sunday schools were as much aimed at bringing basic literacy to the deprived chimney sweeps on Sooty Alley as they were to bringing them salvation. The Gloucester editor assembled his first Sunday school in Mrs. Meredith's kitchen. He paid her for teaching them and later employed others. But he was "outside" the church, and few clergymen gave him encouragement. Among those who did were John Wesley and William Fox. Both gave Raikes early endorsement, even before Raikes revealed to the public what had been going on in Gloucester kitchens for nearly three years. The movement flourished. By the time of Raikes's death in 1811, there were nearly a half million children enrolled in his Sunday schools. William Fox founded the Sunday School Society in London in 1785, and, backed by several wealthy friends, he proceeded to spread the idea.

When the Sunday school movement leaped to America, it became less and

---

13. For more detailed information on children in the church, see Charles B. Eavey, *History of Christian Education* (Chicago: Moody, 1964), and William Barclay, *Educational Ideals in the Ancient World*.

less a literacy program and increasingly a gospel agency. By 1810, the American version of the Sunday school was permitted to come into the churches. As the churches became involved, they became more interested in the content of the teaching, and denominations formed Sunday school boards, or commissions, to supervise the educational work in local churches.

The early twentieth century ushered in more and wider programs aimed at the moral and spiritual education of children. The scout programs were founded between 1910 and 1912. Child Evangelism Fellowship began in 1923. Whereas the scouts were relatively secular in their approach, Child Evangelism Fellowship, working chiefly through Good News Clubs, gathered children in their neighborhoods to lead them to Christ. CEF and a proliferation of other children's agencies continue. Christian Service Brigade, Pioneer Clubs, Awana Youth Association, and Christian Youth Crusaders—each designate growing and well-developed Christian education programs for children; each work beyond denominational lines with a concern for bringing the child to Christ and to discipleship.

REASONS FOR MINISTERING TO CHILDREN TODAY

The sweep of history seems to trace a moving pattern in child training as follows: (1) all training is in the matrix of the home and is informal; (2) child training is shared by parents and relatives and is still informal in nature; (3) training is organized by the tribe or subcultural group to transmit an increasingly complex body of treasured values and is carried on in both formal and informal ways; (4) child training is delegated to education specialists without regard to their values, and procedures are almost entirely formal, both unrelated to the teacher's values and related only with difficulty to the real world.

The church is caught in the magnetic field of education in general, especially with regard to the separation of teaching from active living. In any consideration of the responsibility of the church for the child, the obligation is surely upon us to note carefully what our opportunities and what our motivations are in ministering to the child. Here follow a series of observations about the importance of keeping faith with children in our trust. The sequence may have significance in terms of logic but not necessarily in terms of importance.

1. *Parents are God's "first curriculum."* It is clear from reading any translation of Genesis that the "image of God" of Genesis 1:26-28 is distributed explicitly across the "male and female" spectrum. When one contemplates the very different impacts a father and a mother have on a child, it is clear that the first representation of God which every human "reads" is that one which comes to them in the care and nurture of one adult female and one adult male. Whereas we might want to explore the studies in "father absence" or "maternal deprivation" and to launch a crusade on the platform that every child's first right is to have a resident mother and father, the issue goes deeper. We are all

of us "mothers and fathers" in the sense that the psalmist cried out, "When my father and my mother forsake me, then the Lord will take me up" (27:10). So our church "curriculum" needs first of all to inspire and support positive human parenting, but to move underneath the "orphans in their distress" and to provide parent surrogates in the name of Jesus.[14]

2. *Children are our gift from God.* There is some mysterious sense in which the creation is reechoed in the birth of every child. Whatever intrinsic marks original sin may have transmitted to children, they are uniquely beautiful in their early years. The children of every culture are alike in this way. Their laughter and games, even in the most perverse societies, are reminders that God speaks of His own holiness in the gift of life bestowed on human children. As such, they are at once a rebuke to us and a reminder that God has grand things in mind for the human race. We begin our ministry with children with a vision of helping bring them to fulfillment of God's design for them—a design glimpsed in embryo in the free, creative, joyous beauty of early childhood.

3. *Children are open to God.* Children do not need arguments to prove the existence of God; nor do they need to be convinced that prayer and other acts of worship are important. Beyond this, the evidence is overwhelming that suggests that young children are capable of religious experience.[15] Children are especially capable of such experiences because of the very nature of the development of the human mind. All children pass through growth patterns carefully described by Jean Piaget as "motor" and "egocentric" stages, running from birth up through about age eight. During this time, children have difficulty distinguishing between reality and fantasy. They are creative and imaginative and indulge in magical explanations, inventing a wide range of supranatural persons and events. This capacity makes them highly susceptible to belief both in Santa Claus and in God.[16] We cannot unravel the mystery of this particular stage of development, nor can we separate children's orthodox religious belief from their unbridled fantasy. It will be important that their religious environment be stable during these years and that they have wide

---

14. See Donald M. Joy, *Bonding: Relationships in the Image of God,* especially the chapter "Parents and Children: For Each Other."
15. See, for example, the classic study by Edwin D. Starbuck, *The Psychology of Religon, An Empirical Study of the Growth of Religious Consciousness* (New York: Scribner, 1906), especially chaps. 3 and 15. Strong emphasis to this second of my reasons is given in Frank G. Coleman, *The Romance of Winning Children* (Cleveland: Union Gospel, 1948, 1967), and in Lois E. LeBar, *Children in the Bible School* (Westwood, N.J.: Revell, 1952), especially chap. 1.
16. Jean Piaget, *The Moral Judgment of the Child* (New York: Free Press, 1932, 1965). See also David Elkind, "How the Mind Grows," in his *Children and Adolescents: Interpretive Essays on Jean Piaget* (New York: Oxford U., 1970), and Robert P. O'Neil and Michael A. Donovan, "The Magic Years," in *Sexuality and Moral Responsibility* (Washington: Corpus Books, 1968). Both Elkind and O'Neil are deeply rooted in Piaget. See Donald M. Joy, ed., *Moral Development Foundations: Theological Alternatives to Piaget/Kohlberg* (New York: Abingdon, 1983).

exposure to authentic adult faith. Where these conditions exist, they will separate fantasy from faith naturally and easily as cognitive operations mature.

4. *Jesus placed a high value on children.* Jesus attributed faith and belief to the children who played in His presence and found themselves on His lap and in His stories. Their open credulity became the analogy of commitment to His discipleship. Yet He did not call them to discipleship or chide them for unbelief or draw the net for their conversion. He accepted them at their stage of development for what they were, but He saw beyond that to their potential as full-grown creatures made in the image of God. So He went about seeking to change the life-molding environment of those children. In our ministry, we will do no better than to imitate Him. When we do, we will provide an environment for children in which we (*a*) show respect for their value to God, accepting them at their various stages of development and ministering to them in appropriate ways, (*b*) affirm their childlike faith, and (*c*) develop a rich display of faithful adherence to the traditions, values, beliefs, and life-styles which are thoroughly and honestly Christian.

5. *The church is the "family of God."* The disintegration of family life, which we are presently experiencing in North America, will affect us less if we remember that the true bond of relationship among Christians is faith, not blood. Jesus suggested as much when He posed the question about the identity of His "mother" and His "brothers" (Matt. 12:48-50). Both He and the New Testament writers affirm that the new fellowship of faith is the successor to the old line of Abraham. The congregation, then, ought to be an extended family, a tribe, or a network of intimate circles of mutual concern, sharing, and faith. This feature of congregational life is no doubt the most attractive of the authentic hallmarks of Christian faith. We are created for fellowship, not isolation and loneliness, and fulfillment at the personal level is somehow contingent upon rich interpersonal relationships. If a congregation does not find ways of developing this kind of warmth and support, it cannot hope to nurture its children well. For the very dynamics of relationships in the nuclear family make it imperative that the "tribe" furnish some of the models and reinforce the parental values if they are to prevail. The congregation, through its informal and formal ministries, is uniquely prepared to contribute significantly to the child's Christian decision-making and growth because it is transgenerational in character, relational in essence, and has abundant resources for both didactic and modeling instruction.

6. *Christian faith is never more than one generation from extinction.* Christian faith is not a matter of genes and chromosomes, nor is it transmitted by birthright or inheritance. "God has no grandchildren," someone has quipped, "only children." We must make no assumptions, therefore, about what children know. They know nothing about the acts of God in history unless we share that knowledge. We will carefully plan the learning exposures of our children to unfold to them the mighty acts of God in such a way as to

help them arrive at the same sound faith that we possess—if we are wise.[17]

7. *The early years set the tone for lifelong values.* It is sometimes argued that we should invest our energy in reaching children because we can reach them more easily than adults and because "they have their whole life before them." Both observations are accurate, but a deeper motive should move us. Life's earliest experiences profoundly shape all of life, for this world and the next. Empirically, this axiom is well established by studies on identification and child rearing[18] and in the growing literature on father-absence.[19] A theoretical base is constructed in the model of "satellization."[20] Poetically, the sentiment is underscored by Dorothy Law Nolte's "Children Learn What They Live."[21] The -evidence is rather overwhelming that early sources of consistent value influence are essential if the child is to be formed in such a way as to be an effective, functioning person as an adult.[22] The entire array of church ministries to children must be seen as a major part of this early value influence which has long-range formation goals in mind.

8. *Children deserve to be helped to moral and spiritual maturity.* Just as children pass through cognitive stages in the development of the mind, they also move through identifiable stages of moral thought. Indeed, it seems plausible that the growing mind sets the limits on moral perception. In experiments with children in Christian education settings, Doug Scholl of Harvard University found that there is an upward yearning in the child's mind for more mature modes of moral thought. Using the basic research fabric of Lawrence Kohlberg,[23] he contrived learning experiences using what he called a "plus-

---

17. This mandate is eloquently put by Dora P. Chaplin, *Children and Religion* (New York: Scribner, 1948, 1961).
18. Robert R. Sears et al., *Identification and Child Rearing* (Stanford: Stanford U., 1965). See also his *Patterns in Child Rearing* (New York: Harper & Row, 1957).
19. See E. Mavis Hetherington and Jan L. Deur, "The Effects of Father Absence on Child Development," *Young Children* 36 (March 1971):233-42.
20. David Ausubel develops the satellization model essentially out of dependency and identification clues common to the Sears citations above. See Ausubel's *Theory and Problems of Adolescent Development* (New York: Grune & Stratton, 1954), pp. 167-216. I elaborate on his satellization model in exploring the formation of the young conscience in "How Are Values Formed," chap. 9 of *Meaningful Learning in the Church* (Winona Lake, Ind.: Light & Life, 1969), pp. 110-25.
21. Dorothy Law Nolte, "Children Learn What They Live" (Los Angeles: American Institute of Family Relations, n.d.).
22. Cf. the film, *The Conscience of a Child*, in the Focus on Behavior series (National Educational Television, Bloomington, Ind.: Indiana U., 1963). It chronicles the experiments of Robert Sears and shows resistance-to-temptation experiments with children who come from different qualities of home relationships. Especially significant are the apparent differences in resistance as related to the warmth of boys' relationships to their fathers.
23. For a casual introduction to Lawrence Kohlberg, see "The Child as a Moral Philosopher" *Psychology Today* 1 (September 1968):25-30. A more comprehensive orientation is available in "The Development of Children's Orientations Toward a Moral Order" in M. and L. Hoffman, *Child Development Research* (New York: Russell Sage, 1964) 1:383-431, or in "Stages of Moral Development as a Basis for Moral Education," in *Moral Education: Interdisciplinary Approaches,* ed. C. M. Beck et al. (Toronto: Toronto U., 1971), pp. 23-92.

one-match." In this strategy, the level of moral thinking predominating in the group was noted, then a child with advanced ways of thinking, usually one level above the majority, was used as the model to which other children's thought was elevated.[24] Kohlberg generalizes from his extensive cross-cultural studies that (*a*) each of the six stages he defines is a typology, not an airtight stage, since no person operates exclusively within one typology; (*b*) the stages form an invariant sequence through which all persons pass—the early stages, at least—in relation to age; (*c*) all movement is forward; one never arrives at stage four thinking by way of stage six, but vice versa; and (*d*) a person may stop within any of the typologies or stages; hence, biological maturity does not assure moral development. The Kohlberg observations and his model of typologies may be instructive to evangelical Christians not only because of the profound insights they may stimulate about our effectiveness in promoting growth and maturity in Christian faith, but also in understanding how believers may become arrested at immature levels and fail to grow in Christian faith and behavior. With children, his model may be particularly helpful in assessing a child's actual way of viewing moral events and in thereby coming to his aid in moving to more mature, that is, more fully Christian, ways of thinking and behaving.

9. *Early, consistent saturation in a warm, Christian nurture environment helps children respond personally to Christ's call to salvation.* During the years from birth to age ten, plus or minus two, children need a warm identification environment in which they may develop a strong sense that they are loved by God and by the Christians around them. All the while, they will be interpreting, likely incorrectly, what they see by reducing it to concrete, external, legalistic images and modes. Nevertheless, as children approach the almost simultaneous arrival of sexual awakening, of formal/abstract thinking powers, and of identity awareness, they will sense a deep personal need of God's grace in forgiving, fulfilling ministries if life is to have meaning. Whatever rich childhood experiences children may have enjoyed in their relationship with God, they must eventually come to a distinctly personal response if meaningful discipleship is to take root.[25] We cannot stress too much the importance of an early, positive religious environment for the child, encourage-

---

24. Doug Scholl, "The Contributions of Lawrence Kohlberg to Religious and Moral Education," *Religious Education* 66 (September-October 1971):364-72.
25. For an elaboration of these issues, see my "Children, Salvation, and Drop Out," *Asbury Seminarian* 26 (October 1972):20-35. The Southern Baptists are facing up to issues of early childhood conversion and its attendant baptism and membership, some issues of which are defined and explored in William Hendricks, "The Age of Accountability," in *Children and Conversion,* ed. Clifford Ingle (Nashville: Broadman, 1970), pp. 84-97. Those who have interest in the Anglo-Catholic-Wesley tradition will find rich exploration of the accountability issue in "The Magic Years" and "Sin as Orientation," the opening chapters of Robert P. O'Neil and Michael A. Donovan, *Sexuality and Moral Responsibility* (Washington: Corpus Books, 1968), pp. 1-60.

ment to respond to God's grace, and provision of abundant models whose life testimony affirms the validity of the gospel being verbalized in classes, clubs, and worship.

10. *The child's emerging life needs are best met in the Christian fellowship.* If we hold that Christian faith and life is the means whereby God restores fallen men to fellowship with Himself and to life of highest possible human fulfillment, then we must affirm other truths which derive from that hypothesis. One of these is that Christians are able to take the most honest and realistic view of human needs and that they possess the most useful tools for use in bringing human beings to fulfillment. In the hands of Christian educators, then, any helpful research or models that describe the human condition become torches for lighting our way in identifying persons' needs and in developing ways of meeting those needs. Christians might rightly hold that to the extent that educators and therapists operate from sub-Christian bases, they will be less able to be fully helpful in meeting human need. For example, Erik Erikson makes several announcements: that infants waver in the balance between an orientation of trust versus basic mistrust; that they then proceed to the dilemma of autonomy versus shame and doubt; that by school age, they are caught between the tension of a life-orientation of initiative over against guilt; that the elementary years are predominantly fought out pitting industry against inferiority; and that when pubescence strikes, they will be wavering between positive identity discovery and role diffusion.[26] Christians ought, of all people, to apply Erikson's model to their work and ask whether such life crises are occurring before their eyes. If the model is helpful, as a majority of thoughtful persons now believe it is, we must certainly see that the first named option in each of the crisis pairs is the one Christian growth would opt for. And if we would dare to take the social science approach to Christian education,[27] we would affirm that God has so created humans and human relationships that whatever we sow will be reaped—that there are methodical means of getting desired results through training and childhood education programs in the church. Likewise, even the most superficial glance at Abraham Maslow's hierarchy of human needs, delineated in chapter 3 of this book, will help set the agenda for our Christian education agencies and home ministries.[28] These are only two of today's dominant models, which become a mandate to us as those whose highest objective is to meet human needs—needs that culminate in self-realization as they find themselves recreated in the image of righteousness and true holiness (Eph. 4:24) in Jesus Christ.

26. Erik Erikson, "Eight Stages of Man," in *Childhood and Society* (New York: Norton, 1950), pp. 219-34.
27. See the provocative work of James Michael Lee of Notre Dame University Graduate School, especially his books, *The Shape of Religious Instruction* (1971) and *The Flow of Religious Instruction* (Dayton, Ohio: Pflaum/Standard, 1973).
28. Abraham H. Maslow, *Motivation and Personality* (New York: Harper & Row, 1954), chap. 5. I explore his hierarchy of human needs for implications for Christian education in *Meaningful Learning in the Church* (Winona Lake, Ind.: Light & Life, 1969), pp. 25-36.

11. *Child development is best understood, appreciated, and ministered to in the loving environment of the family of God.* We have noted the distinct opportunity to minister to children across their development of cognitive powers (item 2), their development of moral thought (item 7), and their unfolding developmental needs (item 9). But the church and its children's ministries are capable of responding in superior ways to the physiological-psychological-social development needs of the child as well. Children, for example, who find regular support in the church's programs from birth tend to enter school well ahead of homebound children of similar endowments. The social exchanges, the wider sources of affection, and the regular movement into larger social spheres combine to furnish our children with the benefits eagerly sought for all children through newly launched "early childhood intervention" programs. In our society, children are learning to read earlier than in the past, many reading even before they start kindergarten. The impact of television is largely responsible for the reading acceleration, no doubt. But for reasons not so clearly understood, sexual maturity is also accelerated. It is urgent, therefore, that the church adapt to these accelerations and find ways of meeting the needs which they represent. For example, the onset of puberty has declined for girls from age 17 years 6 months in 1840 to 12 years 2 months in 1980, according to widely publicized reports. The rate has been estimated to be roughly at six months per generation. The effects for those who minister to children become obvious: (*a*) identity needs that accompany biological transition may be expected to strike as early as the middle elementary years; (*b*) awakening moral sense that produces personal guilt and that needs the work of God's grace in healing and forgiveness must be anticipated in some cases well ahead of the prime junior high school years; (*c*) the dropout rate, which seems to be directly related to the onset of puberty, perhaps related to emerging discomfort, embarrassment, or even guilt over sexual feelings and activity, will be striking earlier than ever before.

12. *The educational technocracy obligates us to effective ministry with children.* Never before have we had at our disposal such an array of educational theory and educational hardware to accomplish our tasks in ministering to children. Serious attention to the learning process, still a youthful science, was introduced among the higher concerns of man only in this century. Even now, there is no one satisfactory theory of learning on the horizon. There are tentative theories of instruction now being offered well after earlier theories of learning, which had been thought to contain all that was necessary to observe about instruction. But teaching is not merely learning theory standing on its head; the two seem to have distinctly different characteristics.[29] Beyond the methodologies involved in teaching and learning loom our advanced under-

---

29. See James Michael Lee, "Learning Theory and Teaching Theory," in *The Flow of Religious Instruction* (Dayton, Ohio: Pflaum/Standard, 1973), pp. 39-57. Jerome S. Bruner offers help on teaching in *Toward a Theory of Instruction* (Cambridge: Harvard U., 1966).

standing of how content may be packaged for efficient subsumption in the learner. The intricate steps involved in programming basic packages of information, for example, have formed a new science in itself.[30] This is not even to attempt to profile the arsenal of audiovisual and printed media which is now at our disposal. But finally, and perhaps most hopefully of all, we have now been provided with a detailed analysis of the steps necessary for learning to become internalized and valued. A veritable road map to the transmission of value-laden knowledge and beliefs now exists in an awesome sounding work called a taxonomy of the "affective domain," that is, a classification of teaching objectives based on what pupils should acquire by way of feelings, attitudes, and appreciation.[31] Jesus once sounded a warning and announced a principle to the effect that those who have wide resources at their disposal will be held accountable for equally impressive results (Luke 12:48).

13. *The secularism of our times increases the urgency of providing a rich corrective in the Christian nurture and evangelism ministries.* It is said that Viscount Bryce was once asked what would be the effect of removing Christian ideals and the Bible from public schools. He answered, "I can't answer that until three generations have passed."[32] Public education has been, by any measure, the gift of the Christian heritage to children of the Western world. It is ironic that in our time, Christian expressions have been banned from public school classrooms by judicial processes which have stressed "fairness." It is becoming more obvious that the official state religion of the United States is that of an agnostic secularism—a religion with its own host of priests and temples. While some of those priests still articulate value systems obviously rooted in the Judeo-Christian vision,[33] they are prophets in a culture whose values are sure to erode. Such erosion, as is evident in United States public morality, its tastes in entertainment, its virtually entirely expediency-oriented political climate, and its *Playboy* philosophy, sketches the pervasive and perverse conditions of our secular domain. The child of the late twentieth century is surfeited with value influences which contradict the fundamental values of Christian faith and life. Rarely in the western world, since the days of the young church in the pagan Roman empire, has so much depended on the

---

30. Take seriously, for example, and complete a small programmed sequence to teach a selected body of information using Sivasailam Thiagarajan, *The Programming Process: A Practical Guide* (Worthington, Ohio: Jones, 1971).
31. David R. Krathwohl et al., *Taxonomy of Educational Objectives: Affective Domain* (New York: McKay, 1964).
32. Viscount Bryce, cited in a larger discussion of this issue by Dora P. Chaplin, *Children and Religion* (New York: Scribner, 1961), p. 8.
33. John W. Gardner, former presidential cabinet member, is an illustration. See his *Excellence* (1961) and his *Self-Renewal* (Harper & Row, 1964). Both read like extensions of the Christian gospel; yet, when he was pressed during a question period at an eastern university to state the foundation on which his expressed values rested and from which they were drawn, he is reported to have hung his head and answered, no doubt honestly, that he did not know.

effectiveness of the family of God in infusing the life of Christ and His values into their young.

GOALS WITH CHILDREN

Given sufficient reasons, then, for committing our resources to the effective nurture and evangelism of children, let us conclude our overview by identifying appropriate goals which will mark our achievement of the substantial task ahead.

ULTIMATE GOAL

As ministers to children, we seek to meet their present and unfolding needs, to the end that we bring them to self-fulfillment and maturity in Christian faith characterized by (*a*) personal acceptance of Jesus Christ as Savior and Lord, (*b*) mature decision-making and behavior reflecting internalized Christian values, and (*c*) righteousness, true holiness, and the fullness of the stature of Jesus Christ.

INTERMEDIATE GOALS

The ultimate goal will necessarily require attention to specific subtasks whose accomplishment will be prerequisite to achieving the larger objective, as follows:

1. Reaffirm the primacy of the home as the chief agency of value development, articulation, and transmission.

2. Disciple parents, who in turn will use the "image of God" magnet to form their household in the image of God's Son and present their children and coming generations both to Jesus and to the church.

3. Heighten the congregation's awareness of itself as the "family of God," an extended family consisting of clusters of intimate networks or tribes of faith whose values are shared around a common commitment to Christ, and among whom there is openness and sharing of treasured beliefs, standards, and values.

4. Provide learning and sharing experiences for transgenerational groups composed of entire families, so that children may hear discussions about Christian concerns and expressions of Christian faith from their parents and other adults within the fellowship of the congregation.

5. Arrange for young children to have a wide, systematic, balanced exposure to biblical material, especially narrative accounts which stimulate positive or negative identification responses, as appropriate. It will be important that the teaching stop short of traditional moralistic interpretations, but that children be allowed to form their own moral conclusions (having eyes to see and ears to hear) based on the Word of God through consistent teaching at home and at church.

6. Diagnose persistently the levels of moral thought that are represented in any children's ministry setting, then gear instruction and class activity to minister realistically within that level of thinking. It will be important to advance levels of thought by means of introducing ways of thinking immediately above those most common to the children involved, but short of advanced, mature adult moral thought levels.

7. Make satellization models available to children passing into puberty. Staff members should understand clearly the importance of bringing the young person to Christ. This goal can only be reached in sensitive interplay with the workings of the Holy Spirit in the life and development of this emerging autonomous, identity-seeking, sexually awakened person.

CONCLUSION

There is no question, then. We must effectively "set the child in our midst." In our time, we must resolve not to idolize children, but to see them as next in line beyond us as the custodian of our treasured values, beliefs, and life-styles. It is appropriate that we hesitate in the face of such a task to inquire, How? With this glimpse into some of the opening windows of the world of childhood, of human development, and of the mysterious development of conscience and moral sense, this volume now turns to explore evidences and strategies that will move us forward in meeting our responsibilities.

FOR FURTHER READING

Anderson, Robert H., ed. *Education in Anticipation of Tomorrow.* Worthington, Ohio: Jones, 1973.

Bolton, Barbara J. *Ways to Help Them Learn: Children, Grades 1 to 6.* Glendale, Calif.: Gospel Light, Regal Books, 1972.

Bronfenbrenner, Urie. *Two Worlds of Childhood.* New York: Russell Sage, 1970.

Bull, Normal J. *Moral Judgment from Childhood to Adolescence.* New York: Russell Sage, 1969.

Goldman, Ronald. *Readiness for Religion.* New York: Seabury, 1968.

———. *Religious Thinking from Childhood to Adolescence.* New York: Seabury, 1964.

Ingle, Clifford, ed. *Children and Conversion.* Nashville: Broadman, 1970.

Joy, Donald M. *Bonding Relationships in the Image of God.* Waco, Tex.: Word, 1985.

———, ed. *Moral Development Foundations: Theological Alternatives to Piaget/Kohlberg.* New York: Abingdon, 1983.

Kohlberg, Lawrence. "The Child as a Moral Philosopher." *Psychology Today* 1 (September 1968): 25-30.

LeBar, Lois E. *Children in the Bible School.* Westwood, N.J.: Revell, 1952.

Lee, R. S. *Your Growing Child and Religion.* New York: Macmillan, 1963.

Maier, Henry W. *Three Theories of Child Development.* New York: Harper & Row, 1969.

McCandless, Boyd R. *Children: Behavior and Development.* New York: Holt, Rinehart & Winston, 1967.

O'Neil, Robert P., and Michael A. Donovan. *Children and Sin.* Washington: Corpus Books, 1969.

Piaget, Jean. *The Moral Judgment of the Child.* New York: Free Press, 1965.

Richards, Lawrence O. *A Theology of Children's Ministry.* Grand Rapids: Zondervan, 1983.

Smith, Charles T. *Ways to Plan and Organize Your Sunday School: Children, Grades 1 to 6.* Glendale, Calif.: Gospel Light, Regal Books, 1971.

2

Oscar E. Feucht and
Robert E. Clark

Social and Cultural
Influences on Children

- **Genetics and Culture**
  HEREDITY
  ENVIRONMENT
- **Products of Our Environment**
- **Love in Human Relationships**
- **The Family as an Influence**
  EARLY CHILDHOOD EXPERIENCES
  CHANGES IN MARRIAGE
  CHRISTIAN NURTURE
- **The Church as an Influence**
- **The School as an Influence**
- **The Community as an Influence**
- **Other Influences Affecting Children**
  URBANIZATION
  MOBILITY
  MASS MEDIA
  TELEVISION
  SEX
  DRUG ABUSE

OSCAR E. FEUCHT, D.D., served as secretary of adult education for the Board of Parish Education of the Lutheran Church (Missouri Synod) from 1946 through 1968. He was a consultant in adult and family life education for his denomination. He is now deceased.

ROBERT E. CLARK, ED.D., is professor of Christian education at Moody Bible Institute, Chicago, Illinois, and is co-editor of *Childhood Education in the Church.*

MISSING CHILDREN AND CHILD PORNOGRAPHY
CHILD ABUSE
DIVORCE AND SINGLE PARENTS
LATCH-KEY CHILDREN
HURRIED CHILDREN

The sociological environment of many American children is described by Emma White as follows:

> Children are all around us. Some live in crowded, deteriorating city blocks. Others live in isolated rural areas far from neighbors. Many live on quiet streets of small towns or villages. Children are living in the spreading suburbs and in midtown apartment buildings. Other boys and girls are growing up on farms, ranches, and reservations. Still others are constantly on the move with their families.
>
> All of these children learn through firsthand, day-by-day living. They experience riots, looting, and crime on the streets. They learn the quiet beauty of the natural world near their farm homes, and on occasion, the fury and devastation of floods, tornadoes, and storms. They learn geography as they travel or move to new places. Some know real hunger, while others possess personal TV's or AM/FM radios.
>
> Some children attend excellent schools; others struggle and fail because of poor opportunities for education. Both rich and poor boys and girls feel great emptiness and loneliness because they have no families or friends. Yet many, many children know security and love through happy home lives and rich community experiences.
>
> Some inner-city children may have difficulty visualizing a green meadow, and some rural children may not understand what a busy city is like. All these children know a jet plane as it flies overhead. Today's children learn through split second impressions flashed before them on the television screen. They are aware of peoples, places, events, animals, and objects they have never actually seen. They are aware, in varying degrees, of tensions among groups and nations. These children live in the day of communication satellites and space exploration. Above all, they live in a day of constant and rapid change.
>
> These are today's children!
>
> These are the children the church must serve![1]

GENETICS AND CULTURE

Heredity, or the genetic plan, and the *environment,* or the culture, are the two major forces affecting the lives of children from birth to death.

HEREDITY (GENETICS)

Children are born with traits from their parents through the genetic process. A fertilized cell called a zygote has twenty-three pairs of chromosomes—

1. Emma White, *Let's Do More with Children* (Nashville: United Methodist Church, 1969), p. 1.

twenty-three from the father and twenty-three from the mother. As the zygote divides, each subsequent cell that is formed contains exactly the same number of chromosomes as every other—forty-six. If there are fewer chromosomes than the usual forty-six, particularly in the arrangement of the sex chromosomes, abnormalities occur. Even though thousands of research studies have been done in the field of genetic engineering, we still cannot predict the total development of any given individual.

Thousands of genes are strung out in chainlike fashion on a single chromosome. The genes carry the hereditary potential for all organisms. It is virtually impossible for the same combination of genes to occur twice, for the possibility of any two siblings' receiving the same assortment of chromosomes is about 1 in 281 trillion.[2] We can understand why every person is a unique individual. This is the reason why twins, whether they are identical or fraternal, are so different in their total personalities.

ENVIRONMENT (CULTURE)

Every child is born with hereditary potential, and that potential is shaped by the environment, or culture. A functional definition of culture is "a social group (nation, tribe, or social group) in which attitudes, beliefs, customs, values, roles and expectations are learned and transmitted from one generation or group to another."[3] Culture affects the child from birth.

The process of socialization takes place in the culture. It involves a broad learning process by which a child acquires the attitudes and values of the culture. The family is the basic unit for transmitting cultural practices and values. Socialization is a lifelong process in which children learn to become members of a social group. Through this process, individuals are forced to deal with new situations and adapt to the social group's standards and values.

Heredity and environment both assist in the development of an individual's total personality. Child rearing and training are significant areas in the socialization of the child. Families from different cultural backgrounds will vary greatly in their methods of child rearing and training. The Christian family will approach child rearing and training differently because of the biblical principles governing the parental roles and relationships.

PRODUCTS OF OUR ENVIRONMENT

Each child is born a unified person who acts as a whole, integrated individual in every experience. Through relationships of many kinds, every person undergoes some kind of growth mentally, socially, morally, and spiritually.

2. Grace Craig, *Human Development,* 3d ed. (Englewood Cliffs, N.J.: Prentice-Hall, 1983), p. 117.
3. Craig, p. 125.

Of great significance are the first intellectual and emotional experiences of early childhood. Through the process of attachment or bonding during the first few days and months after birth, the child builds a special relationship with his or her parents or with a primary caregiver. As the parents hold, touch, caress, and talk to the child, a bonding of love and an expression of emotional feelings will be shared through a mutual relationship between the infant and the parents. Attachment is important because it is through this process that the child learns to build a sense of trust in others. This early relationship carries over into later life and will help the child adjust to others more positively as his or her world expands emotionally and socially.[4] Values learned almost automatically become the integrating factors in a child's personality. This takes place as a person internalizes the values which he perceives. These values, psychologists assert, become his conscience. A child closely related to the faith, thinking, and way of life of a conscientious Christian mother and/or father will absorb more of lifelong significance from this source than from any other single source. One pastor put it in these words: "My Christian mother was my real seminary." He absorbed a mass of theological data in college and seminary, but his basic life goals and inner strengths came from his mother. Every child is the product of his most intimate environment. Nothing less than the total life climate makes people what they are.

Too often, we equate education almost completely with the teaching-learning process in a class, a school, or some other institution. Actually, however, people are the products of many experiences in their total environment. Their basic orientation to life is learned through family and cultural influences before going to school.

No one lives in a vacuum. Children are surrounded daily by dozens of factors—both good and bad—that affect and influence their lives. Ultimately, these sociological, cultural, political, and economic factors all have their effect on our nation's morals.

Bettelheim, a distinguished child psychologist, wrote the following regarding the effect of situation ethics not on youth but on *children:*

> The big problem with situation ethics is the havoc it has wreaked in child rearing. We foolishly hope our children will grow up having mature controls when they have never been subject to a stringent morality. The situation ethic view neither equips the child to control his violent desires nor prepares him to act on a basis of long-range goals. The more refined morality that can make distinctions profitably cannot exist unless it has *at its base* a rigid belief in right and wrong, that permits no relativity.[5]

4. Craig, p. 176.
5. Bruno Bettelheim, "Bringing Up Children," *Ladies' Home Journal* 89 (December 1972): 29.

LOVE IS BASIC IN HUMAN RELATIONSHIPS

Problem persons usually reflect inadequate love received from parents, siblings, relatives, teachers, or an environment of one or more negative influences. Psychologists have observed that young children deprived of genuine parental love suffer character difficulties and fail to achieve their potential growth emotionally and intellectually.

Someone must give children more than shelter, food, and nice clothes. Every person needs a proper self-esteem and a sense of worth and direction. To develop such self-esteem, self-confidence, and sense of security, a child needs a happy, hopeful outlook on life. These prevent the aggressiveness and recessiveness of problem children.

Erich Fromm, a distinguished social psychologist, asserts that love for others and love for ourselves are *not* mutually exclusive.[6] Jesus implied the same in His command to love God with all your heart and your neighbor *as yourself* (Matt. 22:37-39). Love includes feeling deeply for others. It shows concern for the welfare, happiness, and development of the one loved.

This kind of love reaches out to all humanity. Like Christ's love, it is universal. Love is not rooted primarily in sexual dynamics, as modern literature and other media erroneously assume. The finest love of a marriage partner flows from the larger springs of true, unselfish, *Christian* love (Eph. 5:25-30).

Genuine love provides basic security; helps us love ourselves and others, interpret and constructively use our culture, and adjust to unpleasant situations; develops group fellowship; fosters warm identification with parents, relatives, teachers, and peers; and works toward alleviation of evils in society.

THE FAMILY AS A SOCIAL INFLUENCE

Many contemporaries are predicting the dissolution of the family and the disestablishment of marriage. Some current university courses openly advocate not only trial marriage but a series of unions with different persons as people tire of each other. However, no society of the past has been able to operate indefinitely with such a system. Children—as well as youth and adults—need a more stable arrangement if life is to be secure and generations are to contribute to society as a whole.

Sociologists point to seven functions that are most effectively carried on within the family. Though they are no longer *exclusively* carried out in the family, they still find their *greatest* fulfillment within the home.

1. Biologically, the home provides procreation, concern for, care of, and feeding of children and other family members.

6. Eric Fromm, *The Art of Loving* (New York: Harper, 1956), p. 58.

2. Educationally, the family is the basic school of life, where we continue to learn from each other from infancy to old age and pass our cultural values from one generation to another.
3. Religiously, all kinds of beliefs have been taught and perpetuated in the family.
4. Economically, gainful employment by various members of the family is necessary to provide the resources for housing and housekeeping.
5. Socially, no one can long live in isolation. The warmth, mutual support, and fellowship of family members are necessary to healthy growth.
6. Recreationally, more than before, families are doing things together: sports, travel, entertaining, celebrating.
7. Affectionally, children need the ties of love which only the family can give. Without this home base, children suffer emotional deprivation. The love between husband and wife, parents and children, brothers and sisters, relatives and friends is essential for our well-being.

We cannot, without considerable loss, relinquish any of these functions exclusively to outsiders. The new policies of foster parents and adoptions, rather than maintaining orphanages, bear witness to the basic need for children to be incorporated into a family. Science has not given us a substitute.

Within the family, children learn physical skills, cultural values, customs, a language, basic housekeeping, and standards of conduct that fit them for society. They also learn religion or irreligion. In this realm there is no neutrality. The decline of family worship and Bible reading in the home is an irreplaceable loss. The absence of personal and family worship further secularizes the home. The welfare of society and the stability of the family are so interrelated that a decline in one almost always involves a decline in the other.

IMPORTANCE OF EARLY CHILDHOOD EXPERIENCES

The child's personality grows out of all the relationships that touch life. That makes parents, brothers, sisters, teachers, and classmates, with their personalites and value systems, part of the child's environment. They give the child a mind-set, a sense of direction, a life-purpose, and goals. In early childhood, we take over the loves and hatreds of our social environment. Children learn what they are exposed to. We adults set the stage for what we call a "rehearsal," which, however, turns out to be the real "play." What is more, the child selects many of the lines of that "play."

Some of our greatest educators have helped us formulate a more adequate concept of education. They indicate that a child's life-style is, to a large degree, set by the time the child enters kindergarten or the first grade; that learning to respond both physically and verbally in preschool days is actually more important than learning to read and count. Pestalozzi, an influential educator of the past, has stated that the basic principle of education is not teaching, but love.

Haim Ginott says, "Only those who communicate daily with children can prevent mental disturbances."[7] In his books,[8] he explains how child care and discipline can be positive. Instead of blaming and shaming, we must convey caring. He warns against humiliating the child and suggests that an ounce of prevention is worth a pound of punishment. Parents can convey to their children that there is no need to lie. They can invite cooperation and teach responsibility, even without rewards or prizes. By the way they handle the child, they can remove harmful fears. Even minor mishaps can create golden opportunities to demonstrate love and better understanding. "To communicate love parents need a language of acceptance: words that value feelings, responses that change moods, replies that radiate respect. The world talks to the mind. Parents speak more intimately—they talk to the heart."[9]

SIGNIFICANT CHANGES IN MARRIAGE

Children in more recent times live in very different environments from children at the turn of the twentieth century. Gesell and Ilg describe the contrast vividly:

> In the more olden times, the world of nature and of human relationships expanded in a rather orderly manner, keeping pace with the maturity of the child. The home was large, the membership of the family numerous, and usually there was yet another child to be born. Someone was always near to look after the preschool child and to take him by graduated stages into his widening world, step by step, as his demands gradually increased. There was free space around his home, a field, a meadow, an orchard. There were animals in barn, pen, coop, and pasture. Some of these fellow creatures were young like himself. He could feast his eyes on them, touch them, sometimes even embrace them.
>
> Time has played a transforming trick with this environment. The apartment child, and to some extent even the suburban child of today, has been greatly deprived of his former companions, human and infrahuman. Domestic living space has contracted to the dimensions of few rooms, a porch, a yard; perhaps to a single room, with one or two windows.[10]

Changes have also taken place in marriage relationships and family living. The following trends in marriage undoubtedly influence children in today's homes.

1. *Marriage is not as binding legally as it once was.* Some states have made divorces easier to obtain through more lax divorce laws such as "no

7. Haim Ginott, "How to Drive Your Child Sane," *Reader's Digest* 102 (January 1973): 89.
8. See Haim Ginott, *Between Parent and Child* (New York: Avon, 1972); *Between Parent and Teenager* (New York: Macmillan, 1969); and *Teacher and Child* (New York: Macmillan, 1972).
9. Ginott, p. 92.
10. Arnold Gesell and Frances Ilg, *Infant and Child in the Culture of Today* (New York: Harper, 1943), p. 260.

fault" divorce or flimsy reasons such as incompatability or "mental or emotional cruelty." Couples can sign marriage contracts, and if the marriage does not work out the partners can find other mates. Many couples do not become legally married but just live together as long as the relationship is functional. In 1984, 1.99 million unmarried couples were living together, up 5 percent from 1.89 million in 1983.[11]

2. *Divorces are on the increase.* Some statistics indicate that one in every two marriages ends up in the divorce court. (Of course, the statistics vary greatly, even in geographical sectors of the country.) In 1984, according to a Census Bureau report, there were. a record 121 divorced people for every 1,000 married people, up from 114 in 1983.[12] Also, some couples are no longer living together, but are not legally divorced. Unfortunately, too, many Christian couples are also being divorced. Selfishness seems to be a major reason couples break up.

3. *The roles of husband and wife are more fluid, especially when both couples work outside the home.* Though stereotypes for husband and wife still exist, many couples share more of the responsibilities of homemaking, parenting, and child care.

4. *Nuclear family living has become more common, particularly in western culture.* Many children now see their grandparents only occasionally because of the distance they live from each other. In years past, many grandparents lived with one of their married children or grandchildren. As a result, nuclear families have become more independent and self-reliant.

5. *The women's liberation movement has affected the family.* Today, more women are seeking self-fulfillment through careers and interests outside the family. Interviews with 3,000 women indicated that 72 percent of women say that marriage is not a prerequisite for happiness. In the same study, 63 percent of women want a career with marriage and family. A decade ago only 52 per cent chose both.[13] Women are becoming more involved in educational, social, community, and political activities outside the home, and those involvements may affect home life.

6. *Marriages are now taking place across all frontiers—national, racial, and religious.* There are many reasons for this change in practice, but the more important are that we live in a more democratic social structure, shifts in cultural practice have occurred, and judicial rulings have declared unconstitutional laws that once prohibited cross-cultural marriages.

Other factors that have affected marriage relationships and family living are also evident. More mothers of young children are working than ever before. The number of women who work outside the home has increased steadily in

---

11. Jack Kelley, *USA Today* (16 September 1985), p. 1D.
12. Ibid.
13. Michelle Healy, *USA Today* (21 October 1985), p. 1D.

recent years. Some 57 percent of married women with children work outside the home—up 31 percent from twenty years ago. By 2000, 75 percent of women will be on the job.[14] For working mothers, child care is a major issue. Corporations and government are providing child care facilities as well as flexible schedules for fathers and mothers to be with their children. Men are playing greater roles in the home and in parenting. Daycare centers, nursery schools, and prekindergartens are also contributing what the average mother cannot provide in child care and educational leadership. (For more on this subject, see chap. 19, "Child Care Programs for Children.")

Shorter working hours make it possible for the father to spend more time with his children. Family outings and vacation trips keep the family together more than in former days.

More and more services have been transferred out of the home: teaching to schools, medical services to clinics or hospitals, care of the disadvantaged to social agencies, and care of the old to nursing homes.

Fewer women in our society are getting married. In fact, according to *U.S. News and World Report,* whereas in 1970 only 10.5 percent of women aged 25 to 29 had never been married, in 1983 that figure had risen to almost 25 percent.[15]

Of those who do marry, the median age for brides is 23, the highest since Census Bureau records began in 1890. The median age in 1983 was 22.8. Grooms are also older. The median age was 25.4 years in 1984, the highest since 25.9 in 1900.[16]

Today, the average number of children per family is smaller. The reasons for that vary. Some couples do not want to have children at all. Other couples would rather establish themselves in a career. Still others feel they cannot afford to have a family in a time of inflation and a high cost of living. And there are those who want their freedom and are not interested in taking on the responsibility of children.

In 1940, the average number of members per family was 3.76. By the early 1970s, the average number had dropped to 3.42. In 1975, the birth expectations of American women showed that young wives 18 to 24 years old expected only an average of 2.2 lifetime births per woman.[17] In 1984, the birth rate per woman was 1.8 children. Projections are that the United States will achieve zero population growth near the midpoint of the twenty-first century.[18]

Another interesting development reflecting the modern trend are new organizations that encourage couples not to bear children.

14. "10 Forces Reshaping America," *U.S. News and World Report* (19 March 1984), pp. 40, 47.
15. Ibid., p. 47.
16. Jack Kelley, p. 1D.
17. Arthur J. Norton and Paul C. Glick, "Changes in American Life," *Children Today* (May-June 1976), p. 3.
18. "When Family Will Have a New Definition," *U.S. News and World Report* (9 May 1983), p. A4.

"None Is Fun" is the slogan of a new organization, the National Organization for Non-Parents" (NON). Its goal: to make being child free a respectable, attractive, even fun alternative to parenthood. "We're not going around saying people shouldn't have children," says Mrs. Ellen Peck, one of the founders. "But we say people shouldn't automatically assume they should have children. Parenthood is a matter to be thought over quite carefully—for both parents' sake and the children's."

The group thinks society is prejudiced toward parenthood. "Everything in our society—from the tax laws to television shows to women's magazines to the most casual conversation—is oriented toward parenthood. It's very difficult to even consider whether you shouldn't have children when everyone is pressuring you to have kids and find out what you're missing."

Two basic questions the group says should be asked before deciding to have children: (1) Are we qualified—emotionally and intellectually, not just physically—for the important job of parenthood in today's complex society? (2) Is a child-centered life what we choose for at least 20 years of our life?[19]

FOUNDATION FOR CHRISTIAN NURTURE

The family is the primary place of Christian nurture. The New Testament summarizes the task of Christian teaching in one comprehensive term: *Christian nurture*. The word *nurture* in Ephesians 6:4 is the Greek word *paideia*. The *Revised Standard Version* translates this word "discipline." J. B. Phillips's phrasing is "Christian teaching," and *The New English Bible* uses "instruction." *Good News for Modern Man* renders this verse, "Raise them with Christian discipline and instruction." The word for "raise" (bring them up) in the Greek is *ektrepho*. It means "to nourish up to maturity." It includes all the environmental factors collectively to which the individual is subjected *from conception onward*.

Note that this directive is given to Christian fathers. The passing on of the Christian faith is to take place in all the interactions of life in the family. William Barclay, in one of his commentaries, remarks that this assignment is given to the family as a major function, because in no other place and under no other set of related functions could full nurture of the total personality really be adequately given.

It is in the home that the "colors are coded" and that the "strands," woven together, form the warp and woof of life. From their own experience, parents can give important insights their children need: words of encouragement and direction, approval and support, love and esteem; and visions of greater goals yet to be achieved.

Samuel Hamilton describes the task of parents in the following words: "All individual personal growth is interpersonal. At every stage of life, from birth to death, the family in the home can provide the setting, the occasions, the

19. James W. Reapsome, *Discern the Times* 2 (15 January 1973):2.

atmosphere, the inspiration, the behavior patterns, the controls, and the dynamic of the most profoundly forming and transforming interpersonal relationships in human existence.[20]

THE CHURCH AS A SOCIAL INFLUENCE

The relationship between the church and the home was succinctly stated by Hamilton:

> The Christian church and the Christian home as institutions are closely bound together. They are like Siamese twins: if you cut them apart you may sever an artery of life and cause one or both to die. The church cannot function as she should in a disordered world unless she employs the home as her main reliance in Christian nurture. And I feel certain that the family cannot be a Christian family or a happy family unless it stays in the circulation of those spiritual influences of which the church is the great custodian.[21]

While the family is not peculiar to Christianity, it is of primary concern to the church, because it is "one of the orders of creation," as Crook calls it.[22] Through the ages, the church has emphasized the Christian pattern of marriage and family living. Increasingly in the last fifty years, church bodies have engaged in biblical research and outlined a positive program of family life education. Unfortunately, many church-centered programs have *blocked* the door to a functional, practical, more relevant ministry *to* families and *through* families. Programs should be church *related* and family *centered*.

The task of the church is to make the whole ethos of the home evangelical in spirit and practice. This task will include areas of concern such as providing premarital counseling, training parents in child care and how to teach their children about sex, helping them learn to conduct family worship and inculcate biblical standards in the home, giving families a God-centered view of the world and the Christian's place in that world.

One Chicago pastor made it a rule of his ministry to visit every new family at supper and demonstrate with a short devotion how meaningful family worship can be. The home is responsible for training children, but the church is responsible for equipping parents in how to train their children.

The influence of the church on children rises and falls as its members everywhere and in every situation live out their faith in Christ. Americans are developing a greater concern for the conservation of our natural resources. But we are equally responsible for the moral and spiritual climate in which our children are raised. Unfortunately, religious influence has declined. After a surge in church membership following World War II, membership and atten-

20. Samuel L. Hamilton, "The Family the Center of Religious Education," *Religion in Life* 18 (Summer 1949): 419.
21. Ibid.
22. Roger Crook, *The Changing American Family* (Minneapolis: Bethany, 1960), p. 133.

dance have now slumped. This is changing the philosophy, life-style, and goals of many families, thus affecting children.

The church program must be attractive and motivating in order to hold people and encourage them to participate meaningfully.

> A well-known educator [John Holt] has suggested that public school children should be given the choice to go to class or not, and teachers should be paid according to the number of children who come to their classes. In the church school, that matter of choice has always been a factor! Both children and their parents must be convinced of the value of the sessions or sooner or later they will stop coming. It does little good to complain that they should come because it is "good for them," just as it does little good to complain that they no longer study their lessons on Saturday night. Our religion classes must have a built-in value demonstration for the learners or we will no longer have a class.[23]

Since our American separation of church and state does not permit religious instruction in public schools, churches must provide that instruction. However, will Sunday, vacation, weekday, or after-school classes meet the need or be equal to the task? What can be covered in such meager time and with parental concern so limited? Let us face this fact: *The common practice in most Protestant churches with once-a-week attendance at worship services is* NOT *equal to the greater task of integrating the Christian faith into all of life!* Three things are apparent: (1) we must strengthen our Christian education ministries to children in the church; (2) churches must give more specific guidance to parents on how to nurture their children in spiritual values; and (3) we must give serious consideration to the need for Christian elementary and high schools.

THE SCHOOL AS A SOCIAL INFLUENCE

The spirit of contemporary society is not overtly anti-Christian; it is merely un-Christian and, in many cases, secular and humanistic. This is an important change that the churches in early America did not face except on the rough frontier, largely because the ethos of the average community was "religious," if not "Christian." Secularization confronts our children as never before.

One of the most potent social forces in America is public education from preschool to university. The quest for higher education has surpassed all previous stages of history. The thirst for knowledge is almost universal, and the things to be learned have increased on an astronomical scale. The community college has brought new learning opportunities to our own back door. However, this new wealth needs to be evaluated not merely scientifically, but

23. Eldor Kaiser, "Kids Are Different Today—Or Are They?" *Interaction* 13 (April 1973):18.

ethically and spiritually. Will our spiritual and ethical growth keep pace with our scientific and psychological growth?

During the academic year, the child spends a major portion of his day at school. The role of the school is far-reaching in its social influences and may have greater effect on the child than his home. One educator has written,

> But students learn much more in school than measures of achievement can detect. The social statuses open to students, the kinds of jobs they will hold, the incomes they can expect, their mental health, their marriage and family life, and their social attitudes and values are all affected by their school experiences. These outcomes may be termed the social impact of education.[24]

In the mid-sixties, a group of elementary educators prepared a list of broad curriculum areas with detailed behavioral goals which elementary schools seek to accomplish.[25] The areas they included in the paper were: (1) physical development, health, body care; (2) individual, social, and emotional development; (3) ethical behavior standards, values; (4) social relations; (5) the social world; (6) the physical world; (7) aesthetic development; (8) communication; and (9) quantitative relationships. A study of these goals would be helpful in discovering what the schools are doing to meet social needs and to influence children.

The outstanding problem in public education is teaching moral and spiritual values. In many cases, the teacher serves as a substitute parent, especially for younger children. Many teachers have high moral standards and are eager to provide the best education for their children. On the other hand, some teachers have godless and humanistic philosophies of education which undermine the ideals and teachings of the Christian home. We recognize the need for separation of church and state, but Christian parents and leaders must assume the responsibility of spiritual teaching. It may be more appropriate for public educators not to teach moral and spiritual values, if biblical principles are so watered down that the Bible becomes nothing more than a great book of literature.

Some church bodies have set up their own Christian elementary schools and high schools at their own expense, in order to give a Christian dimension to all learning and to supply a basic sense of value to all subject areas. (See chap. 35, "The Role of the Christian School.")

THE COMMUNITY AS A SOCIAL INFLUENCE

The moral climate of the neighborhood and permissiveness or tyranny of parents have great effect on children. The influence of the peer group, espe-

---

24. Dorothy Westby-Gibson, *Social Perspectives on Education* (New York: Wiley, 1965), p. 357.
25. Ibid, pp. 97-98.

cially in preteen and adolescent years, cannot be overestimated. A group of delinquents can demoralize a whole neighborhood. The failure of certain housing projects in city slums is directly traceable to the mores of the occupants. This situation is a challenge to the community and has reemphasized the social and welfare ministries of the churches, often ill equipped to deal effectively with the community situation.

Though thousands of children are raised in city slums, ghettos, or rural poverty areas, the vast majority of America's youngsters enjoy the benefits of affluence. Fine homes furnished with the latest gadgets, conveniences, and luxuries—taken for granted by most of today's boys and girls—can corrode children's sensitivity to spiritual interests.

The inner city child is one of the most neglected. His parents lack education and finances to improve their standard of living. Mediocre schools often hinder the educational process. Irregular attendance, poor home conditions, and indifferent parents add frustration to the situation.

> There is a culture of poverty in the United States that is complex and self-propagating. The children of the poor grow up in squalor and filth. They are inadequately nourished, poorly clothed, and often lack adequate parental supervision. They attend inferior schools for a few years, and, under severe economic pressure, drop out as soon as they can. Lacking training, experience, and incentive, they either remain jobless or move from one casual job to another at the lowest pay. Marrying at an early age, they bring up an unrestricted number of children in the same kind of hopeless, deprived life. They may earn enough to provide some sort of food and shelter during their middle years, but in sickness and old age they fall back on relief or charity.[26]

Many inner city children learn to lie, steal, cheat, hate, and shift for themselves. They may feel they have received unfair treatment and may become rebellious toward society, and particularly toward those who have been more successful in material gain.

Some inner city children rise above their circumstances, but many continue to become more entangled and dependent on society. Family counseling services, welfare, and civic groups seek to meet needs, but the struggle for success is overwhelming.

Environmental changes are not sufficient to bring lasting results. Some evangelical groups have done social work in the inner city, but progress is slow and often discouraging. The answer is more than reformation from without. Until a person finds a new way of life in Christ through the gospel, little can be done of lasting value. Through genuine love and concern in practical ways, we

26. Maxwell S. Stewart, *The Poor Among Us—Challenge and Opportunity* (New York: Public Affairs Pamphlets, No. 362, 1964), p. 6.

can show we care, with the ultimate goal being to bring people to Christ as Savior and to give them purpose for living.

OTHER SOCIAL AND CULTURAL INFLUENCES AFFECTING CHILDREN

To reach children effectively in today's society, we need to assess the world in which our generation lives—a world vastly different from apostolic times, the European culture of the middle ages, or even the frontiers of colonial America. A number of social factors that are part of that world greatly affect the way children today live.

URBANIZATION

Thousands of people in past decades have moved from rural to suburban or metropolitan areas. Because there are so many large cities and sprawling suburbs, most youngsters in today's society are urban rather than rural children. The way of life for rural families has changed drastically because of modernization in almost every area of life. Most Americans live in a dozen great metropolitan areas, and it is predicted that 80 percent of us will live in cities by the year 2000.

MOBILITY

It is estimated that at least one in five American families moves each year. Families are uprooted from their homes, jobs, schools, and communities to orient themselves to a new way of life. Children are probably affected more than any other group. Mobility has increased through rapid transportation. The automobile has given us freedom to go almost anywhere we like. The whole world and its way of life is open to us and our children. Many boys and girls have traveled thousands of miles with their parents on family vacations. Job transfers to other cities give families a wider experience with more places and people, and children establish many new, fine relationships. Unfortunately, though, many children become insecure, fearful, and over-anxious as they attempt to adjust to new surroundings, especially in school and in unfamiliar situations. Parents and teachers need to prepare children to make adjustments smoothly from one situation to another.

MASS MEDIA

Newspapers, periodicals, radio, television, including telecasts from Telstar satellites, and a superabundance of literature have made the world one great neighborhood. Entertainment, once expensive and limited, now streams even into the homes of the poor via radio, television, and video tape. Children have the whole wide world in their living rooms. They can get immediate reports on world happenings each day. Social, political, scientific, cultural, and religious happenings add to the vast field of knowledge confronting our children.

TELEVISION

Television has affected children both negatively and positively, according to many research studies. Children learn to be more aggressive and can also practice prosocial behavior through effective role modeling.[27] Unfortunately, the negative effects have been more obvious. Acts of violence, sex, low moral standards, alcoholic beverages, crime, abortion, and drugs have polluted TV.

From a positive viewpoint, some television programs have expanded the child's world. Children can visit almost any part of the world vicariously through television. News broadcasts can be informative and helpful in teaching children about current events. People, places, and things can come alive through TV.

However, television can be desensitizing, demoralizing, and harmful to children. "Preschoolers are the single largest TV audience in America. They spend one-third of their waking hours watching television. In a recent study, 40 percent of four-through-six-year-olds preferred television to fathers."[28]

Preschoolers and school age children cannot help but be influenced in their behavior and moral standards when they watch TV several hours a day. Children can become calloused to crime and sin. They accept low moral standards emulated by role models as "the way things ought to be." Many of the cartoons on television are damaging to young minds.

The Saturday morning cartoons are filled with violence and sex.

> The value systems they teach our children are totally alien to those taught by Jesus Christ. Kids learn nothing about *love your enemy* or *forgiveness.*
>
> Radicki (chairman of the National Coalition on Television Violence) said that twenty-seven of twenty-nine recent studies revealed that cartoons had a detrimental effect on children. One startling finding was that there seems to be little difference in the impact between cartoons, filmed drama, and real life. Young children don't differentiate between what is real life and what is make-believe.[29]

The game Dungeons and Dragons®, for instance, dwells on evil and satanic influences and uses scriptural concepts to carry out mystical, demonic objectives in the supernatural world.

Even so-called family entertainment programs subtly break down the family unit and teach children to disrespect authority and develop life-styles that are contrary to biblical precepts. Many parents are naive as to the effects of TV on

27. Craig, pp. 272-75.
28. C. Sybil Waldrop, *Teaching Preschoolers* (Nashville: Convention), pp. 50-51.
29. "Saturday Morning TV . . . the Devil's Playground," *The Evangelist* (January 1985), p. 26.

their children. Children grow up to be passive listeners and are brainwashed through continual TV viewing. Family togetherness is certainly not encouraged or strengthened. Parents can do much to combat these trends by being effective models—by viewing TV with their children and speaking out against what is contrary to their values, by selecting appropriate programs, and by turning off the TV if the programs are inappropriate. As they read the TV guide, it will not take long for parents to decide which programs are acceptable!

SEX

The American emphasis on sex is described by Crook in this way:

> In recent decades Americans have exploited sex in such a way as to cheapen it and rob it of its real meaning. It is the dominant element in most of our movies and TV shows, our novels and even our jokes. It is used in advertising everything from cosmetics to bulldozers. It has been glamorized by all kinds of artificial adornment . . . Sex is virtually deified, and the beauty queen is its high priestess.[30]

Sex has become a commonplace word in the home, mass media, and in the community. No matter where one goes, sex is a much discussed subject. Unfortunately, many people do not have a wholesome view of sex because of the distorted context in which it is placed. Children need to be taught early in life the biblical meaning of sex, and this teaching should take place in the natural environment of the home.

To counteract the exploitation of sex common in American life today, a wholesome sex education program is needed. Parents are key participants, with the church and school having supplementary roles. Sex education must be taught with the proper spiritual and moral emphases as well as the biological. Parents are in the best position to teach their children the biblical meaning of sex in relation to the whole of life.

DRUG ABUSE

Drug abuse is a continuing and increasingly complex problem in our society. Parents are frightened with stories and reports of the results of their misuse. Drug usage ranges from glue sniffing and marijuana smoking to the use of narcotics, amphetamines, and barbiturates. The number of drug abusers among middle and wealthy classes is rapidly climbing, and the age of abusers is dropping. "It has been estimated that more than 24 million people have smoked marijuana at least once and 8.5 million are full-time users. At the

30. Crook, p. 75.

moment, marijuana use is largely a teen-age and young adult phenomenon."[31] However, some children may be affected by the use of the drug through peer pressure, lack of parental supervision, and a desire to experiment. The effects of the use of drugs can be extremely damaging, as described by Dr. James Dobson:

> There is no more certain destroyer of self-discipline and self-control than the abusive use of drugs. The teen-ager who has begun taking narcotics often shows a sudden disinterest in everything that formerly challenged him. His school work is ignored and his hobbies are forgotten. His personal appearance becomes sloppy and dirty. He refuses to carry responsibility and he avoids the activities that would cause him to expend effort. His relationship with his parents deteriorates rapidly and he suddenly terminates many of his lifelong friendships. The young drug user is clearly marching to a new set of drums—and disaster often awaits him at the end of the trail.[32]

Parts of the body, such as the heart, brain, and eyes, may be damaged by drug abuse. Thought processes and speech habits may be weakened. Emotional depression or imbalance, loss of memory, fear, and recurrence of horrifying experiences, physical exhaustion, personality disorders, mental derangement, and even death may occur. It is evident that those who are drug users have distorted values, are incapable of coping with life, and try to escape reality.

> The drug abuse tragedy occurs at all levels of society; no child is immune to the threat—neither yours nor mine. Every parent must inform himself of the facts regarding drug abuse. We should be able to recognize its symptoms and stand prepared to guide our children should the need arise.[33]

The road to rehabilitation is slow and many times ineffective, depending on the extent and use of drugs. The best treatment is prevention through a drug education program in which children are warned about drugs, their dangers, and effects.

MISSING CHILDREN AND CHILD PORNOGRAPHY

Even though many children are blessed with material goods and have educational opportunities far above other countries of the world, the statistics concerning missing children, sexual child abuse, and child pornography are staggering.

More than 1,000,000 missing children each year are reported, many as

---

31. Craig, p. 380, 382.
32. James Dobson, *Dare to Discipline* (Wheaton, Ill.: Tyndale, 1970), p. 190.
33. Ibid, pp. 193-94.

runaways. Some have been abducted and used for pornographic magazines and illicit practices. Children are used for explicit sex purposes such as child prostitution and homosexuality. The Department of Justice estimates there are over 600,000 child prostitutes in the United States. Many missing children are abused and murdered. Over 50,000 children disappear each year, and their cases remain unsolved. Another 150,000 children are abducted by the noncustodial parent each year.[34]

Many concerned parents and citizens have formed action groups to deal with the problems of missing children and child pornography. National centers and hot-lines have been set up to assist in finding missing children. Television networks, supermarkets, dairy and other commercial establishments have printed literature with pictures and information about missing children. Some children have been found as a result. Child safety tips have been shared wtih parents and teachers. Even though we as Christian parents and teachers believe that "God will take care of and protect us," we also need to be alert to human nature, the wiles of the devil, and evil influences. Certainly we can pray as we never have before for the safekeeping of our children in the midst of "a crooked and perverse nation."

CHILD ABUSE

Child abuse is rising in epidemic proportions each year. Statistics indicate that 1.5 to 2 million children are abused annually. Children in middle and upper class homes are abused as well as children from lower socioeconomic levels. Many of the cases in the middle or upper income levels are never reported. A hard fact in research is that children who are abused come from homes where parents themselves were abused as children. Some theorists say child abuse is caused by the personalities of the parents. Others are convinced that the sociological conditions such as being poor, living in overcrowded conditions, and unemployment cause child abuse. Some psychologists believe that the social situation involving interaction patterns of family members cause children to be abused.[35]

Although there are no simple explanations for child abuse, some contributing factors are inconsistent discipline, uncertain marital roles of husband and wife, the parents' belief that abuse builds the child's character, and parental inadequacies or failures which are blamed on the child. Some children become the brunt of abuse because the child is handicapped, unlovely or homely, unwanted, or has some traits that are undesirable.

Some parents who believe in biblical principles of discipline have misinterpreted and misapplied the Scriptures and have abused their children by beating

34. Cultural Information Service (CIStems, Inc., 1985), p. 2.
35. Craig, pp. 279-83.

them with a rod. The verses in Proverbs that speak of the rod are addressed to rebellious teenagers who were willfully disobedient.

DIVORCE AND SINGLE PARENTS

Although the statistics on divorce vary greatly, we know divorce is on the increase, and consequently many children are left to live with single parents or stepparents. Twelve million children have parents who are divorced. Forty-five percent of children will live with only one parent before the age of 18.[36]

Divorce creates problems of adjustment for adults, but the effects are felt to a far greater extent by the children. Many children grow up with tremendous insecurities, fears, emotional trauma, and irreparable damage that may hinder their total personality development the remainder of their lives.

A child needs support during and after a divorce because he or she may carry awesome guilt. Children tend to blame themselves for the divorce. Parents will need to spend quality time with the children individually to reassure that they are loved in spite of what has happened and that they are not at fault.

Although we may not be able to salvage some marriages, we must be alert to the fact that unless God is at the center of every marriage, there is a possibility that the marriage could break up. Because we are living in a world filled with selfishness, hatred, and turmoil, we must strengthen our faith in God and His Son Jesus Christ to rise above our circumstances and to trust Him to see us through each circumstance in life!

With the disintegration of families (including Christian families) so common, we must do whatever we can to strengthen marriage and family relationships. We must model a biblical concept of marriage; lay foundations very early in life; teach our children biblical concepts and content at their levels of understanding; integrate personal applications with familiar everyday experiences; be good role models in daily life; take our children to church, making the experience a happy and meaningful one; lay precept upon precept as indicated in Isaiah 28:10; and encourage our children to choose friends who provide a positive influence in their lives.

LATCH-KEY CHILDREN

Another problem we are facing in our society as more mothers work outside the home is that of children being left on their own to come home after school to wait for the parents to return from work. Millions of children come home to an empty house every day with no adult supervision for several hours. Children are forced to grow up too soon, are exposed to physical dangers, may experiment with drugs and sex, and could encounter other problems. Many

36. Ibid, p. 278.

children who come home are lonely and fearful and are not old enough to take care of themselves. Some children like to be independent and on their own, especially to be free of babysitters, but these children still need adult supervision.

Many mothers also worry about their children and wonder if they are neglecting them. A mother may have chosen not to have a babysitter because her children do not like their babysitters and think they are too tied down when a babysitter stays with them. But if emergencies arise, to whom do the children turn? What about the children letting other people into the house without adult supervision? Are children safe from child abduction, sexual molestation, and abuse when their parents are gone? How long should children watch TV?

Some families cannot afford to hire babysitters or cannot find competent ones. However, children should not be left unsupervised for long periods of time. Even with an older teen who is more of a companion than a sitter, children may not feel as lonely, fearful, or insecure. Parents need to think about these matters and be concerned that their children are properly cared for. Older children should be able to manage for a short period of time if there is a warm, supportive family relationship, a safe neighborhood, and an adult contact in case of emergency. They need some independence but also adequate supervision as they are developing.[37]

HURRIED CHILDREN

David Elkind in his book *The Hurried Child*[38] emphasizes that children today live under great pressure to grow up too rapidly. Parents put pressure on children scholastically. The mass media, particularly television, imply it is no longer appropriate to be a child. There seems to be a new attitude that says the years of childhood are not to be frittered away by engaging in activities merely for fun. Yet feelings and emotions have their own time schedule and cannot be hurried. A child's behavior and appearance may speak "adult," but their feelings still cry "child."

Certainly we need to give children time to be children. They need time to enjoy and appreciate childhood as a distinct phase or time in life. It is unfair to hurry them through childhood. After all, what is the big rush? They will become adults soon enough in God's own timing. God created the life span the way He did to give people time to develop as human beings so they could receive the maximum benefit from each period or stage of life. As Christian teachers and parents we need to avoid pressuring children and bringing stress in their lives as a result of hurrying them into adolescence and adulthood!

37. Eleanor Berman, "Mommy, I'm Old Enough to Stay Alone—But Is She?" *Working Mother* (September 1984), pp. 84-88.
38. David Elkind, *The Hurried Child* (Reading, Mass.: Wesley Publishing Co., 1981).

SUMMARY

In many ways, children are the same today as children of the past. They are also different. Eldor Kaiser has pointed out some interesting similarities and differences:

> Children are one of the few common denominators in the world. They are much the same from the Orient to Iceland and from the days of Socrates to today. They like to learn. They struggle with growing up, with liking themselves, and they need love from "significant persons." They sin. They need forgiveness. And they believe with a direct and simple faith.

> Kids today are different. They are less submissive and more restless. Rather than work in class, they expect to be entertained. Nothing is new to them and they quickly become bored and apathetic. What they need is a firm adult hand and stricter discipline. Kids question everything and accept nothing as "truth," not even the Bible.

> Kids are all the same. They need love; they need forgiveness; they need to be assured that there is a loving God who holds this crazy, changing universe together.

> Kids are different. No two are alike. What gets through to one doesn't work with the next. Today's kids are different from yesterday's kids—and tomorrow's.[39]

FOR FURTHER READING

Barclay, William. *Train Up a Child.* Philadelphia: Westminster, 1959.

Carlson, Carole. *Established in Eden.* Old Tappan, N.J.: Revell, 1978.

Carter, Velma, and J. Lynn Leavenworth. *Caught in the Middle: Children of Divorce.* Valley Forge, Pa.: Judson, 1985.

Christenson, Larry. *The Christian Family.* Minneapolis: Bethany Fellowship, 1970.

Collins, Gary, ed. *Facing the Future.* Waco, Tex.: Word Books, 1976.

Craig, Grace. *Human Development.* 3d ed. Englewood Cliffs, N.J.: Prentice-Hall, 1983.

Dobson, James. *Dare to Discipline.* Wheaton, Ill.: Tyndale, 1970.

———. *Hide or Seek.* Old Tappan, N.J.: Revell, 1974.

Duvall, Evelyn Millis. *Evelyn Duvall's Handbook for Parents.* Nashville: Broadman, 1974.

Feucht, Oscar, ed. *Family Relationships and the Church.* Rev. ed. St. Louis: Concordia, 1970.

39. Kaiser, pp. 13, 18.

————. *Helping Families Through the Church.* Rev. ed. St. Louis: Concordia, 1971.

Gangel, Kenneth. *The Family First.* Minneapolis: His International Service, 1972.

Getz, Gene. *The Measure of a Family.* Ventura, Calif.: Gospel Light, Regal, 1976.

————. *The Measure of a Marriage.* Ventura, Calif.: Gospel Light, Regal, 1980.

Graendorf, Werner, ed. *Introduction to Biblical Christian Education.* Chicago: Moody, 1981.

Grant, Wayne. *Growing Parents, Growing Children.* Nashville: Convention, 1977.

Grunlan, Stephen. *Marriage and the Family: A Christian Perspective.* Grand Rapids: Zondervan, 1984.

Harvey, Adell. *My Cope Runneth Over.* Nashville: Thomas Nelson, 1984.

Herr, Ethel. *Schools: How Parents Can Make a Difference.* Chicago: Moody, 1981.

Herron, Orley. *Who Controls Your Child?* Nashville: Thomas Nelson, 1980.

Heusser, D-B, and Phyllis Heusser. *Children as Partners in the Church.* Valley Forge, Pa.: Judson, 1985.

Kesler, Jay. *Family Forum.* Wheaton, Ill.: Scripture Press, Victor Books, 1984.

LaHaye, Tim. *The Battle for the Family.* Old Tappan, N.J.: Revell, 1982.

————. *The Battle for the Public Schools.* Old Tappan, N.J.: Revell, 1983.

Logan, Ben, ed. *Television Awareness Training: The Viewer's Guide for Family.* Nashville, Tenn.: Abingdon, 1980.

May, Edward W. *Christian Family Living.* St. Louis: Concordia, 1970.

May, Philip. *Which Way to Educate.* Chicago: Moody, 1972.

MacDonald, Gordon. *Magnificent Marriage.* Wheaton, Ill.: Tyndale, 1976.

MacArthur, John. *The Family.* Chicago: Moody, 1982.

McDonald, Cleveland. *Creating a Successful Christian Marriage.* Grand Rapids: Baker, 1975.

Moore, Raymond and Dorothy. *Home Grown Kids: A Practical Handbook for Teaching Your Children at Home.* Waco, Tex.: Word, 1984.

————. *Home-Spun Schools.* Waco, Tex.: Word, 1982.

Payntner, David. *Must Our Schools Die?* Portland, Ore.: Multnomah, 1981.

Peterson, J. Allen, ed. *The Marriage Affair.* Wheaton, Ill.: Tyndale, 1971.

Phillips, Carolyn. *Our Family Got a Divorce.* Ventura, Calif.: Gospel Light, Regal, 1979.

Rickerson, Wayne. *How to Help the Christian Home.* Ventura, Calif.: Gospel Light, Regal, 1978.

Schaeffer, Edith. *What Is a Family?* Old Tappan, N.J.: Fleming H. Revell, 1975.

Sell, Charles M. *Family Ministry: The Enrichment of Family Life Through the Church.* Grand Rapids: Zondervan, 1981.

Skoglund, Elizabeth. *Your Troubled Children.* Elgin, Ill.: David C. Cook, 1974.

Vigeveno, H. S., and Anne Claire. *Divorce and the Children.* Ventura, Calif.: Gospel Light, Regal, 1979.

Wright, Norman H. *Characteristics of a Caring Home.* Santa Ana, Calif.: Vision House, 1978.

Zuck, Roy B., and Gene A. Getz, eds. *Ventures in Family Living.* Chicago: Moody, 1971.

PERIODICALS

Childhood Education. Association for Childhood Education International, 3615 Wisconsin Ave., N.W., Washington, DC 20016.

Children. U.S. Children's Bureau, Superintendent of Documents, U.S. Government Printing Office, Washington, DC 20025.

Children Today. Children's Bureau, Office of Child Development. U.S. Department of Health, Education, and Welfare, P. O. Box 1182, Washington, DC 20402.

Nation's Schools. McGraw-Hill, Inc., 230 West Monroe, Chicago, IL 60606.

Teacher. CCM Professional Magazines, Inc., 22 West Putnam Avenue, Greenwich, CN 06830.

Today's Child. Edwards Publications, Inc., School Lane, Roosevelt, NJ 08555.

Youthletter, P.O. Box 1132, Dover, NJ 07801

Family Life Today, Box 1971, Marion, OH 43306

Focus on the Family, Box 500, Arcadia, CA 91006

SOURCES FOR INFORMATION

American Association for Childhood Education International, 3615 Wisconsin Avenue, N.W., Washington, DC 20016.

Bureau of Publications, Teachers College, Columbia University, New York, NY 10027.

Children's Bureau, U.S. Department of Health, Education, and Welfare, Washington, DC 20025.

Child Protection Task Force, 305 Sixth Street, Lynchburg, VA 24504.

Child Study Association of America, 9 East 89th Street, New York, NY 10028.

Child Welfare League of America, Inc., 67 Irving Place, New York, NY 10003.

CIStems, Inc. Cultural Information Service, P.O. Box 786, Madison Square Station, New York, NY 10159.

Family Concern, 360 Main Place, Carol Stream, IL 60189.

Focus on the Family, Box 500, Arcadia, CA 91006.

National Center for Missing and Exploited Children, 1835 K Street N.W., Suite 700, Washington, DC 20006.

Parents' Magazine Educational Enterprises, 52 Vanderbilt Avenue, New York, NY 10017.

Public Affairs Pamphlets, Public Affairs Committee, Inc., 381 Park Avenue South, New York, NY 10016.

Superintendent of Documents, U.S. Government Printing Office, Washington, DC 20402.

Part 2

Understanding the Developmental
Stages of Children

3

Mary L. Hammack

Personality Development of Children

- **Influences on Personality**
  HEREDITY
  PRENATAL AND CONGENITAL FACTORS
  ENVIRONMENT
- **Aspects of Personality**
  PHYSICAL
  MENTAL
  EMOTIONAL
  SOCIAL
  SPIRITUAL
- **The Child's Self-Concept**
- **Stress in Children**

All who work with children in the church are involved in a divine program of helping shape young lives. This makes it imperative that those leaders understand how the personalities of children develop. Scripture makes it very evident that our Lord is concerned about each person as an individual, unique from any other individual. Likewise, the teacher must know the personality and characteristics of each student if teaching and counseling are to be individualized to meet specific needs.

Mary L. Hammack, Ed.D., formerly associate professor of Education, Seattle Pacific University, Seattle, Washington, does research and free-lance writing.

Authorities differ in their theories and definitions of personality. To the sociologist, personality is the expression of one's culture; to the scientist and those concerned with medicine, personality is a part of one's physiological and constitutional makeup. The psychologist, on the other hand, emphasizes the behavioral aspects of personality.

In this chapter, *personality* refers to those combined characteristics that make a person unique and different from all other individuals. This includes not only spiritual characteristics but also physical, mental, emotional, and social attributes, as well as congenital and environmental influences.

Though some authors believe that personality development begins at birth, others point out that some characteristics tend to be inherited and that prenatal conditions may affect one's development later. According to this view, personality development begins at the time of conception.

The development of a child's personality cannot be isolated from the influence of environmental, social, hereditary, and motivational backgrounds. Each teacher has the responsibility and challenge to minister primarily to the spiritual needs of each individual. That can be done only in proportion to the amount known about each child, and the love and understanding of the teacher as he prays for spiritual wisdom in meeting evident needs.

Needs are determinants of behavior. The sensitive teacher soon becomes keenly aware of deeper needs, perhaps unrecognized by parents or children. Occasional visits to the students' homes provide insights gleaned in no other way. The wise teacher considers each child an individual case study, unique and challenging.

Teachers should also be aware of children's universal needs that the church can help meet. Those include love, security, sense of belonging, significance, recognition, and interrelated influences.[1] In the church's educational program, teachers can express and exhibit God's love to the child. In Christ, the child can find security. In the fellowship of the church, there is found a sense of belonging. In pleasing Jesus and in serving others, the child can give love, find self-esteem and recognition.

If a child's spiritual needs are being met, many other personal needs will be cared for automatically. Learning in the church must be supernaturally motivated, as all workers pray for the children with whom they work.

---

1. Abraham Maslow's well-known "hierarchy of needs" includes the following, in ascending order of importance: physiological needs (air, water, food, shelter, sleep, sex); safety and security needs (physical and psychological); affiliation needs (love and belongingness); esteem needs (self-esteem and esteem by others); and self-actualization. The latter includes these "growth needs" (which are of equal importance, not hierarchical): meaningfulness, self-sufficiency, effortlessness, playfulness, richness, simplicity, order, justice, completion, necessity, perfection, individuality, aliveness, beauty, goodness, and truth. See Frank G. Goble, *The Third Force: The Psychology of Abraham Maslow* (New York: Grossman, 1970), p. 50, and Abraham H. Maslow, *Motivation and Personality*, 2d ed. (New York: Harper & Row, 1970) pp. 35-51.

The local church is in a unique position to provide opportunity to reach children with the gospel, and thereby to initiate Christian influences affecting the continuing process of personality development. Psalm 32:8, Colossians 3:16, and many other Scriptures concerned with teaching the Word of God give ample incentive to keep this concern uppermost in educational programming.

INFLUENCES ON PERSONALITY

Most child specialists agree that the following factors influence the development of children's personalities.

HEREDITY

A number of inherited traits definitely influence personality. Most obvious among these are certain physical resemblances to parents or relatives, such as the color of eyes, hair, complexion, and one's size. Many scientists feel that certain physical conditions related to health are also transmitted genetically. Some children will accept their inherited traits without concern or desire to change them. Other children may resent the fact that they resemble their parents, brothers and sisters, or other relatives.

Teachers and counselors in the church should be well aware of these concerns and the attitudes of children about them. Prayer is needed for and with each child for acceptance of the inherited characteristics as from the Lord. Counselors may also work with parents in helping them to instill a Christian attitude in children regarding their inherited characteristics. Thus, inherited characteristics affect the child's self-concept and the continued development of personality. Cooperation is needed by parents and relatives in order to help instill a healthy attitude in children toward their hereditary traits, desirable or undesirable.

PRENATAL AND CONGENITAL FACTORS

Various prenatal and congenital factors also contribute to an individual's personality development. A mother's physical condition during pregnancy can bring about in her child endocrine imbalance, dietary deficiencies, and poor health. Nervous instability and a number of childhood abnormalities may result from serious health problems of a mother during pregnancy. At the time the vital organs of the unborn are being formed, some infectious diseases experienced by the mother may affect her child. Deafness, blindness, malformations, and similar disorders may be the result.

In addition, it is known that a well child will have less difficulty adjusting to a normal childhood than a sick child.

Childhood diseases, accidents, and various difficulties, such as allergies, diet, rest schedules, and the like, contribute to attitudes, an important phase of personality development. How these attitudes are accepted by those working with children in the church have positive or negative effects in personality development.

As teachers and counselors better understand some of these conditions, they will be more capable of helping children who are affected unfavorably by prenatal factors. These children need special help in becoming adjusted. They need Christian love and genuine concern from their parents and other teachers.

ENVIRONMENT

The personality development of a child is certainly influenced by environment and conditions affecting daily life. Personality is affected by the way the child is treated by parents and others in the immediate environment. The attitudes of parents and those who care for children make a deep impression on the formation of personality and self-concept.

A child's position in the family constellation also affects character. The youngest child differs from the oldest; an only child differs from a middle child. Dinkmeyer and Dreikurs give this explanation:

> The competition between siblings leads to fundamental personality differences. Frequently as a result of competition, where one succeeds, the other becomes discouraged and gives up; or where one fails, the other moves in. In contrast, alliances between siblings are often expressed in similarity of interests, character traits, and temperament.[2]

Churches must reach out to children from every economic level, regardless of race, color, or a multitude of environmental changes. *All* need to be brought to Christ. However, as children from such varied backgrounds are brought together and many individual needs known, the wise teacher will show equal love and understanding for each child. Realizing that these children are innocent victims of their background and environmental circumstances, special care and patience are essential. How these children are treated in the church will leave a lasting impression on their personalities and on their attitude toward the church, perhaps throughout their lifetime.

Several longitudinal research studies indicate that many personality traits are established early and remain quiet persistent throughout life. Results of research done by the Institute of Human Development of the University of California at Berkeley "probably offer the richest collection of data ever assembled on human beings over a long period."[3] Included in "The Guidance Study"

---

2. Don Dinkmeyer and Rudolf Dreikurs, *Encouraging Children to Learn: The Encouragement Process* (Englewood Cliffs, N.J.: Prentice-Hall, 1963), p. 21.
3. *The Mental Health of the Child* (Rockville, Md.: Public Health Service Publication, No. 2168, 1971), p. 131.

were 252 children born in Berkeley over an eighteen-month period. They were observed for eighteen years.

> The children were weighed, measured, tested, interviewed, and observed at various times through their eighteenth year. Special attention was given to their life at home during the preschool years. Information about them was obtained also from their parents, brothers and sisters, teachers, and classmates. At 30, when they were rearing children of their own, 167 of them were studied again.[4]

This report was supported by and later published by the National Institute of Mental Health. The outcome of these studies in relation to personality development was summarized in this way:

> The child who at five was either reserved and shy or expressive and gay tended to show the same characteristics at 16. The child who was either reactive and explosive or calm and phlegmatic at five was likely to be the same at 16.
>
> The speed of development during childhood, which presumably is determined by both genetic and environmental factors, seems to influence personality characteristics into adulthood. The early talkers (generally those who had received more than the usual amount of parental attention during infancy) were more introspective as adults, perhaps because language rather than action had always been for them the favored response pattern.[5]

The evidence is clear that many personality traits formed in early childhood do follow through for many years. This is confirmed by Maslow's statement: "People who have been made secure and strong in the early years, tend to remain secure and strong thereafter in the face of whatever threatens."[6] This should challenge children's workers in the church to provide Christian experiences that will have deep and lasting impressions on children. These may be offered through the Sunday school, vacation Bible school, the church camping program, youth activities, and various other organizations in the church.

However, each child is more than the production of heredity, prenatal and congenital influences, and environment. Dinkmeyer and Dreikurs explain that a child's "subjective interpretation of all that goes on both within him and around him gives meaning to his actions. The child can take a stand towards what he experiences; he has the ability to interpret and to draw conclusions."[7] They also point out that from a child's contacts with his parents and eventually with others, he "reaches certain generalizations about people and how one deals with them."[8]

4. Ibid.
5. Ibid., p. 134.
6. Abraham H. Maslow, *Motivation and Personality* (New York: Harper & Row, 1954), p. 44.
7. Dinkmeyer and Dreikurs, p. 19.
8. Ibid.

ASPECTS OF PERSONALITY

Specific areas of personalized needs definitely influence a child's personality. Because these are discussed more specifically and chronologically in chapters 5-10, these areas are used here only to point out some of the overall needs, regardless of age, which directly affect the development of children's personalities.

PHYSICAL

The rate of physical growth and development of a child certainly affects self-concept and attitudes. If the child is unusually large or small for that age, if unusually active or inactive, or if there are other deviations from whatever is considered "normal" by the parents, the child's personality will be adversely affected. However, if about the same growth and development characteristics are evident according to other children of that age, there seems to be a positive effect on personality, because self-acceptance is more likely. Very young children soon become aware of whether they are different from other children, and certainly the attitudes of their parents and peers toward them affect their personalities, often permanently. The attitude of Christians about these matters will make a lasting influence.

Consideration should be given in the church to the child who is physically disabled and thus faces a pattern of physical growth different from others. The physically disabled include the crippled, blind, deaf, and others. The attitude physically disabled children have toward themselves and the attitudes others have toward them affect the way personality develops. Some churches plan special activities for physically disabled children, including camping and sports. However, care should be taken that these children are accepted by their peers and treated on an equal basis. Most healthy disabled children want to be treated as other children and not separated or favored because of their disability. How much can be done along this line depends on the types of physical handicaps among children in the church and the number of such children.

Planned activities for physically disabled children can be the means of reaching unchurched children and their parents. For example, a ramp to a side door of the church can encourage children in wheelchairs to attend Sunday school, whereas they might otherwise hesitate to attend. Crippled children are delighted to be included and provided for. Sensing a church's concern for children in need can be an excellent learning situation for the other children in the church. (For more information, see chap. 11, "Teaching Exceptional Children.")

MENTAL

The development of personality is directly related to mental health. A child develops certain attitudes—positive or negative—toward self, family, friends, teachers, and the church.

Personality is correlated with intelligence, at least in the case of boys. Adolescent boys with high I.Q.'s were generally described as friendly, social, and independent—as they had been since the age of four.[9]

Intelligence is a factor contributing to a child's interests, attitudes, and reasoning ability. Most small children are capable of learning more than is often expected of them, although their attention span is short, and they have limited concepts of numbers, time, and space. An experienced teacher quickly senses whether a child is able to comprehend the teachings offered in the church. The intelligence level of the students certainly should affect the manner in which one presents the truths of the Scriptures.

Children need and usually welcome intellectual stimulation and challenge. Maya Pines claims that "millions of children are being irreparably damaged by our failure to stimulate them intellectually during their crucial years—from birth to six."[10]

Jean Piaget, the well-known Swiss psychologist who researched the intellectual development of children for several decades, indicated that children in intellectually stimulating environments advance more rapidly than others. "His theories also explained why environments that restrict children's opportunities to explore, to test their own hypotheses, to have their questions answered and other questions raised, would retard their development."[11] (Piaget's views are discussed further in chaps. 4 and 20.)

Intellectual interests of children at various growth stages should be carefully considered in planning the educational program of the church. Interests reflect personality, and that makes each child unique and a real challenge to every teacher.

The mental development of a child is also greatly affected by vicarious learning experiences. Perhaps the most common are television programs and the general attitude of his parents toward the ones he is permitted to see. The planned curriculum of the church may substitute various meaningful activities to permit child participation and thereby successfully compete for experiences in mental growth and development.

Research also indicates that a "bibliotherapy" (therapy through reading) is a positive influence on social and personal development of young children, especially second graders.[12] Thus it is important that the church be able to

9. *The Mental Health of the Child*, p. 134.
10. Maya Pines, *Revolution in Learning: The Years from Birth to Six* (New York: Harper & Row, 1967), p. 15.
11. Ibid., p. 59. See also these books on or by Piaget: Millie C. Almy, *Young Children's Thinking: Studies of Some Aspects of Piaget's Theory* (New York: Columbia U., Teacher's College Press, 1966); J. McV. Hunt, *Intelligence and Experience* (New York: Ronald, 1961); Jean Piaget, *The Origins of Intelligence in Children* (New York: International Universities, 1952); and Jean Piaget, *The Psychology of Intelligence* (Paterson, N.J.: Littlefield, Adams, 1963).
12. Phyllis Disturce, "The Effect of Bibliotherapy on Personal Development of Second Graders," ED 243099 (master's thesis, Kean College, 1984).

offer books and other literature, for older children especially, that teach Christian concepts and attitudes.

A growing number of churches are recognizing the need to minister to mentally handicapped children. Some churches have found this to be a rewarding experience that has served a number of otherwise unchurched families. (See chap. 12, "Teaching Intellectually Impaired Children," for more on this.)

EMOTIONAL

The love or lack of love shown to an infant by parents indelibly influences his personality. Behavioral psychologists, such as B. F. Skinner, teach that the need for love is an acquired or learned need, whereas other psychologists believe that the love need is innate. The latter seems to be supported by clinical experiments that demonstrate that institutionalized children show psychopathological symptoms when they are not loved, even though all other physiological needs are well satisfied. Montague writes:

> Studies of infants who lived their early lives in hospitals or other institutions have shown that the baby requires much more than routine satisfaction of his physical wants. These children were fed and bathed and cared for in the soundest scientific way. But they lacked the warm personal attention—the cuddling, the carrying, the physical assurance of love—that a mother ordinarily gives her child. They lacked the feeling of support and encouragement, the feeling of being wanted. In short, they lacked love.
>
> Many of these children were found to be retarded even in their physical development. They failed to gain weight properly, they slept poorly, and they suffered longer from respiratory infections than babies who were receiving the personal attention of their mothers.
>
> Moreover, children who have lacked love during their early years very frequently developed emotional difficulties. As they grow up, they may be unsocial and hostile. They usually are insecure, filled with fear and anxiety. And in most cases they are themselves incapable of giving love.[13]

Along this line, Harris comments, "We do not learn to be loving if we have never been loved. If the first five years of life consist totally of a critical struggle for physical and psychological survival, this struggle is likely to persist throughout life."[14] Goble writes:

> In a group of young children, classified from fully accepted to fully rejected, it was found that the partially rejected children behaved in a way which demonstrated their frantic need for affection, but the children who were utterly rejected from

13. Ashley Montague, *Helping Children Develop Moral Values* (Chicago: Science Research Associates, 1953), p. 29.
14. Thomas A. Harris, *I'm OK—You're OK* (New York: Harper & Row, 1969), p. 103.

the earliest days of life exhibited not a tremendous desire for love, but a coldness and apparent lack of desire for affection.[15]

What a challenge this is to teachers in the church to demonstrate genuine love to children, even in those children's earliest years—and earliest months—of life.

The child soon learns that there are different kinds of "love" and ways of expressing it, even though an introduction to it is through the mother or through someone else who cares for the infant. As children hear God's Word, they learn that God is love. They learn also that teachers and others in the church express love for them. Later they learn there is also a love for one's country, neighbors, and even enemies, as well as for parents and friends. The scriptural teachings about love are many and may be applied as appropriate for the various age levels.

Individual personality is also affected by the emotions of others. Some teachers feel that certain emotional expressions are almost contagious because of the part that imitation plays in various circumstances. Children at almost every age tend to imitate others, including their emotional expressions. This is especially important in regard to the negative emotional expressions, such as fear and hate.

Because every individual is unique, each person will express emotions in a different way. If an individual's way is negative, then the teachings of the church, personal example, correction, and prayer can help alter these undesirable personality traits.

Children with aggressive behavior and children who are withdrawn are seeking in those ways to meet their emotional needs. Children with these "behavior disorders" need special attention from their teachers. Ways to handle and help children with these disorders are suggested in many books on child psychology.[16]

Certain behavioral maladjustments among children can be helped by careful planning and the help of Christian teachers. Some children from unchurched homes may display reaction to the church program in an unusual and sometimes undesirable way simply because of their background and lack of understanding. An increasing number of child abuse cases are being reported, and some of these children may come to the church for refuge. Church leaders must accept the challenge and opportunity to help all who need help in times of emotional crisis. Dedicated teachers and counselors need to share informa-

---

15. Frank G. Goble, *The Third Force: The Psychology of Abraham Maslow* (New York: Grossman, 1970), p. 75.
16. See, for example, Katherine E. D'Evelyn, *Meeting Children's Emotional Needs* (Englewood Cliffs, N.J.: Prentice-Hall, 1957), chaps. 7 and 8; and Alfred Adler, *The Problem Child* (New York: Capricorn, 1963).

tion about individual cases and pray for spiritual wisdom in treating children's needs.

Children's emotional needs become even more evident at times of illness and death in the family or during and after divorce. (Note entries in "For Further Reading" at the end of this chapter.) These circumstances leave lasting impressions on their personalities, but the church can come to their aid through trained counselors and teachers who can share the love of Christ.

SOCIAL

Many are the personality influences of social needs. Some children have not been taught to get along well with others. Some are selfish and cannot share toys in the church nursery, for example, without tears. Others are shy and hesitate to play with others their own age. Some prefer to play alongside others rather than with them.

Local churches can provide numerous opportunities for children to socialize in a Christian atmosphere and thereby make friends of lasting influence. Parents should have an active part in this, although providing for the social needs of children does not necessarily mean a round of parties. Sports events and various group activities, as well as contacts outside the church, may contribute to children's social needs. Christlike conduct should be dominant in these activities.

Carefully controlled activities for children in the church should encourage friendships that will have lasting influence on the impressionable personalities of the participants. Children's weekday Bible classes, held in homes, often provide excellent opportunity for sharing and becoming acquainted with those from other home situations.

SPIRITUAL

As human beings, children have more than physical, mental, emotional, and social needs. They also have spiritual needs and problems. How and when a child's spiritual needs are met can have a profound effect on the formation of character. Evangelicals believe that the Bible teaches the personality-transforming power of the gospel (2 Cor. 5:17), even among children. In addition, the sanctifying ministry of the Holy Spirit can produce great changes in one's inner life and outward behavior.

The tender heart of a young child can be directed Godward by parents and others who teach him to love God, Jesus, the Bible, church, and others.

Sensitivity to right and wrong begins to develop at an early age. This enables teachers to show children the awfulness of sin and the need for turning to Jesus for salvation.

Those who teach children in the church are responsible to pray for each one individually, to teach faithfully the Word of God, and to apply scriptural truths to daily living. After children receive Christ as Savior, their roles within the church shift to learning certain concepts of the Scriptures not applicable before salvation. There must be appropriate follow-up for babes in Christ regardless of their physical age.

Childhood years are impressionable ones, and the Christian life is not isolated from everyday living; love and understanding must be an obvious part of the life of his peers and adults. Many children will not see Christ reflected in their parents or relatives. Therefore church workers can help encourage those children to live for Christ.

THE CHILD'S SELF-CONCEPT

An important aspect of the development of personality is the child's self-concept. What do children think of themselves and why? As teachers counsel with students informally and as they see them in their classes, definite impressions of children's attitudes toward themselves become evident.

For the most part, children form self-concepts from those with whom they associate. Soon they learn the attitudes of others toward them and begin to form similar ideas. Obviously, parents play a prominent role in this matter. A child seeks protection, care, and love and thereby learns to love those who respond with love. Many attitudes parents have for a child also reflect their own attitudes about themselves.

Children's attitudes toward themselves are strongly influenced not only by parents but also by culture, heredity, siblings, intelligence, peers, and other factors. For example, a boy who has inherited a strong body may become a capable athlete. This, in turn, builds up his concept of himself. If the same boy had been ridiculed because of his body, he may never have developed it for use in athletics. His concept of himself, influenced by the attitude of his peers, would have prevented him from going into athletics.

Many studies have revealed that a low self-concept and poor academic achievement among children and youth are definitely related.[17] Children's workers do well to ask themselves if their own attitudes in class contribute to or hinder the development of healthy self-concepts among their students. "An endless number of cases can be cited where the praise and encouragement of the child by his teacher has significantly influenced his course and development in life."[18]

---

17. See, for example, William P. Purkey, *Self-Concept and School Achievement* (Englewood Cliffs, N.J.: Prentice-Hall, 1970), and Stanley Coopersmith, *The Antecedents of Self-Esteem* (San Francisco: Freeman, 1967). Also see James Dobson, *Hide or Seek* (Old Tappan, N.J.: Revell, 1974).
18. Goble, p. 152.

STRESS IN CHILDREN[19]

Wise teachers or parents will watch for stress in their children and help them cope. This is a special way to tell children you love them. Children today face many stresses that can cause them to cop out and become discouraged. Events that cause unusual stress are a death or divorce, a remarriage, a move to new city, attending a new school, the birth of a new baby (or adoption), a long vacation, problems at school, participation in a new activity (sports, drama, etc.), an injury or long illness, a parent's being away a great deal (whether for business or personal reasons), the mother's going back to work, loss of friends, loss of family income, and awards for school or community activities. All these cause stress on a scale of 20 to 100. A level of 300 is considered severe stress for a child. It would not take very many of these to add up to difficult stress levels for a child.[20]

Stress comes from all sides. Whether based on facts or feelings, the pain of it is real to children caught in its vise. Stress can make them strong, or stress can make them weak. How the adults in their lives steer the course makes the difference, and in that matter children are helpless.

Children are subject to stress on a routine basis simply by attending school. When other stress events are added they probably need help to find coping methods and techniques. We must let the child know that these events in no way reflect on his own value as a person. He is not bad (nor is he good, necessarily) because this thing happened to him or his family. He is not at fault for the events happening in his life. Teach the child that what he does (or what happens to him and his family) is different from what he is. No matter what happens the child is still worthy of love and affection. Goethe wrote: "Treat people as if they were what they ought to be, and you help them to become what they are capable of." The biggest help a child can receive is trust from an adult; trust that he can handle the situation and trust that you will not forsake him because of this thing that has happened. What an adult *does* in the present becomes what the child *is* in the future.

As church educators we must give the child the dignity he deserves. We cannot control the events that happen in the child's life, but we can value the child and help him cope. Our first prayer should be for protection for the child from the evil one (Satan naturally takes advantage of stress situations), and our second prayer should be for insight to know how to help. A strong relationship between the child and a trustworthy adult is the best help a child can have. Assure him that you are available to help him, and so is God. Teach the child that God loves and accepts him just as he is, no strings attached.

---

19. The section on stress in children was written by Sarah Eberle, a free-lance writer who lives in Huntsville, Alabama. Eberle is the author of chap 9, "Understanding Third and Fourth Graders (Middlers)."
20. Mary Susan Miller, *Childstress!* (Garden City, N.Y.: Doubleday, 1982), pp. 22-23.

Then try to show the child that love and acceptance in your own actions and attitudes. Love the child unconditionally.

Stress is unavoidable. As adults we must support our children and help them learn to cope. We must give children room to grow. Children learn to accept responsibility in order to earn independence; parents have to help them be accountable. Children will learn to cope, to be fair and honest, to work hard only when parents and other adults are strong enough not to protect them from opportunities for this growth.[21] The child is not to be protected from stress; he is to be supported through it. He knows that he is loved because he sees the love of his parents and other adults for him in their actions and attitudes toward him. This means giving up time and other adult pleasures to be interested in the child, but it is worth it when the child grows to be a responsible adult.

SUMMARY

Children's personalities are greatly influenced by their background, environment, and the composite of their physical, mental, emotional, social, and spiritual needs. All the personal experiences which make a child unique contribute to his personality. Observing children at home, school, play, and church can help parents and teachers have a better understanding of children's personality traits, patterns, and needs.

Teachers may be tempted to stereotype individuals according to general personality patterns, but unfounded conclusions must be avoided. If indications of abnormality are evident, it may be better to make referrals to those who are trained to handle such problems.

As a teacher studies the personalities of his students, he will want to pattern his teaching in a way that will appeal to their interests and at the same time will relate scriptural truths to their lives. The better a teacher understands the personalities and needs of children, the better equipped he will be as an instrument of the Holy Spirit to share Christ with children and to help them develop Christlike attitudes and habits.

FOR FURTHER READING

Adams, Jay E. *Christian Living in the Home.* Grand Rapids: Baker, 1972.

Alexander, Olive. *Developing Spiritually Sensitive Children.* Minneapolis: Bethany, 1980.

Borgatta, E. F., and William Lambert. *Handbook on Personality Theory and Research.* Chicago: Rand McNally, 1968.

Chaplin, J. P. *Dictionary of Psychology.* New York: Dell, 1975. Pages 381-82.

Clouse, Bonnidell. "Psychological Theories of Child Development: Implications

---

21. Ibid., pp. 56-57.

for the Christian Family." *Journal of Psychology and Theology* 1 (April 1973): 77-87.

Coleman, William L. *What Children Need to Know When Parents Get Divorced.* Minneapolis: Bethany, 1983.

Dobson, James. *Hide or Seek.* Old Tappan, N.J.: Revell, 1974.

———. *Dare to Discipline* Wheaton, Ill.: Tyndale, 1970.

Haystead, Wes. *Teaching Your Child About God: You Can't Begin Too Soon* Ventura, Calif.: Gospel Light, Regal Books, 1974.

Hearn, Virginia, ed. *What They Did Right: Reflections on Parents by Their Children.* Wheaton, Ill.: Tyndale, 1974.

Hendricks, Howard. *Heaven Help the Home.* Wheaton, Ill.: Scripture Press, Victor Books, 1973.

Hoagland, Joan. "Bibliotherapy: Aiding Children in Personality Development." *Elementary English* 49 (March 1972): 390-94.

Isham, Linda. *On Behalf of Children.* Valley Forge, Pa.: Judson, 1975.

Jenkins, Gladys Gardner, Helen Shecter, and William W. Bauer. *These Are Your Children.* Chicago: Scott, Foresman, 1953.

LaHaye, Beverly. *How to Develop Your Child's Temperament.* Irvine, Calif.: Harvest, 1977.

LaHaye, Tim, and Beverly LaHaye. *Spirit-Controlled Family Living.* Old Tappan, N.J.: Revell, 1978.

LaHaye, Tim. *The Battle for the Family.* Old Tappan, N.J.: Revell, 1982.

Lessin, Roy. *Spanking: Why, When, How?* Minneapolis: Bethany, 1979.

Lyppitt, Peggy, and Ronald Lyppitt. "The Peer Culture as a Learning Environment." *Childhood Education* 47 (December 1970): 135-38.

MacDonald, Gordon. *The Effective Father.* Wheaton, Ill.: Tyndale, 1977.

MacGregor, Malcolm. *Training Your Child to Handle Money.* Minneapolis: Bethany, 1980.

Meier, Paul D. *Christian Child-Rearing and Personality Development.* Grand Rapids: Baker, 1979.

Murray, Andrew. *How to Raise Your Children for Christ.* Minneapolis: Bethany, 1975.

Peterson, J. Allan. *Conquering Family Stress.* Wheaton, Ill.: Scripture Press, Victor Books, 1978.

Rappoport, Leon. *Personality Development: The Chronological Experience.* Glenview, Ill.: Scott, Foresman, 1972.

Rickerson, Wayne E. *Getting Your Family Together.* Glendale, Calif.: Gospel Light, Regal Books, 1977.

Rogers, Fred. *Many Ways to Say I Love You.* Valley Forge, Pa.: Judson, 1977.

Schaeffer, Edith. *What Is a Family?* Old Tappan, N.J.: Revell, 1975.

Swindoll, Charles R. *Home, Where Life Makes Up Its Mind.* Portland, Ore.: Multnomah, 1979.

———. *You and Your Child.* Nashville, Tenn.: Thomas Nelson, 1977.

White, John. *Parents in Pain.* Downers Grove, Ill.: InterVarsity, 1979.

Wilkerson, Barbara. *Childhood—The Positive Years.* Harrisburg, Pa.: Christian Publications, 1982.

Wilt, Joy. *Human Similarities.* Waco, Tex.: Word, 1980.

———. *Human Uniqueness.* Waco, Tex.: Word, 1980.

———. *You're All Right.* Waco, Tex.: Word, 1979.

———. *You're One of a Kind.* Waco, Tex.: Word, 1979.

Yawkey, Thomas, and Kenneth Jones. *Caring: Activities to Teach the Young Child to Care for Others.* Englewood Cliffs, N.J.: Prentice-Hall, 1982.

Doris A. Freese

4

How Children Think and Learn

- **What Is Learning?**
- **How Children Think**
  SENSORIMOTOR PERIOD
  PREOPERATIONAL PERIOD
  CONCRETE OPERATIONS PERIOD
  FORMAL OPERATIONS PERIOD
- **Thinking Related to Learning**
- **Key Factors in Learning**
  PERSONAL OR SUBJECTIVE FACTORS
  SUPRAPERSONAL OR OBJECTIVE FACTORS
- **Moral Development**

Children are in the business of learning. They attempt to put the data of life as gathered through the senses into some logical form. For example, a seven-year-old boy was asked by his father,

"What do you think of when I say, 'Jesus is the light of the world'?"

"The sun."

"Why?"

"Jesus is the Son of God."

Doris A. Freese, Ph.D., is professor of Christian education, Moody Bible Institute, Chicago, Illinois.

Note the logic (inaccurate as it may be) of the child. He related "light" to "sun" in a literal and concrete way. He then confused two different but similar sounding words, "sun" and "Son," in order to explain his logic. The boy was seeking to think through difficult concepts using the resources available to him. He was engaged in the business of thinking and learning.

WHAT IS LEARNING?

If we ask people what learning is, often they will give essentially the definition found in Webster, "To gain knowledge or understanding of or skill in by study, instruction or experience." Even teachers of children may view learning as the simple acquisition of knowledge. Indeed teachers sometimes view their teaching responsibility as that of imparting knowledge and information. A broader definition states that "learning is any relatively permanent change in behavior which occurs as a result of practice or experience."[1] The added dimension in this definition is a change in behavior. In Christian education we are concerned with both acquisition of knowledge (biblical truths) and change in behavior (application of those truths).

Perhaps the term *learning* defies definition because learning, although it occurs in all of us, is complex and involves many variables, such as maturation, readiness, atmosphere, motivation, and a host of other factors. Learning occurs inside the individual, though his environment affects how he responds and reacts. Learning has to do with developing for functioning. It affects the whole person and cannot be separated from human experience and behavior. It involves the acquisition of information, data, and knowledge, as well as changes in behavior.

Pulaski, in explaining Piaget's view, states that "learning occurs when the child deals with the new, the unexpected, and fits it into his already existing framework of knowledge through reflective abstractions."[2] Note that the child builds on what he already knows; he must eventually internalize the new into his existing framework. Bowman adds a dimension in that he sees learning as a kind of creativity. It is an "act of making something that was not there before for the individual."[3]

Ruth Beechick, in her careful work *A Biblical Psychology of Learning*, traces two kinds of learning, cognitive learning and motivation learning, or head and heart learning. Head learning includes both information learning (the acquisition of facts essential to more complex learning) and concept learning

1. Clifford Morgan and Richard King, *Introduction to Psychology*, 3d ed. (New York: McGraw-Hill, 1966), p. 73.
2. Mary Ann Spencer Pulaski, *Understanding Piaget*, rev. ed. (New York: Harper & Row, 1980), p. 201.
3. Locke E. Bowman, Jr., *Teaching Today: The Church's First Ministry* (Philadelphia: Westminster, 1980), p. 43.

(insight and understanding beyond the fact level). Heart learning relates to the self-discipline that comes when one seeks the biblical pattern for discipline and life. The interaction between head and heart are crucial to Beechick's discussion in that heart-set and self-discipline must be active in order for the individual to learn effectively at the mind level. "A heart for learning and the discipline to undergird it are necessary for all learning."[4]

In summary, learning includes both the acquisition of information and knowledge, and a resulting change in behavior as information and experiences are internalized.

How Children Think

Jean Piaget, in his studies of children, saw the child as an "intellectual alien in the adult world."[5] He saw the child as one who "has a host of ideas about the physical and natural world, but these ideas differ from those of adults and are expressed in different linguistic modes."[6] Because the child is a discoverer and acquires many of his notions about his world through his spontaneous interactions with the environment, he is limited only by his abilities and experience.

Piaget suggested four stages, or periods, of cognitive development: sensorimotor (birth to about two years of age), preoperational thought (two to seven years of age), concrete operations (seven to ten or eleven years of age), and formal operations (eleven or twelve and on). (See chap. 20 in this text for further discussion of Piaget's stages.)

The child passes through each stage on his way to a logical understanding of his world. No stage is skipped because each represents both a quantitative and a qualitative change in the child's thinking processes. In other words, the child not only gains ability in processing increasing numbers and complexities of data, but he processes the data differently at each stage.

SENSORIMOTOR PERIOD

During the sensorimotor period the child's chief means of learning occurs through his five senses. He must experience his environment; he touches, holds, looks, listens, tastes, feels, bangs, shakes. For the sensorimotor child his time dimension is now, his space dimension is here, and his orientation is me. When the child adds motor ability through creeping, crawling, and walking, his environment expands a hundredfold. He now explores his surroundings using both his senses and ability to get around. Ask any parent what that means in terms of protection and guidance. This use of the senses continues on

4. Ruth Beechick, *A Biblical Psychology of Learning* (Denver: Accent, 1982), p. 136.
5. David Elkind, *Children and Adolescents: Interpretive Essays on Jean Piaget,* 3d ed. (New York: Oxford U., 1981), p. 108.
6. Ibid., p. 108.

through age twelve but is less acute than in earlier years.

The immediate implications for "teaching" at the sensorimotor level are apparent. The parent or nursery worker will want to provide an enriched environment with freedom and safety factors built in. Things that can be pushed, pulled, banged, nested, stacked, or turned over will be standard equipment in the environment. Books will relate to the child's here-and-now orientation.

PREOPERATIONAL PERIOD

Between ages two and seven the child moves into the preoperational thought stage. (An operation is defined as a means of getting data about the real world into the mind and there transforming the data so they can be organized and used selectively in the solution of problems.) A key achievement at this age level is the acquisition of language, allowing the child to express in words what he is thinking. At this stage the child begins to classify or categorize, but he uses only one attribute at a time. For the kindergartner, his school teacher teaches. It may come as a surprise to him when one day he sees his teacher shopping in the grocery store. "Look, Mommy, my teacher shops, too!"

The preoperational child thinks in specifics and finds it difficult to generalize. He does not understand that an object has many properties. A ball to him will not be "a spherical or ovoid body used in a game or sport." For him, a ball is to throw. It has one specific property. When teaching the preoperational child, it is helpful to move from the specific to the general. For example, rather than begin with "God made everything," let the children identify specific vegetables God made. They can list tomatoes, corn, peas, stringbeans, *spinach* and end up with the idea, "Wow! God made all vegetables!"

Preoperational children especially learn through asking questions. The two- and three-year-old tends to ask "What's that?" questions, whereas the older child asks, "Why?" Elkind states, "Children believe that everything has a purpose and that everything in the world is made by and for man. . . . It is because children believe that everything has a purpose that they ask, 'Why is grass green?' and 'Why do the stars shine?' "[7] The child is not looking for a physical explanation such as the fact that grass contains chlorophyll; he wants a specific purpose such as "Grass is for children to roll in." The wise parent or teacher will answer such questions with a specific purpose and one that relates to the child himself.

The two- to seven-year-old child judges things by how they look to him rather than on the basis of mental operation. He is dependent on appearance. He lacks the concepts of reversibility and conservation. For example, if two identically-sized tall glasses are filled to equal levels with water and then one

7. Ibid., p. 15.

glass is emptied into a short wide container, the child will think the tall container holds more water. He cannot go back in his mind and reconstruct the logic of equal amounts of water; he judges only on the basis of what he sees.

Ask a kindergartner for a recipe of his favorite food, and he may give you the following:

Chocolate Chip Cookies

6 chocolate chips   (Think now. How many chips are there in each cookie?)
a lot of dough
a little bit of milk and water

Mix, make into little circles and put on pan.
Bake at 50 degrees for six hours; take out and eat!
Serves 100 people.[8]

Note several problems in the child's thinking. He judges by appearance— one cookie at a time with six chips. He has some idea of specific ingredients, but the actual quantity is vague. He has no concept of time—"50 degrees for six hours" (it may *seem* like six hours when one is waiting for freshly baked cookies!). He has no concept of numbers—"serves 100 people." Think of the difficulties a preoperational child may have if a Sunday school teacher uses expressions such as "Goliath was nine feet six inches tall," "it rained for forty days and forty nights," or "Jesus fed 5,000 people." Teachers need to help children understand concepts such as "bigness" or "tallness" at their preoperational level. For example, run a tape from floor to ceiling and explain that Goliath's head would still poke through the ceiling. Then measure each child's and teacher's height to show the difference. (I am six feet tall, and the children were quite impressed to learn that Goliath was taller than their "highest" teacher.) Perhaps the beautiful insight will come when one child speaks up (as one did) and exclaims, "But God was bigger."

CONCRETE OPERATIONS PERIOD

Between ages seven to ten or eleven, children move into the concrete operations stage. They begin to manipulate data mentally. They take either what they have experienced or what they have before them and can define, compare, and contrast. They still think concretely, however, in that they use previous experiences or what they have before them as a basis for their mental operations. Ask a preoperational child and a concrete operations child the question, "How does God hear prayer?" The preoperational child who thinks in

8. "Cookery Corner—Through the Eyes of a Kindergartner," *Community Unit Reporter, District* 200 (Wheaton, Ill.) 1, no. 2 (November 1973): 1.

specifics is apt to answer, "He has great big ears." The concrete child with his expanded thinking may say, "God hears my prayers through specially designed earphones." In each case the answer is concrete and based on experience.

Because seven- to eleven-year-olds can manipulate data mentally, they will enjoy classifying the books of the Bible, for example, the books of the law, the books of poetry. Their new memory strategies, such as greater ability to recall and to rehearse, allow them to memorize more readily. They can memorize Bible verses with the references. Up to age seven their reading ability has been limited. Now they can learn the verse *and* locate it in the Bible. Their growing sense of space and distance provides a basis for map studies. Where is Bethlehem in relation to Jerusalem? Where did Paul take his first missionary journey? How long a trip was it?

The concrete operational child is also capable of logical thought. Although he still learns through his senses, he no longer trusts only them to teach him. He also still thinks concretely. According to Beechick, the wise Sunday school teacher will begin every lesson for children at a concrete level and move toward a generalized level. For example, to teach the attribute that Jesus is kind, the teacher should begin with what Jesus did (concrete)—He made the lame man walk. Then he or she should move to the idea that Jesus went about doing good (less concrete, more generalized). From there the children can learn that Jesus is kind (a more generalized concept).[9]

The seven- to eleven-year-old is still literal in his thinking. That means that terms will be taken at face value—what they actually and literally mean. Children at the concrete operations level have difficulty with symbolism or figurative language. To them, Jesus *is* a shepherd rather than one who possesses the qualities of a shepherd, one who loves, cares for, and protects. To children, the expression that Jesus is the Light of the World may have something to do with light bulbs or flashlights. Older children, those ages nine to eleven, often can begin to understand the symbolism but they need much help in order to do so. A class of juniors, for example, would enjoy identifying the qualities of a rock and then try to think through how Jesus is the Rock of our salvation.

FORMAL OPERATIONS PERIOD

Even though children as discussed in this book do not fall into the formal operations period, we will describe the stage briefly in order to note the qualitative differences that begin to occur in late junior level (age eleven) and at the junior high level.

A young person at age eleven or twelve generally moves into the formal operations period. At this time he breaks the barrier of literalism and begins to

9. Ruth Beechick, *Teaching Primaries* (Denver: Accent, 1980), chap. 3.

think in abstract terms. His thinking is no longer restricted to time and space; he is able to reflect, hypothesize, and theorize. He can "think about thinking" in that he can recall and correct his own thinking. Teachers of children, however, must remember that they will not see this stage in children from birth through ten or eleven. Their teaching, therefore, must be geared to the way children actually think, not to the way adults think.

In the formal operations period, individuals will need to develop various cognitive abilities. Bloom and Krathwohl have listed six different cognitive abilities. Beginning with the simplest, the six categories are as follows:

1. *Knowledge of facts and principles* refers to the direct recall of facts and principles. Such knowledge often involves the rote memorization of dates, names, vocabulary words, and definitions—items easy to identify and test. Perhaps, because of its "convenience," this cognitive category has long been the focus of education.
2. *Comprehension* entails the understanding of facts and ideas. Unfortunately, tests that are successful in measuring recall of facts or principles are often unsuccessful in assessing how well the student actually understands the material.
3. *Application* refers to the need to know not only rules, principles, or basic procedures, but also how and when to use them in new situations. This intellectual task is less frequently taught and measured than the previous two.
4. *Analysis* involves the breaking down of a concept, idea, system, or message into its parts, then seeing relationship between these parts. This task may be taught in reading comprehension, math, or science classes. Often, however, the end product of that analysis is taught, but not the analytical process itself.
5. *Synthesis* refers to the putting together of information or ideas; integrating or relating the parts of a whole.
6. *Evaluation* entails judging the value of a piece of information, a theory, or a plan in terms of some criterion or standard. Evaluation is somewhat controversial in education.[10]

We, as adults, may be eager to integrate these six categories into learning experiences with children. However, we will discover that younger children (and even juniors) will have difficulty in applying these cognitive abilities until they have reached the period of formal operations.

Individuals may be able to perform with some measure of success, particularly in the first two categories. The last four categories require intellectual skills which the majority of children are not able to handle in the preoperational or concrete operations periods, except in very limited ways.

10. Grace Craig, *Human Development,* 3d ed. (Englewood Cliffs, N.J.: Prentice-Hall, 1983), pp. 306-7.

THINKING RELATED TO LEARNING

We have discussed how children think. The thinking process arises out of experiences involving exploration, discovery, creativity, adaptation, and interaction. All of these activities lead to learning. Earlier in our chapter we stated that learning includes the acquisition of information and knowledge through experiences and practice with a resulting change in behavior as information and experiences are internalized.

Based on our discussion of the ways children think, let us translate those ideas into how children learn. Keep in mind the relationship between the child's thinking level and what learning may result. Let us also ask the question for each aspect of learning: What can parents or teachers do to promote this kind of learning?

Children learn by experiencing and doing. They must manipulate, play, interact, discover, and experience what is around them in their world. Language becomes important to a child during the preoperational and the concrete periods, but he still needs to experience and do.

Children learn by example. They learn much by observing those in their world—peers, siblings, parents, and teachers. They note which behaviors are rewarded and which are discouraged or even punished. They "try on" various behaviors and eventually internalize certain behaviors into their lives. Watch and listen to a five-year-old as he plays out various roles and observe the accompanying behaviors and language he demonstrates. He identifies with and imitates examples or models who mean something to him.

Children learn by repetition with variation. Repetition is important in the learning process of the child. However, their repetitions often include small—although sometimes large—variations on the theme. Younger children appreciate the security of doing the same thing over and over again. However, as thinking develops and they see other possibilities, they experiment and add new dimensions to their activities.

Children think in specifics and then move to the general. At first, what they do, what they discover, and what they experience as individuals are seen as unrelated facts or experiences. Eventually, they can categorize, classify, and see relationships.

Children learn through concrete language and experiences. They think literally (what the word or term actually means) and concretely (tangibly, not abstractly). They have great difficulty in properly understanding symbolism. Remember, children can readily parrot back "correct" answers, but that does not mean that they understand the concept. Asking children questions helps the teacher assess the actual understanding of children. A good rule of thumb to follow in teaching is this: If we have to explain a term every time we use it, we should choose a term that explains itself at the child's level. For example, if we have to explain "fisher of men" repeatedly, use a more concrete phrase such as "someone who tells others about Jesus."

Thinking and learning are closely related, as we have seen. There are factors, however, that hinder or facilitate learning.

KEY FACTORS IN LEARNING

A child rarely learns in isolation. Learning usually takes place in a setting with others, sometimes with those one's own age, sometimes with those of different ages. The total setting in which the child finds himself not only can facilitate or hinder learning but becomes a means by which the child develops a world view. The environment can be harsh, unyielding, and difficult to manipulate, or the environment can allow the child to explore and discover. Teachers must understand the child's point of view in order to communicate effectively. According to Elkind,

> Most good teachers intuitively recognize the unique world view of the child and gear their instruction and verbalization accordingly. Those who do not, fail to understand the child at crucial moments in the educational process and they in turn may not always make themselves understood.[11]

Factors that affect learning include personal or subjective factors and suprapersonal or objective factors. Personal and subjective factors include those aspects that relate immediately to the child, such as motivation, peer relationships within the group, and communication between the child and the teacher. Suprapersonal (those that are above or beyond the child's control) and objective factors include the environment or physical setting, the emotional atmosphere or climate within the group, and the social and cultural norms a child brings with him.

PERSONAL OR SUBJECTIVE FACTORS

Motivation. According to Beechick, motivation is closely tied in with the heart learning of the child. In her learning model (see Beechick, *Biblical Psychology of Learning,* chap. 4), Beechick relates parental love and discipline and self-discipline to the development of motivation within a child. In Christian education, the training of the child begins in the home, where parents lovingly discipline and teach the fear of the Lord. The natural move for the child is from the home to the classroom, where teachers "step into the parent's place and continue the teaching process."[12] Eventually the child

11. Elkind, pp. 120-21.
12. Beechick, *A Biblical Psychology of Learning,* p. 57.

moves from outer discipline to self-discipline and makes personal choices: "He determines which way his heart will be set."[13]

Motivation ultimately resides within the child. Our first concern is with the child's immediate and eventual desire to walk in the ways of the Lord. On a day-by-day basis, our concern relates to how we can capitalize on the child's inner desire so that continued learning of biblical truths takes place. Both Piaget and Montessori "point out that intrinsic motivation resides in the child and not in methods and procedures."[14] Does this mean that we ignore methods? Hardly. It does mean, however, that the methods we use should allow the child to explore, discover, interact, and adapt. The child must be permitted, encouraged, and guided to learn according to the way he learns. Sitting passively and listening for long periods of time will only serve to deaden motivation.

> When it is said that young children are "active" learners, this must be taken in a literal sense. It is the reason, for example, that Montessori said that "play is the child's work." In play, the child is practicing the various actions that will eventually be internalized as thought. Accordingly, however convenient it may be for grown ups to think of children as learning while they are sitting still, what they learn in this way is likely to be learned by rote and to have little lasting value. In contrast, *what children acquire through active manipulation of the environment is nothing less than the ability to think.*[15]

Peer relationships. In Christian education children are often grouped together with their peers, for example, primaries with primaries. The relationships that develop within a group can have a profound impact on the learning that takes place. It is amazing to discover that a group of children can be involved together for a whole year and yet not know everyone's name in the group. The teacher should find ways to encourage good relationships among the children. He should know and use first names and encourage the children to address one another by name. He can plan activities in which children work in small groups and get to know each other better.

Peer relationships are best developed when a cooperative atmosphere is encouraged. Children today are introduced very early into the competitive aspects of life. They play in little leagues where there has to be a winner—and a loser. They label one another in school according to winner-loser titles: "He's smart," "He's a retard," "He's a dummy," "He's good in arithmetic." Group experiences and peer relationships can have a negative or a positive effect on a child's self-esteem and on his desire and ability to learn. Certainly the Sunday

13. Ibid., p. 59.
14. Elkind, p. 155.
15. Ibid., p. 53.

school, club program, or children's church should be a place where each child feels comfortable and is developing friendships with other children. The very concept of the Body of Christ is predicated on the idea of unity, working together and building up one another in the faith. Whatever we do with children ought to model the cooperative body concept. The child will be more apt to learn in a setting where he is not in competition with everyone else. Benjamin Bloom sees education not as a race but as a group effort "like a team of mountain climbers, straining to reach the summit. Yes, there's still competition, but it's group competition—the group against the mountain."[16] The teacher, therefore, will plan activities that will allow children to work together in conquering a difficult task, such as juniors helping one another to memorize the books of the Bible.

Communication. A third factor that affects learning is how the teacher communicates to the child and how the teacher reads both verbal and nonverbal communications from the child. Earlier we discussed the way children think and how the teacher must teach concretely. The teacher must be willing to discourse at the child's level. For some teachers, that ability seems almost natural, but others must learn how to communicate at the concrete level.

Equally important is the teacher's ability to understand a child's nonverbal communications. The way a child sits and moves, the tone of his voice, and his nervous habits are as much a part of his communication as the verbal responses he gives in class. The teacher who insists that a four-year-old remove his outside jacket when he comes into class may be missing the fact that the child (at this moment in his life) finds security in wearing his jacket in class. The junior girl who sits with her head in her hands may be bidding for attention because she has a genuine fifth-grade problem she would like to discuss with someone. The teacher must be sensitive to all levels of communication if she desires to understand and relate to her students.

SUPRAPERSONAL OR OBJECTIVE FACTORS

Some factors related to learning are above or beyond the control of the child and, in fact, may be beyond the control of the teacher as well. These factors include the environment or physical setting, the atmosphere or emotional climate of the group, and the social and cultural norms the children bring with them to a group.

Environments. All groups meet in some sort of physical setting, a setting that can facilitate or hinder learning. The room may be too large or too small, poorly ventilated, improperly lighted, inadequately equipped; or it may be just right for the group. The teaching staff can do much to make a room more

16. Glenn Heck and Marshall Shelley, *How Children Learn* (Elgin, Ill.: David C. Cook, 1979), p. 12.

appealing to children. Removing clutter from shelves, windowsills, and piano tops; arranging shelves and cabinets neatly; putting up attractive curtains; seeing that the carpet is vacuumed; painting scuffed and chipped furniture; putting up attractive pictures; changing bulletin boards—all these activities will spruce up the room and provide a cheerful place for learning.

Utilization of space should be carefully considered. Does the placement of tables and chairs allow for free movement of children? Are chair arrangements varied? Is there easy access to supplies in cabinets and files? Has consideration been given to moving departments to other rooms to provide for more efficient use of space? With thought and effort, teachers can make the environment more conducive to learning.

Atmosphere. Even the most ideal setting requires a positive climate or atmosphere. Although the physical is important, the emotional setting carries a greater impact on learning. Some groups seem to click together—children know each other, are friendly toward one another, cooperate in accomplishing tasks, and generally enjoy working together. Learning in such an atmosphere flows easily. Other groups seem plagued with conflict, pecking order comments, competitive actions, and overall tension. Learning under these conditions seems strained and forced. The teacher in the second setting tends to spend a large percentage of time keeping order.

What can be done to remedy a negative, tense climate? In many cases, a smaller teacher-student ratio will help provide the individual attention that conflictive children need. The children must first learn to work together in small groups before they will be able to move into a larger group setting. With older children, such as primaries and juniors, it is helpful to discuss feelings— how it feels to be put down by someone. The group can set up guidelines concerning how they will act toward one another. Children can be encouraged to think through how they can practice scriptural truths, such as "Be kind to one another," in the class. Juniors, especially those who know Christ as Savior, can explore what it means to be a part of the Body of Christ and what unity and edification are all about.

The teaching team will model a positive and loving lifestyle. They will praise children for positive behavior and for task accomplishments. They will love all children, even those who constantly grate. They will encourage children to help one another, such as one child's helping another complete an assignment or listening to another say his memory verse. Teachers can provide a secure atmosphere by setting clear rules and quietly enforcing them. Children can feel secure and can learn in an atmosphere where love and discipline are balanced.

Social and cultural norms. Each child brings his family and cultural background with him. In a largely homogeneous group, the teacher may also come from the same cultural setting and find no difficulty in relating to the group and facilitating learning. However, in today's society many urban and suburban churches are comprised of multiethnic groups. No longer are teachers working with children with the same value systems or with similar intellectual ability.

Teachers must keep in mind that any child can be an achiever and can learn. Some may take a little longer, but all have the capacity to learn. Some children may appear to be slower in moving into the next cognitive stage, although chronologically they ought to have reached it. The purpose of understanding the various cognitive stages is not to label a child or even to attempt to push him ahead, but to assess where he is in his thinking process and to select curriculum that will enlarge and enrich his ability.

Understanding a child's social and cultural background helps a teacher in communicating effectively with the child. "Each ethnic and socio-economic group has its own non-verbal signals which must be read if true communication is to occur."[17] For example, a teacher may have a class comprised of several children from the same family. It may be that when one child gets miffed and withdraws from the group, the rest of the siblings also withdraw. Learning ceases for the entire group at that point until the siblings can be reinstated with one another and with the rest of the group. In another situation, a cutting remark may cause a child to lose face, and he may withdraw physically or emotionally or both. Until his self-esteem is reestablished, learning may be hindered for him. The teacher should take time to understand the personal and ethnic backgrounds of his children and plan for learning that considers those norms.

MORAL DEVELOPMENT

Cognitive theorists, such as Jean Piaget and Lawrence Kohlberg, tend to relate the moral development of a person with his cognitive development. "Piaget defined morality as 'an individual's respect for the rules of social order and his sense of justice'—justice being 'a concern for reciprocity and equity among individuals.' "[18] He proposed two stages of development: moral realism and moral relativism. Kohlberg expanded the two stages into six levels.[19] According to Kohlberg, persons proceed through the various levels and do not skip any. However, many persons never reach the higher levels, stages five and six.

Christian parents and teachers must remember that both Piaget and Kohlberg discuss levels of moral *reasoning,* not moral *behavior.* These stages represent the growth of moral concepts or ways of judging intellectually

---

17. Elkind, p. 124.
18. Craig, p. 338.
19. Kohlberg's levels include the following: Premoral, or Stage 0—does not understand about moral issues, good is pleasure, bad is pain; Preconventional, Stage 1—punishment and reward orientation, Stage 2—reciprocity orientation; Conventional, Stage 3—"Good boy" conformity stage, Stage 4—authority-maintaining, law-and-order stage; Principled, Stage 5—social contract concept, Stage 6—individual principles of conscience.

personal actions and the actions of others. *Knowing* what is right does not automatically translate into *doing* what is right. Children can often repeat proper answers, even solid Scriptural principles and Bible verses, and yet not see how those concepts apply in their own lives. For a child to live the principles, both the head and the heart must be involved. Only through the regenerating of the Spirit through faith in Jesus Christ can a child begin to live a life that reflects Christlikeness.

Beechick reminds us that Kohlberg's view of moral developmental stages is a counterpart to "what Paul stated long ago in the spiritual realm, that the law is a schoolmaster to bring us to Christ, who is our righteousness."[20] Christian parents and teachers who wish to make use of Kohlberg's theory must do so by using the Bible first and the theory second.

> At Kohlberg's "premoral" and "preconventional" levels, a Christian parent will already be teaching what he believes to be right, even while realizing that his child has no such high principles but is only responding according to his punishment-obedience orientation. At the "conventional" level, which includes the "good boy" and "law and order" stages, Christian parents and teachers will want to make certain that children are well taught in the "laws" of the Bible. The Bible teaches us things we are supposed to do and not do—we are to love our neighbor, we are not to steal, and so on.
>
> A good grounding at the "law" level is a prerequisite for living later at the principled level. In order to learn to live by his own internalized principles, a person must first have learned to live under the authority of good rules and law.[21]

Children do indeed learn the difference between right and wrong. The awakening of conscience allows for this. Children may even give correct verbal response to questions regarding moral behavior. But ultimately we seek a change of behavior based on a heart-desire to love and follow their Lord.

SUMMARY

Children are engaged in the business of learning, which involves acquisition of knowledge and change in behavior. Children, however, think differently from adults, both quantitatively and qualitatively. Parents and teachers who understand how children think and learn will provide activities and experiences which encourage them to learn at their own levels. Teachers will also be aware of factors, personal/subjective and suprapersonal/objective, that influence learning. Although the teacher may not be able to alter some of the factors, he or she can seek to make learning experiences beneficial to the child.

Ultimately the work of the Christian teacher is the work of God Himself.

---

20. Ruth Beechick, "Lawrence Kohlberg: Why Johnny Can Be Good Without Being Religious," *Christianity Today* 22, no. 6 (30 December 1977): 14.
21. Ibid.

Christian education is a supernatural process. The teacher is communicating a divine message through the Word of God. To effect change in others' lives, he is completely dependent on the ministry of the Holy Spirit. As the Spirit of God works in the lives of the children, He may bring conviction of sin, remind of a truth or a promise, or encourage the child to live for the Lord. A thrilling experience is in store for the Christian teacher who seeks to work both with the Holy Spirit and with children in order to produce eternal results.

FOR FURTHER READING

Beechick, Ruth. *A Biblical Psychology of Learning.* Denver: Accent, 1982.

———. *Teaching Kindergartners.* Denver: Accent, 1980.

———. *Teaching Juniors.* Denver: Accent, 1981.

———. *Teaching Preschoolers.* Denver: Accent, 1979.

———. *Teaching Primaries.* Denver: Accent, 1980.

Bowman, Locke E., Jr. *Teaching Today: The Church's First Ministry.* Philadelphia: Westminster, 1980.

Bruner, Jerome S. *The Relevance of Education.* New York: Norton, 1971.

Collins, Marva, and Civia Tamarkin. *Marva Collins' Way.* Los Angeles: J. P. Farcher, 1982.

Dinkmeyer, Don, and Rudolf Dreikurs. *Encouraging Children to Learn: The Encouragement Process.* Englewood Cliffs, N.J.: Prentice-Hall, 1963.

Elkind, David. *The Child and Society.* New York: Oxford U., 1979.

———. *Children and Adolescents: Interpretive Essays on Jean Piaget.* 3d ed. New York: Oxford U., 1981.

———. *A Sympathetic Understanding of the Child Six to Sixteen.* Boston: Allyn & Bacon, 1971.

Furth, Hans. *Piaget and Knowledge: Theoretical Foundations.* Englewood Cliffs, N.J.: Prentice-Hall, 1969.

Heck, Glenn, and Marshall Shelley. *How Children Learn.* Elgin, Ill.: David C. Cook, 1979.

Moran, Gabriel. *Religious Development: Images for the Future.* Minneapolis: Winston, 1983.

Pulaski, Mary Ann Spencer. *Understanding Piaget.* Rev. ed. New York: Harper & Row, 1980.

Taylor, Robert, ed. *The Computer in the School: Tutor, Tool, Tutee.* New York: Teachers College Press, Teachers College, Columbia U., 1980.

Wilcox, Mary M. *Developmental Journey.* Nashville: Abingdon, 1979.

5

Valerie A. Wilson

Understanding Infants and Toddlers

- **The Importance of the Early Years**
- **Understanding the Infant**
  BIRTH THROUGH THREE MONTHS
  FOUR THROUGH SIX MONTHS
  SEVEN THROUGH NINE MONTHS
  TEN THROUGH TWELVE MONTHS
  MEETING THE INFANT'S NEEDS
- **Understanding the Toddler**
  PHYSICALLY
  MENTALLY
  SOCIALLY
  EMOTIONALLY
  SPIRITUALLY
  MEETING THE TODDLER'S NEEDS
- **The Cradle Roll Department**

Soft, sleepy, red, wrinkled, cuddly, fragile, small: choose any word you want to describe them. Who does not love one of these little people? And to hear proud, happy parents and relatives talk, *their* baby is the most beautiful, the most lovable of all. Indeed, a baby is a miracle. From a fertilized egg (about the size

VALERIE A. WILSON, M.R.E., is editor of Sunday school materials and writer of the Sunday school nursery curriculum, Regular Baptist Press, Schaumburg, Illinois.

of the dot over an *i*) emerges—about nine months later—a fully developed human being. Only the God of creation could have designed such a masterpiece.

It is equally as wonderful to contemplate the fact that God has given this tiny person an immortal soul capable of knowing God. This, then, is the challenge that confronts us: to guide the growth and development of the infant in such a way that one day he will respond to the claims of God upon his life. In order to do this, we must understand the little life which we are seeking to shape, and we must also understand some of the methods that can be used to influence that life.

THE IMPORTANCE OF THE EARLY YEARS

Just as the foundation of a house determines the stability of the superstructure, so the foundation years of life determine the overall direction and characteristics of a life. No period in one's life is as important as the first two years. This is not to say that change and development cannot take place at any other time. Indeed, they must, and they do. But psychologists and educators agree that never again during the whole life will a person learn as fast or as much as he does in these first two years. One educator wrote, "I think it can be said conservatively that a college student in four years does not make proportionately a fraction of the progress the well-trained infant does in his first two years."[1]

To those who are involved in the Christian education of children, this means these first two years of life dare not be neglected or slighted in the church's program. These early years demand the *very best* the church can provide. Neither should these years simply be endured or viewed as unproductive by Christian parents. The basic values and concepts which are communicated to the infant and toddler are the very ones that will determine the course of the child's life. "That child of yours is helpless in the hands of the people around him. He is pliable to their shaping; they set his mold."[2]

Because these first two years are so vital, it behooves us to understand them as fully as possible.

UNDERSTANDING THE INFANT

The term *infant* is used to refer to a child during the first twelve months of his life. The understanding of the infant—or any other age child—involves two areas. First, there are those characteristics that are common to all children of approximately the same age. Second, there are those characteristics that are unique to a particular child. The effective worker will seek to know the general

1. Bernice T. Cory, *The Pastor and His Interest in Preschoolers*, Christian Education Monographs, Pastors' Series, No. 8 (Glen Ellyn, Ill.: Scripture Press Foundation, 1966), p. 2.
2. Anne Ortlund, *Children Are Wet Cement* (Old Tappan, N.J.: Revell, 1981), p. 38.

characteristics of the age group with which he works, but he or she will also do everything possible to know the individual child. Both areas are important. But it is within the scope of this chapter to deal only with the general characteristics.

It is readily evident that no two infants are alike. Each baby is an individual in his own right, with his own pattern and rate of growth and development. However, "Babies grow and develop in certain ways which are fairly uniform. The challenging fact is that they pass through similar stages of growth, but each one grows at a different rate of speed."[3] We need to understand these basic patterns in order to understand individual children.

BIRTH THROUGH THREE MONTHS

The infant "is a bundle of joy and potential. He is a God-given spiritual trust."[4] But he enters the world through a shocking experience—the birth process! He leaves the calm, protected, warm atmosphere of his mother's womb in a traumatic way. And he is encountered at once with the need to function on his own. The advances of modern medicine can provide assistance if life processes, such as breathing, do not function satisfactorily. But eventually, if he is to survive, the infant must take over for himself. The qualifications he brings with him for this momentous task are weakness, helplessness, and complete dependence!

The full-term newborn baby weighs between six and nine pounds and is eighteen to twenty-two inches long. (He has grown 3,500 times in length since conception!) The male infant is usually slightly heavier and a bit longer than the female. The baby is surely a tiny little bit of humanity, but "The chief business of the infant is to grow."[5] And grow he does! His birth weight is usually doubled by the end of six months and tripled by one year.

The newborn baby often appears top-heavy, for his head is one-fourth of his body length. His arms and legs are relatively short, and his abdomen protrudes. His little hands are clenched into fists much of the time, and his legs are often drawn up toward his body. The skin of the newborn infant is red, wrinkled, and thin. In many ways, he resembles an old man more than the cute baby most people picture in their minds.

Physical needs dominate this period of the infant's life. Eating and sleeping are all-important. Sleeping occupies as much as eighteen to twenty hours of the infant's day. When he does awaken, he cries. These early cries are distress signals, reflex responses to discomfort. He cannot tolerate anything that both-

3. Florence Conner Hearn, *Guiding Preschoolers* (Nashville: Convention, 1969), p. 23.
4. Joan Leach and Patricia Elliott, *First Steps: Helps for Workers in the Church Nursery* (Cincinnati: Standard, 1964), p. 10.
5. J. Omar Brubaker and Robert E. Clark, *Understanding People* (Wheaton, Ill.: Evangelical Teacher Training Assn., 1972), p. 22.

ers him; so he responds by being irritable—the only response he can register. The cry of the infant says to the adults around him, "Something is bothering me. I have a need. Meet it."

Since the baby is capable of giving only nonverbal messages, nonverbal messages are what he picks up best. How an adult responds to his cry will teach the baby something about the world he has entered. Each day has its routine of simple acts which meet the physical needs of the baby. "But each simple act carries its own underlying lesson about this world—a lesson the child confronts for the first time."[6]

The senses of sight, taste, smell, and hearing are much keener in the newborn than doctors and psychologists once thought they were. Also, though the baby cannot mentally sort out certain sensations, nevertheless, he is capable of feeling pain, heat, and cold over his entire body. Swiss psychologist Jean Piaget has identified the infant-toddler age as the "sensorimotor period." The term is used "because children solve problems using their sensory systems and motoric activity rather than the symbolic processes that characterize the other three major periods [of development]."[7]

The baby learns much through touch. For instance, he knows different adults by the way he is held. Studies have shown that newborns can also distinguish their mothers' voices from other female voices. Much of baby's sensual gratification comes through the mouth. If the infant does not receive enough gratification at mealtime, he may suck vigorously on a thumb or pacifier. Eventually he begins to explore the world around him, and everything seems to find its way into the baby's mouth!

By the second and third months of life, the infant is attracted by bright, hanging toys and mobiles. The tiny child develops the ability to follow moving objects with his eyes. He will sleep more easily if times of wakefulness are made interesting. By the end of this first three months of life, the infant may begin to gurgle and coo—sounds that bring delight to those around him!

It is highly important during these early months to provide abundant sensory experiences—at home and at church. "Extensive studies indicate that early stimulation of a baby's senses actually increases the child's intelligence."[8]

FOUR THROUGH SIX MONTHS

In his second three months of life, the baby becomes much more active. He rolls and wiggles, and it is not safe to leave him alone on a raised, flat surface for even a moment. During the fifth or sixth month, a baby will begin to enjoy a playpen. He is eager and bold in his approach to new things. By the sixth

6. James L. Hymes, *The Child Under Six* (Englewood Cliffs, N.J.: Prentice-Hall, 1963), p. 6.
7. Ruth L. Ault, *Children's Cognitive Development*, 2d ed. (New York: Oxford U., 1983), p. 22.
8. Grace Ketterman and Herbert Ketterman, *The Complete Book of Baby and Child Care for Christian Parents* (Old Tappan, N.J.: Revell, 1982), p. 149.

month, he usually rolls from his back to his tummy—his first big achievement!

The baby begins early to recognize his mother's face from others; and by six months, he knows his family members from other people. With this new recognition may come tears when family members leave.

Learning to pick up an object is mastered during this time, and a baby will grasp his plaything tightly. He must also learn to let go intentionally. It is frustrating to adults to pick up a dropped object time after time, but the developing infant is enjoying the exercise of this new skill—the ability to let go.

As the infant increases in size, the body undergoes the necessary changes which make for maturity and strength. This is development.[9] Both growth and development are evident during this three-month period, as the world and experience of the infant enlarge.

SEVEN THROUGH NINE MONTHS

Perhaps the most notable "first" of the seven-through-nine-month period is the appearance of the first tooth. This usually occurs after six months, though occasionally a baby will have one earlier, and in rare instances an infant is born with teeth. In the process of teething, the baby is often fretful and fussy; his gums are red and swollen; his appetite may decrease; and he may sleep for shorter periods of time. Adults who care for the child must keep these physical discomforts in mind and continue to provide tender, loving care for a fussy, cranky, runny-nosed baby.

The growing, developing infant is working on his coordination; and he enjoys exercising his muscles. In this period, he struggles to sit up and to pull himself into an upright position. By the eighth or ninth month, he may be crawling.

Toys for this age baby should stimulate his curious mind: small blocks; bright, wooden beads; large spools; nesting toys; bells and balls; large plastic or rubber rings; soft plastic spoons; soft, cuddly toys. Toys should be free of rough edges and tiny, detachable parts. Nontoxic paint should be used on any surface a child might chew.

During this time the infant may develop, as Dodson says, "stranger anxiety."[10] He may be very suspicious of people other than his mother or immediate family. He usually does warm up to people who give him time to become friendly. But these "outsiders" must evidence love and gain his confidence; they cannot force themselves on him. The baby finds increasing amusement in pleasant social contacts, and he enjoys the opportunity to explore. By the time he reaches nine months, he will begin to show active resentment if his interests

9. Brubaker and Clark, p. 22.
10. Fitzhugh Dodson, *How to Parent* (Los Angeles: Nash, 1970), p. 40.

are thwarted. His own distinctive nature and personality are becoming more and more evident.

TEN THROUGH TWELVE MONTHS

A ten-month-old is usually eating solid foods and drinking milk from a cup, though a bedtime bottle may still be given. He sits up without support and is probably crawling quite well. How he loves to explore! He should be kept safely out of trouble, but he needs opportunities for adventure. He needs an environment in which he can maneuver with ease and investigate the world around him.

The baby is able to respond more and more to adult attention. Now he enjoys games such as pat-a-cake and peek-a-boo. His mind needs the challenge of things such as simple pull-apart, put-together toys; several blocks instead of one; boxes, spoons, and nonclip clothespins. This is the time to introduce the child to the world of books. Books with a simple picture and one word on a page help the youngster learn about his world.

The development of nerve and muscle control during infancy starts at the head and moves downward and from the upper part of the arms and legs outward to the fingers and toes. By the end of the first year, the baby can use his thumb and forefinger together—a distinctly human trait, and he shows increasing evidence of coordination. The twelfth month of his life usually finds the baby pulling himself upright, maintaining a standing position and perhaps taking a few steps.

At one year of age, the average child measures from twenty-eight to thirty-one inches in length and weighs, unclothed, from seventeen to twenty-four pounds. He has as few as two or as many as six teeth. He is leaving the world of infancy to embark on a new adventure—the life of a toddler.

MEETING THE NEEDS OF THE INFANT

The needs of the infant can be summarized rather easily: His physical needs must be met, and they must be met in an atmosphere of love and by those who love him. "Spiritual, mental, emotional, and social development hinge upon the ways physical needs are met."[11] As physical needs are met in a gentle, loving way, the infant gains a basic security and a sense of trust which the child will carry through life.

The implications are clear for those who work with infants in the church program. This worker cannot look on his job as routine. He must see it as an avenue of service to the Lord, Who cared deeply for little children (Mark 10:16; Luke 18:15-16). The worker must have for each little child a love that manifests itself in the way in which he cares for the child. The worker in the

11. Hearn, p. 19.

crib nursery has the awesome responsibility of helping the infant form his first and most lasting impression of the place called church. Long before he knows anything about what is *taught*, he will know how he *feels*. And how he feels *now* may influence to a large extent how readily he will expose himself to other aspects of the church's program when he is old enough to decide for himself.

The person who works with infants must be calm and gentle and not easily disturbed. "Handle [a baby] with strength, but practice moving slowly and deliberately. . . . Cultivate a soft tone of voice,"[12] and speak in simple, short sentences. Baby talk is not necessary; simple songs and rhymes, soothing tunes, and gentle humming are much more pleasing and effective. Some curriculum publishers advocate bringing the small baby to the teaching table even before he can sit alone. He is placed in a safety chair or infant seat and listens to the story, participating [with assistance] in "Pat the Bible Book" and other songs.[13]

The role of men in the care of infants is becoming more noticeable. More and more churches are recruiting men for work with young children. James Hymes suggests that a "child's life is richer when, from the beginning, he has the benefit of both a masculine and a feminine approach to the world. . . . Children of both sexes need to feel a hairy hand, a more muscular hand, a bigger hand, a calloused hand."[14] If, from his earliest experiences at church, the child has the awareness of the loving care of a man, he will find it easier to realize and trust the loving care of the Lord Jesus.

The church's provision for the infant includes not only personnel but also a place. The crib nursery must be spotlessly clean and adequately equipped. (See chap. 14, "Leadership for Children," for equipment needed in a crib nursery room.) No parent wants to leave a child in a messy, cluttered, or dirty room. The church wanting to minister to parents as well as infants must do its utmost to provide clean, responsible, efficient, friendly, and loving service to infants and their parents. Such a church is making an investment in lives. No other investment has such rewarding or eternal dividends!

UNDERSTANDING THE TODDLER

Toddler describes the child who is thirteen to twenty-four months old. This designation is a natural one, since some time around twelve months a child begins to toddle. Early adventures in walking are shaky and insecure at best; and they are filled with many tumbles. But little by little, the toddler gains

---

12. Ketterman and Ketterman, p. 344.
13. Palma Smiley, *Early Childhood Curriculum*, Palma Smiley Early Childhood Curriculums (Lubbock, Tex.).
14. Hymes, p. 249.

ability, momentum, and courage. Before long the child is into everything. Perhaps at no other period is so much energy and endurance, insight and courage, required of adults. The toddler can make life fun or frustrating. Adult frustrations, however, can be relieved somewhat if this important year of the child's life is better understood.

In infancy, a child learns basic trust or basic distrust. In toddlerhood, he learns self-confidence or self-doubt.[15] How a child learns to think of himself has far-reaching consequences in the years ahead. We can best understand the toddler by considering the various aspects of his life: physical, mental, social, emotional, and spiritual. (See chap. 33 for more description of children in this age group and how to handle them.)

PHYSICAL CHARACTERISTICS

Physically, the toddler is characterized by his newly acquired ability to walk. At times, especially while walking is still new to him, he may resort to crawling. He is quite proficient at this means of navigation, so it is easy to revert to it when the need arises to get someplace quickly. Some children never do much crawling; others do a great deal. But regardless of how much crawling does or does not precede it, walking is achieved when the child is ready. He cannot and should not be forced to walk. Early walkers are not smarter or better than late walkers. Each child masters this feat when he is ready, commonly between twelve and fifteen months.

The toddler is also gaining ability and dexterity with his hands. He has better coordination in the use of his fingers. He can pull off his cap and socks, open boxes, unscrew lids, put pegs into holes, scribble, turn book pages one at a time, and build a tower with four or five blocks. Dodson has characterized toys as the "textbooks of toddlerhood."[16] Playthings should be chosen carefully, and play activities should be directed toward purposeful ends.

A change is noticeable in the toddler's sleeping habits. He will usually cut down on daytime sleep, needing only one nap a day. He may sleep two or three hours during the day and eleven to twelve hours at night. But he does get weary; so church programs for toddlers need to include opportunities for rest.

As a child approaches age two, the parents begin toilet training. Those who work with the child at church should be aware of this and cooperate with parents in this regard. (It should be noted, however, that it is unusual and perhaps even unwise to have a child trained before the second birthday.)

By the time he reaches the age of two, a child is usually thirty-two to thirty-four inches long and weighs thirty-three to thirty-six pounds. He has come a long way since the time he was only the size of the dot over an *i.*

15. Dodson, p. 53.
16. Ibid., p. 59.

MENTAL CHARACTERISTICS

The mental horizons of the toddler are enlarging even as his physical body is growing. One such area is that of language development. The toddler adds many new words (mostly nouns and verbs) to his vocabulary. He is able to name objects or pictures in a book. He begins to use words in combination and forms simple sentences. He understands commands and prohibitions and comprehends simple questions. By his second birthday, the toddler has a vocabulary of 250 to 300 words. It is interesting to note that a toddler with an older sibling usually has a larger vocabulary and more ability to converse than an only child.

Of all the words he either uses or understands, the toddler's favorite word is undoubtedly *no*. He is seeking autonomy, independence; and *no* is one way to exert himself. The adult should not try to pit his will against that of the toddler. The parent or church worker should let the child know certain things are expected regardless of his response. Negative responses can be reduced by avoiding questions that invite *no* for an answer. If there is, in reality, no choice, the child should not be offered one. Rather than asking, "Do you want to stop playing with the blocks?" the fact should be stated, "When you finish building the tower, we will put away the blocks. Then we will go to the story rug." (Notice that this statement also contains a time element. The toddler is given time to finish an activity before a new one is begun.)

The toddler has a brief attention span and also a short memory. Stories for toddlers must be very short, but they can be repeated often. (A teacher tires of the same thing far more quickly than the child does.) The child's short memory means that directions will have to be repeated several times. Furthermore, they may have to be repeated every week (in a church situation), for the child has forgotten since the last time he was there.

When directions are given, they should be given positively so that the child knows what to do. Negative directions do not tell him what is expected. Rather than saying, "Do not put the book on the floor," the parent or teacher should give a positive directive: "Tommy, let's put the book back on the table."

SOCIAL CHARACTERISTICS

The toddler's world is confined to *me* and *mine*. He has little concept of *you* and *others*. His play is solitary. He has little or no interest in others and has no ability to play with them. But as he nears his second birthday, he gains an interest in being near others. He wants to do the same thing as another child, but he does not want to do it with him. Hence his play is characterized as being parallel but not cooperative.

The church is a good place for the toddler to begin to learn to share, to take turns, and to be kind. But the young child should not be expected to make great gains in these areas. Emotional and nervous systems are not developed to the extent that the child can understand or tolerate social demands. Enough toys and books should be on hand so that a toddler can engage in solitary play.

The toddler treats people in much the same way he treats things—feeling, pushing, trying to manipulate. Many times, the child's actions are misunderstood. An adult may think the child is misbehaving when he is actually only trying to learn about his world. Since the toddler does not have much concept of *person,* he does not realize that one does not poke another child in the same way that one can poke a stuffed animal. When such actions occur, it is usually best to pick up a child and move him to another part of the room. As the child is being moved, the worker should say, "Timmy is our friend. We don't want to hurt Timmy. Here is a book just for you." Such a course of action does several things: (1) it separates the two children; (2) it reinforces the teaching that the other child is a friend; (3) it suggests how not to treat a friend; (4) it diverts the child's attention to something more acceptable.

EMOTIONAL CHARACTERISTICS

Insecurity characterizes the toddler emotionally. Adjustment is difficult. He gets along best in a familiar routine, in a familiar room, and with familiar faces. When toddlers are cared for at church, the room arrangement, the schedule, and the personnel should be the same from week to week. This will help the child feel secure when he comes to church. The person who works with toddlers needs the same characteristics as those suggested for workers with infants—calmness, stability, and gentleness. The toddler needs and responds to the calming influence of an adult.

A child's perception of a situation will vary with physical and emotional states. His reactions are based on whether he is fatigued, insecure, and hungry, or rested, safe, and content. If a child's behavior varies from that which he usually exhibits, such physical and emotional factors may be the explanation.

Often a toddler will act out his feelings in play. The alert worker will watch for indications of how the child feels by the way he treats the dolls, plays with the blocks, and even in the books he chooses.

SPIRITUAL CHARACTERISTICS

Openness and *receptivity* aptly describe the toddler. No walls of doubt or suspicion have yet been raised; no questions concerning rationality or reasonableness have been voiced. The little child will listen with wide-eyed wonder as he is told of God, who makes it rain, or God, who made the doggy. There will be a warm response when the toddler hears of baby Jesus, God's Son. Although the toddler cannot comprehend the same depths of truth as an older child, there is no need to wait until later to begin teaching. Some basic Bible truths can be emphasized repeatedly to the open mind and receptive heart of the toddler. Simple songs about creation, God's love and care, and Jesus, along with a notebook of large but simple Bible pictures, can be used to introduce toddlers to Bible truths.

The church that makes no provision for teaching toddlers is losing precious opportunities. The program for toddlers should be more than a baby-sitting service. A definite teaching program should be carefully planned. (Some publishers include helps for teaching toddlers in their curriculum materials for nursery-age children.) Anne Gilliland suggests the following "desired outcomes" that can serve as a guide in planning a program for toddlers: In regard to *God,* "experiencing happy feelings associated with God"; *Jesus,* "experiencing happy feelings associated with Jesus"; *creation,* "discovering the beauties and wonders around him"; *church,* "developing a growing sense of at-homeness in his room at church"; *Bible,* "becoming familiar with the Bible as a Book"; *family,* "associating experiences he has at home with those he has at church"; *others,* "experiencing happiness in his relationship with others"; *self,* "feeling secure in his environment."[17]

MEETING THE NEEDS OF THE TODDLER

Is a toddler really to be enjoyed and not merely tolerated? It would seem that much enjoyment can result from watching a young life grow and develop. And a sense of satisfaction should result from having a part in shaping that young life for eternity. But to accomplish this and to meet the needs of the toddler require love and patience.

The toddler must be given as much room as possible in which to move around. He must have opportunities to explore. And he must be allowed to practice, for age one is a practice year. The child will improve on everything he started to learn in the first year and will acquire new skills as well.

The church can best meet these needs by providing a separate room, trained workers, and a planned program for toddlers. The toddler-age child does not belong in the crib nursery; nor is he ready to work with two-year-olds. He needs a place, personnel, and program for his particular needs. He is full of energy, activity, and excitement. The church can cooperate with parents in molding this young life for the glory of God.

THE MINISTRY OF A CRADLE ROLL DEPARTMENT

It is impossible to discuss the church's ministry to infants and toddlers without discussing the cradle roll department. No infant or toddler just happens to be in church. The child is there because he was brought there. Therefore, the church that desires to minister to infants and toddlers must do so through a ministry to parents. And this is exactly the function of the cradle

17. Anne Hitchcock Gilliland, *Understanding Preschoolers* (Nashville: Convention, 1969), pp. 86-88.

roll department. It "capitalizes on going into the home, but it also makes provisions at the church for the care of infants and toddlers."[18]

Various slogans have been used to describe the ministry of this department: "A Christian home for every baby"; "Christ-centered homes for times like these"; "Enrolling babies to reach parents for Christ." Each of these points up the fact that this department goes into homes and, in that way, reaches both parents and babies. Perhaps at no other time is a family as easy to reach with the gospel as when a new baby enters the home. The objective of the department "is not to *relieve* parents of their responsibilities for the religious training of their children, but to *help them* fulfill those responsibilities."[19]

The program of the cradle roll department has three facets. The first of this is home visitation. Cradle roll department workers (often called visitors) go to homes where there are children from birth through twenty-four months of age and seek to enroll the baby in the cradle roll department of the church. Once a baby has been enrolled, regular visits are made to the home, and literature is left with the parents.

The second phase of the cradle roll program is providing care for infants and toddlers during Sunday school and church services. The suggestions which have already been offered in this chapter regarding meeting the needs of infants and toddlers apply here. The actual implementation of them would come within the realm of the cradle roll department.

The third phase of the department's ministry focuses again on the parents. An active, vibrant Bible class must be provided for parents when they bring their children to church. In addition to this weekly ministry, special get-togethers should be planned. Some cradle roll departments have a mothers' meeting every month; others have parents' meetings, special banquets, recognition days, or other special events. All of these things are planned to lead parents to Christ and to give them guidance regarding the spiritual training of their children.

A church cannot afford to neglect a cradle roll department and the type of ministry it represents. For one thing, the future of the child is at stake. "The church that deliberately waits to enroll a child until he is three or four years old may never see that child, even though he was born to parents who are church members."[20] Habits are hard to break, especially the habit of sleeping in on Sunday because it is so much trouble to prepare the little one for his morning in the nursery.

But there is another compelling reason for having an active cradle roll department. "The place of the Cradle Roll in the church helps determine not

18. Meryl Welch, *Cradle Roll Handbook* (Schaumburg, Ill.: Regular Baptist, 1979), p. 3.
19. Eleanor L. Doan, *It's Never Too Early* (Ventura, Calif.: Gospel Light, 1967), p. 3.
20. Leach and Elliott, p. 25.

only the future life of the child, but also the future life of the church."[21] Many churches testify to the fact that the cradle roll department is the best of all church-building agencies. "Growths of 35 percent to 65 percent have been attributed to this one department."[22] What an open door of opportunity this presents!

SUMMARY

This chapter identifies the characteristics and needs of children from birth to age two. No other period in one's life is as vital as the very first two years. During these first years, the patterns are established that will affect all the rest of one's life. "As the twig is bent, the tree will grow." This is the time to see that the "twig" is bent toward God. Suggestions are given for meeting the needs of these little ones in the church program. The church desiring to minister to the whole person and the whole family will capitalize on the unique opportunities for reaching and teaching that the years of infancy and toddlerhood provide. Special attention is given to the ministry of the cradle roll department.

FOR FURTHER READING

BOOKS

Aldridge, Betty. *Teaching Toddlers.* Cincinnati: Standard, 1978.
———. *You Can Teach Preschoolers Successfully.* Cincinnati: Standard, 1984.
Ault, Ruth L. *Children's Cognitive Development.* 2d ed. New York: Oxford U., 1983.
Bergen, John, and Ronald Henderson. *Child Development.* Columbus, Ohio: Merrill, 1979.
Biehler, Robert. *Child Development.* 2d ed. Boston: Houghton Mifflin, 1981.
Brubaker, J. Omar, and Robert E. Clark. *Understanding People.* 2d ed. Wheaton, Ill. Evangelical Teacher Training Assn., 1981.
Craig, Grace. *Human Development.* 3d ed. Englewood Cliffs, N.J.: Prentice-Hall, 1983.
Dodson, Fitzhugh. *How to Parent.* Los Angeles: Nash, 1970.
Gangel, Elizabeth, and Elsiebeth McDaniel. *You Can Reach Families Through Their Babies.* Wheaton, Ill.: Scripture Press, Victor Books, 1976.
Harrell, Donna, and Wesley Haystead. *Creative Bible Learning for Young Children Birth—5 Years.* Ventura, Calif.: Gospel Light, 1977.

21. Marjorie E. Soderholm, *Understanding the Pupil: Part I, The Pre-School Child* (Grand Rapids: Baker, 1955), p. 15.
22. Welch, p. 4.

Jenkins, Gladys, and Helen Shacter. *These Are Your Children*. 4th ed. Glenview, Ill.: Scott, Foresman, 1975.

Ketterman, Grace, and Herbert Ketterman. *The Complete Book of Baby and Child Care for Christian Parents*. Old Tappan, N.J.: Revell, 1982.

Leach, Joan, and Patricia St. Louis. *Caring for Babies*. Cincinnati: Standard, 1978.

Meier, Paul D. *Christian Child-Rearing and Personality Development*. Grand Rapids: Baker, 1977.

Neuen, Thelma F. *Toddler Teacher's Guide*. Wheaton, Ill.: Scripture Press, Victor Books, 1977.

Ortlund, Anne. *Children Are Wet Cement*. Old Tappan, N.J.: Revell, 1981.

Strang, Ruth. *An Introduction to Child Study*. 4th ed. New York: Macmillan, 1959.

Strickland, Jenell, comp. *How to Guide Preschoolers*. Nashville: Convention, 1982.

Terrell, Jerry D. *Basic Preschool Work*. Nashville: Convention, 1981.

Uland, Zadabeth. *Bible Teaching for Preschoolers*. Nashville: Convention, 1984.

Waldrop, C. Sybil. *Understanding Today's Preschoolers*. Nashville: Convention, 1982.

Welch, Meryl. *Cradle Roll Handbook*. Schaumburg, Ill.: Regular Baptist Press, 1979.

CRADLE ROLL MATERIALS

These publishers have curriculum materials for use in a cradle roll department or packets available for a visitation program:

David C. Cook, 850 North Grove Avenue, Elgin, IL 60120

Gospel Light Publications, 2300 Knoll Drive, Ventura, CA 93003

Gospel Publishing House, 1445 Boonville Avenue, Springfield, MO 65802

Palma Smiley Early Childhood Curriculums, P. O. Box 64608, Lubbock, TX 79464

Regular Baptist Press, Box 95500, Schaumburg, IL 60195

Scripture Press, 1825 College Avenue, Wheaton, IL 60187

Standard Publishing Company, 8121 Hamilton Avenue, Cincinnati, OH 45231

Sunday School Board of the Southern Baptist Convention, 127 Ninth Avenue North, Nashville, TN 37234

FILMS AND FILMSTRIPS

Babies and Toddlers Do Learn. Filmstrip. Ventura, Calif.: Gospel Light.
How to Use the Bible with Preschoolers. Filmstrip. Nashville: Broadman.

Planning for Effective Teaching of Preschoolers. Filmstrip. Nashville: Broadman.
Reach Out with Cradle Roll. Filmstrip. Nashville: Broadman.
Talking with the Young Child. Filmstrip. Ventura, Calif.: Gospel Light.
Teaching Babies, Creepers and Toddlers at Church. Film or video. Nashville: Broadman.
Teaching Preschoolers Through Activities. Filmstrip. Nashville: Broadman.
Understanding the Preschool Child. Filmstrip. Nashville: Broadman.
You, A Teacher of Preschoolers. Filmstrip. Nashville: Broadman.

PERIODICALS

Living with Preschoolers. Nashville: Broadman.
Preschool Leadership. Nashville: Broadman.
Today's Christian Parent. Cincinnati: Standard.

V. Gilbert Beers

6

Understanding Twos and Threes

- Recognizing Behavior Patterns
- A Comparative Profile
- Spiritual Lessons
- Meaningful Experiences

What *is* a two-year-old?

What *is* a three-year-old?

That depends on the way one looks at this amazing person.

Biologically, a two-year-old is about thirty-five pounds of bone, muscle, flesh, and blood, stretched to almost three feet in height. A two-year-old has a network of plumbing long enough to reach across the country a number of times, carrying blood, water, waste materials, and various other fluids. Add another four or five pounds, stretched up another three or four inches, and you have a three-year-old.

A two-year-old is a live wire from wake-up-time until bedtime. Life is one of self-discovery, gradually becoming acquainted with the big wide world. Even a week or a month can make a significant difference in patterns of growth in

V. GILBERT BEERS, Th.D., Ph.D., is executive director of Christianity Today Institute, Carol Stream, Illinois.

total personality development. Life with the two- or three-year-old is never dull, but can be frustrating for those who may have limited understanding of the process of development.

Mentally, a two- or three-year-old child is like a sponge, absorbing unbelievable amounts of knowledge and understanding—sometimes more knowledge than understanding. This is the time to learn the basics of life, such as good eating habits, good sleeping habits, bladder and bowel control, following directions, getting along with others, and talking well. So much is learned during this period that by the time a child is four, the basic foundations of life have been laid.

Spiritually, a child of this age is a bundle of trust, ready to accept what parents or teachers say. Twos and threes are endowed with a limitless hunger to learn more about the Lord and His Word, but not knowing how to read, he must depend on others, especially parents and teachers, for guidance. This trust makes the child easily pliable and is both an opportunity and a responsibility to those who teach.

Socially, the two-year-old is a loner, even in a group. By three, the child has begun to mingle with the group. Family ties are very strong at these ages, and it is best not to pull too hard at these ties when introducing the child to a new group. In reaching out, a two-year-old will feel much more comfortable keeping a strong hold on family, especially on mother.

Temperamentally, a two-year-old, especially about midpoint between two and three, is sometimes called a "terrible two." There is a strong reason for such a label, for here is a bundle of frustration to anyone searching for peace and quiet.

A "terrible two" may be terrible because of "terrible" things, such as thumb sucking, bedwetting, nose picking, showing off, getting into everything, tearing up things just to see them torn up, and a number of other creative frustrations. Life is a two-way street on which the child travels in both directions at the same time. Powers of choice have not developed enough to show which way is best, so the child often tries both ways, "shifting gears" constantly from go to stop, this way to that, pushing and pulling forward and backward, in and out, and up and down.

The frustrated parent may find it easy to say "terrible two" or even "naughty child" and may even be tempted to say, "Why can't my child be like others?" not realizing that this child *is* like others of that *same age*. What one may really mean is, "Why can't my child be like an adult?"

But twos and threes are not adults. In our rational moments, we realize that we want them to behave exactly the ways twos and threes should behave, not as adults. The burden of understanding is on our part, not theirs. We must understand how twos and threes are made, how they behave, and how they learn at this particular point in their journey through life. Then we will enter with a new enthusiasm into our task of guiding them.

RECOGNIZING BEHAVIOR PATTERNS

The following case studies will acquaint the reader with some of the typical behavior patterns which one might expect from twos or threes, depending on their maturity. We must recognize that some twos are more mature than some threes, so there may be a rather wide range in the maturity level among individual twos and threes.

Karen. On a rainy day, Karen comes into Sunday school with her new umbrella open. As the teacher helps her fold it and then take off her raincoat, Karen bubbles with excitement about the new umbrella.

"Mommy and I went to the store yesterday. She got me my new umbrella. Isn't it pretty?"

"Karen, that's a very pretty umbrella. Did it help to keep the rain from getting you wet?"

"Yes, and Mommy says I must not forget it. She said she won't buy me another one."

"I'll help you remember to take it home, Karen. We don't want you to get wet, do we? God made the rain so the flowers will get wet and grow. But you don't need the rain to make you grow."

"But God doesn't have an umbrella, does He? Will He get wet?"

What characteristics are evident in the conduct of twos and threes as revealed through Karen's experiences?

Karen relates herself to her mother. "Mommy and I went to the store." Even though she is growing accustomed to her Sunday school and her teacher, there is a strong tie to home and mother, and she is anxious to tell about it.

Karen seeks assurance that her umbrella is all right. "Isn't it pretty?" Children of this age need assurance that their shoes are nice or that they look pretty or that they did something good.

Karen is very candid about her home relationships. She tells the disciplines as well as the delights of her relationship with mother.

God is very specific to Karen. He is capable of having an umbrella and of getting wet. He is a personal being, and Karen shows concern for His welfare.

Ken. When Ken's cousin comes to visit, he has trouble sharing and playing with him.

"That's *my* horsey. *I* want to ride it."

"Ken, why don't you let Bobby ride your horsey now?"

"No, *I* want to ride it. It's *mine!*"

"Ken, look at these pretty blankets. Why don't you put them over these chairs and make a barn with them? Bobby can ride out on the horsey to get the cows."

Ken is ready for something new and runs to put the "barn" together, while cousin Bobby quickly jumps on the horse and rides. But the two play with their "own things," doing little in playing together.

What have you discovered about Ken that indicates he may be typical of twos and threes?

Ken has trouble sharing. He feels that because his toys belong to him, he should play with them.

Ken's interest span is short. When directed to something else, he is ready to go.

Ken is a loner. Even when his cousin Bobby comes to play with him, Ken plays with his choice of toy and lets Bobby play by himself. Sometimes they play together, but often their togetherness is really each doing his own thing.

Ken and Bobby use some imagination in their play. Chairs with blankets over them can become a barn. A rocking horse can ride out to a pasture to round up some cattle.

Kevin. It is almost time for lunch and Kevin is impatient to get something to eat.

"I'm hungry, Mommy. Isn't it time to eat yet?"

"Almost, Kevin. Why don't you play awhile until we're ready."

"I don't want to play. I'm hungry."

"Kevin, you can be my helper. Then we can eat soon. Will you help me put the things on the table?"

Kevin is glad to help Mother. He is happy that he can be a helper and happy too that he can help get lunch ready earlier. He hurries back and forth, putting on the things the way Mother tells him.

What does Kevin reveal about twos and threes?

Kevin is impatient when he wants something. He is not ready to wait the necessary time to get what he wants.

Kevin resists a suggestion to "go do something" while Mother finishes preparing lunch. He insists on his wants.

When Kevin is given a new and happy experience, he is willing to give up his demands temporarily. He is happy to help Mother, especially when he realizies that his work really is helping her and indirectly is helping him too.

A COMPARATIVE PROFILE OF TWOS AND THREES

The following tables will help you point out how the characteristics of twos and threes relate to each other. One must recognize that a two-year-old is technically any child from two years and zero days through two years and 364 days. There is continuous growth throughout the year toward the third birthday. Hence, when we speak of a two-year-old in this profile, we are, of necessity speaking in a rather broad sense. A child of two years and 300 days is more akin to a three-year-old. But the profile should help to give some orientation to the general characteristics of the age and learning levels considered here.

TABLE 6.1

PHYSICAL CHARACTERISTICS OF TWOS AND THREES

CHARACTER-ISTIC	TWOS	THREES
Height	About 33-38 inches	About 35-40 inches
Weight	About 25-35 pounds	About 27-40 pounds
Posture	Slightly stooped, not fully erect; knees and elbows somewhat bent, leans forward while running	Walks upright now, swings arms more like an adult
Sleeping habits	Needs about twelve hours at night plus a two-hour nap in the afternoon; tires easily; is upset by confusion	May begin staying awake during afternoon nap time, but should "rest" during that time anyway
Toilet habits	Does not yet have complete control; is still subject to accidents, especially at night during sleep	Should have good control now, except may need to be put on the toilet before going to bed
Eating habits	Schedule is important, adds to security; a snack may be necessary between meals, but should be small and simple; foods may include such things as slices of fresh fruit (oranges, apples), bananas, fruit cups, milk, eggs, toast, meat or fish in easy-to-chew form, cooked vegetables (peas, beans, carrots), pudding, graham crackers, juices, small sandwiches, soups, and lettuce	Schedule is still important; the same foods could be used with some variation
Dressing ability	Is beginning to dress self; does best with familiar clothing that pulls on or off or buttons in front	Has learned to button and unbutton front and side but not in back; can remove shoes and can slip in and out of some boots; has not yet learned to tie shoes

TABLE 6.2

MENTAL DEVELOPMENT OF TWOS AND THREES

ACTIVITY	TWOS	THREES
Reading	"Reads" pictures by telling what is in them; likes to listen to stories or poems; interest span is three to four minutes; enjoys repetition in stories; may ask to have one story read again and again; often adds own thoughts, especially if encouraged by parent or teacher; Bible storybooks are good because they are true, and child will believe everything he hears	Still "reads" pictures by telling what is in them; enjoys rhymes, nonsense verse, and making up own stories; likes some exaggeration; alphabet books begin to hold interest, although has not yet learned to read; teacher or parent should ask questions while reading to child to stimulate thinking
Drawing	Can use crayons but does not stay within lines; likes to show off work to parent or teacher; can make simple things from clay or sand—cakes, roads, tunnels; can begin to use finger paint but makes crude designs	Is beginning to draw distinguishable objects, designs, and letters, though sizes may be disproportionate; has begun to use paint brush; crayon work is less crude than at two
Singing	Rhythm is important, especially to act out something; may be able to sing short choruses learned in Sunday school; may sing in a group but does not carry a tune; enjoys listening to records with music and stories	Some threes are beginning to stay on pitch; may sing alone but sings better in a group; still enjoys records
Playing habits	Simple wood puzzles, building blocks, simple construction sets, sandbox, stuffed animals, large wood beads or spools to string, clothespins, and plastic bottles are good now	Still enjoys many of the same toys; also likes dolls, punching bag, small wagon, and rocking horse; likes to play stories and act out parts; likes to imitate others

TABLE 6.3

SOCIAL RELATIONSHIPS OF TWOS AND THREES

SITUATION	TWOS	THREES
Playing with others	Is a loner and may play by self even when with a group; needs to play with others to develop social consciousness; is extremely possessive of own toys and must be encouraged (not forced) to let even closest friends play with toys	Has learned to take part in group activities more than at two; may also try to bully or dominate others; is more group minded; more willing to share toys and will play with others in a group
Living with parents	Gets into everything around the house; can be encouraged to help but needs supervision; if left alone, can create chaos	Is learning not to get into everything; is eager to help mother or father when asked; enjoys being appreciated for helpfulness
Going to Sunday school	Needs contact with others and needs to hear Bible stories and music	Learns to sing with others; learns simple Bible truths; needs to share ideas with others

SPIRITUAL LESSONS FOR TWOS AND THREES

Twos and threes are ready to learn such important truths as these: God loves me. God made the world. God made me. God takes care of me. God wants to help me. God is always with me. Jesus loves me. Jesus is my best Friend. Jesus is the Savior. Jesus is God's Son. God gave me a family. Father and Mother take care of me. Father and Mother love me. God wants me to love brothers and sisters. God wants me to help my family. I get my clothing from plants and animals God made. I get my food from plants and animals God made. I can talk to God. I can please God. I can listen to God's Word. My church is God's house. (Chap. 21, "Teaching Theological Concepts to Children," lists other spiritual truths children can be taught at this age.)

Twos and threes are ready to express their love to God and talk with Him. They are ready to listen to Bible stories and learn Bible facts and truths. They may at times find it hard to distinguish between God and Jesus. They will see many illustrations of God's love in their early home-life. If they have bad experiences with their father in the home, it may be difficult for them to think of God as a loving Father.

Twos and threes are happy to sing about God and things associated with God. They like to come to Sunday school and develop friendly thoughts toward God's house, God's people, and God's Book. This age level is vital for laying an early foundation for a strong Christian life.

MEANINGFUL EXPERIENCES FOR TWOS AND THREES

One approach to the understanding of twos and threes is through an understanding of those experiences that are meaningful to them. Experiences which may have special meaning to a child of this age may often be overlooked by the adult conditioned to a different way of life.

The experiences given here have come from actual reports by parents of twos and threes.

Twos and threes often involve themselves in parents' everyday activities. Washing the dishes, a trip to the store, a trip to the laundromat, driving the family car, filling the car with gasoline, washing the car, and taking care of household chores are all of interest for the developing child. Often they will imitate these activities and pretend that they are part of the adult world, especially the world of their father or mother.

Twos and threes have developed an interest in planting, gardening, and cultivating plants. They are usually delighted to be included in digging, watering, planting seeds and in pulling weeds. But since their interest span is short, they will soon find that this is "work" and lose interest in it. They are also curious about the color and texture of leaves and flowers and their fragrance. They may find a special delight with a plant in their room.

Twos and threes have an early interest in simple tools, such as hammers, pliers, and screwdrivers. It is not surprising to find that toymakers manufacture wood or plastic tools for young children so that they may imitate father in household maintenance.

Making a scrapbook is fun for two- or three-year-olds. If parents will involve themselves in this activity, helping the child go through old magazines, clipping pictures out with the child's suggestions, and helping the child mount them in a scrapbook, they will find that the child has a growing imagination in the selection and use of this material. Pictures are chosen on the basis of the child's interests at this age level, such as pets, homes, farm animals, families, and other related subjects.

The child's room and home are of special interest. The world of activity is small, compared to older children, and the room and home form a large proportion of it. Thus experiences that center on room and home are of special interest.

Pets provide meaningful experiences for two- and three-year-olds. They may either be their own pets or the pets that they would like to have.

Twos and threes are interested in the care of a baby in the family or neighborhood. They learn how Mother and Father hold the baby, feed it, and care for it. This may develop a natural curiosity in the child's own time spent as a baby.

Young children develop a natural curiosity and interest in thunderstorms. They often learn fear or courage from parents' reaction to the storm.

Men who serve the home and community, such as milkmen, mailmen, policemen, firemen, and garbage collectors, attract the interest of young children. Since these occupations touch the lives of the twos and threes more than accountants, executives, or teachers, it is understandable that they should develop an early interest in them.

The family atmosphere is an important factor in the young children's attitudes toward God and His Word. If they live with a family suffering from undue stress, it is more difficult to appreciate a God of love and kindness. Parental relationships, with one another and with the children, leave lasting impressions on the young child as they form early concepts about spiritual things.

The world of books is an important part of the child's vicarious experiences. At this early age level, of course, children become acquainted with books through parents who read to them. This in itself is an important experience, bringing child and parent close together physically and mentally. Twos and threes are ready to listen to short, simple Bible stories and react to them.

SUMMARY

This discussion has been purposely general because no two children are alike. A parent reading this will automatically compare a child with the characteristics given and will discover that in some ways, his toddler is ahead of what has been mentioned, or perhaps, that a certain child is not as tall or heavy or active as the average descriptions given here. This should cause no alarm.

It would prove helpful—and certainly very interesting—for a mother to keep a diary of her child: how the day was spent, likes and dislikes, reactions to various situations, food enjoyed, toys that are favorites, special gifts, and many other little details. As she looks back over the previous entries, she will notice problems or needs that did not seem apparent when they occurred; she will then be able to see what areas her child is proficient in and in what areas she needs to concentrate more attention. She could also alert the Sunday school teacher or dayschool worker to be aware of certain habits the child may be forming or ways in which they can encourage and help.

FOR FURTHER READING

Ames, Louise B. *Your 2-Year-Old.* New York: Delacorte, 1976.

———. *Your 3-Year-Old.* New York: Delacorte, 1976.

Ames, Louise B., and Joan Chase. *Don't Push Your Preschooler.* Rev. ed. New York: Harper & Row, 1980.

Barbour, Mary A. *You Can Teach 2's and 3's.* Wheaton, Ill.: Scripture Press, Victor Books, 1974.

Beechick, Ruth. *Teaching Preschoolers.* Denver: Accent, 1979.

Brubaker, J. Omar, and Robert E. Clark. *Understanding People.* Wheaton, Ill.: Evangelical Teacher Training Assn., 1981.

Church, Joseph. *Understanding Your Child from Birth to Three.* New York: Random, 1973.

Clark, Robert E. *Teaching Preschoolers with Confidence.* Wheaton, Ill.: Evangelical Teacher Training Assn., 1983.

Craig, Grace. *Human Development,* 3d ed. Englewood Cliffs, N.J.: Prentice-Hall, 1983.

Dobson, James. *The Strong-Willed Child:* Birth Through Adolescence. Wheaton: Tyndale, 1978.

Gesell, Arnold. *The First Five Years of Life.* New York: Harper, 1940.

Gesell, Arnold, and Francis L. Ilg. *Infant and Child in the Culture of Today.* New York: Harper, 1943.

Gilbert, Sara D. *Three Years to Grow: Guidance for Your Child's First Three Years.* New York: Parents Magazine Press, 1972.

Gilliland, Anne Hitchcock. *Understanding Preschoolers.* Nashville, Tenn.: Convention, 1969.

Harrell, Donna, and Wesley Haystead. *Creative Bible Learning for Early Childhood: Birth Through Five Years.* Ventura, Calif.: Gospel Light, Regal Books, 1977.

How to Do Bible Learning Activities: Early Childhood. Ventura, Calif.: Gospel Light, Regal Books, 1982.

Hymes, James L. *Teaching the Child Under Six.* Columbus, Ohio: Merrill, 1981.

Marzollo, Jean. *Supertot: Creative Learning Activities for Children from 1 to 3.* New York: Harper & Row, 1977.

McDiarmid, Norma J. *Loving and Learning: Interacting with Your Child from Birth to 3.* New York: Harcourt, 1975.

Pomeranz, Virginia E. *The First Five Years: A Relaxed Approach to Child Care.* Garden City, N.Y.: Doubleday, 1973.

Soderholm, Marjorie E. *Understanding the Pupil: Part 1, The Pre-School Child.* Grand Rapids: Baker, 1955.

Margaret M. Self

7

Understanding Fours and Fives

- **Tasks and Needs**
  TRUST
  AUTONOMY
  INITIATIVE
- **Age-Level Characteristics**
  PHYSICAL
  MENTAL
  SOCIAL
  EMOTIONAL
  SPIRITUAL

Those who guide young children often become so absorbed in providing adequate materials and equipment, establishing a workable schedule, and arranging for other elements of a teaching/learning program that they overlook the initial step in planning—understanding the child.

All children at given age levels follow a certain general pattern of growth and development. Understanding specific characteristics of this pattern makes it possible to predict how a child will most likely respond. Although a five-year-old is generally like most other fives, he is so influenced by his environment,

MARGARET M. SELF, B.A., an early childhood specialist and author, lives in Oak Harbor, Washington.

health, heredity, and other factors that he proceeds through his pattern of development at his own unique pace, different from all others. The range of normality is wide; no two children develop at exactly the same rate and in exactly the same way. So those who guide young children need also to be aware of the specific personality traits, needs, and abilities of each individual child—each one's own inner timetable.

Having a knowledge of the stages of development within a generally predictable pattern and recognizing the developmental tasks a child is ready to accomplish enables teachers to know the kinds of behavior to expect from most children. This knowledge encourages teachers to plan activities during which children can experience success and at the same time be challenged to extend their learning. For example, the teacher who guides a group of just-turned fours will choose books with a shorter portion of the story on each page than those selected for a group of older fives. The teacher who is aware of the group's attention span will limit group time (when all children assemble on the rug) to ten to twelve minutes. As fours grow older, the teacher will increase the group time in relation to the group's maturing ability to sustain interest in such a setting. With older fives, for instance, the teacher will plan learning experiences in which children may sequence several story pictures, answer simple comprehension questions, or make up a new phrase for a familiar song.

Teachers who recognize stages of development are able to deal with most behavior problems in an easy, matter-of-fact way. The four-year-old who was seemingly well adjusted and outgoing yesterday and who turns shy today may be going through a typical stage. Of course the staff member will observe the child to see if the shyness passes in a short time. If not, the teacher will examine possible causes. A child's growth pattern is often a series of mountains and valleys, ups and downs. Very rarely does growth proceed consistently on a smoothly rising incline.

TASKS AND NEEDS

During their early years all children must begin accomplishing several basic tasks, the completion of which is essential to adequate personality development. They began working on these tasks immediately after birth and continue throughout their life span. During these years, each child must begin to develop a sense of trust, a sense of autonomy, and a sense of initiative.[1] These tasks are not independent of each other. The accomplishment of any one of the three is dependent on the successful achievement (to a degree) of each of the other two.

Related to this life-long learning comes the need for children to develop a

---

1. Erik H. Erikson, *Childhood and Society* (New York: Norton, 1963), chap. 7.

strong concept of self-worth. They also need to achieve an appropriate measure of independence, relate successfully to peers and adults, and acquire feelings of acceptance, as well as develop a measure of self-control.

Unfortunately, these developmental tasks and needs are often the least obvious to the casual observer. However, a teacher's knowledge and understanding of this vital aspect of early childhood and its importance to the child's total personality development is essential. With this information as a background, the teacher can then plan specific ways to help children accomplish these tasks.

TRUST

Learning to trust is the first task in the development of a healthy personality. Children begin this task as newborns. They learn to trust as they discover they are kept safe, are fed when they are hungry, and are given attention when they want it. By the time they near their second birthday, they learn to trust their environment, the people in it, and themselves. This sense of trust is the basis on which Christian faith can grow. As children learn to trust the adults in their lives, a foundation is being laid for trust in God.

The relationships children have with the adults around them at church can contribute significantly to developing a sense of trust. The presence of a different worker each week means the child and that adult must begin a new relationship. This is too much to require of a child. Trust relationships are more easily built when the same adults are seen regularly.

Another way for the church staff to help children develop a sense of trust is to listen attentively to what they have to say. Keep the secret shared, no matter how cute or trivial it may seem.

Love is an important ingredient in the task of learning to trust. Children need love that is unconditional and ever available. That love must express a concern to give what is required for all areas of growth and development. Children need to know that they matter very much to someone and that someone cares what happens to them. They can tolerate many deprivations, but never total rejection.

Children need to feel loved and accepted regardless of what they do or do not do. A teacher's actions, smile, even tone of voice can say, "I love you." A smile across the room or a friendly pat on the shoulder is often enough to let the child know he is important to you. Use the child's name often as you talk with him. Appreciate each child as an individual. Often the child who seems the least lovable is the one who needs love most. Pray for that child and ask God to show love to him through you. Offer honest praise and encouragement. Listen to the child when he speaks to you. Kneel down to his eye level. Show a genuine interest in what he has to tell you. "Let us not love with word or with tongue, but in deed and truth" (1 John 3:18, NASB).

Fours and fives need to feel they are acceptable just the way they are, all the time, regardless of the way they look, the clothes they wear, or whether they are "good" or "bad." Children who feel loved and accepted for themselves—not for what they do—will gain self-confidence and feel valued. If they feel acceptance must be earned, they may feel insecure and unworthy. Rebellious or aggressive behavior might be a means of attracting attention to a need for acceptance.

Children who feel loved and accepted by adults will find it easier to feel accepted by God. Help them know they are acceptable to God at all times. Avoid giving the impression that God will not love them if they are naughty. God's love is a free, unconditional gift. God never withholds love in order to secure obedience. "For by grace you have been saved through faith; and that not of yourselves, it is the gift of God (Eph. 2:8, NASB).

The young child is taking those important first steps toward finding himself as a person. When he is five, he usually begins kindergarten and moves beyond the circle of his family. The child needs to know that though he may reach out for new and exciting adventures, he can depend on his own world to remain familiar and comforting—that he can trust what he has come to know.

Knowing and feeling he is loved is essential to a child's feeling of security. Show him through your actions that you love him. Show him that he is important to you because he is himself, not because of the way he compares with other children. It is through experiencing your love that the child begins to understand God's love. When he feels secure and comfortable in your love, he will begin to feel secure in God's love.

Children find security in familiar surroundings and procedures; therefore, plan a program that follows the same general routine each session. They also find security in limits. They need to know what is expected of them and what they can and cannot do. Set limits for the appropriate use of equipment and material. Avoid forbidding certain behavior at one time but allowing the same behavior later under the same circumstances. Consistency helps the child to be able to predict what will happen. Consistency builds trust in the environment and people in it. Allow as much freedom as possible with these limits.

AUTONOMY

Developing feelings of autonomy (independence) is another developmental task fours and fives are in the process of accomplishing. This is an area in which they need the assistance of understanding adults.

"Let me do it" are familiar words to those who guide young children. This plea is evidence of a child's first steps toward independence. He is attempting to discover his own abilities. The child needs to know he can do things on his own but with the assurance there is an understanding adult nearby on whom he can depend if he needs assistance.

Careful, thoughtful guidance will help young children attain independence. Allow freedom in choosing materials and activities. Free choice requires that materials be readily accessible. Arrange materials so the children know where they are and can reach materials without asking for assistance and return them when through.

In order to grow in independence, children must be allowed to assume the appropriate amount of responsibility when they show they are ready. Give as much independence as they can handle. Encourage their efforts and praise their accomplishments. Because children's skills vary, the teacher needs to know the ability of each child in the group.

Children are not born with the ability to control their own actions. They must develop self-control with the careful guidance of adults they trust. Developing this self-control does not happen overnight. It takes time. Fours and fives first need to know what adults expect of them. After they have tested these limits and found them to be consistent, they begin to develop their own system of self-control. By adhering to a well-organized routine and enforcing a few rules of conduct, adults encourage children in their efforts to be responsible for their own actions.

To develop self-control, fours and fives also need consistent, positive guidance. They need a balance between rigid authority and total permissiveness. They need limits—but freedom to move about within these limits. As children receive thoughtful and careful guidance, a learning process takes place. They become responsible for their own behavior. From this responsibility grows self-control, discipline from within.

INITIATIVE

Learning to develop a sense of initiative—the desire to go ahead and discover—is the third in a young child's developmental tasks. "What will I become?" he asks himself. He wants to discover what his place in the world will be. He wants to plan and organize, to put his own ideas into practice. He is eager to "get the show on the road."

Dramatic play offers a child opportunities to "try on" different roles. It takes initiative to explore the possibilities of becoming a fireman or a doctor.

Daring to try out new ways and to take on new responsibilities requires an atmosphere conducive to experimenting. A climate in which everyone must do the same thing at the same time and in the same way stifles a child's initiative. He soon learns that attempting new ideas (the results for which he might be blamed) is too much risk for him to take. Encouraging a child's initiative generates healthy personality growth.

Children can usually withstand other deprivations, if only the adults in their lives help them to develop feelings of self-worth. The importance of a positive self-concept is deeply rooted in biblical teaching. Jesus taught that a good self-concept is necessary if we are to be capable of loving others. So He linked love of self and love of others in the second of His great commandments, "You shall love your neighbor as yourself" (Mark 12:31, NASB).

This kind of self-image definitely affects a child's ability and desire to learn. It allows him to give his attention to the business of learning. It encourages him to explore and experiment.

All children need to be assured of their own unique place in the world of people. They need assurance of worth as individuals. Helping children feel good about themselves is not building conceit. It is, rather, enabling them to try, to be creative, to make use of their world.

Recognition of worth depends largely on the child's experience of love, security, and acceptance expressed by adults. How can a child feel acceptable unless someone accepts him? When he feels secure in the love and acceptance of adults around him, he can begin to feel good about himself. When he realizes that he has certain rights and dignity as an individual, he can more readily recognize the rights and dignity of others.

AGE-LEVEL CHARACTERISTICS

Although Christian educators are concerned primarily with the spiritual development of children, they dare not overlook the physical, mental, emotional, and social aspects of the total personality. Teachers who are aware of this multifaceted growth pattern have increased opportunities to relate the gospel of God's love to every part of the child's being—to relate the whole of life to the God who designed man with a physical, mental, emotional, and social, as well as a spiritual, dimension of life.

"For everything there is an appointed season, and there is a proper time for every project under heaven" (Eccles. 3:11, Berkeley). The right time for a child to behave like a four-year-old is during the time he is four years old. Being four is not simply a time to get ready for five!

The qualities that come with being four or five are not imperfections or flaws. Early childhood is not a disease to be endured or cured like measles or the common cold. Instead, early childhood is the "appointed season" and the "proper time" to behave like a young child.

In their study of age-level characteristics, teachers of fours and fives need to be aware of the readiness concept—those "teachable moments" when a child shows he is ready for the next learning step. The alert teacher provides a variety of learning experiences at the child's level and then identifies that next step in light of his success and interest. For example, before introducing the idea of missions to fives, the aware teacher will observe the ability of the child to see the relationship between two events. He will watch for children's interests in others and in the world beyond home and church. Before introducing a game using a variety of colors, the teacher will be sure children can easily recognize primary colors. The teacher alert to the readiness concept will lengthen story time when children's increasing attentiveness is noted. "The single most significant secret to good education . . . is *timing*. The trick is to teach when someone is able to learn, and when he wants to be taught. Good education is the art of striking while the iron is hot."[2]

PHYSICAL CHARACTERISTICS

Four-year-olds are in a period of rapid growth. They are a whirlwind of activity, running, jumping, climbing, twisting; they are noisy and boisterous. They seem to be constantly on the go. They use both feet going up and down stairs; they hop on one foot, turn and run, stop and start quickly. They are stronger and more confident than they are at three.

Their rapidly developing large muscles need exercise. Leg and arm muscles are developing more than those in their fingers. Their bodies demand movement. They actually hurt when required to sit still for more than five or ten minutes. Wise teachers alternate physical activities with quiet experiences so that the child is not required to sit still for long periods.

Fours are gaining in their control of small muscles. Although use of these muscles is often not dependable, they enjoy attempting activities that involve coordination. They like to practice zipping, buttoning, and cutting, but they have difficulty coloring within lines.

Constant activity causes the four-year-old to become easily fatigued, tense, or confused. Tiredness may result in unacceptable behavior. Teachers need to be alert for the child who is becoming overstimulated in order to redirect his attention to a quiet activity.

Five-year-olds are in a leveling off period in their physical development, but are still full of energy and vim. They are beginning to lose their chubbiness. They are getting taller—with longer arms and legs. Coordination is much better than at four. However, large muscles are still developing. Although they are less restless than at four, they still need exercise. They are becoming more and more skilled at all motor activities, and play is increasingly purposeful. A five-year-old hits the beanbag target more often now than when four. Eye-hand coordination is improving noticeably. He enjoys using his physical skills. Often he wants to demonstrate his physical skill. "I can stand on my toes. Want to see me do it?"

While the growth rate of five-year-olds is slowing, girls are maturing more rapidly than boys in their physical development. Boys who become restless during a large group activity might be reflecting their physical inability to sit motionless for more than a few minutes.

Fives are increasing in their ability to sing a tune, although they often do not

2. James L. Hymes, Jr. *The Child Under Six* (Englewood Cliffs, N.J.: Prentice-Hall, 1963), p. 117.

sing on pitch. They enjoy assembling construction toys, and can handle small objects and tie shoelaces. They may still have difficulty in coloring within lines or cutting accurately.

Most fives are learning to print in public school kindergarten. Wise teachers praise their accomplishments but are careful not to embarrass the child who is not yet able to write. They find other areas in the child to commend and praise.

What does this brief overview of physical characteristics imply for those who work with fours and fives?

• Arrange the room with open spaces to provide for moving about without bumping into tables and chairs. When space is at a premium, remove some of the furniture. Work on the floor.

• Offer both large and small muscle activities. Block-building with unit blocks, puzzles (some with a few large pieces; others with ten-to-twelve smaller pieces) home-living play, and collage-making provide opportunity for muscle stretching.

• Include frequent changes in activities, from quiet to active then quiet again, in order to meet the children's physical needs.

MENTAL CHARACTERISTICS

Fours and fives are hungry for stimulation! They are curious. They want to know and are eager to learn.

Four-year-olds have discovered they can put thoughts and ideas into words. And people will listen. A powerful tool, indeed! They use their new-found language skills almost constantly, liberally punctuated with "Why?" and "How?"—sometimes to get information, sometimes to gain attention. They have discovered that experimenting with words, such as making up silly rhymes, is fun. Often they need assistance in distinguishing between what is real and what is imaginary. They have a foot in both worlds. And the tactful adult can offer guidance that allows them to save face. When a child relates an event that is obviously a product of his imagination, the teacher can say, "That was really interesting! Have you ever seen the real lions we have at the zoo? How do they look?"

Limited comprehension of time and space is typical of four-year-olds. They understand "today" and "yesterday." Such expressions as "a long time ago" and "far away" are adequate for both fours and fives in Bible story settings.

Fours and fives are literal-minded. They accept the words they hear to mean exactly that. Symbolism and other figures of speech are extremely confusing and misleading. When a shy child is asked, "Has the cat got your tongue?" he presumes that to be a normal occurrence! Equating misdeeds with a "black heart" is also beyond a child's comprehension.

Five is the age of intellectual growth. Although rooted in reality, they have an active imagination. They know the difference between real and pretend in their world of "I'm the daddy and you're the mommy" dramatic play. However, they are not always sure when adults are pretending. Five-year-olds are honestly curious about the world around them. They ask questions because they want to know. Chatting with five-year-olds can be a delightful experience. Their increasing vocabulary allows them to use complete sentences. They are beginning to understand cause-and-effect relationships.

Adults are often fooled by the five-year-old's seemingly accurate use of words. They assume that because he uses certain words, he understands their meaning. This is not always the case. Five-year-olds are great at parroting what they have heard on TV or from adults. They often think they understand the words. Adults too may think they understand, but they need to remember that words are not yet the best criterion of what a five-year-old knows or understands.

Teachers should be especially careful in helping the four- and five-year-old learn Bible verses. The goal for these ages is to build understanding. Be certain they understand what they are repeating. Again and again, with conversation, explanation, and pictures, build a groundwork of familiarity with understanding. Memorization may then be the eventual result, but do not make it the aim.

Five-year-olds are able to use equipment and materials in an increasingly varied way. Blocks become complex buildings or a launching pad. Collages take on creative designs. When they draw a picture, they usually make the important parts the largest. The five-year-old likes to have something to show for his efforts. He demonstrates an increasing interest in letters and numbers. "What does this say?" and "How do you make a W?" are familiar questions.

Both fours and fives enjoy stories. Fives especially thrive on answering questions and talking about the story they had just heard. Older fives like to have the teacher begin a simple story for them to finish.

The concept of time for five-year-olds is confined to the span of a day. They are likely to tell the teacher accurately what happened that morning or what they anticipate that evening. They also recall past events quite well, but not in terms of the time that has elapsed since they occurred. Avoid asking five-year-olds, "What was last Sunday's memory verse?" Rather, say, "Our Bible tells us to 'Love one . . .' " Pause to let children complete the verse. Then repeat it with the children several times.

The attention span of four-and-five-year-olds is sustained when they are actively involved. Listening experiences need to include related pictures and objects to illustrate the words they hear. They learn most effectively through firsthand experiences. Since they do not read to learn, they must depend on other avenues. They look, listen, and explore. They learn by active involvement as well as by sitting still, listening.

What does this say to those who work with fours and fives? "Let me do it!" is the familiar plea of the young child. By all means let them do it.

• Plan lesson-related activities so that fours and fives are actively involved in discovering and practicing ways to know and to understand God's Word, His world, and His love.

• Avoid symbolism! Use words and phrases that mean exactly what they say.

• Ask questions requiring more than a yes or no answer.

SOCIAL CHARACTERISTICS

Four-year-olds are making a wonderful discovery—friends! At three, they still enjoy playing alongside others. Now, they often consciously seek out one or two children with whom to play. They form little groups and exclude others, often quite rudely! Sometimes fours are shy about entering a group and wait until they are invited. They feel left out if others do not accept them. Teachers need to plan activities in which fours have repeated opportunities to take turns and share materials with perhaps three or four others. Like many other concepts in Christian living, this one is not learned in a single Sunday. Fours (and fives) need repeated opportunities to practice scriptural truths, such as, "Share what you have with others" (Heb. 13:16, *20th Cent.*).

In spite of their newfound enthusiasm for others, four-year-olds need guidelines on how to get along together. A simple suggestion from a teacher to a quarrelsome group often redirects the play that has deteriorated. "These blocks are ours. And you can't have them!" can be turned by suggesting, "It looks to me like your road needs a tunnel. Here are two boards just right for a tunnel."

Although a four-year-old enjoys interaction with other children, his keenest interest lies in himself. This self-centeredness shows in his greeting. "Look at my new shoes!" "I'm going to the park after church." "My mother bought me my new dress." The four-year-old uses personal pronouns overtime. Almost all his conversation turns back to himself.

One of the four-year-old's most heartfelt desires is to win the approval of those about him, particularly the adults in his life. Often he feels that the end justifies the means. Grabbing, showing off, wanting to be first, and interrupting are frequently his tools to get attention.

Four-year-olds test their world. They are often brashly confident, and may exhibit unacceptable behavior just to see how far they can go. They find security in the very limit they defy. Yet they need the security of limits that do not hinder their freedom to experiment. Teachers should be consistent and positive in their guidance, emphasizing the behavior they desire. For example, they may say, "We keep the clay on the table," rather than, "Don't put the clay in the book rack."

Fives are delightful children! They are usually friendly, enjoy playing with others, are interested in taking turns and sharing, although they may not always do so. Generally, they want to be helpful. They seem content with themselves and those about them.

Their play is still limited to small groups. Improved language skill allows them to offer suggestions and share ideas. They have fewer conflicts with others than they did at four. Often they can resolve their problems without adult assistance. However, when such assistance is necessary, five-year-olds usually understand what is fair. They are learning to respect the rights and feelings of others. With guidance, they can develop a genuine interest and concern for those about them.

The child of five exhibits a strong spirit of conformity. When one child says, "This juice tastes sour," immediately others agree. Teachers can use this "strength-in-numbers" to foster consideration for the feelings and needs of others. For example, "Susan hasn't been able to come to Sunday School because she is sick. I think getting some "get-well" pictures from our class would make her feel glad. Let's draw her some pictures so she'll know we love her."

Adult approval is important for five-year-olds to possess. They actively seek praise and are willing to cooperate to get it. They identify with the adults they most admire—feeling with those adults, wanting to be like them, and emulating their actions. When adult-child relationships are warm and friendly, identification can grow. What an opportunity for teachers to put their Christian beliefs and teachings into practice!

Although five-year-olds are becoming friendly social beings, their world still centers on themselves. Their authority is "my mommy and my daddy." They interpret the actions of those about them in terms of their own needs and desires.

How does this overview of social characteristics affect a teacher's procedures?

• Reinforce a child's positive behavior. "Bob, I like the way you moved over to make room for Meg in our circle."

• Plan learning experiences in which children have repeated opportunities to take turns and share materials.

• Be consistent and positive in guiding behavior. Tell a child the behavior you desire rather than the kind you want to discourage.

EMOTIONAL CHARACTERISTICS

The four-year-old often exhibits his emotions quite intensely. At a moment's notice, he can burst into a rage. "I'm mad at him!" he will exclaim, usually with decisive gestures. His feelings of love and hate, joy and sorrow, fear and pleasure are all very close to the surface. But these emotional outbursts are usually fleeting. In a few minutes, all is forgotten, and he is busy with a new interest. Fives also continue to display their emotions, but their outbursts are becoming less frequent. They are beginning to discover other ways to solve their problems.

When a child exhibits strong feelings, consider these suggestions: Help him know it is all right to have strong feelings. Help him recognize their validity. Mirror his feelings by saying, "When Timmy knocked over your blocks, you were pretty mad." Avoid, "You shouldn't be mad at Timmy. That's not nice." Rather, say, "Tell me what happened. . . . Did you tell Timmy how you felt? . . . Maybe he knocked over your blocks by accident. Maybe he didn't mean to." Teach the child that he cannot employ the "eye for an eye and tooth for a tooth" concept. Assure him that an adult nearby can be trusted to protect him from his own hostile actions. "I cannot let you hit Timmy. And I cannot let anyone hit you."

Fear is probably the outstanding emotion fours and fives have to live with. Fear is part of a child's growing-up process. It is an unfortunate child whose teachers or parents use fear as an instrument of discipline. (Of course, a child needs to fear some things for his own protection.)

A child's fear can be lessened somewhat by a teacher's thoughtful planning. For instance, avoid the details of the crucifixion story. These awesome events tend to overwhelm the child emotionally. Emphasize the joy that "Jesus is living, and we are glad!"

Young children often reflect emotions of the adults about them. When a teacher appears worried or uneasy, children tend to mirror these feelings. Children also reflect a teacher's calm, unhurried manner.

Not all children's intense feelings are negative. They can experience intense feelings of joy and happiness and sympathy for others.

Attitudes of young children are of far greater consequence than their factual knowledge. Developing positive feelings and values should be of greater concern to teachers than a child's ability to recount information. Surrounding a child with loving, secure, and understanding Christians, who have a faith that makes a difference in the quality of their lives is a powerful teaching and learning tool.

Being aware of the emotional dimension in a child's personality allows a teacher to

• Help a child handle his strong feelings in a positive manner.

• Avoid using fear as a disciplining technique.

• Express feelings of joy with a smile and an optimistic attitude, knowing children will generally reflect these emotions.

SPIRITUAL CHARACTERISTICS

Spiritually, fours and fives think of the Lord God in a personal way. These children can sense the greatness, wonder, and love of God when His attributes are translated into specific terms within their experience. Simply telling fours and fives, "God made the world," is not nearly so meaningful as displaying natural objects for them to examine. Then, "God made everything in our world, even these beautiful shells," takes on great significance.

Fours and fives can think of the Lord Jesus as a friend who loves and cares for them. Jesus' love needs to be interpreted in specific terms. Since His love is often expressed through His provision of a loving family, guide the child by saying, "Debbie, who cooked your breakfast for you this morning? . . . Did you know the Lord Jesus planned for your mother (tailor your conversation to each child's family situation) to care for you? . . . He did! The Lord loves you, Debbie."

Children of four and five have a simple trust in God, the Lord Jesus, and in the adults about them. They are ready to accept all you tell them about God and the Lord Jesus. It is imperative that information be accurate; make sure the child does not misunderstand words, attitudes, or actions.

Fours and fives can be taught to talk to God, to thank Him, and to ask Him for the things they need. Assure the child that God answers in the way that is best—with "Yes," or "No," or "Wait."

Worship experiences—a response of heart and mind to the greatness and goodness of God—can be very real to fours and fives. Worship for young children is not limited to the time designated on the morning schedule. Moments of spontaneous worship arise most often as a teacher and one or two children are involved in an activity. For example, as Brian was working with salt-flour dough, Mr. Ross called Brian's attention to his fingers. "Just look at what your fingers are doing! I'm glad God made your hands to make such an interesting structure." Brian stopped and looked at his hands as if he had never seen them before. When Mr. Ross saw Brian's expression of wonder, he said softly, "Let's thank God for your hands." Together they prayed.

Wonder, joy, and gratitude are emotions closely related to worship. But they are not in themselves worship. A teacher, sensitive to a child's feelings, can help associate those feelings with God's goodness.

Fours and fives are beginning to recognize right and wrong. Their developing conscience is not only feeling what is right and wrong for themselves, but what is right and just for others. Fours and fives can know that disobeying is doing wrong. Children need to be assured that God *always* loves them and is ready to forgive when they are truly sorry.

A child's spiritual growth is somewhat dependent on his emotional maturity. Fours and fives think in terms of the personal, as they relate to Christlike people around them. The love and care of God the Father and of the Lord Jesus become real as children sense love from Christlike adults in their lives. Teachers who live their faith in a warm, caring relationship with children are channels through which God and His love can be made known.

In considering these spiritual characteristics,

• Plan learning experiences that translate God's (Jesus') love into the fabric of everyday living.

• Do not expect maturity beyond that which a child possesses.

• Use words a child understands; avoid symbolic phrases such as "fishers of men" or "give your heart to Jesus."

SUMMARY

There is a wide range of differences among four- and five-year-olds. Each child is an individual and develops at his own rate. However, there is enough similarity among children of the same age that specific characteristics can be noted. A teacher using these behavior traits as a general guide for planning can provide learner-centered experiences enabling young children not only to understand and retain Bible truths, but also to respond with appropriate attitudes and actions.

Knowing and understanding the ways children grow and how to work with each stage of their development is not something that is learned once and for all. Leaders and teachers must continually refer to age-level characteristics and developmental tasks as they evaluate curriculum content and procedures. They must be sure their program is attuned to the God-oriented timetable the Lord has established for each child's growth and development.

FOR FURTHER READING

BOOKS

Baker, Katherine Read, and Xenia F. Fane. *Understanding and Guiding Young Children,* 3d ed. Englewood Cliffs, N.J.: Prentice-Hall, 1975.
Beechick, Ruth. *Teaching Kindergartners.* Denver: Accent, 1980.
Bergan, John, and Ronald Henderson. *Child Development.* Columbus, Ohio: Merrill, 1979.
Biehler, Robert F. *Child Development.* 2d ed. Boston: Houghton Mifflin, 1981.

Brophy, Jere, et al. *Teaching in the Preschool.* New York: Harper & Row, 1975.

Clark, Robert E. *Teaching Preschoolers with Confidence.* Wheaton, Ill.: Evangelical Teacher Training Association, 1981.

———. "The Learner: Children." In *An Introduction to Biblical Christian Education,* edited by Werner C. Graendorf. Chicago: Moody, 1981.

Craig, Grace. *Human Development.* 3d ed. Englewood Cliffs, N.J.: Prentice-Hall, 1983.

Gregg, E. M., and J. D. Knotts. *Growing Wisdom, Growing Wonder: Helping Your Child Learn from Birth Through Five Years.* New York: Macmillan, 1980.

Harger, Grace B., and Arline J. Ban. *Teaching and Learning with Young Children.* Valley Forge, Pa.: Judson, 1979.

Harrell, Donna, and Wesley Haystead. *Creative Bible Learning for Early Childhood: Birth Through Five Years.* Ventura, Calif.: Gospel Light, Regal Books, 1977.

Haystead, Wesley. *Teaching Your Child About God.* Ventura: Calif.: Gospel Light, Regal Books, 1983.

Hildebrand, Verna. *Guiding Young Children,* 3d ed. New York: Macmillan, 1985.

———. *Introduction to Early Childhood Education.* New York: Macmillan, 1981.

How to Do Bible Learning Activities: Early Childhood. Ventura, Calif.: Gospel Light, Regal Books, 1982.

Hymes, James L. *Teaching the Child Under Six.* Englewood Cliffs, N.J.: Prentice-Hall, 1981.

Jenkins, Gladys, and Helen Shacter. *These are Your Children.* 4th ed. Glenview, Ill.: Scott, Foresman, 1975.

LeBar, Mary, and Betty Riley. *You Can Teach 4s and 5s.* Wheaton, Ill.: Scripture Press, Victor Books, 1981.

Linam, Gail. *Teaching Preschoolers.* Nashville: Convention, 1977.

Rudolph, Marguerita, and Dorothy H. Cohen. *Kindergarten and Early Schooling.* Englewood Cliffs, N.J.: Prentice-Hall, 1984.

Smart, Mollie Stevens, and Russell C. Smart. *Preschool Children: Development and Relationships,* 4th ed. New York: Macmillan, 1982.

Strickland, Jenell. *How to Guide Preschoolers.* Nashville: Convention, 1982.

———. *Reaching Preschoolers.* Nashville: Convention, 1979.

Terrell, Jerry. *Basic Preschool Work.* Nashville: Convention, 1981.

Todd, Vivian, and Helen Herreran. *The Years Before School,* 3d edition. New York: Macmillan, 1977.

Waldrop, C. Sybil. *Understanding Today's Preschoolers.* Nashville: Convention, 1982.

Wand, Zadabeth. *Bible Teaching for Preschoolers.* Nashville: Convention, 1984.

JOURNALS

Children. U.S. Children's Bureau, Superintendent of Documents, U.S. Government Printing Office, Washington, DC 20025.

Preschool Leadership. The Sunday School Board, Southern Baptist Convention, 127 Ninth Avenue North, Nashville, TN 37234.

The Young Child. National Association for the Education of Young Children, 1834 Connecticut Avenue, N.W., Washington, DC 20009.

Elsiebeth McDaniel

8

Understanding First and Second Graders (Primaries)

- Who Are the Sixes and Sevens?
- Who Is Six?
- Who Is Seven?
- How to Teach First and Second Graders

Six- and seven-year-olds come to a teacher with distinctive personalities, but with a general eagerness to learn, an unlimited curiosity, and a variety of growing skills and abilities to help them learn through what they discover themselves. Some of them are shy, soft-spoken, and quiet, while others are active, talkative, and outgoing. But all are in their believing years. These first and second graders believe that a teacher is to be trusted and followed.

When a teacher looks at these children, he cannot help but think, *Look, you are important to me. I am going to do my best for you!* A public school teacher may say this to a child and mean that he will help the child acquire a great deal of factual information in the classroom and apply it to himself. However, when a Christian teacher says, "I am going to do my best for you!" he is committing himself to prayer, preparation, time, and personal interest. He

ELSIEBETH McDANIEL, M.A., is director, early childhood publications, Scripture Press Publications, Inc., Wheaton, Illinois.

is promising to give a child one of the greatest gifts that any individual can give to another. That teacher is promising to be one of the few people in the community dedicated to helping the child come to know, love, and obey the Lord.

WHO ARE THE SIXES AND SEVENS?

First and second graders come in assorted sizes, weighing forty to seventy pounds and standing forty-five to fifty inches tall.

Thoughtless adults tend to classify them according to size. If this were a good method of classification, the tallest and heaviest children ought to be the most mature. But size is only one method of identification. A very small boy may be intellectually ahead of a husky, tall boy. Or a six-year-old may have more spiritual insight than a seven-year-old. Therefore, if we are to help children learn, we must realize that observable physical growth is only one way to measure maturity. Children are also growing mentally, spiritually, and emotionally. We are teaching the whole child. "Learning experiences need to involve the total child if we are to avoid fragmented learning. If we are to ensure the most effective learning possible, we must be aware of all areas of growth and plan for needs in each area to be met."[1]

The whole person, or total child, is involved in true learning, and true learning makes a difference in the whole person. Christian educators who see children mostly in church-related activities must realize that they see only one facet of the children's lives. Is the Sunday-school Jimmy the same boy as Little-League Jimmy or playground Jimmy? How can a Christian educator discover that Jimmy is the boy with a pet dog, a fear of the dark, a protective attitude toward a younger sister, and a growing appreciation for fairness and justice?

Next to knowing the Lord and His Word, a teacher must know his students. It is not enough to know names and addresses. The teacher must know a child and his problems—and all children do have problems. What are a child's likes and dislikes? What are his fears, strengths, and weaknesses? How does this child think, and what skills can he perform? Answers to these questions make a difference in the teaching-learning experience.

Any list of characteristics for this age group is only a number of generalizations. Books will be helpful, but a teacher learns most about his class by becoming personally involved with each one. However, even personal involvement is not enough. Children change, and the effective teacher will be aware of this. The gullible six-year-old of September becomes the wiser and more skilled seven-year-old of June. All children are in the process of becoming: they are not finished products. Do not let your mental description of children or of a

---

1. Barbara J. Bolton, *Ways to Help Them Learn: Children, Grades 1 to 6* (Glendale, Calif.: Gospel Light, Regal Books, 1972), pp. 3-4.

particular child become rigid. Change your thinking about a child as he changes mentally, socially, physically, and spiritually. Keep up with him!

One easy and perhaps humorous means of identifying a first grader is by his teeth. Pete may have white, even, attractive teeth one Sunday and have a wide gap the next week because he has lost his two front ones. All children of this age are losing baby teeth and growing permanent ones.

One can also identify sixes and sevens by their built-in need to wiggle. The growing muscles of these children must have opportunities to move. How important it is to provide a change of pace during a learning situation! It is important too that Christian educators recognize the variation among these children in the control of smaller muscles. Some children enjoy writing, coloring, cutting, and other craft activities. Still others become impatient if their efforts fall short of the standards they set for themselves. Art and craft activities are good ways of teaching as long as the children are interested, learning, and enjoying their work. However, no child should be pushed beyond his ability and enjoyment.

First and second graders are entering the "doing age." A first or second grader will learn far more by doing than by listening to his teacher talk. He will learn more by doing than by observing. His teacher, on the other hand, will learn a great deal about a child by being both an observer and a listener. "Children tell more about themselves through their behavior than through verbalization."[2]

A six or seven often expresses his attitude about himself and others through his bodily movements. Notice the way a self-confident child walks and handles himself. Then study the downward glance of a shy child, and note the small, close-to-his-body movements of his hands and arms. Boisterousness and giggling are at times the result of embarrassment, but at another time, they may be cries for attention. These attitudes may indicate frustration over something that seems impossible. Or high spirits can be merely a response to another child's sense of humor and the joy of a shared joke. As you observe children, you will notice that some behavior demonstrates a child's immaturity, whereas other behavior is the warning light of an emotional need.

Based on specialized study made by educators, we can make generalizations about each age. However, teachers must realize that children are not better at something just because they are a year older. The whole child must be regarded as a different person. An effective teacher continually revises his description and understanding of each child.

Children mature at different rates. Some sevens act like sixes and some sixes appear to be seven or older. But understanding some of the general characteristics of each year will help a teacher understand the developing children he teaches.

2. Marjorie Stith, *Understanding Children* (Nashville: Convention, 1969), p. 5.

Who Is Six?

Six is an age of transition. This child is moving from his preschool years of accomplishment. Probably at no period of life does a child accomplish as much as during the preschool years.[3] He is now eagerly looking forward to being recognized as a schoolchild who can read.

A six-year-old is entering a wider world. He is more eager than previously for the approval and acceptance of his peers. Educators should be aware of him as a person who is sensitive to criticism and is concerned about being left out of the group. A teacher may criticize unconsciously if he comments on one child's drawing and fails to comment on another child's work.

Many sixes are quite immature, even though they may be as tall as second or third graders. Emotions are very near the surface. A six may cry as easily as a preschooler. He still maintains a close hold on home and the familiar as he tentatively reaches out to the unknown. He vacillates between the need for security and the desire to try new experiences.

Sixes may or may not be competent readers because eyes have not attained full growth nor ease in left-to-right movement. Therefore, the Christian educator is careful not to make reading demands on sixes. Teachers must use visuals and methods that communicate clearly without reading ability.

Movement is one of the outstanding traits of six-year-olds! These young children must have plenty of opportunity to move. Sixes jump, rush about, and run instead of walking. They may try hard to sit still, but it will be difficult, Many of them seem unconscious of foot-tapping, twisting a lock of hair, shifting in a chair or moving it, or making facial movements. It is well to overlook this movement unless it is a disturbing factor to other children.

Though sixes enjoy activity, it does not always have to be purposeful. They will run, push, pull, jump, skip, or walk because it is more exciting than sitting still. To run for the joy of movement is more important than running a race with other children. Sixes do not enjoy competition. They are poor losers, and it is very difficult for them not to win, be first, be the best, or be the leader. Sixes need help in getting along with others and respecting others' rights and feelings. Though first graders are trying to leave babyhood behind, it is hard for many of them.

Sixes move as quickly mentally as they do physically. Their attention span is short. Do not expect them to listen to long explanations, descriptions, or narrations. Give them one idea at a time. Keep things simple! Help them thoroughly understand one new idea at a time.

Most first and second graders have very little understanding of spatial distances. It is hard for them to distinguish between Old Testament and New

3. Gladys Jenkins, Helen S. Shacter, and William W. Bauer, *These Are Your Children*, 3d ed. (Glenview, Ill.: Scott, Foresman, 1970), p. 81.

Testament events, because anything beyond their experience is simply "long, long ago." Do not try to develop Bible chronology during these years. Some very mature children may begin to grasp sequential events, but most will not. As Dorothy Cohen says,

> The existence of this very moment in time is so strong in the consciousness of children that the existence of a time before the important now is really hard for them to conceive. Even in relation to their own growth, they feel that they are as they always were, although they take it on faith that they were indeed once babies. The future, too, seems remote. . . . The same confusion holds true of space as of time. . . . Adults take this kind of knowingness about space and time as something that has always existed and assume that it exists in children, too. But careful study reveals that it does not emerge until a certain amount of maturing has taken place.[4]

Sixes are trying to determine the difference between reality and fantasy. Christian educators must be sure to teach the Bible clearly as reality. Television programs are a continuing influence in the lives of children, but sixes are not able to distinguish between reality and fantasy in TV programs. Furthermore, if adults on a telecast or in life do wrong acts, it is difficult for a six to believe it is wrong. Six-year-olds believe that adults are generally right!

Most sixes cannot divorce the church and goodness. If a person is in church, even though the person may not be a Christian, a six believes the person is OK. These children find it unbelievable that some Bible people (Pharisees and Sadducees, for example) could be wicked, since they knew Jesus and were closely associated with religion. Sixes tend to believe that anyone with religious connections must be good.

WHO IS SEVEN?

Sevens are very much like sixes. Many of the same characteristics apply to both age levels. Sevens grow out of many of these characteristics as they approach eight. A second grader usually has a very high standard of performance. That is why seven has sometimes been called the "eraser age." A seven-year-old wants to do perfect work to earn the approval of adults, his peers, and himself. He has learned in school how writing should look, how books should be read, and how assignments should be done. Now he wants to achieve that standard. Help him accept himself and his limitations. Do not minimize his attempts at perfection by urging him to hurry or by saying, "That's good enough." See the problem from his point of view, perhaps saying, "I know you want to do good work. Why don't you finish your work the best you can? Doing the best you can is more important than doing absolutely perfect work."

---

4. Dorothy Cohen, *The Learning Child* (New York: Random, 1972), p. 140.

Do not criticize a child for taking a long time. Estimate how long an activity will take and allow time for it, or change the activity. Avoid the use of involved and intricate projects which may cause frustration.

There are physical changes that occur at seven. For one thing, the sheer size and weight of the brain increases: by seven, the brain has 90% of its total weight, compared to 25% at birth. Around seven, children become more physically coordinated and graceful than they were before. At seven most children are beginning to identify themselves as to their personhood and know something of their abilities and inabilities.

Sevens worry! They worry about not being liked, being late for school, meeting new people, and not getting things done on time. Do not set impossible standards, but anticipate that in their desire for perfection, sevens will work more slowly than sixes. Be sensitive to the needs of sevens because they are sensitive people who need more praise than criticism.

Eye-hand coordination is improving at seven. If children are competent readers they will enjoy reading. Seven is a cautious age for some children. Do not shove them into new experiences until they are ready for them. Maintain a friendly, helpful attitude as you present opportunities to try writing poetry, composing a song, drawing, or using a filmstrip projector.

Seven-year-olds are more ready to fight with words than fists, though they will fight with complete physical involvement. They usually stand up for their own rights and have a growing sense of justice for themselves. Sometimes they will argue for the rights of others. Help them see that in the Bible and other stories—behavior brings its just reward. Children love the story of Jonah because he disobeyed, was punished, received forgiveness, and did right. However, they find it hard to understand how David could be just in pouring out the water from the well of Bethlehem when his men went to so much trouble to get it (2 Sam. 23:14-17).

How to Teach First and Second Graders

Many guiding principles for working with children in the first two grades of elementary school may be found in chapters 1 through 4 and 19 through 31 of this book. Suggestions here refer directly to the characteristics of first and second graders and how those characteristics influence the teaching-learning process.

Children are more likely to learn from what they can experience in a concrete, physical way than from verbalization—merely talking at them. They are very much aware of their physical senses, and they use them to discover new ideas and information. That is why it is very important to use visuals, tapes, records, role playing, and dramatization. A child learns more by playing the part of a boy who must make a choice than he does from a teacher's saying, "We must all choose what God wants us to do." When a child sees a filmstrip of God's people going through the Red Sea, he learns more than from a verbal description of the event.

These children love stories! What an opportunity to teach the Bible, which is filled with the best of stories! Be sure to emphasize that the events really are in the Bible. If the event is unfamiliar, a perceptive child may say, "Is that really in the Bible?" It is a good rule not to tell imaginary stories with Bible backgrounds unless it is absolutely necessary. There are many Christmas legends and myths that are interesting to an older child but that confuse first and second graders.

As a general rule, do not use object lessons. These children think in concrete, literal terms. It is impossible for them to understand that a lighthouse can represent the Bible, or rocks represent sin. Older children are intrigued with symbolism, but not sixes and sevens. (See chap. 20, "Children and Their Theological Concepts," for a discussion of Piaget's views on children's conceptual development.)

The Bible is the source book for all Christian education. Every lesson should be based on the Bible. However, unless you are planning to write curriculum—not an easy task!—you will do well to follow the material written for these children. Curriculum writers usually do a great deal of research before deciding what Bible lessons are suitable for first and second graders. They choose Bible material that will be easily understood and effectively related to a child's experiences. There is little for a child to apply in the story of Jephthah's vow because it is an adult situation and the consequences of the main character's actions are emotionally upsetting. Then too, because a child will learn most through stories, curriculum writers select Bible events that have a story quality about them. Principles expounded by Paul in the New Testament are generally best left for study in later years.

What do first and second graders need? As do other children, they need worship, study, expression, and Christian fellowship. Particular chapters on these and related topics should be read and related to the material in this chapter. (See chaps. 20-26.)

First and second graders are ready for all the basic truths of Scripture if they are presented on the children's level and related to their lives. When they feel guilty, lonely, or frustrated, they need to understand and experience the Lord's help. When they are happy, they need to associate the Lord with the good things in this world.

What specifically should we teach? We cannot teach children what we have not learned ourselves. Remember, "Religion is more caught than taught." Probably most of these children think about God in a physical form. Their understanding of Him is related to their experiences with adults. They respond readily to the idea of God as Creator, but the thought of God still at work in His creation is difficult for them to grasp. If Christian educators emphasize such attributes of God as love, kindness, wisdom, perfection, and goodness, then maturity will bring about the fuller realization that God is Spirit. When a child asks, "What does God look like?" the teacher may say, "God does not need a body as we do. The important thing to know is that He loves us and wants us to love Him."

At six or seven, many children are ready to receive the Lord Jesus Christ as Savior. At this age, a child begins to put together a connected story of the life of Jesus—from the baby in the manger to the risen Savior. He can understand that he has a personal responsibility to God. He can feel secure in God's love and forgiveness.

How should we teach these children? In the ways they learn best. We tell them Bible stories because they like stories and can easily follow the action. We ask them to answer questions in order to test their knowledge and understanding of how what they know applies to them. We ask them to express themselves through role playing, assignments, art, and writing activities, because *im*pression—our teaching—must always be followed by *ex*pression. Expressional activities help a child put into practice what he has learned. Teachers learn through these activities what a child has understood and is willing to make his own experience.

More important than a rigid schedule is a variety of experiences. Storytelling, filmstrips, and singing can be accomplished in a large group—up to fifty children. However, original skits (or any dramatization), creative activities such as composing a song, writing poetry, handwork, or discussion, should be used in smaller groups of five to ten pupils.

Remember that each child enters the learning experience as a total person. Some activities demand his use of seeing and hearing; but other activities demand bodily movement, creative thinking, and small muscle control. Children need a change of activity—a variety of learning experiences. It is seldom justifiable to spend an hour in any one activity. Gauge the interest of the children, and change activities to meet their needs. About twenty minutes is long enough for most activities, and sometimes, a shorter period is advisable. Some children will learn more through role playing, others through seeing a filmstrip. Vary your teaching methods to reach the various learning styles of your students.

It is much easier to read a book about children than it is to teach them. However, working with live boys and girls in their world will be ever so much more helpful and beneficial than reading. Let your reading be a guide and a means of providing as much information as possible. But the test of teaching is teaching! Even as the children learn through doing, so must you!

SUMMARY

The teacher's concept of the whole person, or total child, makes a difference in learning. Teachers must view each child as an individual and yet recognize age-level characteristics, attitudes and needs. An effective teacher continually revises his understanding of each child.

First and second graders need a variety of experiences. These children can generally engage in one activity for about twenty minutes, although their attention spans will vary according to their interest and individual responses. Teaching methods should be varied to reach the different learning styles of the students.

FOR FURTHER READING

Bergan, John, and Ronald Henderson, *Child Development.* Columbus, Ohio: Merrill, 1979.

Biehler, Robert F. *Child Development.* 2d ed. Boston: Houghton Mifflin, 1981.

Bolton, Barbara J., and Charles T. Smith. *Creative Bible Learning for Children.* Ventura, Calif.: Gospel Light, Regal Books, 1977.

Brubaker, J. Omar, and Robert E. Clark. *Understanding People.* 2d ed. Wheaton, Ill.: Evangelical Teacher Training Assn., 1981.

Cohen, Dorothy. *The Learning Child.* New York: Random, Pantheon Books, 1972.

Craig, Grace. *Human Development.* 3d ed. Englewood Cliffs, N.J.: Prentice-Hall, 1983.

How to Do Bible Learning Activities: Grades 1-6. 2 vols. Ventura, Calif.: Gospel Light, Regal Books, 1982, 1984.

Ginott, Haim. *Teacher and Child.* New York: Macmillan, 1972.

Jenkins, Gladys G., Helen Schacter, and William W. Bauer. *These Are Your Children.* 4th ed. Glenview, Ill.: Scott Foresman, 1975.

Lichtenwalner, Muriel, and Arline Ban. *Teaching and Learning with Early Elementary Children.* Valley Forge, Pa.: Judson, 1979.

McDaniel, Elsiebeth, and Lawrence O. Richards. *You and Children.* Chicago: Moody, 1973.

Price, B. Max. *Understanding Today's Children.* Nashville: Convention, 1982.

Schimmels, Cliff. *The First Three Years of School: A Survivor's Guide.* Old Tappan, N.J.: Revell, 1985.

Shelly, Judith Allen. *The Spiritual Needs of Children.* Downers Grove, Ill.: InterVarsity, 1982.

Smith, Charles T. *Ways to Plan and Organize Your Sunday School: Children, Grades 1 to 6.* Glendale, Calif.: Gospel Light, Regal Books, 1971.

Stith, Marjorie. *Understanding Children.* Nashville: Convention, 1969.

Sarah Eberle

9

Understanding Third and Fourth Graders (Middlers)

- **Who Is a Middler?**
- **Aspects of Developmental Skills**
  PHYSICAL
  SOCIAL
  INTELLECTUAL
  EMOTIONAL
  SPIRITUAL
- **Loving the Middler**

WHO IS A MIDDLER?

Hello, I am a middler boy. My name is Robert. I am 8 years old and in the third grade in school. I can read pretty good but my favorite subject is mathematics. The thing I like best in school is recess because that is when we play games and my team wins sometimes. I like to win. The boys don't usually play with the girls. The girls have their own games to play and they don't want us to play with them. I don't know why, but I feel strange when I am with girls. I sometimes wonder if they feel the same way. They sure act "stupid" sometimes. I also take drama lessons on Saturdays. They have the third and fourth grades together. I have a small part to learn in the play we are preparing. I hope I

SARAH EBERLE is a free-lance writer living in Huntsville, Alabama. She has written Bible school curriculum for middlers and preschoolers and is the author of the children's book *What Is Love?*

don't goof it up. The girls giggle every time someone makes a mistake. Next year I will take the course on lighting so I won't have to be with the girls. Last summer my "T-ball" team won our league championship. I have a trophy. I am also in cub scouts. I have worked very hard to earn my first badge, the Bobcat. My parents are helping me on the Wolf badge. Sometimes I worry about my dad. He travels a lot with his work and I miss him very much. I fight with my sister more when he is gone. Dr. J is my hero. He is awesome. I love to watch him jump and dunk the basketball. Someday, maybe, I'll be able to do that. My mother says he is a Christian. That makes me glad to know that someone like that is also a Christian.

*   *   *

My name is Wendy. I am 9 years old and am in the fourth grade. We moved to this town last summer. This is a new school for me. I like my teachers. My favorite subject is reading. My teacher at the other school said I was the best reader in her class. I also enjoy being in campfire. It is a good way to make new friends. Some of the boys in my new school are really "stupid" when we have gym class. They think they have to be better than the girls. They make me feel funny sometimes so I stay away from them. My parents said I could be on the soccer team. I like sports because it is a way to keep healthy. On Saturdays I go to a drama class, which is where I met Robert. I was surprised that a boy was interested in dramatics. I thought only girls did that. We will learn a play and give it for our parents at the end of our lessons. I hope we can stop giggling so we will do a good job. I can't wait to put on all that make-up. When we first moved I was a little scared, but I have made some friends in my neighborhood and at school. I love Mary Lou Retton. She is my favorite person. When she smiles I feel like she is smiling right at me. Maybe someday I can be like her. My parents said if she comes somewhere near where we live they will take me to see her. I can hardly wait.

Aspects of Developmental Skills

Middlers are just exactly what that name implies. They are in the middle of childhood. Perhaps this can be visualized best by saying that they are in a valley between two mountains. This time is probably the most peaceful time of childhood (if any time in childhood can be called peaceful). By the time a child has started third grade he has attained certain developmental skills that cut down on frustration levels associated with academic learning. This is the time, according to Piaget, that children are acquiring concrete operations in their learning abilities. Concrete operations are simple logical operations such as classifications, seriations, symmetry (balance), and one-one or one-many correspondences; but their use is limited to actual objects or materials, or to ones that can be easily imagined.[1] During the middle years, children seem to be integrating, focusing, and validating what they have learned. Much time and effort was spent acquiring many new developmental skills in the first two grades of elementary school. This knowledge they now expand on as they apply it to further their learning in more areas of concrete operations. In fact, children probably have the capacity to deal with the world, at least on simple terms, by the time they are in the third grade. Even if they learn no more, they can at least function with the skills they have already achieved. Some educators even recommend keeping children at home until they have developed these abilities and are ready to function at the third grade level.

The concept of reversibility is used in learning mathematics skills as well as some music skills. Reversibility means that the child can retrace the steps to solve a problem, actions can be cancelled or reversed, and the original situation can be restored. For instance, $2 + 1 = 3$ and $3 - 1 = 2$. Or, musically, the child can learn to go up the scale or down the scale to return to where he started. The understanding of rhythm is based on this skill. In $4/4$ time there are always four beats to the measure no matter how they are expressed—in quarter notes, half notes, whole notes, or corresponding rests. The concept of reversibility is usually learned by the time a child enters third grade. That is one reason many children start music lessons then. If the child has taken lessons earlier he has probably learned by rote. He will now be able to understand better what he is learning, and music will be more meaningful. A wise teacher will use this new interest in music to advantage. In fact, at this time children are very interested in writing songs or setting Bible words to music because they want to use their new skills to express their own innate creativity. Try setting an entire Bible verse to a certain rhythm. Middlers will enjoy this kind of activity because it has meaning to them. To teach Bible verses, use the concept of reversibility in leaving out a word and having the child put in the correct word. Or, print the verse backwards and let the children reverse it to make it correct. Use other word games that have to do with the order of the verse. Children enjoy using this new skill.

PHYSICAL DEVELOPMENT

Middlers have certain developmental skills that help them accomplish goals they have set for themselves and that parents and teachers have set for them. This is the time in a child's life when he especially begins participating in sports activities. Boys and girls are about equal in their ability at this point in developmental growth. However, during the next two years most boys will attain a more muscular body and more graceful large muscle movements.

1. Ruth M. Beard, *An Outline of Piaget's Developmental Psychology for Students and Teachers,* (New York: Basic Books, 1969), pp. 12-13.

Girls' bodies will also become stronger, but the development of the small muscle movements will be their gain. Girls will be able to write cursive better than most boys because it is natural for them to do this task. Girls are usually able to learn to play the piano or violin earlier because of the small muscle gains they have made. A boy's muscle growth naturally leads him to participate in sports activities. Often, girls in third grade can play on the same level as boys, but by the time they reach the fifth grade there is a marked difference in their abilities. Perhaps it is programming from our society, but it is certainly caused in part by the basic body structure and development of the child.

Children at this stage should be able to learn rules and participate according to those rules. They should understand that breaking those rules results in some sort of "punishment" for their team. Throwing the bat in "T" ball is an automatic out, for instance. Junior football and soccer teams are started at this age. Soccer teams often have both boys and girls participating together. This co-participation lasts sometimes until sixth grade when boys have become stronger and have learned to play with a certain degree of roughness. Since girls no longer care to be on the teams, they will then start their own teams and compete with each other.

It is important for parents and other adults to understand that participation in sports can be a fulfilling activity for children if it is kept in perspective. There will be some who excel at sports, but all children will not, nor should they be expected to by adults. Unnecessary pressure to perform beyond ability will frustrate the child during a time when he should be at peace. Sports can be a good method of helping children learn certain coping skills they will need to use later in life. Unfortunately, adult attitudes quickly rub off on children. Never berate a child for not winning. Applaud him for doing his best or just for making an effort. Help the child learn that participating well is important—not winning. This is valuable especially when a child wins. The winning child is actually no "better" just because he won. In fact at this age, winning has a lot to do with luck and the bounce of the ball. That is not an excuse—it is the truth. Help middlers learn this truth and they will be happier as they participate in sports activities.

SOCIAL DEVELOPMENT

General social characteristics. Up to the age of about eight, sex is ignored in play grouping. Boys and girls play together without any tension. However, at approximately eight years, attitudes seem to change and associations with members of the opposite sex decrease sharply. By the age of eleven to twelve, boys and girls in American culture are almost entire segregated.[2] As a teacher or parent it would be unwise to insist that boys and girls get along together.

2. Paul Mussen, *The Psychological Development of the Child,* 3d ed., edited by Richard S. Lazarus, (Englewood Cliffs, N.J.: Prentice-Hall), p. 108.

Though this is often the time for first girlfriends or boyfriends, do not plan activities or games that force the sexes to interact closely. Such plans can be upset easily.

Children in middle childhood develop more intense friendships among those of the same sex. "Best friends" usually come from their own neighborhoods or classrooms and possess valued personality characteristics.[3] Since children who work together come to like each other better, it would be wise to include new students in activities as soon as possible. That is a good way to integrate a new person into the group, whether it be a Sunday school class, youth group, or neighborhood group.

Middlers are able to play together as a group better and for longer periods of time than younger children. They are willing to sacrifice individual wants for the good of the group. They are able to work out compromises when problems arise to avoid breaking up the group. They will even make up their own rules for clubs or games and abide by them strictly.

Even though they are growing away from their families, the family is still the most influential structure in the middler's life. The importance of the father is growing as the mother's role is diminishing somewhat. The child is beginning to see himself as an individual in a family now. He can spend time away from home, even for several days at a time, without experiencing homesickness. He will soon have his first experience with summer camp. Prepare him for it by telling him truthfully what kinds of experiences he will have. It would help if a friend went with him the first time. As parents and teachers we should help the child accomplish his independence with as little difficulty as possible. This will actually help ease some of the tension the child will cause when he reaches adolescence.

Significant others and hero worship. Children at this age still have an almost mystical attitude toward adult authority. Until about ten years of age rules are still believed to be decided by adults and so to be kept. To violate these rules is considered absolutely unfair. Adults in the middler's life are very important. Middlers recognize leaders and want to be like them. But, even more important, they want them to be good people. They cannot have the significant adults in their lives be less than perfect. They still see life as good or bad, no in-between. Attachments to certain adults can be very strong. Often this attachment is to the parents, but not always. In fact, it is healthy for children to find other adults who are willing to interact with them. It broadens their base of identification. Modeling and identification have significant effects on the development of various facets of moral behavior that are related to conscience. Identification is a learned motive to be similar to another individual. The person or group with whom the child identifies is referred to as the model.[4] Thus, it is important that church leaders set good examples for these

3. Ibid., p. 119.
4. Ibid., pp. 84-85.

young people to see. These "significant others" can become role models for the child to copy. No one has to tell the child to be like "so-and-so"; he will naturally want to be.

Hero worship, which grows out of the middler's mystical attitude toward adult authority, is an important facet of the personality of the middler child. He chooses a certain sports or entertainment figure and decides that person is worth his attention. He will spend his allowance on books, magazines, records, or pieces of clothing that will help him identify more closely with this hero. Early middler children will change their heroes often. As the child matures, he tends to identify more closely with a limited number of heroes; however, he can have three or four heroes at the same time. As teachers and parents, we should use this need to identify with someone "bigger" to teach the child about real heroes found in the Bible. Also, there are many Christian athletes and entertainers who could easily become heroes to the middler child. Make magazines and newspaper articles about these performers available to the children. Encourage them to write to these Christian personalities. Often special relationships are developed between a child and an athlete that are good for both. And finally, you may need to help middlers develop some criteria for selecting heroes. Help them understand that people are just human beings. In spite of what it looks like on the outside, everyone has problems, even the heroes we like so very much. There is only one real Hero who ever walked on earth, and that man was Jesus. Any other hero must be compared to Him in the final analysis.

INTELLECTUAL DEVELOPMENT

Third graders can now express themselves through the written word with greater ease. In school they can write stories and spell many new words. The development of their writing and vocabulary skill allows them more freedom to explore the world and express what they have learned. They can answer questions by writing and can use this new skill in workbook activities. Short answers can be written or copied with relative ease. Children this age enjoy using this new skill, for they are developing the ability to write in cursive. Let the children practice writing on the chalkboard. It is good for them, and they sense that you, as their teacher, understand something special about them.

Middlers can remember a number of things at the same time. Multiple directions may no longer be frustrating to them. They have learned to think in terms of steps or processes. Middlers enjoy projects with more than one step involved. They can learn new games easily. Use games in your teaching. Club ministries and team sports allow the middler child to use this new skill and expand it. These are programs that are made up of many different steps and projects to accomplish a goal. The child has to learn or accomplish one step before going on to the next step. If a child cannot verbalize what he is supposed to be learning, he is not learning it. Piaget claims that language serves mainly to communicate that which is already understood.[5] Most children can and want to verbalize new concepts. Test your child's learning in this way.

Middler children have a better concept of time than younger children. Most children are present-oriented. They feel and act in response to experiences in the here and now. They live in the present moment, with all its spontaneity, impulsiveness, and unpredictability. Formal schooling suppresses the present in favor of the future, with due respect paid to the past. Teaching a child future-orientation is obviously a necessary part of mature development. However, we object to its over-reaching sphere of influence that deprives children (and grown-ups too) of the ability to laugh at nothing, to see beauty in a ladybug's ambling, and to experience exquisite delight in just being close to one's best friend.[6] Learning things that happened in the past is necessary, but the concepts must be applied to the present situation of the child. In school they are learning about things that happened two hundred years ago. They can also understand time relationships on a time line that extends from the time of Abraham to the time of Jesus if these events are marked clearly and defined precisely. For instance, they can understand that the Exodus took place about 400 years after Jacob and his sons went to Egypt if both events are clearly marked on the time line. They probably can't comprehend 400 years (most adults cannot do so, either), but they can understand that so much time has passed because there are four inches between the markers on the time line.

Even when this concept is learned, children still must be helped to make application to the present that can also be understood for the future. Acting out Bible stories with the help of simple costumes makes them very present. This is one way of helping children overcome the distance of time involved in the Bible stories that are so important to their spiritual growth. Costumes, though simple, are important because they help the child "put on" the character he is to enact. They remove the Bible story one step from the child himself and let him be a more willing participant in the drama.

Reading is another skill that is important to middlers. They can now read and comprehend short stories and answer questions about the story. Also, they draw conclusions from hints and clues in the story. Bible teachers can use this ability to help their students make application of Bible stories to their lives. They can also distinguish between true and false statements about a story just read. They can remember these facts for longer periods of time. Teachers can expect the middler child to be able to retell last week's Bible story and be able to remember the application. Curriculum materials are written in units so that

5. Mary Ann Spencer Pulaski, *Understanding Piaget* (New York: Harper & Row, 1980), pp. 94-102.
6. Philip G. Zimbardo and Shirley L. Radl, *The Shy Child* (Garden City, N.Y.: Doubleday, Dolphin Books, 1982), p. 129.

one story builds on another to help children retain information and meaning.

An obvious help in the classroom would be Bibles that your middler children can read easily. Also, make Christian books available to your children to read in their leisure time. This is the age at which a child will decide to continue reading or drop it altogether. Parents and teachers must be aware of this need and try to fill it.

Middlers can memorize with ease. They can learn entire Bible verses in a short period of time. However, care must be taken to make sure that children understand what they are memorizing. Rote memorization is merely an achievement rather than true learning. Learning occurs when children understand and can apply what they have learned to everyday life. Perhaps it would be preferable to have the children learn to paraphrase a Bible verse and then memorize their own paraphrase. The teacher can correct misunderstandings found in the paraphrase before the work of memorizing begins. This is a way to see if the children are really assimilating what is being taught. Each child could have an entire book of paraphrased Bible verses from a group of lessons. Display the children's paraphrases where everyone in the church can read them, or have them printed in the church newsletter. Try to do this during one quarter of the year to see if the children respond positively to it. Parents could have their child paraphrase some verses and present them for family devotions. It is good for a child's self-esteem to participate in this way in a family time together.

EMOTIONAL DEVELOPMENT

The middler child is a "can-do" child. He believes he can do anything he sets his mind or body to do. Middlers have a good sense of worth because they have been learning to control their bodies and minds. They have accomplished many things and think they can accomplish many more. Their frustration level is at an all-time low, which gives them a sense of peace. Self-esteem should be at an all-time high during these years of middle childhood. They want to take on challenges at this time. Interests vary from sports, to drama, to church activities. The middler child may look and act like a shotgun going off. There is so much to do, and he wants to do it all—by tomorrow, if possible. He is sure he can do it. This is the time the child should be allowed to stretch his interests. He should be involved in many different experiences. In doing this he will become aware of his own individual uniqueness. He will find things he especially likes to do and does them well. He will also discover things he does not like to do at all. It is best to let him find out for himself, rather than for an adult to tell him. Adults should be there to praise the effort as well as the success. Encourage the child where it is obvious that he is interested and does well, even if it is something you would not expect of your child. This is one of the greatest gifts you can give a child: acceptance when he is different. The child will appreciate his own unique personality even more if the adults in his life appreciate it, also.

Third graders are starting to develop a sense of humor. They are learning what jokes are and want to participate in joke-telling. Many of their first efforts may be difficult to understand, but bear with and encourage middlers in this. Help them memorize good jokes; it is a good memory stretcher. Allow them to make up new jokes. They may surprise you with some very funny stories. Most of all, laugh with them. The gift of laughter is important to give a child. We need to learn to laugh with and at ourselves more often. When you listen to your child tell a joke you are giving him time and attention. This is important to the middler child. It shows that he is still a vital part of your life.

The middler has learned some control over emotional outbursts. Since children feel things deeply but don't know how to handle these feelings, they "explode." It is not wrong for children to have these feelings—it is natural. During these two years the child will learn to handle these explosive feelings in more constructive ways. Because their vocabulary is expanding at a rapid rate, they can express how they feel verbally rather than violently. Some children become highly talkative during this time. There is so much to tell about how they feel about life and how they are being treated by it. Listen, adults, listen. Also, middler children are better able to draw or create something to work out these intense feelings. Sometimes they will write just a word or two to express how they feel. Help your child discover constructive ways to express his feelings. Never insist that the child hide the feeling. An emotionally healthy child will be able to handle life situations better than one who cannot express his feelings, whether those feelings are good or bad.

Middlers know and experience difficult feelings: fear, anger, confusion, hurt, guilt. It is wise to let the child know that these feelings are a normal part of growing up. Everyone feels them at some time. Fear is a normal feeling given to us by God to keep us from harm. If we were never afraid we would put ourselves in dangerous and harmful situations. But some children experience abnormal fear. A fear is abnormal when it keeps a child from participating in everyday situations. Most fears can be dealt with easily if the child can express them to his parents. If a child is afraid of the dark, install a nightlight. If a child is afraid of a noise outside his window, find out what is making the noise and get rid of it, or explain it to the child if it cannot be removed. If a child is afraid of heights, do not force him to go up tall buildings. Using common sense can help most situations. If the fear is keeping the child from participating in the normal activities of life, find help. Emotional illness in adults is often related to some sort of fear in childhood that was never dealt with effectively.

Sometime during the middle childhood years the child will begin to experience guilt. Guilt is not a popular topic because we think of it as a negative feeling. But guilt is what leads us to God. When a child becomes aware that what he did was wrong, feelings of guilt follow closely. God lets us feel guilty so that we can recognize our need of His grace.[7] At first the guilt feelings will be slight, but they will grow with the child's awareness that he does lots of wrong things. By the age of nine most children have a fairly large storehouse of guilt. Teachers and parents do not usually have to make the child feel guilty; he already does. It is our job to explain God's forgiveness to the child and let the child make a decision.

It is normal for children to be confused about new things, especially when those new things change their lives. A move to a new town or city can cause confusion. The child has to reorient himself to the new surroundings. The house is unlike his old one. The school is in a different location. There will be new surroundings in the classroom. The new teacher will do things differently and explain things differently, and that can cause confusion. Divorce and remarriage usually cause a great deal of confusion for a child. Even when the child is fully aware of the circumstances, he will still be confused for a time. Let the child have time to work through this confusion.

Middler children are also aware of many social issues of the day that affect their feelings. Third and fourth graders know that children are kidnapped and murdered. They know that children are abused. They know that children have diseases that cause pain. They know that thousands of children die each year of hunger. They know all this and more and usually want to help in some way. Children are not logical; they do not think about what to do. They just want to do something to remove some of the hurt in the world. A wise teacher or parent will plan some sort of project for their middlers to participate in to alleviate the suffering.

Probably the most important feeling the middler child has is the need to belong to a group. Every child feels that he wants to belong to something bigger than himself. A child will identify himself by the group(s) with whom he belongs. He is a cub scout, she is a campfire girl, they are thespians. One of the most important relationships to build in life is to help the child feel like he belongs in the family of God. An excellent way of creating a bond of belonging is to do things together. As a class or group have parties, plan projects, visit shut-ins, participate in a clean-up day.

Middler children experience a need to worship God in the here and now. They need to be able to plan and carry out their own worship services when possible. They will need adult guidance and help, but they can create a worshipful experience for themselves. In churches where there is children's worship let the children help plan what will happen. Even the order of what they do can be planned by them. Middlers will still worship spontaneously, even though much of their worship is planned informally. They will stop on the way to school to thank God for spring, or for parents, or for whatever caused the feeling to well up in their hearts. As adults we have learned to quench those

7. Paul Tournier, *Guilt and Grace* (San Francisco: Harper & Row, 1962), pp. 181-88.

feelings before they are expressed. Children are still open to them. Adults need to re-learn this and encourage them to continue worshiping God with spontaneity.

SPIRITUAL DEVELOPMENT

To middler children, spiritual development is a natural part of their lives. They are interested in the God who made the world in which they live. They want to know all they can learn about this God and perhaps get to know Him personally. They can feel a personal closeness to God and talk to Him as naturally as they would to their parents or friends. They pray for friends and for their needs and they expect answers. They need to learn about prayer so that it does not become a "give-me" conversation. Teach the middler children that prayer is more than just talking to God. It is also learning to listen to what God wants to say. A good teaching tool is to let the middlers write out prayer thoughts in a prayer diary. When God answers the prayer they are to enter the answer. They should also write what they think God is telling them in their prayer time. This could become a prayer journal that children may want to keep for the rest of their lives. Middlers take prayer seriously. Perhaps adults should learn from them.

God is the supreme authority and power in the universe to middler children. They can accept the fact that God knows what is best for them. However, they do not understand where God came from or when He was "born." They are curious about these things and want truthful answers to their questions. In truth, we can tell them that God is, He *just is*. That is what He told Moses when he asked who God was during the burning bush episode. When Moses asked God what answer he should give the Israelites when they asked who sent him to deliver them, God told Moses to tell them *"I AM"* sent him. God has no beginning and no end. He *just is*. That is difficult for the middler to understand (it is difficult for the adult to understand) because everything he knows about has a beginning and an end. God is different from everything else in the universe.

They want to know why God loves people, especially people who are bad. It does not make sense that God would love bad people as well as good people. It is difficult for middlers to understand that God (whom he looks upon as a giant parent) would love bad people. They can almost understand that God would love good people; that makes sense to them. The important teaching for the middler here is to know that God loves people. God loves all people no matter what they have done. Whether a person goes to heaven or not depends on that person's response to God's love—whether he receives His offer of salvation from sin.

Middler children also have some curiosity about death. They have probably experienced the death of a family member or pet that they knew fairly well.

They want to know if dying hurts, if it is permanent, where a person goes when he dies, and how it feels. Most importantly, if the person was close to the middler, they will ask "Was it my fault?" When someone in the church dies, their natural curiosity is awakened. Tell children the truth about the circumstances surrounding the death. There is no need to tell the details, but answer their questions truthfully. Help children look in the Bible for answers to those questions. Also, ask how they feel about the death of that person. Sometimes that will start an important conversation that will clear up some misconceptions the middler might have.

The most important thing in the spiritual development of these children is to be truthful in all things. Middlers do not think lying is excuseable, no matter what the reason. Things are all black or all white. There are still no gray areas in their thinking. Something is either good or bad. It cannot be good and bad at the same time. People are either good or bad. They cannot imagine a good person doing something bad. As they learn about guilt and forgiveness, this will change.

Most children in the third and fourth grades are aware of the spirit world as shown in cartoons on television on Saturday mornings and in some movies. They recognize good and bad spirits. Help them realize that God is not just a "good spirit" to save them from dangerous situations like those that happen to cartoon characters. Satan is not just a "bad spirit" who goes around getting boys and girls into trouble. God lives in people by the Holy Spirit and helps them make choices and be strong even when they are weak. Help the middler child learn the difference between the two kinds of spirit worlds. One is make-believe, the other is true. Do not let the entertainment industry take this concept away from our children.

LOVING THE MIDDLER CHILD

The middler child is no longer a "baby," and he will remind you of the fact the moment you try to treat him as such. You can no longer take this child into your arms and soothe the hurts and take away the rejection he feels. Only in the privacy of his own home will the middler allow such show of affection and caring to take place. As teachers in the church we need to discover ways in which we can let middler children know that we do indeed care and are willing to help bear the pain and rejection they feel. The other side of this coin is also true. We need to create an atmosphere of caring that allows these children to share their joy and happiness.

First, we must recognize the uniqueness of each individual. Children are not put together on an assembly line. They are not all alike. In fact, no two children are exactly alike, not even identical twins. One secret of real caring is to get to know your children as the unique individuals they are. Helping your children develop a sense of self, of who they are becoming, is vital to a deepening relationship. One key to this is acceptance of the child just as he is, without having to make changes or improvements before we are willing to accept him. Regular affirmation of the child is a must. This is done by praising the child when he has made an effort whether it is a success or not. Noticing improvements in behavior or in skills is important to the child. Making children feel like they have to earn acceptance and love is deadly. Even God does not require that, how can we?

As church educators, we need to help children incorporate spiritual values into what they are becoming. Help your children find a workable set of guidelines to base their lives on. Of course, they will expect you to live by these same guidelines you are setting up for them. Children sense that you care about them when you set guidelines and expect them to stay within them. When children test the guidelines, they are really testing the one who set them up, asking what is really important. "Am I important enough for you to be firm with me even though it causes you discomfort?" It is the wise adult who stays within the set guidelines.

Spend time with the children outside the classroom. Be sensitive to what each child says when he is in a group and when he is alone. A trip by car can be a very revealing opportunity. The children will talk with each other about what they really care about without realizing that an adult is listening in and taking mental notes. Plan times to be alone with each child, too. When you have a chance to be alone with the child, let him tell you about school work, home life, sports, or whatever. It usually takes only a few minutes to let the middler know that you are really interested in what he thinks and how he feels as an individual. Children need good listeners.

Contact tells the child that you care about him. Make eye contact with each child whenever you can. Just a few seconds of eye contact communicates your care and concern. Sometimes a touch of your hand on his shoulder or rubbing his head is all the physical contact needed to tell the child that you care. Some children will shrink from physical contact, so be patient and depend on eye contact alone to establish a relationship. When a child knows that he can trust you, he will let you touch him physically. These contacts make contact on a deeper, spiritual level possible. You are letting the child know that he is important to you.

Summary

Middler children are a joy to work with because they are excited about learning new things. Their development has allowed them to be more independent of their families, and they enjoy the new freedom this gives them. Encourage middler children to be involved in as many activities as they can. Help them discover the unique persons that they are becoming. And never forget that their spiritual development is not a separate part of their lives. It is an integral part of all of life. If you have the opportunity to become a "special other" in a middler's life, take the job seriously. You can have a profound effect on the life of a child. Encourage all the children in your church to grow into responsible Christian men and women by being one yourself. The strength of a Christian's character is the best teacher in the world.

FOR FURTHER READING

Bolton, Barbara J., and Charles T. Smith. *Creative Bible Learning from Children.* Ventura, Calif.: Gospel Light, Regal Books, 1977.

Button, Alan Dewitt. *The Authentic Child.* New York: Random, 1969.

Chapin, Alice. *Building Your Child's Faith.* San Bernadino, Calif.: Here's Life, 1975.

Elkind, David. *The Child and Society.* New York: Oxford U., 1979.

————. *The Hurried Child.* Reading, Mass.: Addison Wesley, 1981.

Grant, Wilson Wayne, M.D., *The Caring Father.* Nashville, Tenn.: Broadman, 1975.

Haystead, Wesley. *Teaching Your Child About God.* Ventura, Calif.: Gospel Light, Regal Books, 1974.

How to Do Bible Learning Activities: Grades 1-6. 2 vols. Ventura, Calif.: Gospel Light, Regal Books, 1982, 1984.

Kellerman, Jonathan. *Helping the Fearful Child.* New York: Norton, 1981.

Ketterman, Grace H., M.D., *You and Your Child's Problems.* Old Tappan, N.J.: Revell, 1983.

Kiley, Dan. *Nobody Said It Would Be Easy.* New York: Harper & Row, 1978.

Klein, Carole. *The Myth of the Happy Child.* New York: Harper & Row, 1975.

MacDonald, Gordon. *The Effective Father.* Wheaton, Ill.: Tyndale, 1984.

Ortlund, Anne. *Children Are Wet Cement.* Old Tappan, N.J.: Revell, Power Books, 1978.

Young, Leontine. *Life Among the Giants.* New York: McGraw-Hill, 1966.

10

Marjorie E. Soderholm

Understanding Fifth and Sixth Graders (Juniors)

- **Abounding Activity**
- **Hero Admiration**
- **Loyalty**
- **Competition**
- **Justice**
- **Excellent Memory**
- **Humor**
- **Hobby-Loving**
- **Relational Thinking**

Building clubhouses, playing football, experimenting with chemistry sets, wrestling with their friends—juniors enjoy them all. Juniors are active and noisy and full of life. And they do not leave their interests and liveliness at home when they come to the church for Sunday school, worship, or club meetings. Juniors bring all of themselves along, sometimes to the dismay of the adult leaders. But to know junior-age children is to love them. They have a keen sense of loyalty, and if they know adults who appreciate them, they identify with those adults, are loyal to them, and learn much from them.

MARJORIE E. SODERHOLM, M.A., formerly taught at Trinity College, Deerfield, Illinois, and presently serves as a consultant and instructor in Christian education and Bible study.

Juniors are in the fifth and sixth grades in school, and most juniors are ten or eleven years old. Though there is no one junior who is average on all counts, there are some characteristics that one can expect to observe and interact with when working with juniors.

ABOUNDING ACTIVITY

Juniors are on the move. They want things to do. Suggest that the books need to be distributed, or that someone is needed to lead the next song, or that you want to send someone with a note to the office, and you will have plenty of volunteers. They like doing things that mean going places—going on a field trip, going to camp, going fishing with Dad. This is true of girls as well as boys. One girl, now a grown woman, appreciatively recalls the times she used to go hunting with her father, and even now, recalling these experiences seems to strengthen her relationship with her father.

Juniors enjoy making things, but projects chosen must be those which will demand of the pupils what they can do. Otherwise, they will respond with "This is baby stuff," and they will do a careless job. On the other hand, a project such as making simple puzzles for younger children is not considered babyish because it is a service project for someone else. One group of juniors enjoyed making the crafts in the leftover vacation Bible school craft kits the church had purchased, knowing that these would be used as awards for attendance and Scripture memory in another Sunday school. Never once did the leaders hear those juniors complain about making something too easy for them. But if the leaders had chosen those crafts for the juniors themselves, serious discipline problems would have arisen.

Juniors like Bible stories of people in action. Hero stories are among their favorites. Juniors like to have a part in telling stories they have heard before. They like to act out the stories. They like the "guess who" part of a Bible story review at the end of a series, in which each group of children acts out one of the stories for the others to identify. This is in keeping with juniors' love for action.

HERO ADMIRATION

The foregoing leads into the characteristic of juniors called hero worship. They admire people who do things they would like to do, people who are strong, people who help others. While ten- and eleven-year-olds admire good qualities in others, they may also identify with someone who is not of high moral character simply because that person is popular and persuasive. Juniors may be carried away by some TV drama, often along with their parents, into heroizing people and then wanting their heroes to reach their goals, which may even be that of taking another's spouse.

Juniors need help from parents and teachers in distinguishing between what is right and what is out of harmony with God's principles for living. Without this direction, the tolerance level of juniors for divorce, drugs, killings, defiance of authority, and so on, will stretch to accept these things as a part of normal living. Then it will be God's principles of life, rather than the violation of those principles, that will sound strange to them. It used to be said, "Many philosophies of life are in competition for the minds of high school students." But the battle for the mind is being fought earlier now. Therefore, the teacher of juniors must realize he is entrusted to use God's Word, the Sword of the Spirit, for the purpose of influencing the minds of children to follow God's principles.

LOYALTY

Juniors have many loyalties. As their interests expand, they want to take part in more activities. Thus they face conflicts. If the boys' club at church meets the same time as the junior band at school, the child may want to do both, yet must make a choice. Parents and teachers should give principles on which to make this and other choices. It is not sufficient for adults merely to give juniors the impression that they think the best children are the ones who choose the club at the church over a school-sponsored group. Adult sponsors of junior activities need to get together to see if some schedule conflicts can be resolved in order to allow children who wish to, to participate in several activities.

Juniors' loyalties should be directed to the Lord. Juniors need to understand that harmony in their lives comes only if they allow the Lord to be in control of each area of their lives. It would be good for adults to reevaluate their own relationship with the Lord, for if juniors are to see the Lord's power to bring harmony within a life, they will have to see it in those adults who influence them. For instance, if a junior girl wants to go to summer camp, and her parents say she cannot, the club leader—or whoever is encouraging her to go to camp—should not say, "Now, you'll have to put God first. He has to come before your parents, so we'll pray that God will let you go to camp."

Juniors need to be taught that God says they are to obey their parents, and that God uses their parents to show them what to do. If their parents say they cannot go someplace, it is not the place of other adults to stimulate friction between the children and their parents.

If friction exists in a home between parents and children, the church worker who can help bring harmony to the home is active in one of God's prime concerns. God made the family the basic institution of society, but many of today's children are growing up in fractured homes. A person who encourages a child to obey his parents is building in the child a respect for the principle of authority in his life. The child who catches this principle in his home understands what it means to obey the Lord more realistically than a child who has not experienced the authority of his parents in his life.

COMPETITION

Juniors like to compete. They like team games in which they learn to cooperate with others, although at the same time they enjoy competing with others. Competition is good when it encourages them to do better than they might do otherwise. It can be overdone if they work to gain for themselves at the harm of others. Bible drills and contests can be used to help juniors know how to find the books of the Bible and to know what the Bible says. However, a Bible drill leader needs to determine ways to keep a drill from becoming a contest between the fastest one on each side, with all the others acting as a cheering team.

Here is how one teacher conducted a Bible drill that kept all the juniors "in the running" rather than sitting back and letting a few take part. The juniors had studied the Ten Commandments, one lesson on each, for ten weeks. For the eleventh week, the teacher printed the Ten Commandments (Ex. 20:3-17) in short form on a large chart, which was placed at the front of the room.

Then she selected several New Testament verses to be used in the Bible drill. For each of the verses, a team was able to make three points. The first child who found the verse earned a point for that team. The team on which five children had found the verse before five on the other team had done so earned another point. After that, the child who had found the verse first was given the opportunity to make another point for that team. To do so, the child was to tell which of the Ten Commandments the New Testament verse was most like.

This drill was helpful in accomplishing several things:

1. It helped the children learn the location of the books of the New Testament.

2. It helped all the children get into the practice of finding the books. The slower ones did not give up because of a "Johnny always wins, so why try?" attitude.

3. It caused the juniors to think of what the verses used in the drill said. The child who found the verse the first time had time to read and think while the others were working on the "five first" part.

4. The juniors were seeing relationships between the Old and New Testaments. This helped keep the children from thinking that the Old Testament had no relevance today, or that the God of the Old Testament differs from the God of the New Testament.

5. The children were reviewing without having a "dry old review."

JUSTICE

Juniors have a keen sense of justice, which helps them feel more responsible for their own wrongs. They are not so likely as younger children to blame someone else. At least if they do blame others, they do not easily rest with the idea that the incident is cared for. They still sense some responsibility for their own wrong. This makes it easier for them to understand that God must punish sin, that Jesus took that punishment, and that they need to give their lives to the Lord.

The junior age is a time when children are responsive to the gospel message. Teachers should not push juniors into a decision of accepting Christ as Savior, but they should be alert to their growth in understanding who Jesus Christ is and the claims He makes on a person's life. Many persons who say they accepted Christ as Savior when they were children also say that they did not really understand what it means to have a personal relationship with Him, to have Him as the manager of their lives, and to be free from doubts about their childhood decision. This is not to say that children cannot make a meaningful response to the Lord, but rather that they need more than a few stories to serve as a foundation for that response.

Because juniors have heard many stories in which the good side wins, some may interrupt the Bible storyteller with the words, "Oh, Stephen will win; the good guys always do." Then when they hear that Stephen was killed, they may say, "How come God let him die? Stephen was good." Juniors can grasp the concept that the "good" person is the one who stands for what is right even if it costs him something.

Though juniors have a sense of justice, many of them have been influenced by the lax attitude of our culture and have only a vague understanding of the significance or consequences of wrongdoing. In one class, the teacher was trying to point out that although David was forgiven for his sin against Bathsheba and Uriah, he did experience some consequences for his sin. In trying to explain *consequences,* the teacher asked, "What happens if you don't study for your spelling test?" The group of juniors did not seem to think much would happen. They said they would have a chance to try again, and if they did not make it, it really would not matter much.

This shows how students bring all of themselves to the teaching-learning situation in the church. They interpret what they hear there in the context of their experiences at home and at school. One teacher, trying to explain the idea of judges at the city gates in Jerusalem in Old Testament times, said, "Where is it that decisions are made today in our town? When we have problems to be settled, where are these settled?" The answer given was, "At the psychiatrist's." Children today are familiar with home friction, broken homes, and psychiatrists.

Juniors recognize sin as sin when they hear stories of people doing wrong, but to see sin in their own lives is not so easy. This is not just because they are children but because they are human. Juniors do not easily make applications into specific areas of their lives on the basis of a general application made at the end of a story. They need help in seeing how the principle applies. It is too general to aim to teach the juniors that they should be honest. They knew that before they came to the class. They consider themselves honest because they would not rob a bank, or steal a car, or take another person's coat. Juniors need to be confronted with specific illustrations showing what real honesty is. What about keeping five cents extra change? What about saying we are ten years old if we are really twelve in order to get half-fare prices?

Parents need to see what they teach their children when they fail to practice honesty. At a plane ticket office, a mother was purchasing tickets for herself and two children. When she gave the ages of the children, the younger one's mouth dropped open. The other, being "wiser" and having caught onto the mother's reason for giving false ages, just looked at his sister with an air of disgust which said, "Keep your mouth shut." The next time, the daughter too will understand the "advantages" of lying. If teachers will use illustrations like this, children cannot accept a general notion of honesty without thinking of areas where they are being dishonest.

Parents also need illustrations that will cause them to realize that they are the most influential teachers of their children. One day, a pastor who taught a course once a week at a nearby school was driving to that school. Enroute, he was thinking about his class and did not notice a fifty-mile-an-hour speed limit sign. Soon a patrol car stopped him, and the officer began writing out a ticket. When he looked at the pastor's driver's license, he said, "Oh, I'm sorry; I didn't know you were a preacher. If I had, I wouldn't have given you a ticket, but now that I've started it, I have to finish it." The preacher responded with, "I'm just as guilty as if I weren't a preacher; go ahead and finish it." That patrolman had an unusual experience that day: he met a man who accepted responsibility for what he did and did not try to get himself out of it. That evening, the pastor said to his nine-year-old son, "Your dad's name is going to be in the paper tomorrow. I was driving too fast, and I got this ticket." The father gained much more respect with his son that day than if he had come home bragging about getting out of a fine.

Excellent Memory

Many teachers of juniors have realized that juniors have a good memory, when a child comes up with, "But last week you said *I* could do it this week." The teacher of juniors cannot brush a child aside by glibly saying, "You can do it next time." For the child will remember that "next time" and will claim those rights, even if it means taking it out some way on the other child who was allowed to do what was promised.

Juniors can memorize Scripture, but they need help in understanding what the passages mean and how they apply to them. If they have been coaxed or paid for doing what they ought to do, they may have their price for Scripture memorization, too. If rewards are given, children should not receive them for haphazard jobs. Otherwise, when the students work harder and do a better job, they may want a greater reward than the one that came easy for less work. The reward should be within the reach of all. If children know they will receive an illustrated New Testament on completion of a certain number of verses memorized, they know they can reach the goal no matter how long it takes. If only the first one to memorize that amount of Scripture receives the prize, the others will quit early, knowing that they cannot win anyway.

HUMOR

Jokes and tricks are favorites with juniors. They make funny remarks to get the attention of others in the class. If someone gives an answer that is wrong, others will repeat it several times just to make fun. If a teacher twists up some words, juniors are alert enough to catch it and make some comment about it.

One teacher asked a class of girls to sign their names on a paper she sent around the table. They were to include name, address, and birthday; thus it took some time for the children to do this, and the paper was still being sent around when the teacher was ready to tell the Bible story. She said, "Now I want you to pay attention to the story even if that paper is still going around. You'll have to listen with one ear, and write with the other." Quick as a flash, the juniors were saying, "Ha! You can't write with your ear." Some juniors might have even demonstrated what it looks like to write with one's ear! This kind of happening is not necessarily a fault of the teacher, but it shows what juniors consider funny. If the teacher understands this, he will not take this fun-making personally.

Juniors need to be taught that some things are not funny. It is not a funny thing to have a big scar on one's face, or to have the problem of stuttering, or to wear a brace on one's leg. They need to realize that to mimic and mock persons with these problems is hurting the person who needs acceptance rather than rejection. They can be taught to be grateful to God for the healthy bodies they have. They need to realize that often it is people with physical limitations who develop inner qualities that make them more like Christ than those who have it easy because of their good looks and abilities.

HOBBY-LOVING

Advertisers recognize that juniors love hobbies. They offer pictures of baseball players and coupons toward the purchase of model autos along with the purchase of their products. Juniors are collectors—stamps, models, ribbons from fair entries, sports equipment, and charms for bracelets. As a teacher visits the homes of his students, his interest in their hobbies will contribute to a mutual appreciation between teacher and student. It is wise to encourage juniors to relate some hobbies to the Bible, if possible. For example, if a boy has some stamps depicting different aspects of the Christmas story, he may like to bring them to class. The teacher could ask the group to determine the order of the incidents in the pictures on the stamps. A stamp could be assigned to each student and the group could retell the Christmas story, each contributing the part represented by the assigned stamp.

RELATIONAL THINKING

By studying history in school, juniors are learning to fit events of the past in sequential order. This helps juniors appreciate the historical sequence of Bible stories, which in their earlier years were isolated accounts. Juniors can now understand that Abraham was before Moses, and Moses before David. Maps and time charts help students place Bible accounts in order.

One Christmas season, a teacher of juniors took old Christmas cards to class. The children were asked to sort them into two piles: one pile was to contain cards showing the real Christmas story, and the other pile was to contain other cards. Cards with pictures of Santa Claus, reindeer, fireplaces, and so on, went into one pile; cards showing shepherds, angels, and manger scenes went into the other pile. Next the teacher asked the children to sort cards with the real Christmas story into two piles—one depicting events recorded in Matthew and one depicting events mentioned in Luke. Bibles came out at this point, as the children needed help in separating the pictures into these two piles. Then the teacher divided the class into two groups and gave one group the set of Matthew pictures to put in order and the other group the Luke pictures. Now they were looking at the Scriptures more closely. For handwork that day, they each made a Christmas card with the real Christmas message. They were invited to use any of the pictures, greetings, or Scripture passages printed on the cards they had been working with. Each left with a card to send to someone in order to share the message of Jesus' coming to earth. After Christmas, one of the boys in that class said, "I looked at all our Christmas cards, and we didn't get many with the real Christmas message on them." This boy was not from a Christian home, and his parents may have heard more about Jesus Christ's coming to earth to give His life for them than that Sunday school teacher ever thought of when gathering old Christmas cards for that lesson. This was a good use of juniors' interest and ability in the chronology of events.

Readers will notice recurring references to parents in this chapter. This is because work with juniors means work with parents. It is difficult for a teacher who has a child in a class for an hour or less a week to build discipline into a child's life if the child is undisciplined at home. If children attend Sunday school every Sunday for a year, which is unlikely for most children, and if the actual teaching time each Sunday is forty minutes, they would receive less than thirty-five hours of instruction in the Bible in a year's time. The junior may also be in a worship service and in a club program, but even that hardly doubles those thirty-five hours for most children, as far as actual Bible teaching is concerned. If those few hours supplement and reinforce what the parents are taking responsibility for, they can be of great significance in the child's life. If not, one certainly cannot say it is useless, but it is much more difficult to have an effective ministry in the child's life.

Churches must place greater emphasis on the role of the father in the home. To have classes and clubs for children and missionary meetings for women is not enough to accomplish the work of the church in the lives of children. Fathers are the key. They are to be the spiritual heads of their homes. Junior age children need someone to give them direction, someone to guide their loyalty to Christ, someone whom they can admire, someone to provide security through discipline, someone to give them an example of serving the Lord and depending on Him. The best "someone" to provide these things is the child's own dad.

Sunday school teachers, club leaders, and other adult leaders with juniors can supplement, but not supplant, the role of Christian dads in the home.

Churches that minister not only to juniors but also to the junior's family, will find that their ministry to the pupils themselves will be far more effective.

SUMMARY

Juniors are in the fifth and sixth grades in school, and most of them are ten or eleven years old. They are active and they want to do things and go places. They admire men and women who do things they would like to do. Conversely, they want to do what people they admire are doing. Thus they are not always wise in choosing which heroes to follow, and they need help in choosing that which is in line with biblical principles of life. They have a wide range of interests, and because they want to participate in many, they face conflicts between one interest and another. They need clear teaching about obeying their parents, need to know that obedience to parents is commanded by God and is His way of guiding them into what is best for them.

Juniors like competition, whether in sports or Bible games. They have a keen sense of justice, which helps them feel more responsible for their own wrongs than they did when they were younger. It also helps them understand God's justice in punishing people for their sins. They can relate God's justice to the death of Christ and to their need to receive Him. They are able to memorize Scripture quite easily, but they need help in understanding and applying what they memorize. They have a sense of humor and enjoy teasing. They need to be taught to discern between what is funny and what is not. They are hobby lovers and collectors at heart.

Working with Juniors is most effective when teachers and parents work together. Teachers cannot supplant the role of parents, but they can supplement what the parents are doing in guiding juniors in their relationship to God.

FOR FURTHER READING

Ban, Arline. *Teaching and Learning with Older Elementary Children.* Valley Forge, Pa.: Judson, 1979.

Beechick, Ruth. *Teaching Juniors.* Denver: Accent, 1981.

Bergan, John and Ronald Henderson. *Child Development.* Columbus, Ohio: Merrill, 1979.

Biehler, Robert F. *Child Development.* 2d ed. Boston: Houghton Mifflin, 1981.

Bolton, Barbara J., and Charles T. Smith. *Creative Bible Learning for Children.* Ventura, Calif.: Gospel Light, Regal Books, 1977.

Brubaker, J. Omar, and Robert E. Clark. *Understanding People,* 2d ed. Wheaton, Ill.: Evangelical Teacher Training Association, 1981.

Clark, Robert E. "The Learner: Children." In *Introduction to Biblical Christian Education.* Edited by Werner C. Graendorf. Chicago: Moody, 1981.

Craig, Grace. *Human Development.* 3d ed. Englewood Cliffs, N.J.: Prentice-Hall, 1983.

Dobson, James. *Dare to Discipline.* Wheaton, Ill.: Tyndale, 1970.

Gibson, Joyce, and Eleanor Hance. *You Can Teach Juniors and Middlers.* Wheaton, Ill.: Scripture Press, Victor Books, 1981.

How to Do Bible Learning Activities: Grades 1-6. 2 vols. Ventura, Calif.: Gospel Light, Regal Books, 1982, 1984.

Jenkins, Gladys, Helen Shacter, and William W. Bauer. *These Are Your Children.* 4th ed. Glenview, Ill.: Scott, Foresman, 1975.

McDaniel, Elsiebeth. *How to Become God's Child.* Wheaton, Ill.: Scripture Press, 1970.

Nichols, Charles. *Teaching Children with Confidence.* Wheaton, Ill.: Evangelical Teacher Training Association, 1983.

Soderholm, Marjorie E. *Explaining Salvation to Children.* Minneapolis: Free Church, 1962, 1972, 1979.

———. *Salvation—Then What?* Minneapolis: Free Church, 1968.

Various authors. *Stories of Faith and Fame.* Fort Washington, Pa.: Christian Literature Crusade, various publication dates. About 95 pages each. This is a series of over twenty-five biographies of Christians. They give the reader good insight into the development of Christian character and the faithfulness of God. The series is a good one for juniors to read and to keep rereading during the teen and adult years. Some of the books included in the series are these:

Batten, J. R. *Golden Foot.* (About Judson of Burma)
Davey, Cyril. *The Monk Who Shook the World.* (About Martin Luther)
Erskine, John T. *Millionaire for God.* (About C. T. Studd)
Martin, R. G. *Knight of the Snows.* (About Wilfred Grenfell)
Reason, Joyce. *Searcher for God.* (About Isobel Kuhn)
Robbins, Nancy E. *God's Madcap.* (About Amy Carmichael)

Part 3

Meeting Special Education Needs

11

Julie Hight

Teaching Exceptional Children

- **Who Are They?**
- **The Basis for Ministry**
- **Defining Exceptionalities**
  PHYSICALLY DISABLED
  HEARING IMPAIRED
  VISUALLY HANDICAPPED
  COMMUNICATION DISORDERS
  LEARNING DISABILITIES
  BEHAVIORAL AND EMOTIONAL DISORDERS
- **Classroom Management**
- **The Teacher of Exceptional Children**

All children have the need to be trained in Biblical standards, including the exceptional child: those with physical disabilities, sensory impairments, communication disorders, learning disabilities, emotional and behavioral disorders, and some other health impairments. Until recent years the availability and the opportunity for children who have disabilities to participate in our Sunday school programs and worship services have been minimal. Today, however, we are seeing an increasing awareness on the part of church leaders and educators

JULIE HIGHT is a free-lance writer, instructor, and consultant in special education. She lives in Addison, Illinois.

regarding the importance of a spiritual ministry to children who have special needs. Doors which were once closed are opening, providing a Christian education to these youngsters through the local church.

WHO ARE THE EXCEPTIONAL CHILDREN?

There have been many attempts to define the term *exceptional children.* This term has been used when referring to a particularly gifted child or a child with an exceptional talent. It has also been used with children who deviate from the "norm." In the field of education, the term *exceptional children* has generally been accepted to include both the gifted and the disabled. Specifically, "A child is considered educationally exceptional if his deviation is of such kind and degree that it interferes with his development under ordinary classroom procedures and necessitates special education, either in conjunction with the regular class or in a special class or school, for his maximum development."[1]

In this chapter, the exceptional child is a child who deviates from the average or normally developing child due to a physical disability, a sensory impairment (such as deafness or blindness), a communication disorder, a learning disability, a behavioral or emotional disorder, or any of a wide range of other health impairments (i.e., muscular dystrophy, multiple sclerosis, heart disease, and so on). The extent and degree of impairment determines what modifications of teaching methods and curriculum are necessary as well as the possible need for changes in the physical structure of the classroom to assist the exceptional child to function at maximum capacity. In addition, we shall define and briefly examine the various disabilities; however, our discussion will focus mainly on modifications and techniques for an effective spiritual ministry to children with special needs.

A disability shows no favoritism as it cuts across all racial, cultural, and religious barriers. "Disabled people now comprise about 13% of the entire U.S. (and world) population."[2] Table 11.1 indicates the approximate number of handicapped children in the public school system as reported by the Department of Education, Special Education Programs.[3]

THE BASIS FOR MINISTRY TO EXCEPTIONAL CHILDREN

Prior to any discussion of teaching methods, curriculum, or structural changes, it is of utmost importance to establish the *need* for a spiritual ministry to the disabled. Unlike their able-bodied peers, the labels *exceptional,*

---

1. Samuel A. Kirk, *Educating Exceptional Children,* 2d ed. (Boston: Houghton Mifflin, 1972), p. 5.
2. Stephen Monjar, "What Do You Say After You See They're Disabled?" The Rehabilitation Institute of Chicago, July 1983.
3. U.S. Division of Educational Services, Special Education Programs, October 1, 1985.

TABLE 11.1

HANDICAPPED CHILDREN IN THE PUBLIC SCHOOLS DURING THE 1984-85 SCHOOL YEAR

TYPE OF DISABILITY	TOTAL
Learning Disabled	1,818,308
Speech Impaired	1,112,249
Mentally Retarded	623,507
Emotionally Disturbed	330,408
Hard-of-Hearing and Deaf	48,081
Multi-Handicapped	54,063
Orthopedically Impaired	47,511
Other Health Impaired	61,849
Visually Handicapped	20,749
Deaf-Blind	987
Total of all conditions	4,117,712

handicapped, impaired, and *disabled* often automatically trigger the thought that these individuals have little capacity for spiritual growth. It is necessary to emphasize that a brain does not cease to function, nor does a spirit lack insight, simply because a particular part of a body is impaired.

The teacher of children with disabilities must be convinced that God did not make a mistake when He created those with impairments but has a specific purpose in allowing the disability. Scripture clearly reveals the care God used in His creation of us (Ps. 139:13-16). Furthermore, God also demonstrates His control over various disabilities. After Moses spoke to the Lord of his own slowness of speech and tongue, the Lord said to him, "Who has made man's mouth? Or who makes him dumb or deaf or seeing or blind? Is it not I, the Lord?" (Ex. 4:11, NASB). Our ministry to children with special needs is not based on feelings of pity or simply the desire to be helpful. Our basis comes from the realization that youngsters with disabilities have the same spiritual needs and potential as their able-bodied peers.

DEFINING THE VARIOUS EXCEPTIONALITIES

In this section we will be examining the various areas of exceptionalities. For this purpose, the terms *disability, impairment,* and *handicap* will be used interchangeably with the word exceptionality. " 'Disability' means that one or more things that most people can do, a disabled person can't do as easily, or sometimes, at all. It's important to remember that a disability is almost never 'total' and usually affects a surprisingly narrow range of activity."[4]

4. Monjar.

PHYSICALLY DISABLED CHILDREN

Physical impairments are conditions which primarily limit a child's physical abilities. These handicaps are usually visible, because of the awkward manner in which a child may move or because of the special devices such as wheelchairs, braces, or artificial limbs he must use to achieve mobility.

Definitions and causes. A physically handicapped individual is one who has a physical disability resulting from a neurological impairment (such as cerebral palsy or epilepsy), an orthopedic impairment (such as brittle bones or arthritis), or other health impairments (such as heart disease or asthma). The degree of involvement ranges from minimal afflictions to severe, crippling afflictions that force an individual to be totally sedentary.[5] The *neurologically impaired* are those children whose handicapping condition is due to incomplete development of or injury to the central nervous system.[6] The *orthopedically impaired* are those who have a crippling impairment that interferes with the normal functions of the bones, joints, or muscles to such an extent that special arrangements must be made by the school.[7] Regardless of the type of physical disability, it may be necessary to modify the physical structure of the classroom where they attend.

Physical impairments may result from birth defects (such as a defect in development during the prenatal period), diseases (such as poliomyelitis or muscular dystrophy), or accidents (such as falls, accidents, or a traumatic injury to the brain).

Points for consideration. Although there are many types of physical disabilities, ranging from mild to severe impairments, the teacher should be aware of a number of basic guidelines when he or she teaches children with physical handicaps.

1. Physical impairment is not synonymous with mental retardation. Often, we link the functioning of the body with the functioning of the brain. Do not assume that children in wheelchairs are mentally handicapped. Instead, presume that the mental ability of the child is normal unless you are informed otherwise. In some cases a mental impairment does accompany a physical handicap; however, this is not always the case.
2. Learn as much as possible about the disabilities of the physically disabled children you are teaching. Parents can provide the needed information regarding their child's specific strengths and weaknesses. In addition, find out what you can expect in relation to a child's motor abilities. In knowing this, you can determine how to structure activities and study time to best suit students with special needs. Specialists—such as teachers, physical

5. Joni and Friends, *All God's Children* (Woodland Hills, Calif.: Joni and Friends, 1981).
6. Kirk, p. 351.
7. Ibid., p. 367.

therapists, and social agency representatives—are available to provide additional information. When questions arise, just ask!
3. Avoid being overprotective. Children who are physically impaired need reassurance and stability, not shielding from exposure to regular classroom involvement. Provide opportunities for participation by disabled and able-bodied children together.
4. Special classes for physically handicapped children are not necessary. Wherever possible, unless an additional impairment would warrant the need for a special class, mainstream (include in the existing Sunday school class).

Above all else, remember that these are *children* who happen to have a physical impairment. They have similar desires, needs, and concerns as those of their able-bodied peers. God sees past the "broken" outside to the spiritual needs of the heart. As teachers, we must follow His example.

Modifications. Despite the fact that special classes are not usually necessary, teachers of the physically handicapped would be unprepared if they did not plan for some special modifications in their class. The following are guidelines for making the educational setting a comfortable and accessible environment for those children who experience difficulty in mobility.

1. Wheelchairs, walkers, and braces require extra space. Make certain that the classroom can accommodate this equipment. In addition, the room should be free of clutter or any debris that would impede safe movement.
2. Seat the child near a helpful friend or teacher. This arrangement makes it possible for the child to acquire assistance easily when needed.
3. Children who are in wheelchairs have an eye level different from that of children seated at desks or tables. When teaching or presenting any material, compensate for this difference.
4. If additional adaptive equipment is needed for these children to participate actively, make sure that it is placed in a location where it is readily available. This includes a wrist orthosis for eating or writing.
5. Enlist the help of other children to assist in transporting or adjusting the position of the wheelchairs. Such an activity can be valuable interaction for both the disabled and the able-bodied student.

In any classroom situation, it is crucial to call attention to the many similarities between the children and not the differences. In so doing, teachers who have children with physical disabilities in their class will build understanding and acceptance into the lives of their able-bodied students.

HEARING IMPAIRED CHILDREN

Individuals with hearing impairments may have difficulty hearing in one or both ears. There are no obvious markers that automatically draw attention to hearing impaired children. Often they are lonely because of the tremendous barrier their impairment presents. Helen Keller once stated, "Blindness separates an individual from things, but deafness separates an individual from people."

Definitions and causes. The Committee on Nomenclature of the Conference of Executives of American Schools for the Deaf has made the following definition:

1. Deaf: Those in whom the sense of hearing is nonfunctional for the ordinary purposes of life. This general group is made up of two distinct classes based entirely on the time the loss of hearing occurred. These include:
   a. Congenitally deaf—those who were born deaf.
   b. Adventitiously deaf—those who were born with normal hearing but in whom the sense of hearing became nonfunctional later in life through illness or accident.
2. Hard of Hearing: Those in whom the sense of hearing, although defective, is functional with or without a hearing aid.[8]

The causes of hearing impairment in children can be placed into four categories.

1. *Hereditary deafness.* Deafness can be inherited by the baby as a result of certain genetic deficiencies.
2. *Congenital deafness.* Deafness can be caused either by illness in the mother (the mother's developing rubella, commonly known as German measles, during the first trimester of pregnancy) or an injury at birth.
3. *Deafness caused by childhood illnesses.* Meningitis, severe ear infections, typhoid fever, diphtheria, scarlet fever, viral infections such as mumps or measles, and encephalitis (a disease that in many cases affects the brain) can cause deafness in children.
4. *Deafness caused by childhood accidents.* A blow to the head, explosions, or other loud noises can cause deafness.[9]

There are many degrees of hearing loss. Hearing impairments range from the minimal (where speech is heard but there may be some difficulty in discriminating certain sounds) to severe loss (which requires the use of a hearing aid if the person is to receive any sound at all).

Characteristics. Although it is impossible to state a list of characteristics that apply to all deaf children in all situations, the list developed by John A. Cooper gives insight for understanding the deaf child.

8. Committee on Nomenclature, Conference of Executives of American Schools for the Deaf, 1938, *American Annals of the Deaf,* p. 83.
9. John A. Cooper, *Working with Deaf Persons in Sunday School* (Nashville: Convention, 1982), p. 28.

- The deaf child may have an emotional dependence on a person who can communicate with him. He will not want to leave that person. He may cling to his mother, his teacher, or a friend who can communicate with him. The deaf child may be shy and have nothing to do with people who cannot communicate with him. The deaf child may not play with other children.

- The deaf child may be socially immature. He has not had many of the experiences outside the home that a hearing child has. The deaf child may not know how to act in Sunday school. He may not know how to work with other children. The deaf child has to depend on others longer than the hearing child.

- The deaf child may be spoiled. The parents may let the child do anything he wants to do. This is especially true if the parents cannot communicate with their child.

- The deaf child may have temper tantrums. This is a way of showing he is unhappy or frustrated. He cannot tell why he is unhappy. He gets attention by kicking and screaming.

- The deaf child may show his feelings by physical actions. Love will be shown with lots of hugs and kisses. Anger will be shown with hitting, biting, and kicking.

- The deaf child may make throat noises or other noise. This is one way he has of keeping in touch with himself. The hearing child does this with his voice.[10]

According to *Webster's New Collegiate Dictionary*, "to communicate means to impart, to convey knowledge of or information about: make known." It is the responsibility of the church to communicate the love of Jesus Christ regardless of the method or the type of language used. In so doing, those children with hearing impairments are given the opportunity to experience God's love, find acceptance, and serve the risen Savior.

Points for consideration. Children with hearing impairments have the same need to know God as their hearing peers; however, teachers of deaf and hard of hearing children must be familiar with some general guidelines. This information is important in successfully sharing the Gospel of Jesus Christ.

1. Hearing impaired children are frequently isolated and lonely because of their disability. Often they are misunderstood, appearing to be unfriendly or unlovable. They are the silent minority. The inability to communicate with the majority leaves feelings of frustration and rejection.
2. Children who are deaf or hard of hearing are not mentally handicapped; however, they may fall behind their hearing counterparts in academic areas due to the language barrier.
3. Not all hearing impaired children can read lips (referred to as speech-

10. Cooper, p. 118.

reading). The ability to do this may indicate how involved they become in class activities.

4. The majority of hearing impaired children use the "total communication" approach to language. That philosophy advocates the use of any and all means of communication to provide unlimited opportunity to develop language competence. Included are the following: speech, hearing aids, speech-reading, gesturing, signs, finger-spelling, pantomine, reading, writing, pictures, and any other possible means of conveying ideas, language, and vocabulary.[11] But be aware that not all children use this approach and may only communicate by speech-reading.

5. Most deaf persons have the ability to use their voices. Usually they prefer not to do so because of the poor quality of their speech. Hearing affects the manner in which we speak. Without it, there is no control over tone quality, inflection, or speed.

6. Regardless of the degree of impairment, teachers must communicate to students in a language that they understand. In the event that you have a deaf child in your class or are a teacher of a deaf Sunday school class, it is necessary to have good command of their language. This may require your learning signs and finger-spelling.

7. When communicating, do not yell or shout. Increasing the volume does not guarantee that you will be heard. Besides, shouting distorts the natural movement and shape of the lips and therefore can make speech-reading difficult.

8. Avoid ignoring a deaf individual when you are conversing with a hearing one. Courtesy would dictate that you not leave the handicapped child out. In addition, deaf children may feel as though you are talking or joking about them.

A sensitive teacher will realize that these students are children who happen to be deaf. It is inappropriate to refer to those with hearing impairments as "deaf and dumb," "deaffie," or "deaf mute." These phrases are an affront to their functioning ability. The correct terminology is "deaf," "hard of hearing," or "hearing impaired."

Modifications. Although there are curriculum and other published materials to be used specifically by the deaf, it would be unwise to assume that these could meet everyone's need. An important word to remember is *adapt.* Jesus adapted His spiritual lessons to meet the needs of those He was teaching. He is our perfect example. The following are some modifications to be used when working with deaf children in the Sunday school.

11. Lottie L. Riekehof, *The Joy of Signing* (Springfield, Mo.: Gospel, 1978), p. 7.

1. Remember that deaf and hard of hearing children learn with their eyes. This means that *all* lessons should be visual. The following items can be used to help visualize the lesson:
   a. overhead projector
   b. chalkboard
   c. pictures
   d. maps
   e. filmstrips (when used wisely)
   f. flannelgraphs
   g. dramatization
   h. storytelling
   i. displays and interest centers
   j. puppetry
   This list is not comprehensive, but gives various ways to teach a lesson visually.

2. A teacher must be aware that the language of the deaf is different from that of hearing children. The lessons must be adapted to fit the language level of the deaf or hard of hearing.
   a. Use short, simple sentences.
   b. Use words with one or two syllables. They are easier to read than larger words. On the average, deaf children have reading levels that are two to five years behind that of their hearing peers.

VISUALLY HANDICAPPED CHILDREN

Educational procedures rely heavily on the sense of vision. *Blindness* covers a fairly wide range of visual defects and refers to severe limitations either in the sharpness of sight or in the size of the area that can be seen at one time. Children with severe vision loss will not have enough sight to serve them in the ordinary activities of life for which sight is essential. Blind children or children with severe visual impairments lack an extremely important group of learning experiences, those which depend on sight.

Definitions and causes. The National Society for the Prevention of Blindness Fact Book defined blindness and partial sight as follows:

   a. Blindness is generally defined in the United States as visual acuity for distance vision of 20/200 or less in the better eye with best correction; for visual acuity of more than 20/200 if the widest diameter of field vision subtends an angle no greater than 20 degrees. (In simpler terms, a person is considered "legally blind" if he can see no more at a distance of 20 feet than someone with normal sight can see at a distance of 200 feet.)

b. The partially seeing are defined as persons with a visual acuity greater than 20/200 but not greater than 20/70 in the better eye with correction.[12]

However, recent data have resulted in a revision in terminology. For educational purposes, Kirk suggests two definitions: *the visually impaired,* which refers to those who can learn to read print; and *the blind,* who cannot read print, but who need instruction in braille.[13]

There are several causes of blindness: prenatal influences, eye diseases (such as glaucoma, cataracts, or diabetes), poisonings, infectious diseases, and injuries.

It is estimated that there are about 6.4 million persons in the United States with some kind of visual impairment: that is, persons who have trouble seeing even with corrective lenses. Of these, 1.7 million are severely impaired. This means that they are either "legally blind" or that they function as if they were "legally blind" even though their vision does not fall into that definition.[14]

Points for consideration. Children with visual impairments can function within the normal Sunday school class. Below are listed some guidelines for teachers working with the blind or visually impaired.

1. Children with visual handicaps sometimes may seem to be unresponsive and to lack curiosity. They sometimes hold their heads down, because they don't need to hold them up to see: or it may be easier for them to hear with their heads bent slightly downward. Being unable to see, they cannot react to others' facial expressions. Therefore, they have no need to look into the face of the person with whom they are speaking. This makes them seem uninterested. It is important to keep this trait in mind and recognize that when you present information to the visually impaired child, you cannot use appearance as a barometer of level of interest.[15]
2. Blind children are inconvenienced, not incapable. With minor adaptations, the blind child can participate in most activities.
3. Persons with severe visual impairments become accustomed to the environment of a particular classroom. Therefore, when changes in the room are made (such as the moving of furniture or other objects), it is important to reorientate the children to the room.

---

12. National Society for the Prevention of Blindness, *N.S.P.B. Fact Book: Estimated Statistics on Blindness and Visual Problems* (1966), p. 10.
13. Kirk, p. 293.
14. Joni and Friends, p. 64.
15. Patricia Porter and Grace Lane, "Programming to Meet the Needs of Handicapped Children: Curriculum and Environmental Adaptations," in *The Exceptional Child: A Guidebook for Churches and Community Agencies,* ed. James L. Paul (New York: Syracuse U., 1983), p. 96.

4. Inform individuals who are blind of possible hazards, such as slippery floors, sharp inclines, or uneven surfaces.
5. When walking with a visually-impaired student, do not grab his arm—let him take yours. He may want to walk a half step behind you: from the motion of your body he can tell when you come to curbs, steps, or turns.
6. Blind and visually impaired students need to have love and acceptance demonstrated to them as much as their sighted classmates. In addition to verbal praise, show your feelings through the sense of touch (a hand on the shoulder or arm, or a hug).

Modifications. The primary objective when teaching blind and visually impaired children is to present concepts in a mentally vivid, yet concrete manner. With minor adaptations in the materials being used and a teacher who is committed to providing Biblical instruction to those with visual handicaps, these children can not only "see" spiritual truths from the Word but can also apply the Word to their daily lives.

1. Because blind students are unable to acquire information visually, the teacher should use the senses of hearing, touch, taste, and smell when she or he presents materials. The teacher should use as many of the sense avenues as possible when teaching a concept. He should not limit the instruction to one particular avenue but should use a combination of senses.
2. The teacher should remember that humor and voice inflection are important when teaching visually impaired children.
3. The verbal explanations the teacher gives should be clear and direct. The teacher should be specific when giving directions or asking for a response. He should avoid vague descriptions or questions.
4. Because some blind children use braille, there should be Bibles, curriculum, and other materials available to them in braille.
5. The teacher should use music to help blind children develop the sheer joy of sharing, by singing with and listening to those in his class. Music can create security and can stimulate thought and help the blind student develop an understanding of God's Word and message. Music can also provide opportunities for mental, spiritual, and social growth. (See also chap. 25.)
6. Crayons, paper, pencils, clay, and watercolors can all help visually handicapped children express emotions. This expression of emotions will help the children indicate and share their individuality. Many times when a child cannot verbalize adequately, expression can be achieved through arts and crafts. Although the work will need further guidance than the child with sight, it will allow the handicapped child to express himself and show his individual talents in ways that might not be expressed by a seeing child. These crafts should be of interest to the child and should be a step toward learning about God and life in its fullest. (See also chap. 32).

7. Role playing can help children become familiar with and remember events, ideas, and situations from Bible stories, incidents in their homes, and other situations. Any experience can be acted out, even those from real-life situations that the child has experienced during the preceding week.

Visually handicapped children as much as sighted children need Jesus Christ and the church. Through participation in the worship and instruction of the church, children who are visually impaired may come to know and love the Lord Jesus and to have their lives enriched.

COMMUNICATION DISORDERS

Communication affects every aspect of our lives. Social interaction, learning, and job achievement are all dependent on our ability to communicate. Our communication involves essentially three parts: (1) a message sender, (2) a message, and (3) a message receiver. A breakdown can occur in the expression of the message or in the reception of the message. When adapting methods, the teacher will find it practical and useful to view the child's difficulty as affecting either "information in" or "information out." Children with hearing handicaps have difficulty receiving the message—information in. Children with speech difficulties have trouble expressing the message—information out.[16]

Children with language disorders have difficulty processing the message. That is, the message can be heard and spoken; the breakdown lies in what happens to that message when it gets past the hearing mechanism and before it reaches the speech mechanism.[17]

Communication disorders include many specific problems. Among the most commonly found are those children with cleft palate (failure of the bone and tissue of the palates to fuse), stuttering, delayed speech, language disturbances, auditory perception problems, or hearing loss.

Definitions. Defective speech is any speech that draws unfavorable attention to itself, whether through unpleasant sound, inappropriateness to the age level, or interference with communication.[18] Included in the area of speech disorders are problems with articulation (how a child puts speech together), stuttering, and voice disorders (problems that involve the quality, tone, and volume of speech).

Language disorders affect the way children understand directions and their ability to communicate a reply. Often there are problems in selecting the correct words to express what they want or there is an inability to put words together into the proper sequence to form sentences. Language difficulties

16. Ibid., p. 89.
17. Ibid., p. 87.
18. Kirk, p. 74.

often cause problems in the areas of reading, spelling, and writing.

Communication disorders may occur in combination with other handicapping conditions. Cerebral palsy (an injury to the neuromuscular system that causes a lack of motor control), hearing loss, and mental retardation are often accompanied by communication difficulties. The degree of involvement differs with each individual.

Points for consideration. The teacher who works with children with language disorders will be more successful if he or she keeps the following points in mind.

1. Children with communication disorders vary from ones whose speech is understandable to some who are almost totally unintelligible.
2. Most children with communication difficulties are undergoing speech therapy. It is not the responsibility of church workers to attempt remediation of these problems. Concentrate on *what* is being said, not *how* it is being said.
3. Children with defective speech may be apprehensive about sharing verbally in class. Avoid forcing a child to read aloud or pressuring him to participate.
4. Do not pretend to understand a child's speech if you do not. Instead, ask for the child to repeat the statement. Explain that you are having difficulty understanding but that you will listen more closely when the statement or question is repeated.
5. Avoid interrupting the sentence of a child who is stuttering. Allow the child to speak at his own rate. Be careful not to finish sentences for him.
6. When speech becomes a problem, such as in stuttering, do not ask the child to "stop and start over again" or "slow down and take a deep breath." Again, let the child speak at his own rate.
7. There are some children who have a total absence of speech. This only occurs in connection with another disability such as mental impairment, physical handicap, or an extreme emotional disturbance.

Children with communication disorders may feel frustrated at their difficulty in communicating with others. In addition, they may become embarrassed about their difficulties, which could lead to isolation. Church workers need to be aware of these feelings and strive to make the environment one filled with acceptance and love, demonstrated through patience.

Modifications. Understanding the limitations of communication disorders will better equip teachers to make the necessary modifications in their teaching methods. For children with defective speech or language difficulties, the Sunday school class can be one of anxiety or one of joy and anticipation.

1. When asking these children questions, limit the need for a multi-word answer. Whenever possible, structure questions so that they can be answered in one or two words. For instance, say, "Steven, do you want to use

the green crayon or the blue?" rather than, "Steven, what do you want?"

2. Teach the lesson using as many visuals as possible. In this way, if a child cannot answer verbally, he may point to a correct answer or express a sequence of thought by using visuals.

3. Flannelgraph stories allow children with language disorders to follow the sequences of events in a story. It also helps them visualize the progression of the story.

4. Encouraging a child to verbalize about what has just happened, or to express what he is thinking or feeling, will help the child develop vocabulary as well as assist him in the sequencing of sentences.

5. Children can often sing, participate in choral readings, and recite verses without stuttering. These are excellent opportunities for a child to share in group activities and achieve a measure of success.

6. Children with language disorders may have difficulty reading or writing. Do not insist that they perform in these areas, but provide other opportunities for group participation.

Teachers in the church who display genuine love and concern for children with these special needs will find that the children and their parents will respond with appreciation. Here is an opportunity to display the patience, kindness, and selflessness of God-given love (1 Cor. 13:4-5).

CHILDREN WITH LEARNING DISABILITIES

Throughout the years, a growing concern has emerged for children who have difficulty learning. As a result, since about 1960, another form of exceptionality has appeared in the professional vocabulary, specifically, children with learning disabilities.

Definition. In an attempt to define the term *learning disabled,* several committees were formed consisting of professionals from the fields of medicine, psychology, education, and language. A definition was formulated by the National Advisory Committee on Handicapped Children in their annual report to Congress in 1969:

> Children with special learning disabilities exhibit a disorder in one or more of the basic psychological processes involved in understanding or using spoken or written languages. These may be manifested in disorders of listening, thinking, talking, reading, writing, spelling or arithmetic. Learning disabilities do not include problems which are due primarily to visual, hearing, or motor handicaps, to mental retardation, emotional disturbance, or to environmental disadvantage.[19]

19. National Advisory Committee on Handicapped Children, *Special Education for Handicapped Children: First Annual Report* (Washington, D.C.: U.S. Department of Health, Education, and Welfare, 31 January 1968), p. 4.

These children carry various labels, such as hyperactive, brain injured, minimally brain damaged, and many others. Learning disabilities are usually caused before, during, or shortly after birth.

Points for consideration. The following points will be useful to remember when working with children who have learning disabilities.

1. Children with learning disabilities may be of any intellectual level. Some are below average in intelligence, whereas others are gifted in intelligence. These disabilities differ from child to child, and it is difficult to identify characteristics that are typical in all children.
2. Discrepancies will exist in their abilities and functioning levels. They may be able to complete a task in one area, but a simpler task requiring them to use processes in which they have a deficit will be difficult, if not frustrating, to complete. For instance, a child may have difficulty reading the most simple material yet excel in art; another may read well but be poorly coordinated.
3. Behavior may be a problem in class when the activities these children must complete are too difficult for their ability level. Teachers must be careful in what they ask such children to do.
4. Learning disabled children often have low self-esteem. They are aware of their difficulties and that they have failed to meet the expectations of their parents and teachers.
5. Provide opportunities for these children to experience success. The accomplishment of a job well done will aid in raising a child's self-esteem.
6. Give genuine praise to the child for the work he has done well.

Modifications. Learning problems are frustrating to the children who have them. Sensitive teachers will adapt their lessons to provide successful learning experiences with quality Bible instruction. The goal is to present material that is challenging to a learning disabled child and yet not at such a high level of difficulty that the child becomes frustrated and loses interest in the program.

1. Give detailed instructions. Because of the difficulty these children have in sequencing, you may need to repeat directions or to give new instructions as each section of an assignment is begun. For instance, instead of reading a series of instructions to be followed, give the child one or two instructions at a time. When he has completed those, proceed with additional ones.
2. Employ all of the senses when teaching. If possible, find out from the child's parent or teacher which sense avenue the child learns through best. If a child learns best visually, then provide the majority of his learning experiences through the visual channel. Reinforce your instruction using the other senses.
3. Make sure that you teach the main idea of your lesson. Your learning

disabled student may give you the details of the lesson but not have any idea of the main point.

4. Free the classroom from distractions as much as possible. These children are easily distracted, and unnecessary pictures, toys, and materials may tend to confuse them.

5. Teach the lesson using concrete examples. A learning disabled child will grasp the meaning if he can see and feel what you are explaining. For instance, during the Bible story talk about and show items that relate to that time period. Encourage the children to imagine how the people functioned in their daily activities.

6. Be aware that some children with learning disabilities may appear hyperactive or overactive. They have short attention spans and seem to be involved in constant movement. Attempt to keep these children near you. Physical contact, such as an arm around the shoulder or a hand on the student's arm, may briefly increase the attention span.

In spite of the difficulties that children with learning disabilities encounter, they can successfully participate in educational programs. The only requirement necessary is that the atmosphere of the class be one that fosters acceptance and self-worth because of God's great love for all of His children.

CHILDREN WITH BEHAVIORAL AND EMOTIONAL DISORDERS

Children who have been identified as having a behavioral or emotional disorder are often regarded with apprehension. The label itself may immediately produce uneasiness in the teacher; however, it is a priority to realize that these children have the need to know Jesus Christ as Savior and have the capacity to grow in Him.

Definitions and causes. Attempts to find a type of maladjustment characteristic of all children with emotional and behavioral disabilities have failed completely. Among children with learning problems, one can find a few who are emotionally healthy, some who are very inhibited, and some with neurotic symptoms. Children with behavioral and emotional problems may be identified as withdrawn, immature, overly dependent, excessive daydreamers, excitable, restless, lacking in self-confidence, easily distracted, or unable to get along with peers.

Behavioral and emotional disorders can be defined as a deviation from age-appropriate behavior that significantly interferes with (1) the child's own growth and development and/or (2) the lives of others.[20]

There are many causes of behavioral and emotional disorders. Among them are physical and sexual abuse, broken homes, and extreme criticism. Many studies have shown that parents' inconsistencies in discipline or their rejection

20. Kirk, p. 389.

of or hostility toward their children are positively correlated with conduct disorders in those youngsters.

Points for consideration. Keeping the following points in mind will be helpful in dealing with children who have behavioral and emotional disorders.

1. Many children with emotional or behavioral disorders have never experienced the security of a loving home. In addition, they lack a correct perception of the family unit. Often there has not been a positive role model available. Children with these disturbances need men and women to demonstrate Christ's love to them.
2. Children with emotional or behavioral disorders are not "crazy." They exhibit the same behaviors as other children, only to an excess.
3. The teacher of these children should not attempt to be a therapist. Only a professional counselor, psychologist, or psychiatrist should assume that role.
4. Many children with emotional or behavioral problems also have difficulty learning. This increases the frustration they experience. In preparing to teach them refer to the adaptations discussed above for working with learning disabled children.
5. If a child exhibits aggressive behaviors, do not make any materials available to him that could be destroyed, tampered with, or used to injure someone.

Modifications. Significant but low-key modifications in classroom practices can make a difference in the teacher's ability to deal successfully with children who have behavioral and emotional disorders.

1. Emotionally and behaviorally handicapped children may learn better in small, closely supervised groups, or on a one-to-one basis. It is a good idea to provide individual attention for these children. A teaching assistant would be a tremendous asset in such cases.
2. Puppets and stuffed animals work well in helping these children act out feelings. Also the use of role playing and drama could be beneficial.
3. The learning environment should be one in which the child will experience success.
4. Children with behavioral and emotional disorders should be taught that God did not make a mistake when He made them. Additionally, they should be taught that God loves them so much that He sent Jesus to die for them.
5. If and when a behavior problem arises, confirm to the student that you do not accept the inappropriate behavior but that you do accept and love him.

Finally, there are two elements that must remain *consistent* in the lives of children with emotional and behavioral disorders: *love and discipline.* The teacher's consistency in love and discipline with these children will be an example of the unconditional love their heavenly Father has for them.

CLASSROOM MANAGEMENT

In addition to the methods suggested under *Points for consideration* in each section of disabilities, classroom management is an important aspect of teaching exceptional children, to ensure that the learning environment provides for optimal growth.

Basically, classroom management is a means of structuring a class in a manner that enhances learning at the same time it discourages inappropriate behavior. The following suggestions can be implemented or added to existing class structure.

1. Establish guidelines for the class. Regardless of their impairment, children must be knowledgeable of their limits. They will not know what is acceptable behavior if you do not tell them. It is helpful to explain "why" you require a certain type of behavior. For instance, explain to the child that there will be no hitting allowed in your class because God wants us to be loving and kind.
2. Expect the same behavior from a disabled child as you would from an able-bodied one.
3. Be a model of the desired behavior as a teacher.
4. Be consistent. If you establish a guideline, make certain that the children obey it.
5. Anticipate potential problems. Act before they occur or get out of control.
6. Make the punishment consistent with the offense.
7. Do not attack the character of the child when you are correcting him or her. Many children with impairments already have a low self-esteem.
8. Emphasize the fact that the child's sin can be confessed and that God will cleanse him (1 John 1:9). Encourage the child to pray.
9. Do not continue to remind the child of a specific misbehavior after he has been punished by displaying a poor attitude toward him, excluding him from activities, or ridiculing his inappropriate behavior in front of his peers.

Use the points above as guidelines only. Adapt them to fit in with what is best for the particular class.

THE TEACHER OF EXCEPTIONAL CHILDREN

A parent of an exceptional child once commented, "I don't think teachers necessarily need to be trained in special education. They just need to have the ability to feel, to reach out, knowing that even though a child's behavior may not be acceptable, he is still precious to God." That parent was correct.

Teachers of exceptional children do not have to be specialists. They must have a desire to see disabled children come to know Christ and be determined to work toward that result.

Just as important is having a commitment to the children. It takes time to become acquainted with the students and their special needs. In addition, the more familiar the teachers are with the students, the more capable they will be in teaching them. That makes it particularly sad when teachers lose interest in a program once it has been in existence for some time. Get people who support a ministry to exceptional children to pray for you and to assist you in whatever way they can.

Not only are the children affected by the special education ministry; so are the families of those children. Teachers of exceptional children can open the door for the entire family to participate in the function of the church. Often, when there is no class available for a child with special learning needs, the entire family misses the opportunity for worship and growth. Many families feel isolated because of a handicapped child. A study revealed that four out of five marriages which contained a disabled child were ending in divorce. When teachers are willing to adapt materials and consider the special needs of exceptional children, they also have a chance to share the love of Christ with the families involved.

SUMMARY

In summary, it must be restated that our basis for working with exceptional children is found in the Scriptures. God took great care when creating us and demonstrated control over handicapping conditions. Jesus ministered to those who by the world's standards were unlovely. We must see beyond the outside of disabled children to the spiritual need of their hearts.

Special classes are not always necessary because exceptional children can and should be mainstreamed into regular church programs whenever possible. With appropriate modifications, sensitive teachers can provide an environment that allows disabled children the opportunity for spiritual growth.

In ministering to exceptional children, teachers may find it possible to reach out to the families involved. In so doing, many more individuals may have the opportunity to experience the love of Jesus Christ through the local church.

FOR FURTHER READING

OVERVIEW

Dunn, Lloyd M. *Exceptional Children in the Schools.* 2d ed. New York: Holt, Rinehart and Winston, Inc., 1973.

Kirk, Samuel A. *Educating Exceptional Children.* 2d ed. Boston: Houghton Mifflin, 1972.

Physically Disabled Children

Eareckson, Joni. *Joni.* Grand Rapids: Zondervan, 1976.

Joni and Friends. *People Plus: The Christian Church's Responses to Persons with Disabilities: A Curricula for the Individual Church Family.* Agoura, Calif.: By the author. P.O. Box 3333, 1981.

Hearing Impaired Children

Cooper, John A. *Working with Deaf Persons in Sunday School.* Nashville: Convention, 1982.

Yount, W. R. *Be Opened! An Introduction to Ministry with the Deaf,* Nashville: Broadman, 1976.

Visually Impaired Children

Kemper, R. D. *An Elephant's Ballet: The Story of One Man's Successful Struggle with Sudden Blindness,* New York: Seabury, 1977.

Kerr, J. S. "The Visually Handicapped: Our Blind Spot." *Spectrum,* Spring 1973.

Children with Learning Disabilities

Carpenter, Robert D. *Why Can't I Learn?* Glendale, Calif.: Gospel Light, 1974.

Cherne, Jacqolyn. *The Learning Disabled Child in Your Church School.* St. Louis: Concordia, 1983.

Hill, Charles H. "The Learning Disabled Child Goes to Church School." This article, published in January 1974, is available from *Learning With,* 2900 Queen Lane West, Philadelphia, PA 19129.

General Insights for Working with Exceptional Children

Joni and Friends. *All God's Children,* Agoura, Calif.: The Author. P.O. Box 3333, 1981.

Paul, James L., ed. *The Exceptional Child: A Guidebook for Churches and Community Agencies.* New York: Syracuse U., 1983.

Ross, Bette M. *Our Special Child: A Guide to Successful Parenting of Handicapped Children.* Old Tappan, N.J.: Revell, 1984.

Wheeler, Bonnie. *Challenged Parenting: A Practical Handbook for Parents of Children with Handicaps.* Ventura, Calif.: Gospel Light, Regal Books, 1983.

Wilke, Harold H. *Creating the Caring Congregation: Guidelines for Ministering with the Handicapped.* Nashville: Abingdon, 1980.

12

Roberta L. Groff

Teaching Intellectually Impaired Children

- Historical Background
- Definition
- Causes
- Classification
- Characteristics
  TRAINABLE RETARDED
  EDUCABLE RETARDED
- How They Learn
- Religious Consciousness
- Religious Concepts
- The Teacher of the Intellectually Impaired
- Teaching Methods
  STORYTELLING
  ROLE PLAYING
  PUPPETRY
  MUSIC
  CRAFTS

Every year approximately 130,000 babies are born in the United States with some degree of mental retardation. In Canada, approximately 17,000 babies

ROBERTA L. GROFF, M.A., is principal of the Horizon School, Alberta, Canada.

each year are born mentally impaired. In both countries, 3 percent of the population are intellectually impaired. In the U.S., this is 6½ million people— *twice* as many as those who are affected by blindness, polio, cerebral palsy, and heart disease *combined.*

In the past, churches have lacked concern, care, and programming for those who are intellectually impaired and their families. However, in the last decade or so, churches, as well as the general public, have awakened to the fact that mental disability is a serious problem. A growing spate of literature is being written on the Christian education of the mentally impaired, and an increasing number of churches are developing classes for this special population. These teaching programs include Sunday school classes, weekday programs, after-school instruction, vacation Bible school, and resident and day camps.

The needs of the handicapped person are the needs that motivate us all. He longs to love and to be loved. He longs for warmth, home, friends. He suffers bewilderment, frustrations, hurts, and pains. These indicate his needs as a person. The term *mentally impaired* tells us that his ability to satisfy these needs will be slow in developing.

The church can help meet the spiritual needs of these exceptional children in a way that no community program can possibly do. A concerned parent has suggested two specific ways in which local churches can minister to the mentally impaired. First, churches, realizing that the mentally impaired are individuals for whom Christ died, can provide classes in Sunday school and vacation Bible school and boys and girls weekday activities for the disabled. Second, churches can show concern for each disabled child's family members. Brothers, sisters, grandparents, and other relatives are deeply affected by the discovery that a child in their family has mental disability. The parents of these children have heavy burdens. The church can share in these burdens through the gift of understanding. All members of the family need to know that their church and their minister care for them in this additional burden which they carry.[1]

HISTORICAL BACKGROUND

Jacob Rodrigues Pereire, Jean Marc Itard, Johann Jacob Guggenbuhl, Edward Seguin, Samuel Howe, and Marie Montessori belong in the roster of pioneers who have made valuable contributions to the study of mental retardation and the care and training of the retarded.

Ancient history records that the retarded were known as "defectives." Wealthy Romans kept a "fool" in the household as an amusement for guests. Later they became playthings for princes.[2] Retarded persons received the

1. Dorothy L. Hampton, "Retarded Children and Christian Concern," *Christianity Today* 8 (31 January 1964): 12-14.
2. Leo Kanner, *A History of the Care and Study of the Mentally Retarded* (Springfield, Ill.: Thomas, 1964), pp. 5-6.

worst treatment during the Reformation; many Reformers regarded them as something less than human, void of a soul.[3]

In 1799, a boy, believed to be around the age of twelve, was captured in the forest of Aveyron, France. This boy, whom they called Victor, revealed more animal characteristics than human. He lacked speech, selected his food by smell, and in general did not respond like a human being. Jean Marc Itard felt that Victor (called the "wild boy of Aveyron") was an example of a completely untutored human being and that, with proper training, this boy could respond as a human being. Itard was successful in getting the boy to control his actions and to read a few words. Itard's method of teaching was "repeated rewarding trials." Although he felt his experiment was a failure, educators are recognizing his methods as important in teaching mentally handicapped children.

Edward Seguin (1812-1880), continued the search for methods of training retardates. He established the first public residential facility in France for the mentally retarded and did extensive writing relating to the care, treatment, and curriculum for the retarded. His philosophy of education was not too different from many principles advocated today. He emphasized education of the whole child, individualized instruction, the importance of rapport between student and teacher, and the principle of beginning with needs and concerns of the child before proceeding to the unknown.

During our century, Marie Montessori and Ovide Decroly have built on the work of Itard and Seguin. These researchers all worked on sensory-motor development of the brain because of their conviction that all learning comes through the senses.

The first step taken in the United States toward providing care for the retarded was the introduction of a bill in the Massachusetts legislature in 1846 providing for the establishment of a state asylum for "idiots." This bill was defeated, but, as an outcome, an experimental school for teaching "idiots" was opened in Massachusetts in 1848. Other states followed, and the nineteenth century witnessed a promising beginning of scientific work on behalf of the mentally retarded. Educational programs were developed, state institutions were established, and social responsibility was recognized.

DEFINITION

Current definitions of mental retardation are numerous. Most of them are valid because they cover some aspect of the condition.

Dybwad called mental retardation "a condition which originates in the developmental period and is characterized by markedly subaverage intellectual functioning, resulting in some degree of social inadequacy."[4]

3. Ibid., p. 7.
4. Gunnar Dybwad, *Challenges in Mentally Retarded* (New York: Columbia U., 1964), p. 3.

According to the American Association on Mental Deficiency, retardation is "a group of conditions which renders the individual unable to compete in ordinary society because of impaired or incomplete mental development."[5] Simply stated, mental retardation is the result of injury to or disease of the brain either before, during, or after birth.

The terms referring to the mentally retarded vary according to historic precedent as well as to the physical, emotional, and social implications. Some terms for the least serious retardation are *marginally dependent, feebleminded, moderate,* and *educable* (meaning they can benefit from some education and eventually hold jobs under supervision). More severely mentally handicapped persons have been labeled *semi-dependent, imbecile, trainable retarded* (meaning they can be taught self-care).

Historically, the profoundly retarded have been referred to as idiots, low grade, and defective. Today's terminology refers to them as *severely* and *profoundly retarded.*

CAUSES

Mental disability is no respecter of persons. The intellectually impaired are born to average, brilliant, and dull parents alike, and into highly educated families as well as illiterate families. More than two hundred causes have been identified. Generally, they can be classified as (1) heredity; (b) prenatal, perinatal, and postnatal trauma; and (c) social-cultural factors.[6] Pediatricians estimate that more than 90 percent of mental impairment occurs in the prenatal stage.[7] Such genetic factors as defects in endocrine functioning, blood incompatibilities, and virus illnesses in pregnant women are also suspected as contributing to mental disability.

Injury at birth also causes brain damage. For example, when oxygen is accidentally cut off during the birth process, some brain cells are killed. Incomplete mental development results when the dead cells happen to be those controlling the intelligence.

Postnatal causes of retardation fall into three groups: acute illnesses, traumatic events, and progressive disorders which were not recognized at an early age.[8] Any illness which produces a long-lasting high fever can cause brain damage, as can severe head injuries and convulsions. Some other factors

---

5. Edward L. French and J. Clifford Scott, *Child in the Shadows* (New York: Lippincott, 1960), p. 40.
6. Bernard Faber, *Mental Retardation: Its Social Context and Social Consequences* (Boston: Houghton Mifflin, 1968), p. 6.
7. Harriet E. Blodgett, *Mentally Retarded Children: What Parents and Others Should Know* (Minneapolis: U. Minnesota, 1971), p. 15.
8. Ibid., p. 18.

include nutritional deprivation and metabolic disturbances. Toxic agents may poison the brain cells and prevent their functioning.

CLASSIFICATION

Mental impairment is a broad category that includes persons who are functioning at numerous levels of efficiency. It means that intelligence and physical growth are subaverage to some degree.

In the realm of persons with normal intelligence, we assign the levels of average, above average, and genius. So the intellectually impaired have similar levels, known in the descending order as educable, trainable, and those requiring custodial care. Schools use these categories as general guidelines for assigning intellectually impaired children to given classrooms.

We have suggested that an enormous number of factors contribute to classifying the level of an intellectually impaired person. Not everyone in the field agrees as to how those factors should be classified. As a result, the several national organizations use slightly differing classifications.

The American Association on Mental Deficiency classifies measured intelligence of the retarded into five categories: borderline, mild, moderate, severe, and profound. The American Psychiatric Association puts the retarded into three groups: Mild, moderate, and severe. "Mildly retarded" would include individuals with an IQ in the 75 to 85 range; "moderately retarded" includes those in the 50 to 75 range, and "severely retarded" designates those in the 0 to 50 range.[9] This classification, however, tends to lead to oversimplification of a complex problem. Within each of these levels there is a wide range of abilities, especially among the severely handicapped.

The National Association for Retarded Children suggests this classification: marginal dependent (or educable), semi-dependent (or trainable), and dependent (or custodial or nursing). The marginal dependent (or educable) are those in the IQ range of 50 to 75. They are persons who have learning difficulties in the regular grades.[10] The semi-dependent (or trainable) have been defined as having an IQ from 30 or 35 to 50 or 55. The dependent (or custodial or nursing) retardates are those with IQs below 30. These individuals are totally dependent, and many of them require nursing care throughout life.

CHARACTERISTICS

The mentally handicapped can be identified by a definite set of mental, physical, social, and emotional characteristics. Each person, of course, does not possess every characteristic. But each one does have learning problems to

9. Louis Rosenzweig and Julia Long, *Understanding and Teaching the Retarded Child* (Darien, Conn.: Educational Pub., 1960), p. 12.
10. Ibid., p. 13.

varying degrees. In addition, the mentally impaired have poor language communication skills, physical handicaps and illnesses, lack of motivation, limited experiences, and behavior problems. Some other general characteristics are listed below:[11]

TRAINABLE RETARDED

Physical: Can have oddly shaped skulls; some have cerebral palsy; tend to have smaller physiques and growth abnormalities in height and weight; may have dazed conditions, odd body and facial mannerisms, excessive fondling of others and unusual emotional states.[12] May have hypotonia (lack of muscle tone), be subject to epilepsy, be microcephalic or hydrocephalic. A study of the etiology will reveal the characteristics prevalent in specific syndromes.

Mental: Have poor reasoning, ineffective use of language, inability to think abstractly, low concentration level, lack of motivation; have trouble carrying a task to completion; lack imagination and creativity; IQ is between 30 and 50; rate of academic development around one-half to three-fourths that of the average person; is slower in conceptual and perceptual abilities.

Social: Have interests corresponding more closely to those of children of equal mental ages than those of chronological peers.

Emotional: Are quiet and introverted; sometimes loud and physically offensive; possess little motivation outside of their own needs and are sometimes oblivious even to their own needs.

EDUCABLE RETARDED

Physical: Are more like normal children physically than mentally, socially, or emotionally; have poorer motor coordination and higher incidence of sight, speech, and hearing difficulties.

Mental: Have limited vocabulary and poor reasoning ability; IQ ranges between 50 and 75.

Social: Today's attitude toward the mentally handicapped has created an awareness of their social needs; they are able to attend school with "normal" peers, can profit from community activities as well as benefit from church and Sunday School programs; their social needs are similar to normally developing individuals, but a great deal of guidance and instruction is required if we are to meet these needs; churches must respond and accept these people, and provide social and spiritual experiences for the handicapped.

11. Adapted from John W. Howe and Thomas W. Smith, *Characteristics of Mentally Retarded Children* (County Superintendent of Schools, Los Angeles Board of Education, Bulletin No. 3, 1950).
12. *Exceptional Children in the Schools*, ed. Lloyd M. Dunn (New York: Holt, Rinehart, & Winston, 1963), p. 141; and Harry J. Baker, *Introduction to Exceptional Children* (New York: Macmillan, 1959), p. 261.

Emotional: Many of the same traits are prevalent in the educable, as listed above for trainables; many of the educable mentally handicapped (EMH) suffer from depression as a result of their frustration from being slow; the church needs to be in tune to meet the needs of this special group.

How They Learn

Researchers have found no evidence that the mentally impaired learn by a process different from the way nondisabled persons learn. The mentally impaired assimilate information by the same mechanical means. But since they have incurred mechanical damage known as brain injury, they do not take in the same impressions as others. Normally developing persons learn as they react to their environment through sight, touch, taste, hearing, and smell. But in the mentally handicapped, brain damage has blocked or dulled some of the senses. All such persons have the added emotional handicap of knowing that their learning and behavior differ from those around them. They see and feel their own clumsiness and incoordination, but they are powerless to help themselves.[13]

Along with dulled sensory perception, the intellectually impaired have limited use of logic and reasoning because their thinking does not pass easily from the concrete, see-and-feel world to the abstract. For example, trainables cannot grasp the abstract meaning of numbers and thus cannot come to the deductive conclusion involved in telling time. When no logical, reasoning, thought-building process is involved in a learning procedure, the person will likely succeed if all other positive factors (including a comfortable, secure environment and approving, undemanding teachers) are provided.

Another adjustment concerns the language the teachers use. They must be overly conscious that learning success for intellectually impaired students depends on how well they speak in words that can be understood. The effective teacher begins at the language level of the students, works at that level, and then slowly introduces new words.

Mentally handicapped children cannot be expected to wait with their questions. Their learning must be immediate and spontaneous; they need much preacademic learning. In church-related teaching situations, children need to learn to follow directions, to sit still, to communicate with others. The Sunday school teacher must continually repeat instructions as well as lesson points. Disabled children must practice even minor things before they can perform them well. This is especially true of trainable students. In fact, they can excel at tasks they learn by rote. Teachers should allow them to distribute papers, books, and supplies and must be prepared to reward students who have

---

13. *Mental Retardation*, ed. Alfred E. Baumeister (Chicago: Aldine, 1967), p. 185.

successfully completed tasks with something pleasurable, even the teacher's own smile. No endeavor should go unrecognized.[14]

RELIGIOUS CONSCIOUSNESS

The ability of the intellectually impaired to have spiritual awareness and to become spiritually regenerated has been questioned by some educators, and some have denied it completely. However, this denial places such special needs persons below the level of human beings. Another attitude intimates that the mentally disabled need carry no spiritual responsibility because they are "heaven's very special children," and thus are instruments of an unusual mission for God.[15] Some sincerely believe that the mentally handicapped are beyond spiritual experience and responsibility. However, in some cases, this view may simply be an excuse to justify withholding religious education. The rationale some follow is this: the disabled can't understand anyway, so why try at all?

As a result of her experience in teaching mentally impaired children and adults, the author is very reluctant to deny their basic human nature. Evidence of this fact was recorded by one of the early researchers. Edward Seguin wrote that mentally retarded persons "have a moral nature. No one who has had the happiness of ministering to them will deny" that.[16]

The mentally handicapped should not be considered religiously unaware, nor should they be labeled spiritually irresponsible. Responsibility always depends on mental and physical age. We do not expect the child who is a Christian to handle adult spiritual problems. But we do teach him simpler concepts and expect some spiritually motivated behavior from him. So it is with mentally disabled persons; some will achieve greater knowledge and responsibility than others. If the mental age is six years, then all functioning—including spiritual—will likely be at that level. Mary Theodore concurs:

> A severely retarded person with mental age from three to seven, has a limited concept of goodness and wickedness. He can absorb some moral training, but his degree of responsibility will be small. He fails to see implications and foresee consequences of his actions.[17]

RELIGIOUS CONCEPTS

The ability of a mentally impaired person to grasp spiritual concepts depends entirely on his mental age. Jesus, God, the Holy Spirit, sin, death,

14. Ibid., p. 191.
15. Parents sometimes hold this view, such as is described by Dale Evans Rogers in her book *Angel Unaware* (Westwood, N.J.: Revell, 1953).
16. Edward Seguin, *Idiocy and Its Treatment by the Physiological Method* (New York: Columbia, 1907), p. 47.
17. Mary Theodore, *The Challenge of the Retarded Child* (Milwaukee: Bruce, 1959), p. 153.

forgiveness, and eternal life are primarily abstract concepts. Intellectually impaired children and adults, particularly at the trainable level, are able to think only in the here-and-now, feel-and-touch world. Thus the paramount consideration is not to debate their spiritual consciousness and responsibility but to discover the degree to which their knowledge and responsibility can extend. The degree differs with each individual as it does with the normally developing person.

The author feels that the opportunity for salvation is important for the disabled, especially for those going beyond the (mental) age of accountability. The consequences are too great not to present salvation. While it is true that some of the mentally handicapped are manipulated into religious experience, others have made intelligent decisions for God. The following is the simple, scriptural formula for discussing God's plan of salvation.

1. Most mentally handicapped can understand some degree of right and wrong, that everyone has done wrong things and that he himself has done wrong things. These displease God or make Him unhappy (Rom. 3:23).

2. The result of wrong behavior is being put away from God forever; but if we are sorry for our sin, He will take us to His home in heaven (Rom. 6:23). If the handicapped person does understand sin or wrongdoing, he must ask forgiveness, though it be in the very simplest terms.

3. God took punishment for his sin when He allowed men to kill His Son by nailing His body to a cross. Christ died because He loved us so much and didn't want God to punish us (John 3:16).

4. The disabled person should respond and can respond when his mental capacity permits. He must be sorry for his sin and come to the point where he can say with his mouth and feel with his heart, "Jesus is my Friend. He died to take my sin away" (Rom. 5:8).

THE TEACHER OF THE INTELLECTUALLY IMPAIRED

The success of the church teaching situation for the intellectually impaired comes in direct proportion to the ability of its teacher. Certain competencies— spiritual, social, and emotional—are necessary if his work with the disabled is to prove effective. As a priority, the special education teacher must be a Christian in order to accomplish spiritual results. He must have patience, respect for, and sensibility to human need,[18] plus love for the student who is "different."

Leaders in the church's special education program should have professional competence in addition to Christian character. The teacher needs a good working knowledge of mental deficiency or at least familiarity with learning

18. Elmer L. Towns and Roberta L. Groff, *Successful Ministry to the Retarded* (Chicago: Moody, 1972), p. 61.

disorders. No teacher will ever be effective unless he works from a basic knowledge of learning problems.[19]

He must be patient. His classroom atmosphere should be informal but have established routines. He must be creative, able to present lessons with a variety of methods, thereby more nearly meeting the needs of individual students.

To the following checklist of attitudes, every teacher and worker with the mentally handicapped should give prayerful and careful consideration.[20]

1. Am I comfortable with this person? The ideal teacher of the mentally disabled is relatively free of the fear that would prohibit him from being relaxed with the disabled. Many mentally impaired persons have offensive and annoying mannerisms. The teacher accepts the mentally impaired as he is and works within the limits of his disability.

2. What are my feelings toward him? Do my feelings change? A person may seem perfectly comfortable with the intellectually impaired and yet never experience a change of attitude about them. Some adults see these disabled people as a group that never grows or matures in any way. Teachers must recognize the humanity of the mentally impaired and be willing to provide them with learning opportunities.

3. Can I accept the student where he is and not show irritation at his efforts to learn? The effective teacher combines patience with a sensitivity to the needs of each student. One cannot teach the mentally handicapped as a group, for each student manifests his learning problems differently within the large framework of disorders.

4. Am I rigid in my approach? No intellectually impaired youngster is able to respond to an unbending, unaccommodating attitude from his teacher. Flexible methods and expectations are necessary in order to have an ideal learning situation.

5. Am I satisfied with him? The honest teacher will ask himself, "Does the quantity and quality of the student's learning growth show that I am doing my job?" Because the work of the intellectually impaired always falls behind the norm of children his age, the teacher's goal is always that both learning and ego-building will take place. He must pattern learning tasks in such a way that the student succeeds and thereby feels good about himself.

6. Can I set limits? This involves two things: establishing clear behavioral bounds, and determining the goal for a given learning experience. Students must learn what is appropriate behavior. They need a structured learning situation, a given task which they can successfully complete through predetermined and precise steps.

7. Have I been careful to discuss his problems at an appropriate time? The

---

19. Ibid.
20. Bernice Baumgartner, *Helping the Trainable Mentally Retarded Child* (New York: Columbia U., 1967), pp. 77-78.

mentally disabled person's feelings go as deeply as anyone else's. Some problems need to be discussed with him privately. Others should be dealt with in his absence, and some may need to be shared in the presence of others. In any situation, the best type of counseling for the betterment of the individual should be given.

8. Do I feel and express my love to him?

9. Can I help fellow church members understand intellectual impairments and the need to extend social acceptance to the mentally disabled?

TEACHING METHODS

STORYTELLING

Storytelling is one of the world's oldest artistic forms. Mentally handicapped children love stories because they help kindle their meager imagination. Also stories help mold ideas. Intelligent choice of stories plus expertise in telling them will assist the disabled in understanding healthy moral behavior. Such concepts as "Thou shalt not steal" take root in the mind far more easily when the teacher uses a story rather than a lecture. Bible characters become human, and children see that Bible people faced problems similar to ours. They thought about stealing and lying. They did these things, but God forgave them and is also willing to forgive us.

"Whatever the teacher tells the trainable pupil, he accepts as true; therefore he accepts fairy tales just as he does Bible stories, for he can make no distinction between the real and the unreal, between fact and fancy, or between Cinderella and David and the giant."[21] The teacher must explain the difference every time he tells a story. (For more on storytelling and story playing, see chaps. 30 and 31.)

Those who teach these special-needs children should use visual aids abundantly. The spoken word alone leaves a clouded impression on the mentally impaired, so the use of visual aids to supplement the spoken word is of utmost importance. Flannelgraph is an excellent visual aid. Lap flannelboards are effective in helping children learn Bible stories. Each child should have his own board to use. Lap flannelboards can be made by covering sturdy cardboard boxes (with hinged lids) with contact paper and covering the lid with flannel material. Children can cut figures from magazines and papers and create their own visualized story. Flash cards, records, strips, and show-'n–tell records and filmstrips are other effective audio and visual aids.[22]

21. Towns and Groff, pp. 77-78.
22. An 8mm. Stori-Strip Projector may be purchased from Gospel Light Publications, Glendale, California 91204. Show 'n' Tell records and filmstrips on Bible stories, produced by General Electric, can be purchased from David C. Cook Publishing Company, Elgin, IL 60120, or from a GE dealer. For more on visuals and audio aids, see chap. 28.

ROLE PLAYING

Students will grasp differing roles more easily if they can perform them. (See again chaps. 30 and 31.) For example, children learn something about the role of father or mother by acting out that role. Almost any kind of experience can become the subject for role playing. It may bring about controlled, emotional releases. It can give children an opportunity to learn the art of social cooperation. And it can help reinforce concepts they have learned.

In using role playing with the mentally impaired, start with something very simple. For example, have all the children pretend to gather baby Moses in their arms, put him in his basket, and place him in the water. Do not attempt any role-play situation until a story is clear in the children's minds.

PUPPETRY

Puppetry has great value for use with the mentally handicapped. It helps them become cooperating members of a group and to adjust socially to their peers. Through a puppet, the child assumes a new identity. The teacher thus gains a new understanding of any behavior maladjustments. If the children have little or no speech ability, they can be taught to act out recorded stories with puppets.[23] The teacher can use puppets to tell a story, to lead a song, to ask a child to cooperate, to teach a memory verse.

MUSIC

Although music is effective in teaching any child, it is of particular value in the teaching of the mentally handicapped. Learning experiences can be made more pleasant if the teacher associates them with the use of music. Through music, children hear of God's love and can verbally and emotionally respond to it. What children are learning becomes more permanent in their minds if they are able to sing about it.

Music has a calming effect on the mentally impaired child. Soft, slow music may calm a group of excitable children. Conversely, stirring music may stimulate an unresponsive child into class participation. Joyful music may bring happiness to an unhappy child. It can also be an aid in developing the sense of hearing.[24]

Perry suggests other values that music may have for the retarded. It can—

set a mood;
provide a tool for learning ideas;

23. A catalog of puppets, scripts, and backdrops for use in Christian education can be obtained from Higley Press, P. O. 2470, Jacksonville, FL 32200.
24. Natalie Perry, *Teaching the Mentally Retarded Child* (New York: Columbia U., 1960), p. 93.

enhance social growth because they learn to do something together such as singing or clapping;

stimulate physical coordination because they can march or keep time in other ways;

stimulate spiritual growth because they hear spiritual ideas in the words of songs and can be led into worship.[25]

Perry suggests the following criteria for selecting music. It must—

have a simple melody, no longer than twelve measures with a limited and repetitious range of notes;

have familiar, interesting words, not baby talk;

have a clear rhythm with prominent beats;

have slow tempo because the retarded need more time to pronounce words;

have a definite Christian message;

meet a wide range of needs within the class.[26]

Record and cassette players are valuable means for developing the handicapped child's appreciation and awareness of music. Many mentally impaired persons have difficulty with sound discrimination; thus records can help refine their hearing sense. Teachers can use this tool with a group or with individuals.

The rhythm band is a good means of encouraging social growth in mentally disabled children. They realize that though each one has a different instrument, no one instrument is more important than the other. They also learn cooperation by realizing that they cannot always play the instrument they desire.[27] (See chap. 25 also.)

CRAFTS

Craft activities for intellectually impaired children need to be selected carefully if they are to serve their designated purpose. Each activity chosen should reinforce the lesson and help meet the teaching aim. Any craft project must be explained carefully to the students with regard to the process and the end result. When students understand the end result, they will work toward it in methodical, slow steps. Teachers must analyze the steps beforehand and ex-

25. Ibid.
26. Ibid., pp. 159-61.
27. For additional information on music for retarded children, consult these sources: Bernice W. Carlson and David R. Ginglend, *Play Activities for Retarded Children* (Nashville: Abingdon, 1961); David R. Ginglend and Winifred E. Stiles, *Music Activities for Retarded Children* (Nashville: Abingdon, 1965); Doris Driggers Monroe, "Music Has Charms for the Retarded, Too," *Church Training* 1 (November 1971): 36-41; Ferris and Jennet Robins, *Educational Rhythmics for Mentally and Physically Handicapped Children* (New York: Association, 1968).

plain each step clearly. Otherwise, students may become confused and give up. Molloy suggests these criteria for selecting crafts. They must—

> be useful to the child;
> be simple enough to be learned with directed instruction and practice;
> have an added degree of difficulty in successive crafts which will teach a new manual skill;
> be interesting to the child.[28]

In Sunday school, crafts usually cannot be put to optimum use because of limited time. However, churches with weekday or extended sessions for the mentally handicapped can make better use of crafts. (See chap. 32 also.)

SUMMARY

Twenty years ago there were virtually no special church-sponsored classes for the intellectually impaired. Today Christian educators are recognizing this long-neglected ministry and are opening their arms in love for these special-needs children. It is a wide open door, and if entered, will bring enrichment to many lives. The teacher, helper, and director of the activities will have his life enriched by knowing and responding to the needs of these children and their families. Parents and families of the mentally impaired will be strengthened through the knowledge that the church cares, and the children will understand the love of God through the love and concern of the church.

Christian education of the intellectually impaired calls for skill. Conferences and workshops on ministering to these children will help teach a congregation about mental impairment, about community services available for the disabled, and about the learning potential of the intellectually impaired.

The pastor and congregation working together can be a real force in reaching the mentally impaired and their families for Christ.

FOR FURTHER READING

BOOKS AND PERIODICALS

Agee, J. Willard. "The Minister Looks at Mental Retardation." *Pastoral Psychology* 13 (September 1962): 12-22.

Ashman, Adrian, and Ronald Laura, eds. *The Education and Training of the Mentally Retarded.* New York: Nichols, 1985.

Bauer, Charles E. *Retarded Children Are People.* Milwaukee: Bruce, 1964.

Baumgartner, Bernice. *Helping the Trainable Mentally Retarded Child.* New York: Columbia U., 1967.

28. Julia S. Molloy, *Trainable Children* (New York: Day, 1961), p. 334.

Blodgett, Harriet E. *Mentally Retarded Children: What Parents and Others Should Know.* Minneapolis: U. Minnesota, 1971.

Bogardus, LaDonna. *Christian Education of Retarded Children and Youth.* Nashville: Abingdon, 1963.

Buck, Pearl S. *The Gifts They Bring.* New York: Day, 1965.

Buscaglia, Leo. *The Disabled and Their Parents: A Counseling Challenge.* Thorofare, N.J.: Slack, 1983.

Carpenter, Robert D. *Why Can't I Learn?* Glendale, Calif.: Gospel Light, 1972.

Deiner, Penny L. *Resources for Teaching Young Children with Special Needs.* New York: Harcourt Brace Jovanovich, 1983.

Egg, Marie. *Educating the Child Who Is Different.* New York: Day, 1968.

———. *When a Child Is Different.* New York: Day, 1960.

Hadley, Gloria. *How to Teach the Mentally Retarded.* Wheaton, Ill.: Scripture Press, Victor Books, 1978.

Hahn, Hans R., and Werner H. Raasch. *Helping the Retarded to Know God.* St. Louis: Concordia, 1969.

Kemp, Charles F. *The Church: The Gifted and the Retarded Child.* St. Louis: Bethany, 1957.

Ketterman, Grace H. *You and Your Child's Problems.* Old Tappaan, N.J.: Revell, 1983.

McConnell, Nancy P. *Different and Alike.* Colorado Springs, Colo.: Current, 1982.

Monroe, Doris D. *A Church Ministry to Retarded Persons.* Nashville: Convention, 1972.

Organizing Religious Classes for Mentally Retarded Children. St. Louis: Lutheran Church (Missouri Synod), n.d.

Palmer, Charles E. *The Church and the Exceptional Person.* Nashville: Abingdon, 1961.

Perske, Robert. *New Directions for Parents of Persons Who Are Retarded.* Nashville: Abingdon, 1973.

———. *Hope for the Families: New Directions for Parents of Persons with Retardation or Other Disabilities.* Nashville: Abingdon, 1981.

Peterson, Sigurd D. *Retarded Children: God's Children.* Philadelphia: Westminster, 1960.

Sieving, Hilmar A., ed. *The Exceptional Child and the Christian Community.* River Forest, Ill.: Lutheran Educ. Assoc., 1950.

Schultz, Edna. *They Said Kathy Was Retarded.* Chicago: Moody, 1963.

Stair, Ernest R. "Religion and the Handicapped Child." *Religious Education* 62 (1968): 352-54.

Stubblefield, Harold W. *The Church's Ministry in Mental Retardation.* Nashville: Broadman, 1965.

Theodore, Mary. *The Challenge of the Retarded Child.* Milwaukee: Bruce, 1959.

Thomas, Janet K. *How to Teach and Administer Classes for Mentally Retarded Children.* Minneapolis: Denison, 1968.
Towns, Elmer L., and Roberta L. Groff. *Successful Ministry to the Retarded.* Chicago: Moody, 1972.
Valett, R. E. *Modifying Children's Behavior: A Guide for Parents and Professionals.* Belmont, Calif.: Fearon, 1978.
Your Child and the Mentally Retarded. Nashville: Baptist Sunday School Board., n.d.
Welborn, Terry, and Stanley Williams. *Leading the Mentally Retarded in Worship.* St. Louis: Concordia, 1973.
Wilke, Harold H. *Creating the Caring Congregation: Guidelines for Ministering with the Handicapped.* Nashville: Abingdon, 1980.
Wood, Andrew H. *A Manual for Reaching Retarded Children for Christ.* Union Grove, Wis.: Shepherds, n.d.

JOURNALS ON THE INTELLECTUALLY IMPAIRED OR INCLUDING ARTICLES ON THE SUBJECT

American Association on Mental Deficiency. 5101 Wisconsin Avenue, Washington, D.C. 20016.
Bold (Bolder Opportunities for Learning Disabled). 9451 West Broadview Drive, Bay Harbor Island, FL 33154.
Exceptional Children. 1411 South Jefferson Davis Highway, Arlington, VA 22202.
Journal of Religion and Health. 16 East 34th Street, New York, NY 10016.
Pastoral Psychology. Manhasset, NY 11030.
Today's Health. 535 North Dearborn Street, Chicago, IL 60610.

SOURCES OF LESSON MATERIALS

Abingdon Press. 201 Eighth Avenue, South, Nashville, TN 37203.
BCM International. 237 Fairfield Avenue, Upper Darby, PA 19082.
Concordia Publishing House. 3558 South Jefferson Street, St. Louis, MO 63118.
David C. Cook Publishing House, 850 North Grove, Elgin, IL 60120.
John Knox Press. 801 East Main Street, Richmond, VA 22309.
Milwaukee County Association for Retarded Children. 1426 West State Street, Milwaukee, WI 53233.
Scripture Press Publications, 1825 College Avenue, Wheaton, IL 60187.
Shepherds, Inc. P. O. Box 1261, Union Grove, WI 53182.
    Shepherds has a wide selection of lesson materials for the mentally handi-

capped. They also have guidebooks on developing church programs for the mentally handicapped.

Sunday School Board, Southern Baptist Convention. 127 Ninth Avenue, North, Nashville, TN 37203.

OTHER SOURCES OF INFORMATION

Association for Childhood Education International. 3615 Wisconsin Avenue, N.E., Washington, DC 20017.

Canadian Association for Retarded Children. 4700 Keele Street, Downsview, Ontario, Canada.

Child Study Association of America. 9 East 89th Street, New York, NY 10028.

Compassionate Friends. P. O. Box 1347, Oak Brook, IL 60521.

Down's Syndrome Congress. 1640 West Roosevelt Road, Chicago, IL 60608.

Federation for Children with Special Needs. 312 Stuart Street, 2d Floor, Boston, MA 02116.

National Association for Retarded Children. 910 17th Street, N.W., Washington, DC 20006.

National Education Association. 1201 Sixteenth Street, N.W., Washington, DC 20006.

Special Education Information Center. Box 1492, Washington, DC 20013.

U.S. Department of Health, Education, and Welfare. Washington, DC 20025.

Charles T. Smith

13

Teaching Gifted Children

- History of Education for the Gifted
- Identifying the Gifted
  DEFINITION OF GIFTEDNESS
  IQ—THE STANDARD MEASURE
- Causes of Giftedness
  FAMILY BACKGROUND AND INFLUENCE
  HEREDITY VERSUS ENVIRONMENT
- Characteristics of the Gifted
  GENERAL
  RELIGIOUS
- Education of the Gifted
  ORGANIZATIONAL PROCEDURES
  IMPLICATIONS FOR CHRISTIAN EDUCATION
  CURRICULUM PROCEDURES
  INSTRUCTIONAL PROCEDURES
  THE TEACHER OF GIFTED CHILDREN
  THE CHURCH'S ROLE

Special education for the intellectually gifted dates back to at least the seventh century before Christ. Nebuchadnezzar, the great Babylonian king, had besieged and crushed the city of Jerusalem, deporting many of its citizens. He

CHARLES T. SMITH, M.R.E., is minister of Christian education at the College Avenue Baptist Church, San Diego, California.

ordered the chief of his officials to bring some of the sons of Israel, including members of the royal family and of the nobles to serve in his palace. In order to qualify, they were to be those "in whom was no defect, who were good looking, showing intelligence in every branch of wisdom, endowed with understanding, and discerning knowledge, and who had ability for serving in the king's court" (Dan. 1:4, NASB). Once selected, these candidates entered a vigorous three-year education program involving the "literature and language of the Chaldeans" (Dan. 1:4, NASB). Daniel and his three friends became the king's top students.

HISTORY OF EDUCATION FOR THE GIFTED

History reveals definite efforts to educate the gifted and to utilize their talents. Over 2,000 years ago, in ancient Greece, Plato advocated that young children of superior intellect be selected for education in specialized forms of science, philosophy, and metaphysics. The survival of Greek democracy was seen by Plato to be contingent on the eventual use of these superior citizens in leadership roles in the state.[1]

In the sixteenth century, special efforts were promoted by Suleiman the Magnificent to identify the gifted Christian youth in the Turkish empire and educate them in Islam, philosophy, science, art, and war. Surveillance of the population at regular intervals led to the selection and education of a large group of superior individuals who, after one generation, made the Ottoman Empire a great power in science, art, culture, and war.[2]

In the seventeenth century, the bishop Comenius made frequent reference to the special education of students with exceptional aptitudes for learning. He advocated financial aid to those bright students from poor homes.[3]

Thomas Jefferson, early in the eighteenth century, proposed that the state of Virginia "strengthen its natural aristocracy of virtues and talents by establishing rigorously selective tests in the grammar schools through which 'the best geniuses will be raked from the rubbish annually' and sent to William and Mary College at public expense."[4]

During the nineteenth and twentieth centuries, little organized effort was made in Europe and the United States to select the gifted children for special education. In Europe, secondary schools and universities were generally keyed to educate those of higher social class and family influence from which the more intelligent were believed to come. Now there is a growing trend to base such education on the academic achievement and interests of the children.[5]

1. Samuel A. Kirk, *Educating Exceptional Children,* 2d ed. (Boston: Houghton Mifflin, 1972), p. 105.
2. Ibid., pp. 105-6.
3. Gertrude H. Hildreth, *Introduction to the Gifted* (New York: McGraw-Hill, 1966), p. 42.
4. Ibid., p. 43.
5. Kirk, p. 106.

The United States has concentrated its efforts on the education of all children, through mass education procedures, believing that all men are created with equal potential and thus worthy of equal educational opportunities. Until recently, however, special educational provisions for gifted children (such as special classes and programs) did not receive wide public support. The present interest in the education of the gifted is due to a number of national and international situations: (1) the sharp conflict of ideology between nations; (2) the knowledge explosion; and (3) complaints about the place of the gifted child in the American educational system.[6]

IDENTIFYING THE GIFTED CHILD

There are various opinions among educators as to what constitutes a gifted child. Many use the word *gifted* synonymously with "high IQ" (intelligence quotient—the ratio between mental age, determined by tests, and chronological age). Others believe that the use of intelligence tests as the sole measure of giftedness is inadequate. They point out that intelligence tests fail to measure sufficiently a broad range of cognitive abilities (convergent thinking rather than divergent is the main emphasis, thus nullifying the creative abilities) and cannot adequately account for school achievement and academic performance (a child with a high IQ may do poorly in school, and one with a low IQ may do well).[7]

A BROADER DEFINITION OF GIFTEDNESS

Sometimes individuals are thought to be gifted because of the extent of their proficiency in music, art, drama, or mechanics, and many other areas, as opposed to strict academic giftedness. For this reason, the National Society for the Study of Education defined giftedness thus: "A talented or gifted child is one who shows consistently remarkable performance in any worthwhile line of endeavor. Thus, this definition includes not only the intellectually gifted but also those who show promise in music, the graphic arts, creative writing, dramatics, mechanical skills, and social leadership."[8]

Gardner enthusiastically supports this broader view of giftedness. He has identified seven forms of intelligence: linguistic and logical-mathematical (the two most highly valued in our society), spatial (the visualizers, artistic), musical, bodily-kinesthetic (personal movement and handling of objects—the athletes, dancers, and some engineers), and two forms of personal intelligence—interpersonal (knowing how to deal with others) and intrapersonal (knowledge

---

6. Ibid., pp. 106-7.
7. Jacob W. Getzels and Philip W. Jackson, *Creativity and Intelligence* (New York: John Wiley and Sons, 1962), pp. 2-3.
8. *Education for the Gifted:* Fifty-Seventh Yearbook of the National Society for the Study of Education (Chicago: U. Chicago, 1958), 2:19.

of self). None of these ought to have priority over others, and Gardner believes we waste much human potential by focusing only on the linguistic and logical-mathematical. The gifted have varying blends of intelligences that need to be channeled and nurtured into appropriate roles.[9]

Sumption and Luecking define the gifted as "those who possess a superior central nervous system characterized by the potential to perform tasks requiring a comparatively high degree of intellectual abstraction or creative imagination or both."[10] Most studies have established a substantial relationship between creativity and intellectual aptitude, though a few have supported the creativity-intelligence distinction.[11]

The first definition is broad, allowing for achievement in any area; whereas the latter considers the potential to achieve. Perhaps Neff's eclectic definition is best since it combines the best of both aspects: "The gifted person is one whose performance, or potential to perform, in worthwhile human endeavors requiring a comparatively high degree of intellectual abstraction and/or creative imagination is consistently remarkable."[12]

IQ—THE STANDARD MEASURE OF GIFTEDNESS

Despite the current efforts to depend less on IQ in identifying the gifted, most schools and educators continue to rely on standardized intelligence tests, due primarily to the fact that there are few other measuring devices. Kirk admits that superior intelligence is only one way of determining success and achievement but believes it still remains the basic ingredient of what is called giftedness. For practical purposes, he narrows giftedness to a few general terms: *"superior ability to deal with facts, ideas, or relationships,* whether this ability comes from high IQ or a less well-defined creativity." He then proceeds to refer to those with special aptitudes (mechanical, artistic, musical, physical, linguistic, social) as talented, rather than gifted. He realizes that there is considerable overlapping between those who are talented and those who are gifted; the very talented may also be intellectually gifted.[13]

When IQ is used for identifying giftedness, authorities set different standards, ranging from an IQ of 115 to an IQ of 180 and above.[14] Keller defines the academically talented as those with IQ's of 116 and above (Binet test), constituting 20 percent of the school population. Among this group are "most of the creatively talented, many of the psychosocially talented and a good

9. Howard Gardner, "Human Intelligence Isn't What We Think It Is," *U.S. News and World Report* (19 March 1984), p. 75.
10. Sumption and Luecking, quoted in Kirk, p. 108.
11. *Education of the Gifted and Talented,* Report to the Congress of the United States by the U.S. Commissioner of Education (Washington, D.C.: U.S. Gov. Printing Office, 1972), p. 20.
12. Herbert B. Neff, *Meaningful Religious Experiences for the Bright or Gifted Child* (New York: Association, 1968), p. 29.
13. Ibid., pp. 109-10.
14. Kirk, p. 109.

portion of the kinesthetically talented."[15] Federal education officials list two gifted levels. The gifted are those with IQs of 132, and they comprise approximately 3 percent of the school population. The highly gifted are those with IQs of 148, and they comprise only 1 percent of the school population.[16] Kirk prefers to make the standard for giftedness higher, beginning with IQs above 148. "Superior" children are those with IQs from 116 to 132, and the "very superior" have IQs ranging from 132 to 148.[17]

CAUSES OF GIFTEDNESS

FAMILY BACKGROUND AND INFLUENCE

According to Keller, there is a growing resource of information on gifted children. They tend to come from small families (frequently the first child), from well-educated and productive parents (30 percent of children from gifted parents are also gifted), from high socioeconomic background (40 percent do not need college scholarships), from certain ethnic-cultural origins (first are English, German, and Jewish families), and from particular religions (first Jews, then Protestants, and then Catholics).[18]

Mounting evidence points to the strategic role of the parents and family in the development of gifted children. "Considering that most persons concerned about raising the intellectual level of Americans concentrate on improving the schools, this may well be the most significant oversight in American education."[19] Pressey points up the importance of early training and postulates that "a practical genius is produced by giving a precocious, able youngster early encouragement, intensive instruction, continuing opportunity as he advances, a congruent stimulating social life, and cumulative success experiences."[20]

On the other hand, undue parental pressure on children to learn and succeed may be harmful to children; intellectual growth depends largely on intellectual readiness, intrinsic motivation, and an accepting, encouraging environment.

HEREDITY VERSUS ENVIRONMENT

Heredity as well as environment has an impact on intellectual ability. Jensen has concluded that about 80 percent of intelligence is determined by heredity, although others estimate that the inherited factor is only from 25 to 45 percent.[21] In a Congressional report by the United States Commissioner of

15. William P. Lineberry, ed., *New Trends in the Schools* (New York: Wilson, 1967), p. 47.
16. Ibid.
17. Kirk, p. 113.
18. Lineberry, p. 48.
19. Ibid., p. 48.
20. Kirk, p. 114.
21. Cassidy, Robert, "Can Our Schools Survive?" *Parent's Magazine* 48 (May 1973): 10-14.

Education, the inherited factor rates high. "Various estimates of the proportions of intelligence variance due to heredity and environment, based on twin studies over a twenty year period, ascribe from sixty to eighty percent to heredity. All of the researchers agree that some part of the variance must be attributed to the effect of the environment in which children are reared."[22]

The preschool years are particularly important in the development of intelligence. Bloom believes that half of a seventeen-year-old's mental ability is developed in his first four years of life.[23] Furthermore, in Bloom's analysis of major studies, he concluded, "The greatest impact on IQ from environmental factors would probably take place between the ages of 1 and 5, with relatively little impact after age 8."[24]

These facts have become part of the rationale for public and private thrusts in preschool education.

CHARACTERISTICS OF GIFTED CHILDREN

Although no two gifted children are alike, they do tend to possess certain characteristics that distinguish them from other children. Observant teachers will be able to spot these characteristics or abilities both in and out of the classroom.

GENERAL CHARACTERISTICS

According to a recent study on the education of mentally gifted minors (based on 132 IQ as the beginning of giftedness), such children are likely to possess the following abilities:

1. They learn to read earlier and with greater comprehension. Kindergarten teachers need to discover which of their pupils already read, and arrange curriculum accordingly.

2. They learn basic skills faster and need less practice. If parents and teachers persist in teaching the gifted child at the same speed and with the same amount of repetition as a normal child, the advanced one will become bored and careless, and will lose his motivation.

3. They can understand abstract ideas that other children at the same age level cannot.

4. They pursue interests beyond the usual limitations of childhood.

5. They can comprehend implications and nuances which other children need to have explained to them. Gifted ones pick up more information and do so faster.

6. They can take responsibility at an earlier stage in life and assume it more naturally.

22. *Education of the Gifted and Talented,* p. 18.
23. Lineberry, p. 133.
24. *Education of the Gifted and Talented,* p. 24.

7. They can maintain much longer concentration periods. They often become immersed with the facts and content of a subject for its own interest, not because it was presented entertainingly.

8. They can express thoughts readily and communicate with clarity in one or more areas of talent.

9. They read widely, quickly, and intensely in one subject or in many areas.

10. They have seemingly limitless energy to expend.

11. They can manifest creative and original verbal or physical responses.

12. They employ a more complex processing of information than the average child their age.

13. They can respond and relate well to peers, parents, teachers, and adults who likewise function easily in the higher-level thinking processes, depending on a balance in their emotional adjustment.

14. They can have many projects going, particularly at home, so that they are either busily occupied or looking for something to do.

15. They often assume leadership roles because of an innate sense of justice that is often noticeable in them, and youth gives them strength to which other young people respond.[25]

There are some additional characteristics which may also evidence themselves in gifted children. They may have a highly developed sense of humor and creative wit. Their nonconformity may be a troublesome characteristic to their parents and teachers and is generally related to their highly original and creative nature. Socially the gifted child may find himself in a dilemma, wanting to be loved and share love, but being critical, snobbish, and even intolerant of others with less talent. Nevertheless, he is often found to be cheerful, thoughtful, sympathetic, generous, and conscientious.[26]

In physique and general health, gifted children surpass the best standards for American children.[27] Coupled with their excellent physical development is their superior muscular coordination (though their handwriting may be poor anyway).[28]

One of the activities they enjoy is collecting things, frequently of unusual or complicated nature (stamps, butterflies, chemicals, archaeological artifacts). Hobbies are numerous and precocious when compared to those of other children the same chronological age.[29]

RELIGIOUS CHARACTERISTICS

Neff, writing from a religious perspective, adds the following general characteristics:

25. *Education of Mentally Gifted Minors* (Sacramento, Calif.: California State Department of Education, 1971), pp. 11-12.
26. Neff, pp. 42-43.
27. Kirk, p. 124.
28. Neff, pp. 41-42.
29. Ibid.

1. The gifted child has an earlier and greater degree of religious develop-ment. By reading over the general characteristics of gifted children, it is necessary only to transfer them into a Christian education setting to see the type of student the parent and the teacher in the church has to teach. His ability to learn and understand the Bible and its abstract doctrinal concepts and principles for living is great. The gifted student will begin earlier to ask searching questions about the universe, the purpose for life, the reason for creation, the effects of man's fall, the means of salvation, the destiny of man, the nature of angelic creatures, the nature of God and the Trinity, and ques-tions on ethical principles, problems, and solutions. His higher intelligence provides the need and reason for earlier religious instruction. And the higher the intelligence, the greater the demand for such Christian teaching.[30]

Monroe states that a child's ability to understand abstract concepts (which is basic to understanding theological concepts) depends on (1) his innate mental ability; (2) the nature of his environment; and (3) his particular pattern in rate of growth.[31]

It is obvious that gifted children will understand abstract theological con-cepts (e.g., Jesus is the same as God, or Jesus had to die to obtain our salvation) much sooner than the normal child, due to their exceptional intellec-tual ability.

2. Neff's second characteristic of gifted children is a reasoning ability that allows children to perceive subtle relationships and to observe inconsistencies. It is this quality that makes gifted children seem so adult-like. Their early use of the words *like* and *as* indicate their ability to generalize (a process resulting in the use of similes and metaphors as they see similarities and make compari-sons).[32] After the father of a bright four-year-old read from a Bible storybook the story of David and Goliath, the daughter, with all sincerity, asked, "Daddy, did God like David to kill Goliath?" The question was loaded. Only recently had the mother exhorted her not to hit other children in the neighborhood. The child was confronted with an apparent conflict in morality that perplexed her. The father's explanation failed to satisfy her, so she repeated the question two more times. The gifted child will be quick to note subtle relationships and point up any inconsistencies.

3. Gifted children have a highly developed moral and spiritual awareness with the unusual ability to translate this into conduct. Their interest in reli-gious things coincides with their mental age rather than their chronological age. Therefore, when gifted children reach the mental age of about twelve, according to Hollingworth, they are ready for full admittance to religious participation (church doctrinal orientation and active church membership).[33]

30. Neff, pp. 57-58.
31. Doris Monroe, *Integrative Review of Research Relating to Concept Development in Children* (Nashville: Baptist Sunday School Board, 1964), pp. 69-71.
32. Neff, p. 40.
33. Ibid., pp. 37-38.

Therefore, an understanding of the gospel of Christ and personal response to it in conversion will logically accompany the gifted child's early spiritual awareness. It is probable that this decision will easily precede the child's twelfth year, depending on the nurture received and readiness factors other than intellect. His spiritual maturity in understanding and behavior are likely to set him apart from his peers and may result in social separation—something to be guarded against.

4. The gifted child has a tendency toward self-criticism and moral anxiety. The gifted child's keen insight, critical judgment, knowledge, and unusual ability to make evaluations have both good and bad points. With his sense of moral values developing earlier than other children, he becomes disturbed over the mistreatment of others (e.g., a preschooler watching a boxing match on TV with his father) and may accept personal responsibility, even guilt, for group actions. The gifted child tends to set high standards for himself, his family, and his church group. He may become disillusioned with the group if they fail to measure up to his standards.[34]

5. The gifted child searches for purpose and meaning in life. He seeks a reason for being and exerts considerable energy to accomplish something of real worth. It is Neff's conviction that in the religious realm, this quest for meaning generally turns out to be a baffling and frustrating experience. The child becomes confused by unacceptable answers to his questions about God, bored with the traditional methods of Christian instruction, disgusted over the inconsistencies, frustrated over his own unresolved spiritual conflicts, and senses guilt because of injustices. Soon a feeling of alienation from God sets in, due to his lack of appropriate, harmonized, theological information.[35]

The gifted child's search for eternal purpose becomes stalled, and he often rejects Christianity. In time he either becomes involved in some fanatical endeavor or lives out his life in meaningless, unfulfilled existence. Only a few are fortunate enough to be guided into a constructive and reasonable faith in God.[36] The challenge of meeting the gifted child's need for purpose and meaning in life within existing structures of Christian education is one to which the Christian teacher should forthrightly and intelligently respond.

EDUCATION OF THE GIFTED

After the Soviet Union launched Sputnik, national interest was created for the special education of the gifted children in the United States. At that time, the prevalent idea was the acceleration of federally sponsored education programs for the gifted. Soon special provisions were being made to adapt the school program to the abilities of the gifted children, including "1) accelerating, enriching, or grouping children, 2) devising a curriculum suitable to

34. Ibid., pp. 37-38, 43-44.
35. Ibid., p. 59.
36. Ibid., pp. 59, 60.

children with high abilities, and 3) utilizing appropriate instructional procedures."[37]

ORGANIZATIONAL PROCEDURES

The first of these provisions relates to the organizational procedures commonly used in providing an appropriate learning environment for gifted students in public schools.

Acceleration. A method frequently employed is known as acceleration, which involves stepping up the learning pace for the gifted student. Acceleration takes on several forms: (1) early admission to kindergarten or first grade; (2) skipping grades; and (3) telescoping grades.

Frequently acceleration involves the early admission of children to kindergarten or the first grade. Intellectual readiness of students for such a step is determined by individually administered IQ tests, and social readiness is determined by interviews with school officials and observation of the children in informal group play. Early admission has the value of adapting to the readiness of children and providing a greater likelihood that the entrant will pursue an undisturbed course in elementary school; further acceleration is rarely necessary.[38]

A second form of acceleration is skipping grades, which involves completely eliminating one grade of school. Gold believes there is little justification for skipping grades, since it is employed as the simplest solution to the obvious boredom of a bright child. Initially, skipping is a challenge to the child, but soon the problem repeats itself and demands more skipping, and may eventually place the child out of reach of his friends and in a class where he is the smallest student.[39] Kirk disagrees and cites research that demonstrates that "children who have skipped grades have shown social, educational, and vocational adjustment superior or comparable to that of equally intelligent nonaccelerates."[40]

A third form of acceleration is telescoping grades, which enables gifted children to cover the same material provided in a regular curriculum but in a shorter time.[41] The nongraded elementary class is a good example. For some three years, children remain in a basic group (either primary or intermediate) and are helped to make individual progress toward specific, individual, learning goals. If academic progress leads to an early completion of the class (in two years rather than three), promotion from the ungraded class may occur.[42]

37. Kirk, p. 135.
38. Milton J. Gold, *Education of the Intellectually Gifted* (Columbus, Ohio: Merrill, 1965), p. 336.
39. Ibid.
40. Kirk, p. 136.
41. Ibid.
42. Gold, p. 337.

Students are frequently grouped according to ability within a class or placed in separate classes for brighter learners.[43]

Enrichment. The second organizational procedure involves providing special opportunities for the gifted student to broaden and deepen his interests and insights through many activities and experiences within the regular school class or program. *Enrichment* has been tried through the following procedures: (1) challenging children in regular grades with additional reading assignments and outside class activities; (2) grouping children within the class for activities that fit their abilities and interests; (3) employing a special teacher who helps identify the gifted, assists the regular teachers in the instruction of their gifted students, counsels these children regarding their study activities, and holds some special study seminars with them; and (4) encouraging the maintenance of high standards in the instruction of the gifted.[44]

According to Gallagher, enrichment has often failed to meet educational anticipations due to the additional work required of the teacher. Special assignments must be worked out for the gifted child on top of those already required for the rest of the class. The teacher must also be well oriented in advanced subject matter to provide effective student guidance. Furthermore, appropriate methods of stimulating the high-level concept realization and productive thinking capable of the gifted students again strains the teacher's knowledge.[45] The use of assistant teachers or teacher's aides especially oriented to meet some of these special enrichment needs may be one way to bring about greater success.

Grouping. Another organizational procedure used in teaching the gifted involves grouping them in one of the following ways: (1) within regular classrooms (for academic subjects); (2) in special sections for the study of academic subjects (e.g., English, science, mathematics, and social studies); (3) in modified special classes (special instruction with other gifted students as a part of each school day); (4) in special classes (progressing from grade to grade but with a special curriculum adapted to their interests and abilities); and (5) in special schools (separate institutions for the gifted). The first two provisions are the most widely accepted, while the last three are more controversial.[46]

"The fundamental argument for such grouping rests on the belief that it drastically reduces the wide variation in achievement found in a heterogeneous group."[47] But Burns and Johnson contend that research does not support the practice of sectioning bright students into classrooms for the purpose of attaining a homogeneous learning group. They point out that the achievement differences between a normal group of students and a gifted group is not of a

43. Hildreth, p. 290.
44. Kirk, p. 139.
45. James J. Gallagher, *Teaching the Gifted Child* (Boston: Allyn & Bacon, 1964), pp. 80, 82-83.
46. Kirk, pp. 140-41.
47. Paul C. Burns and A. Montgomery Johnson, *Research in Elementary School Curriculum* (Boston: Allyn & Bacon, 1970), p. 478.

significant magnitude to have a practical influence in the classroom. Every group of students has high, average, and low achievers (the bright child may be in any of these categories) in any particular achievement area. "If ability grouping based upon intelligent quotient is to be used with students of average to very superior ability, the justification, for such grouping will have to depend on reasons other than homogeneity of achievement."[48]

Glasser believes that keeping classes grouped heterogeneously rather than homogeneously has at least three advantages: (1) they eliminate early segregation of various types of students; (2) they keep communication open between the potential student failures and the successful students; (3) the faster learners can help motivate and assist the slower ones.[49]

Glasser contends that virtually all subjects are easily and best taught in mixed groups. The heterogeneous class will succeed except when there is a great disparity in reading levels accompanied by behavior disturbances. Homogeneous reading groups are then employed, meeting about one and one-half hours each day. These groups are evaluated at least twice a semester so that rapidly progressing students may be moved on to a more advanced group.[50]

IMPLICATIONS FOR CHRISTIAN EDUCATION

The Christian school generally follows the organizational procedures commonly practiced in public education, and the Sunday school may follow in a somewhat similar way. If a particular child is entering kindergarten or the first grade early, the child will obviously do so in the graded Sunday school program. The same procedure will follow if a grade is skipped.

If the child is in a nongraded primary or intermediate class, he may be placed in his chronological age Sunday school department or class or an older department or class that fits his level of social and intellectual maturity. Since the child is in Sunday school only an hour a week, his sense of social acceptance and comfort is of significance. Therefore, teachers should be careful not to accelerate him to a group where he is hindered in developing friendships.

Group-graded departments of children will offer a child contact with his peers and also the opportunity to progress, according to his ability, with children who are older. In this case, teachers must be alert to the fact that the gifted child should be encouraged to go to an older class or group that fits his ability or to choose a learning activity that challenges his interest and capabilities.

Closely graded departments may have as much as a four-year span of

48. Ibid., p. 480.
49. William Glasser, *Schools Without Failure* (New York: Harper & Row, 1969), pp. 88-89.
50. Ibid., p. 91.

abilities represented among their one-year chronologically grouped students. Care should be given in placing the gifted child among students with whom he can successfully work and learn; a capable teacher is of paramount importance.

Enrichment is a logical means of keeping the bright child challenged in the Sunday school, but the department superintendent and teacher are the key to its success. Additional activities and assignments may be initiated by the student or suggested by the teacher. Independent work or collaboration with other students in researching and completing certain creative, Bible-learning activities will certainly be a productive procedure to follow.

Such small group collaboration may represent ability grouping within a graded department or class, similar to that which Glasser recommends, when a homogeneous grouping proves unsatisfactory. For example, the gifted child who is six years old may already be reading on a third grade level. The child may therefore have to work independently or in collaboration with one or more students who are able to read well. But the worship, music, and discussion activities will generally suit both the gifted and the average child.

Special classes or modified classes for superior and gifted children may be put to use either on Sunday or during the week for educational purposes. No church should feel locked into a heterogeneous grouping of children if particular needs may be better met in a more homogeneous grouping. Churches that are running a two- to three-hour Sunday morning educational schedule may find the modified special class fits perfectly into their schedule. Gifted and superior-ability students may meet together for forty-five minutes to an hour with an able teacher for special studies utilizing library resources for research, exploring Bible subjects of interest to them.

CURRICULUM PROCEDURES WITH GIFTED CHILDREN

The discussion of the characteristics of gifted children and organizational procedures in providing adequately for their education has already provided some insight into the type of curriculum and instructional approach needed.

The curriculum plan must fit the gifted child's needs and capabilities. Kirk suggests five ways the elementary school curriculum may be expanded for the gifted. These ideas can be adapted easily into the church educational program.

Exploring structure and principles. First, there needs to be an emphasis on the overall structure and basic principles of subject content rather than on mere facts. Gifted elementary students will particularly benefit from understanding the underlying scheme—structure, ideas, theories—of the subjects they study. Once this underlying scheme has been found, the advanced students will be more freely motivated to absorb new knowledge and grasp the specific facts of the field. Gifted students are able to handle the theoretical aspects of the various fields of knowledge and, in a sense, emulate the scientist in the investigation of the phenomena behind the product.[51]

The gifted child will become bored if his teachers only tell the familiar Bible stories and do not give him opportunity to explore the entire background of a particular event and to find and investigate the biblical principles behind God's actions. The preadolescent student may want to compare the ethical teachings of the Old Testament with the New Testament, explore the geological evidence for a worldwide flood, or search out the theories on the origin of the Bethlehem star. The Bible itself may be a wonder to this child, and he may want to examine the evidences for its validity. The child's curiosity—even doubts— must never threaten the teacher but serve to motivate further study and instruction.

Searching the method as well as the facts. Second, there needs to be an emphasis on the methods used to gain information rather than on the information itself. Again, the student is to act as a scientist in his exploration of assigned problems, using plans of operation provided by his teacher. Explanations by the teacher on cause and effect are to be avoided, since the objective in his approach is for the student to discover these relationships on his own.[52]

As gifted children are led in the study of the Bible, they may soon desire an understanding of how the Bible was written, including information about the authors of the various books, dates the books were composed, how they become canonized, and how they have been preserved. A simplified study of the Dead Sea Scrolls may be particularly appreciated by the gifted student. The study of elemental biblical hermeneutics may even interest the older elementary student. The exploration of biblical manners and customs and archaeology may also prove an effective study for the students who wish to know how biblical people lived, worked, and traveled, and how such information sheds light on our understanding of Scripture.

Capitalizing on interests and readiness. Third, there needs to be an emphasis on being aware of the interests and readiness of the gifted child. Frequently the child asks questions and expresses interest in discussing subjects which parents and teacher may feel he is totally unprepared to understand. But the gifted child is able to understand concepts traditionally reserved for high school students when taught in a simplified form. Bruner advocates this approach in his "spiral curriculum," in which children are taught and then retaught, in an expanded form, the great issues, principles, and values of society in a manner consistent with their form of thought and frame of reference.[53]

The Jewish fathers practiced this principle in the instruction of their children

51. Kirk, p. 146.
52. Ibid., pp. 146-47.
53. Ibid., p. 147.

through the annual feasts (i.e., Passover, Pentecost, Atonement, Tabernacles). Their small children would not understand the deep significance of the Passover lamb or the symbolism of the Day of Atonement. But each year their understanding was deepening, and, for the bright Jewish child, a comprehension of the abstract meaning of these concrete observances was increasing each time they were experienced.

Sunday school teachers will be presenting significant biblical personages and events to their children which the gifted child will have comprehended at a much younger age. Each coverage should bring something new to light for the students, and the gifted child will soon explore the stories to their depths. The teacher should be alert to each child's interests and readiness to further explore biblical doctrines and subjects and be able to give guidance in following these interests to bring intellectual satisfaction and encourage Christian nurture.

Expanding content, depth, and breadth. Fourth, there needs to be an emphasis on expanding the depth and breadth of the curriculum. Special classes for the gifted tie directly into meeting this need, but regular class enrichment is certainly a key means of expanding subject content for the gifted student. Enrichment may be accomplished either through additional reading and assignments in a subject (breadth), or through a more intensive study of some aspect of the curriculum (depth) rather than a superficial approach to it.[54]

Christian education within the church program must be characterized by flexibility in approach to studying the Bible. Teachers who have a gifted child in their group should be prepared to lead the child more deeply or broadly in the subjects, issues, and people of the Scriptures. In studying events in the life of the apostle Paul, the gifted child may wish to trace Paul's life from beginning to end or concentrate on one aspect of his life, such as his strict Jewish upbringing and training as a Pharisee. If the gifted child is expected to be content with studying the same material and in the same fashion as the other students, boredom is sure to result.

Using resource persons. Fifth, there needs to be an emphasis on using special teachers or resource persons to assist in meeting the far-flung interests of the gifted child. It is frequently necessary to call such persons into the class or send the gifted student or group to such persons to gain further information and guidance. Team teaching is sometimes used to provide instruction in specific areas by competent teachers. Academic guidance may also be provided through a special teacher who is able to ascertain a gifted student's interests and abilities and direct the child into a challenging and need-fulfilling area of study.[55]

54. Ibid., p. 148.
55. Ibid., pp. 148-49.

Those who are teaching a gifted child will find using resource persons to be particularly rewarding when they reach the limitations of their own knowledge in a technical, theoretical, doctrinal, historical, or philosophical area of student inquiry. Admitting one's lack of knowledge in an area and then calling on others (the pastor, education director, seminary student, adult teacher) for special assistance will help hold the gifted child's interest and satisfy his budding curiosity and hunger for spiritual knowledge and guidance.

Older preschool as well as elementary gifted students can ask some profound questions and launch out into some heavy subjects. Such inquiries may be converted into learning activities, placing the students in the exploratory learning role and directing them to the persons who may provide just the information needed. At times, the students should be led to share their discoveries with the entire class or department for the group's stimulation and benefit.

INSTRUCTIONAL PROCEDURES WITH GIFTED CHILDREN

A broad range of instructional procedures needs to be employed in teaching gifted children including the use of (1) creative teaching principles; (2) creative teaching methods and activities; and (3) flexible groupings and scheduling. These procedures will be discussed as they relate to Christian education.

Creative teaching principles. When the teaching of gifted children is approached in ordinary, traditional ways, student dissatisfaction may result. More progressive or creative principles must be employed, which lead to the direct involvement of the student in satisfying learning experiences. Some of the important principles are as follows:

1. The gifted child must be presented with a constant intellectual challenge both at school and at home.
2. The gifted child must be exposed to large bodies of knowledge.
3. The gifted child's curriculum should be characterized by breadth, depth, and flexibility.
4. The gifted child requires adequate time for exploration of knowledge and critical thinking.
5. The gifted child's independence, originality, and creative expression in learning must be encouraged and utilized.
6. The gifted child must have the freedom to initiate or suggest learning ideas and activities and to choose the specific activities he desires to pursue.
7. The gifted child learns easier with less repetition, drill, and routine.
8. The gifted child must have a receptive learning environment that assists him in meeting his needs of affection, independence, approval, and self-esteem.

9. The gifted child must be stimulated to further study to avoid underachievement and to realize fully his potential.
10. The gifted child needs guidance in the rational and creative use of his knowledge.
11. The gifted child must have his individual achievements oriented socially and spiritually.
12. The sum total of the gifted child's learning experiences must fit his religious as well as general characteristics.

Creative teaching methods and activities. It is quite obvious that the effective teaching of the gifted child will require a greater variety of methods; the standard methods (storytelling, flannelgraph, discussion, workbook activity, memory work) will not by themselves fit the principles already outlined. Many of the traditional methods result in more teacher activity than student activity; this is just the opposite of what is needed.

Ten categories of creative methods may serve as avenues of learning for the gifted child: (1) art (painting, clay modeling, etc.); (2) writing; (3) drama (pantomime, role playing, picture posing); (4) group vocals; (5) interviewing (biblical and contemporary persons); (6) music; (7) map study; (8) construction (tabernacle, Palestinian home); (9) learning games and puzzles; and (10) research (field trips, using resource books and visual aids).

The preschool child will find art, construction, music, and puzzle activities particularly useful. The various interest centers in the Christian education setting may contain the materials necessary for good learning. A book rack may contain books with more detailed Bible story pictures and captions which the older, bright preschooler may be able to read. An easel and paints may provide the child with tools necessary for painting pictures of Bible events or people. Play dough or clay may be the means of "making" his church or the bread and fishes Jesus used to feed the people. Puzzles should naturally be more complicated than those used with less gifted in the same age group. While the child is physically engaged, he will be more fluent in conversation with his teachers about God's world, church, book, people, and acts.

Enrichment of the children's curriculum will also be made easier through the use of creative methods. Bible stories and correlated music will naturally accompany the Bible learning activities that the children suggest and/or choose. Any one of the avenues or methods may serve as a challenging approach, if it leads to the impression and expression of an appropriate breadth and depth of Bible knowledge. The gifted child will participate earlier in creative writing activities and research than the average child, due to a rapidly developing vocabulary (i.e., writing contemporary versions of Bible stories, diaries of Bible personalities, Bible times newspapers using the Bible and other resource books for important information). Contributions in art, modeling, and construction activities will be more detailed and complicated.

Research projects (using books, cassette tapes, programmed materials) will be particularly rewarding, and with guidance, factual findings may be worked into a game form to be used by the child's peers.

Flexible groupings and scheduling. Flexibility of approach is essential in dealing with the varied differences in individual needs, interests, backgrounds, and aptitudes in the average class. In such an environment, the gifted child is more free to investigate and pursue personal interests. Furthermore, the entire class or department may benefit considerably from special reports and presentations by the gifted child.[56]

If a church is following plans the major Christian education curriculum publishers recommend for preschool education, adequate flexibility in groupings and schedule is generally provided. Children are free to roam from group to group as they participate in interest centers of their choice, each stressing some aspect of the Bible story and theme. Teachers at each center guide the informal participation of the children and may enrich the learning activity for the gifted child. These children may desire to stay with an activity for a longer period, pursuing the subjects in greater detail with the teacher.

On the middle and older children's level, traditional plans and schedules do not generally provide the flexibility desired for the gifted child. Children are placed for thirty to forty-five minutes in permanent class groups in which each child is expected to participate in the same teacher-led experiences. When few, if any, learning activity options and choices are provided, a sterile atmosphere for the gifted child exists.

Plans that are most conducive to the gifted child include temporary groupings of students (those which only last as long as a unit of study, usually a month), which are organized around Bible learning activities chosen by the students. This arrangement allows the gifted child's interest and curiosity to be channeled into an area of study which he may suggest or be led into according to his ability. Such activities may either be individualized (something frequently preferred by the gifted child) or carried on with a group of students who may represent a wide range of intellectual capabilities (where the gifted child may spearhead the study and indirectly assist in teaching the slower students).

The type of learning activity will generally determine how successfully the gifted child may collaborate with slower students. Does the activity challenge his abilities? Does it tap his curiosity or interests? Does it include study procedures and skills that both the average and gifted child can perform on their own level? Is the nature of the activity such that it constitutes a meaningful learning experience both for the average and gifted student? Frequently the gifted child will enjoy doing the technical research necessary for the construction of a model of the tabernacle, whereas other children may enjoy gathering

56. Ralph L. Pounds and Robert L. Garretson, *Principles of Modern Education* (New York: Macmillan, 1962), p. 231.

the materials and making the objects that will go into this project. Thus, collaborative learning between a wide range of student abilities is possible.

THE TEACHER OF GIFTED CHILDREN

The teacher is the key figure in the Christian education of the gifted. He is not only the trusted and wise guide and adviser but a model of intellectual interest and achievement. His basic role is to stimulate intellectual interest in Bible study and to structure effective learning experiences, rather than being merely a conveyor of facts and information. His approach and methods are flexible and creative rather than authoritarian and traditional. He maintains a positive attitude in teaching that encourages the creativity and spontaneity of the gifted in learning.

The best teacher for gifted children will not necessarily be the most learned and educated, but the one who has the ability to stimulate the gifted student to maximum achievement.

The teacher's qualifications which assist in accomplishing this end will include the following, some of which are adapted from Hildreth's discussion of this subject:[57]

1. He is enthusiastic about God and His Word, and possesses a vital, growing relationship with Christ and the Body of Christ.
2. He possesses a healthy emotional, mental, and social state of being with which the gifted child may identify.
3. His training includes not only experience in creative teaching but a broad range of subject knowledge, including a competent grasp of Bible doctrine, history, and customs.
4. He understands and loves children and possesses a keen knowledge of the gifted child's general and spiritual characteristics.
5. He has the ability to discern the special interests and talents of the gifted (musical, artistic, mechanical, etc.) and is likely to arouse and utilize them in the teaching-learning process.
6. He has the ability to manage teaching in a small group as well as on an individual basis.
7. He encourages original thinking and intelligent problem solving.
8. He possesses skill in listening to children's questions and helping them seek out answers.
9. He is skilled in the techniques of intelligent conversation, questioning, and answering.
10. He develops a meaningful relationship with the gifted child and his parents and assists the parents in meeting the intellectual and spiritual needs of their children.

57. Hildreth, pp. 531-33.

The training of the gifted child will include the normal orientation and experience necessary for regular Christian day school or Sunday school teachers. Additional preparation will be necessary in the areas already discussed in this chapter. Furthermore, the educational resources and supplies which are so vitally related to the enrichment or acceleration of the gifted child's Christian education must be available and employed by the teacher.

THE CHURCH'S ROLE IN TEACHING THE GIFTED

It is the local church's responsibility to make adequate provisions for the Christian education of gifted children. In the average-size church, the number of gifted children will be small, and, as a result, they may constitute an overlooked minority. Yet these children offer a great deal of promise in their contributions to Christianity in its mission in the world.

The following are suggested steps which the church should follow in carefully planning and developing a ministry to the gifted. First, the church should determine the need in the church and in the community by the following procedures: (1) it should discover who the gifted ones are; (2) it should gather information from teachers and parents which may reveal the giftedness of a particular child; (3) it should consult with public school officials as to which children score in the upper 5 or 10 percent of students of a particular age (those who gather this information must keep it in strict confidence); (4) it must not administer intelligence tests; (5) it should seek to identify the gifted by uncovering their talents.

Second, the church should institute a program for gifted children, using the following guidelines: (1) it should study the effectiveness of the education presently being provided for gifted children in the elementary or church school; (2) it should determine the acceleration or enrichment needed; (3) it should evaluate the teacher changes or adjustments required; (4) it should seek out the teachers most suited to teach gifted children and approach them for this ministry; (5) it should prepare the teachers through regular training procedures, extra curriculum study, and observation of gifted children in classroom learning activity; (6) it should determine the suitability of the regular church curriculum and decide what enrichment and special groupings will be necessary; (7) it should accumulate educational resource materials needed for enrichment utilizing the church and public library; (8) it should follow the educational procedures most suited to the gifted in order to meet their intellectual-spiritual needs; (9) it should guide the gifted children in the constructive, Christian-oriented use of their abilities and talents; (10) it should work closely with the parents of gifted children, realizing that God has given them the primary responsibility for the Christian nurture of their children.

SUMMARY

The challenge facing both churches and parents in the Christian education of their gifted children must be intelligently and enthusiastically responded to. Far too little attention has been given to the life of the gifted to make any claim that they are being adequately provided for. The God-given abilities and talents of this exceptional group must be conserved and developed through special Christian education.

FOR FURTHER READING

Baskin, Barbara, and Karen Harris. *Books for the Gifted Child.* New York: R. R. Bowler, 1980.

Bruner, Jerome S. *The Process of Education.* Cambridge, Mass.: Harvard U., 1960.

Colangelo, Nicholas, and Ronald Zaffrann, eds. *New Voices in Counseling the Gifted.* Dubuque, Iowa: Kendall/Hunt, 1979.

Dunn, Lloyd M., et al., eds. *Exceptional Children in the Schools.* New York: Holt, Rinehart, & Winston, 1963.

Feldhusen, John, and Donald Treffinger. *Creative Thinking and Problem Solving in Gifted Education.* Dubuque, Iowa: Kendall/Hunt, 1977.

Fleigler, Louis A., ed. *Curriculum Planning for the Gifted.* Englewood Cliffs, N.J.: Prentice-Hall, 1961.

Freehill, Maurice F. *Gifted Children: Their Psychology and Education.* New York: Macmillan, 1961.

Gallagher, James. *Teaching the Gifted Child,* 2d ed. Boston: Allyn & Bacon, 1975.

———. *The Education of the Gifted and Talented Students.* Washington, D.C.: Council for Basic Education, 1979.

Gardner, Howard. *Frames of the Mind: The Theory of Multiple Intelligence.* New York: Basic, 1983.

Gowan, John C., and George D. Demos. *The Education and Guidance of the Ablest.* Springfield, Ill.: Thomas, 1964.

Hill, Mary Broderick. *Enrichment Programs for Intellectually Gifted Pupils.* California Project Talent, publication no. 4. Sacramento, Calif.: California State Dept. of Ed., 1969.

Kemp, Charles F. *Church: The Gifted and the Retarded Child.* St. Louis: Bethany, 1958.

Kirk, Samuel, and James Gallagher. *Educating Exceptional Children,* 4th ed. Boston: Houghton Mifflin, 1983.

Laubenfels, Jean. *The Gifted Student: An Annotated Bibliography.* Westport, Conn.: Greenwood, 1977.

Morse, William C. *Humanistic Teaching for Exceptional Children.* Syracuse, N.Y.: Syracuse U. Press, 1979.

Narramore, Clyde. *Is Your Child Gifted?* Grand Rapids: Zondervan, 1976.

Passow, Harry A., ed. *The Gifted and Talented, Their Education and Development: Seventy-eighth Yearbook of the National Society for the Study of Education.* Chicago: U. of Chicago Press, 1979.

Readings in Gifted and Talented Education. Guilford, Conn.: Special Learning Corporation, 1978.

Robeck, Mildred C. *Acceleration Programs for Intellectually Gifted Pupils.* California Project Talent, publication no. 3. Sacramento: California State Dept. of Ed., 1968.

Seligman, Milton. *Strategies for Helping Parents of Exceptional Children: A Guide for Teachers.* New York: Macmillan, Free, 1979.

Strang, Ruth. *Helping Your Gifted Child.* New York: Dutton, 1960.

Swanson, B. Marian and Diane Willis. *Understanding Exceptional Children and Youth.* Chicago: Rand McNally, 1979.

Torrance, E. Paul. *Gifted Children in the Classroom.* New York: Macmillan, 1965.

Tuttle, Frederick. *Gifted and Talented Students,* Rev. ed. Washington, D.C.: National Education Assn., 1983.

Part 4

Organizing, Administering, and Supervising Children's Ministries

14

Robert E. Clark

Leadership for Children

- What Leadership Is
- Rationale for Leadership
- Styles of Leadership
- Theories of Leadership
- Leadership and Management
- Biblical Leadership
- General Qualities of Leadership
- Specific Qualities
- General Responsibilities of Personnel
- Specific Responsibilities
- Major Tasks in Managing Children's Ministries
- Setting Up Superior Facilities and Equipment
- Using Facilities and Equipment Productively
- Facilities and Equipment for Departments
- Finances
- Records

Dynamic and effective adult leadership is imperative in every agency or ministry for children in the local church. Children deserve the best leadership a church can provide. Some well-meaning but naive adults think that almost

ROBERT E. CLARK, Ed.D., is professor of Christian education, Moody Bible Institute, Chicago, Illinois, and is co-editor of *Childhood Education in the Church.*

anyone can lead or teach children. They think of children as small adults who are immature and rowdy. The children need someone to make them behave and keep them quiet while the adults are busily engaged in their own activities.

Childhood is a distinct period in life as much as the youth years and adulthood. We need to take every opportunity to minister to children and meet their needs. They are in the most impressionable years of life and develop rapidly in their total personalities. It is amazing how much children learn during the first eleven years of their lives!

One of the greatest needs in the church today is to provide dedicated and trained adult leaders who have a vision to work with children at all levels. Since children are pliable and easily molded, they need good, positive, and consistent adult role models—adults who love them and are willing to train and minister to meet their needs.

If trained leadership is a key need in the church, why is so little being done to prepare leaders for their responsibilities? Why are volunteer staff members placed in positions to work with children without adequate preparation? Many individuals want to be involved, and are eager to serve, but have little or no training when they assume their positions. Take Harry Dixon for example:

Harry Dixon is a dedicated layman at First Avenue Church who sincerely desires to serve the Lord. Last month he was asked to superintend the junior department of the Sunday school. Harry reluctantly accepted, because Jim Hatch, the general superintendent, was desperate for someone to take the position. The woman who had been in charge resigned because, she said, juniors are unruly, disrespectful, and uninterested in studying God's Word, and she was tired of trying to keep them quiet.

Harry loves children and appreciates the enthusiasm of vivacious juniors. He is challenged with the potential of these energy-filled, abounding, adventurous, and fun-loving youngsters. Harry readily admits that he was not selected on the basis of training or his knowledge of the position.

In fact, Harry felt quite the opposite! He had not even had one hour of formal training or experience in working with juniors. His "exposure" was his experience with his own two junior-age children. At the time he was approached, he was not involved in any other responsibility in the church, and he thought he should at least be doing something to help out in an emergency.

Jim assured Harry that the position was only temporary and that he would assist him in whatever way he could. Jim was new at his responsibility, and he said that Harry and he could learn together. Little did Harry realize the great challenge in store for him! Perhaps it was best he did not know, for, otherwise, he may never have accepted the position.

What an introduction to such an important ministry! With circumstances like these, is it any wonder that there is such a high attrition rate among church leaders? What kind of training or experience was needed to prepare Harry for his new position? What are some of the basics he should know to function efficiently as a department superintendent? How can Harry succeed in his leadership role without becoming discouraged and disillusioned?

Many a worker has found himself in a predicament similar to Harry's. If staff members are to perform effectively, they need careful preparation, training, and guidance. It is essential that a staff member know his qualifications and responsibilities. He needs to view himself in relation to other people and their responsibilities. He must be sensitive to human relations and be a diplomatic problem-solver. He needs to recognize himself as the leader of a team. All the available training and experience he can gain will profit in guiding others toward desired goals.

Leadership at any level demands our best, especially in the children's division, where exemplary leadership is of prime importance. Leaders of children should strive for excellence in their ministries. John W. Gardner, former Commissioner of Education, said, "Whoever I am or whatever I am doing, some kind of excellence is within my reach." George Sweeting, president of Moody Bible Institute, expanded the idea by saying, "The pursuit of excellence is not just for a privileged few . . . nor is excellence reserved for the superstar or genius. It is for you—whoever you are, wherever you are, whatever you do."[1] This kind of attitude should be our goal as we work with children in the church.

WHAT LEADERSHIP IS

Webster indicates that a leader is a person who guides, conducts, or directs; he is a person who holds first place or is fitted to do so.

Dwight Eisenhower is credited with saying, "Leadership is the ability to get a person to do what you want him to do, when you want it done, in a way you want it done, because he wants to do it."[2]

Effective leadership requires a willingness to follow directions and a cooperative spirit on the part of group members. The effective leader spends much of his time motivating his staff to do what needs to be done. One of his greatest challenges is to encourage his workers to *want* to do their tasks. Carefully laid plans based on needs, clear-cut and realistic objectives, and efficient organization to put plans into operation are required for effective leadership. The leader must be in control of the situation so that efforts are directed toward desired shared goals.

RATIONALE FOR LEADERSHIP

Effective leadership is essential for progress. Someone must be responsible for planning, organizing, directing, and making decisions. Some groups oper-

1. George Sweeting, *You Can Climb Higher* (Nashville: Thomas Nelson, 1985), p. 19.
2. Dwight Eisenhower, in Bradford B. Boyd, *Management-Minded Supervision* (New York: McGraw-Hill, 1968), p. 113.

ate in a leaderless structure with group members sharing in the responsibility equally. However, unless individuals are skillfully trained and experienced, they need leaders to motivate them toward goals to be accomplished. The leader acts as a guide to show the way and to coordinate activities.

Many people are eager to study and to serve, but they need guidance in what to do and how to do their work well. The effective leader will want the group to accept the challenge of dependability, responsibility, and decision making, but it will be his role to give the direction needed. Leadership which focuses on people provides security, encouragement, and progress.

STYLES OF LEADERSHIP

Styles of leadership will vary in every situation, depending on one's definition and philosophy of it. Basically, leadership styles can be divided into four major categories:

AUTOCRATIC

Autocratic leadership is dictatorial. The leader makes most of the decisions, policies, and plans. He may be aggressive and even hostile. Initiative and independence from group members may be stifled. One-way communication is preferred.

LAISSEZ-FAIRE

The leader with a laissez-faire policy assumes a passive or permissive role. He refuses to make decisions for the group and may refrain from giving counsel or even stating his opinion. The group may become frustrated and insecure because positive, active leadership is lacking.

BUREAUCRATIC

The problem with bureaucratic leadership is that it requires too much "red tape." Rules and regulations are handed down through lines of authority. The leader refers to what "they" want, without clearly defining who "they" are. The organizational structure is formal with much routine and mechanics involved. Decisions may be postponed indefinitely, and progress is likely to be slow.

DEMOCRATIC

Democratic leadership is invested in the group. In the church democratic leadership must be under God's authority and follow scriptural principles. In this type of leadership, the leader acts as a guide and offers suggestions when they are needed. He provides positive direction and encourages each member of the group to participate. Decisions are made by the group and the vote of the majority rules. Teamwork is evident, and a feeling of interdependence of group members and togetherness is stressed.

Rush[3] identifies the styles of leadership in a different way. He says leadership style focuses on how you use authority. In the *dictatorial* style, he says the leader operates as a dictator. The leader makes all decisions and determines who will carry them out. In the *authoritative* style, the leader makes most of the decisions and considers his views to be most valid. He frequently uses others for his own benefit. The *consultative* style leader considers using the skills and ideas of others in formulating plans and making decisions. The leader still retains final decision-making power, but before he makes a final decision, he consults those affected by the decisions. The *participative* team style leader gives most of his authority to the team, though he remains as the team's leader. The leader acts as a team facilitator, and focuses on stimulating creativity and innovation.

In determining which style of leadership is best, Ted Engstrom suggests[4] that

> leaders are different. But so are followers! Which is another way of saying that some situations demand one style of leader, [whereas] others demand a different one. . . . At any given time the leadership needs of an organization may vary from another time . . . it follows that those leaders will need different styles at different times. The appropriate style depends a great deal on the task of the organization, the phase of life of the organization, and the needs of the organization."

In children's work in the church, each of the above styles of leadership may need to be exerted at times. *Autocratic* leadership may be needed when the group lacks ability to make decisions, is not united, or is insecure, or when immediate decisions must be made by the leader. *Laissez-faire* leadership may be helpful when the leader is eager for the group members to think for themselves and assume the responsibility of decision making. Proper lines of authority, as suggested by *bureaucratic* leadership, must be followed so that decisions can be made at the proper levels. Various kinds of decisions need to be made by the group, and *democratic* leadership will encourage team spirit, unity, and loyalty. A combination of different types of leadership provides healthy balance in planning and decision making.

THEORIES OF LEADERSHIP

Kraus[5] has suggested three basic theories of leadership, which can function in various situations. These are trait leadership, situational leadership, and functional leadership.

3. Myron Rush, *Management: A Biblical Approach* (Wheaton, Ill.: Scripture Press, Victor Books, 1983), pp. 221-25.
4. Ted W. Engstrom, *The Making of a Christian Leader* (Grand Rapids: Zondervan, 1976), p. 78.
5. Richard Kraus, *Recreation Today: Planning and Leadership* (New York: Appleton-Century-Crofts, 1966), pp. 54-57.

TRAIT

Trait leadership consists of certain personal qualities which are essential to successful performance of a leadership task. Traits such as intelligence, courage, enthusiasm, sensitivity, energy, and responsibility may be inborn or learned. The emphasis in this type of leadership is on what sort of person the leader *is*.

SITUATIONAL

The person who becomes a situational leader is chosen because of the requirements for the task at hand. There seems to be a great divergence of leadership behavior in different situations. This type of leadership emphasizes superior competence or knowledge. What the leader *knows* in the situation is significant.

FUNCTIONAL

The emphasis in functional leadership is more on what a person *does* than on what he is or knows. Leadership is not exclusively invested in an individual leader but is viewed as a function of group structure. The effectiveness of leadership acts is judged in terms of meeting functional group needs.

Perhaps the most logical position to take in the children's division is that a composite of these three theories of leadership is most effective. In any situation, varying qualities and abilities are needed. Leaders must know their responsibilities in order to function effectively. Leadership is also a shared process and, at times, will be in the hands of individuals other than the appointed leader. General personality characteristics, proper attitudes toward people and ability to work with them, and the qualities of functional importance are all essential aspects of effective leadership.

LEADERSHIP AND MANAGEMENT

Leadership is a broad term which emphasizes the need for direction and guidance by individuals who are committed to serving others. A good leader is a good manager. The leader works with people for the purpose of meeting their needs as well as accomplishing the objectives of the organization. The leader as manager has several significant tasks. Some of the tasks which will have priority are planning, organizing, staffing, directing, controlling, delegating, supervising, and coordinating responsibilities so the work can be done efficiently. Each of these functions will need to be thought through carefully to achieve desired maximum results. The leaders of children must remember they are ministering to children and their needs and the focus must be on the children, not the leaders.

BIBLICAL LEADERSHIP

Biblical leadership is a distinctive kind of leadership. The basic definition of leadership does not change, but a dimension is added. Biblical leadership requires that a leader know Jesus Christ as his personal Savior. The individual depends not on his own abilities and talents in leadership but on Jesus Christ who can strengthen him for any kind of responsibility (Phil. 4:13). Jesus Christ said, "Without me ye can do nothing" (John 15:5). It is not by personal might, nor by human power, but by the Spirit of God that spiritual results are attained (Zech. 4:6 b). Leadership is a spiritual gift—one of administration, supervision, or management (Rom. 12:8). Christ gives this gift to individuals whom He chooses in His body, the church.

Henrietta Mears, founder of Gospel Light Publications, said that we are all leaders. Either we lead people *to* the Lord or *away* from Him by the way we live. Our personal example is extremely important as we relate to people in leadership. Everyone has the responsibility to lead an exemplary life, but some individuals are given greater responsibility in leading and guiding others so that the work of God may flourish and bring eternal results. Any leader is only an instrument in the hand of God. It is God who does the work and brings the results.

GENERAL QUALITIES OF LEADERSHIP

John Stott raised some questions about the general qualities of leadership in a recent article in *Christianity Today.*

> What, then, are the marks of leadership in general, and of Christian leadership in particular? How can God's gifts be cultivated and leadership potential developed? And what is needed to blaze a trail that others will follow?

He then suggests five essential ingredients:

> *Vision*—a deep dissatisfaction with what is and a clear grasp of what could be. . . . *Industry*—thinkers, planners, and that demands industry or hard labor. Men of vision must become men of action. . . . *Perseverance*—the resilience to take setback in stride, the tenacity to overcome fatigue and discouragement, and the wisdom to "turn stumbling blocks into stepping stones." . . . *Service*—among the followers of Jesus, leadership is not a synonym for lordship. Our calling is to be servants not bosses, slaves not masters. . . . True greatness, true leadership, is achieved not by reducing men to one's service but in giving oneself in selfless service to them. . . . *Discipline*—the final mark of a Christian leader. Not only self-discipline in general . . . (in the mastery of passions, time, and energies), but in particular the discipline with which one waits on God. The leader knows his

weakness. He knows the greatness of his task and the strength of the opposition. But he also knows the inexhaustible riches of God's grace.[6]

Staff members will need to develop each of the above qualities as they minister to children. These qualities will enable leaders and teachers to be much more effective in their ministry for Christ.

SPECIFIC QUALITIES OF LEADERSHIP

In addition to these general qualifications, there are specific qualifications each staff member should consider in order to become more effective in working with children.

PHYSICALLY

Has good health to attend to responsibilities
Is alert and active; exercises in order to keep his body in good condition
Is neat and attractive in appearance and dress
Seeks to get proper physical rest and maintains an adequate diet in order to
    function effectively

INTELLECTUALLY

Is well organized, can plan, and give directions to staff
Is eager to learn and keeps alert
Is current in thinking, ideas, and practices
Is resourceful, creative, and flexible
Is able to adjust to the level of children
Has an awareness of characteristics, needs, and potential of children

EMOTIONALLY

Has good emotional control
Is able to empathize with those being led and seeks to understand them as
    people
Is able to find constructive ways to release emotional energy
Is relaxed and secure in position

SOCIALLY

Is friendly, cheerful, sociable, and relates well to others
Is concerned about others and their needs
Practices acceptable social habits and courtesies in daily life
Is a friend of children

6. John R. W. Stott, "What Makes Leadership Christian?" *Christianity Today* 19, no. 11 (9
    August 1985): 24-27.

SPIRITUALLY

Is a growing Christian, exemplifying a close spiritual fellowship with Christ
Is obedient to the Word of God in daily life
Is pursuing defined spiritual goals
Is enthusiastic about the Lord's work and about his own position
Is dependable, punctual, and regular in attendance in church activities
Is dedicated to the work of God through the church
Is a good Christian model for others to follow
Is dependent on the Lord Jesus Christ for strength to do work

No one individual possesses all these qualifications to the same degree. Though some traits may be more difficult to attain than others, the list can serve as a standard by which to encourage leaders to improve in their service for Christ. The Christian life is a continuous growing process.

Quality leadership in the children's division does not just happen. Because of the importance of child life and the tremendous responsibility we have in ministering to children, we must provide enthusiastic, well-trained, and dedicated leadership. Effective organization, administration, and supervision are necessary in guiding children step by step in developing the potential God has given them. We are not babysitting children but assisting them to become all that God has planned for them!

GENERAL RESPONSIBILITIES OF PERSONNEL

The position of the worker determines the worker's specific responsibilities. However, in any agency or activity in the children's division, all staff members have some of the following general responsibilities:

Be regular in attendance and on time for presession activities.
Be well prepared and flexible to change plans if necessary.
Take care of routine matters efficiently.
Supervise and have control of your own area of responsibility.
Enroll in training opportunities provided by the church and other sources.
Follow up present and absent students.
Attend all workers' conferences and other meetings scheduled for workers.
Know how to lead students to Christ and how to guide them in Christian growth.
Provide social activities.
Participate actively in the program whether it is the opening worship, the lesson, the presession, or another activity.
Be alert for new ideas, be creative, and use variety.
Use teaching tools provided.
Correlate activities with other workers, agencies, and departments.

SPECIFIC RESPONSIBILITIES OF PERSONNEL

Every agency may not utilize all the positions listed below, but the specific responsibilities listed can serve as a brief description of each position.

LEADER (superintendent, sponsor, director of a particular agency or ministry)

Is responsible for activities of the department or agency
Is responsible for recruiting personnel with approval from the children's division committee or board of Christian education
Does long-range planning with staff
Delegates responsibility to each worker
Prepares each activity for which he or she is responsible
Is responsible for arrangement and provision of rooms and equipment
Sees that materials and supplies are ordered and available when needed
Gives guidance, assists in problem solving, and counsels
Provides training and supervision of workers
Conducts conferences with workers
Evaluates the situation and the workers periodically

TEACHER

Is responsible for the group assigned and prays regularly for students
Is well prepared for responsibilities
Gets acquainted with students through personal contact, home visitation, and social activities
Keeps the room and equipment in good order and reports needed repairs
Attends meetings for which he or she is responsible and reports on progress made

ASSOCIATE, ASSISTANT, OR HELPER

Assists in specific responsibilities assigned by the leader
Prepares for specific responsibilities assigned
Is cooperative and helpful in every way possible

PIANIST

Is responsible to be proficient in the music used in the agency or department
Spends time in practice to improve skills
Finds music selected by the leader and builds a loose-leaf book of selections
Arrives early and sees that everything is in readiness

SECRETARY

Becomes acquainted with types of records and procedures used
Is responsible for maintaining the records in his or her area of responsibility

Keeps cupboards clean and neat

Orders supplies for the agency or department

Helps in whatever ways he or she can to make the work of the department
more pleasant

Every staff member needs a written job description. The job description
should include a definition of the position, its qualifications, specific responsibilities, and how the position relates to other parts of the children's division
and total church program. Written job descriptions are effective only as they
are implemented.

To keep job descriptions current, ask staff members to evaluate their position in view of their job descriptions and to submit an evaluation in writing.
Then compare those suggestions from the staff member with the job description, discuss the job description with the individual and determine what revi-
sions need to be made.

Major Tasks in Managing Children's Ministries

Leaders in the children's division will discover that some major tasks will be
involved in the management of their work. The tasks which are most significant are *organization, administration,* and *supervision.* Each of these areas
can be sub-divided into several categories. However, a treatment of only the
major tasks will be given here. Additional suggestions for a more thorough
study of leadership and management tasks are given in the "For Further
Reading" section at the end of the chapter. Supervision will be discussed in
depth in chapter 15.

ORGANIZATION

Organization refers to the framework, structure, or plan to be followed. It
involves the order or arrangement of people or activities and the relationships
which exist between people or things. It may be an outline of what the leader
plans to do. Organization is what is seen as one draws a diagram or writes an
outline. Organization is the first step toward progress in any situation. The
individual must visualize how people and things fit together in a total pattern.
Organization involves deciding *who* will do *what.* It may include a list of
general and specific duties staff members are to perform, or it may include
steps involved to get a particular job done. One of the problems in organization
is that flowery or ivory-tower plans can be drawn theoretically, but implementation must become a reality in order for the plan to be effective.

Lois LeBar[7] suggests that organization should be *simple,* with every non-

7. Lois E. LeBar, *Focus on People in Church Education* (Westwood, N.J.: Revell, 1968), pp. 70-
72.

Childhood Education in the Church

essential eliminated; *flexible;* and *democratic,* under God's authority. If too much red tape is required to arrive at a decision or to complete a job, little progress will be evident and staff members may become discouraged and stop trying. It is also important that adults be flexible and willing to change their plans if necessary in order to meet children's needs.

In effective organization, workers with children must function as a team. Staff members should be consulted for their ideas. Changes should be discussed and decisions made by the group. An atmosphere of acceptance and rapport encourages staff members to feel at ease in expressing themselves. It is important for leaders to keep in mind the following principles of organization:

1. Organization is a means to an end and not an end in itself.
2. Organizational structure must be based on the characteristics and needs of children.
3. Changes in organization should be thought through carefully and carried out systematically.
4. Individuals involved in the situation should be consulted before organizational changes are made.
5. Organizational plans will vary according to the needs and size of the church.

ADMINISTRATION

Administration is organization in action. It means carrying out plans and decisions made in organization by managing or directing in order to accomplish stated goals. Administration is the process of putting people to work in service.[8]

Gulick and Urwick indicate that effective administration includes planning, organizing, staffing, directing, coordinating, reporting, and budgeting. Each of these functions, properly carried out, encourages efficiency and more effective results. The ministry of the church deserves to be carried on by competent and trained personnel who know what they are doing and have a vision to carry the program to desired goals. Adequate directions enable workers to know their responsibilities and how to follow through efficiently. Efforts to coordinate the work are necessary in order to avoid omitting, overlapping, or duplicating responsibilities.

The following are some basic principles in administration:

1. Every worker needs a clear, written description of the position he or she holds.
2. Lines of authority must be clearly established.

8. Luther Gulick and L. Urwick, "POSDCORB," in *An Introduction to School Administration: Selected Readings,* ed. M. Chester Nolte (New York: Macmillan, 1966), pp. 223-24.

3. Responsibilities must be delegated and accountability should be expected.
4. Significant policies and procedures need to be written out.
5. Every problem must be solved at the level where it ought to be solved.
6. The plans of the workers and of the leaders must be integrated.
7. Lines of communication must be kept open in effective administration.

Many administrative problems are due to the failure to define responsibilities or lines of authority, unwritten plans, poorly stated policies and procedures, resistance to change, negative attitudes, lack of purpose, lack of communication, lack of vision and initiative, or lack of dedicated personnel.

SETTING UP SUPERIOR FACILITIES AND EQUIPMENT

Do the facilities in which children meet affect their learning? Rooms may not be as important as people who teach or what is being taught, but if maximum learning is to be attained, the environment is one of the most important factors to consider.

Children are sensitive to atmosphere, color, and beauty. Much of their learning is through the five senses, and attitudes are developed through what is "caught" as well as what is taught. The personalities of children are easily molded, pliable, and affected by their environment. They respond to a reverent, quiet atmosphere and are eager for happy learning experiences in the church.

Children need a comfortable, secure atmosphere that is very clean and attractive. *A good rule to keep in mind is that the younger the child, the more space is needed.* First floor arrangements are best for younger children, but basement rooms can be decorated with delightful color schemes and furnished with suitable equipment to provide the kind of atmosphere needed. Churches must work with what they have; but with little cost, ingenuity, soap and water, and a willingness to work, rooms can be transformed into beautiful and acceptable environments for children.

Facilities and furnishings must be planned for children, not for the adults who work with children. The standards Heim suggests for church buildings—beauty, utility, comfort, economy, and adaptability[9]—have been applied below to children's rooms.

1. *Beauty*—order, symmetry, strength, grace, and color should be considered when planning facilities for children. Since children have keen senses, the surroundings should appeal to their senses and bring pleasant experiences and memories.

2. *Utility*—facilities should be useful and functional. The purpose for each room determines how it should be planned.

9. Ralph Heim, *Leading a Sunday Church School* (Philadelphia: Muhlenberg, 1950), pp. 259-62.

3. *Comfort*—proper heating, cooling, lighting, ventilation, acoustics, safety—all are important for children. Rooms can serve as places of worship, instructional centers, and as places where children want to come.

4. *Economy*—true economy—accomplishing the maximum service with minimum space—comes from careful planning. Christian stewardship requires making every dollar buy the most in permanent values while avoiding elaborateness.

5. *Adaptability*—a building or room that can be enlarged or modified is the ideal. Sometimes the same rooms can be used for multiple purposes, although policies need to be established concerning the use of the facilities by different groups to reduce conflicts of purpose and care.

Using Facilities and Equipment Productively

The following suggestions are given to help ensure more productive use of facilities and furnishings.

1. Use the same facilities for various activities of each department of the church.
2. Be aware of age-group characteristics and needs when planning buildings and purchasing equipment.
3. Buy durable equipment that will stand up with normal wear and tear.
4. Buy adjustable folding tables to serve multiple purposes.
5. Provide cupboard and closet space for each department. Encourage workers to keep cupboards and closets in good order.
6. Redecorate periodically to keep the appearance of the building fresh and clean. Departments can do redecorating with approval from the supervisory board or committee in charge of facilities and furnishings.
7. Keep an accurate and current inventory of the equipment and supplies.
8. Remove unnecessary items from the room. Store items that are used only periodically to keep the building neat, attractive, and free of fire hazards.
9. Replace worn-out equipment and repair broken or damaged equipment.
10. Install good lighting, heating, and ventilation systems.
11. Set up a fire alarm plan in the building so that people know how to evacuate in case of fire.
12. Periodically evaluate the use of the total facilities of the church to determine if the best use of building space is being made. Discourage departments from claiming "lifetime leases" on any particular room or furnishing in the church. Get people to understand that departments, rooms, and facilities may have to be changed to make better use of the available space.

Facilities and Equipment for Department Groups

In each department of the children's division, the following guidelines will prove helpful to those responsible for facilities and planning.

CRADLE ROLL

The cradle roll department needs facilities at the church for parents who bring their children to be cared for during Sunday school, church services, and other special activities. The room should be located on the first floor near the sanctuary and the parents' classroom(s). The facilities should be spacious and attractively decorated and carpeted. They must be very clean and neat, with equipment suitable for meeting needs of very young children. It is best to have separate rooms for crib babies and for toddlers and walkers.

Desirable furnishings include a built-in sink, toilet facilities, cupboards for storage, a secretary's desk, platform rockers, adult-size chairs, a playpen, cribs, baby-size chairs and tables, refrigerator, washable and unbreakable toys, a toy box, a bottle warmer, a basket for babies' belongings, and a wastebasket. Also, clean sheets, towels, diapers, and first-aid supplies are necessary. A dutch-door and a built-in diaper changing table are also desirable. Cradle roll staff workers should be the only personnel allowed in the cradle roll facilities for sanitary and safety reasons.

TWOS AND THREES

The room for twos and threes should be located on the first floor (preferably in the southeast corner of the building) near the parents. It should be accessible by an outside entrance with a door at the rear of the room. The room should be large enough to accommodate fifteen to twenty children. The ideal space per child is twenty-five to thirty square feet. Small classrooms should be eliminated to provide a more flexible room arrangement and to make better use of the space. The walls should be soundproof and decorated with bright, cheerful, and warm colors and with light woodwork. Low windows with clear glass, equal to one-fourth of the wall space and on the children's eye level, are desirable. Attractive drapes and carpets aid in absorbing sound in the room and provide a warm, homelike atmosphere. Chairs should be eight to ten inches high and made of solid oak or Fiberglas®. Tables may be rectangular or round with adjustable legs and should be ten inches higher than the seat of the chairs. Coat racks and toilet facilities should be on the level of the children. Story rugs and individual resting mats, a secretary's desk, a department Bible, offering receptacles, record players, a toy center, interest centers, supply cupboards, and closets are some of the essential items of equipment.

FOURS AND FIVES

The items mentioned for twos and threes should also be provided for fours and fives. However, the height of chair seats should be ten to twelve inches from the floor. The room should be large enough to provide space for twenty to twenty-five children. A chalkboard, bulletin and flannelboard, a piano, a portable library with a round book table, visual files with flat pictures, and permanent pictures hung at the children's eye level are also needed to furnish the room.

Primary children can occupy a basement, first, or second floor room, with a door in the rear. Soundproofing should be included in order to reduce noise. At least fifteen to twenty square feet of space are needed for each child. The equipment should be primary size, with the chair seats twelve to fourteen inches in height and the tables ten inches higher than the chairs. A large, flexible room is necessary with movable partitions so that it can be used for multiple purposes. The maximum number of children for one room is forty in the department plan and twenty-five in the closely graded setup (where there is a separate room for each grade). A toy center is not essential, but objects, curios, and the American and Christian flags should be part of the equipment.

JUNIOR

The junior department room should have space for a maximum of fifty students in the department plan and twenty-five students per grade in the closely graded plan. Facilities and equipment mentioned in the previous paragraphs for younger age levels are needed in the junior department and geared to the junior level. Chair seat height should be fourteen to sixteen inches. Hymn books are appropriate for this department. Since juniors love adventure and the outdoors, and have exuberant energy, they need plenty of playground space for play activities and release of excess energy.

FINANCES

The agencies and departments in the children's division, as part of the total program of the church, merit adequate financing to enable them to accomplish their goals.

Usually it is best to finance the children's work through the Christian education budget. The budget is planned by the board of Christian education in conjunction with the agencies and departments involved. Each year at the appropriate time, the board of Christian education asks each agency and department to submit a budget for approval for the next year. All items, including redecorating or remodeling, equipment, materials, and supplies, are considered in the budget. One advantage of this kind of budgeting is that it necessitates advance planning. Funds need to be allocated wisely and used efficiently, but workers should be trusted to use funds with discretion in order to meet the needs of childen without having to pinch pennies.

It is helpful to require workers to secure permission from the proper authority for purchasing equipment, materials, and supplies. By having one person in a department or agency responsible for ordering equipment and supplies, proper control can be exercised. Any changes needed in the physical plant should be submitted in writing to the appropriate board for approval before work is done. Also, projects that are undertaken should be completed to conserve finances and keep the building in good condition.

It is important that children be taught Christian stewardship in the use of time, talents, and treasures. (Practical suggestions as to how to do this are given in chap. 26, "Teaching Missions, Stewardship, and Vocational Education to Children.") Adults can set a good example for children by the way funds are handled and used. Many churches operate on limited budgets and cannot afford elaborate furnishings. However, if proper care of facilities and equipment is encouraged, children can be taught to respect and care for personal and church property. Involvement in caring for the building and equipment will teach children far more than verbalizing negatively when they do not care for things as they should.

Special financial projects can be sponsored by departments and agencies in the children's division. One caution must be kept in mind, however: special projects ought to be approved by a central committee, whether it be the board of Christian education, the children's division committee, or the Sunday school board or council. Otherwise, some projects may overlap others or may not be within reach of the goal.

When children see how their money is spent in practical ways—such as replacing burned-out lightbulbs, redecorating a room, buying a new filmstrip projector or chairs for the department, or giving a file cabinet to a missionary—their sense of responsibility is increased and they enjoy the blessing of giving. We must always remember that the foundations for teaching Christian stewardship are laid during childhood years!

RECORDS

Enrollment, attendance, visitation, follow-up, personnel, and progress reports are some of the kinds of records a church may find helpful. Record systems are available for purchase from several of the Christian education publishers listed at the end of this chapter.

Keeping an accurate record of attendance for regular students, visitors, and staff members will enable workers to know attendance trends and to know what follow-up contacts need to be made. The system should be simple and require little time. Also, follow-up records for absentees and regular visitation on all regular attenders and visitors will help systematize the follow-up procedures. Prospect and survey records will enable visitation workers to make new contacts for the church. A permanent enrollment file, with basic information about each individual who attends the church, is of tremendous help to new workers. Records on the personnel working in the children's division may be a part of the records developed by the board of Christian education or the children's division committee.

Some tips to follow in developing and using a record system are as follows.

1. Provide sufficient secretarial help.
2. Have a convenient place for the secretarial staff to work.
3. Provide storage for records in a file or cupboard.
4. Have sufficient forms for maintaining records.
5. Keep the record system simple in procedures and policies.
6. Maintain the records neatly and efficiently according to approved procedures.
7. Keep records current and well organized in the filing system.
8. Use information from records in various ways.
9. Evaluate the record system often to see how it may be improved.

SUMMARY

Effective leadership and management for ministries with children are essential. A leader is one who guides a group toward desired shared goals. Management refers to the tasks leaders perform as they work with people to meet their needs. Some of the important tasks in management are planning, organizing, administering, directing, delegating, controlling, decision making, and implementing and supervising.

Styles of leadership are determined by personality characteristics, tasks to be performed, and needs to be met. Various styles of leadership will be employed at different times and in a variety of circumstances.

Qualities such as dedication, vision, purpose, and servanthood describe what a leader *is*. Though some leaders may be born with certain leadership qualities, most leaders develop their qualities as they work with people and carry out their responsibilities.

Leaders of children will be concerned about providing proper facilities and equipment, finances, and efficient records to meet the needs of staff members and children.

FOR FURTHER READING

Blanchard, Kenneth, and Paul Hersey. *Management of Organizational Behavior.* Englewood Cliffs, N.J.: Prentice-Hall, 1982.

Blanchard, Kenneth, and Spencer Johnson. *The One Minute Manager.* New York: Berkley, 1984.

Drucker, Peter F. *Managing in Turbulent Times.* New York: Harper & Row, 1980.

———. *The Effective Executive.* New York: Harper & Row, 1966.

Eims, Leroy. *Be the Leader You Were Meant to Be.* Wheaton, Ill.: Scripture Press, Victor Books, 1975.

———. *Be a Motivational Leader.* Wheaton, Ill.: Scripture Press, Victor Books, 1981.

Engstrom, Ted W. *The Making of a Christian Leader.* Grand Rapids: Zondervan, 1976.

Gangel, Kenneth O. *Building Leaders for Church Education.* Chicago: Moody, 1982.

———. *The Church Education Handbook.* Wheaton, Ill.: Scripture Press, Victor Books, 1985.

———. *So You Want to Be a Leader.* Harrisburg, Pa.: Christian Publications, 1973.

Getz, Gene. *Sharpening the Focus of the Church.* Chicago: Moody, 1974.

Graendorf, Werner C., ed. *Introduction to Biblical Christian Education.* Chicago: Moody, 1981.

Hendrix, Olan. *Management for the Christian Leader.* Milford, Mich.: Mott Media, 1981.

Kilinski, Kenneth K., and Jerry C. Wofford. *Organization and Leadership in the Local Church.* Grand Rapids: Zondervan, 1973.

LeBar, Lois E. *Focus on People in Church Education.* Westwood, N.J.: Revell, 1968.

McDonough, Reginald M. *Working with Volunteer Leaders in the Church.* Nashville: Broadman, 1976.

Rush, Myron. *Management: A Biblical Approach.* Wheaton, Ill.: Scripture Press, Victor Books, 1983.

Sanders, J. Oswald. *Spiritual Leadership.* Chicago: Moody, 1980.

Sisemore, John T., ed. *Vital Principles in Religious Education.* Nashville: Broadman, 1966.

Sweeting, George. *You Can Climb Higher: The Christian's Pursuit of Excellence.* New York: Thomas Nelson, 1985.

Swindoll, Charles R. *Improving Your Serve.* Waco, Tex.: Word, 1981.

———. *Strengthening Your Grip.* Waco, Tex.: Word, 1982.

Towns, Elmer. *The Successful Sunday School and Teachers' Guidebook.* Carol Stream, Ill.: Creation, 1976.

15

Robert E. Clark

Supervising Children's Ministries

- Historical Perspective
- Purposes and Functions
- Personal Qualities of the Supervisor
- Staff Recruitment
- Staff Development
- Teacher-Supervisor Conferences
- Evaluation of Personnel
- Team Teaching
- Curriculum for Children's Ministries
- Planning the Curriculum Unit
- Selecting Curriculum Materials
- Evaluating Curriculum Materials
- Using Curriculum Materials

Supervision is undoubtedly one of the most significant functions to be performed in working with staff members who minister to children. Although organization and administration provide important foundations in leadership and management, supervision deals with the "strengthening of human re-

ROBERT E. CLARK, Ed.D., is professor of Christian education, Moody Bible Institute, Chicago, Illinois, and is co-editor of *Childhood Education in the Church.*

sources, with emphasis on the development of teachers (and leaders) in service."[1] Supervision also encourages improvement in the quality of leaders and teachers personally and professionally.

Supervision focuses on people and their effectiveness in carrying the program toward its goals. Staff members can be caught up in the busyness of activity in the church, and in the final result see little progress in the lives of individuals. Quality is more important than quantity. The number of activities or personal involvements does not determine success. What occurs in the lives of people as a result of careful planning, organization, instruction, and follow-through is far more significant in producing lasting results.

HISTORICAL PERSPECTIVE OF SUPERVISION

From the historical perspective, supervision has undergone many changes. In the eighteenth, nineteenth, and early in the twentieth centuries, supervision was more of an inspection made of teachers' personal lives and their effectiveness.

The inspection was done by laypersons and underprepared administrators. In the 1920s and 1930s, supervision was considered to be "scientific supervision." This kind of supervision was done by supervisors who were thought to be better prepared in the subject matter, and who were aided by tests, initial research efforts, and courses of study.

In the 1940s and 1950s, "democratic supervision" was oriented toward human relationships, with emphasis on commendation and encouragement.

In the 1960s and 1970s, and continuing, supervision has been referred to as "neoscientific supervision," with concern for exact and measurable instruction, and competency-based or performance-based education as the theme.

Since the beginning of the 1980s, supervision has been for the purpose of strengthening human resources, with emphasis on development of teachers in service.[2]

Today, some negative connotations of supervision are still being emphasized in church education. Some people think of supervision as "snooper-vision." They have a mistaken conception that supervision looks through "the little window" in the classroom door to see what the teacher is (or is not) doing.

Some individuals think of supervision as "inspection." The supervisor checks up on teachers and other staff members to see if they are doing their jobs according to set standards. Weaknesses are most significant and become the major focus in evaluation. The outcomes tend to be negative and discouraging.

---

1. Ronald C. Doll, *Supervision for Staff Development: Ideas and Application* (Boston: Allyn & Bacon, 1983), p. 10.
2. Ibid.

Supervision is not merely setting a good example or exerting a positive influence. Supervision requires more than the creation of a good feeling. There are actual problems to which attention must be directed with positive suggestions and corrections made.

As we examine the historical perspectives of supervision, we can profit from past developments in evaluating our philosophy of supervision. We certainly do not want to interpret supervision negatively. A more healthy approach is to emphasize many of the positive aspects of supervision practiced over the years.

PURPOSES AND FUNCTIONS OF SUPERVISION

Purposes and functions are interrelated in supervision. Some significant purposes are to improve instruction, build better and more effective interpersonal relationships, develop team spirit, build group morale and encourage staff members, motivate and stimulate staff to attain goals they have set for themselves, provide counsel and assistance for staff members, demonstrate specific skills and "show how" to do particular tasks, orient workers to new positions, and learn how to evaluate positively.

Wiles and Lovell[3] suggest seven functions of supervision. They include goal development, program development and actualization, control and coordination, motivation, problem solving, professional development, and evaluation of educational outcomes. The functions of supervision are based on the definition and purposes of supervision, and vary according to the local church situation and needs.

Supervision includes a variety of functions; because of space limitations, we will concentrate only on selected ones. Those included for more in-depth study are these: the personal qualities of supervisors, staff recruitment, staff development, supervisor-teacher conferences, evaluation of personnel, team teaching, and curriculum development.

PERSONAL QUALITIES OF THE SUPERVISOR

The same qualities emphasized in the chapter on leadership are applicable for supervisors. The Christian supervisor certainly should know Christ as Savior-Lord. The fruit of the Spirit should be evident in his life. The role of the supervisor is that of a servant. He or she should act as a resource person with a commitment to help others.

Lois LeBar wisely suggests that the person of the supervisor is very important.

> As the supervisor helps workers improve their work, he himself must of course be proficient in both principles and practice. In all his contacts he must demonstrate

3. Kimball Wiles and John T. Lovell, *Supervision for Better Schools*, 4th ed. (Englewood Cliffs, N.J.: 1975), p. 8.

Scriptural methods, be a good administrator, a good communicator, provide recognition for work well done, and help teachers continually evaluate. . . . More difficult than these skills, and more important, are his personal relations—with God, with himself, and with others.[4]

Role modeling is especially important for leaders of children. The biblical life-style is "caught" as well as "taught." Children are careful observers, and tend to imitate or identify positive or negative qualities they see in adults.

From early childhood on, we observe the actions of those around us and copy whole behavior patterns, often down to the most minute detail. As many an embarrassed parent will testify, young children have a remarkable talent for capturing Mommy's or Daddy's actions, words, and mannerisms and mimicking them publicly.[5]

The same application can be made of those who work with children in the church.

By the time a child is six, his basic personality structure is formed. Spiritual concepts, attitudes, and actions are taught in childhood, and they may affect a person the remainder of his life. In addition, children are eager to learn and will learn rapidly if sound educational principles and methods are applied. By the time children start school, they may have learned as much as they will the rest of their lives. This means that staff members who work with children should be carefully and prayerfully recruited. Not everyone can or should teach children.

Muriel Blackwell, in *Called to Teach Children,* emphasizes that teachers are called by God to teach children. She suggests several questions that teachers can answer to determine whether they have been "called to teach."

1. Have I had a personal experience of faith in Christ as my Savior?
2. Do I feel committed to accept the Bible as God's authoritative Word for my life and to share this truth with children?
3. Do I feel a love and concern for children and the belief that they need to know and understand God's Word?
4. Am I willing to help children know and understand (at their level of understanding) the Bible as God's plan for their lives?
5. Am I willing to learn and accept the truth that children learn and understand at levels different from adults and that a teacher of children must work with this truth and not contrary to it?
6. Do I have some abilities for organizing, planning, studying, and cooperating as a team member?

4. Lois LeBar, *Focus on People in Church Education* (Westwood, N.J.: Revell, 1968), pp. 208-9.
5. Grace Craig, *Human Development,* 3d ed. (Englewood Cliffs, N.J.: Prentice-Hall, 1983), p. 130.

7. Am I a fairly stable person who can accept normal energies of children and work with them without becoming unduly stressed?
8. Am I willing to go on learning as I go on teaching?[6]

These questions are not comprehensive, but they can serve as a basis for self-evaluation for a teacher or leader who desires to know the kind of person God calls to be a teacher or leader of children.

STAFF RECRUITMENT

One of the greatest challenges leaders have in church ministry is to discover and recruit competent people who are dedicated and willing to be equipped for service.[7] Because the majority of workers are volunteers, we cannot expect individuals to spend countless hours in preparation or service. Our expectations must be realistic and attainable. On the other hand, we do not want to do a mediocre job in serving the Lord in whatever position we have. We should be willing to do our best, even though our time and efforts may be limited.

Recruitment procedures need to be thought and prayed through carefully. We are enlisting men and women in the most important service they can render to God and humanity. Standards need to be high but possible to reach. Recruiting needs to be done in a businesslike manner with a positive thrust for spiritual service. The guidelines given below should help in strengthening recruitment procedures in any situation.

RECRUITING MEN

The importance of recruiting men to work with children cannot be treated lightly! Boys, early in their educational experiences, need to identify with men. Many boys in our society come from fatherless or broken homes and need to relate to a male image. Men can understand and communicate with children better than women in some situations, especially as children grow older. Many times, potential discipline problems can be solved through responsible men. Even in the cradle roll department, men can exemplify a father image and begin to build positive attitudes that church is for men and boys as well as women and girls.

IDENTIFYING NEEDED STAFF MEMBERS

What staff members are needed in the children's division of the church? The following list shows the wide variety of personnel, though not every church will need all these workers.

6. Muriel Fontenot Blackwell, *Called to Teach Children* (Nashville: Broadman, 1983), pp. 30-31.
7. For excellent ideas on recruitment, see Mark Senter III, *The Art of Recruiting Volunteers* (Wheaton, Ill.: Scripture Press, Victor Books, 1983).

Department superintendents for
Sunday school and vacation
Bible school
Teachers for Sunday school, weekday
classes, and summer ministries
Leaders for children's churches
Helpers and assistants
Pianists

Training hour leaders (sponsors)
Club workers for weekday clubs
Recreational leaders
Visitation workers
Camp counselors and teachers
Committee members
Prayer partners
Secretaries

DISCOVERING STAFF MEMBERS

How can a church discover workers who can serve effectively with children? These are some suggestions:

1. Pray earnestly for the Lord's guidance in discovering workers (Matt. 9:38). So often we try everything but prayer and consequently see few results.
2. Use talent surveys or interest finders.
3. Interview individuals to discover their gifts, abilities, and interests.
4. Check membership applications for areas of interest, abilities, past training, and experience.
5. Be a good listener; be on the lookout for key ideas or clues in talent discoveries.
6. Set up a card file on people in the children's division who are potential for service. Each card could include personal data, qualifications, training, experience, types of service for which the individual is best suited, age-group interests, and records of interviews or contacts.
7. Keep a current list of personnel needs. The children's division of the board of Christian education or other responsible committee can compile a list of persons needed, the qualifications and responsibilities required, and the date the position is to be filled.
8. Encourage the pastor to challenge individuals for service through his sermons.
9. Ask other staff members for names of potential workers.

ENLISTING STAFF MEMBERS

As workers are discovered, they need to be recruited for specific ministries. Here are some basic principles to consider in enlisting people:

1. Have a personnel committee who will contact and follow up prospective workers.
2. Keep the church informed as to personnel needs through bulletin newsletters, sermons, and personal contact.
3. Make contacts in a businesslike manner. Do not make the person feel he is

a last resort or the only one left. Stress also the importance of the position.

4. Emphasize spiritual service rather than a job to be filled, a duty to perform, or an obligation to fulfill.

5. Explain carefully the position and provide materials necessary for efficient operation.

6. Write a letter of invitation after the person has been interviewed.

7. Conduct impressive installation services, stressing the importance of spiritual service.

8. Have a standard for each enlisted leader to sign as he joins the staff. Be sure to explain the standard as a goal. Emphasize important responsibilities, such as thorough preparation and attendance at workers' conferences.

9. Set a positive example in leadership that is worth emulating.

10. Have an "Opportunities for Service" night in the church. Give a brief survey of positions available, qualifications, types of training needed, and the contribution the positions make to the total program.

11. Encourage workers, answer their questions, and seek to assist in whatever way you can after they have been appointed to their positions.

12. Encourage workers to attend conferences, leadership seminars, and other in-service activities for personal and professional growth.

The strength of any educational enterprise lies in the quality of leadership recruited. One of the greatest challenges of the church is to enlist staff members who are dedicated, willing to learn, and eager to grow. A careful and well-planned program of enlistment will pay great dividends in building a quality staff.

STAFF DEVELOPMENT

Staff development is a continuous and comprehensive process essential to the personal and professional growth of volunteer staff members.

Staff development has several characteristics that can be beneficial to all workers. A leader or teacher does something to improve as a person or in his or her work. The most successful staff development experiences occur when staff members realize that they need the experience. By participating in the training they will be able to grow and to benefit in a personal way. The emphasis should be growth-oriented. It should be assumed that people will grow and develop in their responsibilities. Staff development emphasizes the needs for teachers and leaders to change as persons. It encourages leaders and teachers to help other persons. They can take an active role in planning their own in-service activities and individualized programs that meet their specific needs. They can set objectives for themselves and plan activities to accomplish those objectives.

Well-planned staff development encourages individuals to expand their horizons in academic learning, ability to work with others, constructive emotional outlets, and spiritual maturity. Every church can provide opportunities for growth in all areas of personality development, in particular to equip leaders and teachers spiritually to help them communicate a biblical life-style to their students.

Staff development strategies can take many different forms. The following are some of the more common ways of assisting leaders and teachers in their personal and professional growth.

FORMAL TRAINING CLASS

The sources listed at the end of the chapter give useful information concerning a formal leader/teacher training class. In addition, the following should be considered.

What it is: A class conducted regularly for a specified length of time and with specific requirements, in which various topics are discussed, information is shared, and individuals are taught to make application to specific situations.

For whom: All workers in the children's division, depending on the content of the course.

When: During Sunday school, Sunday evening, a weekday, or a weeknight.

Areas of study:
Choose courses that will provide foundations for effective ministry with children. Some courses will be more general in nature, whereas others may be more specialized. Some areas to consider are these:

Bible survey	Teaching/learning	Christian living
Bible analysis	Children's ministries	Missions
Doctrine/theology	Leadership development	Music
Christian education	Psychology	

Principles to apply:
Plan a continuous, systematic program based on the needs of people.
Set attainable standards and requirements for courses.
Consider both prospective and experienced workers and their needs in planning courses to be offered. Offer refresher and advanced courses as well as foundational courses.
Schedule the courses at the most convenient times for the majority of people.
Begin with a limited program and expand as interests and needs emerge.

Encourage (or require) staff members to enroll in a minimum number of classes each year.

Grant leaves of absence from teaching and other responsibilities so that workers can take refresher courses.

Select qualified teachers who can give quality instruction related to practical situations.

WORKERS' CONFERENCE

What it is: Regularly scheduled meetings to instruct and inspire, and to help workers find practical solutions to problems they encounter in their ministries.

For whom: Workers of a particular agency, department, or group in the church.

When: Depends on type of meeting and people involved; should be scheduled regularly at the same time each month or quarter.

Topics: Chosen according to the needs and interests of the group.

Principles to apply:
Plan the meetings six months or a year in advance.

Schedule meetings at times most workers can be present.

Expect workers to be present at meetings; promote and publicize well in advance.

Plan time limits of one to one and one-half hours.

Be well prepared with an agenda, program outline, and time schedule.

Keep business to a minimum; provide more opportunity for inspiration and interaction.

Discuss topics of greatest interest to workers.

Vary the format and methods used; make meetings interesting and informative.

Involve members of the group in presentation of topics.

Follow through on decisions made by the group.

APPRENTICESHIP OR ON-THE-JOB TRAINING

What it is: First-hand experience on the job in which an inexperienced or prospective staff member works under the supervision of a more experienced leader/teacher.

For whom: For inexperienced and prospective workers who need to learn a particular responsibility.

When: Any time; any agency, department or position in the children's division.

Types: Leaders, teachers, assistants, helpers.

Principles to apply:

Select leaders/teachers who are adequately prepared to be effective models in guiding others in quality experiences.

Encourage those who supervise others to try new ideas and to serve as resource people.

Provide brief courses in interpersonal relationships for those who plan to be supervisors.

Encourage supervisors to develop effective "team relationships" through which all workers feel part of the team.

Help the in-training worker develop the skill of appraising and evaluating his or her own work.

Have periodic conferences in which the supervisor and the trainee evaluate progress, set new goals, and plan for improvement.

Encourage the apprentice to become increasingly less dependent on the supervisor until he can function without the help of the supervisor.

Take a positive attitude in helping others develop; try to see the apprentice's potential.

CONVENTION

What it is: A planned program of general meetings and workshops in which workers from several local churches meet for inspiration, instruction, and fellowship.

For whom: Active and prospective workers of a particular denomination or association or group of churches.

When: Usually during fall or spring; may range from one to several days; may be a Sunday school or Christian education convention.

Principles to apply:

Plan to take workers to a convention at least once a year.

Help workers select workshops that will be most beneficial to them.

Encourage workers to visit displays, to get acquainted with workshop leaders, and to ask questions.

Encourage workers to take notes on workshops they attend and to share ideas with others as they return home.

Arrange a time for workers to share ideas with those who could not attend the convention.

Follow up suggestions with practical implementation in the church.

CHRISTIAN EDUCATION CONFERENCE

What it is: Key Christian education leaders invited to a local church or churches to encourage, stimulate, instruct, and challenge the workers.

For whom: Workers and prospective workers in the local church.

When: Usually an all day or weekend conference; fall and spring usually the best times of the year.

Types: Program geared either to a specific agency, such as the Sunday school, the total church program, or children's division.

Principles to apply:
Contact key speakers and leaders who can minister to the specific needs of staff members.
Confirm dates and schedules with leaders well in advance.
Plan general sessions and workshops.
Build enthusiasm for the conference through prayer, long-range planning, and varied publicity.
Plan programs that meet the needs of workers and give solutions to some of the problems they are trying to solve.
Expect workers to attend as many of the sessions as possible.
Schedule sessions when most of the workers can attend.
See to it that the schedule is not too full.
Follow up suggestions for improvement which leaders have presented.

IN-SERVICE STRATEGIES

Lloyd Dull suggests some additional in-service strategies that will encourage participation of group members.[8]

Case studies—individual cases can be discussed and analyzed.

Demonstration teaching—teaching principles and methodology can be put into practice by a demonstrating teacher. Preparation for and evaluation of the exercise would be helpful.

In-service interest centers—in these centers a variety of audio or visual materials and equipment are put on display.

8. Lloyd W. Dull, *Supervision: School Leadership Handbook* (Columbus, Ohio: Merrill, 1981), pp. 115-19.

Project technique—major problems and issues are analyzed and summarized, and conclusions and recommendations are made.

Role-playing—here dramatization of situations takes place; then come follow-up discussions, related research, and the generation of possible solutions to the dilemmas presented in the role-playing.

Intervisitation—classrooms in one's own church or in another church are visited.

Videotape feedback—this technique helps teachers to understand and to change their teaching behavior by analyzing and evaluating a videotape of their teaching.

Microteaching—in this method a short lesson from five to twenty minutes is presented in which the teacher practices a particular teaching skill. The teaching is done once, critiqued, and then repeated for comparisons. The complete cycle is to teach, critique, reorganize, reteach, and critique.

Modeling—the learner observes the model who demonstrates a particular skill or set of skills; then learners shape their own techniques after those of the model.

Professional resource aids—these sources are used as subjects or problems are being considered during an in-service session.

Research and experimentation—leaders/teachers engage in research activities and projects as individuals or as teams. They follow the steps in the scientific method: define problem, draw up hypotheses, do research and gather data, conclude and make recommendations for further study.

The library resource center can be one of the most helpful facilities in the church in providing training tools for staff members and in encouraging involvement in in-service strategies. Many staff members can work on projects on their own schedule, at their own pace, and on projects that are beneficial to them. The resource center needs to have flexible hours so that the services are available for the greatest number of staff members, and it should have functional check-out procedures so that workers can borrow materials for study at home.

It is important, too, that the center is well-organized so that workers can easily find the resources they need. The center should have on hand current resources in books, periodicals, reference works, curriculum materials, cassettes, and videotapes. Therefore, it is imperative that the resource center be included in the church budget so that up-to-date materials can be purchased.

TEACHER-SUPERVISOR CONFERENCES

Although most volunteer staff workers need and appreciate guidance, they may seldom let their need be known. Their reasons for not asking for help are varied: they may not be aware of what they need, they may feel foolish asking for assistance, or they may want to leave things as they are because of a lack of time or concern. The supervisor must be alert to determine the real needs of the individual and begin where the person is.

Clinical supervision is an interesting concept that may be helpful in supervisor-teacher conferences. The steps in the process are described as a cycle of clinical supervision. Because we are working with volunteer staff members in the church, we may not be able to apply all the steps in their entirety, but we can follow the general pattern.

The clinical supervision cycle involves the supervisor at two levels of work with the teachers: helping them to understand and improve their professional practice and helping them to learn more about the skills of classroom analysis needed in supervision.

Morris Cogan identifies eight phases in the cycle of supervision:

Phase 1: establishes the teacher-supervisor relationship.
Phase 2: requires intensive planning of lessons and units with the teacher.
Phase 3: requires planning of the classroom observation strategy by teacher and supervisor.
Phase 4: requires the supervisor to observe in-class instruction.
Phase 5: requires careful analysis of the teaching-learning process.
Phase 6: requires planning the conference strategy.
Phase 7: is the conference.
Phase 8: requires the resumption of planning.[9]

A simplified plan may be a combination conference-observation, in which the supervisor observes the teacher in action and then confers with the teacher about the session observed. Before the observation, the supervisor should discuss with the teacher the purpose of the observation, agree on a definite date and time for the observation, and talk over what the teacher plans to do in some detail. The supervisor should help the teacher think through the plan and should make any suggestions that he believes will strengthen the teaching-learning experience and make the teacher be more at ease during the observation. Then the supervisor and teacher should have prayer together and commit the session to the Lord for His blessing and direction.

Some basic principles and procedures to help teachers and supervisors improve their skills in teacher-supervisor conferences are given below:

9. In Thomas J. Sergiovanni and Robert J. Starratt, *Supervision: Human Perspectives* (New York: McGraw-Hill, 1979), pp. 309-11.

Arrive *before* the session begins.
Sit where the teacher feels most comfortable.
Ask the teacher to introduce the supervisor as a visitor.
Take part in the session as the teacher suggests.
Stay for the entire session if possible.
Take notes inconspicuously or wait until later to record observations.

Immediately after the session, the supervisor should thank the teacher for the privilege of observing. Mentioning some positive things noted about the session will help put the teacher at ease. Then the supervisor should schedule a conference to discuss the session in more detail. At this conference, the following should be done:

Establish rapport through a comfortable atmosphere and informal greetings.
Have prayer together and seek the Lord's direction in the discussion.
Ask the teacher to express himself about the situation, beginning with positive feedback.
Commend the teacher for evident strengths.
Discuss areas that may need improvement, without dwelling on the insignificant.
Discuss practical ways the needs for improvement can be made.
Suggest some possible resources the teacher can use for follow-up.
Leave the situation in a positive manner, mentioning that the supervisor is available for further assistance.
Follow up with future opportunities to encourage growth and enrichment.

The same procedure can be used with other staff members as well as teachers. The principles can be adapted to the type of situation. If we want to be effective counselors, we need to assist staff members in becoming more independent in solving their own problems and better able to help themselves.

EVALUATION OF PERSONNEL

WHAT EVALUATION IS

Evaluation is the culmination of the educational process. It means to appraise, to assess, to measure progress in view of stated objectives, and to determine strengths and needs for improvement. Actually, our work is incomplete unless we take time to evaluate.

Staff members can evaluate themselves or they can be evaluated by their peers or supervisors. Supervisors can also be evaluated by staff members. Self-evaluation may be more effective when staff members and supervisors formally evaluate their own work and make suggestions for self-improvement.

Evaluation should always begin with the strengths of the individual. Also, the focus of the attention should be on the work, rather than the worker. After the strengths have been observed, then needs for improvement can be suggested. If we begin with needs for improvement, workers can become discouraged by having their weaknesses pointed out, since human frailties and shortcomings tend to be more glaring or threatening than strengths. It is imperative that positive attitudes exist in evaluation, with the desire to make progress and accomplish anticipated objectives for self-improvement.

PURPOSES OF EVALUATION

As wise supervisors we will assess progress and determine what direction we should take. Evaluation helps us discover emerging needs and decide what steps should be taken and in what sequence. Evaluation must be done regularly and systematically for us to derive the greatest benefits. As we discover the progress we have made and analyze our strengths and needs for improvement, then we can suggest and implement specific recommendations to make necessary changes.

STEPS IN EVALUATION:

The following steps in evaluation and follow up are positive and constructive:

List strengths and needs for improvement.
Determine specific ways to strengthen each need discovered.
Implement suggested ideas.
Evaluate progress and, if necessary, make new recommendations.

CRITERIA FOR EVALUATION

Here are questions that can be used in evaluating a leader/teacher in any area of children's ministries:

Is the teacher/leader:
growing as a person in spiritual relationships?
organized in his or her work?
prepared?
enthusiastic about his or her work?

Does the teacher/leader:
have clearly defined goals?
give clear directions and assignments?
relate well to those under his or her leadership?

welcome suggestions from the group?
provide training for staff members?
set a good example for others to follow?

Staff members may ask the following questions in evaluating themselves:

Am I growing in my relationship with the Lord?
Am I prepared for my task?
Do I have a clear concept of my responsibilities?
Am I organized in my work?
Do I have vision and enthusiasm for my work?
Do I have initiative?
Am I dependable and faithful in my work?
Am I a good listener?
Do I take advantage of in-service opportunities?
Do I get along well with others?
Am I developing my creativity?
Am I growing as a whole person?
Am I genuinely interested in each child in my class or group?

TEAM TEACHING

A concept currently gaining momentum in Christian education is team teaching. The concept can be used in supervision to improve the skills of leaders and teachers and make more effective use of gifts and talents. Areas of expertise in subject matter can also be utilized. Leaders and teachers can learn to work together in large and small groups. Individual learning experiences can also be integrated.

Many children are exposed to team teaching in elementary school. Because of the interest in and apparent success of team teaching, leaders of children's ministries will profit from knowing how team teaching functions. Not every church should have team teaching. The fact that this approach is popular in educational settings outside the church is not sufficient reason for introducing the concept in the church. However, when many students experience team teaching during the week, they may become more easily bored by the traditional patterns of education in the church. To be effective, team teaching takes time, effort, careful planning, supervision, and evaluation.

WHAT TEAM TEACHING IS

Several variations of team teaching are currently practiced.

1. *The master-associate-helper arrangement.* A lead teacher is usually a more experienced person who is responsible for the leadership of the group. The associates and helpers work with the supervisor in a team effort. Responsi-

bility is shared under the guidance of the lead teacher. This plan is especially helpful in apprenticeship programs to train inexperienced teachers.

2. *Co-teaching.* The time is divided between two teachers with equal responsibility. Each teacher conducts his own activities and teaches his specialty in the time allotted.

3. *Equal sharing.* This type is a daring enterprise in which two or more teachers equally plan, conduct, and evaluate a specific learning situation. A coordinator is usually designated to give directions to the group and to correlate activities. The teachers volunteer or are assigned activities according to their abilities and interests. A team spirit is developed in which each teacher contributes to the whole.

Adaptations or combinations may be made in these three types, but the kind and quality of staff members available will determine the program best suited for a local setting.

ADVANTAGES AND LIMITATIONS OF TEAM TEACHING

Advantages	*Limitations*
Brings life and vitality to teaching and learning	May lack clear and well-defined goals
Provides variety in the use of methods and materials	May not have roles and responsibilities clearly established
Allows for more flexible scheduling	May cause some team members to be too dependent on others
Utilizes teaching strengths and specialties	May be difficult to find a time to meet or allow sufficient time for preparation
Builds enthusiasm and morale	
Provides variety in teacher personalities	May have unresolved conflicts in personalities and teaching philosophies
Encourages effective teamwork	
Encourages more pupil involvement	May have inadequate facilities and equipment to do the job well
Allows for large groups, small groups, and independent study	
Is excellent training for new teachers	May not have sufficient leadership to function effectively

Teaching teams can capitalize on their strengths and continue to improve apparent weaknesses. For those weaknesses that are outstanding, specific and practical ways of overcoming the need should be suggested and implemented by the team members. Each of the limitations listed above *can* become strengths if positive steps are taken to improve the situation.

SUGGESTIONS FOR EFFECTIVE TEAM TEACHING

Careful, long-range planning and detailed preparation are essential in successful team teaching. A basic philosophy of team teaching must be developed by those involved in the process. A teaching team cannot work effectively if there is lack of definition, rationale, or knowledge of how the team is to function.

Here are some steps the leader may follow, which may create a positive climate and aid in preparing for this teamed instructional experience.

1. Determine what kind of team teaching is to be done.
2. Decide who will be involved: coordinator, teacher, assistants, resource people.
3. Organize several training sessions (as many as are needed to be thoroughly prepared) that are conveniently arranged in time and length. Cover the following aspects of team teaching:
    Develop a clear understanding of what is to be done.
    Identify and discuss the roles and responsibilities of each team member and how each one relates to the others on the team.
    Select and study the curriculum materials to be used.
    Determine the characteristics and needs of students to be taught.
    Write out aims to be accomplished based on student needs and content.
    Develop a functional schedule which includes activities, methods, and materials, time to be allotted for each activity, and individuals responsible. The same kind of planning needs to be done for each session.
    Work out detailed plans for each activity. (This may be done on an individual basis rather than in group work.)
    Evaluate progress; check all details to be sure everyone is prepared.
    Carry out plans in actual teaching.
4. Meet weekly as a team to evaluate the session to plan long-range goals.
5. Evaluate the complete process periodically to determine whether goals are being accomplished and are meeting emerging needs.

Team teaching can be exciting if team members meet together to plan, if someone is responsible to coordinate the process and encourage progress, if resources are available, and if student needs are being met through the experience.

CURRICULUM FOR CHILDREN'S MINISTRIES

Curriculum is one of the most important functions of supervision in children's ministries. In fact, it is the starting point in planning the Christian education program for children. Certainly, planning and selecting the curriculum is one of the most important responsibilities of workers in the children's departments.

DEFINITION OF CURRICULUM

Traditionally, curriculum has been thought of as a course of study, a prescribed program to follow, or a lesson to be taught. The teacher or department superintendent studied his quarterly and followed it meticulously. Many teachers became frustrated because they could not do everything the lesson plan suggested. Some resorted to the reading of the manual because they believed they could not present the material as well as the writer said it. Others spent so little time in preparation that they could not present the ideas without reading them. Curriculum materials have often become crutches or hindrances because of misuse.

In contemporary usage, curriculum has become broader in meaning. In public education, Doll indicates the trend toward a more inclusive definition: "The commonly accepted definition of the curriculum has changed from content of courses of study and list of subjects to all the experiences which are offered to learners under the auspices or direction of the school."[10]

Paul Vieth has suggested that "in the broadest sense of the term . . . all life is the curriculum. There is no experience which does not have an influence on what people become."[11] However, curriculum can be so broad in its meaning that it becomes vague and difficult to define. Boundaries must be determined in order for the workers to use the term intelligently and develop a functional curriculum.

Curriculum for children's ministries may be defined as the total program for children, including integration of content (subject matter) and experiences utilized by Christian leadership, in accord with biblical principles in the written Word and centered on Jesus Christ, the living Word, under the guidance of the Holy Spirit.

PURPOSES OF CURRICULUM

The curriculum in the Christian education of children should accomplish three basic purposes: (1) lead children to Jesus Christ as Savior from sin; (2) guide children in continued growth toward Christlikeness; (3) equip children for effective service in the will of God. These purposes are what God has intended. They are accomplished when children see their need of a Savior and accept Him, when they are becoming more like Christ in daily living and are growing up in Him (Eph. 4:15), and when children are being challenged to equip themselves to do what God wants in their everyday experiences. A child does not have to wait until he is grown up to serve Jesus Christ effectively.

BIBLICAL FOUNDATIONS FOR CURRICULUM

In evangelical Christian education, we have a body of content or subject matter we believe is of utmost importance to teach our children. The Bible is our textbook and main source for what we teach. Other relevant subject

---

10. Ronald C. Doll, *Curriculum Improvement: Decision-Making and Process* (Boston: Allyn & Bacon, 1970), p. 21.
11. Paul Vieth, *The Church and Christian Education* (St. Louis: Bethany, 1947), p. 134.

matter may be taught, or secondary sources may be used, but the Bible is the foundation and the final authority.

Thus, the curriculum for children must be Bible based and Christ centered. In laying the foundation, we must be careful that what we teach is accurate and true to the Scriptures and glorifying to Jesus Christ. We want our children to know facts and principles from the Word of God and to have a thorough understanding of what the Bible teaches. We also want our children to apply the Bible to their lives and to obey it. Experience is an essential part of growth and is provided through activities in the classroom and carry-over outside the classroom. It is our responsibility to arrange significant experiences for the children so that the Bible can be meaningful in everyday life and applied to encourage change in behavior.

Those who are in places of responsibility in children's ministries (superintendents, teachers, secretaries, assistants, pianists) have tremendous responsibility in leading children to the Savior and in guiding them in continued growth after they accept Christ. Only dedicated Christian leaders can provide the example necessary to guide children in the church, for God has chosen human vessels to communicate His message of a living Savior and Guide for life. They must be enabled and led by the Holy Spirit to do their work in His strength and wisdom. Competent, well-trained leaders who are yielded to the Holy Spirit are essential in producing life-changing curriculum.

PRINCIPLES IN CURRICULUM DEVELOPMENT

Curriculum includes more than lesson materials. It involves the total ministry with children in the church. It includes what, when, where, and how subject matter is to be taught. Curriculum is determined by the characteristics, needs, interests, capacities, backgrounds, and goals of the learners. Objectives (aims, purposes, goals) must be determined by needs so that we know what we want to accomplish. The schedule to follow, staff members who teach or have other responsibilities, grouping of students, facilities and furnishings, methods (ways of doing) and materials[12] (tools in doing), and the administration and supervision of the program, are all parts of the curriculum of Christian education for children.

The need for correlation of curriculum from one agency or department to another is a perennial problem in the church. Sunday school teachers should be concerned not only with what *they* are teaching but also with what is being taught their students in church time, club work, and vacation Bible school. It would be well for leaders to meet together and share what they are using in order to avoid duplication and omissions. A curriculum chart indicating what is being studied in each agency and department of the church may be helpful in beginning to correlate curriculum.

12. For a more in-depth discussion of methods and materials, see chap. 27.

Long-range planning in curriculum is also essential. Those working with children need to be concerned about articulation, that is, building progressively from one age level to another. As children progress through the foundation years, Bible content and theological concepts need to be taught when they are most meaningful (see chap. 20). As a child grows in experience, his knowledge needs to be expanded and enriched, and he should begin to find answers to his life problems in the Word of God. He must begin to obey the truth as well as know it.

PLANNING THE CURRICULUM UNIT

In order to select and adapt materials that will most effectively meet specific needs, it is essential to understand the basics of curriculum structure.

UNITS OF LEARNING

A unit of learning is one way to organize and integrate content and experience to bring about changes in behavior. A unit may be defined as a series of two or more lessons which are related to the same topic, and which integrate content and experience to bring about a change in behavior. In effective unit planning, both subject matter and experience are essential. Emphasis is given to three kinds of objectives—knowing, feeling, and doing—with the ultimate goal being a change of behavior.

A unit of learning has many advantages. It encourages long-range planning, emphasizes a central theme or focal problem, focuses on the learners and their needs, allows time for accomplishment of objectives and meeting of needs, provides variety in use of methods and materials, and gives opportunities for review and application. A unit provides opportunity for better introduction to a new study and culmination at the conclusion of a study with possible carry-over into life.

Lois LeBar suggests four steps in effective unit planning: the teacher's preplanning, planning with the students, finding and sharing the answers, and planning a culminating activity to consummate the unit.[13]

The teacher's preplanning. In the "teacher's preplanning" stage, the individual needs of students are studied and prayed through, and teaching aims are formulated. Bible content is selected on the basis of those needs, and the teacher lives with the selected portions until he or she is totally absorbed with the content and is excited about the possibilities for the class. Then the teacher is ready to set the stage for an experience with the Word that will lead the students to that same vision and action.

Planning with the students. In step two, the students assume responsibility for the solution of the problem. With the assistance of the teacher, a plan of attack is decided on, and the group is organized to work on the problem.

13. Lois LeBar, *Education That Is Christian* (Westwood, N.J.: Revell, 1958), pp. 207-19.

Flexibility and continual evaluation of plans are important if real needs are to be met.

Finding and sharing answers. In step three, finding and sharing answers, energies are mobilized to find answers. The teacher supervises research and other methods of investigation for students who can read. Younger children will listen to a Bible story. The role of a teacher is that of one who guides while students discover for themselves Biblical answers to their problems.

Culminating the unit. The final step, or culminating activity, should be the learners' use of their new-found truth in new situations, or at least a realization of the difference that truth ought to make in their daily lives. The activity may take a variety of forms, such as a demonstration program, a report, an art project, creative writing, or a service project.

SELECTING CURRICULUM MATERIALS

Curriculum materials play a vital role in curriculum planning because they provide ideas that can stimulate lay workers' thinking and doing and can assist in organizing units for teaching and learning. Selection of materials is, therefore, very important. Since so many materials are available currently, the frustration comes in selecting the *best* materials for a particular local church. No publisher can produce exactly what every church needs, for each publisher serves a wide constituency. Some churches have ventured to write their own curriculum materials, but the task is tremendous, and unless one has much training in writing and editing and time and resources in abundance, the process can be very discouraging. Adapting already published materials is a more feasible plan for most churches.

If you decide to adapt already published materials, a word of caution needs to be stated about changing from one publisher to another. Publishers give much thought and planning to the preparation of their materials so that important omissions or repetitions do not occur. If a church changes publishers too often, the correlation between age levels will become extremely complicated. It is best, therefore, to use one publisher's materials at least through the children's division.

Several types of curriculum materials are published: closely graded—a separate lesson for each age or grade; group (or departmentally) graded—the same lesson for two or more ages or grades; uniform—a lesson based on the same Scripture for all departments; unified—all departments study the same basic theme; elective—the department or group chooses what it wants to study. Some of these types may be combined in materials from the same publisher. Most agencies beyond the Sunday school use some type of group-graded materials. It is important for a church to know the type of curriculum materials a publisher produces, since correlation and articulation are important factors in curriculum development.

Evaluating Curriculum Materials

In selecting materials, it is necessary to develop criteria for evaluating what is best for a local situation. Naturally, the size of the church and department or agency; the staff members' background, experience, and training; the type of community in which the church is located; the philosophy of the church in selecting and using materials; and financial resources will affect curriculum selection. Doll has developed a list of twenty questions (given below) that teachers should ask themselves as they decide which materials to use.[14] These questions must be interpreted in view of the age, grade or department to be taught.

THEOLOGICAL CONSIDERATIONS

1. Are the materials based on the Scriptures as the major instructional source for Christian education?
2. Do they provide a faithful record of and a friendly commentary on biblical events and teachings, rather than an interpretation of events and teachings that is actually or potentially negative?
3. Do the materials speak with assurance of God's power and goodness in performing miracles, including the great miracles of Christ's virgin birth and His resurrection?
4. Do they uphold the Bible's validity in helping people solve problems today?
5. Do they emphasize the stable, dependable values that the Scriptures teach?
6. Do the materials encourage the learner to commit himself to Jesus Christ as his personal Savior?
7. Do they make it clear that the learner's right relationship with God is a necessary precondition to his having right relationships with others?
8. Do they help those learners who have given themselves to Christ to increase their faith and trust in Him?

SUBSTANCE AND ORGANIZATION

9. Do the materials state understandable and acceptable objectives?
10. Do they contain specific data, main ideas, and key concepts in balanced proportion and arrangement?
11. Do they achieve a focus on main ideas and key concepts to which all other content clearly contributes?
12. Are the materials appropriate to learners' abilities, needs, and interests?
13. Do they cause learners to repeat important experiences and review important ideas?

14. Ronald C. Doll, "Twenty Questions to Ask About Sunday School Materials," *Christianity Today* 16 (3 March 1972): 7-8.

14. Do the materials increase in difficulty throughout the span of years they cover?

FEATURES HELPFUL IN LEARNING

15. Do the materials provide a variety of ways to stimulate learning?
16. Do they contain and suggest supplementary aids to learning?
17. Do they make thrifty use of the time available for learning?

FEATURES HELPFUL IN TEACHING

18. Are inexperienced teachers able to use the materials without difficulty or confusion?
19. Are teachers' guides or teachers' editions of the materials genuinely helpful, suggesting procedures that make teaching easier and more effective?
20. Do they contain suggestions for teacher planning and growth and for ways of evaluating teaching and learning?

USING CURRICULUM MATERIALS

After selecting curriculum materials, the work has just begun. The staff members need to become thoroughly familiar with the layout, content, aims, and helps provided and suggested, and to adapt the ideas to their own situation. Teachers must remember they are teaching students, not lessons. They need to ask themselves, "What can we do to derive maximum benefit from these materials in making them relevant to our situation and to bring about change in the behavior of our students?" Several questions may be asked by children's workers as they seek to adapt materials:

What changes, if any, must be made in doctrinal emphases to be able to use the materials according to our doctrinal position?

What adaptations are necessary to use the materials in the community setting?

What are the current practices of the church in the use of curriculum?

What are the present needs of our students?

What objectives do we need to accomplish in our church?

How can we adapt the materials to meet the needs of the less advanced and more advanced students?

What facilities do we need to change in order to derive maximum benefit from the materials?

What additional resources should we purchase?

What, if any, changes in our schedule are necessary in order to use the materials most effectively?

What kind of training do our leaders or teachers need?

Should we meet with the leaders and teachers in order to plan our use of the materials?

What suggestions made in the teachers' or leaders' manuals must we implement?

Which visuals and other aids suggested by the publisher should we use?

How can we effectively use students' manuals and activities suggested?

How can we correlate the activities suggested in the materials with the activities of other agencies?

SUMMARY

Supervision is a key word in children's ministries. The concept of supervision has undergone many changes historically. Today, supervision is thought of as the "strengthening of human resources" with an emphasis on the development of individuals for more effective service. Supervision is concerned with building quality in ministry. The purposes and functions in contemporary supervision encourage staff members to develop their own strategies which will enable them to improve.

Supervision has many facets. Some of those discussed in depth in this chapter are recruiting staff, developing staff, evaluation, team teaching, and curriculum development. If each of these areas is considered seriously, the children's ministries in the church will undoubtedly be strengthened and the results increased!

FOR FURTHER READING

Blackwell, Muriel. *Called to Teach Children.* Nashville: Broadman, 1983.

Boyan, Norman, and Willis Copeland. *Instructional Supervision Training Program.* Columbus, Ohio: Merrill, 1978.

Boyd, Bradford B. *Management-Minded Supervision.* New York: McGraw-Hill, 1968.

Colson, Howard, and Raymond Rigdon. *Understanding Your Church's Curriculum.* Nashville: Broadman, 1981.

Doll, Ronald C. *Curriculum Improvement: Decision Making and Process.* 5th ed. Boston: Allyn & Bacon, 1982.

————. *Supervision for Staff Development: Ideas and Application.* Boston: Allyn & Bacon, 1983.

Dull, Lloyd W. *Supervision: School Leadership Handbook.* Columbus, Ohio: Merrill, 1981.

Graendorf, Werner C., ed. *Introduction to Biblical Christian Education.* Chicago: Moody, 1981.

Griggs, Donald. *Basic Skills for Church Teachers.* Nashville: Abingdon, 1985.

Hunkins, Francis. *Curriculum Development: Program Improvement.* Columbus, Ohio: Merrill, 1980.

LeBar, Lois E. *Children in the Bible School.* Westwood, N.J.: Revell, 1952.
———. *Education That Is Christian.* Rev. ed. Westwood, N.J.: Revell, 1981.
———. *Focus on People in Church Education.* Westwood, N.J.: Revell, 1968.
Sergiovanni, Thomas, and David Elliott. *Educational and Organizational Leadership in Elementary Schools.* Englewood Cliffs, N.J.: Prentice-Hall, 1975.
Sergiovanni, Thomas, and Robert J. Starratt. *Supervision: Human Perspectives.* 2d ed. New York: McGraw-Hill, 1979.
Towns, Elmer. *The Successful Sunday School and Teachers' Guidebook.* Carol Stream, Ill.: Creation, 1976.
Westing, Harold J. *Make Your Sunday School Grow Through Evaluation.* Wheaton, Ill.: Scripture Press, Victor Books, 1976.
Wiles, Jon, and Joseph Bondi. *Curriculum Development: A Guide to Practice.* Columbus, Ohio: Merrill, 1979.
———. *Supervision: A Guide to Practice.* Columbus, Ohio: Merrill, 1980.
Wiles, Jon, and John Lovell. *Supervision for Better Schools.* 4th ed. Englewood Cliffs, N.J.: Prentice-Hall, 1975.
Unruh, Glenys, and Adolph Unruh. *Curriculum Development: Problems, Processes, and Progress.* Berkeley, Calif.: McCutchan, 1984.
Zuck, Roy B. *The Holy Spirit in Your Teaching.* Wheaton, Ill.: Scripture Press, Victor Books, 1984.

SOURCES FOR TRAINING MATERIALS

The following organizations and publishers have leadership and teacher training materials available. Write for samples:

Accent B/P Publications, Box 15337, Denver, CO 80215
Awana Youth Association, 3201 Tollview Drive, Rolling Meadows, IL 60008
Convention Press, 127 Ninth Avenue North, Nashville, TN 37203
BCM International, 237 Fairfield Avenue, Upper Darby, PA 19082
Child Evangelism Fellowship, Warrenton, MO 63383
Christian Service Brigade, Box 150, Wheaton, IL 60189
Concordia Publishing House, 3558 South Jefferson Avenue, St. Louis, MO 63118
David C. Cook Publishers, 850 North Grove, Elgin, IL 60120
Evangelical Teacher Training Association, Box 327, Wheaton, IL 60187
Gospel Light Publications, 2300 Knoll Drive, Box 3875, Ventura, CA 93006
Lowell Brown Enterprises, 717 Lakefield Road, Suite F, Westlake Village, CA 91361.
Pioneer Clubs, Box 788, Wheaton, IL 60189
Regular Baptist Press, 1300 North Meacham Road, Schaumburg, IL 60195

Scripture Press Publications, 1825 College Avenue, Wheaton, IL 60187
Standard Publishing Company, 4121 Hamilton Avenue, Cincinnati, OH 45231
Success With Youth, Inc., Box 27028, Tempe, AZ 85282
Youth Specialties, 1224 Greenfield Drive, El Cajon, CA 92021

16

Ruth C. Haycock

Church Agencies and Ministries for Children

- **The Beginnings**
- **Distinctives**
  SUNDAY SCHOOL
  CHILDREN'S CHURCH AND EXTENDED SESSION
  TRAINING HOUR
  RELEASED TIME CLASSES
  WEEKDAY BIBLE CLASSES
  ACTIVITY CLUBS
  VACATION BIBLE SCHOOL
- **Organization**
  THE NEED FOR COORDINATION
  SUGGESTED ORGANIZATIONAL STRUCTURE
  SUCCESS FACTORS
- **Innovations and Trends**
  INCREASING CHURCH-CENTEREDNESS
  LESSENED DISTINCTIVENESS AMONG AGENCIES
  SPECIAL CLASSES OR GROUPS
  VARIETY OF ORGANIZATIONAL PATTERNS
  NEW GROUPINGS OF STUDENTS

RUTH C. HAYCOCK, Ed.D., was part-time professor of Christian school courses at Piedmont Bible College, Winston-Salem, North Carolina, and served as consultant for the Association of Christian Schools International. She is now deceased.

THE BEGINNINGS OF CHURCH AGENCIES

Through seventeen centuries of church history, we read of no agencies designed especially to meet the spiritual needs of children. Then in 1780 came Sunday schools, first in England, and then in the Christian world at large. Here was an organized effort to teach the Bible to children. Sunday schools arose in response to a need for general and Bible instruction. They began independently of churches and were opposed by them on the bases of misuse of the Lord's Day and the futility of teaching poor children.

Sunday schools multiplied. The Wesleys urged every new Methodist church to institute a Sunday school. Other denominations were slower to respond, and it was about 1900 before Sunday schools had general denominational acceptance.

This pattern was repeated again and again in the history of Christian education: a need became evident; churches tended to be unresponsive; outside groups organized to meet the particular need; a coordinating agency arose to provide direction and materials; the organization strived for recognition of the need and for recognition of itself as a valid arm of the church; gradually acceptance came from one or both. In some cases the result was a joint sponsorship of a specialized agency for children; in others, churches or denominations developed their own programs patterned after the independent ones.

In the following sections, the distinctives of the Sunday school and other agencies with a primary interest in children will be discussed; then, how to coordinate those agencies within a church will be considered.

DISTINCTIVES OF SPECIFIC AGENCIES

SUNDAY SCHOOL

The Sunday school, in addition to having the longest history of any church educational agency, is also the most comprehensive. In Bible-believing churches, it has the largest attendance, covers the widest span of years, has available the richest curriculum resources, is graded most carefully, and has the most influence on the church's decisions about facilities.

The choice of a Sunday school curriculum is of utmost concern. Both teachers and pupils learn Bible content and doctrine largely through this curriculum. A good curriculum should, therefore, be thoroughly biblical, agree with the church's doctrine, be carefully graded, and furnish the teacher with helps adequate for a well-conducted class.

The major purpose of the Sunday school is to teach the Word of God in order that lives may be changed. Thorough Bible instruction will result in worship, expression, and service. If instruction does not lead to such response, it is incomplete.

The children's division of a Sunday school is generally divided into departments and classes. In most churches, preschool children are divided into three departments: infants and toddlers, birth to age two; nursery, ages two and three; and beginners, ages four and five. In some churches, this latter department is referred to as the "fours and fives"; in others, it is called the kindergarten department, the beginner department, or the preprimary department. In larger churches, there are six preschool departments, one for each year.

School-age departments often include three years for primaries (grades 1 to 3) and three for juniors (grades 4 to 6); however, some churches use two-year departments (grades 1 and 2; 3 and 4; 5 and 6); and large churches provide a separate department for each school grade.

Within each department, students are placed into groups of four to eight children for at least part of the period. These small classes allow for discussion, memory time, and expressional work. The departmental sessions stress worship, fellowship, and promotional activities, and, in the elementary grades, Scripture memorization and missionary education. Whether the Bible lesson is taught in the assembly or in smaller groups depends largely on the teaching methods considered desirable.

A departmental staff consists of a superintendent, secretary, pianist-helper, and several teachers. (The general qualifications and specific responsibilities of each department worker are discussed in chap. 14, "Leadership for Children.") The department staff meets for prayer, planning, and specialized training.

Although there have been critics of the Sunday school, God has honored and used it to the salvation and spiritual growth of many, many children, as well as youth and adults.

CHILDREN'S CHURCH AND EXTENDED SESSION

When a church makes no special provision for children during the morning service, the youngsters develop the habit of turning off the service and thinking about more interesting things. Once this habit develops, it often lingers into youth and adult years and accounts for the slowness of adults to learn from regular worship services.

"Junior church" was the first effort to provide meaningful worship for children, but the term *junior* often included those of junior age and below. More churches now use the term *children's church* and grade the groups using Sunday school terminology, nursery through primary or junior.

A children's church usually meets simultaneously with the adult service. Some meet separately during the entire hour; others meet with the adults for part of the service and are then dismissed for their own program. Children may plan and participate in graded worship. School-age children may gain understanding of the church and its services, government, missionary program, and distinctives; they as well as preschoolers can profit from the added Bible teaching.

When this second hour elaborates in various ways on the Bible teaching of the Sunday school, it is called "extended session." Several publishers provide church-time materials that build on their Sunday school curriculum. This feature can be helpful, since, in order to handle an extended session otherwise, a local worker must plan supplementary materials to add depth and breadth to the Sunday school topic each week.

A children's church program needs at least two workers, with one additional person for every eight or ten children. Also, a pianist and secretary are needed. Men should be included on the staff to help emphasize the relevance of God and church to men and boys.

Children's church can teach saved children to worship the Lord and to appreciate what He has done, and it can help unsaved ones to see their need of Christ. Graded sessions can provide instruction on subjects that might otherwise be omitted, while at the same time removing distractions from adult services and releasing space in a crowded sanctuary.

TRAINING HOUR

When Francis Clark organized his first Society of Christian Endeavor in 1881, he did not know that one day there would be youth groups in most churches. Neither could he foresee training hour sessions on Sunday nights for *every* age level.

Training hour before or after the Sunday evening service is a regular function for many Christian families, though the term *training hour* itself may not be used. To make adult attendance possible, there must also be sessions for children of all ages.

There are certain advantages in such an all-family hour: it promotes attendance at evening services; it gives additional time for the instruction of believers; it permits a high degree of student involvement; it allows participation in leadership to some who attend their own Sunday school classes.

Historically, the training hour has emphasized learning how to live the Christian life and gaining experience in carrying responsibility. Participants learn to speak, preside, lead singing, share their faith, and discuss contemporary problems in the light of Bible teaching. The training hour should not be another preaching service or Sunday school class but a situation in which children are guided to think through problems and to express themselves. Application receives more stress here than learning Bible stories.

Each age-group for which a church sets up a training hour program needs a staff of two to four persons, depending on the size of the group, preferably including at least one married couple. When departmental groups exceed twenty-five children, they should be divided by school grade. The suggested minimum of four staff members permits the children to be grouped, each group with a leader, for planning, preparing programs, or for Bible study.

In choosing curriculum materials for the children's training hour, a committee must make several decisions: (1) Do we want a theme which continues through the total program? Several publishers produce such materials, capitalizing on children's interest in space travel or animals. (2) Do we desire an individual achievement program with awards or ranks? (3) What emphasis do we want on Scripture memorization? (4) Do we prefer the same routine from week to week? Children sense security in familiar routines, yet routines can be deadening. (5) To what extent should we use or try to develop the children's creativity? (Choosing curriculum materials is also discussed in chap. 15, "Supervising Children's Ministries," and in chap. 27, "Methods and Materials for Children.")

For many children, a well-executed training hour provides an extra experience, enabling them to meet the problems of everyday life and to use the Bible in solving them.

RELEASED TIME CLASSES

As American public education has become increasingly secular, church leaders and many educators have recognized that, in some way, the public school must show its students the contribution of religion to life. If schools ignore religion completely, they tell children, in effect, that it is unimportant.

In an effort to highlight the significant nature of religion, many states have authorized schools to release students each week to go to their churches, or to other off-campus locations, for religious instruction. Parents give permission for their children's attendance. In some cases, the church is responsible to the school for attendance records, since the instruction is considered part of the school day. In other situations, students are dismissed early, either to attend the special classes or to go home.

Released-time programs have certain advantages: attendance is regular because, once parents have given permission, the students must attend; many children from unsaved homes will participate; students and parents tend to be serious about the classes, as an extension of the school.

In spite of these plusses, however, a church should consider carefully before starting a released-time program. Success depends on a staff adequate to teach classes simultaneously, to escort children to and from the church, to keep records, and to handle the program on a regular basis over an extended period. Sufficient classroom space is also crucial. Good discipline is important, too, because a church's reputation is not improved when children go from an orderly school to a disorderly church.

The curriculum should be grouped by school grades, if possible, so that learning activities may be suitable and each year may build on the preceding ones. Many churches, however, have satisfactorily grouped children over a two- or three-grade range and have used a rotating curriculum. Because many children receive no other solid Bible instruction and others have learned much in church and home, the curriculum decision is often a difficult one. Long-range planning should, therefore, precede the initial classes.

Released time is meant primarily for instruction. Learning experiences should be planned using large and small groups, individual work, testing, and evaluation. Any expressional work and worship should relate to the content being studied.

Staff needs of such a program vary according to the number of children expected and the grades included. This in turn depends on the proximity of the public school, the reputation of the church, and the number and strength of competing groups. In addition to a teacher and assistant for each class, a director and secretary are needed. Their responsibilities include counseling children and leading them to the Lord. In many situations, children may not remain after class for counsel and must return to school for dismissal and bus transportation.

Released-time classes are not for every church, but where they are permitted and where other factors indicate the Lord's leading, they can provide many new contacts for church follow-up.

WEEKDAY BIBLE CLUBS OR CLASSES

Home Bible classes for children go by several names: Good News Clubs, Bible Clubs, and Joy Clubs, among others. Certain characteristics are true of all: (1) they gather neighborhood children into a Christian home for a one-hour club; (2) they serve kindergarten and elementary school children, often without grading, sometimes with two separate groups for the Bible lesson; (3) they stress chronological, visualized Bible study; (4) they emphasize evangelism and encourage children to bring friends.

Because such classes meet after school, children are already dressed suitably. Because they are neighborhood groups, the economic and social level of the host home is comparable with that of the attending children. Because the classes are informal, they are a welcome change from the school day.

Weekday classes are usually staffed by a teacher, a helper, and a hostess (or the hostess may also be the helper).

An effective ministry in children's Bible classes depends on careful preparation and on workers' showing love for the children in club, casual contacts, and home calls. Clubs with a church's prayer backing reach many children and homes for the Lord. Any affiliation with an outside organization must not overshadow the fact that God has given the local church responsibility to reach out into the community.

ACTIVITY CLUBS

Psychologists often point out that we need new experiences if we are not to go stale. Doing something different is a thrill and a challenge at any age. In all preparation for children's sessions, we strive for variety and freshness, but most youngsters need more than we give them in the classroom. They need cookouts and field days; they respond to learning to build campfires and to tie knots; they enjoy crafts and projects. Here they can learn lessons that relate Bible truths to life; they can see their leaders informally; they can learn to express themselves and to discipline themselves; they can learn Christian sportsmanship.

Earlier generations engaged in some of these experiences at home with older family members; some were members of scouts or Camp Fire Girls. It was to young adults who had known the enthusiasm and thrill of these secular organizations that God gave a vision for Christ-centered clubs sponsored by Bible-believing churches. Christian Service Brigade began for boys, with Pioneer Girls (now Pioneer Clubs, with both boys' and girls' groups) following. Then came the Awana Youth Association, Sky Pilots, and others.

All activity clubs are somewhat similar: they meet weekly for two hours; they include games and crafts as well as Bible study; their members work for badges and ranks; they exist as an integral part of a church program, with emphasis on evangelism and Christian growth; they require leadership training before a group is formed; they have divisions for several age-groups. Historically, it is the elementary grades for which activity clubs have existed, but recently several programs have added groups for four- and five-year-olds.

The specific leadership needed depends on which program a church chooses. Each organization publishes an array of guidebooks for leaders and manuals for members. Careful study should precede the adoption of a club program. Persons likely to be involved should visit other clubs and discuss their effectiveness with the clubs' leaders. They should send for materials and examine them prayerfully. If possible, they should invite a field representative from the organization to present the program and answer questions. Conviction based on thorough preparation can lead to a wise decision and a fruitful ministry.

VACATION BIBLE SCHOOL

Vacation Bible school provides time for concentrated Bible study and varied activities. The maintenance of a high degree of enthusiasm and continuity is difficult in sessions that are spaced a week apart, but here is an agency meeting several hours a day for five to ten consecutive days.

The results can be fantastic in spirit, achievement, and depth of study. Children can become involved in projects for which there is little time in shorter sessions. They can play together under the direction of adults and teenagers who exemplify Christian virtues and teach biblical attitudes.

Most schools are organized into departments and classes, following the grading of the Sunday school. Classification should be by school grade just completed to avoid mixing children who do not read and write with those who have had school training. In schools with limited space for departmental activities, all school children can meet for an assembly, which helps build school spirit and center attention on the Lord Jesus Christ.

Since the day's session is divided into a number of periods, team teaching is preferable. (For more on team teaching, see chap. 15, "Supervising Children's Ministries.") When a teacher is responsible for only the Bible lesson, or only the Scripture memory work, or the handwork, that teacher can prepare adequately; as a result, more workers are willing to serve. An experienced teacher should present the Bible lesson, the basis for the day's work. As inexperienced workers observe others teach and lead, they too learn and grow.

In order for children to use workbooks comfortably and do creative projects, they need table space and tools. Although boys and girls must learn to share, it is unreasonable that they should spend half of their work period waiting for scissors or paste.

The most familiar curriculum materials are probably the departmentally graded lessons available from major Sunday school publishers. Each publisher chooses an overall theme for the year and relates the various departmental lessons to that theme, rotating the lesson series over a three-year period. Correlated with the Bible lessons are worship plans, games, songs, handwork, and special features. Student manuals and visual materials enable a staff with limited training to work effectively.

In addition, uniform series, with all grades studying the same Bible content, are available from some Sunday school publishers, from some missionary agencies that do children's work, and from individual churches. Some series are planned well and provide excellent graded material for students and teachers. Others provide little supplementary helps but have been used effectively by trained workers in low-budget situations.

Closely graded lessons, with a separate series for each school grade, are produced by a few publishers and may be used year after year.

ORGANIZATION OF THE CHILDREN'S DIVISION

THE NEED FOR COORDINATION

Mrs. James needed help! She was teaching a released-time class of fifth-graders and getting nowhere. What was she doing wrong? In desperation she came, seeking a solution. The lesson series she used was a good choice. Her plan for the teaching period was one others had used successfully. She was known as an effective teacher.

Investigation showed these facts: the children attended Sunday school, junior youth group, church-sponsored home clubs, an after-school junior missionary meeting, as well as her released-time classes. In most sessions, the teacher used a flannelgraph Bible story; in Sunday school, home clubs, and released time, lessons were from the Pentateuch; in the junior youth group, the lessons were based on the Pentateuch, though they were not direct Bible study; the home clubs taught the identical series used in released time and were two weeks ahead! Every agency taught a weekly memory verse. Except for the missionary group, no children could remember learning any new song.

It was evident that these juniors were learning. They were learning to occupy themselves otherwise when the Word of God was taught. They were convinced that no teacher expected them to learn very much because of the constant repetition. They were also learning that only the Pentateuch is important.

Whatever the combination of agencies a church uses in its efforts to reach and teach children, coordination is necessary for meaningful accomplishment.

SUGGESTED ORGANIZATIONAL STRUCTURE

When a new church begins, coordinating church functions is relatively easy. The same few people are involved; the number of agencies is limited; the pastor is in close touch with what goes on. It is often he and his wife who train workers for their responsibilities.

As a church grows, these factors change. Agencies multiply; leadership expands; the pastor cannot supervise all that goes on. As he works with his board, it soon becomes apparent that their responsibilities cover too many other areas to include coordinating all the areas of the church's ministry.

The next step in organizational structure is a board (or committee) of Christian education. Such a board usually includes the head of each educational agency, the pastor or director of Christian education, a representative from the church board, and sometimes a member elected from the church at large. It often meets monthly to recommend or set policy, approve personnel and curriculum, and coordinate the educational program in general.

Growing out of this board, several committees prove helpful: children's work, youth work, adult work, and leadership development.

The children's-work committee, for instance, may consist of the leader of or an elected representative from each agency (Sunday school, children's church, vacation Bible school, training hour, weekday clubs). Another way to organize the children's-work committee is to have a representative from each of the age groups in the children's division (cradle roll, twos and threes, fours and fives, primaries, and juniors). These representatives meet together to organize, administer, and supervise the work of the children's division.

At times, the committee may call all workers in the children's division together for the consideration of needs or for inservice training. The amount of responsibility given to the committee will determine how often it should meet. The chairman of the committee may be appointed by the board of Christian education or elected by the committee to serve a designated length of time.

TABLE 16.1

CHILDREN'S AGENCIES

LEVEL	SUNDAY SCHOOL	CHILDREN'S CHURCH	TRAINING HOUR	VACATION BIBLE SCHOOL	WEEKDAY BIBLE CLASSES	RELEASED-TIME CLASSES	ACTIVITY CLUBS
Birth to age 2	Cradle roll	Nursery (baby care)	Church nursery if adult training hour meets	Nursery for children of workers			
Ages 2 and 3	Nursery or twos and threes	Nursery church	Church nursery if adult training hour meets	Nursery			
Ages 4 and 5	Fours and fives	Kindergarten church	Kindergarten training hour	Kindergarten	Preschool classes	Kindergarten	Fours and fives
Grades 1, 2, 3	Primary	Primary church	Primary training hour	Primary	Grades 1 to 6 often together in one club in each neighborhood	Grade 1 / Grade 2 / Grade 3	Primary
Grades 4, 5, 6	Junior	Junior church	Junior training hour	Junior		Grade 4 / Grade 5 / Grade 6	Junior

The responsibilities of the committee should be delineated in the church constitution or by-laws, so that as members change, a functional committee continues. Some of the specific responsibilities of the committee are as follows:

Prepare a list of needs in the children's division.

Write realistic goals that can be accomplished within specified times.

Give guidance in organizing, administering, and supervising the departments.

Correlate the work of the departments and agencies.

Provide a balanced program in instruction, worship, fellowship, and expression-service.

Seek to improve specific activities in music, worship, memorization, recreation, and teaching-learning.

Publicize and promote the work of the children's division.

Discover, enlist, and provide training for workers with children.

Suggest and recommend curriculum for use in the children's division.

Develop wholesome human relations and build a cooperative team spirit among the workers.

Evaluate the work of the children's division periodically; set new goals.

Table 16.1 shows children's agencies and the age groups they most often serve. Although a particular church seldom includes every agency, careful planning is needed to provide adequate staff and curriculum for each age level and effective progress from one level to the next.

SUCCESS FACTORS

The effectiveness of a church program is not measured by the number of agencies; neither is it judged by quantity of Scripture verses memorized or the number of times the children go through the Bible. The factors that really count relate to objectives the church seeks to achieve.

Clear objectives. In chapters 5 through 10, the needs of each age group were discussed. Those chapters pointed out that because certain things are happening in the lives of primaries, for example, these boys and girls have particular needs. Some are common to people of all ages; others are specific developmental tasks of the primary years. If each agency ministering to primary children takes responsibility for all those needs, leaders will have more goals than they can achieve, with resultant discouragement and frustration.

One task of the children's work committee is to study pupils' needs and then determine which agency should accept specific responsibility for which needs. Some overlapping is unavoidable and probably desirable, but a clear understanding of agency objectives provides for leaders a basis for selecting materials and activities and makes evaluation and progress possible.

TABLE 16.2
COORDINATING CURRICULUM

	SUNDAY SCHOOL	CHILDREN'S CHURCH	WEEKDAY CLUB	TRAINING HOUR	MISCELLANEOUS
Objectives					
Curriculum, Year 1 — 1 2 3 4					
Year 2 — 1 2 3 4					
Year 3 — 1 2 3 4					
Memory work					
Songs or bases for selection					
Special activities					

Coordination of curriculum. A departmental curriculum chart, such as Table 16.2 illustrates, can help children's workers coordinate their activities. The table shown is only a possible skeleton. The actual chart should be on a large sheet of paper.

Some church publishers have available a prospectus, outlining their long-range curriculum. To find the three-year cycle of memory work, one must often study the manuals for the three-year span.

If for some agency the materials used are not satisfactory, the chart for that agency should be prepared last. Out of a study of the total curriculum, the lack of need for the agency may become evident. On the other hand, gaps may appear that indicate the necessity for a program different from what has been used. To leave the selection of lesson content to each leader is to invite chaos.

Before any new agency is introduced, the need for it should be established. Somehow it is easier to start something else than to make what we have function at the top level. The result of adding agencies is competition for children, attention, workers, curriculum, time—an ineffective but busy program.

Growing leadership. Ministries to children grow when their leaders grow. This statement is true whether we are concerned with children's development in spiritual dimensions or in enthusiasm and attendance. Youngsters are quick to take advantage of the situation.

Growth in leaders must begin in their personal lives with the Lord and then in their relationship with others. It must include responsibility to their church in capacities other than teacher or leader. Growth should result in wholesome influence in the neighborhood and at work.

All those who work in one agency must understand their objectives and the way in which their program relates to others. This understanding comes through group study of agency materials, attendance at area rallies, training sessions, and local staff meetings, and time for united prayer and planning. Lack of this knowledge leads to branching out at the whims of leaders until everyone does "that which is right in his own eyes."

Prospective workers for all agencies should be approved by the board of Christian education. New workers should visit sessions before they take responsibility; they should serve as apprentices before they become leaders.

Profitable presessions. It has been repeatedly said that a Sunday school teacher is late if he is not present fifteen minutes early. Teachers should be ready for students in order to capitalize on those precious minutes with the early birds before the session officially begins. In addition to providing a get-acquainted and counseling time, many departments plan specific projects which involve one or several youngsters and which relate to the Bible lesson. The use of presession adds to the teaching time, but it also prevents the discipline problems that develop when children are unsupervised.

The same principle may be applied to other agencies. The shy child may open up in this period; any child may reveal his understanding; the teacher may behave less formally; special interests may reveal themselves. In longer sessions, as in vacation Bible school, when the weather is favorable, outdoor activities will work better than indoor ones.

In their teacher's manuals, many curriculum writers suggest presession activities related to the lessons. Activities should be simple enough to be completed in a short time or suitable for continuation from session to session without too much handling of materials.

Two- to five-year-olds can look at picture books, draw pictures, listen to records or tapes, explore a nature center, play a story, participate in finger plays, present their offering, help with a bulletin board, listen to a story or review information in a variety of ways.

Primaries and juniors are less limited because they can read and write. In addition to the above activities, they can sing around the piano; learn new songs; review memory verses; prepare scrapbooks or posters; look at Bible stories using View-Masters, filmstrips, or a phonoviewer; play Bible games; write letters to missionaries, absentees, or shut-ins; drill on vocabulary; prepare something special for the opening assembly; read books; prepare a diorama or a box movie; examine a missionary display; or make a tape recording.

The uses of presession time are limited only by the imagination of the adult leaders. The informality of smaller groups makes possible unusual supplementary activity.

Communication with the church. The success of church agencies is never merely a matter of a top-notch program, excellent leadership, and superior organization. Our ministry is a spiritual matter; we are interested in seeing boys and girls trust the Savior and grow in him. Those results come only as the Holy Spirit is active both in the leadership and in the hearts and minds of children. If we see no results, perhaps we have not asked God to change our lives and those we teach. He delights to respond as we look to Him.

Not only does God respond to individual prayer, but in a special way, He honors group prayer and agreement in prayer. Because that is true, a church must be kept up-to-date about its children's work. When there are victories, church members should join in praise to God; when there are needs wisely shared, they should join in petition. Prayer partners are always an asset but especially so when problems should not be publicly reported.

Communication with the church has other values. When people know what goes on, they are more sympathetic; they supply needs rather than wonder what costs so much; they consider helping instead of relegating responsibility to others; they promote the *whole* church program.

INNOVATIONS AND TRENDS

Church agencies are constantly, though slowly, changing in response to developments in the school system, new community conditions, and further insights into scriptural teaching.

INCREASING CHURCH-CENTEREDNESS

With an increasing emphasis on the establishment of indigenous national churches on the foreign field and new churches at home has come a general acceptance of the importance of the local church in New Testament teaching. Churches that once operated no weekday children's work but often encouraged their members to work with extrachurch groups now provide a church-related program.

The result is improved coordination with other church agencies, better opportunity for follow-up, and a more solid status for the weekday classes because of the church's reputation. Children are learning that their church is concerned about them. As they outgrow a particular agency, the church still has a place for them.

LESSENED DISTINCTIVENESS AMONG AGENCIES

When each church agency began, it was out of a conviction that children had particular needs that it could meet. Therefore, each group within a church was distinctive. As time went on and each agency sought to improve its program and materials, it dipped into other areas where it had not previously worked. As a result, each program has increased in breadth, and some of the earlier distinctives have been lost. A problem arises when we seek to make each agency complete in itself for the benefit of those who attend only one and when we also want each program to be part of a coordinated whole.

SPECIAL CLASSES OR GROUPS

Contemporary churches are probably doing more than at any time in history to consider the needs of special groups: the mentally impaired, the physically handicapped, the deaf, and others (see chaps. 11 through 13). A church's provision for such children recognizes the fact that God loves them and that they need the Savior. It proves to the community that a church cares.

VARIETY OF ORGANIZATIONAL PATTERNS

No longer must vacation Bible school be two weeks long and two-and-a-half hours each forenoon. VBS may operate for five days or eight; it may meet in the evening or both morning and evening; it may meet in backyards all around the community; it may run one evening a week for ten weeks. Day camp or Indian village Bible camp may be substituted for the more formal VBS.

Some Sunday schools meet longer than one hour; some combine with children's church for a longer session. Some have no opening assembly but meet for a closing session instead.

NEW GROUPINGS OF STUDENTS

Whereas controlled class sizes have been rather consistently recommended for each age group, now it seems there are no rules. With an increase in team teaching, the trend is to meet in larger groups for parts of each period, breaking into small groups for specific activities. As individualized instruction and small group projects have become common in public schools, adaptations are being made in church classes. There seems to be a widespread recognition that the use of various sized groups provides variety for the children and more effective use of leaders and that children should not be grouped in the same way for all activities.

Church agencies for children are, first, *church* agencies. They are part of a church's ministry to people. Second, they are *for children* and must therefore provide for the needs of youngsters, both saved and unsaved. Together they must offer understanding and experience to enable a believing child to grow into a mature follower of the Lord Jesus Christ.

SUMMARY

The needs of children from birth through the elementary grades include many areas of life. Because biblical teachings relate to all of them, no one children's agency operating for one hour a week can hope to be a sufficient supplement to the Christian home to do all that is needed. As a result, a church must determine what kinds of instruction and activity will best provide for its own families as well as for the unchurched children of the neighborhood.

The New Testament does not specify particular agencies for Christian education; neither does it mention the teaching of children in the church. It does command parents, fathers in particular, to bring up their children "in the nurture and admonition of the Lord." It leaves self-governing local churches to determine what they will provide to assist parents in fulfilling God's command.

FOR FURTHER HELP

ACTIVITY CLUBS

Accent Publications, P. O. Box 15337, Denver, CO 80215-0337. Eager Beavers, grades 1-3; Junior Astronauts, grades 4-6.

Awana Youth Association, 3215 Algonquin Road, Rolling Meadows, IL 60008. Coed clubs for preschoolers; graded boys' clubs and girls' clubs through high school; Awana Friends program for mentally retarded.

Christian Service Brigade, P. O. Box 150, Wheaton, IL 60187. Tree Climbers for fathers and sons, grades 1, 2; Stockades for boys in grades 3-6, at two levels.

Joy Club Youth Ministries, P. O. Box 455, Elyria, OH 44036.

Pioneer Clubs, Box 788, Wheaton, IL 60187. Separate boys' and girls' clubs for school-age children and youth, grades 1-12. Two-year spans for children.

Success with Youth Publications, P. O. Box 27028, Tempe, AZ 85282. Space

Cubs for 4's and 5's; Whirlybirds for primaries; Jet Cadets for juniors.
Word of Life Fellowship, Inc., Schroon Lake, NY 12870. Olympian Program
for primary and junior levels.

AGENCIES AND THEIR ADMINISTRATION AND COORDINATION

Graendorf, Werner C., ed. *Introduction to Biblical Christian Education*. Chicago: Moody, 1981.

Everest, Norma J. *Education Ministry in the Congregation*. Minneapolis: Augsburg, 1983.

Hakes, J. Edward, ed. *An Introduction to Evangelical Christian Education*. Chicago: Moody, 1964.

Richards, Lawrence O. *A Theology of Children's Ministry*. Grand Rapids: Zondervan, 1983.

Trouten, Donald J., et al. *Church Educational Ministries*. Wheaton, Ill.: Evangelical Teacher Training Assn., 1980.

CHILDREN'S CHURCH

Freese, Doris. *Children's Church: A Comprehensive How-To*. Chicago: Moody, 1982.

Huttar, Leora W. *Church Time for Pre-Schoolers*. Denver: Accent, 1975.

Johnston, Dorothy Grunbock, and Kathleen Abbas. *Churchtime for Children*. Denver: Accent, 1980.

Larson, Jim. *Churchtime for Children: Developing a Successful Churchtime Ministry for Children in the Elementary Grades*. Glendale, Calif.: Regal Books, 1978.

Lebar, Mary E. *Wonder Programs for 4s and 5s*. Wheaton, Ill.: Scripture Press, 1973.

Nursery Learning Programs and *Primary Adventure Programs*. Wheaton, Ill.: Scripture Press.

Rock, Louise H., and Robert A. Allen, eds. *Children's Church for Kindergartners*. Elgin, Ill.: David C. Cook, 1974. Also *Children's Church for Nursery*.

Welcome to Super Church: A Children's Church Manual. Kingsport, Tenn.: Super Church Ministries (P. O. Box 905, 37662).

HOME BIBLE CLUBS

Child Evangelism Fellowship, Inc. (Warrenton, MO 63383). Source for Good News Club information.

Freyermuth, Virgil. *Joy Club Leader's Guidebook*. Elyria, Ohio: Fellowship of Baptists for Home Missions, 1978.

Jordan, Bernice C. *Guidebook to Better Teaching*. Upper Darby, Pa.: BCM International (Formerly Bible Club Movement, 237 Fairfield Avenue, Upper Darby, PA 19082).

Prichard, Pamela R. *How to Conduct Backyard Bible Clubs.* Chicago: Moody, 1977.

SUNDAY SCHOOL

Blackwell, Muriel, and Elsie Rives. *Teaching Children in the Sunday School.* Nashville: Convention, 1976.

Blazier, Kenneth D. *A Growing Church School.* Valley Forge, Pa.: Judson, 1978.

Byrne, H. W. *Christian Education for the Local Church.* Grand Rapids: Zondervan, 1973.

Calhoun, Mary. *Adventures with Children.* Nashville: Abingdon, 1978.

Cully, Iris. *New Life for Your Sunday School.* New York: Seabury, 1976.

Davis, Ginny. *Reaching Children Through the Sunday School.* Nashville: Convention, 1979.

Haystead, Wesley. *Ways to Plan and Organize Your Sunday School: Birth to Age 5.* Glendale, Calif.: Gospel Light, 1971.

Malehorn, Harold. *Over 200 Ways to Improve Your Sunday School.* St. Louis: Concordia, 1982.

Richards, Lawrence O. *A Theology of Children's Ministry.* Grand Rapids: Zondervan, 1983.

Rives, Elsie. *Basic Children's Sunday School Work.* Nashville: Convention, 1980.

Smith, Charles T. *Ways to Plan and Organize Your Sunday School: Grades 1-6.* Glendale, Calif.: Gospel Light, 1971.

Towns, Elmer. *The Successful Sunday School and Teacher's Guidebook.* Carol Stream, Ill.: Creation, 1976.

Understanding Sunday School. Wheaton, Ill.: Evangelical Teacher Training Assn., 1981.

Westing, Harold J. *Make Your Sunday School Grow Through Evaluation.* Wheaton, Ill.: Scripture Press, Victor Books, 1976.

VACATION BIBLE SCHOOL

Daniel, Eleanor. *Vacation Bible School Ideas: How-to's for a Successful Summer Ministry.* Cincinnati: Standard, 1977.

The ABC's of Vacation Bible School. Cincinnati: Standard, 1984.

Freese, Doris. *Vacation Bible School: A Current Approach to a Proven Program.* Wheaton, Ill.: Evangelical Teacher Training Assn., 1977.

Getz, Gene A. *The Vacation Bible School.* Chicago: Moody, 1962.

Jenkins, Jerry B., and W. Arthur Blakely. *VBS Unlimited.* Wheaton, Ill.: Scripture Press, Victor Books, 1974.

Self, Margaret M., ed. *Year-Round Bible Ministries.* Glendale, Calif. Gospel Light, Regal Books, 1976.

17

Jean Fisher

Managing the Classroom Effectively

- **What Is Classroom Management?**
- **What Is the Biblical Basis?**
- **What Are Some Significant Problems?**
  THE FACILITIES
  THE TEACHER
  THE LEARNER
  THE HOME
- **Principles of Classroom Management**
  INSTRUCTION OR NURTURE
  INDIVIDUALIZATION
  DEVELOPING SELF-DIRECTION
  MOTIVATION
  CORRECTION OR CHASTENING

WHAT IS CLASSROOM MANAGEMENT?

A look into the primary department at First Church finds the children busily working at various learning centers. Teachers stationed at each learning center are also busily at work as they ask questions, offer suggestions, praise accomplishments, redirect energy being used unproductively, remind of accepted

JEAN FISHER, M.A., is associate professor of Christian education at Cedarville College, Cedarville, Ohio.

classroom behavior, enjoy the children, answer questions, and help children to show respect for others and to work cooperatively together. These teachers are practicing classroom management as they maintain a teaching-learning environment in which teachers can teach and learners can learn.

Classroom management is a means toward several ends. The means is the teacher's provision of a learning environment with boundaries. Those boundaries are the teacher's expectations regarding student behavior. They are clearly communicated to the students and thus provide structure and security. The teacher's careful planning and organization of the learners and materials also provide structure. Learners experience security in knowing how to work within the organizational structure of the classroom. Order and nonthreatening control and an atmosphere permeated by the mutual respect of teacher and children relieves anxiety and frustration and allows everyone to concentrate on the work at hand.

The ends toward which classroom management are directed are effective learning in group situations, the development of self-discipline, and the building of positive character traits. Certainly, the ultimate end is to bring lives into conformity with the image of God's Son, for that pleases and glorifies God the Father.

What Is the Biblical Basis for Classroom Management?

Teacher and learners are engaged in interpersonal relationships that have the potential to be either destructive or edifying. If these relationships are to be profitable for all, it is necessary to understand certain biblical principles. First, the teacher must appreciate the worth and dignity of each child, for the child has been created in the image of God (Gen. 1:27) and is loved by God (Mark 10:13-16). In spite of man's depravity, he is of worth to his Creator, who has lavished him with mercy, grace, and love. Consequently, the child should always be treated as a person of worth and dignity. He is never to be deprecated or told he is "no good" or "worthless," for that is not true; he is never to be demeaned or slighted, for he has dignity and worth.

Second, the teacher must understand that contrary to some modern psychological theories, the child is a responsible agent created with intellect, emotion, and will who, within the limitations of his fallen nature, can make choices (Josh. 24:15, John 7:17). This means that the child can be held accountable for his behavior (Rom. 3:19). His behavior is not simply his response to the stimulus of others or his environment. "One should be held accountable to the degree to which he possesses both the insight into the particular behavior expected of him and the ability to respond as he should."[1] A redeemed child, indwelt by God's Holy Spirit, will undoubtedly have greater understanding

---

1. Jack Fennema, *Nurturing Children in the Lord* (Philadelphia: Presb. & Ref., 1977), p. 15.

regarding biblical truth than the child who has not received Christ as Savior. Be aware of each child's understanding and hold him accountable in those areas.

Third, the child must understand the biblical response to those who are in authority over him (Heb. 13:7). The teacher has been given the responsibility for spiritual leadership in the classroom, and he should therefore expect the child to respond with respect; conversely, the Christian teacher should be a person who earns the respect of the child.

Fourth, the teacher must understand Christ's injunction about the exercise of authority. The disciples had an ongoing argument about which of them would be the greatest in the kingdom (Mark 9:33-37; 10:35-45). Jesus taught them that they were not to be autocratic in the exercise of authority; rather, they were to become servants to others, even to young children. Authority was to be exercised in humility and love as they followed the example of Christ, for He came to serve and not to be served (Mark 10:45). Humility and love, however, do not rule out the exercise of authoritative leadership, as is evident in Paul's epistles, especially in 1 Corinthians. Most children will ultimately respond to authority that is tempered by humility and love.

Fifth, the teacher must remember that the Scriptures instruct those in authority to discipline children: "And ye fathers, provoke not your children to wrath: but bring them up in the nurture and admonition of the Lord" (Eph. 6:4). What does it mean to bring up children in "the nurture and admonition of the Lord"? The Greek word for nurture, *paideuō* (verb form) or *paideia* (noun form), is derived from *paia,* meaning child, and can be translated either nurture or discipline. The Scripture makes no distinction between the terms. To discipline is to nurture and to nurture is to discipline. Intrinsic to nurture and discipline are instruction and correction, terms that are themselves synonymous with education and chastening.

The Greek word for admonition, *noutheteō* or *nouthesia,* brings out a different aspect of training. *Noutheteō* and *nouthesia* are derived from *nous,* meaning mind or intellect, and involve admonition, counseling, and confronting. As such, they relate more to older children who can think through problems because of their increased understanding and ability to reason. Thus instruction and chastening *(paideuō* or *paideia)* are probably best directed toward young children and should gradually be replaced by reasoning or admonition *(noutheteō* or *nouthesia)* as the children mature.[2]

These biblical principles provide the basis for classroom management in church education. The teacher who builds classroom management procedures on them can avoid unbiblical behavioral theories that focus on manipulating outward behavior instead of addressing the child's inner nature.

2. Ibid., pp. 51-55.

What Are Some Significant Classroom Management Problems?

THE FACILITIES MAY BE A SIGNIFICANT PROBLEM

Although environment does not determine behavior, it has the potential to influence behavior. An adult ushered into a spacious, beautifully appointed room usually responds in appreciation of that beauty by moving more sedately, by handling objects carefully, perhaps even by speaking more quietly. Likewise, children also can respond positively to order and beauty. Yet some church facilities for children leave much to be desired in the way of order, beauty, and space.

Many churches struggle with inadequate space for students and materials, with poor ventilation and lighting, and with unattractive rooms desperately in need of redecorating. Such facilities make an unintended but eloquent statement about the importance those churches place on teaching children the Word of God. That statement is not lost on impressionable children. The overcrowding, the decreased opportunity for meaningful physical activity, and the physical discomfort caused by such facilities frequently result in behavior problems.

The administrative and teaching staffs should objectively evaluate the facilities, recognize the problems, and determine how to resolve them. Although administrators need to encourage a flexible attitude regarding utilization of space, their concern must always be the welfare of the children and not a sense of ownership felt by any group. Classes or whole departments should be moved when the result provides more adequate space for the younger learners in the church.

Teen volunteers plying paint brushes and rollers can transform dreariness and gloom into cheeriness and beauty, even on a limited budget. The children's delight in their new surroundings will amply pay the volunteers. Curtains or drapes will add a homey touch. Carpet will eliminate noise caused by the movement of feet and furniture on hard surfaces. A quieter classroom is a more easily managed one. Storage space for materials for teachers and students will assist in bringing orderliness into the classroom. Children may respond by becoming more orderly in their behavior. Facilities are not neutral.

Problems in the physical appearance of a church building are the most easily remedied, but teachers must also be aware of the psychological atmosphere of the learning environment. Do the children consider their classroom a happy place to be? Is it a place where they are accepted and loved as they are, not as the teacher wishes them to be? Is it a place where they can learn without having their self-esteem assaulted? Can they leave feeling a sense of joy and accomplishment? If so, to God be the glory, for concerned and loving teachers are doing their work in a manner that glorifies God.

THE TEACHER MAY BE A SIGNIFICANT PROBLEM

The teacher's prayerful and thorough preparation for each session is an essential ingredient to classroom management. Yet a teacher may arrive for class unprepared for the awesome responsibility that lies before him (James 3:1). That teacher is behind before he even begins, and he never catches up. His unpreparedness makes it difficult for him to give full attention to the children. His insecurity and apprehension can cause him to be inflexible. He tends to respond to even the slightest hint of misconduct with a raised voice and the demand for instant obedience. It is hard for such a teacher to discern what can be ignored and what demands attention—is the finger tapping only annoying, or is it really disturbing?

The more thorough a teacher's preparation is, the more at ease and flexible he can be, and the more he will enjoy his students. His teaching materials will be organized and ready for use when they are needed. The teaching time will be structured, yet an attitude of flexibility will be maintained when the unexpected occurs. The unexpected may be a teachable moment when children are ready for a particular learning experience, yet the unprepared teacher may let it escape unnoticed. The prepared teacher can give his attention to the learners and show sensitivity to their response by adjusting his teaching plan. The prepared teacher teaches learners, individual learners, and does not simply cover content. Learners are encouraged by this personal interest to be more active in the learning process and more responsible in their behavior.

Every child is entitled to unconditional love as an image bearer, but every child does not seem equally lovable to the teacher. The teacher must be spiritually mature and dependent on God for help to love the unlovable as God Himself loves the child. Teachers need to spend much time in 1 Corinthians 13 in order to understand that expertise in methodology is to no avail without love.

Paul instructed the Corinthians, "Be ye followers of me, even as I also am of Christ" (1 Cor. 11:1). He exhorted the Philippians, "Those things, which ye have both learned, and received, and heard, and seen in me, do: and the God of peace shall be with you" (Phil. 4:9). Teachers will not need to instruct children, especially young ones, to imitate them, for the children will naturally imitate the teacher. They must see love, respect, consideration, sympathy, cooperation, and other biblical attitudes modeled by significant adults before they will demonstrate the same qualities in their lives. It is within this context that the Word of God becomes vital truth to be lived and not just facts to be learned.

Teachers who communicate to a child that he is not expected to achieve—that he is indeed expected to fail, to misbehave, and to make a general nuisance of himself—will probably experience the self-fulfilling prophecy. Children discern teacher expectations and often live up—or down—to them. Love "beareth all things, believeth all things, hopeth all things, endureth all things" (1 Cor. 13:7), even of the most discouraging, difficult, and demanding child.

THE LEARNER MAY BE A SIGNIFICANT PROBLEM

Perhaps the reader is exclaiming, "Well, at last! We are finally getting to the crux of the problem in classroom management—the learner!" Yet as we recognize that problem learners have a significant part in the disruption of the learning environment, let us not forget that we as teachers will ourselves be a significant part of the problem unless we are building classroom management on biblical principles.

The nature of the child has already been discussed. Because the child has been created in the image of God and has been endowed with intellect, emotion, and will by his Creator, he is a spiritual being who is capable, following redemption, of making God-honoring choices. Even the unsaved child can make choices in accord with biblical truth. However, all children will inevitably make choices that are not in accord with truth, and all children will indeed experience both the constructive and the destructive influences of their environment. They are not immune to them. Consequently, classroom management is necessary.

In discussing the learner as a significant problem in classroom management, a group of public school teachers listed in order of priority those concerns that were representative of the problems discussed in classroom management literature:

1. Individualization. Dealing skillfully with the wide range of abilities found in the average classroom so that the slower students are not still working long after the more able ones are finished. Giving the less able extra help and the more able additional challenge. Using time effectively so that an increased amount of individual help is provided for all students.

2. Developing self direction. Helping students become responsible for their own behavior and completion of assignments. Enabling students to work independently.

3. Motivation. Stimulating students' interest and curiosity in learning so that they will all work close to their capacity.

4. Reaching disruptive students. Helping children who do not seem to care to learn or to cooperate. Changing their negative behavior to positive behavior.

5. Disciplining students. Controlling students in a way that is consistent and positive.[3]

All five of these concerns will be considered later in this chapter under the heading "Principles of Classroom Managing." Concerns one through three will be discussed in that section under the subheading "Principles of Instruction and Nurture." Concerns four and five will be discussed under the subheading "Principles of Correction or Chastening."

---

3. Carl J. Wallen and LaDonna L. Wallen, *Effective Classroom Management* (Boston: Allyn & Bacon, 1978), p. 2.

Classroom management problems do not surface as broad categories, however, but as individual children with behavior problems. Ask a veteran teacher, "In what ways do children disrupt the learning environment?" and he will run out of breath before he will run out of descriptions of disruptive behavior. The list might include the child who seldom does what he is told, the hyperactive wiggler, the "you can't make me" child, the chatterbox, the class clown, the bored child who bothers others, the child who is desperate for any kind of attention, the withdrawn child who never gets involved, the creator of annoying noises or faces, the asocial child who is aggressive, the child who doesn't listen to directions, the immature child who clings or cries easily, the child who constantly introduces ideas extraneous to the discussion, children with short attention spans, the tattler, the child with low self-esteem, and the "octopus" who cannot keep hands and feet to himself.

TABLE 17.1
NEGATIVE INFLUENCES AND THEIR RESULTS

INFLUENCE	RELATED BEHAVIOR OFTEN OBSERVED
1. Malnutrition	Hyperactivity Drowsiness Easy loss of temper Irritability
2. Lack of sleep	Inattentiveness Short attention span Irritability Inability to complete assignments
3. Child abuse or neglect	Withdrawn, sullen Aggressiveness; takes out anxiety on peers and teacher Poor attendance record Excessive seeking of attention
4. Excessive TV viewing	Short attention span Extreme aggressiveness Difficulty in following directions Inability to complete work assignments
5. Violence in the home	Extreme anxiety level Withdrawn and very depressed Poor attendance record Constant seeking of attention

SOURCE: Kevin Sivick, *Disruptive Student Behavior in the Classroom* (Washington, D.C.: National Education Assn., 1980), p. 7.

Churches ministering to inner-city children or to children from lower income or unstable homes may encounter other types of disruptive behavior. Some of these problems cut across economic and social levels, however.

THE HOME MAY BE A SIGNIFICANT PROBLEM

Table 17:1, "Negative Influences and Their Results" makes it apparent that children who live in disruptive homes in which they are abused or neglected may demonstrate disruptive behavior in the classroom. It cannot be assumed that all such homes are non-Christian; even children from Christian homes experience mistreatment. Nor can it be assumed that children from stable homes who receive consistent, loving discipline will never demonstrate disruptive behavior in the classroom.

Some children may be over-indulged and under-disciplined. They expect every whim to be granted and seldom know what it means to be thwarted in doing what they please. Parental indulgence, indifference, and inconsistency may result in a total lack of self-control, extreme self-centeredness, or insecurity on the child's part. This inevitably leads to disruptive behavior when teachers attempt to guide or correct them.

Teachers who acquaint themselves with each child's home can gain insight regarding the child's behavior. They may need to intervene in ways provided by the local law enforcement agencies if they suspect that children are being neglected or abused. Their prayer for the problems of individual children and their loving concern and involvement in the lives of these children can help to curb disruptive behavior patterns. Christian teachers must love not only in word, but in deed, for they can only be used by God to accomplish His purposes when they are willing to count the cost of investing their lives in the lives of those they teach.

PRINCIPLES OF CLASSROOM MANAGEMENT

INSTRUCTION OR NURTURE

It has, of course, been impossible to reach this point without constant reference to the teacher, the one who is responsible for classroom management. The principles of classroom management given thus far relate to instruction and nurture rather than to correction and chastening. The following principles have been suggested:

- Demonstrate unconditional love for each child, even those who seem unlovable, for all are loved by God.

- Respect each child, for he is created in God's image and therefore has dignity and worth.

- Communicate to the child that he is responsible for the choices he makes and is accountable both to God and to the teacher, who is exercising God-given authority (given by God to parents who in turn delegate it to church administrators and teachers).

- Exercise authority in a biblical manner—tempered with love and humility.

- Provide a learning environment that meets the physical and psychological needs of children.

- Demonstrate growth as a teacher by putting teaching-learning principles into practice and improving methodology.

- Undergird preparation for the classroom with specific prayer for the learners.

- Organize learners, materials, and time toward the end of effective learning.

- Know and manifest the truths of 1 Corinthians 13 to the learners.

- Model the truth in attitudes and actions.

- Communicate positive expectations regarding the child's achievement and behavior.

- Become knowledgeable about each child's home background.

- Be ready to invest time, energy, and concern in each child's life, especially those from unstable homes.

These principles emphasize the quality of the interpersonal relationship between the teacher and the children that is so essential. This positive relationship results in meaningful formal and informal instruction in God's Word, for the teacher is always teaching, either directly or indirectly, by word or by deed. It is the actual instruction in the Word of God, discussed throughout this text, that provides the principles of instruction or nurture by which both teacher and learner should govern their thoughts, attitudes, and behavior.

INDIVIDUALIZATION

Christ, our Creator, demonstrated His understanding of individual differences when He distributed amounts of money "to every man according to his ability" in order for each to invest it and to earn more (Matt. 25:14-30). The two who faithfully used their abilities received this commendation from the Lord: "Well done, good and faithful servant." Christ did not demand the same level of performance, but what He did expect was faithfulness in using God-given abilities.

Christian teachers will want to be just as aware of individual differences. Comparisons teachers make that cause pride in more capable learners and a sense of defeat, self-doubt, and self-hatred in less capable ones violate the principle of individual worth and dignity. They foster rivalry with and dislike for those to whom the child is unfavorably compared. Instead, teachers should concentrate on the accomplishments of each, commending what is done well and focusing on what is done correctly, rather than on mistakes. During each session the teacher should praise each child, perhaps for a positive attitude or action, a thoughtful answer, or for doing the work of which he is capable. The teacher should encourage the child to continue striving for improvement in work and behavior when he becomes discouraged, and he should communicate his confidence in the child and recognize with appreciation even the effort toward improvement. All of these things should be done to affirm the child's worth, not to manipulate his behavior. Thus, each child learns how to develop his abilities and to face any limitations realistically. And in the process, behavior usually does improve.

The more capable students need opportunities to use their abilities without feeling they are being penalized by being given more work. Discover their special interests and provide materials that challenge them to explore those interests. (See chap. 13.) The less capable child who truly needs special time and assistance must be given both, and a low teacher-learner ratio enables the teacher to give that needed assistance. Teen helpers rotating in and out of the department on a quarterly basis, or older adults, can provide the required attention.

DEVELOPING SELF-DIRECTION

The child's dependency should gradually be replaced by a growing independence. Control by others should decrease as self-control develops. Learners should assume increasing responsibility for their own work and behavior. Because the Lord requires faithfulness at every level of accountability, it is the teacher's task to assist the child in developing self-direction within the absolutes of Scripture. Even preschool children can manifest independence by getting out materials and putting them away, by using materials properly, and by settling interpersonal problems without the constant intervention of the teacher. Although the younger child makes such choices on the basis of reward and punishment, he is nonetheless learning to make right choices. However, a child should not be expected to perform above his maturity level. Instead of expecting a two-year-old to share, it is better to have enough materials for everyone.

Commend the positive behavior of one child to the others. "Joshua is ready to listen. He is sitting with his legs crossed. His hands are in his lap. Now Marty is ready to listen, too." "Jessica obeyed the Bible words, 'Share what you have,' She gave Rachel a doll." This understanding of expected behavior helps the child in making decisions about his own behavior, and self-direction or discipline develops as the child makes his own decisions and experiences the consequences of those decisions.

As the child understands his increasing responsibility, he must learn to accept it by saying:

1. I am responsible. I have been given a task. I am both able and called to respond.

2. I have freedom to choose. My actions are not caused or predetermined for me.

3. I am accountable. I do not have license to do as I please. There are expectations placed on me, standards with which I am to comply, and structure within which I must perform.[4]

Since children can be accountable when standards are clearly delineated, word standards positively and keep them to a minimum. It is better to develop broad guidelines that can be applied to specific situations, rather than to construct an unending list to cover every possible problem. For example, "Treat others as you want them to treat you," is applicable to every kind of interpersonal problem. Or paraphrase biblical commands that have broad application. "Use your time wisely" (Eph. 5:16). "A soft answer turns away anger" (Prov. 15:1). "Be kind to each other" (Eph. 4:32). Appropriate adult guidance enables the child to consider possible ways to apply standards, and in the process he will learn self-direction or discipline, for he is the one who must evaluate, decide, act, and live with the consequences of decision. Self-control or discipline based on biblical standards leads to the development of Christian character.

MOTIVATION

The biblical and interpersonal principles reviewed at the beginning of this section speak to the teacher's motivation of the learners. The learner is also motivated to learn when he understands the purpose for learning. Learning activities can be fun and have purpose at the same time. Even preschoolers comprehend the importance of learning about God and obeying His Word when truth is applied to specific, concrete life experiences. Older children can explore, with the teacher's guidance, the relevance of biblical truth to their daily lives.

Nothing succeeds like success—success is a motivating factor.

4. Fennema, pp. 70-71.

They learn best when they feel successful as learners, when they have evidence that they are mastering the material taught.

In a teacher-centered class, information passes one way—from teacher to learner. This doesn't give the students a chance to test their learning, to find out if they really understand the truths.

But when students have a chance to participate, they can express their ideas and in this way test their learning. They prove to themselves that they understand.[5]

Interaction not only helps children to test their understanding, but it also reduces behavior problems. However, the teacher must avoid the tendency to interact with some children while ignoring others. Children who feel they are neglected find it difficult to remain interested and may create their own diversion.

Rewards are frequently used in church education not only to motivate learning but also to motivate changes in behavior. This is a basic method of those who espouse behavior modification. The Christian teacher should carefully evaluate Fennema's view of this practice.

There are certain limitations to the using of rewards as motivators which the Christian teacher ought to be aware of. Reinforcement can be disrespectful to the child because it tends to promote dependency. Reinforcement assumes that the child cannot and should not direct his own behavior, that he cannot make good choices once he becomes aware of norms, direction, accountability, goals and mandates from God. Reinforcement can be harmful, first of all, because it tends to endorse unbiblical motivations for conduct. It teaches the instant gratification philosophy of hedonism and the what's-in-it-for-me philosophy of materialism. Reinforcement can be harmful also because it seeks to limit the response of the child rather than to expand it. It seeks to elicit only one response, a response which has been predetermined by another person. God calls for a voluntary and personal response. Creatures who bear the image of the Creator are called to respond in a creative way.[6]

Teachers who implement the instruction and nurture principles in order to manage the classroom effectively should have no great difficulty in motivating learners. The teacher's purpose in seeking to manage the classroom effectively is that God will be glorified as children learn and obey His Word. This must also become the purpose of the redeemed child—that his attitudes and conduct will bring glory to his Heavenly Father.

CORRECTION OR CHASTENING

It is inevitable, however, that all children will not respond at all times to the principles of instruction and nurture in classroom management. Since the child

5. Lawrence O. Richards, *Creative Bible Teaching* (Chicago: Moody, 1970), pp. 134-35.
6. Fennema, pp. 24-25.

is a sinner by nature and choice, he will not always make right choices. The teacher must then use correction or chastening principles of classroom management to reach and discipline disruptive or misbehaving students.

Correction or chastening is forward-looking, whereas punishment is backward-looking. The purpose of correction is to direct the child lovingly in the right way. The purpose of punishment is to inflict retribution for wrongdoing. The writer of Hebrews speaks about God's chastening.

> For whom the Lord loveth he chasteneth, and scourgeth every son whom he receiveth. . . . For they [earthly fathers] verily for a few days chastened us after their own pleasure; but he for *our* profit, that *we* might be partakers of his holiness. (Heb. 12:6, 10; italics added)

The Christian teacher seeks to chasten or correct, not to punish. The goal of chastening is not mere outward conformity to established standards, but an inner commitment of the heart and will to obey biblical mandates because it is right to obey.

The teacher who implements the following principles of correction or chastening will be greatly helped to manage the classroom effectively.

- Clarify classroom standards.

- Develop a regular classroom procedure or structure.

- Remember that children do forget at times. Ask, "Which classroom standard (or procedure) did you forget?"

- Determine what can be ignored and what demands attention.

- Be consistent and fair. That is every child's right.

- Encourage children to help each other. Make right behavior everyone's responsibility.

- Reason with the child mature enough to reason.

- Listen oḃ ˙vely to the child's viewpoint.

- Avoid ultimatums and threats.

- Warn regarding the consequences of behavior and then follow through.

- Recognize the difference between firmness and harshness.

- Pray with the child that he will exercise self-control.

- Maintain eye contact.

- Lower your voice rather than raising it.

- Use nonverbal correction. Finger to lips, or pointing to work, arms folded and stern look of disapproval.

- Walk toward the disturbance—do not shout across the room. The problem may be corrected before you arrive. If not, restore order calmly.

- Be aware of changing weather patterns, anticipation of holidays, and other breaks in routine that may affect classroom management.

- Assess the situation, and change plans if following them portends disaster.

- Rearrange seating and explain why.

- Name the child who needs to correct his behavior. "John, do you know what Noah. . . ?"

- Touch the child gently to make him aware that you see his behavior problem.

- Specify the wrong behavior, who is involved, and what they are to do. "Sue and Mary, you cannot talk and listen to directions. Please stop talking and listen."

- Remove the child who persists in misconduct. This may be a temporary removal until he is ready to accept responsibility for his behavior, or it may be removal to sit with his parents.

- Praise the Lord with the child when victory is gained.

- Guide the child in making necessary restitution.

Christian parents must be a part of the correcting and chastening process, yet the teacher sometimes fails to include them. Parents need to view the church as an extended family genuinely interested in their child. In a firm and loving way the parents must make clear to their child that they expect the teacher to inform them of any misconduct. Church policy might be that after one warning an usher will take a primary or junior child to sit with his parents.

Children whose parents do not attend may be assigned to a couple willing to assume this responsibility. The usher may request parents of younger children to go to their child's classroom if a problem persists.

When children understand that the entire church family loves them and wants to see them making right choices and demonstrating responsible behavior, teachers will find that much of the work of managing the classroom effectively has already been accomplished.

Summary

Classroom management involves setting standards and developing a structure that assists children toward self-discipline and growth in Christian character. It is to be built on biblical concepts concerning the nature of the child, the exercise of authority, and right discipline. Effective classroom management can be hindered by inadequate facilities, unprepared teachers, disruptive learners, and problems created by inept parental care and discipline. Classroom management that provides boundaries and organizational structure can overcome these hindrances. It should be guided by principles of instruction or nurture that recognize individual differences and the need for self-direction and motivation in the learner, and by principles of correction or chastening that curb disruptive behavior and promote self-discipline. These principles should focus on future behavior—the commitment to obedience in attitude and action that will bring God glory.

FOR FURTHER READING

Beechick, Ruth. *Teaching Juniors.* Denver: Accent, 1981.

Dobson, James. *Dare to Discipline.* Wheaton, Ill.: Tyndale, 1970.

Dollar, Barry. *Humanizing Classroom Discipline: A Behavioral Approach.* New York: Harper & Row, 1972.

Fennema, Jack. *Nurturing Children in the Lord.* Philadelphia: Presb. & Ref., 1977.

Ginott, Haim G. *Teacher and Child.* New York: Avon, 1972.

Hancock, Maxine. *Confident Creative Children.* Burlington, Ontario: G. R. Welch, 1978.

Jones, Vernon F., and Louise S. Jones. *Responsible Classroom Discipline.* Boston: Allyn & Bacon, 1981.

LaMancusa, Katherine C. *We Do Not Throw Rocks at the Teacher.* Scranton, Pa.: International Textbook, 1967.

Marshall, Hermine H. *Positive Discipline and Classroom Interaction.* Springfield, Ill.: Charles C. Thomas, 1972.

Meier, Paul D. *Christian Child Rearing and Personality Development.* Grand Rapids: Baker, 1977.

Narramore, Bruce. *An Ounce of Prevention.* Grand Rapids: Zondervan, 1973.

Richards, Lawrence O. *Creative Bible Teaching.* Chicago: Moody, 1970.
Sivick, Kevin. *Disruptive Student Behavior in the Classroom.* Washington, D.C.: National Education Assn., 1980.
Wallen, Carl J., and LaDonna L. Wallen. *Effective Classroom Management.* Boston: Allyn & Bacon, 1978.

18

*Richard E. Troup and
J. Omar Brubaker*

Recreation and Camping for Children

- **Recreation**
  WHAT RECREATION IS
  HISTORY
  VALUE
  SCRIPTURAL BASIS
  MEETING AGE-GROUP NEEDS
  KINDS OF RECREATION
  PLANNING FOR RECREATION
  KINDS OF PARTIES AND PICNICS
  PLANNING CHILDREN'S PARTIES
  PICNICS
  GAME LEADERSHIP
  RESOURCES
  ORGANIZATION, ADMINISTRATION, AND SUPERVISION
- **The Christian Camp**
  WHY CAMP?
  WHY CHILDREN'S CAMP?
  KINDS OF CAMPS
  PLANNING A CHILDREN'S CAMP
  LEADERSHIP FOR CHILDREN'S CAMPS

RICHARD E. TROUP, M.R.E., is associated with the Denver Technical Center, Denver, Colorado.
J. OMAR BRUBAKER is professor of Christian education, Moody Bible Institute, Chicago, Illinois.

RECREATION

Children have a great amount of free time. Even after they enter first grade, school involves only about thirty hours a week. A child's afternoons, early evenings, Saturdays, and Sundays are normally his to use as he wants.

Much of his free time, however, may be under the secularizing influence of non-Christian friends or adults, television, clubs, or other groups. One way in which churches can counteract those influences is by a program of meaningful leisure and recreational activities.

WHAT RECREATION IS

Recreation usually occurs during one's leisure time when he is free from his occupation or work, after the practical necessities have been met. Webster defines recreation as "a means of refreshment or diversion." Recreation is enjoyable, pleasureful, and can be free from financial involvement. It restores the body or mind, recreates, and refreshes.

A functional definition of recreation is, "a voluntary activity or experience which one pursues in his leisure time and which brings personal satisfaction and enjoyment." Meyer, Brightbill, and Sessoms indicate nine basic characteristics of recreation: (1) it involves activity; (2) it has no single form; (3) it is determined by motivation; (4) it occurs in unobligated time; (5) it is entirely voluntary; (6) it is universally practiced and sought; (7) it is serious and purposeful; (8) it is flexible; (9) it has by-products.[1] One little boy said recreation is "what you do when you don't have to."

Recreation for children will vary according to individual interests, needs, and capacities. Those who conduct recreation activities with children must recognize these variations and not force every child into the same program. For recreation to refresh, build up, and encourage happy and worthwhile experiences, individualization is important.

HISTORY OF RECREATION

The outlook on recreation has changed considerably over the years. From the earliest times, man has had leisure moments in which he has engaged in pottery making, sculpture, painting, music, drama, and athletics. In Bible times, much recreational benefit came from various feasts and festivals of the Jewish people. During the Middle Ages, contests and tournaments were held by the knights. The Renaissance created new interest in the great works of art and literature from the Roman and Grecian empires. In Colonial America, recreation was not held in high esteem. In fact, idleness was associated with

---

1. Harold Meyer, Charles Brightbill, and Douglas Sessoms, *Community Recreation: A Guide to Its Organization,* 4th ed. (Englewood Cliffs, N.J.: Prentice-Hall, 1969), pp. 34-38.

evil, loose morals, and personal degeneration. It should be recognized that there was a recreational value in working together. In spite of the general feeling in that era, individuals participated in sleigh rides, skating, outings in parks, circuses, taffy pulls, and the like.

The twentieth century has brought about drastic changes in recreation. The industrial revolution, affluence, urbanization, and travel have allowed more time and opportunity for leisure and recreation. Tourist trade has become a major economic pursuit. A return to the artistic and cultural values, the linkage of recreation with education and spiritual goals and programs have been some of the underlying elements in the growing concern for recreation.[2]

The National Recreation and Park Association (formerly known as the National Recreation Association) was established in 1906. The scouting movement, Campfire Girls, YMCA and YWCA, and other service organizations have all contributed to recreation.

For today's children, recreation has become an integral part of life. As we view the future, the problems in providing worthwhile recreation may increase in volume and depth. Parents and leaders in churches have the responsibility to meet the needs of children in recreation and to guide them in the wise use of leisure time.

VALUES OF RECREATION

Much value can be derived from recreation, with fellowship being basic. Tensions can be released and excess energies used in worthwhile ways. Children can be taught how to be good sports in various activities, and individual skills may be developed and improved through recreation. Children need to learn to relate to others on the playground as well as in the classroom or home. Creativity can be encouraged and developed, and new ways of doing can be introduced. One of the outstanding benefits of recreation is to develop character. It has been said that "children work at their play." Through a constructive and well-planned recreational program, children can learn to enjoy making the best use of time. The challenges for effective teaching in natural settings are unlimited for leaders and teachers of children.

SCRIPTURAL BASIS OF RECREATION

Sometimes Christians develop a list of dos and don'ts but fail to apply Scripture in considering recreation as part of the development of the total personality. Psalm 122:1 should apply to our total church program: "I was glad when they said unto me, 'Let us go to the house of the Lord' " (NASB).

2. Richard Kraus, *Recreation Today: Program Planning and Leadership* (New York: Appleton-Century-Crofts, 1966), pp. 3-27.

Proverbs 17:22 tells us, "A merry heart doeth good like a medicine." In Ecclesiastes 3:1-8, we note there is a time for everything. Christ developed as a total person "in favour with . . . man" (Luke 2:52). He told His disciples, "Come away yourselves to a lonely place and rest awhile (Mark 6:31, NASB). Paul used the athletic contest as an analogy to the Christian life (1 Cor. 9:24-27). Timothy was instructed, "Bodily exercise is all right" (1 Tim. 4:8, TLB).

Though no specific Scripture states, "Thou shalt have recreation," we must be aware that man is a total personality and a social as well as a spiritual being. Children need to develop wholesome attitudes toward life and a broad perspective on the whole of life.

MEETING AGE-GROUP NEEDS

Many of the needs of children can be met in recreation if we select activities according to several principles:

1. Provide opportunity to develop the physical life normally and naturally.
2. Emphasize balance between active and quiet activities and between indoor and outdoor activities.
3. Use variety in activities with short duration according to the attention span.
4. Provide activities that are purposeful and lead to a learning experience.
5. Select activities that meet the need of particular age levels.
6. Give adequate adult supervision in *all* activities.
7. Set a good example to follow.
8. Give careful, clear directions; if necessary, demonstrate what to do.
9. Provide opportunities for use of imagination and creative expression.
10. Enlist youthful and fun-loving leaders who are able to relate to children.

A thorough understanding of the characteristics and needs of children is basic to a successful recreation program. (Chaps. 3-10 present the characteristics and needs of children.) Only as the nature and needs of children are understood can the best kinds of recreational activities be selected in developing well-rounded personalities.

KINDS OF RECREATION

Recreation is as diversified as the individuals who participate. Below are some of the general categories with specific activities which may be used in recreation with children.

Social Recreation

Parties	Games-outdoor	Eating together
Games-indoor	relays	banquets
icebreakers	races	desserts
musical chairs	tag	picnics
table games		potlucks
writing games		progressive dinners
musical		

Outdoor Recreation

Nature activities	Sports	fishing
bird walks	badmiton	horseback riding
field trips	baseball	hunting
hiking	basketball	lawn darts or "jarts"
scavenger hunts	bicycling	skating
Camping	boating	snow activities
day	climbing	swimming
resident	croquet	volleyball
trip		
weekend		

Cultural and Creative Recreation

Drama	Literature	Arts and crafts
charades	choral speaking	cartooning
pageants	poems	ceramics
pantomimes	Scripture reading	drawing
play readings	story hour	jewelry craft
plays	story reading	junk crafts
puppets	Audiovisual	metal craft
role plays	films	mounting
shadow plays	filmstrips	painting
story plays	TV	papercraft
tableaux	videocassettes	printing and
Storytelling		lettering
humorous		woodcraft
sacred		
seasonal		
secular		

Hobbies			
collecting	creating	doing	learning
by age	creative writing	games	field trips
by composition	drama	photography	museums
by colors	music	sports	reading
by design	sewing	taking trips	
by shapes	woodworking		

The interests, abilities, and needs of children are significant factors to be considered in selecting recreational activities. Focus must be on the children as individuals. Activities that are above the children's level of comprehension or are too difficult for them to perform should be avoided due to frustration, discouragement, and failure.

PLANNING FOR RECREATION

In planning recreational activities, six basic questions need to be answered:

Who: the people involved in the activity, their characteristics, needs, interests, and capacities
What: the type of activity, the theme, or main emphasis of the activity
Why: the specific, clearly stated purpose or aim for the activity
When: the month, day, year, hours for the activity
Where: the location and directions on finding the location
How: the outline, plan, and arrangement of the program; what is to be done, the activities, methods, materials, time schedule, and leadership needed

KINDS OF PARTIES AND PICNICS

A well-developed program of recreation for children may include the following kinds of parties and picnics:

Seasonal. Children enjoy attending parties at Halloween, Christmas, Easter. This give opportunities to reach unchurched neighborhood children and to teach children of believers the true meaning of special days.

Birthday. A large children's department could have a monthly party for those with birthdays that month. Some churches have a once-a-year birthday to celebrate all the children's birthdays for that year. For such an annual event, it is best to choose a month when no regular holiday exists, such as January.

Special emphases. If many children are gone for the summer, plan a "before-you-leave" party in the spring or a "welcome back" September party.

PLANNING CHILDREN'S PARTIES

Successful parties can be planned by applying these ideas:

1. Plan each social around an interesting theme, with each phase of the party coordinated into this theme.
2. Vary the time and place of the activity from month to month, according to the season of the year and the theme selected.
3. Rotate the responsibility of social chairman. This will help assure new and fresh ideas.

4. Use a variety of promotional media, such as postcards, brochures, bulletin boards, skits, and puppets.
5. Plan decorations that are not expensive but relate creatively to the theme.
6. Use a variety of games, including opening ice-breaking games, more active games (perhaps of a partner or team variety), and transitional games of a quieter nature (perhaps while seated in a circle).
7. Have a brief devotional period, if appropriate, while the group is still seated in the circle for the last game or while the children are seated at tables. Correlate the devotional to the theme.
8. Relate refreshments to the theme. Also, at each social, have a different committee or person plan the refreshments in order to avoid having the same things repeatedly.
9. Be sure that clean-up responsibilities are delegated.
10. Send invitations to the visitors who were present, encouraging them to attend other activities of the church.[3]

To avoid duplication and to coordinate activities, it is helpful for the children's leaders to plan a year's social activities together. A typical once-a-month program schedule might look like this:

September:	Welcome-back party
October:	Halloween party
November:	Trip to museum, zoo; special event
December:	Christmas party
January:	All-church, all-age social (birthdays)
February:	Valentine party
March:	Teacher's institute picnic
April:	Easter (vacation) party
May:	Before-you-leave party
June:	Sunday school picnic
July:	Family Independence Day camp
August:	Beach party

PICNICS

1. *Annual picnic.* Many churches have an all-church picnic with separate activities for each department. Larger churches may have several picnics, each for a separate department.

2. *Holidays.* Obtain a public school calendar and plan an outing on the date of the teachers' institute or convention. A long holiday weekend makes an

---

3. Richard E. Troup, "Church Recreation for Adults," in *Adult Education in the Church,* ed. Roy B. Zuck and Gene A. Getz (Chicago: Moody, 1970), p. 207.

ideal time for a children's all-day field trip with a picnic. Other long weekends from which to choose are Labor Day, Lincoln's birthday, Washington's birthday, Memorial Day, Independence Day.

3. *Regular day, plus.* A teacher may wish to have a picnic breakfast on a Sunday morning with his class at a picnic site, returning to the church in time for Sunday school or the morning service. Others may prefer a Sunday afternoon picnic right after church. Or a picnic could be held on a weekday immediately before the regularly scheduled, weekday club activities, with the meeting being held outdoors. The picnic may replace the club activities for that one week.

GAME LEADERSHIP

All leaders in recreation will have opportunity to lead games. For each game, they need to be familiar with the basic rules and how to explain the game to children. Thorough preparation for the game enables them to lead it smoothly, efficiently, and flexibly. Also, better control of the group is possible, and discipline problems may be avoided or kept to a minimum. Leaders should be so familiar with the games that they can be absorbed in leading and enjoying them without undue concern for technique. Many leaders find it helpful to write the steps of the game on a three-by-five-inch card.

The following questions will assist the leaders in evaluating themselves regarding their game leadership:

Did I know my group in selecting the game?
Was I familiar with the basic rules and regulations?
Did I prepare the best room arrangement?
Were necessary equipment and materials available?
Did I secure the attention of the entire group before trying to explain the game?
Did I name the game?
Were my explanations clear and concise?
Did I demonstrate the steps in logical order?
Did I answer questions to clarify and correct mistakes?
Was the game concluded while interest was high?
Did the group enjoy the game?
What changes would I make if I were to lead the game again?

RESOURCES FOR CHILDREN'S RECREATION

Church libraries are expanding to include more than books and periodicals. Projected materials, catalogs of sources, packets and notebooks or file cabinets of visual nonprojected aids, mimeographed items, and pamphlets are changing many church libraries into full Instructional Materials Centers (IMC).

The recreation section of an IMC could include materials in the categories suggested earlier in this chapter under "Kinds of Recreation." At the end of each quarter, any new materials purchased by the children's agencies should be turned in to the IMC, filed by topic, to be used as often as needed.

Community resources include such places as public libraries, museums, park district headquarters, schools, and bookstores.

ORGANIZATION, ADMINISTRATION, AND SUPERVISION OF RECREATION

Successful recreation programs do not just happen! Careful planning, prayer, and work are essential. *Organization* is the first step—planning the program, schedules, and activities. *Administration* is related to carrying out the plans the leaders have made. Administration is organization in action. In organization, we plan the work, and, in administration, we work the plan. Personnel, buildings and equipment, finances, and publicity are vital areas to consider in administration. *Supervision* has to do with building a quality staff and program. In supervision, we are concerned with training, guiding, counseling, developing effective human relations, and evaluating.

Here are some general principles in organizing, administering, and supervising recreation for children:

1. Plan the program with the children's needs in focus.
2. Set realistic goals which can be accomplished.
3. Begin with fewer activities and expand as needs emerge.
4. Make long-range plans. Schedule activities on a calendar and correlate them with activities in the total church program.
5. Discover and enlist those who have potential in leadership.
6. Provide training for workers to assist them in developing leadership ability.
7. Provide sufficient housing, equipment, and materials to do the work.
8. Make funds available through the church budget or other means.
9. Publicize recreation activities well in advance and in various ways.
10. Evaluate the program periodically to determine strengths and needs for improvement.

The above principles can be stated in question form to serve as criteria for evaluating recreation for children.

Recreation programs can be carried on through Sunday school classes or departments, clubs, vacation Bible school, or camp. The board of Christian education or children's division committee may supervise and guide recreation, but specific activities will be conducted by those who work with children.

If a local church has no recreation program for children, it may begin small, but it should begin. Even a biweekly hobby club led by the pastor or a Sunday school teacher is a step in the right direction.

A church may evaluate its situation by asking these questions: How many children are now attending our church activities? How many are within walking distance of our church building? How do these children spend their after-school hours? What are their interests and desires?

If a church does not have a ball field, gymnasium, or game area, it may consider using a nearby field, hall, or public park.[4]

Persons who are not Bible teachers or public speakers could possibly function as leaders or helpers for games, sports, or crafts. Many high schoolers and college-age youth can be trained, supervised, and utilized with great effectiveness.

After school is often a good time for a recreational program. Having activities then will not pressure the child or invade the evening hours when family, school, and usual church activities already function.

Few churches have a consistent program of recreation for boys and girls. Only a few of these programs are developed with distinctively Christian purposes in mind. Weekday club activities help add a recreational dimension.

Too many of the adults involved with children in recreational activities have a guilty conscience. They feel they are not engaged in a legitimately "spiritual" activity. However, as those adults recall their childhood, they must admit that many of their warmest recollections are of recreational activities. Often the adults who made the deepest impression on them are those who were involved with them in fun times. This underscores the fact that Christ-centered recreation is one of the most productive areas of the church's ministry.

THE CHRISTIAN CAMP

Camping is one of the church's most effective programs for accomplishing its biblically developed objectives. It offers a well balanced program of teaching, worship, fellowship/recreation, and expression.

WHY CAMP?

Evangelism, Christian commitment, Christ-centered character development, vocational direction from the Christian perspective, Spirit-led person-to-person relationships, skills for practical Christian living—all these are developed in children through Christian camping to an extent that exceeds many, if not all, other ministries of the local church.

Evangelism. "Camp's great! Not only did I have fun here and make a lot of friends, but I learned about God and accepted Christ as my personal Savior." This is a typical response of many boy and girl campers! The pastor of the largest church of his denomination reported that every one of the teenagers

---

4. For excellent suggestions on ways to utilize limited facilities, see Edward L. Hayes, "Recreational Activities," in *Youth and the Church*, ed. Roy G. Irving and Roy B. Zuck (Chicago: Moody, 1968), p. 250.

who had joined the church during that year had trusted Christ as Savior at their camp.

A large Arizona conference grounds, with a highly developed evangelistic program featuring several directly evangelistic services in its chapel each day, reported that one out of ten campers received Christ as Savior. Later, this conference developed a pioneer satellite camp, featuring trained counselors who directed a smaller number of campers in a decentralized activity program. An average of one salvation response was reported by each counselor for every six campers. This program included no chapel services, no professional Bible teacher, and no overtly evangelistic outreach. Instead, the emphasis was on personal influence and guidance, with open Bible discussions, led by the counselor, with his handful of junior or junior high campers drawn from churched homes.

Challenge to Christian service. An evangelical denomination of more than one thousand churches has reported that more of its pastors responded to God's will to enter the ministry in a summer camp than in any other setting. An independent mission society serving in the Orient discovered that more of its personnel felt called to missionary service in a camp than through any other means.

Christian growth. Few camps make an attempt to determine how Christian attitudes and habits are developed within their programs. A survey in one liberal denomination disclosed that, of those persons who had attended camp, 87 percent felt that they had had a "rich and lasting experience," the best proportionate response to any activity except "ecumenical" meetings, and double or triple the response to its traditional agencies of Christian education.

Richard Doty did extensive evaluation of character development in a camp and reported exceptional levels of growth when specific goals are aimed for with measurable techniques.[5] Christ-centered camping has yet to develop such tools, but, even so, increasingly greater results are evident.

Some of the changes experienced in campers' lives include dishonesty being replaced with honesty, reliance on parents' directions for religious habits giving place to a direct response to God, mechanistic conformity to church rules yielding to a Spirit-produced morality. One camper said, "At Sunday school they teach you about these things, but at camp they expect you to do them."

WHY CHILDREN'S CAMP?

Families, senior adults, as well as teens can benefit tremendously from Christ-centered camping. But camps for children have their own distinctive values in addition to those values mentioned earlier for all camps.

Christian peer relationships. Many children ages six through eleven uncon-

5. Richard S. Doty, *The Character Dimension of Camping* (New York: Association, 1960), p. 15.

sciously pass judgment on their peers, thereby excluding those whom they dislike and even hate.

Proper relationships with peers can be encouraged and developed in a Christian camp. To help accomplish this, the camping program for elementary children should be built around the cabin group of four to seven campers. As the counselor and his cabin or tent group spend time together, the campers can learn to function in a Christ-centered way. This kind of opportunity for building Christ-honoring attitudes toward peers is unique to camping.

Christian intergenerational relationships. Few children have a relationship with an adult in which each has the opportunity to discover the personality and ability of the other and to relate to the other within a mutually accepting and supporting Christ-centered spirit. Even Christian parents often find it difficult to develop such a relationship with their children.

Most elementary teachers in secular schools are not Christians, and those who are believers are prohibited by law from functioning in the classroom as Christian leaders. This makes it difficult—if not impossible—for the public school to develop Christian adult-child relationships. This is frequently a problem also in the typical Sunday school class because of time limitations.

Many elementary education classes are taught by women. A boy can go from kindergarten through grade six without ever having a male teacher, much less a Christian father-hero-model figure. Whenever dedicated Christian men are used in junior boys' camps, they can have an unusual impact on young boys' lives.

Christian skill development. "What did you do to our son?" This question stopped the camp director in his tracks. Then he breathed with relief and thanksgiving as the parents continued, "We sent you a boy and you returned to us a man."

After camp, a boy spent a Saturday afternoon chopping up a fallen tree into fireplace-size pieces and stacking them in a neat pile—without even being asked. Before camp, however, he had detested his parents' requests to help with the woodchopping. When another junior returned from a wilderness camp, he proudly told his mother, "Mom, at camp I learned to pray on my own."

How to enjoy the Bible, how to share with others what Christ means to them, how to trust the Lord in difficult times—these are some of the many Christian skills children can learn at camp.

KINDS OF CAMPS

At least six kinds of camps are possible with children.

1. *Trip camping.* Campers travel by bus or van from site to site. (It is usually best not to travel by car because of the cost, insurance problems, not enough drivers, etc.) Because of the tedium of travel for children, this type of camp is

normally not used extensively with boys and girls.

One camp in Arizona has a modified trip camp which includes juniors. The week is divided between two sites, with the camp moving in the middle of the week to the second location by bus. When state and national parks and forests are used for trip camping, tents are needed for sleeping, and a mobile kitchen and supply trailers complete the facilities.

2. *Trail camping.* On foot, bike, minibike, horse, or canoe, the trail moves as a trip camp does, except that it goes by "camper power." An advantage of both trail and trip camping is that expensive facilities are not needed.

Public lands contain thousands of miles of developed trails. A topographical or "quad" map, such as those published by the U.S. Geological Survey (normally available at office supply stores, blueprint stores, or camping stores), indicates foot trails by single dotted lines or jeep trails by double dotted lines. These maps are ready-made for rough trail hikes.

Children enjoy backpack camping as a family, with mother and father doing most of the detailed planning, carrying, cooking, and shelter construction.

Though most camps do not provide this type of program for children, some trail camps are conducted for older juniors who are involved in outdoor skill achievement through an organized boys' or girls' weekday club program.

3. *Weekend camping.* Campsites are increasing rapidly, with facilities for year-round camping. By including winter and spring school vacations plus long weekends, a camp can add up to one hundred days to its ninety-day summer season.

Family weekends, couples' conferences, and leadership workshops are naturals for this off-season thrust. Children can participate as they come with adults to the above kinds of camps. The camp can provide separate activities for children, and they sleep in the same cabin with their parents at night. Father-son and mother-daughter outings or weekends are other options.

Church organizations for older children can include a carefully structured twenty-four-hour weekend camp as a highlight of its activities. The time of year should be chosen carefully so that weather and activities will not be overly strange to the campers. If the church is located in a city where January weather is sunny and gets up to eighty degrees, and the desired campsite usually has snow and below-zero temperatures in January, then the weekend "campspiration" should be scheduled two or three months later. A church with an evangelistic children's club outreach may offer such a twenty-four-hour outing as a reward for children who have earned points by attending regularly, bringing visitors, and memorizing Scripture verses and songs.

4. *Family camping.* In a family camp, children attend with their parents as family groups. Long weekends are desirable for family camps. All (or most) activities are conducted by families. At mealtimes, one or two families are seated at each table; table devotions are led by the parents; family Bible studies are conducted, using special resources provided. Depending on the ages and

number of children, activities may include swimming, with parents responsible for their children; crafts; table games; hikes by families; and even tournaments, with family units or with representatives competing, such as father-son Ping-Pong doubles and four-member-family volleyball. Separate game sessions may be conducted for children, while other camp sessions are held for youth and adults.

A growing number of campgrounds are providing this kind of camping for families who are not attending the traditional summer Bible conference with its age-segregated meeting-oriented program. A church can rent facilities and operate its own program with a full family emphasis or an age-level conference or an adaptation of the two.

A church in Phoenix had such an enthusiastic response to such a ministry during the week including Independence Day, that the Sunday services at the church were canceled and the services were held at the campgrounds.

5. *Day camping.* This is one of the most rapidly expanding outreaches of today's aggressive church. Day camping is ideal for primaries and juniors and can also be used occasionally for four- and five-year-olds.

In contrast to traditional resident camps, a day camp operates only during daylight hours, with the exception of youth day camps held in the evenings or an overnight special event toward the end of a day-camp period for older children.

Children usually bring their own bag lunch, and the camp provides the drink for lunch and treats for midmorning and/or midafternoon. With no sleeping or eating facilities needed, the costs are held down, so that this type of camp can be not only financially self-supporting but in some cases can even provide a source of income to the director or sponsoring agency.

Some churches hold day camp at their church site. Other day camps are held at city parks or on lawns of large residences (be sure to check with neighbors and to check on insurance, rest-room facilities, etc.) or county or state forests, meeting each day at the same location or rotating between several locations.

Some resident camp properties were originally located too close to towns, but what has handicapped outdoor camping now becomes an open door to converting all or part of the grounds to a day camp.

In some areas special day camp facilities are being developed where farmland or county park areas are available. If children meet at a city location (such as the church building) the day-camp site should be no more than a thirty- to forty-five minute bus ride away. A church that meets near an expressway may find within twenty-five miles a highly usable site or a variety of sites.

Vacation Bible school materials may often be easily adaptable to day camp for Bible study, crafts, and game times. Curricular materials for day-camp use are being published by the Southern Baptist Sunday School Board.

What are the values of day camping? Two pastors, Dale Cowling, of Little

Rock, Arkansas, and W. A. Criswell, of Dallas, Texas, cite advantages of their day camping:

> Our day camping program gives our church a two-fold opportunity: (1) it enables us to do an intensive job of character building in lives of boys and girls, relating them to God through normal experiences in the out-of-doors; (2) it provides an opportunity for graduating high school students and college students to minister through small group involvement to boys and girls of unstable background.

> Our church uses day camping to share Christ and develop Christian character in campers and counselors. This year we had forty decisions for Christ the first eight days of camp. Day camping has become an indispensable part of our church program.[6]

6. *Resident camping.* Overnight camps, lasting from five full twenty-four-hour periods to as long as a full summer-long session of ten weeks (with the summer's first weeks for staff training), have been a part of the church's ministry for a century. Usually age-graded, separate sessions are held for juniors, children who have completed school grades four to six.

Often separate sessions are conducted for boys and girls, but successful coed junior camps are common. Segregation by sex is determined by whether the other church agencies provide adequate association in coed or boy-girl groupings.

Some camps do not accept campers until they have completed grade five, unless they have been active in church weekday clubs during grade four. Some camps combine third and fourth graders into one camping program and fifth and sixth graders into another.

Rather than one large, junior boys' camp one week of the summer (along with other one-week single age-group sessions), some camps are developing summer-long programs (or at least several weeks) for one age or several ages.

Instead of two hundred junior boys in one mass program, utilizing all facilities for one week, and two hundred girls the next, a camp could take fifty juniors a week for eight weeks. Some campers would want to come for two-week periods and would be housed and led in separate subunits. Thus the same two hundred campers might involve two hundred and fifty camper weeks.

Living facilities would need to be separated from those of other older ages because of the difference in rising hours (juniors later) and lights out (juniors earlier), rest hour after lunch (longer and quieter for juniors), and activity period lengths (shorter for juniors with less free time between).

Meeting rooms, dining rooms (or subdivisions of a room by planters, screens, folding walls, etc.), outdoor activity areas (softball; volleyball; individ-

6. *Day Camping*, brochure, Baptist Sunday School Board, Nashville, Tenn., p. 4.

ual games, such as tetherball; swimming; crafts; archery; riflery, etc.) can be assigned to various groups or ages sharing the grounds. Otherwise the facilities can be used on a rotating basis: for example, juniors may eat at 11:15, teens at 12:00 noon, and families at 12:45; juniors may be in chapel at 10:00, while teens are in cabin Bible study and family camp is using the activity area.

Principles of camp programming[7] true for all ages need to be adjusted to the needs of younger campers. Growing bodies need longer periods of rest at night and after lunch. The menu in a junior camp will contain different vegetables, desserts, and hot drinks, more milk, and less salads than a teen or adult camp. The intensity of the spiritual thrust will be geared to the emotional level of children as well as to their less developed spiritual concepts.

It is generally best to have one counselor for every four children in an activity camp and one for every seven in a conference camp. Counselors need to be especially aware of the needs of the children nearing adolescence, some of whom are already involved in adolescent-level questions.

Sixteen- and seventeen-year-olds make effective children's camp counselors if they (1) are experienced campers; (2) are proved leaders in church club programs or youth groups; (3) possess unquestionable references from pastor, teacher, and parent; (4) have received a week of on-site camp leadership training; (5) are in a camp with continuing in-service training and counselor supervision; and (6) can be given a two-hour duty-free rest period each day completely apart from camper observation. These young people should be especially mature socially and emotionally.

A number of experimental camps are being conducted for children. Under adequate controls, where there is a reasonable hope for success and almost no possibility for any harm, a church or camp could try some "growing edge" camping. A Rhinebeck, New York, secular camp conducted a two-week trial session for ten metropolitan New York children under the age of six from deprived homes. The director was assisted in the specialized program by fourteen counselors.

Each Monday of July and August, five boys of elementary age were driven from the Phoenix inner city to the high mountains two hours away. Here a second counselor waited at their tent site to lead them in a five-day unstructured camp of their own planning, scheduling, cooking, and woods-land-mountains-oriented pioneer camp. A similar wilderness camp is held by a Dallas, Texas, church several weeks each summer on an island in Tennessee.

PLANNING A CHILDREN'S CAMP

A successful camp begins with a well-worked-out plan of activities. This schedule should be posted in the leadership room for the camp staff to know

7. See, for example, Joy Mackay, *Creative Counseling for Christian Camps,* chaps. 5-7; Lloyd D. Mattson, *Camping Guideposts,* chaps. 1-4, 8; Floyd and Pauline Todd, *Camping for Christian Youth,* chaps. 16-17.

what is projected. As the week progresses, however, and the weather changes or the spiritual tempo accelerates or slows, the reason for the schedule being written in *pencil* becomes apparent. Planned flexibility is a basic programming principle.

The following are *possible* schedules for three kinds of camps, to be *modified* by the individual camp within legitimate limits.

WEEKEND

FRIDAY P.M.

	4:30	buses leave church building
	6:30	arrive at camp
		bunks assigned
	7:00	supper
	7:30	orientation hike
	8:00	game time
	8:45	campfire
	9:30	fireside devotions
	9:45	clean up for bed
	10:15	cabin sharing
	10:30	lights out (unusually late for children, but acceptable on Friday in a one-night camp)

SATURDAY A.M.

	7:30	rise and clean up
	8:00	breakfast
	8:30	cabin devotions
	9:00	choice of outdoor activities
	10:00	chapel
	10:30	team activities (or by cabin)
	11:30	leisure

SATURDAY P.M.

	12:00	lunch
	12:30	cabin sharing (rest hour)
	1:30	activities
	2:30	all-camp sharing time
	3:00	cabin cleanup, snack
	3:30	bus departs

DAY

9:00   buses leave church building (if buses pick up children at their homes, begin pickups as early as necessary)

9:30	arrive at site
	orientation
9:45	activity 1 (crafts, games, missions project, Bible study)
10:15	activity 2 (same as above or chapel)
10:45	snack time
11:15	activity 3 (same as above or special event)
11:45	cleanup, leisure
12:00	lunch
12:30	planned rest
1:00	activity 4 (slower paced)
1:45	activity 5 and group meeting
2:30	leave site by bus
3:00	return to church building
	staff meeting

RESIDENT

7:00	rise, cleanup
8:00	breakfast
8:30	personal devotions
	cabin cleanup
9:15	activity 1[8]
10:30	activity 2
	(If a chapel is desired, the first activity period may be from 9:15 to 10:15, chapel from 10:15 to 10:45, and activity 2 from 10:45 to 11:45.)
11:45	cleanup
12:00	lunch, and table fun time
1:00	rest hour
2:00	cabin activities
3:30	choice of unstructured activities
5:30	supper
6:30	all-camp special activity[9]
7:30	cabin time—sharing, planning, devotions
8:30	lights out

8. A staff meeting for half the counselors may be held at each of the first two activity periods.
9. The final activity should be varied each day. Normally, each day, provide an all-camp and a cabin (or two-cabin) activity, one of which is spiritual in nature (campfire, testimony meeting, musical program, missions seminar, dedication service) and the other recreational (watermelon hunt, scavenger hunt, treasure hike, moonlight hike without flashlights, wiener and marshmallow roast, skit night, film).

LEADERSHIP FOR CHILDREN'S CAMPS

The single most important element in a successful camp is leadership. *Every* leader must meet basic qualifications, have the special skills required by his position, be trained in camp leadership, have proper orientation to this camp and its distinctives, and be adequately helped throughout the camp.

Table 18:1 shows the basic staff requirements for an ideal-size camp of fifty-six to eighty campers (four pairs of cabins with seven campers each, or eight pairs of five cabins with five campers each).

TABLE 18.1

BASIC STAFF REQUIREMENTS

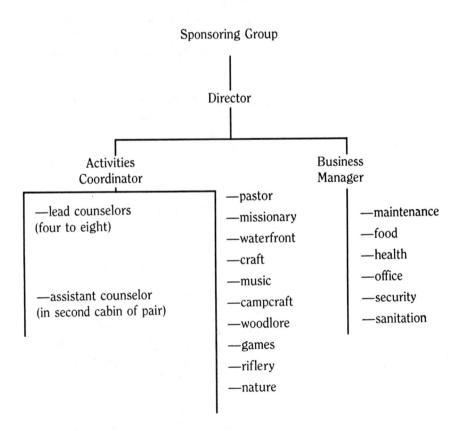

Sponsoring Group	
Director	

Activities Coordinator

—lead counselors (four to eight)

—assistant counselor (in second cabin of pair)

—pastor
—missionary
—waterfront
—craft
—music
—campcraft
—woodlore
—games
—riflery
—nature

Business Manager

—maintenance
—food
—health
—office
—security
—sanitation

Some staff members may hold more than one position, so long as the total staff is at least on a one-to-five ratio with campers.

In order to reach the unsaved, the church must depart from its "Come to our meetings in our buildings at our times and hear the message as we know it and want to define it" format. We need to communicate to our potential "customer" where he is and in the setting he prefers. Outdoor leisure-time settings, involving activities that are fun, offer ideal evangelistic opportunities.

Small groups, unhurried pace, and close relationships with skilled and dedicated leaders all add up to an ideal educational camp setting.

Camping resembles the work of an Evangelist-Educator who taught on a mountainside, who counseled in a boat, who admonished by a campfire, who preached as He led a day's hike to Emmaus. In the name and spirit of Christ, using a setting He loved and mastered, let us adventure outdoors for Christ.

SUMMARY

Childhood education in the church will be greatly enhanced through the ministries of recreational activities and camping. There is a natural appeal to children through fun, games, and activity in a nature setting. These activities can be carried out in connection with many of the church's agencies for ministry to children.

The results will be rewarding as those who participate are refreshed and renewed in mind, body and spirit. Positive attitudes and relationships can be developed. Boys and girls can be glad and enjoy going to the house of the Lord. Children will more likely remember the teachers and leaders who "did stuff" with them. What an opportunity for influencing young lives for the Lord!

FOR FURTHER READING

RECREATION

BOOKS AND ARTICLES

Books on Parks, Recreation and Leisure 1973, 16th ed. Arlington, Va: National recreation and Park Assn., 1973.

Cassendre. *Making All Things Beautiful.* Valley Forge, Pa.: Judson, 1979.

Conner, Ray. *A Guide to Church Recreation.* Nashville: Convention, 1977.

Cox, Claire. *Rainy Day Fun for Kids.* New York: Association, 1962.

Eisenberg, Helen, and Larry Eisenberg. *The Handbook of Skits and Stunts.* Martinsville, Ind.: American Camping Assn., 1984.

Epp, Margaret. *Come to My Party.* Grand Rapids: Zondervan, 1964.

Gale, Elizabeth W. *Children Together.* Vol. 2. Valley Forge, Pa.: Judson, 1980.

Games and Self-Testing Activities for the Classroom. Washington, D.C., U.S. Government Printing Office, 1961.

Gardner, Ann, ed. *The Best of Church Recreation Magazine.* Nashville: Convention, 1982.

————. *The Best of Church Recreation Magazine II.* Nashville: Convention, 1984.

Handbook for Recreation. Washington, D.C.: U.S. Government Printing Office, 1960.

Harbin, E. O. *The New Fun Encyclopedia.* 5 vols. Revised by Bob Sessions. Nashville: Abingdon, 1984.

How to . . . Recreation for the Small Church. Nashville: Convention, 1975.

Jackson, Neil. *How to Organize for Recreation.* Nashville: Convention, 1970.

Kay, Evelyn. *Games That Teach for Children Three Through Six.* Minneapolis: T. S. Denison, 1983.

Kraus, Richard. *Recreation Today: Program Planning and Leadership.* New York: Appleton-Century-Crofts, 1966.

Maness, Bill. *Recreation Ministry.* Richmond, Va.: John Knox, 1983.

McCay, Gracie, and Virginia Sargent. *Children Together.* Vol. 3. Valley Forge, Pa.: Judson, 1985.

Meyer, Harold, Charles Brightbill, and Douglas Sessoms. *Community Recreation: A Guide to Its Organization.* 4th ed. Englewood Cliffs, N.J.: Prentice-Hall, 1969.

Mitchell, Leon. *How to . . . Sports.* Nashville: Convention, 1970.

Mulac, Margaret. *Fun and Games.* New York: Harper, 1956.

————. *Games and Stunts for Schools, Camp, and Playgrounds.* New York: Harper & Row, 1964.

————. *Party Fun for Holidays and Special Occasions.* New York: Harper & Row, 1960.

Myers, Gail Anderson. *A World of Sports for Girls.* Philadelphia: Westminster, 1985.

————. *Fun Sports for Everyone.* Philadelphia: Westminster, 1985.

Opie, Iona, and Peter Opie. *Children's Games in Street and Playground.* London: Clarendon, 1969.

Richart, Genevieve. *The Master Game and Party Book.* Grand Rapids: Baker, 1973.

Smith, Frank Hart. *How to . . . Social Recreation.* Nashville: Convention, 1970.

————. *Reaching People Through Recreation.* Nashville: Convention, 1973.

————. *Social Recreation and the Church.* Nashville: Convention, 1977.

Spiker, Louis. *Children Together.* Vol. 1. Valley Forge, Pa.: Judson, 1982.

Stuart, Sally E. *The All-Occasion Game Book: A How-to Book for Parties and Holidays.* Cincinnati: Standard, 1981.

Wackerbarth, Marjorie, and Lillian S. Graham. *Games for All Ages and How to Use Them.* Grand Rapids: Baker, 1973.
———. *Successful Parties and How to Give Them.* Minneapolis: Denison, 1961.
Yukie, Thomas. *Fundamentals of Recreation.* New York: Harper & Row, 1970.

MAGAZINES

Child Life. 1100 Waterway Boulevard, Indianapolis, IN 46202.
Church Recreation. Department of Church Recreation, Southern Baptist Convention, 127 Ninth Avenue North, Nashville, TN 37203.
Highlights for Children. Highlights for Children, Inc., P. O. Box 269, Columbus, OH 43216.
Pack-O-Fun. 14 Main Street, Park Ridge, IL 60068.
Recreation. National Recreation and Park Association, 1601 North Kent Street, Arlington, VA 22209.

SOURCES OF GAMES AND INFORMATION

American Art Clay Co., Indianapolis, IN 46222.
American Association for Health, Physical Education and Recreation, 1201 Sixteenth St., N.W., Washington, DC 20036.
American Crayon Co., Sandusky, OH 44870.
Awana Youth Association, 3201 Tollview Drive, Rolling Meadows, IL 60008.
Berea College, Berea, KY 40403.
Bible Games, Inc., P. O. Box 1049, Stockbridge, MA 01262.
Burgess Publishing Co., 426 South Sixth Street, Minneapolis, MN 55415.
Christian Service Brigade, Box 150, Wheaton, IL 60187.
Church Drama IDEAS, P. O. Box 1861, Arvada, CO 80001-1861.
Church Recreation Service, Baptist Sunday School Board, 127 Ninth Avenue North, Nashville, TN 37203.
Church Recreation Specialists, 4262 Cadiz, Ft. Worth, TX 76133-9990.
Color-Graphics Division, D. C. Harris Company, Wooster, OH 44691.
Cooperative Recreation Service, Inc., Delaware, OH 43015.
Dennison Manufacturing Co., Framingham, MA 01701.
Flaghouse, Inc., 18 West 18th Street, New York, NY 10011.
Fun Books, 5847 Gregory, Hollywood, CA 90028.
League of Federal Recreation Association, 927 Fifteenth Street, N.W., Washington, DC 20005.
National Association of County Park and Recreation Officials, 1001 Connecticut Avenue, N.W., Washington, DC 20036.
National Recreation and Park Association, 3101 Park Center Drive, Alexandria, VA: 22302.

Pioneer Clubs, Box 788, Wheaton, IL 60187. A Division of Pioneer Ministries.
Pioneer Drama Service, 2172 South Colorado Blvd., Box 22555, Denver, CO 80222.
Rainbow Crafts, Inc., Cincinnati, OH 45212.
World Wide Games, Inc., Box 450, Delaware, OH 43015.

CAMPING

BOOKS AND ARTICLES

Barnett, Timothy L., and Steven R. Flora. *Christian Outdoor Education.* Duluth, Minn.: Camping Guideposts, 1982.
————. *Exploring God's Web of Life: A Handbook for Christian Outdoor Education.* Duluth, Minn.: Camping Guideposts, 1982.
Cowle, Irving M. *Day Camping.* Minneapolis: Burgess, 1964.
Donaldson, George W., and Oswald Goering. *Perspectives on Outdoor Education . . . Readings.* Dubuque, Ia.: Wm. C. Brown, 1972.
Doty, Richard S. *The Character Dimension of Camping.* New York: Association, 1960.
Fabian, Leonard. *The Family Book of Camping.* New York: Stadia Sports, 1973.
Graendorf, Werner, and Jerry Crosby. *Christian Camp Counseling.* Chicago: Moody Correspondence School, 1979.
Graendorf, Werner, and Lloyd Mattson, eds. *Introduction to Christian Camping.* Chicago: Moody, 1979.
Haslam, Larry. *How to . . . Retreats.* Nashville: Convention, 1971.
LaNoue, John. *A Guide to Church Camping.* Nashville: Convention, 1977.
————. *Day Camping Director's Guide.* Nashville: Convention, 1976.
LaNoue, John, and Kaywin LaNoue. *Children's Camp Resource Book: Day Camps and Retreat Camps.* Nashville: Convention, 1976.
Mackay, Joy. *Creative Counseling for Christian Camps.* Wheaton, Ill.: Scripture Press, 1966.
————. *Raindrops Keep Falling on My Tent.* Wheaton, Ill.: Scripture Press, 1972.
Mattson, Lloyd D. *Camping Guideposts.* Chicago: Moody, 1972.
————. *Family Camping.* Chicago: Moody, 1973.
————. *Foul-up or Follow-up?* Wheaton, Ill.: Scripture Press, Victor Books, 1974.
Mattson, Lloyd D., ed. *God's Good Earth—Christian Values in Outdoor Education.* Duluth, Minn.: Camping Guideposts, 1985.
————. *Way to Grow!* Wheaton, Ill.: Scripture Press, 1973.
Mattson, Lloyd, and Elsie Mattson. *Rediscover Your Family Outdoors.* Wheaton, Ill.: Scripture Press, Victor Books, 1980.

Mitchell, Grace L. *Fundamentals of Day Camping.* New York: Association, 1961.

Nelson, Virgil, and Lynn Nelson. *Retreat Handbook: A Way to Meaning.* Valley Forge, Pa.: Judson, 1976.

Reichter, Arlo, et al. *The Group Retreat Book.* Group Books, Loveland, Colo., 1984.

Sanders, Marjorie L. *Getting Away: Resources for Directors of Christian Camps and Retreats.* Nashville: Broadman.

Smith, Frank Hart. *A Guide to Planning and Conducting a Retreat.* Nashville: Convention, 1978.

The Day Camp Director's Package: American Heritage. Nashville: Convention, 1985. Package includes Director's Guide, Counselor's Guide, Unit A, B, and C Camper's Books.

To the Activity Specialist. Wheaton, Ill.: Pioneer Girls, 1964.

Todd, Floyd, and Pauline Todd. *Camping for Christian Youth.* New York: Harper & Row, 1963.

MAGAZINES

Camping Magazine. American Camping Association, Bradford Woods, 5000 State Road 67 North, Martinsville, IN 46151-7902.

Journal of Christian Camping. Christian Camping Int., Box 646, Wheaton, IL 60189.

19

Elsiebeth McDaniel

Child-Care Programs for the Church

- Types of Child-Care Programs
- Reasons for Day-Care Programs
- Basic Considerations
- Characteristics of a Good Program
- Qualifications for Workers
- A Typical Day
- Curriculum
- Parental Involvement
- How Should a Church Begin a Child-Care Program?

In the last twenty years, at least three factors have contributed to the rapid development of child-care programs in the United States. First, Head Start, a government-sponsored program of early childhood education for children in poverty areas, has focused attention on the needs of young children. Second, the growing number of working mothers has emphasized the need for child care. And third, research in human development has revealed that the first four or five years of life are the period of most rapid physical and intellectual growth and that quality care during those years is therefore very important.

ELSIEBETH McDANIEL, M.A., is director of early childhood publications, Scripture Press Publications, Inc., Wheaton, Illinois.

The number of working mothers in the United States has more than doubled in the last twenty years. In 1982 there were 6 million mothers working outside their homes. In 1983 there were "8.5 million children under six whose mothers [were] in the work force. . . . By 1990 it's predicted that half of all preschool children, or 11 million, will have mothers in the work force."[1] Yet, though mothers are solving financial problems and perhaps fulfilling their own need to make contributions to society beyond that of a homemaker, they are creating other problems. The most common problem is that of finding adequate day care for their children. It has been stated that the "supply of child care lags so far behind the need that as many as 6 to 7 million children 13 years old and younger, including many preschoolers, may go without care for significant parts of each day while their parents work."[2] In every community the number of children who must fend for themselves is growing. Perhaps most of the children needing day care are from the inner city, but many small town and suburban communities are also interested in day care.

Day-care centers and nursery schools do far more than solve the working mother's problem. Good day-care centers and nursery schools provide a child with many learning experiences during his most impressionable years. A good day-care facility gives a child more than custodial care. It is also dedicated to the development of vigorous minds and bodies.

It should be understood that a day-care center is not a substitute for a strong family life. The vast majority of children are better off in the care of their own parents twenty-four hours a day whenever possible.

However, a day-care program can provide these advantages: (1) intellectual stimulation at the child's level and suited to his capacity; (2) activities that promote healthy physical growth; (3) opportunities for maximum social growth in relationship to adults and other children; (4) assistance in sound emotional development; and (5) help for each child in building self-confidence and awareness of his unique, creative potential. A church day-care facility also provides spiritual nurture.

TYPES OF CHILD-CARE PROGRAMS

What types of church child-care are available? In the last few years, many churches have begun child-care programs, called either nursery schools, pre-schools, church kindergartens, or church day-care centers. *U.S. News and World Report* observes that "churches operate or provide space for the bulk of

1. Ellen Goodman, "Who Cares?" *Young Children* 38, no. 3 (March 1983): 9, 10. © 1983, Washington Post Writers Group, reprinted by permission.
2. Helen Blank, "The Need to Expand the Dependent Care Tax Credit: An Important Source of Assistance to Many Families," *Young Children* 38, no. 5 (July 1983): 78. Copyright © 1983, by the National Assn. for the Education of Young Children. All rights reserved. Reproduction in whole or in part without written permission is strictly prohibited.

day-care centers and preschools, serving more than 3.5 million children," and it further notes that "the demand is so great for centers that accept infants that some churches let couples reserve spaces even before a baby is born."[3] The conditions the magazine describes reflect the fact that the fastest growing element of child care in the past decade has been the demand for group care for infants and toddlers. The current emphasis on providing for child care in their programs is a significant trend among churches and is evidence of a national concern for young children. Most churches, of course, are challenged by the opportunity to add a spiritual dimension to child care.

Nursery schools, in contrast to day-care centers, are designed for a portion of the day—either five, three, or two mornings or afternoons a week, serving children ages 3-5. Nursery schools are designed to promote experiences manageable by young children. Because it is basically a structured program with planned activities, a shorter time—two or three hours—is advisable. Young children cannot function well in a structured program for a full school day. That is why the day-care center program, often lasting eight or ten hours each day, emphasizes more free play and rest.

Nursery school introduces variety into a child's environment. It expands his horizons and experiences beyond the home. Nursery school supplements the home; it is not a substitute for the home experiences a child and his parents need.

The longer the day for children in group care, the more the program should try to incorporate a homey atmosphere. Both at home and at school, children need opportunities to solve real problems—to learn to cope with one's self, with other children, with adults, with natural environment (the outdoors), and man-made environment (furniture, stairs, and so on).

The church kindergarten is similar to the nursery school. However, a child is usually enrolled for half-day sessions throughout the five-day week. The program is structured with definite physical skills and mental achievements built into its goals. Any church considering a kindergarten needs to be aware of the curriculum offered in public school kindergartens. Church kindergartens should achieve the same educational goals as the secular kindergarten, adding spiritual objectives suitable for this age-level.

The church kindergarten is limited to children who are four or five years of age. Like the church nursery, the kindergarten has special concern for the spiritual growth of the children it serves. Its faculty members, in addition to having teacher certification, should be dedicated Christians. Its curriculum provides opportunities for worship and other experiences that help broaden a young child's spiritual understanding.

3. Jeannye Thornton, "Threading Your Way Through the Preschool Maze," *U.S. News & World Report* (1 Oct 1984), 76.

The church day-care center has a less structured program than either the nursery school or kindergarten. However, it should incorporate the elements of a good preschool in its program, usually in the morning session. Its sessions are five days a week, from early morning till late afternoon, to accommodate the working hours of parents. Though few day-care centers are able to do so, there should be some consideration for school-age children who need supervision before or after school. When possible, these children should come to the church facilities for free play and planned activities.

REASONS FOR DAY-CARE PROGRAMS

What are some of the reasons for day-care centers? In 1981 it was estimated that there were more than 16,000 licensed day-care centers. But the Department of Health and Human Services says that in the same year only about 1.9 million children were enrolled in these centers, whereas over 5 million were cared for in homes by older children, a neighbor, a relative, or in an unlicensed facility. An unlicensed facility often makes little attempt to maintain standards of health and hygiene, to say nothing of offering the children experiences that are mentally, spiritually, and physically stimulating.

There is no doubt that the need for adequate day care can scarcely be overestimated. But in addition to what the secular day-care center offers, the church can reach both the child and the parents with spiritual truth. However, the local church must decide whether child care is a ministry it wishes to undertake. The answer cannot be a simple yes or no. Churches operating day-care centers indicate that there are benefits to the church. But these benefits should be regarded as by-products and not motivating factors for establishing a day-care center. The underlying reason for providing child care should be a ministry to meet crucial human need in the name of Christ.

What are the by-product benefits to the church? One benefit is stronger ties with church families whose children are cared for in the center. Another benefit is a greater Christian influence in the community. One denomination has estimated that 17 percent of the children enrolled in child care eventually came into the church, bringing their families.

Whatever child-care program is undertaken, the ministry should be regarded as an integral part of the church's total program in the same sense as that of the Sunday school or youth program. Not only must the child-care program have facilities and staff, it should also have the united prayer support and interest of the church!

BASIC CONSIDERATIONS FOR A CHILD-CARE PROGRAM

What are some basic considerations for a child-care program? Though additional criteria for evaluating child-care programs appear elsewhere in this chapter, eight basic guidelines are listed here to provide an overview of specifications and considerations for child care:[4]

1. The ratio of children to teacher should be as follows:
   For two-year-olds, three children per teacher
   For three- and four-year-olds, five children per teacher
   For five- and six-year-olds, seven children per teacher
   (Although state guidelines may call for fewer teachers, the ratio presented here is ideal.)
2. Space should include 75 square feet outdoors and 35 square feet indoors for each child.
3. Safety and hygiene considerations should include fire protection, adequate heating and ventilation, lighting, protection from safety hazards, liability insurance, first-aid equipment, clean kitchen facilities and toilets (at least one toilet and wash basin for every 15 children).
4. A medical report for each enrolled child should be required.
5. Both indoor and outdoor play apparatus should include blocks and other toys; raw materials for creative expression—wood, sand, clay, crayons, and paints; an ample supply of books, records, and homemade or manufactured rhythm band instruments.
6. The educational program should have understandable and measurable goals, adapted to the age groups served.
7. Teachers should be well-adjusted personalities with the necessary educational background. They should hold to the same basic beliefs as the church which administers the program.
8. The church child-care center should be especially concerned about parental involvement. If the church neglects communication with parents, it weakens its ministry to parents. More will be said about this later in the chapter.

As indicated earlier, many children not in child-care centers are left to fend for themselves. It is not farfetched to assume that a significant percentage of these children will some day require rehabilitative services, whether by a probation officer, social worker, or psychiatrist. Good care now may reduce costs in the future.

Day care involves children at the most impressionable time of their lives. Caroline Chandler, a medical doctor, recognizes the importance of these early years. She says,

> The early years are important years because on them rests the entire span from childhood to old age. During early childhood, development comes about through

---

4. Adapted from *Some Ways of Distinguishing a Good School or Center for Young Children* (Washington, D.C.: National Assn. for the Education of Young Children).

two processes—maturation and learning. Although learning can be accelerated by people and things in the child's environment, the steps in maturation can be neither telescoped nor skipped. All children go through the same pattern of development even though there may be wide variation in the rate of development among individual children. This holds true for physical and emotional (or personality) development.[5]

Because early childhood years are important, a child must have the best environment possible. For many children, that is the child-care center. Educators are increasingly endorsing day care because of the benefits to the children themselves. Ideally, the mother creates the preconditions for the development of human intelligence, the foundation on which public school education builds. However, not all mothers have the time or inclination for doing this properly, and even those who are expert may need some help. The mothers who would welcome help may find it in the church nursery school or kindergarten.

The need for adequate child care is undebatable! However, the local church must do more than recognize the general need. The church must see its own vision, determine its own dedication, and declare its own involvement.

Does the local church care about day care? The alert and progressive local church cares about day care, because through an adequate program the church can accomplish these goals: (1) guide the child's physical, intellectual, emotional, social, and spiritual growth, (2) make better use of buildings and facilities during the week; (3) reach families for Christ and church membership. Through day care, families will be reached that would never open their doors (and hearts) for any other reason.

CHARACTERISTICS OF A GOOD PROGRAM

What characterizes a good child-care program? Consideration for the physical, mental, emotional, social, and spiritual needs of the young child is more important than church facilities or even the opportunities of counseling with parents. A good child-care program must be geared to the needs and potential development of young children. Though originally designed to care for only the physical needs, current child-care programs seek to become interested in the *whole child.*

Any church contemplating child care must meet state and local regulations. Information is available from each state's Department of Children and Family Services at the state capital or through a regional office. Regulations will specify minimum standards. Some states will also provide budget guides for day-care centers. A state budget guide will suggest the necessary items to be purchased on a limited budget. Other helpful publications, such as suggested

5. Caroline Chandler, "The Importance of the Early Years," *Early Childhood—Crucial Years for Learning* (Washington, D.C.: Assn. for Childhood Education, 1971), p. 3.

menus and lists of free or low-cost materials to equip the center, may be obtained.

The following items must be adequate before a church considers opening a day-care center:

Space: Is there space for running about freely for active play and still other space where quiet play may go on undisturbed, both indoors and out?

Hygiene: Is there adequate and approved fire protection? Are heating facilities adequate and officially approved? Is there protection against drafts?

Equipment: Are there large pieces of apparatus to climb? Are there ample raw materials that will stimulate the child's initiative and self-expression?

Personnel: Are there enough teachers both to guide the group and to take care of individual children's needs?

Method: Is each child helped to gain increasing power in concept development? Instead of always being shown or told, is he encouraged to use materials creatively? Does the teacher realize that patterns to follow or models to copy usually hamper creativity?

Attitudes: Are the teachers well adjusted? Do they realize that human feelings are important? Do they give children a feeling of adequacy, stability, and belonging, without showing favoritism?

> Without question the intangibles for every nursery school or child care center program depend on the quality of the staff—particularly the director. He creates the atmosphere in which the children live and breathe and have their being.
>
> There are clues by which the effects of the "intangible atmosphere" on the children can be measured. Just watch them. Are they absorbed in their activities? Do they behave like people or like puppets awaiting orders? Are their faces alive and expressive or bored and listless? Is there a natural hum of normal activity and conversation or is there the enforced quiet that waits for a pin to drop with a loud clang? Are questions being asked, heard, and honestly answered? Are children feeling good about themselves? Are they valued as persons or only as automatons? Have they opportunities to experiment, make mistakes, use their own best judgment as well as improve their skills and their controls? Is their feeling of independence being encouraged? May they express individual differences or is there always only one right way—the teacher's? Can minds and bodies and feelings stretch themselves or are they kept too neatly confined by expectations of convenient conformity?[6]

QUALIFICATIONS FOR WORKERS

What are the qualifications for workers in a church-sponsored center? State certification regulations change. Therefore, it is advisable to check on current standards. However, some qualifications do not change. Love and concern are

---

6. Cornelia Goldsmith, "Begin Early," *Childhood Education* 40 (March 1966):344.

important factors, but mere affection is not enough. Some government-sponsored day-care centers have received criticism because of the affection displayed by the workers. The attitude of these workers is: "You poor deprived child. Your mommy can't be with you. So you may do whatever you want to make up for it." These workers are not expressing genuine love for the child. If they were, they would work to give him their love while making him a self-reliant and self-respecting individual in his particular set of circumstances or environment.

Because each member of the staff has a direct or indirect influence on each child, it is important that staff members respect each other and respect the children. The issues of physical and emotional abuse, neglect, and sexual abuse are of concern to parents and to child-care teachers. In the mid-eighties several cases of secular day-care abuse came to public attention. It goes without saying that the church day-care center—pre-kindergarten, or kindergarten—must never offend in these danger zones. However, the workers need to discuss these areas and know that even in church families neglect and abuse can occur. The staff must be well informed concerning abuse and must be prepared to handle instances of abuse they become aware of. Generally they should not try to handle these cases by direct confrontation with a parent. Books on the subject are available. Each center needs to discuss the problems of abuse and neglect and possible solutions to them. The staff members must consider the child's well-being as most important.

In addition to education and experience, every worker in a church-sponsored child-care center should use the following personal checklist.

1. I am dependable and consistent with the children.
2. I practice patience, love, and understanding.
3. I learn from the children and other sources.
4. I know the Bible and bring its concepts into the curriculum.
5. I do my best to be physically attractive.
6. I am available to the children, meaning I respond with curiosity, enthusiasm, and enjoyment, as the need demands.
7. I enjoy children and have a growing understanding of them.
8. I know the world in which each preschooler lives—his family, home, and activities away from the church.
9. I regularly attend courses or read books helpful to my work.
10. I realize that I will never get to the place where I know all the answers.

A TYPICAL DAY

What is a typical day like in a child-care program? The daily schedule differs for each type of child-care facility, depending on the length of the day, climate, building arrangements, the children's ages, and the abilities and interests of both the children and the staff. The program suggested here is for a day-care center operating for a full day. Nursery schools and church kindergartens could follow a similar schedule. However, the church kindergarten would include more structured activities with less emphasis on choice of activity or outdoor play. Both the nursery school and kindergarten would be in session from about nine o'clock till noon or from one o'clock to three-thirty.

If the day-care center operates only a half day, its basic program would follow the suggested program for either the morning or afternoon session. A morning day-care center would begin as does the full day program. However, it would end with a fifteen-minute period planned to prepare the children for going home. The following is a suggested schedule for a full-day day-care center:

7:30-9:00	admission, morning health inspection, toileting period, if necessary
	breakfast, if this is a regular part of the program
	choice of activity—for example, dramatic play in the housekeeping corner; quiet play, such as working puzzles, using crayons, stringing beads, looking at books, block building; active play with indoor climbing equipment; easel painting; caring for small pets and plants
9:00-9:30	morning juice, usually a social sit-down period
9:30-10:30	outdoor play (In inclement weather portable outdoor apparatus may be brought indoors.)
10:30-10:45	clean-up, toileting, washing
10:45-11:30	stories, music, conversation periods
11:30-11:45	rest or quiet period
11:45-12:15	noon meal
12:15-12:30	preparation for nap, toileting, washing, undressing
12:30- 2:30	nap
2:30- 3:00	dressing, afternoon snack
3:00- 4:00	choice of activity and perhaps some planned activities— music, stories, games
4:30- 5:30	indoor or outdoor play and preparation for going home.

CURRICULUM

What are some possibilities for a curriculum? The curriculum for the church-sponsored child-care center would have spiritual emphases not found in the secular program. These would include more learning experiences planned to develop concepts about biblical truths. Children would have opportunities to hear both Bible stories and modern stories that emphasize Christian beliefs. Prayer would be used whenever it seemed to fit into the conversation—thanksgiving for good times and God's gifts; petition for family and personal needs; and thanks before snacks and meals. Some of the songs, rhymes, finger plays, and other teacher-directed activities would focus on spiritual truth. Creative handwork would be more than mere fun or development of skills.

Currently, child-care staffs seem to be writing their own curriculums, adapting from a variety of published sources—both secular and religious. (Some of the religious sources are listed in the bibliography.) But there is a need for publishers to produce curriculum guides for church-sponsored child-care centers. Some denominations have established curriculum guidelines, such as the following.

1. Surround a child with Christian love—both in materials and attitudes.
2. Use many opportunities to point a child to God:
   Thank God before snacks and meals.
   In conversation, express appreciation for God's goodness in weather, new clothing and experiences, new babies and pets. A child's discovery of God's handiwork in nature usually provides an opportunity to direct his thinking to the Creator and Sustainer of the universe.
3. Stories, songs, poems, and action rhymes which are not Bible stories must never be contrary to Christian beliefs. The Bible stories used should be coordinated with those used in Sunday school and other church agencies.
4. The curriculum and daily program must meet the following needs of the child:
   (a) The need for a sense of security—of feeling liked and cared for as he is; of feeling that he knows what is expected of him and that he can depend on the adults around him.
   (b) The need for a sense of adequacy—of feeling that he can do what is expected of him and that he can make a contribution to others—children and adults.
   (c) The need for a sense of belonging—of feeling that he is accepted as part of the child-care group or as a part of a small group.
   (d) The need to discover and express individuality in the way a child uses materials—of feeling that he can often express his own ideas in the way he responds to and uses materials.

PARENTAL INVOLVEMENT

Parental involvement is crucial to a successful child-care ministry. An open-door policy should be maintained that encourages parents to visit the center. They should feel free to talk with teachers and ask questions. Parents need assurance that their child is receiving the best possible care and attention and that the atmosphere of the center is warm and nurturing, with loving adults attuned to the responses of children.

Curriculum highlights should be sent home along with periodic newsletters. Parents should receive information updating them on their child's development. Parental help can be enlisted with trips, special programs, and other support services.

How Should a Church Begin a Child-Care Program?

The steps a church might take in setting up a child-care program should include at least the following:

1. First discover the needs of the church and community.
2. Then survey church members to discern their feelings about a child-care ministry.
3. Contact agencies for information about zoning regulations, building requirements, enrollment levels, tuition, policies.
4. Evaluate the church's facilities in light of state requirements and the standards agreed on by the committee.
5. Study the community, agencies, and groups now providing this service.
6. Prepare a tentative financial plan that shows income sources and expenses.
7. Submit the information and a recommendation to the church.

The study committee or day-care board should perform the following duties to begin the school and when the school is in operation.

1. Determine policies and procedures for operating and administering the program.
2. Determine staff qualifications and enlist personnel to direct and teach in the program.
3. Lead in complying with legal and licensing requirements.
4. Organize efforts to involve church members and parents.
5. Lead in an aggressive public relations program to keep church members informed and educated about activities and happenings in the school.
6. Review reports and records regularly to insure proper operation of the center.
7. Oversee the financial position and budget of the center.
8. Make regular reports and recommendations to the church about the work and activities of the program.
9. Coordinate the program with other preschool ministries of the church.

Summary

A child-care center is not a substitute for a strong family life. Most children are better off in the care of their own parents twenty-four hours a day whenever possible. However, church child-care programs—day care, pre-kindergarten or nursery school, and kindergarten offer advantages over similar secular programs. These child-care programs should achieve the same educational goals as the secular counterparts, but add objectives for spiritual knowledge and behavior.

This chapter describes the reasons for child-care programs—the underlying reason should be *ministry* to meet crucial human needs in the name of Christ. The suggested outline of a typical day, as well as checklists for equipment and teacher evaluation, will assist in developing a child-care ministry.

FOR FURTHER READING

A Lap To Sit On . . . and Much More. Washington, D.C.: Assn. for Childhood Ed. Int., 1966.

Barry, James C., and Charles F. Treadway. *Kindergarten Resource Book.* Nashville: Broadman, 1965.

Croft, Doreen J., and Robert D. Hess. *An Activities Handbook for Teachers of Young Children.* Boston: Houghton Mifflin, 1975.

Decker, Celia, and John Decker. *Planning and Administering Early Childhood Programs.* 2d ed. Columbus, Ohio: Merrill, 1980.

Early Childhood: Crucial Years for Learning. Washington, D.C.: Assn. for Childhood Ed. Int., 1966.

Evans, E. Belle, and George E. Saia. *Day Care for Infants.* Boston: Beacon, 1972.

Evans, E. Belle, Beth Shub, and Marlene Weinstein. *Day Care: How to Plan, Develop, and Operate a Day Care Center.* Boston: Beacon, 1971.

Flemming, Bonnie M., and Darlene S. Hamilton. *Resources for Creative Teaching in Early Childhood Education.* New York: Harcourt Brace Jovanovich, 1977.

Gilliland, Anne Hitchcock. *Understanding Preschoolers.* Nashville: Convention, 1969.

Green, Arthur S. *The Kindergarten Arts and Crafts Book.* Minneapolis: Denison, 1962.

Halbert, William H. Jr. *Church Weekday Early Education Director's Guide.* Nashville: Convention, 1972.

Hammond, Sarah Lou. *Good Schools for Young Children.* New York: Macmillan, 1963.

Hemphill, Martha. *Weekday Ministry with Young Children.* Valley Forge, Pa.: Judson, 1973.

Hicks, JoAnne Deal. *Resources for Creative Teaching in Early Childhood Education.* New York: Harcourt Brace Jovanovich, 1977.

Hoover, F. Louis. *Art Activities for the Very Young.* Worcester, Mass.: Davis, 1961.

Hutchens, Elizabeth G. "The Future of Preschool Education." *Church Administration,* June 1969.

Huttar, Leora W. *Jack and Jill Stay for Church: How to Lead a Churchtime Nursery.* Chicago: Moody, 1965.

Implications of Basic Human Values for Education. Washington, D.C.: Assn. for Childhood Ed. Int., 1964.

LeBar, Mary E. *Wonder Programs for 4s and 5s, Yearbook 1.* Wheaton, Ill.: Scripture Press, 1972.

———. *Wonder Programs for 4s and 5s: Yearbook 2.* Wheaton, Ill.: Scripture Press, 1973.

LifeWay Bible Curriculums for Kindergarten and Pre-kindergarten. Wheaton, Ill.: Scripture Press, 1984.

Lifson, Allan. *101 Funshop Favorites.* Fountain Valley, Calif.: Educational Consultant Group, 1978.

Lindner, Eileen, Mary Mattis, and June Rogers. *When Churches Mind the Children.* Ypsilanti, Mich.: High-Scope, 1984.

Newbury, Josephine. *Nursery-Kindergarten Weekday Education in the Church.* Richmond, Va.: John Knox, 1960.

Reynolds, Jean Kirk. *How to Choose and Use Child Care.* Nashville: Broadman, 1980.

Robison, Helen F. and Bernard Spodek. *New Directions in the Kindergarten.* New York: Columbia U., Teachers College Press, 1967.

Tobey, Kathrene McLandress. *The Church Plans for Kindergarten Children.* Philadelphia: Westminster, 1959.

Young Children. Journal of the National Assn. for the Education of Young Children. 1834 Connecticut Avenue, N.W., Washington, D.C. 20009.

Part 5

Helping Children Develop Spiritually

20

*Norman Wakefield and
Robert E. Clark*

Children and Their
Theological Concepts

- Factors Influencing Theological Concepts
- The Process of Concept Development
  PRECONCEPTUAL PERIOD
  CONCRETE CONCEPTS PERIOD
  ABSTRACT CONCEPTS PERIOD
- Discovering Children's Theological Concepts
- How Misconceptions Occur

During the years of childhood, children are confronted with an awesome task. They must draw from bits and pieces of information and experiences and construct a world of reality. At birth, they are tiny, responding creatures, knowing little of the world. By the time they have completed high school they will not only have amassed a remarkable fund of information, but this information will have been organized through cognitive processes into an unbelievably complex data bank.

An understanding of how children form concepts from images and precepts is vital to the Christian educator. He must appreciate how crucial it is that the

NORMAN WAKEFIELD, Ed.D., is a free-lance writer and consultant in family life education and Christian education, living in Phoenix, Arizona.

ROBERT E. CLARK, Ed.D., is professor of Christian education at Moody Bible Institute, Chicago, Illinois, and is co-editor of *Childhood Education in the Church.*

growing child gain clear, accurate concepts related to God, Christ, the Holy Spirit, sin, death, and such. The educator should understand the process whereby concept formation occurs. He needs to ponder why theological misconceptions occur and what Christian parents and teachers can do to aid the child in accurate concept formation.

One might define a concept as "an image or representation whereby objects, events, or experiences may be classified and distinguished." Thus, when input from various sources and experiences is analyzed, one observes characteristics which tend to be common to all situations. These common attributes are incorporated to develop a concept.

Figure 20.1 illustrates the range of information that is used in concept building. Through the wide range of experiences with his own father, through visual representations of God the Father, and through stories and interpretations, a concept of God the Father gradually emerges. It may be grossly distorted or remarkably accurate, depending on a number of factors to be discussed later.

Figure 20.1
How A Child's Concept of God Is Formed

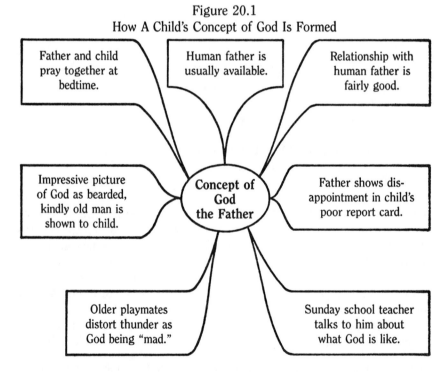

FACTORS INFLUENCING THEOLOGICAL CONCEPTS

Significant factors create a wide range of differences in the theological concepts of children. Two children in the same Sunday school class may have such a diverse background of personal experience and Christian training that one grasps the rudimentary elements of the Trinity, whereas the other has no concept in this area. Thus one might well ask, What influences the development of theological concepts?

1. Definite theological concepts do not appear to develop until later in childhood. However, *impressions* and *awarenesses* early in childhood are very influential in forming the foundation for theological concepts later on. Erikson has pointed out that the child develops his basic sense of trust and mistrust in the first eighteen months of life.[1] Before children understand what it means to trust God, they have formulated feelings and attitudes about trust. Children who from infancy have experienced an emotionally warm, dependable home environment are better able to develop healthy attitudes toward life. They gain positive impressions of interpersonal relations, a sense of orderliness toward life, and an awareness of a harmonious world. These impressions are not rationally thought through, but felt within. As such, they are inner, unseen forces which shape future concepts toward God, the Bible, the universe, self, and others.

2. *Parents* possess great power to influence the roots of theological concepts. Erb notes, "The goodness of God can be learned by analogy from the goodness of father, the comfort of God from the comforting of a dear mother."[2] Christian parents have the privilege of conveying the reality of God as a living person who is vitally concerned about individuals. Parents interpret life events to the young in ways which reveal the many-faceted nature of God.

The parents' role is crucial for two reasons. First, they largely control the quality of affective relationships in the early years. These relationships are the experiential structure on which the later concepts rest. Second, parents can most effectively stimulate the child intellectually as well as interpret the world to the child. Both mother and father can enrich the child's early precepts through conversation about God, reading well-chosen Bible stories, singing unto the Lord, praying with the child, and observing the wonders of God's world. Through these impressions, the young child builds up a valuable supply of positive, accurate images and precepts from which concepts will emerge.

"Though some parents would like to deny it, their children's concept of God is largely determined by what they as parents are."[3] An excellent example of the impact parents—and grandparents—can have upon their children's spiritual development is found in 2 Timothy 1:5. Paul indicates that the vital faith of both mother and grandmother had been communicated to son Timothy. Doctrine must be impregnated with a living experience of the reality of those truths.

Other significant persons also influence a child's understanding of spiritual

1. Erik H. Erikson, *Childhood and Society* (New York: Norton, 1963), p. 247.
2. Alta Mae Erb, *Christian Nurture of Children* (Scottdale, Pa: Herald, 1955), p. 97.
3. Armin Grams, *Children and Their Parents* (Minneapolis: Denison, 1963), p. 77.

concepts. His Sunday school teachers regularly confront him with Christian theological concepts embodied in songs and choruses, Bible stories, prayer, and related learning activities. Either through the communication process or in the actual content of the materials, children often pick up faulty ideas and images. For example, one young child is reported to have tearfully exclaimed, "Oh, Mommy, I am so frightened that the Lord Jesus will come out of my heart, it is beating so hard!"[4] Thus the quality of teaching within the children's agencies of the local church is a contributing factor to theological concept development.

3. Another factor influencing concept formation is the child's *intellectual development.* The Lord appears to have built a timetable within man whereby his intellectual development unfolds progressively. Studies by Jean Piaget and others have stressed that the young child does not have the mental structure to handle abstract concepts. The infant begins with a small number of impressions and gradually builds an ever enlarging network of experiences and impressions. Overstimulation to facilitate a more rapid intellectual development does not appear profitable. It amounts to pouring in data more rapidly than the computer is programmed to assimilate. From the Christian perspective, overstimulation of the young child with too many Bible facts and "advanced" concepts will likely lead to confusion and distortion on the part of the child. One is reminded of the counsel of Garrison, "It should be emphasized that if the church is to be effective in character training, the teaching must follow the fundamental principles of learning set forth in educational psychology."[5]

4. A fourth factor that influences concept formation is the child's *level of language development and enrichment.* The ability to use words provides the youngster with symbols by which he can "handle" images and precepts. This is a necessary step before the child can generalize and comprehend objective concepts. In fact, Chomsky has noted that children often do not know the grammatical construction which is necessary to understand or interpret concepts.[6]

When the child's environment is void of conversation concerning spiritual topics, his development in this area is stunted. In many non-Christian homes, the child hears ideas and attitudes which are distortions of spiritual truth. It is unrealistic to expect a child coming to Sunday school from a non-Christian home to have an adequate and accurate vocabulary of biblical ideas related to God, Christ, and salvation.

---

4. Johanna L. Klink, *Your Child and Religion* (Richmond, Va.: John Knox, 1972), p. 116.
5. Karl C. Garrison et al., *Educational Psychology* (New York: Appleton-Century-Crofts, 1964), p. 308.
6. Carol Chomsky, "Language Development After Age Six," in *Readings in Child Behavior and Development,* ed. Celia Lavatelli and Faith Stendler (New York: Harcourt Brace Jovanovich, 1972), p. 273.

The Process of Concept Development

"A person's relationship to God does not come within the bounds of human measurement. Nor can it be quantitatively known to what extent a faith has become vital enough to be shared with others. The inner core of Christian motivation is known only to God."[7]

The Christian educator must always respect the inner supernatural working of the Spirit of God in the life of the child. Christian educators should be careful not to limit what they think a child can do, because of research by behavioral scientists. At the same time, the discerning Christian educator may be aware of human behavior and child development.

The research of Jean Piaget has provided much insight into the process of concept development. Piaget has pointed out that the newborn enters the world with little more intellectual ability than mere reflex mechanisms. The infant's intellectual development consists of a progressive capacity to differentiate and integrate, utilizing the reflex mechanisms in his experience. Incoming external data is assimilated with existing internal data through an enlarging mental capacity. Until approximately eighteen to twenty-four months of age, the child is not able to produce a symbolic representation which make possible a memory of past events as well as an anticipation of future events.

In these first eighteen to twenty-four months, infants are gaining very influential awarenesses about the world they have entered. In the early months, they have no distinct sense of time, space, distance, or relationships. Through the slow process of experimenting with their environment and constantly assimilating new sensory data with existing impressions, the most basic structuring of their experiences begins.

The Christian educator should not minimize the seriousness of the infant's task. He is being forced to begin piecing together his design of reality. Taking bits and pieces of data from personal experimentations, parents, and other persons, he must come to understand his world. Too often adults hold a simplistic view of childhood ("he's just playing"), failing to realize the consequences of the early impressions and awarenesses. Each event in the child's life is an occasion for learning whereby the child's world of reality is enlarged and verified.

Following this foundational birth-to-two-year-old period, there appear to be three periods in the development of the child's maturity in forming concepts. Using age divisions suggested by Piaget, the following periods are identified: two to seven years, preconceptual period; seven to eleven years, period of concrete concepts; eleven to fifteen years, period of abstract concepts. The reader is encouraged not to view these as rigid divisions but helpful approximations. Concept development actually is a progressive development moving

---

7. Iris V. Cully, *Children in the Church* (Philadelphia: Westminster, 1960), p. 56.

from disorganized to organized, formless to form, concrete to abstract, literal to symbolic.

The preconceptual period ranges from ages two to seven. When the young child begins to talk, he gains a valuable tool for exploring his world. He is not restricted to action alone but can probably seek explanations. Language ability provides opportunity to explore ideas. Parents frequently are overwhelmed at the persistent questions that are voiced by the preschooler. "Where is Jesus?" "Who is God?" "Where does He live?" "Where is heaven?" One study of 6,000 children between the ages of three and twelve revealed that four- and five-year-olds asked more questions about God than any other age group.[8] The parent who can patiently respond to the youngster's inquiry both provides information and builds a relationship with the child.

Several characteristics of the child's thinking process at this age are important for parents and teachers to understand. First, there is little capacity to grasp concepts of *time, distance, numbers,* and *reversibility.* To speak of

Figure 20.2
The Difference Between Preconceptual and Conceptual Thinking

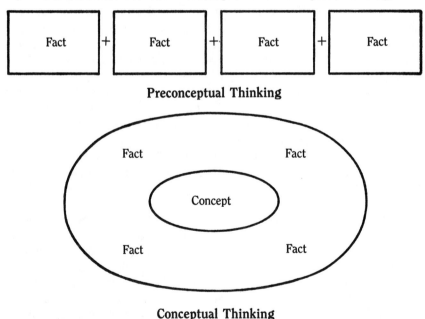

Preconceptual Thinking

Conceptual Thinking

8. Alice L. Goddard, "Children Ask About God," *International Journal of Religious Education,* 40 (January 1964):20.

Jesus as having lived on earth 2,000 years ago is meaningless to the young child who has no concept of 2,000 years. Even though the five-year-old may say that he is five-years-old, he is repeating information that he has been given without grasping its meaning. Even brief periods of time, say thirty minutes, are not understood. The young child can better understand time in relationship to another event. "After Mother finishes the dishes, she will take you for a walk."

Concepts of distance and number have little meaning to the child unless they are transferred into measurement that can be seen. For this reason, biblical data must be expressed in statements such as, "There were many, many, people listening to Jesus," rather than indicating a specific number.

Second, the child's preconceptual thinking during this period is *transductive*. (See Fig. 20.2.) Children tend to relate ideas on a one-to-one basis. They have difficulty making mental comparisons, but must build them up one at a time. They cannot group ideas together and draw a central principle. Each incident is taken separately because the child has such limited conceptual framework.

One important application of transductive thinking focuses on the child's response to what he learns from the Bible. Since he cannot generalize his learnings, application must be made specifically to a tangible situation. "Studies in honesty among children have shown that young children must learn moral behavior in specific situations; such learnings are later integrated into a unifying concept."[9]

The limitations of transductive thinking have implications for theological concepts. It is very difficult for the child to integrate information into an overall concept of Jesus Christ, sin, or death. As children develop in the later part of this period (four to six years), they will have an increasing capacity to generalize their intellectual experience, to formulate the rudiments or relationships necessary for a conceptual hierarchy, and to assimilate ideas and preconcepts on a broader scale.

Parents and teachers often fail to grasp the importance of the child's inability to think conceptually. The youngster hears such statements as, "God made the world," "God is everywhere," "God lives in heaven," "God sent Jesus to earth," "God can see us." He lacks the ability, however, to focus this information into a meaningful, unified whole. Thus, the statements remain disjointed, even to the point that two statements, one immediately after the other, are in direct conflict.

Third, during the preconceptual period, the child's thought is characterized by *syncretism*. Syncretistic thinking links items and events or experiences that do not belong together. This may occur partly because the child cannot classify many relations. Susan may ask Mr. Jenkins, "Where is your mother?" Upon

9. Garrison, p. 294.

questioning, it is discovered that because Susan cannot grasp the husband-wife concept she is actually referring to Mr. Jenkins's wife. From a theological standpoint, the child may link ideas of God with ideas which are not related to God.

Fourth, preconceptual thought is dominated by *centering*. Centering refers to the tendency of the child to focus attention on one characteristic or feature of an idea or experience and fail to see other important aspects. Thus, young children may listen to a Bible story and miss some aspects because their attention is focused on only one aspect. The young child has difficulty seeing the pattern or scope of an event. The same is true of visual experiences. A teacher, for example, may be visualizing the account of Jesus' triumphal entry, but little Johnny is so intrigued by the donkey that he misses other aspects of the account that the teacher considers more important.

Fifth, the thinking of children during this period is *artificial* or *humanistic*. That is, they tend to assert that events in the natural world are caused by people. For example they think of lightning or the movement of clouds as caused directly by people. Being highly imaginative, children cannot distinguish clearly between the world of reality and the world of make-believe. Therefore their preconcepts of God may not only be poorly related, but may also have dimensions that reflect their world of fantasy.

The following account reflects how much artificialism can influence a youngster's behavior: "A little boy hasn't eaten up his plums. It thunders that night. He comes downstairs in his pajamas to eat up his plums; he is afraid that God is angry with him."[10]

Sixth, the young child is *egocentric* in his thinking. *Egocentricism* should not be equated with selfishness. Rather it reflects the child's inability to see an idea, event, or experience from another person's perspective. For this reason, it is difficult to convey the concept of sharing, or help the child to understand how another child may feel.

One may well ask, "What are the implications of these limitations in the thinking ability of the two-to-seven-year-olds?" One obvious point is that parents and teachers must not expect too much of children at this age. Strictly speaking children may have difficulty developing and relating theological concepts during the preconceptual period. They have images and preconcepts, but their thinking is fragmentary and discrete. They are endeavoring to understand who God is, but their intellectual powers are not sufficiently developed to piece all the information together.

A second point is that the biblical information children are given must be accurate and broken down to their level of comprehension. In spite of the limitations in the young child's thinking, parents and teachers must not neglect the opportunity to teach the Bible. According to Richards, "Whatever ap-

10. Klink, p. 46.

proach we take to preschool Christian education, it cannot neglect the Word and words of God, made understandable to tots on the threshold of learning."[11] It is an excellent time to create an awareness of God, as well as providing clear, accurate data concerning Bible events and truths. As parents endeavor to express the reality of Christ in the home, the young child can sense that God is a real person—though unseen—one who is powerful, compassionate, and concerned about the child, his family, and others.

A third implication is warranted. Young children gain a preconceptual awareness of the nature of God through observing others who express the love of God through their behavior. It is interesting to note that many of the young child's questions concerning God relate to his activity, which may be the child's way of investigating the nature of God as a *person*. For example, a five-year-old girl asks her mother, "God watches over us, doesn't he, Mother? He won't let anything hurt us?" This child is exploring the person of God in a most practical manner.[12]

CONCRETE CONCEPTS PERIOD

Between the ages of seven and eleven, the child begins to think in literal, or concrete, terms. The transition from the preconceptual period to the concrete concepts period is a movement from perceptions to intellectual operations. The level of development is significant because it represents a period when a form of conceptualization is possible. However, limitations accompany this advancement, and it is good to understand what they are.

During this period, children are limited in their verbal reasoning. When asked to use verbal propositions rather than objects, they must consider one statement at a time in reasoning the proposition through. This would suggest that the ability to manipulate theological concepts becomes very difficult as the concept becomes more abstract.

Related to the above limitation, seven-to-eleven-year-olds are poor at generalizing beyond particular situations or examples. Their intellectual abilities are restricted to physical actions which they can internalize. Thus, their understanding of theological concepts is limited to generalizations of specific incidents or information before them. Children within this age group wrestle with the concept of the Trinity, but find it difficult to grasp, because it is hard to conceive concretely. One must be careful to distinguish between a child's affirmation of belief in the Trinity and a conceptual understanding of the truth. Adults often mistakenly believe that because a child verbally acknowledges a theological concept, he genuinely understands what it means. A child's re-

11. Lawrence O. Richards, *Creative Bible Teaching* (Chicago: Moody, 1970), p. 150.
12. Mary E. Venable, "Little Children Ask Big Questions," *International Journal of Religious Education,* 40 (Oct., 1963):4-6.

sponse, "Father, Son, and Holy Spirit" to the question, "What is the Trinity?" is not evidence that he has a concept of the Trinity. More likely, it demonstrates his ability to answer a question with facts he has previously acquired.

Probably the most significant advancement in the child's development during this period is an enlarging ability to classify data. This is a significant development toward forming theological concepts, for the youngster is formulating structures to categorize and identify common elements. As skill at grouping common relationships becomes greater, the ability to form concepts grows.

Now that the child is gaining skill at grouping information, notable features become evident. At about nine years of age, children are becoming more competent at developing hierarchies of classes and relationships. For example, they can now begin to grasp divisions in the Bible, such as the minor prophets, the gospels, and the epistles. As they mature, they gain facility at working with multiplication of classes, such as the second of the Pauline epistles.

Grouping skills are invaluable for concept formation for two reasons. First, the child begins to comprehend what is included in that particular concept. When data can be classified according to certain relationships it is more easily categorized. Second, however of equal importance, the person has the power to determine what is to be excluded. He can ask, Is this information consistent with other facts I know about the topic?

At least six classifying operations are needed for concept building. The activities included are: (1) combining information; (2) distinguishing or separating; (3) dividing information into subgroupings; (4) organizing by placing in order; (5) substituting; and (6) repeating. Through these processes, the learner consolidates his expanding reservoir of learning by discovering common associations, identifying elements and principles of identity. These skills are very important as a basis for developing sound concepts of God, Christ, salvation, and other doctrinal concepts.

At this point, the reader is cautioned to recall an important limitation in thinking at the seven-to-eleven-year-old period: Conceptual abilities are rooted in concrete situations. Grouping of relationships and classifying of information are limited to specific, concrete situations that the seven-to-eleven-year-old can manipulate. In forming an understanding of divisions in the Bible, the child could "see" the divisions because they could be outlined on paper and illustrated from the Bible. To comprehend a theological concept of sin would be more difficult, because it is more abstract and must draw from a less definitive, less concrete basis.

ABSTRACT CONCEPTS PERIOD

During the four-year period, between the ages of eleven and fourteen, the individual develops the mental ability for mature conceptual thinking. Especially important is the capacity to think in abstract terms, utilizing the world of propositions. Problems can be approached in a systematic manner and solved by using logical procedures which are expressed in abstract form. In addition, the classifying abilities which were emerging in the earlier period become more refined, better integrated, and more flexible. Whereas the seven-to-eleven-year-old is occupied with the immediate and the real, the eleven-to-fourteen-year-old is concerned with the theoretical, the remote, and the future.

This period is vitally important to the development of theological concepts. First, the older child is endeavoring to incorporate earlier learnings into broader, more abstract principles and concepts. Parents and teachers should expect the eleven-to-fourteen-year-old to be reflective. Also, the individual in this period can range beyond the tangible, finite, and familiar, to conceive of hypothetical situations and infinite possibilities. From the perspective of Christian education, this period offers great opportunity for the formulation of a biblical foundation for Christian living.

How Adults Can Discover Children's Theological Concepts

Unfortunately, most adults have lost the precious memory of what it was like to be a child. They cannot recapture the intense feeling a child experiences of waiting two weeks for Christmas to arrive—while seeing those mysterious gifts under the tree. Adults fail to remember a world of words and ideas which were unclear, having to ask again and again, "What does that mean?" An essential task of parenthood and teaching children is to rediscover the world of childhood. Only then can the adult sense the meaning of what the youngster does, as well as act most wisely to guide the child toward insight.

In rediscovering the world of the child, the adult becomes aware of his concepts related to Christian truth. Teachers who neglect this task frequently demand more of children than they are able to produce. The world is interpreted to them from an adult perspective on the assumption that they perceive and think as adults. Thus, Jesus Christ is described as the light of the world, the bread of life, or the way, the truth, and the life—all concepts too difficult for the young child to grasp.

Parents and teachers of children can discover children's concepts by deepening their understanding of child development. Insight can be gained as one better understands the mental, emotional, and spiritual characteristics of a certain age. This insight can be enhanced by an alert observation of children in various settings. In this way, the information can be observed in actual life situations.

Also, the adult who desires to understand the child's world of thought must develop disciplined, perceptive skill in listening to children's conversations. One should note their choice of words. It is enlightening to observe how they sing songs, recite verses, and describe Bible stories. As one listens to the meanings a child gives to events, he realizes more fully the extent to which a child grasps a biblical truth. For example, the adult who asks the young child,

Why? will probably be told, "Because," or "Because he did." What one discovers is that the child does not have the intellectual maturity to reason out a cause. Thus, a simple "because" is used in reply.

In addition to perceptive listening, the adult should converse with and question children in informal, friendly situations. Asking an eight-year-old "What is sin?" will demonstrate where that individual is in his concept of sin. One who desires to discover the child's theological concepts can ask such questions as, "Tell me what you think of when you think of God"; "Who is Jesus?" "What does it mean to be born again?" One should purposely use commonly spoken terms to see if they really are understood: born again, gospel, heart, love, share, pray. Soon the adult will sense the range of understanding the individual child possesses. As more and more children are questioned, a more generalized awareness of the potential of age levels will emerge.

One, however, must be alert to two dangers. The first is the danger of generalizing from too small a group of children. Conversing with children in a primary class is not adequate to make definitive statements about the theological concepts of children in grades 1 through 3. For one thing, all the children might be from Christian homes where conscientious guidance had taken place. Or, a large number may have received little Christian education. The results would be noticeably different.

The other danger arises when the adult settles for pat answers as evidence of insight and understanding. Isolated biblical facts are not valid indicators of Christian concepts. The child must take objective facts, learn their meaning, and then realize for himself the implications of those facts.

Another way to discover children's theological concepts is to allow children to express their religious ideas through such means as art, music, and role play. By taking advantage of these forms, the child can often descriptively conceptualize his understandings. The results may sometimes be humorously revealing. A child, who was asked to draw a picture, produced a work depicting two adults in the back seat of an automobile and one person in the front. When asked what his picture was about, the youngster replied, "That's God driving Adam and Eve out of the garden." However humorous, the story vividly portrayed the child's understanding of the event.

Parents and children's workers should utilize as many means as possible to discover the concepts their children have of biblical ideas. Only as one perceives where the child is in his own development will he be able to guide the child to more mature concepts. Through personal investigation, the adult will realize the wide range of individual differences which exist among children.

How Misconceptions Occur

Many children formulate wrong precepts and concepts because of intellectual overstimulation. Two sources may be especially harmful. The first is the intense input of information from mass media. The child's mind may become cluttered with images and ideas which he cannot assimilate because he does not have the ability to organize them. Such data may be linked transductively with another idea so that two incompatible ideas exist side by side.

The other source of overstimulation is the eager parent or teacher who mistakes quantity for quality. Thus the child is prodded to memorize numerous Bible verses which are not understood; is confronted with a volume of facts, incidents, and problems which can never be mastered; and is taught hymns and choruses which contain concepts too advanced to comprehend. The child is given too much data and/or too advanced data. This results in confusion and misconceptions. A far better principle is to provide the child with smaller units of information and experience which can be digested healthily. It is wise not to push theological concepts on children before they can intellectually comprehend them.

Children also gain misconceptions because they have no accurate means to check their own observations and inferences. Russell notes that errors in concepts occur because of "overconfidence in the results of one's observations and conceptual thinking."[13] Children are also basically trusting of adults, feeling that whatever the adult says must be true. Thus, if they process their information incorrectly, or are given wrong ideas and attitudes by adults, they have little ability to correct the error without adult guidance.

Errors in concepts can also result when the preconcepts on which the concepts are built are faulty. This may also result when childhood experiences are in opposition to biblical concepts. The child who has experienced a very distorted father-son relationship may have difficulty building an adequate Father-son relationship.

Misconceptions result when misleading visual aids are used in teaching biblical concepts. One well-known Bible storybook portrayed Satan in a garb complete with horns, tail, and pitchfork. Such faulty images make lasting imprints in the child's mind. How many children conceive of angels with wings because of pictures visualizing them as such? Yet, is this biblically accurate?

By hearing words incorrectly, children gain inaccurate information for concept building. This often occurs in children's songs when the combined effects of poor adult pronunciation, group singing, and musical accompaniment distort or blur the words. One child wondered what "Jesus loves me, the sigh no," meant. In addition, children's songs are sometimes theologically confusing or heavily symbolic. For a very interesting learning experience—for the teacher—ask the students what such things as "He's the lily of the valley" mean.

Misconceptions also occur as a result of peer conversation. The child can easily gain incorrect impressions and information from playmates, especially those of different faiths. If other children are untaught in Christian truth, they

13. David H. Russell, *Children's Thinking* (Boston: Ginn, 1956), p. 246.

may introduce the child to distortions or untruths which he readily integrates into his fund of data on the topic.

Since misconceptions can so readily occur, the following principles should be practiced:

1. Avoid teaching symbolic concepts before children can understand them.
2. Clarify your own theological concepts before teaching children. What do I believe about the Holy Spirit? How can I state these truths in simple, nonmisleading terms?
3. Match words with experience and experience with words. Each reinforces and clarifies the other. Experience expresses the deeper meaning of words, and words clarify experience.
4. Teach nothing which shall later have to be unlearned.
5. Attempt to move theological concepts beyond "inert ideas" to principles of daily living. Children may accept that God is all powerful, yet they may not know how to apply the concept to their own lives. Parents can help by demonstrating the reality of Christian truth.
6. Enrich rather than advance. Help the child gain an enriched meaning of basic truths rather than a cyclopedic understanding. For example, the concept of honesty could be built through many channels: life situations, life-related stories, Bible stories, songs, pictures, Bible verses.
7. Deal with one concept at a time.
8. Adjust information to the child's intellectual level.
9. Integrate information with the child's experience in a manner which allows him to test and comprehend its meaning.

SUMMARY

If children are born into a Christian family, they will very likely be introduced to concepts in theology early in life. Their parents and others often attempt to teach basic theological truths through Bible verses, music, and activities.

An understanding of how children form concepts from images and precepts is vital to parents and Christian educators. There are many significant factors which influence the teaching of theology to children. Even before children are ready to learn formally, impressions and awarenesses are taught by parents and teachers through attitudes and actions.

The child's intellectual and language development are also important factors to consider. The process of concept formation must be understood as theological concepts are introduced and taught. Adults need to be well-grounded in their own biblical and doctrinal beliefs so they can teach children accurately.

Adults can discover children's theological concepts in various ways. Misconceptions may occur in the process of teaching theology, and so parents and teachers should be prepared to correct misunderstandings, clarify truth, and teach simply and clearly as opportunities arise.

FOR FURTHER READING

Almy, Millie C. *Young Children's Thinking: Studies of Some Aspects of Piaget Theory.* New York: Columbia U., Teachers College Press, 1966.

Beadle, Muriel. *A Child's Mind.* Garden City, N.Y.: Doubleday, Anchor Books, 1971.

Brearly, Molly, ed. *The Teaching of Young Children.* New York: Schocken, 1970.

Eastman, Frances M. "Was Jesus Born Like Me?" *International Journal of Religious Education* 40 (December 1963):16-17, 37.

———. "What Is the Bible?" *International Journal of Religious Education* 41 (October 1964):8-9, 38-39.

Elkind, David. *Children and Adolescents: Interpretive Essays on Jean Piaget.* Paperback ed. New York: Oxford U., 1971.

———. "The Development of Religious Understanding in Children and Adolescents." In *Research on Religious Development.* Edited by Merton P. Strommen. New York: Hawthorn, 1971.

Fitzgerald, Annie. *Dear God Books.* Sets 1 and 2. Minneapolis: Augsburg, 1983, 1984.

Goldman, Ronald. *Readiness for Religion.* New York: Seabury, 1968.

———. *Religious Thinking from Childhood to Adolescence.* New York: Seabury, 1964.

Halverson, Delia. *Helping Your Child Discover Faith.* Valley Forge, Pa.: Judson, 1982.

Haystead, Wes. *Teaching Your Child About God.* Ventura, Calif.: Gospel Light, Regal Books, 1981.

Hendricks, William L. *A Theology for Children.* Nashville: Broadman, 1980.

Holm, Marilyn F. *Tell Me Why: A Guide to Children's Questions About Faith and Life.* Minneapolis: Augsburg, 1985.

Lichtenweiner, Muriel. "Children Ask About Death." *International Journal of Religious Education* 40(June 1964):14-16.

McMichael, Anne. "As Children See the Church." *International Journal of Religious Education* 40(March 1964):10-11, 40.

Phillips, John L., Jr. *Origins of Intellect: Piaget's Theory.* San Francisco: Freeman, 1969.

Piaget, Jean. *The Construction of Reality in the Child.* New York: Basic Books, 1954.

———. *The Origins of Intelligence in Children.* New York: International Universities, 1952.

Venable, Mary E. "Little Children Ask Big Questions." *International Journal of Religious Education* 40(October 1963):4-6.

————. "Religious Concepts Affect Daily Living." *International Journal of Religious Education* 40(July-August 1964):16-17, 37.

Waldrop, C. Sybil. *Guiding Your Child Toward God.* Nashville: Convention, 1985.

Wilcox, Mary M. *Developmental Journey.* Nashville: Abingdon, 1979.

21

V. Gilbert Beers

Teaching Theological Concepts to Children

- **Laying the Right Foundation**
  KNOW WHAT YOU ARE TO TEACH
  KNOW THE CHILD YOU WISH TO TEACH
  KNOW HOW YOU PLAN TO TEACH
- **God's Truth Is for Everyone**
  NEEDS CHANGE WITH GROWTH
  WHAT IT MEANS TO LEARN DOCTRINE
  A GUIDE TO DOCTRINE FOR DIFFERENT LEARNING LEVELS
- **Know the Child You Want to Teach**
  YOUR CHILD IS AN INDIVIDUAL
  YOUR CHILD IS NOT A LITTLE ADULT
  YOUR CHILD IS A TOTAL PERSON
- **Some Methods to Use in Teaching Doctrine**

Here is a child—transparent, uncomplicated, understandable, and accessible. A child is human, like the rest of us.

There is theology. To many, it seems opaque, complicated, scholarly, and remote. It may seem philosophical, dealing with another world.

Are the two incompatible? "Theology" and "child" seem to be made of different stuff. Some are tempted to ask, Is theology really for a child? Isn't it more for a theologian?

V. GILBERT BEERS, Th.D., Ph.D., is executive director, Christianity Today Institute.

Theology is complicated only when we make it so. It is as simple as the song nursery children sing, "Jesus loves me, this I know, for the Bible tells me so."

The Bible provides the truth about God and those subjects related to God. People have organized that truth and called it theology. It usually encompasses the truth about God, Jesus, the Holy Spirit, the church, sin, salvation, man, angels, the Bible, heaven, hell, death, the last times, and Satan. These are topics that touch our eternal destinies, both here and in the hereafter.

Some theological concepts are admittedly beyond the thought and conversation level of the typical child. But most of the great truths of the Bible which we organize into theology can be stated in such a way that a child can understand them. It is a matter of putting the subject matter into the communications and learning level of the learner.

Peter and the author of Hebrews spoke of "milk" as being truths for those who are spiritually young and of "meat" as being for those who are spiritually more mature (1 Pet. 2:2; Heb. 5:14).

In this chapter, we are concerned with milk, truth which can be assimilated into young lives. Whether we speak of theological concepts, doctrine for children, or biblical truth, we are speaking of the same—those concepts of God and related subjects which can be learned by a child.

LAYING THE RIGHT FOUNDATION

The basic foundation for this kind of teaching lies with you, the teacher. Whether you are a teacher or parent, you must first understand those truths yourself if you wish to communicate them to a child. It is vital also that you understand your child, at his or her present learning level and as an individual, and you must understand the processes which you will use in your teaching.

KNOW WHAT YOU ARE TO TEACH

We evangelicals are often guilty of exchanging words without clarifying them. Do you find yourself using such words as *sin, salvation, repent, dedicated,* and *Savior* with your child, but not really teaching what these words mean?

Have you ever tried to explain these words to yourself as if you were the four-year-old or six-year-old you teach? Try it. You may find that you are not sufficiently clear yourself as to the meaning of these terms.

Teaching is not merely the bartering of words. It is the clarification of ideas and the shaping of attitudes and lives. Clarify these truths in your own mind first; then help them become crystal clear to your child.

KNOW THE CHILD YOU WISH TO TEACH

Age-level characteristics are explained in chapters 5 through 10 in this book. Study those characteristics carefully for the age level you are teaching, for they are important keys to that learning level.

You will recognize that each individual child does not fit exactly into the expected learning level. There are some ten-year-olds who think like six-year-olds and some sixes who think like tens. But most children do fit into their proper learning level, and it is important for you to know what to expect at that level.

As you learn the characteristics of a certain age level or learning level, study also the individual characteristics of your child. "There is only one you" is a truth basic in good teaching. You must know your child as an individual as well as a representative of a certain learning level.

If you are the child's parent, or frequent teacher, you may be tempted to think that you do know that child because you see him or her often, or live under the same roof. However, that does not guarantee that you genuinely know this child, any more than husbands and wives know each other because they live together.

Communication is the road to understanding. If you would know your child, you must communicate with that child. Conversation will lead you into your child's mind and heart and help you to know the child as a person. Then you will be ready to teach as you should.

KNOW HOW YOU PLAN TO TEACH

Why are you trying to teach that child? What do you hope to accomplish? Do you simply want the child to know more about Bible truth? Or do you want the mind, heart, attitudes, and actions to change in response to that teaching?

True learning never ends with the head. It proceeds into the heart and hands also.

How do you hope to accomplish this change in your child? What processes will you use? These are all elementary considerations, but they do lay the proper foundation to the kind of learning you will want for your child as you share Bible truth.

GOD'S TRUTH IS FOR EVERYONE

A child is a total person growing toward eternity. He is not a little adult. Nor is the child a big infant, although there may be times when you may be tempted to think so. The child is in a constantly changing pattern of development. Each day, week, month, and year sees a newer maturity than before.

It is easier to see this change when we jump across the years. Today's adult was once yesterday's child. Each minister or criminal was once a child—growing through each age level. Each child today will become tomorrow's adult. What that person does as an adult will depend much on the childhood years.

Growth is the road that leads through life toward the hereafter. It is God's provision for the gradual change of infants into children, children into youth, youth into adults, adults into old people, and old people into inhabitants of another world. Each person passes through identical periods of life, although under very different circumstances.

How you teach God's truth to a child depends on where that child is in the level of growth, what kind of an individual he or she is, and a number of other factors. One important factor in teaching doctrine to children is the recognition of the changing needs in that child's life.

NEEDS CHANGE WITH GROWTH

Teachers and parents alike recognize that a child's personal needs change as he or she grows. Some of these basic personal needs include the need for love, the need to belong, the need for approval, the need for care or concern, the need for security, the need to succeed, and the need to serve others. Table 21:1, showing the growth in the need for love, represents the change in almost any of these basic needs.

It is important that you, the parent or teacher, recognize not only the

TABLE 21.1

THE GROWTH OF LOVE

AGE LEVEL	FOCAL POINT OF LOVE	ASPECT OF LOVE NEEDED
Infant	Parents, especially the mother	To be held in parent's arms, to be nursed
Preschool child	Parents, some close friends	To be secure in the family circle
Elementary school child	Parents, school friends, neighbor friends	To be a part of home, school, and friends
Junior high young person	Friends, parents, other sex	To be accepted by friends, parents, and other sex
High school young person	Friends, other sex, parents	To date, but also to be part of original family
Young adult	Other sex, friends, parents	To marry and/or to enjoy secure relationships with friends
Parents	Children, mate, friends	To enjoy a secure marriage and to give oneself in love to children
Other adults	Mate, children and grand-children, friends	To have a mature marriage, acceptance by children and grandchildren, and friends

learning level of your child, but also the need level. When you do, you will be able to bring God's truth to work on specific needs in that child's life. We must not be satisfied to teach subject matter without reference to daily living, and that includes daily, personal needs.

WHAT IT MEANS TO LEARN DOCTRINE

Too often parents and teachers associate learning with head knowledge. The child has "learned" something when he can repeat it. But that does not fulfill the child's needs for daily living. It is a start, but it is not enough.

There are four steps necessary for the effective learning of truth. Head knowledge is the first one. Knowing is a necessary step, for one must see clearly what Bible truth *is* or *says* before he can understand it.

The second step is understanding, or seeing clearly, what that Bible truth *means*. It is not possible to move on to the next steps in learning until the learner first understands what he or she is trying to put into his life.

The third step is applying. In applying Bible truth, the learner sees clearly what the truth means to *me*. The learner understands more than the meaning of the truth, but also that meaning in relationship to his own life.

The fourth step is practicing. When a child learns what the truth is, then what it means, and then what it means to him or her, it is time to put it into practice in life.

When someone wants to make Bible truth vital to a child, it is essential to help the child incorporate the truth into life. That reaches all the way through the four steps to good learning.

A GUIDE TO DOCTRINE FOR DIFFERENT LEARNING LEVELS

The charts on what children can learn suggest theological concepts which can be taught at each learning level.[1]

TABLE 21.2

WHAT A CHILD OF TWO AND THREE CAN LEARN

ABOUT GOD	God loves me. God takes care of me. God loves and cares for my family. God provides sun and rain. God does good for people. God is all about me. God wants me to talk with Him. God made the world.

1. Adapted from V. Gilbert Beers, *Family Bible Library* (Nashville: Southwestern, 1971), 10:14-15, 18-19, 22-23, 26-27.

	God made me. I can praise God by singing and praying. I can tell God I am sorry for the bad things I do. I should please and obey God.
ABOUT JESUS	Jesus loves me. Jesus once lived on earth, but now is in heaven. Jesus is God's Son. Jesus is a Friend. Jesus said good things which are in the Bible. Jesus was once a child like me.
ABOUT THE BIBLE	The Bible tells about God. The Bible is a good Book. The Bible is a special Book. I should love the Bible.
ABOUT HOME AND PARENTS	God gave parents. I should obey my parents.
ABOUT CHURCH AND SUNDAY SCHOOL	Church is a place to learn about God. Church is a place to see friends. Church is God's house. I should like to go to church. I can give money to God's house to help buy things.
ABOUT OTHERS	God gives grownups to care for me. Others may be good friends. Others may sometimes be unkind. Jesus wants me to be kind to others and share with them.
ABOUT ANGELS AND LAST THINGS	Angels came to tell people when Jesus was born. Angels love God and praise Him.

TABLE 21.3
WHAT A CHILD OF FOUR AND FIVE CAN LEARN

ABOUT GOD	God loves me and others. God cares for all who love Him. God cares for and loves families. God made all things. God is to be trusted and depended on. God is everywhere. God will hear prayer anytime. God sent Jesus to die for sin. God wants me to be thankful for all He has made. God wants me to obey Him by obeying my parents. God loves me.

About Jesus	Jesus loves me and is my best friend. Jesus came to be the Savior. Jesus is now living in heaven. Jesus will help me obey and share. Jesus wants all children to love Him. Jesus is always with me. Jesus died for me. Jesus can help me do hard things.
About the Bible	The Bible tells about God. The Bible is God's Word. God tells me what He wants me to do in the Bible. The Bible helps me know what to do. The Bible is a Book of true stories.
About Home and Parents	God gave parents to care for me and teach me. God gave parents to pray for me. I should obey my parents. I should want to love and please my parents. I sin when I disobey my parents or am unkind.
About Church and Sunday School	Church is a place to learn, sing, and worship God. Church is a place to meet with others who love the Lord. Church is a special place. Church is a place where we learn about God.
About Others	God made all people. God loves everyone and wants all to love Him. God wants me to tell others about Jesus. Others may not share as I do. Others may be loving and kind to me. I am to be kind, share, and pray for others. God wants me to share my money. God wants people to help others.
About Angels and Last Things	Some angels are good and some are bad. Satan (the devil) is a bad angel who did not want to please God. Satan and his angels want us to do bad things.

TABLE 21.4
WHAT A CHILD OF SIX AND SEVEN CAN LEARN

About God	God loves me and my family and my friends. God loves all the people of the world. God wants people to love Him too. God wants people to give their lives to Him.

	God provides food for people by letting plants grow. God takes care of the world He made. God is good, but He is also against evil. God wants us to pray and read our Bibles. God is holy and cannot fail. God has all power to help me.
ABOUT JESUS	Jesus is the Son of God. Jesus came to earth to die for sin. Jesus wants us to accept Him as our personal Savior. Jesus wants to help people go to God. Jesus wants to take sin from our lives. Jesus never did anything wrong. Jesus rose from the dead and lives in heaven. Jesus loves us and wants to be our friend. Jesus did many wonderful miracles while on earth. Jesus can help me choose to do the right things.
ABOUT THE BIBLE	The Bible is God's Book, for it tells about Him. The Bible tells us what God wants. The Bible tells how God worked with others. The Bible tells much about us. The Bible is a good Book to study, for it helps us. The Bible should be read and memorized. The Bible contains sixty-six books. The Bible has two major parts, called the Old and New Testaments.
ABOUT HOME AND PARENTS	Parents are God's leaders for us on earth. Parents want to help us, so we should obey them. Parents love us, so we should love them too. Parents provide food and clothing and home for us. God is an important guest in our home at all times.
ABOUT CHURCH AND SUNDAY SCHOOL	Church is God's house. Church is a place where God's people go. Church is a happy place. Church is a place for songs and prayer and Bible study. Church needs our help to keep it clean and quiet. Church is not just a building but also the people in it. I can give to the Lord's work through the church.

ABOUT OTHERS	Others may want the same thing I do; I must share.
	Others may not want to do the same thing I do; I
	   must learn to give in halfway.
	Others may need something very much; I must learn
	   to give.
	Others may be in trouble; I must learn to pray.

	Others may be unkind; I must learn to forgive.
	Others may not know Jesus; I must learn to tell them about Him.
ABOUT ANGELS AND LAST THINGS	Satan tempts us to sin and disobey God.
	Good angels worship and praise God.
	Good angels are God's servants.
	Jesus has gone to heaven to prepare a place there for all who love Him.
	Jesus is coming to take us to live with Him forever.

TABLE 21.5

WHAT A CHILD OF EIGHT AND NINE CAN LEARN

ABOUT GOD	God is all powerful, and wise, and everywhere.
	God is present with me at all times.
	God wants to help me as I grow.
	God loves me and wants me to love God.
	God made the universe and all in it.
	God wants me to pray each day.
	God always answers prayers with yes, no, or wait.
	God loves people all over the world.
	God the Holy Spirit is a person who is spirit.
	When I receive Jesus as my Savior, the Holy Spirit comes into my life.
ABOUT JESUS	Jesus is the Son of God, the Savior.
	Jesus died on the cross for sin.
	Jesus can give salvation to those who ask.
	Jesus can forgive sin.
	Jesus loves me even when I sin.
	Jesus wants me to be a disciple and follow Him.
ABOUT THE BIBLE	The Bible is an exciting Book to read.
	The Bible is a true Book, not fiction.
	The Bible is God's Word.
	The Bible should be read each day.
	The Bible has many important verses to be memorized.
	The Bible is God's truth.
	The Bible tells what God wants us to know.
ABOUT HOME AND PARENTS	Parents have rules for me to follow, but they also have God's rules to follow.
	Parents are to me what God is to my parents.
	Parents want me to be a part of the family group.
	Home is a secure place where I can find my strength.

	Home is a happy place. Home is a place where I can talk over my problems with my parents. Home is a place where I can learn to follow rules.
ABOUT CHURCH AND SUNDAY SCHOOL	Church is like a school, except that I learn about God and the Bible. Church is a place where I can worship God. Church is a place to sing about God. Church is a place for families. Church is a happy place where I want to go. Church needs my help to be all that it should.
ABOUT OTHERS	Others include a wider world, far beyond the community. Others include foreign boys and girls across the sea. Others need help, which I can give. Others need the gospel, which I can share. Others need my prayers. Others need my money, which I can give.
ABOUT ANGELS AND LAST THINGS	Satan is a beautiful angel who sinned against God. Satan is the most wicked of all created beings. Satan tempts Christians and leads them astray. Good angels protect God's people. Good angels are God's messengers to people and carry out God's judgments. Heaven is for those who have accepted Christ as their personal Savior. People who do not accept Christ as their Savior will be separated from God forever.

TABLE 21.6

WHAT A CHILD OF TEN AND ELEVEN CAN LEARN

ABOUT GOD	God is Spirit, who is everywhere, but whose home is in heaven. God is all powerful, but He permits evil things to happen. God is all wise, but He permits people to choose between Him and sin, even though He knows what is best. God is one, but He is a triune being: Father, Son (Jesus Christ), and Holy Spirit. God is absolutely perfect, holy, and just. God hates all sin. God cares for and protects His children. God wants to show me His will for my life.

About Jesus	Jesus took on Himself the body of a man so He could do what God had planned. Jesus fulfilled part of God's great plan for me, to bring me to God; I must fulfill the other, to accept what Jesus did on the cross. Jesus shows me how to live for God, for His perfect life is a pattern for all. Jesus took the punishment for the sins of all people on Himself at Calvary. Jesus became alive again and lives in heaven. Jesus Christ was born of a virgin.
About the Bible	The Bible has the answers to all my everyday problems. The Bible can help me live a happy life. The Bible tells the history of God's work among people. The Bible is God's Word, the authority for life. The Bible is set in the culture of another kind of people. I need to understand that culture to understand the Bible. The Bible is without error. The Holy Spirit guided the writers of the Bible books. The Bible is a Book to honor and to memorize. It is God's truth to put into everyday practice. The Bible is God's truth for all people. I need to share it with others. The Bible, which is God's Word, is to be obeyed.
About Home and Parents	My home and parents are part of God's plan for me. My home and parents function as part of God's plan, but I should do my part too. I should show loyalty to my home and parents. I should show honor to my home and parents. I should accept correction from my parents, for this will help me become a strong leader. I should begin to see what makes a Christian home, looking toward the day when I will start one.
About Church and Sunday School	The church is a fellowship of believers in Christ. The church brings me in contact with Christian leaders. The church trains me in worship, study, prayer, witness, service, and fellowship. The church is a place where I can serve God. The church is a place where I can learn to practice Christian giving and outreach. I can learn about the ordinances.
About Others	Others need my respect for their thoughts, their possessions, their rights. Others need my understanding.

	Others need my help. I must show others honesty, loyalty, and fair play. Others need my forgiveness. Others need my prayers. Others fit into God's plans, just as I do.
ABOUT ANGELS AND LAST THINGS	Satan is the ruler of spiritual wickedness. Satan wants to keep people from coming to God. God has a plan for the future, which will come to pass. People who have trusted Christ as their Savior and have died will be raised from the dead when Christ returns. Satan and his angels will be cast into the lake of fire for eternal punishment. People who have not trusted Christ as their Savior will spend eternity in hell.

These are some of the many theological concepts, or Bible truths, which a child can learn. Some of these truths will need to be simplified for the very young child. Other children can understand more advanced concepts. These concepts are discussed more in *Leading Little Ones to God* and *Family Bible Library*.[2]

KNOW THE CHILD YOU WANT TO TEACH

YOUR CHILD IS AN INDIVIDUAL

Fingerprints, voiceprints, and other measuring devices show what we have known all along: there is nobody else exactly like your child. He or she is a unique creation. God made your child different from all other children, even those of the same age.

While it is important for you to know the general characteristics of children of that same age or learning level, you cannot escape your responsibility to know your child as an individual. Talk with him in depth. Try to understand what he thinks and why. You will teach him doctrine more effectively as you understand who he is and how he functions.

YOUR CHILD IS NOT A LITTLE ADULT

Teaching a child is not merely downgrading adult concepts. It is "customizing" those concepts to the learning level of the child. The teacher who "talks down" to a child will lose his interest.

A teacher should not expect maturity beyond what the child possesses. Too

2. Marian M. Schoolland, *Leading Little Ones to God* (Grand Rapids: Eerdmans, 1962); Beers, 10:9-38.

often we hear parents or teachers say, "I don't know why he doesn't show more interest in praying or in reading his Bible." Sometimes we simply expect that child or young person to have a maturity that comes with later years.

Remember that your child may have distractions from learning which are not apparent to you as an adult. Home atmosphere and the security generated in it, relationships with parents and other family members, the climate at school during the week, his health and sleeping habits—these all affect interest in learning Bible truth. It may not be that the child is disinterested in spiritual things. That child simply may have too many distractions to be interested. You cannot know this until you know that child as a person.

YOUR CHILD IS A TOTAL PERSON

Your child is a complex mixture of body, soul, mind, heritage, experiences, reactions, attitudes, thoughts, and associations with others. You are teaching a total person, not merely mind or soul.

Some of these things are beyond the child's control. He did not choose family or heritage. She did not select her own body, soul, or mind. Many of his experiences are planned by those with whom he lives.

A child who stays up too late on Saturday night to watch TV may not be too interested in your Bible teaching on Sunday morning. A child who has come to Sunday school from an unfortunate home situation may not be as quick to understand the delights of the family of God.

Doctrine is taught best in the context of daily living. You cannot isolate yourself from the child's experiences, heritage, homelife, and other determining factors, and expect to teach that child successfully. Know your child, but know him as a total person. Then you can teach him doctrine that will change his life.

SOME METHODS TO USE IN TEACHING DOCTRINE

Teaching a child is clarifying truth to him, not seeking to control his mind. If we seek to shape the child in our own image, we are trying to play God. Our task is to make truth so clear and so inviting that the child will become a happy student of the Word and, having given his life to Christ, will shape that life in the image of God.

This places on us, the parents and teachers, a responsibility which may sometimes seem frightening. But when we accept this responsibility as partners with God, it becomes a rich and rewarding experience.

Too often the word *teaching* forms in our minds the image of a direct transmission of knowledge to a learner. "Here are some truths for you to learn. Now learn them and practice them." This is a direct, or propositional approach.

We as parents and teachers should be aware of what is being taught biblically and theologically to our children as they move from one grade or department level to another in the church program. Even as we think of meeting the needs of the total person, we need to consider the total ministry to children—what they are being taught in Sunday school, church time, club ministries, vacation Bible school and other ministries that touch their lives.

Some areas of theology are best taught or emphasized at certain age levels in childhood. Foundational truths taught in early childhood are expanded and enriched as the child develops through the years. Different ministries can emphasize various aspects of theology so children will have well-rounded and balanced teaching. A survey of what is being taught at all levels in childhood would be helpful. Some theological teachings may need greater emphasis, while others may not be appropriate for the level being taught.

It is imperative that the teaching is done literally and concretely. Symbolism, generalizations, and abstractions should not be used, particularly at the earlier levels of childhood. Careful explanations of theological truth related to everyday living should be part of the total teaching.

A consistent and articulated program of Bible and theology should be developed from early childhood through the junior department level. Plans should be made to bridge the gap for those who lack background in biblical teaching through new enrollees classes, reading at home and individualized programs.

Parent-teacher meetings may be helpful for sharing information and keeping the lines of communication open as parents and teachers seek to work together. The church should *supplement* home training, not assume the spiritual responsibility of parents.

Some have found a degree of effectiveness in the direct approach, both in general education and in Christian education. But there is another effective way of doing the job.

Some favor an indirect approach. In it, education is accomplished not through propositions but through motivation. A child will learn more when he or she wants to learn, when truths are presented in such a way that they are interesting and delightful to the child.

Dr. Seuss, "Sesame Street," and Walt Disney have shown the effectiveness of this approach in general learning. Not much has been done with this approach in Christian literature for children.

Some methods that may be helpful in the indirect approach are:

1. *Example.* What you the parent or teacher do may speak louder than what you say. If you put the doctrine to work in your own life, it will show forth to the child as he observes you. You are really a living textbook.

2. *Reading.* Gladys Hunt has written an excellent book about the rewards of good reading with children and the learning values which come from that

reading.[3] As she points out, we must not limit our reading to those books which are "biblical" or "religious." Many life-building values come from the great children's books of today and yesterday, often supporting some important doctrines which we teach.

3. *Shared experiences.* A hike in the woods, a trip in the family car, a walk around the block, or a dozen other experiences involving the learner and the teacher, can be rewarding. In the context of these experiences, much can be taught about God and His plans for us. Claudia Royal points out the values of associating nature with the God who made it all.[4]

Experiences are everywhere. They are waiting for the teacher and child to participate in them and learn.

4. *Conversation.* Conversation is a pipeline between your mind and heart and the mind and heart of your child. To know your child thoroughly requires conversation. There is no other effective way to discover the innermost thoughts and attitudes. Ask the child questions that require more than just yes or no answers. Help her to reveal her own thoughts and ideas, to tell why she thinks as she does.

Conversation comes naturally through experiences which the teacher and child share. What is more natural than to talk about God the Creator as you walk through the autumn woods together or sit by a campfire and look up at the stars?

5. *Music and singing.* Christian songs are filled with important theological concepts for children. The songs for children, the great hymns, gospel songs—these are in themselves a course in doctrine.

There is something about singing doctrinal concepts that makes them stick in the mind and impress themselves upon the heart. Who does not remember the songs you learned as a child in Sunday school? They are theology. They touch the mind and heart of the child. But because they are sung, they are remembered better.

There is something wonderful about singing as a family. Singing together not only teaches, but helps to weld the family together.

6. *Picture reading.* Long before a child begins to read words, he learns to "read" pictures. The parent or teacher may point out many things in the pictures to focus the child's attention on the activity there. But the child will find more than the adult will. He will spontaneously find things the adult may miss.

Kenneth N. Taylor uses this method in *The Bible in Pictures for Little Eyes*.[5] By asking questions that focus attention on certain things, the parent or teacher helps the child learn many important Bible truths. A Bible story

3. Gladys Hunt, *Honey for a Child's Heart* (Grand Rapids: Zondervan, 1969).
4. Claudia Royal, *Teaching Your Child About God* (Westwood, N.J.: Revell, 1960), pp. 144-46.
5. Kenneth N. Taylor, *The Bible in Pictures for Little Eyes* (Chicago: Moody, 1956).

book with questions at the end of the story is *The Victor Family Story Bible,* by V. Gilbert Beers and Ronald A. Beers.[6]

Many other methods can be used, but these more obvious ones will stimulate you to think of others. The creative teacher or parent will build quite a list of indirect methods which can help the child learn doctrine.

It is very important that you look for opportunities in everyday living which can help your child learn the great truths of the Bible. This was the kind of education that God told His people to practice in the time of Moses, "And these words, which I command thee this day, shall be in thine heart: And thou shalt teach them diligently unto thy children, and shalt talk of them when thou sittest in thine house, and when thou walkest by the way, and when thou liest down, and when thou risest up" (Deut. 6:6-7).

SUMMARY

Is theology for the child or for the theologian? We *can* teach theology to children, but it must be taught simply and clearly with the "milk of the Word." The subject matter chosen must be on their levels of comprehension.

In laying foundations in teaching theology, we must know what we are to teach, know the child we wish to teach, and know how we plan to teach the child.

God's truth is for everyone, but we must make it applicable to children and their changing needs. There are four steps necessary for learning truth. These steps are knowing, understanding, applying, and practicing.

There are basic concepts that can be taught at each age level in childhood. The charts given in the chapter will provide guidance for teachers and parents to know what to teach at particular levels through childhood.

It is especially important that teachers and parents consider children as individuals, teach them as children and not as little adults, and as total persons.

There are many ways to teach theology, and we should use the best methods for each age level to communicate the truth and incorporate it into the lives of our children.

FOR FURTHER READING

Baker, Dolores, and Elsie Rives. *Teaching the Bible to Primaries.* Nashville: Convention, 1964.

Beers, V. Gilbert. *Family Bible Library.* Vol. 10. Nashville: Southwestern, 1971.

---

6. V. Gilbert Beers and Ronald A. Beers, *The Victor Family Story Bible* (Wheaton, Ill.: Scripture Press, Victor Books, 1985).

Bye, Beryl. *Teaching Our Children the Christian Faith*. London: Hodder & Stoughton, 1965.

Chamberlain, Eugene. *Preschoolers at Church*. Nashville: Convention, 1969.

———. *When Can a Child Believe?* Nashville: Broadman, 1973.

Edwards, Mildred Speakes. *Opening Doors of Faith: Guidance for the Christian Home When Children Are One to Five*. Kansas City, Mo.: Beacon Hill, 1953.

Fitzgerald, Annie. *Dear God Books*. Sets 1 and 2. Minneapolis: Augsburg, 1983, 1984.

Furnish, Dorothy Jean. *Exploring the Bible with Children*. Nashville: Abingdon, 1975.

Gleason, John J., Jr. *Growing Up to God*. Nashville, Abingdon, 1975.

Halverson, Delia. *Helping Your Child Discover Faith*. Valley Forge, Pa.: Judson, 1982.

Haystead, Wes. *Teaching Your Child About God*. Ventura, Calif.: Gospel Light, Regal Books, 1981.

Hendricks, William. *A Theology for Children*. Nashville: Broadman, 1980.

Holm, Marilyn F. *Tell Me Why: A Guide to Children's Questions About Faith and Life*. Minneapolis: Augsburg, 1985.

Hunt, Gladys. *Honey for a Child's Heart*. Grand Rapids: Zondervan, 1969.

Mow, Anna B. *Your Child from Birth to Rebirth*. Grand Rapids: Zondervan, 1963.

Royal, Claudia, *Teaching Your Child About God*. Westwood, N.J.: Revell, 1960.

Schoolland, Marian W. *Leading Little Ones to God*. Grand Rapids: Eerdmans, 1962.

Smith, Judy Gattis. *Developing a Child's Spiritual Growth Through Sound, Taste, Touch and Smell*. Nashville: Abingdon, 1983.

Trent, Robbie. *Your Child and God*. New York: Harper & Row, 1952.

Waldrop, C. Sybil. *Guiding Your Child Toward God*. Nashville: Convention, 1985.

Wilcox, Mary M. *Developmental Journey*. Nashville: Abingdon, 1979.

SERIES OF BOOKS TO USE IN THEOLOGY

Lindvall, Ella K. People of the Bible Series. Chicago: Moody, 1982, 1984.

Nystrom, Carolyn. Children's Bible Basics. Chicago: Moody, 1978-84.

22

Elizabeth Gangel

Using the Bible with Children

- Place of the Bible in Teaching Children
- Principles in Using the Bible
- Ways to Use the Bible
  IN THE CLASSROOM
  IN THE HOME
- Learning About the Bible
- Memorization of the Bible
  PRINCIPLES OF MEMORIZATION
  STEPS TO FOLLOW
  PROGRAMS FOR MEMORIZATION
  PORTIONS FOR MEMORIZATION
  CRITERIA FOR SELECTING MEMORY PASSAGES
- Relating the Bible to Life

Evangelical Christians are very quick to say that the Bible is the most important Book ever written. They believe it from "cover to cover," but in the reality of daily living, experience does not always support creed. The Bible is picked up on Sunday morning and carried to church and then returned to the shelf, not to be picked up again until the following Sunday. Many children are not seeing their parents reading and living God's Word. Martha Aycock suggests,

ELIZABETH GANGEL, B.S., is a Christian education consultant and author, residing in Rockwall, Texas.

Most educators and theologians agree that the most effective way for children to begin to know and understand the truths recorded in the Bible is to live with adults whose lives express these truths. When they do, children catch the spirit of Christ long before they can read or understand words about Him.[1]

Some objectives worth consideration while using the Bible with children are: (1) that the child may show a growing love for the Bible; (2) that the child may understand that the Bible is the basis of the Christian faith and the final authority on faith and conduct; (3) that the child may understand how Bible truth applies to daily living; (4) that the child may understand the origin of the Bible, including the preparing and preserving of it; (5) that the child may understand Bible content, customs, history, and geography; (6) that the child may commit Bible passages to memory.

THE IMPORTANCE AND PLACE OF THE BIBLE IN TEACHING CHILDREN

When we say the Bible is a special Book, that it is very important and should have a prominent place of recognition, exactly what do we mean? Do we mean we should have a special location in which to put the Bible in our homes or Sunday school rooms? Do we mean one must be careful how he handles the Bible? Do we mean that a teacher should always be sure the children understand that the stories he is telling and the verses he is teaching are taken from the Bible?

All of these things may be important, but we must go beyond them and teach our children that the Bible is a "God-breathed," written message, which gives us the answers to questions about God, ourselves, and the Christian life. Children need to know that the Bible is our final authority—a Book without error in its original languages. It shows us the way to God through Jesus Christ, helps us to know how to live the Christian life, and gives us guidance for making everyday decisions.

The best reason that the Bible is important comes from the Bible itself. "All Scripture is God-breathed and is useful for teaching, rebuking, correcting and training in righteousness, so that the man of God may be thoroughly equipped for every good work" (2 Tim. 3:16-17, NIV).

The following passages of Scripture give just a few of the reasons we teach the Bible.

"How can a young man keep his way pure? By living according to your word. . . . I have hidden your word in my heart that I might not sin against you. . . . I am a stranger on earth; do not hide your commands from me. . . . Your word, O Lord, is eternal; it stands firm in the heavens" (Ps. 119:9, 11, 19, 89, NIV). "For everything that was written in the past was written to teach us, so that through endurance and the encouragement of the Scriptures we might

1. Martha B. Aycock, ed., *Understand* (Richmond, Va.: John Knox, 1972), p. 115.

have hope" (Rom. 15:4, NIV). "Jesus did many other miraculous signs in the presence of his disciples, which are not recorded in this book. But these are written that you may believe that Jesus is the Christ, the Son of God, and that by believing you may have life in his name" (John 20:30-31, NIV). "But as for you, continue in what you have learned and have become convinced of, because you know those from whom you learned it, and how from infancy you have known the holy Scriptures, which are able to make you wise for salvation through faith in Christ Jesus" (2 Tim. 3:14-15, NIV).

Second Timothy 3:15 is the key to our understanding of the task which we have while teaching the Bible to children. Even though the Bible was written by adults, we, as adults, have the responsibility of training our children according to God's plan, and this must happen primarily in the home.

PRINCIPLES IN USING THE BIBLE WITH CHILDREN

When using the Bible with children, we should keep in mind these three principles. The first principle is that children should be able to have and use their own Bibles. Many Sunday schools encourage this by counting the Bibles brought every Sunday morning and putting the number on the register. Other churches try to solve the problem by having extra Bibles in the pew racks and in each Sunday school class. Providing Bibles may be a step in the right direction, but the most important aspect of this principle is to teach the children how to *use* their *own* Bibles. In order to do this, we must have cooperation between parents and teachers.

The big family Bible is fine but will not lend itself to individual study and the feeling of ownership by each member of the family. Parents can be of great assistance to their children if, during family worship, they take the time to help each child find the Scripture passages and generally to encourage him to become more familiar with his own Bible.

Teachers can help by doing the same things in the classroom. Many children become discouraged about taking their Bibles to Sunday school because they are not given the opportunity to use them and, therefore, decide it is not worth the effort to carry their Bibles back and forth each week. Later in the chapter, we will come back to this subject with some specific suggestions.

The second principle to keep in mind is that we must teach the Bible as God's whole revelation and not build a doctrine or teaching from one passage of Scripture to the exclusion of others.

One guideline of hermeneutics, the science of interpretation, is that of progressive revelation. Our children must be taught to understand that God was constantly revealing more of Himself and His plan all through biblical history. Today we can understand more of God's plan of redemption than Moses was able to comprehend.

Another guideline is that of the proportion of the Bible which deals with certain themes. Because God chose to have four books with eighty-nine chapters given over to the life and ministry of Jesus Christ, we can be sure that it is a very important theme in God's total revelation.

Another guideline is that of context. We must teach our children that they cannot build a doctrine of prayer on one verse such as, "You may ask me for anything in my name, and I will do it" (John 14:14, NIV), without looking at the verses which precede or follow. All the passages in the Bible must be considered when we form our beliefs on a particular subject.

The third principle in using the Bible with children is that children should realize the Bible is their final authority. Children tend to follow much more readily and naturally the example of parents and teachers than the teachings of the Bible. They need to be guided away from this tendency.

J. Omar Brubaker and Robert E. Clark remind us, "It is important to be absolutely truthful in answering a child's spiritual questions and not take advantage of his trusting spirit."[2] They also suggest, "The primary child is God-inclined, with a tender conscience, a strong impulse to obey, and implicit faith. He still believes what he is told, but is already beginning to seek proof and certainty."[3]

Because of these facts about children, parents and teachers must be careful to live what they teach and to teach only biblical truths. Then at the proper time, children can begin to understand that the authority for all of spiritual truth has come directly from God through His Word.

By the time students reach their teens, they should not be claiming beliefs because a church teaches them or even because parents hold to those truths. Teens need to develop their own set of convictions and beliefs based on the teachings of Scripture. David put it well: "Your word is a lamp to my feet and a light for my path" (Ps. 119:105, NIV).

Ways to Use the Bible with Children

Because it is important for children to begin to use their own Bibles, we might ask how parents and teachers can help to bring this about. The situation can be approached from two aspects, with some ideas and suggestions for each.

IN THE CLASSROOM

Nursery and kindergarten children can grasp that the Bible is a special Book which tells us about God and Jesus. They can understand that from this Book come the stories that they love and the Bible words they have memorized.

2. J. Omar Brubaker and Robert E. Clark, *Understanding People,* 2d ed. (Wheaton, Ill.: Evangelical Teacher Training Assn., 1981), p. 38.
3. Ibid., p. 46.

The teacher should always have a Bible in hand as he tells the Bible story, referring often to the fact that the Bible is true. A Bible should always be kept at some important place in the classroom for quick use and reference as the source of authority.

If children at these ages begin to bring their own Bibles, the teacher should be sure to give them an opportunity to "pretend read" from them. The teacher could help the children to find the Bible story of the day, or he could underline the Bible verse lightly in pencil.

By the time a child has reached his primary years, he is beginning to read. Now many activities can help him begin to learn the joy of using and studying the Bible. Because primary children are eager to use their new skill, a teacher should have no difficulty in getting volunteers to read certain verses or passages during classroom teaching or discussion.

A modern paraphrase such as *The Living Bible* can help children read the Bible with more ease and understanding.

Children also enjoy group reading. This approach will help a shy child to get involved. Group reading can be done in several ways: reading in unison, taking turns, choral reading. Some teachers record a Bible passage on a tape recorder and then during classtime, allow the children to join in and read along with the teacher, or the teacher could lead the group in alternate reading.

Wise teachers encourage primary children to investigate the Bible individually. This can be done by utilizing the students' manuals printed by Sunday school publishing companies or by asking specific fact or thought questions to which the students must find answers in a certain passage.

Early elementary children will need help with the basic skill of locating an assigned Bible book, chapter, or verse. Teachers can make this process easier by encouraging the children to memorize the books of the Bible in order and by giving plenty of opportunity to use this new information.

Juniors are ready for increased opportunities to use their Bibles. They are able to expand into areas such as problem-solving and research. Perhaps during class discussions, a question might come up which no one is able to answer. What a marvelous opportunity for personal Bible investigation! The students are sent home with an assignment to find the answer to the question in their Bibles.

A teacher may decide to spend some class time guiding students in solving a life-situation problem similar to experiences which they are facing at school or home. It could be a fictitious story with several possible endings. The students would investigate the Bible to decide on the right solution and then tell what passages of Scripture helped them solve the problem.

Juniors will also enjoy the competition of quizzes and sword drills. These activities will give them more opportunities to use and become familiar with their Bibles.

"Expressing" a Bible verse or passage has a lot of possibilities. Students may rewrite a verse in their own words, or verses may be expressed through art. The message in Romans 9:20-24 about the potter and the clay, for example, could be effectively taught with the use of clay modeling.

Rives and Sharp, in *Guiding Children,* say, "Today, a new emphasis is placed on providing the opportunities for children to experiment, research, think through, and to discover truths for themselves. Creative writing is one of these avenues."[4] Their chapter on "Learning Through Creative Writing" contains many helpful suggestions on how to write litanies, poems, stories, newspapers, and letters.

Barbara Bolton's book *How to Do Bible Learning Activities* also has many fine ideas on how to teach the Bible through art, drama, oral communication, creative writing, music activities, and Bible games.[5]

IN THE HOME

A group of fourth graders in a Christian school were asked some questions about the Bible. It was very interesting to evaluate their answers. When asked, "Do you ever read the Bible yourself?" 86 percent said "yes" or "I try," and only 14 percent said "not very much" or "not often."

When they were asked, "Do your mom and dad ever read the Bible to you?" 43 percent said "yes," and 57 percent said "no" or "sometimes."

In some homes, children may be more interested in reading and knowing about the Bible than are their parents. Some parents have the idea that the spiritual training of their children is the responsibility of the church or the Christian school. But God says, "These commandments that I give you today are to be upon your hearts. Impress them on your children. Talk about them when you sit at home and when you walk along the road, when you lie down and when you get up" (Deut. 6:6-7, NIV).

Family worship, training, and sharing will not just happen; it must be planned and worked into the family schedule. During family worship, each member should feel an openness to ask questions about the Bible that he might never ask in Sunday school. It is a time to share prayer burdens and lean on the Lord as a family. As Dorothy Martin says, "We can raise children to walk with the Lord day by day through each year. How is this possible? By following God's methods outlined in His Word and bringing the family to God every day for His blessing. This is what the family altar can do if we really work at it."[6]

Allowing children to help in the planning of family devotional times will increase their interest. They may tire of always hearing the parents do the Bible

---

4. Elsie Rives and Margaret Sharp, *Guiding Children* (Nashville: Convention, 1969), p. 100.
5. Barbara Bolton, *How to Do Bible Learning Activities,* Glendale, Calif.: Gospel Light, Regal Books, 1984.
6. Dorothy Martin, *Creative Family Worship* (Chicago: Moody, 1976), p. 19.

reading and "preaching." Older children can help plan which subjects to discuss, which songs to sing, whether printed material should be used, and which Bible story to use. They can also help assign responsibilities to family members. (For more on children's personal devotions, see chap. 23, "Teaching Children to Worship and Pray.")

Many books are available for use in family devotions. A list of Bible story-books and devotional books that children can read in personal and family devotions is given at the end of this chapter.

LEARNING ABOUT THE BIBLE

The same group of fourth-grade students referred to earlier were asked, "What is the Bible to you?" The answers varied from "It is a good Book," "It is love," "It is everything," to "It's the truth, the Word of God."

Most fourth graders are ready to explore such questions about the Bible as, How did we get our Bible? Who wrote it? How long ago was the Bible written? How was it protected all these years? In what languages was it originally written? What did those languages look like? How many people helped write the Bible? Is it one Book or many books?

By the time children reach middle elementary years, they are beginning map study in school. We need to begin at the same time to acquaint them with maps in connection with certain Bible stories. How can they fully understand the story of the good Samaritan, the account of the woman at the well, the wanderings of the children of Israel, or Paul's missionary journeys without some map study? Yet Sunday school teachers are themselves embarrassed at their own inability to draw a simple map of the land of Palestine.

The Victor Handbook of Bible Knowledge by V. Gilbert Beers is a marvelous source of information.[7] It contains maps, illustrations, and descriptions of life in Bible times.

Older children are also ready to learn how to use a Bible dictionary or concordance. Perhaps in the study of a certain passage of Scripture, a term is used which is unfamiliar to the children or which they find difficult to explain in their own words. Here is an opportunity to take time to help the children see how to consult a Bible dictionary to find the meaning of such terms.

A pictorial Bible dictionary can be a very interesting way to study proper names and a most helpful tool for students preparing a class report.

The concordance is basic to effective word study. Let's return to the word *prayer* for an example of a word study. Bring several concordances to class and pass them out among your students. The students may work in teams or individually, depending on the number of concordances available. Each team

---

7. V. Gilbert Beers, *The Victor Handbook of Bible Knowledge,* Wheaton, Ill.: Scripture Press, Victor Books, 1981.

can be assigned to several books of the Bible. The team's responsibility would be to look up the verses in those books that talk about prayer and to write down what they teach. After reporting what they have found, the class will have a much better knowledge of what the Bible has to say about prayer.

Older children can also be taught how to use a commentary as an aid to understanding a Bible verse.

Using your imagination, make the study of God's Word an exciting adventure for your students in class and your children at home. May we never make the Bible seem boring.

MEMORIZATION OF THE BIBLE

Christ is our example in showing us the importance of memorizing Scripture. When Christ was tempted by Satan, He was able to defeat him by the authority of God's Word. This victory was possible because He knew the Scriptures from memory. To the extent children know the Scriptures they can overcome Satan's temptations against their young lives. "I have hidden your word in my heart that I might not sin against you" (Ps. 119:11, NIV).

Clark suggests several reasons for having children memorize Bible verses:

> God uses His Word not only to convict of sin but to guide in right and holy living. Memorized Scripture can help children obey authority, find encouragement, resist temptation, witness, make decisions to glorify the Lord, express their thoughts to God, claim God's promises and prepare for the future.[8]

Children can also be encouraged to memorize Bible portions as a means of being able to answer their friends' questions about God and the Bible. "But in your hearts acknowledge Christ as the holy Lord. Always be prepared to give an answer to everyone who asks you to give the reason for the hope that you have" (1 Pet. 3:15, NIV).

Many Christian young people and adults, while hospitalized or undergoing other troubles, have been blessed by recalling many Bible verses which they had committed to memory when they were children.

PRINCIPLES OF MEMORIZATION

For many people, memorizing is only a repetition of words which are soon forgotten. Some ways to make Bible memory work more meaningful and lasting are suggested in the following paragraphs.

1. Help the children understand the meaning of the verse(s) to be memorized. After a verse is understood, it is easier to memorize. Comprehension aids memorization.

---

8. Robert E. Clark, "Helping Children Memorize Scripture," *Moody Monthly* 72 (July-August 1972):66.

2. Review the verses memorized. Most people have experienced the type of rote learning done exclusively to pass a test or to receive a certain recognition. Without periodic review, such "learning" fades rapidly. Referring to the memory verse several times throughout the lesson helps the children retain it.

3. Use visual aids when teaching memory verses. Flash cards, overhead projection, tape recorders, puppets, pictures, posters, puzzles, secret codes, and songs are tools that can help children remember Bible verses. (Scripture Press publishes suede-backed Scripture-text cards for such passages as Luke 2:8-14, 16; Rom. 10:9-15; Ps. 23; and Matt. 6:9-13.)

4. Consider having the children memorize occasionally from a modern Bible version or paraphrase. Suppose a memory verse for juniors is 2 Timothy 2:15. Which one of these translations would be most meaningful for a junior?

"Study to shew thyself approved unto God, a workman that needeth not be ashamed, rightly dividing the word of truth" (KJV).

"Be diligent to present yourself approved to God as a workman who does not need to be ashamed, handling accurately the word of truth" (NASB).

"Do your utmost to present yourself to God approved, a workman who has no cause to be ashamed, correctly interpreting the message of the truth" (Berkeley).

"Work hard so God can say to you, 'Well done.' Be a good workman, one who does not need to be ashamed when God examines your work. Know what his word says and means" (TLB).

"Do your best to present yourself to God as one approved, a workman who does not need to be ashamed and who correctly handles the word of truth" (NIV).

Should all memorization center on the King James Version? This is a debated question. If a child can understand and apply the verse more easily from a modern version, perhaps we should not allow tradition to stand in the way. On the other hand, if all of the children in the class have the King James Version, it may be less confusing to teach from it than to teach from a version or paraphrase owned by only a few students in the class.

5. Enlist the cooperation of parents in memory work. Parents can be a great help in encouraging the memorization of Scripture. They have the entire week to review the verse and to help their children become aware of situations in which the verse applies.

6. Weave the memory verse into the lesson. Clark suggests,

> One of the best ways to teach a memory verse is to weave it into the lesson where it fits naturally. The verse may be repeated several times throughout the session and by the end of the period the pupils will be acquainted with the basic content and meaning of the verse.[9]

9. Ibid.

7. Help the children comprehend how the verse applies to their lives.

It is important to memorize Bible verses and entire passages, but if the memorized verses have no meaning or bring about no change in the lives of the children we teach, then they are of little value.

If a preschooler is able to recite "Be ye kind one to another." and is constantly found hitting, biting, kicking, and grabbing toys, he has not really learned that verse. If a seven-year-old is able to say, "Children, obey your parents in the Lord; for this is right," but continues to ignore his parents' commands to turn off the television or get ready for bed, he has not truly learned that verse.

Are these children just very difficult and incorrigible? Not necessarily. Perhaps the problem lies with the teacher or parent. All too often, memory verses are handled like this:

Teacher: How many of you boys and girls know your memory verse this week? (Several hands go up.) OK, Billy, you say it first.

Billy: "It is a good thing to give thanks unto the Lord," Psalm 92:1.

Teacher: Very good, Billy, you may put a star on the chart. Susan, you are next.

By the time the three or four children who know the verse have said it, there are probably three or four more children who are ready to say it just from listening to the others repeat it. The children are very pleased that they are able to perform and to put a star on the chart. The teacher moves on to another activity, but when it comes time to have prayer, there is no connection made between the verse and giving thanks to God. Even helping the children grasp the meaning of the verse is not enough; they must understand how that verse applies to their lives. Verses can be used that illustrate different aspects of a child's life at home, school, playground, church, and in his relationships with his parents, brothers and sisters, and friends.

STEPS IN MEMORIZATION

In teaching children to memorize Scripture, it is helpful to follow these steps:

1. Be sure to select Scripture according to the characteristics and needs of the students being taught.
2. Learn the material well yourself.
3. Present the material in a setting. Weave the verse or passage naturally into the lesson, teach with a melody or song, tell a story in which the Scripture is repeated with variety, use pictures to illustrate the Scripture, or relate the verse or passage to a natural setting, such as the creation.
4. Introduce the whole passage before analyzing its parts.

5. Break the selection into parts and analyze each part carefully: vocabulary, concepts, relationships, illustrations for clarification.
6. Repeat the whole verse or passage.
7. Show specifically how the selection can relate to daily life.
8. Drill for fun, and in a variety of ways.
9. Use the verse or passage in department or class activities. Review often and meaningfully.
10. Encourage practice in real life with follow-up as to how God has used His Word.

It is far better to help children learn a few verses or passages well than many poorly.

PROGRAMS FOR MEMORIZATION

Most evangelical publishers of curriculum materials include a memory verse correlated with each lesson. When used properly, these passages are excellent teaching tools. The Bible verse helps reinforce the truth of the lesson.

Memory work is an important part of the programs of the Awana Youth Association, Christian Service Brigade, Pioneer Clubs, and denominational club programs. In these programs, awards encourage the children to memorize Scripture.

In some churches, children are required to memorize verses in each of several educational ministries, including Sunday school, children's church, Sunday evening children's group. This demands careful supervision in order to avoid overloading the children with more than they can retain, and to avoid needless repetition of the same verses.

The Bible Memory Association produces age-graded materials that encourage Bible memorization on a regular basis.[10] Children ages three through six may participate in the "ABC plan," which includes three stages, one stage per year for the three years. The plan includes twenty-four verses altogether. Stage 1 is for ages three or four, in which the child learns a short verse each week for twelve weeks. Stage 2 is for ages four or five, in which the child learns two short verses a week for twelve weeks. And stage 3 is for ages five or six, in which the child learns two short verses with references each week for twelve weeks. Each year, the child builds on what was learned the previous year, reviewing the twenty-four short verses.

The "Beginner plan," for children in grades 1 through 5, includes memorizing four or five verses each week during January, February, and March.

Success with Youth, Inc., publishes "Power Flight 52," a memorization program for juniors.[11] It is designed to be completed in fifty-two weeks or less.

10. Write to Bible Memory Association, Box 12,000, St. Louis, MO 63112.
11. Write to Success with Youth, Inc., Box 27,028, Tempe, AZ 85202.

Of course, it is always possible for teachers or parents to work out their own particular memorization programs. The following section contains suggested verses or passages for each age level.

PORTIONS FOR MEMORIZATION

For preschoolers. Generally a portion of a verse is best to use in teaching memory work to preschoolers. The following are some verses suitable for young children, given here to illustrate that portions of verses are sufficient.

THEME	BIBLE WORDS	REFERENCE
A child's behavior	"Love one another."	1 John 4:7
	"Be kind to each other."	Eph. 4:7 (TLB)
	"Don't forget to do good."	Heb. 13:16 (TLB)
	"Children, obey your parents."	Eph. 6:1
Creation	"He has made everything beautiful."	Eccles. 3:11 (NIV)
	"God created the heavens and the earth."	Gen. 1:1
The Lord's attitude toward us	"The Lord is my Helper."	Heb. 13:6 (TLB)
	"He cares for you."	1 Pet. 5:7 (NIV)
	"He loved us, and sent his Son."	1 John 4:10
Our attitude toward the the Lord	"We love him, because he first loved us."	1 John 4:19
	"I will love you, O Lord."	Ps. 18:1 (NIV)
	"I will sing unto the Lord."	Ps. 13:6

For primaries. Because many of the passages used for preschoolers are parts of verses, the primary years are a good time for children to learn the complete verses. For example, all of Ephesians 6:1 is as follows: "Children, obey your parents in the Lord: for this is right." The words for preschoolers from Psalm 13:6 can be expanded as follows for primaries: "I will sing unto the Lord, because he hath dealt bountifully with me."

Some older primaries are able to learn passages that are fairly short and easy to understand. Several examples are Psalms 23; 100; 136:1-9; and John 14:1-6.

For juniors. Juniors are capable of tackling large sections of Scripture (in addition to the weekly verse with the Bible lesson.) Some passages on selected themes are these: love, 1 Corinthians 13; faith, Hebrews 11; salvation, John 3; Ten Commandments, Exodus 20; Beatitudes, Matthew 5:1-12; Christ's return, 1 Thessalonians 4:13-18.

CRITERIA FOR SELECTING MEMORY PASSAGES

The following questions can be kept in mind when selecting Bible passages for memorization:

1. Is the content of the passage or verse within the range of ability for comprehension?
2. Is the meaning of the passage or verse given in literal and concrete terms that children can grasp?
3. Can the vocabulary be explained for understanding?
4. Is the passage or verse appropriate in length for the attention span?
5. Can the passage or verse be applied specifically to their everyday experiences?

RELATING THE BIBLE TO LIFE

A fine Sunday school teacher I know is always trying something new and creative with her fifth-grade students. Her students could recite several verses on prayer, including these: "Pray always with all prayer and supplication"; "Men ought always to pray"; "Pray for one another." But she could not get any of her students to lead in prayer.

She decided on a behavioral objective for her class: each student will learn to pray orally during this quarter. Then she set about to accomplish that objective. The next Sunday, when they came into class, she brought an extra chair and placed it in the circle. She told the students that Jesus was sitting in that chair, even though He could not be seen with human eyes, and she wanted each of them to say something to Him as if He were really there. Slowly, awkwardly, each child began to say something. One boy, who had tried very hard not to get involved, said, "I love You, Jesus." What a breakthrough! Over a period of time, this teacher saw her objective accomplished, and the students were beginning to see how the Bible related to their individual lives. They began to understand that the Lord was right there with them and that they could talk to Him about anything just as easily as they could talk to their teacher or their friends.

One night, when our daughter was nine years old, she said she was afraid to fall asleep. A couple of days later, we were reading from the book of Psalms, "I will lie down in peace and sleep, for though I am alone, O Lord, you will keep me safe" (Ps. 4:8, TLB). Julie looked up at me, smiled, and said, "I didn't know the Bible said that." She had discovered that the Bible had something to say about the problem she was facing.

When we begin to see changes in the lives of our students as a result of Bible stories, Bible study, and memorization, we have begun to accomplish our goal.

SUMMARY

All biblical Christian education, whether it takes place in the home, the church or the school, must be based on the teachings of Scripture. The Bible is the focal point of everything we do. The Word of God is the Christian's guide for faith and practice. If we fail to communicate its truth properly to our children, little else matters.

Christian leaders must not only believe and teach that the Bible is the infallible Word of God but must live out biblical principles as an example before children. It is not sufficient to merely teach *about* the Bible; rather, it is essential that Christian leaders be able to say with the psalmist, "I have not departed from your laws, for you yourself have taught me. How sweet are your promises to my taste, sweeter than honey to my mouth!" (Ps. 119:102-103, NIV).

FOR FURTHER READING

GENERAL STUDIES

Adam, Ernest R., and Mavis Allen. *How to Improve Bible Teaching and Learning in Sunday School.* Nashville: Convention, 1976.

Aycock, Martha B., ed. *Understand.* Richmond, Va.: John Knox, 1972.

Bible Background Booklets. Minneapolis: Augsburg, various dates, 1980 on.

Bible Background Learning Kit. Minneapolis: Augsburg, 1981.

Books of the Bible Learning Kit. Minneapolis: Augsburg, 1981.

Bolton, Barbara J. *How To Do Bible Learning Activities.* Glendale, Calif.: Gospel Light, 1984.

———. *Ways to Help Them Learn: Children, Grades 1 to 6.* Glendale, Calif.: Gospel Light, Regal Books, 1972.

Brubaker, J. Omar, and Robert E. Clark. *Understanding People.* 2d ed. Wheaton, Ill.: Evangelical Teacher Training Assn., 1981.

Coleman, Lucien E., Jr. *How to Teach the Bible.* Nashville: Broadman, 1979.

Duvall, Evelyn M. *Faith In Families.* Nashville: Broadman, 1972.

Edge, Findley B. *Helping the Teacher.* Nashville: Broadman, 1959.

———. *Teaching for Results.* Nashville: Broadman, 1956.

Furnish, Dorothy. *Living the Bible with Children.* Nashville: Abingdon, 1979.

Gangel, Kenneth O. "Teaching for Memorization." *The Sunday School Times and Gospel Herald* 70 (15 July 1972):28-29.

Gibson, Joyce, and Eleanor Hance. *You Can Teach Juniors & Middlers.* Wheaton, Ill.: Scripture Press, Victor Books, 1981.

Griggs, Donald. *20 New Ways of Teaching the Bible.* Nashville: Abingdon, 1983.

Harrell, Donna, and Wesley Haystead. *Creative Bible Learning for Young Children.* Ventura, Calif.: Gospel Light, Regal Books, 1977.

Haystead, Wesley. *Teaching Your Child About God.* Ventura, Calif.: Gospel Light, Regal Books, 1981.

Kiethahn, Mary N., and Marilyn H. Dunshee. *How to Teach Bible Stories: For Grades 4-12.* Nashville: Abingdon, 1978.

Klausmeier, Robert. "Make the Bible a Children's Book, Too!" *Evangelizing Today's Child* (January-February 84), pp. 6-7, 58.

Klink, Johanna L. *Your Child and Religion.* Richmond, Va.: John Knox, 1971.

LeBar, Mary E., and Betty A. Riley. *You Can Teach 4s & 5s.* Wheaton, Ill.: Scripture Press, Victor Books, 1981.

Liu, Sarah, and Mary Lou Vittitow. *Creative Bible Activities for Children.* Wheaton, Ill.: Scripture Press, Victor Books, 1977.

Martin, Dorothy. *Creative Family Worship.* Chicago: Moody, 1976.

McDaniel, Elsiebeth, and Lawrence O. Richards. *You and Children.* Chicago: Moody, 1973.

McDaniel, Elsiebeth. *You Can Teach Primaries.* Wheaton, Ill.: Scripture Press, Victor Books, 1981.

Rice, Shirley. *The Christian Home.* Norfolk, Va.: Norfolk Christian Schools, 1967.

Rives, Elsie, and Margaret Sharp. *Guiding Children.* Nashville: Convention, 1969.

Rood, Wayne R. *On Nurturing Christians.* Nashville: Abingdon, 1972.

Rowen, Dolores. *Ways to Help Them Learn: Early Childhood, Birth to 5 Years.* Glendale, Calif.: Gospel Light, Regal Books, 1972.

Short, Beth. *Memorizing Bible Verses With Games & Crafts.* St. Louis: Concordia, 1984.

Smith, Judy Gattis. *20 New Ways to Use Drama in Teaching the Bible.* Nashville: Cokesbury, 1981.

Trent, Robbie. *How the Bible Came to Us.* Nashville: Broadman, 1964.

Weatherly, G. "The Bible and Your Children." *The Sunday School Times and Gospel Herald* 70 (15 November 1972): 22-23.

Westerhoff, John. *Will Our Children Have Faith?* New York: Seabury, 1976.

BOOKS FOR CHILDREN'S DEVOTIONS

Beers, V. Gilbert, and Ronald A. Beers. *Choosing God's Way.* Wheaton, Ill.: Scripture Press, Victor Books, 1983.

———. *My Favorite Things.* Wheaton, Ill.: Scripture Press, Victor Books, 1984.

Daily Bread. Warrenton, Mo.: Child Evangelism Fellowship.

Dienert, Ruth Graham. *First Steps in the Bible.* Waco, Tex.: Word, 1980.

Freeman, Margaret. *Hidden Treasure Parables for Kids.* Cincinnati: Standard, 1982.

Hook, Martha, and Tinka Boren. *Little Ones Listen to God.* Grand Rapids: Zondervan, 1971.

Jahsmann, Allan Hart, and Martin P. Simon. *Little Visits with God.* St. Louis: Concordia, 1957.

———. *More Little Visits with God.* St. Louis: Concordia, 1961.

Jay, Ruth Johnson. *Selected Devotions for Pre-teens.* Chicago: Moody, 1983.

LeBar, Lois E. *Family Devotions with School-age Children.* Westwood, N.J.: Revell, 1973.

Merrell, Jo Ann. *Bible Stories For Family Devotions.* Minneapolis: Bethany House, 1980.

Schoolland, Marian M. *Leading Little Ones to God.* Grand Rapids: Eerdmans, 1962.

Shibley, David, and Naomi Shibley. *Special Times with God.* Nashville: Thomas Nelson, 1981.

———. *More Special Times with God.* Nashville: Thomas Nelson, 1984.

Taylor, Kenneth N. *Stories for the Children's Hour.* Rev. ed. Chicago: Moody, 1968.

Webb, Barbara O. *Devotions for Families: Building Blocks of Christian Life.* Valley Forge, Pa.: Judson, 1976.

Whitehouse, Donald, and Nancy Whitehouse. *Pray and Play: A Guide for Family Worship.* Nashville: Broadman, 1979.

BIBLE STORYBOOKS FOR CHILDREN

Adcock, Roger. *God's Early Heroes.* Wheaton, Ill.: Scripture Press, 1971.

———. *Stories of Jesus.* Wheaton, Ill.: Scripture Press, 1971.

Barrett, Ethel. *It Didn't Just Happen.* Glendale, Calif.: Gospel Light, Regal Books, 1967.

Beers, V. Gilbert. *A Child's Treasury of Bible Stories.* New York: World, 1971.

———. *Family Bible Library.* Nashville: Southwestern, 1971.

———. *My Picture Bible.* Wheaton, Ill.: Scripture Press, Victor Books, 1982.

———. *Walking With Jesus.* San Bernandino, Calif.: Here's Life, 1984.

Beers, V. Gilbert, and Ronald A. Beers. *The Victor Family Story Bible.* Wheaton, Ill.: Scripture Press, Victor Books, 1985.

Egermeier, Elsie E. *Egermeier's Bible Story Book.* Rev. ed. Anderson, Ind.: Warner, 1969.

Fletcher, Sarah. *Bible Story Book—Old Testament.* St. Louis, Mo.: Concordia, 1983.

———. *My Bible Story Book.* St. Louis, Mo.: Concordia, 1974.

———. *My Stories About Jesus.* St. Louis, Mo.: Concordia, 1974.

Gross, Arthur W. *Concordia Bible Story Book.* St. Louis, Mo.: Concordia, 1971.

Haan, Sheri Dunham. *A Child's Storybook of Bible People.* Grand Rapids: Baker, 1973.

———. *Good News for Children.* Grand Rapids: Baker, 1969.
Lindvall, Ella K. *Read-Aloud Bible Stories* Vols. 1 and 2. Chicago: Moody, 1982, 1985.
———. *The Bible Illustrated for Little Children.* Chicago: Moody, 1985.
Marshall, Catharine. *Story Bible.* Lincoln, Va.: Chosen, 1982.
Mills, Brenda. *My Bible Story Picture Book.* Eugene, Oreg.: Harvest, 1982.
Reid, John Calvin. *30 Favorite Bible Stories.* Cincinnati: Standard, 1982.
Taylor, Kenneth N. *Taylor's Bible Story Book.* Wheaton, Ill.: Tyndale, 1970.
———. *The Bible in Pictures for Little Eyes.* Chicago: Moody, 1956.
Van Ness, Bethann. *The Bible Stories.* Nashville: Broadman, 1963.
Vos, Catherine F. *Child Story Bible.* Grand Rapids: Eerdmans, 1969.

23

Edward L. Hayes

Evangelism of Children

- The Child and the Church
- The Concept of Conversion
- The Age of Accountability
- Evangelistic Appeals
- Conversion and the Concepts of Moral Development
- Discipling a Child's Decision
- Christian Nurture
- Christian Discipleship

Sparkling with controversy, the subject of child conversion prompts debate and discussion. The issue is one of theology as well as methodology. It is one of faith as well as feeling, dogma as well as response, crisis as well as process. It is at the core of our faith and is the root of true Christian education.

Jesus Himself said, "Except ye be converted, and become as little children, ye shall not enter into the kingdom of heaven" (Matt. 18:3). To Him, the recovery of one lost child was top priority, and those who offended children were marked for judgment. Turning to Jesus was turning to God.

Leading the young child to Christ has only within recent times become a specialized ministry in churches. This is due, in part at least, to particular viewpoints toward the concept of the soul, original sin, baptism, the nature of

EDWARD L. HAYES, Ph. D., is executive director of Mount Hermon Association, Mount Hermon, California.

church membership, and the psychology of human maturation. For instance, the belief that infant baptism is not only legitimate but preferred over believers' baptism forestalls the necessity of evangelistic instruction to the young. Furthermore, concepts of grace in relationship to the depravity of human nature have led to at least two dominant positions on the nature of the soul and the necessity of early conversion. One view holds that a child's depravity demands an early conversion, as early as age three. Another holds that God's grace is operative in a child's innocence; until an age of accountability, no stress ought to be placed on crisis conversion. Of course, the issue of church membership as it relates to baptism either fosters child evangelism or forbids it.

Another major area of human investigation sheds both light and confusion on the subject. Moral development theories[1] posed by Jean Piaget, Lawrence Kohlberg, and others basically hold that the normal socio-psychological developments of a person preclude any necessity of conversion. While not denying the existence of religious developments, these theories hold no brief for what Kohlberg calls "Divine Command Theorists" who call for exclusive moral education within church, school or home.[2] At best, however, these theories give insight into what might be called normal behavioral development.

Finally, since the rise of the religious education movement at the turn of our century, the wedding of psychological insights with traditional or biblical truths has led to skepticism toward some evangelistic tactics with the very young. These and other issues combine to form a confusing mosaic. A theology of conversion, particularly as it relates to the child, is desperately needed.

The rise of child evangelism efforts can be traced to a vacuum which existed in Reformation theology. To be sure, the child was not ignored. Luther himself placed great value on the education of the young, but the matter of conversion was largely an adult concept. In the nineteenth century, revivalists stressed the necessity of a crisis conversion. Fired by the zeal of Sabbath school proponents, church leaders recaptured something of a primitive evangelistic fervor.

Augustus H. Strong, a leading theologian, was captive to an idea that the conversion of children was vital to Christian expansion. In a sermon preached in 1865 at the Baptist church in Haverhill, Massachusetts, Strong sanctioned the rise of the Sunday school, or Sabbath school as it was called. "Its beginning," he pronounced, "marks an era in the history of the church. It seems that God is fulfilling one of His last words of prophecy by turning the hearts of the fathers unto the children." He went on to recognize a renaissance in freedom. "At long last it is now believed that Christ died for the woman, the

---

1. Jean Piaget, *The Moral Judgment of a Child* (New York: Free Press, 1965).
2. Lawrence Kohlberg, *The Philosophy of Moral Development* (San Francisco: Harper & Row, 1981), pp. 311-15.

Negro, and the child. Only in recent centuries have men come to believe that any of these actually had a soul."[3] Strong, along with few others of his time, looked upon children as mortal, responsible spirits, capable of sin and just as capable of receiving salvation. With Augustus Strong, this teaching was tempered by a rising spirit of independence from either of the extremes of forced guilt by evangelistic excesses or by evasion of the responsibility for and validity of child conversion.

Today, child evangelism efforts are marked by increasing institutionalization and agency expansion. Specialization has entered the Christian marketplace, and organizational efforts abound. Reaction and counteraction call for sound formulations and standards for proper assessment of their worth. This chapter attempts to answer at least six fundamental questions: Should the child be evangelized? What is the proper age for declaration of faith? Do children differ from adults in response? What is the relationship of evangelism to nurture? How do theories of moral developments relate to the theology and praxis of child evangelization? What implications does a theology of conversion have to church, home, and community evangelistic strategy?

The Child and the Church

There are comparatively few references to children in the New Testament. "This fact," says William B. Coble in *Children and Conversion,* "can easily lull us into the false assumption that children are to be treated in the same manner as adults."[4] But even so, children are of first-rate importance, according to William Barclay in *Train up a Child.*[5]

In the Old Testament, the concept of covenant carried with it the fundamental relationship of the child to the community. It is precisely this dimension that is often missing in contemporary evangelical approaches to child evangelization. And it is exactly at this point that Horace Bushnell, whose fundamental work *Christian Nurture*[6] still continues to influence Christian education, made his controversial contribution. His idea of an "organic unity" between Christian parent and child grew out of his Theology of the Covenant.

The concepts of inherited guilt and inherited faith have been thought to be Old Testament ideas. The sins of the fathers were indeed thought to be visited upon the children, but an optimism accounting for inherited faith finds little warrant in the Bible. Although a corporate solidarity was evident between

3. Augustus H. Strong, "The Conversion of Children," in *The Watchman-Examiner* 53 (23 September 1965): 583.
4. William B. Coble, "New Testament Passages About Children," in *Children and Conversion,* ed. Clifford Ingle (Nashville: Broadman, 1970), p. 36.
5. William Barclay, *Train Up a Child* (Philadelphia: Westminster, 1959), p. 234.
6. Horace Bushnell, *Christian Nurture* (New Haven, Conn.: Yale University, 1916).

father and son particularly,[7] and between Israel and the child corporately, this does not explain the necessity of the call of the prophets to repent. There was, and still is the need for a radical break between the past and the future between Kohlberg's "is" and "ought" dimension of moral development. That break we call conversion.

Our bondage to sin is not something we can free ourselves from unaided. It is also impossible for communities to do it for us. Dykstra asserts: "In traditional theological language, we have said that such salvation depends upon God's grace."[8]

It is clear that the New Testament builds on the Hebrew ideal of the father training the child. This assumption may explain in part at least the relative absence of instructional material in the New Testament regarding children. It is also clear that Jesus was never too busy for children. On the occasion when His disciples tried to hold back the children, Jesus allowed them to come to Him (Matt. 19:13; Mark 9:36; Luke 18:15). On the way to Jerusalem, Jesus had time to hold the children. His reference in Matthew 18:10 to angels guarding children clearly refers to God's special place for children in the kingdom.

Fathers, in particular, were to care for the child in spiritual matters (Matt. 7:11; Mark 11:13). This primary human duty was absolutely binding. To receive a child was to receive Jesus Himself (Matt. 18:5; Mark 9:36; Luke 9:48). The fate of a man who provides the wrong example to a child is a more bitter fate than that which many other sins deserve. Jesus taught that it would be better for a man to have a great millstone hung around his neck and be drowned than to cause a child to stumble (Matt. 18:6-14; Mark 9:42; Luke 17:2).

We must conclude from Jesus' teaching on the kingdom that children were important. The false sophistication of adults was placed in stark contrast to the simple faith of a child. "Whosoever shall not receive the kingdom of God as a little child, he shall not enter therein" (Mark 10:15). The child, according to Barclay, "is the very pattern of the citizen of the Kingdom."[9]

The child was a lesson on true greatness in Matthew 18:1-5; Mark 9:33-37; and Luke 9:46-48. When the disciples asked who was the greatest in the kingdom of heaven, Jesus called a little child to Him. Conversion, or turning around, was the one essential requirement for entrance to heaven. Becoming as a little child was a natural way of saying two things: children are important in

---

7. Kohlberg, pp. 101-89. The author gives an extended treatment of the facts of moral development (the "is" dimension) and the ideal content or epistomological status of moral development (the "ought" dimension). Here the door of opportunity is opened for the formulation of a revelational-based view of Christian conversion.
8. Craig Dykstra, "What Are People Like: An Alternative to Kohlberg's View," in *Moral Development Foundtions,* ed. Donald M. Joy (Nashville: Abingdon, 1983), p. 161.
9. Barclay, p. 235.

the kingdom, and adult faith must bear the marks of childlike simplicity. The child was not to imitate adult belief; instead the adult was to discover the simplicity of trust.

Although the gospel passages do not indicate a methodology for child evangelism, they do emphasize the worth of the individual. We are reminded that every reference to children in the gospels adds to our understanding of the gospel message. It is for all mankind, rich or poor, great or small, adult or child. "Even so," said Jesus, "it is not the will of your Father which is in heaven, that one of these little ones should perish" (Matt. 18:14).

The meager references in the Acts of the Apostles and in the epistles lend little help in building a strong case for child evangelism as such, other than to build the case that the gospel is for all mankind. For instance, the promise in Acts 2:39 makes reference to "you and your children." The entire nation of Israel is in focus, not children. In the instance when Paul baptized the Philippian jailer, "he and all his house" (Acts 16:33), apparently the whole family believed (v. 34). No support may be given for household faith, that is, an organic link between an adult believer and a child in a spiritual relationship. The children made their own decision.

The New Testament gives guidelines for the nurture of children (Eph. 6:4; Col. 3:21). Barclay concludes:

> The New Testament lays down no kind of curriculum of training for the child; the New Testament knows nothing about religious education and nothing about schools; for the New Testament is certain that the only training which really matters is given within the home, and that there are no teachers so effective for good or evil as parents are.[10]

For at least two centuries, the early church apparently did not allow children to be baptized or enter the church. By A.D. 400, the doctrine of original sin had come to justify infant baptism. The issue of evangelizing children cannot be fully answered by direct references to the gospel or to the epistles. Certainly no methodology is implied. The tension between accepting a gospel for all and the scriptural teaching of universal sin transmitted from Adam to the present keeps Christians searching for a theology of child evangelism.

THE CONCEPT OF CONVERSION

What do we mean when we speak of conversion? The question hinges on a theological term which has social, developmental, and psychological implications. Emile Griffin in *Turning* has given us a working definition.

---

10. Ibid., p. 236.

By conversion I mean the discovery made gradually or suddenly, that God is real. It is the perception that this real God loves us personally and acts mercifully and justly toward each of us.[11]

To us it is the direct experience of the saving power of God. His premise is the knowledge of universal sin, and its consequences. It accounts for moral and religious growth, consistent with human development. It also recognizes a gap between language development and experience and it recognizes individual differences.

The necessity of the conversion of children is based on the reality of mankind's inherent sinfulness. "Each child," writes William Hendricks, "is born into a sinful humanity. All individuals eventually confirm themselves as sinners. It is God's purpose to save all."[12]

The issue of child conversion takes seriously the issue of the sinful nature and the radical nature of saving faith.

The practice of the church must conform to the theology of conversion. A turning from sin is required, but we dare not force adult norms of behavior on the very young. Unwarranted anxiety toward children should be avoided. Childhood is a time to establish a foundation for a strong faith. Such a foundation of meaning will aim for the establishment of a credible faith, freely chosen, and one which can then be nurtured throughout life.

THE CHILD AND THE AGE OF ACCOUNTABILITY

The notion that a child is capable of sin and just as capable of receiving salvation leads to questions. When should a child be held accountable for his sin? When should a child accept Jesus Christ as Savior? When should he cope with divine grace?

An "age of accountability" is not taught in the Scriptures. In fact, there is no basis for it other than a logical inference. If we accept the biblical teaching of original sin as related to an Adamic nature, we infer that the infant is born in sin, needs divine grace, and is ultimately accountable for that sin. The observation that men are sinners by nature as well as by choice throws a burden upon an early concern for infants.

Advocates of infant baptism assume a covenant relationship between the child and the family of God. They argue from the silence of the New Testament on the issue, not from any direct teaching. The "unsafe" status of the child propounded by Augustine introduced the emergence of the concept of baptismal regeneration. Belief that the sacrament of baptism conveyed to the infant

---

11. Emile Griffin, *Turning* (Garden City, N.Y.: Doubleday, 1982), p. 17.
12. William Hendricks, "The Age of Accountability," in *Children and Conversion,* ed. Clifford Ingle (Nashville: Broadman, 1970).

all the benefits of grace solved the logical problem, at least, of what to do with original sin.[13] It remained for another rite, confirmation, to emerge. Confirmation conveyed the intent of personalization of faith and entrance to the church as an active member.

When children joined the catechumens during the time of Augustine (c. A.D. 400), the long tradition was begun that eventually led to complete sacramentalism in regard to child salvation. It was not until the Reformation that any dominant mood of dissent appeared, although "believers' baptism" was practiced from the earliest of Christian times.

Accountability had to be reckoned with by those who resisted infant baptism on grounds that personal faith was essential. How to account for this indispensable faith element in the New Testament led to the notion of an age of accountability. Denying the notion that the church is an hereditary body, in which fleshly birth rather than the new birth qualifies for membership, a personal act of faith and repentance would seem necessary. And if a personal act of faith would be necessary, then a rite with an infant would be insufficient.

What then is necessary for child conversion? The same thing that is essential in adult conversion: a conscious turning from sin and a turning toward God (Acts 9:35; 11:34-35; 26:20).

But when is a child accountable for his sin? We do not know for sure. A. H. Strong urged those who worked with children to heed several propositions: (1) the age of possible conversion begins with the first moment of moral consciousness; (2) the natural possibilities for good are greatest at the moment of that first unfolding and are less and less every moment thereafter; and (3) a character changed in early years is more promising of growth and power in the world than one dragged for years through the mire of sin.[14]

These propositions seem pertinent and reasonable. They imply a ground for both belief and action. However, they give no light on an exact age. From a central text such as Romans 14:12, "So then every one of us shall give account of himself to God," we conclude that accountability, not an exact age, is the issue. Harold Frazee declares,

> The age at which a declaration of faith is possible and to be expected is a relative matter. It is almost as difficult to assert that a given age is the proper one for a declaration of faith as it is to declare a particular age is the correct one at which to be married.[15]

---

13. See Robert P. Lightner, *Heaven for Those Who Can't Believe* (Schaumburg, Ill.: Regular Baptist, 1977) and John Inchley, *Kids and the Kingdom* (Wheaton: Tyndale, 1976), p. 33, for a discussion of the salvation of infants or others who die before an "age of accountability."
14. Strong, pp. 584-85.
15. Harold B. Frazee, "The Proper Age for a Declaration of Faith," *Religious Education* 58 (September-October 1963): 439.

THE CHILD AND EVANGELISTIC APPEALS

Accountability and a concept of age need not be linked together. Perhaps because we have attempted to tie the two together, excesses have been experienced in well-meaning attempts to convert the young. It is a mistake to set an arbitrary age for conversion. It is equally a mistake to set a certain day for "decisions." Somehow, God's sovereign Spirit does not evidence His regenerative work according to fixed days and years.

William Hendricks, writing in *Children and Conversion,* asserts, "It is highly doubtful that many children below the age of nine can express or have experienced despair for sin as radical separation from God." He continues with the emphatic declaration, "One cannot be 'saved' until he is aware he is 'lost.' "[16] His concern is that we not risk serious problems for the future by continuing to invade the preschool and children's departments for evangelistic prospects. As a Baptist theologian, his primary concern is that an adequate perspective be maintained regarding believers' baptism.

Indeed, he has a point, if baptism should follow conversion as closely as possible. The time lag between an early conversion and entrance into church is a problem in many instances.

Those who hold that the evangelism of the child is to be as early as possible because of the damnation of the infant have not been altogether consistent. They would maintain that saving the child saves a life. But why the time lag from birth to, say, age five or six? Is not the child captive to his sin nature during that period as well? If an age of accountability occurs between ages three to five, or thereabouts, why not urge full obedience to our Lord and baptize at that early age of response? But most church leaders refuse to do this on pragmatic grounds. Few children, if any, know the demands of meaningful participation in the life of the church. One might also argue that few very young children know the demands of Christian discipleship as well.

Early conversions often lead to recommitments in later childhood or early adolescence. Also, they may lead to outright defections from the faith. But that is true of individuals who were converted later in life as well. The outward response to an inner conviction is difficult to assess. Only God knows the human heart. We are limited to external assessment, which is faulty at best.

What happens between an early response to an appeal for salvation and a later "rededication," as many would call a recommitment? Often a child responds to a gospel appeal out of a deep desire to gain approval. It is part of the identity struggle within each of us to desire the approval of a parent or teacher. Winning the child according to this set of psychological principles may be little more than instilling into the child the mysterious codes and mores of our society. Thus, willingly obedient, a child may gain his rightful place in the

16. Hendricks, p. 95.

family or other adult institutions. Such a crass assessment, I recognize, is surely not the case in every instance. For God even uses these faulty, inadequate steps of faith. Surrounded by love and continued teaching from the Scriptures, the childish response may indeed lead to salvation. But to say that every child who indicated a desire to receive Christ was actually "saved" may be outright presumption.

Left to falter on his own with partial nurture, a child may drift into sin during his childhood or early adolescence. Without a concept of "lostness" at the time of his "conversion," the individual may thus be a candidate for delusion and some despair. Fortunately for some, the repeated proclamation of the gospel bears its fruit. Guilt, remorse, and finally repentance coupled again with faith may lead the individual back into the fold. Adults often register some shock to see children repeatedly "walk the aisles" in evangelistic meetings. Have they not already been converted?

All of this discussion is meant to demonstrate the fact that when we seek to integrate a doctrine of salvation with a behavioral concept of evangelistic methodology, we encounter difficulty. Would it be better not to attempt an integration? Would it be better to leave unanswered the questions of when and how evangelistic appeals are to be made?

To do so is to evade a basic responsibility of integrating our faith with our actions. To do so is to admit to irrationality. What, then, are we to do in fulfillment of our Christian duty to proclaim the gospel to every creature? Here are my suggestions:

1. Incline the child to put his faith in Christ by sound Christian teaching surrounded by Christian love from birth onward. Such preevangelism, as it may be called, builds a proper foundation for intelligent faith and active discipleship. We find good support for this in the New Testament. Paul wrote to Timothy reminding him of his early heritage, "And that from childhood you have known the sacred writings which are able to give you the wisdom that leads to salvation through faith which is in Christ Jesus" (2 Tim. 3:15, NASB).

2. Avoid anxiety-producing appeals to both parents and children. Here I speak of excesses and not the faithful teaching of the Scripture as it relates to both sin and salvation.

In any effort to evangelize children, youth, or adults, the Scriptures give us the clues. We are to balance our zeal with confidence in the sovereign God. Faith comes by hearing and hearing by the Word of God (Rom. 10:17). Faith is the end, not the method, of providing the "hearing." Faith comes by the instrumentality of the Word. Excessive human motivation may work against the faith-prompting work of the Holy Spirit through the divine Scriptures.

3. Teach accountability as an action toward God, not toward men. Differentiating between the two is a primary point of maturity. Autonomy from the Christian perspective accounts for relationships between self, God, and others. When confronted with the claims of Jesus Christ on the life, each individual

must give an account for what he knows. In childhood, accountability is invariably toward parents, as commanded by God (Eph. 6:1-2). Moving from childlike credulity to responsible autonomy involves transferring one's accountability to an authority higher than his parents. Of course, wise parents and leaders will instruct the young that all authority belongs to God and that any human authority is allowed by His permission. The power of the godly example in exercising authority prompts response toward God.

It is difficult to resolve the age-old problem of what happens when human authority—say, a parent's desire for a child not to go to church, make public profession of Christ, or be baptized—comes in conflict with divine authority. Do we appeal to the scriptural directive, "We ought to obey God rather than men" (Acts 5:29)? Does our duty to see the child converted, even against parental wishes, take precedence over the commandment of Ephesians 6:1? I believe it does not in most instances. Every reasonable effort should be made to enlist the parent in providing a climate for spiritual response. When that is impossible, no undue pressure should be placed on the young child to disobey. Older children are perhaps in a different category. Certainly, youth and young adults should have the freedom to believe, just as all men have freedom to reject Christ. But accountability is to be taught. Conflict between a desire to obey God rather than parents may find its resolution in time. God knows the heart, and its inward response is what counts.

4. Make appeals for young children to receive Christ that are prompted by pure motives and are given simply and in a nonpublic manner. The notable success of various child evangelism efforts cannot be denied. But the motive must never be numbers or outward response, nor should appeals be accompanied by offers of gifts, recognition, or special privileges. The abuses are not even worth mentioning, but they exist. Offers of free books, even a Bible, to children who accept Christ are questionable, if made in public. Any child would make a decision in order to receive a gift. The gift of salvation stands far above gimmickry. The offer of salvation is not an offer of silver and gold (Acts 3:6).

Public decision days, long popular among some Sunday schools, fail to account for the individuality of conversion. But at the same time, a wise attitude would be, "Forbid them not."

The key to successful evangelism for children is bringing truth to their own level, unmixed with argument. In presenting Christ to children, we must keep the message simple. Soderholm suggests several key principles to follow in presenting the gospel to children.[17]

> 1. The teacher should be clear in explaining what the child should know in order to appreciate the significance of Christ's death. God loves you; you have sinned; Christ died to pay for your sin; you must admit to Him

17. Marjorie E. Soderholm, *Explaining Salvation to Children* (Minneapolis: Free Church, 1962), pp. 10-14.

that you are a sinner and ask Him for forgiveness. Then you are in God's family and have everlasting life.

2. The teacher should be familiar with Scriptures that will help lead children to Christ. These include John 3:16; John 3:36; Romans 3:23; and Romans 5:6.
3. The teacher should be careful to explain the terms he uses.
4. The teacher should depend on the Holy Spirit. A decision prompted by the Spirit is the only genuine decision.
5. The teacher should use the Bible in sharing the gospel message.
6. The teacher should let the children ask questions. Questions open the windows of the mind and help prevent forcing the message on children.

The simplicity of salvation is evident in the following Bible stories, which can be used to help explain salvation to children: Nicodemus (John 3); the woman at the well (John 4); the lame man and Peter and John (Acts 3); Philip and the Ethiopian (Acts 8); the Philippian jailer (Acts 16).

Giving an invitation is a natural and normal part of the gospel presentation. How it is done is quite another thing. Teachers are wise not to force or push for decisions. The gospel, rightly presented, has its own appeal. The Savior has His own drawing power. This is the divine work of the Holy Spirit in wedding human need and response to the winsomeness of Christ. Though there is no formula to follow in giving invitations, several ideas may prove helpful.

1. Ask children to respond "inside" before asking for outward response. A teacher might say, "If you want Jesus to be your Savior, say to yourself, 'Yes, Jesus, I want You to be my Savior.' "
2. Make the invitation clear. A child's mind wanders easily. Ask the child, "Can you tell me why you came to talk to me?"
3. Use natural situations to talk to children about receiving Christ. When a child asks, "Can I accept the Lord?" that is the time to stop and lead the child to Christ. Another simple and effective way is to invite children to remain after class if they desire to accept Christ.
4. Avoid making the invitation so easy that acceptance is not genuine. Some human response is necessary. Open "confession" of acknowledgment that they desire to accept Christ often fixes the decision in the mind of a child.
5. Avoid group decisions with the young. Better results are obtained at the time of decision if the teacher deals with the child individually and personally.

A word of caution is necessary regarding the use of symbolism in explaining the gospel. Although the Bible contains metaphors, and similes, and symbols,

these terms can be explained simply. Insights gained from child-learning research seem to indicate that the young learn symbolic terms and words if they
are accompanied by meaningful adult actions, interpretive moods, and tones.
Speaking the truth in love, according to the apostle Paul (Eph. 4:15), enhances
maturity. And love wins children to the Savior.

Such terms as *heart, saved,* and even *sin* need to be explained. In fact, the
New Testament often supplies alternative words such as the image of joining a
family (John 1:12) or the analogy of birth (John 3:3) to explain "receiving
Jesus into the heart." The concept of salvation is extremely rich in supportive
concrete ideas, such as being set free from a prison, being bought like a gift, or
receiving a prize or gift. Sin carries with it the notion of disobeying a law,
wrongdoing, or not living up to what God expects.

Words alone will not win. Words—meaningful terms—combined with love,
rich and deep feeling, make the gospel come alive in a child's experience. God
stands ready to save the child on the exercise of the child's faith. If the child is
a five-year-old, God will be pleased to accept a five-year-old's response. If the
child is ten, then God will accept a ten-year-old's faith response.

CONVERSION AND THE CONCEPTS OF MORAL DEVELOPMENT

In recent years, the significant character development research of Jean
Piaget and Lawrence Kohlberg have added a new dimension to the issue of
child conversion. How do the social and psychological theories of normal
human development relate to religious conversion? The answers are not simple, but at least an approach to a solution is needed. (See chaps. 4 and 20 for
further information on Piaget and Kohlberg.)

The theories of Lawrence Kohlberg are formidable. In his magnum opus,
The Philosophy of Moral Development, Kohlberg establishes six basic stages
of moral development. In an unusual mix of social, scientific, philosophical,
and educational writing he traces the moral development of a child. While his
naturalistic presuppositions do not allow him to account for the valid phenomenon of religious conversion, his findings must be taken seriously.

Scholarly responses to the moral theorists, particularly Kohlberg, are to be
found in several important works.[18] In summary, it seems plausible to assume
that God's redemptive work with mankind, including children, works in harmony with how He has created us. The issue of child conversion is not so
disjunctive as to preclude any acceptance of moral development theories.
Richards asserts that "transformation is a progressive reshaping of the believer
toward that pattern of life revealed in Scripture as God's ideal man, His special

18. See Donald M. Joy, ed., *Moral Development: Foundations* (Nashville: Abingdon, 1983); Craig
    Dykstra, *Vision and Character: A Christian Education Alternative to Kohlberg* (New York:
    Paulist, 1981; and Cedrick B. Johnson and H. Newton Malony, *Christian Conversion: Biblical
    and Psychological Perspectives* (Grand Rapids: Zondervan, 1981).

creation."[19] In a later work specifically dealing with conversion, Richards concludes: "Our emphasis needs to be on the growth process which both comes before and continues after conversion."[20]

Resolution of tensions between conversionists and moral theorists will not be easy. Serious scholarship is needed rather than, as Ted Ward, a leading character education theorist, warns, "using Kohlberg's research and its theory of moral development as a point of departure."[21]

DISCIPLING A CHILD'S DECISION

The responsibility of leading the born-again child into normal, healthy, spiritual growth is primarily the task of parents. But if a child's parents do not possess spiritual life or know how to nurture spiritual growth, the whole community of the church needs to become involved. This is especially important for the child who comes from a non-Christian home. Several suggestions may help:

1. Explain to the child's parents what he has responded to and encourage them to provide a home environment that includes regular church attendance, prayer, and Bible reading.
2. Make sure the child has a Bible and knows how to find simple verses to read.
3. Provide a "This New Life of Yours" class for primaries and juniors to explain salvation more thoroughly. This may last several weeks and may be held during children's church, Sunday evening children's groups, or sometime during the week.
4. Offer help and encouragement if you are a friend, but not the parent. Above all, pray and trust the Holy Spirit to continue the good work begun in the new child of God.

In the context of this chapter, words on discipleship may be too brief to give much more than a direction, a course, or a route to take. All that a church attempts to do, if it is following a biblical pattern, is designed to build up the child. Adequate provision for competent teachers, care by a loving pastor, and the surrounding concern of every church member will go a long way in assuring the child of normal spiritual growth.

W. O. Cushing's children's hymn, "When He Cometh," portrays the reward of children's work.

> Little children, little children,
> Who love their Redeemer,

19. Lawrence O. Richards, *A Theology of Christian Education* (Grand Rapids: Zondervan, 1975), p. 47.
20. Lawrence O. Richards, *Helping My Child Know Jesus* (Cincinnati: Standard, 1975), p. 6.
21. Ted Ward, foreword to *Moral Development Foundations*, p. 10.

Are the jewels, precious jewels,
His loved and His own.

Like the stars of the morning,
His bright crown adorning,
They shall shine in their beauty,
Bright gems for His crown.

THE CHILD AND CHRISTIAN NURTURE

Horace Bushnell's insistence "that the child is to grow up a Christian, and never know himself as being otherwise,"[22] has sparked controversy ever since it was written. Bushnell made that statement in opposition to the practice among the New England Calvinists at that time (1846) of expecting the child to grow up in sin and to be converted at maturity.[23] His attitude toward revivalism was not as one-sided as it may appear. To quote from the man himself:

> I desire to speak with all caution of what are very unfortunately called revivals of religion; for, apart from the name, which is modern, and from certain crudities and excesses that go with it—which name, crudities, and excesses are wholly adventitious as regards the substantial merits of such scenes—apart from these, I say there is abundant reason to believe that God's spiritual economy includes varieties of exercise, answering, in all important respects, to these visitations of mercy, so much coveted in our churches. They are needed.[24]

Bushnell recognized that not all conversions would be by Christian nurture, so that other evangelistic efforts would be advisable and necessary. Nor was he opposed to a crisis experience as a matter of principle. Rather, he believed that they should be, in the case of children in the Christian home, prompted in the natural surroundings of Christian teaching.

Bushnell was vulnerable, it seems, in pushing for an organic link between parent and child. Presumptive grace, that is, the grace of God operating through the Christian parent, can be expected to bring the child to his own commitments. Infant baptism, he felt, was consistent with apostolic practice.

Regardless of a theology which had the effect of deemphasizing conversion, Bushnell pioneered children's work in churches. He was one of the first to insist on the importance of the first three years in formation of the child's basic outlook on life. He pointed out that learning takes place before the development of language. His emphasis on parental guidance was without parallel in

22. Bushnell, p. 4.
23. See Peter Slater, *Children in the New England Mind* (Hamden, Conn.: Archer, 1977), for a full documentation of ideas about children between the seventeenth and mid-nineteenth centuries. The Puritan belief in infant damnation in large measure prompted the writings of Horace Bushnell in 1847.
24. Bushnell, p. 46.

his time. Only the home permeated by a Christian spirit, he contended, provides adequate Christian nurture. Mere outward and occasional observances of religion are self-defeating. If Bushnell's observations are correct, the home is the center of Christian education, whether the churches plan it that way or not.

Implications of a nurture approach are several. On the one hand, we cannot believe in any organic unity of the child with the parent by which the faith of the parent is the faith of the child. Latent faith is a contradiction in terms. Until a child knows the difference between sin and holiness, he cannot trust Christ who came to handle the sin question. On the other hand, let us guard against the opposite extreme of imagining that a course of doctrinal instruction is necessary before a child can apprehend the sufficiency of Christ. There are two simple demands of the gospel—renunciation of sin and trust in Jesus. A child can meet both of these demands.

THE CHILD AND CHRISTIAN DISCIPLESHIP

Christian discipleship is based upon the belief that both the parent and the community of faith have responsibility to nurture growth in spiritual things. Both of the dimensions of parenting and church education are treated elsewhere in this text (see chapters 16 and 33). However, it is important to understand the scope of duty and opportunity. Child conversion cannot be treated in isolated fashion from either a theology of conversion affecting all persons, or from moral development of the human personality. Nor can it be treated apart from the valid discipling approaches commonly proved effective in local church ministries.

It is sufficient to say that the credulous, conscious choice of a child to have faith in Christ is only a part of a series of developments leading to an integrated faith. The believer in God sees the divine work in the growth of persons from infancy through adulthood. Discipleship, seen in the Bible as primarily an adult process of learning, holds valid claim to all in the commission of Christ. It remains for parents and church leaders to develop specific programs for value clarification, modeling, and decision-making based on the Scriptures.

SUMMARY

In this chapter, I desire to tread cautiously between extremes. I am convinced that churches have neglected family education and have tended to emphasize a highly individualistic approach to evangelism. A return to parental guidance in evangelism is needed. But churches must minister to fragments of society as well as whole families. In the history of Christian witness, the gospel has fallen on all kinds of soil. Any attempt to dogmatize away from early efforts to lead the young to the Savior are fruitless. But the cautions are there. No exact strategy is to be found in the New Testament. Indeed the weight may well be on the side of adult evangelism over child and youth evangelism. But in regard to spiritual influence and training, the weight of effort is to be directed toward work with children. It is the duty of Christ's church, the faithful, to proclaim the gospel, to trust the power of Christ to preserve His own, to hold out all the help it can to aid the spiritual maturation of the young. Emphasis should be on the grace of God as preeminent over the sinfulness of mankind.

Theologian Augustus Strong wrote before the turn of the century what many firmly believe:

> Sometimes the conversion of an important worldly man in the community is thought of as a great proof of God's divine grace, but that worldly man, fettered by lifelong sinful habits, will probably do far less for Christ than a boy of twelve who is converted and consecrates his life to the Savior. . . . There is no good reason to doubt the fact of the importance of conversion in childhood.[25]

Maybe Martin Luther was correct when he wrote, "If Christendom is to be helped, one must begin with the children."[26]

FOR FURTHER READING

Barclay, William. *Train Up a Child.* Philadelphia: Westminster, 1959.
———. *Turning to God.* Philadelphia: Westminster, 1964.
Best, W. E. *Regeneration and Conversion.* Grand Rapids: Baker, 1975.
Burkhardt, Helmut. *Biblical Doctrine of Regeneration.* Downers Grove, Ill.: InterVarsity, 1977.
Bushnell, Horace. *Christian Nurture.* New Haven: Yale U., 1916.
Bye, Beryl. *Teaching Our Children the Christian Faith.* London: Hodder & Stoughton, 1965.
Chamberlain, Eugene. *When Can a Child Believe?* Nashville: Broadman, 1973.
Dobbins, Gaines Stanley. *Winning Children.* Nashville: Broadman, 1953.
Downs, Perry. "Child Evangelization." *Christian Education Journal* 3 (1983).
———. "Christian Nurture: A Comparison of Horace Bushnell and Lawrence O. Richards." *Christian Education Journal* 4 (1983).
Dykstra, Craig. *Vision and Character: A Christian Education Alternative to Kohlberg.* New York: Paulist, 1981.
Frazee, Harold B. "The Proper Age for a Declaration of Faith." *Religious Education* 58 (September-October 1963).

25. Strong, p. 585.
26. *What Luther Says,* ed. Ewald M. Plass (St. Louis: Concordia, 1959), 1:141.

Griffin, Emile. *Turning.* Garden City, N.Y.: Doubleday, 1982.

Inchley, John. *Kids and the Kingdom: How They Come to God.* Wheaton, Ill.: Tyndale, 1976.

Ingle, Clifford, ed. *Children and Conversion.* Nashville: Broadman, 1970.

Johnson, Cedrick B., and H. Newton Malony. *Christian Conversion: Biblical and Psychological Perspectives.* Grand Rapids: Zondervan, 1981.

Joy, Donald M., ed. *Moral Development Foundations: Judeo-Christian Alternatives to Piaget/Kohlberg.* Nashville: Abingdon, 1983.

Kohlberg, Lawrence. *The Philosophy of Moral Development.* San Francisco: Harper & Row, 1981.

———. *The Psychology of Moral Development.* San Francisco: Harper & Row, 1984.

LeBar, Lois E. *Children in the Bible School.* Westwood, N.J.: Revell, 1952.

LeBar, Mary E. *Living in God's Family.* Wheaton, Ill.: Scripture Press, 1957.

Lightener, Robert P. *Heaven for Those Who Can't Believe.* Schaumburg, Ill.: Regular Baptist, 1977.

Munsey, Brenda, ed. *Moral Development, Moral Education, and Kohlberg: Basic Issues in Philosophy, Psychology, Religion, and Education.* Birmingham, Ala.: Religious Education, 1980.

Piaget, Jean. *Moral Judgment of the Child.* New York: Free, 1965.

Plass, Ewald M., ed. *What Luther Says.* St. Louis: Concordia, 1959.

Poling, David. *To Be Born Again: The Conversion Phenomenon.* Garden City, N.Y.: Doubleday, 1979.

Prince, John. *Early Harvest: Leading a Child to Christ.* London: Falcon, 1976.

Richards, Lawrence O. *A Theology of Christian Education.* Grand Rapids: Zondervan, 1975.

———. *Helping My Child Know Jesus.* Cincinnati: Standard, 1975.

Shoemaker, Samuel Moor. *How to Become a Christian.* New York: Harper, 1953.

Slater, Peter Gregg. *Children in the New England Mind.* Hamden, Conn.: Shoestring, 1977.

Soderholm, Marjorie E. *Explaining Salvation to Children.* Minneapolis: Free Church, 1962.

Strong, Augustus H. "The Conversion of Children." *The Watchman-Examiner* 53 (23 September 1965).

Swanson, Lawrence F. *Evangelism in Your Local Church.* Chicago: Harvest, 1959.

Trent, Robbie. *Your Child and God.* Rev. ed. New York: Harper & Row, 1952.

Waterlink, Jan. *Leading Little Ones to Jesus.* Translated by Betty Vredevoogd. Grand Rapids: Zondervan, 1962.

Yoder, Gideon G. *The Nurture and Evangelism of Children.* Scottdale, Pa.: Herald, 1959.

24

Eleanor Hance

Teaching Children to Worship and Pray

- **What Is Worship?**
- **Scriptural Basis**
- **Worship and Spiritual Growth**
- **Contribution of Worship to the Total Program**
- **Types of Worship**
- **Time for Worship**
- **Planning a Worship Service**
  PRINCIPLES FOR BUILDING
  FORM FOR GROUP WORSHIP
  ELEMENTS OF WORSHIP
  STEPS IN PLANNING
- **The Leader's Part**
- **Aids to Effective Worship**
- **Criteria for Evaluating**
- **Teaching Children to Pray**
- **Answering Questions About Prayer**
- **Private Worship**
  FOR PARENTS
  FOR CHURCH LEADERS AND TEACHERS
- **Family Worship**

ELEANOR HANCE, M.A., is a curriculum writer for juniors, residing in Sarasota, Florida.

What Is Worship?

Do the following phrases produce mental images of any children's "worship" you have observed? Chairs askew, crumpled papers, tattered songbooks, chalkboard scribblings, outdated posters; children scuffing, poking, squeaking chairs; teachers chatting, thumbing materials; pianist asking pages, shuffling music; leader calling for order, raising voice; loud singing, mumbled prayer, hohum announcements, noisy offering, Bible teaching, dismissal scramble.

Worship is the highest calling of Christians, and yet, judging by the atmosphere of the average worship experience, the least understood. Perhaps it is because some Christian adults have not examined the meaning of worship themselves that they do not value it more for children.

Worship is easier to discuss than to define. In the broad sense, it is the whole reason God redeemed us through the sacrifice of His own Son—for communion with Him. It involves a person-to-Person relationship. When we realize that God is vitally alive, present, loving and seeking us, we respond with an outpouring of love and honor for Him. We do not seek this fellowship with the Lord for what we can get out of Him in benefits to ourselves— although there are residual benefits—but we seek Him because of who He is, because we are impelled to tell Him how wonderful He is. Worship is not primarily self-getting (subjective) but self-giving (objective).

In the narrow sense, worship is the specific act of adoring contemplation of God. R. A. Torrey believed this is indeed the biblical use of the word.[1] So conceived, hearing the Scripture, singing, praying, listening to the sermon, are not worship in themselves, although they may lead to worship.

In this chapter, the term *worship* is extended to the whole communion experience, with adoration the climax. God reveals Himself and thus extends an invitation. Those made holy by the redemption of Jesus Christ fulfill the joy of their personal relationship by entering into close communion. Such awesome encounter produces a response of adoration, which is surely the essence of worship and, as stated previously, is often used as the limited definition of worship. But this response may be accompanied by other responses, as was often true of people as recorded in God's Word:

> Praise to God for His goodness and love; confession of sin and unworthiness in the presence of God's holiness; thanksgiving to God for his blessings of forgiveness and new life; petition to God with prayer for ourselves and intercession for others; dedication of self, personal commitment, the offering of one's whole self to God.[2]

It is difficult to express sublime experience in words, but the following statements show something of the different aspects of this experience:

1. R. A. Torrey, *What the Bible Teaches* (Westwood, N.J.: Revell, 1898), p. 472.
2. R. Harold Terry, "A New Look at Worship," *Church School Worker* 13 (June 1963):11.

Worship is love, admiration, awe, reverence, adoration. It is "man's heart reaching out to, and communicating with, his Creator." It is "the loving response of an individual's heart to a consciousness of God's presence." It should involve my emotions and my will. I will not worship unless I have a positive attitude toward God.[3]

Worship is an activity that includes, when complete, six components: an outreach of the self toward God; a felt inreach of God toward the self; resultant communion; some thought about things of God and godliness; an emotional reaction to the same; and, above all, some response in peace, purpose, or action.[4]

Worship is man's movement toward God because of God's prior movement toward man. We love Him because He first loved us. God has revealed Himself extensively: in the mighty acts of history, redemption, and providence, in the loving sacrifice of His Son, in the written Word, in the giving of the Holy Spirit. God makes the first move, showing His power and love. This then invites our positive reaction of rendering exultant homage because of who He is and what He has done.[5]

SCRIPTURAL BASIS OF WORSHIP

There is only one authoritative source for an understanding of worship and that is the Word of the Person whom we worship. God has given us a spiritual banquet of information which we can only sample here.

John's exalted vision underscores the highest goal of worship. "The twenty-four Elders fell down before him and worshiped him, the Eternal Living One, and cast their crowns before the throne, singing, 'O Lord, you are worthy to receive the glory and the honor and the power, for you have created all things. They were created and called into being by your act of will' " (Rev. 4:10-11, TLB). The created ones worship their eternal living Creator because He alone is worthy. Indeed, the word *worship* derives from the earlier word *worthship*, giving reverence and honor to that which is worthy.

Scripture after Scripture, from the beginning of God's Word to the end, exhorts us to give the Lord the glory due His name (Ps. 96:8-9) and simply because He is worthy. Not to worship is to disobey God. It follows that not to teach children to worship is also to disobey God.

Not all worship is acceptable. God lays down certain principles. Only those whose sins have been purged by the blood of Christ may be bold to enter the presence of the holiest (Heb. 9:7, 14; 10:19). In Exodus 34:14, God commands that our worship be singlehearted, because God claims absolute loyalty and exclusive devotion. And in John 4:23-24, Jesus explains to the Samaritan woman that although the place of worship is not important—nor the man-

3. Mary E. LeBar, *Children Can Worship* (Wheaton, Ill.: Scripture Press, Victor Books, 1976), p. 11.
4. Ralph D. Heim, *Leading a Church School* (Philadelphia: Fortress, 1968), p. 187.
5. Leslie B. Flynn, *Worship: Together We Celebrate* (Wheaton, Ill.: Scripture Press, Victor Books, 1983), p. 29.

ner—the quality of worship is. It must be "in spirit"—not in man's own strength and to his credit, but Spirit-inspired with no confidence in the flesh. It must also be "in truth"—real and sincere, without pretense of form or mere profession.

When our worship is pleasing to the Lord, something happens. In Exodus 34:5-8, we find God revealing who He is to Moses on Mount Sinai and Moses worshiping God. When Moses finally came down from the mountain with the tablets of the Ten Commandments, his face glowed from being in the presence of God (v. 35). Although God's Shekinah glory does not manifest itself in the physical body of the worshiper, something of God's glory does shine through in the worshiper's radiant spiritual life.

WORSHIP AND THE SPIRITUAL GROWTH OF CHILDREN

Although worship experience is an objective end in itself (glorification of God), it has a subjective result (change in the worshiper). We cannot have true communion with the high and holy One, the Lord of lords, without some personal reaction. The change starts inwardly and manifests itself outwardly. Change in the direction of growth toward Christian maturity is the central concern of Christian education. Paul says, "We all, with open face beholding as in a glass the glory of the Lord, are changed into the same image from glory to glory, even as by the Spirit of the Lord" (2 Cor. 3:18). So, although spiritual changes are not the purpose of worship, they can be expected as results of worship in the lives of children as well as adults.

Worship produces awareness of personal need. When we are confronted with God's perfection, then our own weaknesses, failures, omissions, and sins become more evident. In contrition, we submit our needs, enjoy His loving forgiveness, and receive His assurance of help. Both Isaiah 6:5 and Job 42:5-6 describe the impact of personal encounter with the Lord. A child can sense his own need if he is given opportunity to have personal fellowship with the Lord through worship.

Worship strengthens faith. It would be impossible to have contact with the real, living God without believing more firmly who He is and what He is like. (Witness again the experience of Moses in Exodus 34.) Children have simple faith and can express that faith through worship.

Worship results in commitment. Worship is indeed adoration of God, but adoration is expressed through more than the lips; it involves the whole being. Such adoration would be hollow mockery without total commitment of self. Thus, a worshiper's intellect, emotions, and actions all reflect this identification of his own will with the Lord's. Romans 12:1 instructs the believer to give himself in total commitment. The concept of commitment may be very simply presented to a child by saying, "Jesus wants me to love Him more than anyone or anything else and to tell Him that I do."

Worship brings personal fulfillment. Since the creature was created for relationship with His creator, as so well expressed in Revelation 4:11, there is inner satisfaction in communion experience. Fulfillment of that for which we were created results in the only true inner peace and joy we experience. The child can be led to worship and to experience this peace and joy by singing, listening to and reading God's Word, and by talking to God.

Worship provides power. Isaiah 40:29-31 attests to the spiritual power which results from waiting on the Lord. We can soar in our Christian life with wings like eagles. Even children get tired and discouraged with their spiritual failures, but worship impels and encourages the new life of Christ through the power of the Holy Spirit.

CONTRIBUTION OF WORSHIP TO THE TOTAL PROGRAM

The total Christian education program is all the learning activities under guidance of mature Christians which maximize Christian growth. Those activities have been variously classified, but traditionally they include instruction, worship, fellowship, and service. Sometimes these are all understood to include the element of evangelism; sometimes evangelism is listed separately to heighten its importance.

Instruction in the Word is usually limited to formal teaching-learning activities. By instruction, we communicate God's standard of perfection through the precept and example of His Word, and we indoctrinate, convince, convict, and guide. *Fellowship* includes all informal activities which lend themselves to interaction with others. Fellowship is the practical laboratory of example and relationship through which Christians gain insight, shape attitudes, test actions. *Expression-service* opportunities are outlets for fulfilling God's command to love one another. They serve as an athletic field for the exercise which strengthens, and provide the God-given reward of joy.

Worship fits in most appropriately after instruction. "Good teaching should call for a response in worship, a response of the heart and will."[6] The Godward response comes before the manward response of expression-service. It provides the impetus of love and concern demonstrated in practical living. To adore God is to submit wholly to His will. To submit to His will is to carry it out— inwardly and outwardly. As its contribution to Christian growth, worship provides incentive for spiritual change and energizes for that change. "With eyes wide open to the mercies of God, I beg you, my brothers, as an act of intelligent worship, to give him your bodies, as a living sacrifice, consecrated to him and acceptable by him" (Rom. 12:1, Phillips). The practical admonitions set forth in the rest of Romans 12 flow from this submission to the Lord which is designated an act of worship.

6. Mary E. LeBar, p. 13.

TYPES OF WORSHIP FOR CHILDREN

Worship experiences are often classified by contrasting private and public worship, formal and informal, planned and spontaneous. For children, each of these must be considered by more than definition. The factor of maturity level figures to a large degree.

Chapters 5-10 of this book deal with developmental characteristics of children with their many implications for worship. Vieth[7] and McGavran[8] have much helpful material on worship needs of children of various ages. Doris A. Freese's chapter on "Worshiping at Different Age Levels" provides excellent guidance.[9]

Worship for twos and threes is best characterized as spontaneous. One of the mistakes of well-meaning adults is to plan worship for younger children patterned after that of older children. But twos and threes have attention spans of only a couple of minutes for a listening activity. Because they are limited in vocabulary and concept, they respond better to experience than to verbal content. Their activity is incessant, directed by the inner urge to move, explore, manipulate, question. And they are better oriented to individual or parallel activity than cooperative activity. It is clear, then, that group worship with a set program may not be fruitful. This does not mean that nursery worship is not planned at all. It is planned to the degree that the leader provides materials and experiences which may lead to moments of informal worship—a conch shell to help the youngster who shares its wonder say thank You to God; recorded songs about the Lord's love for those who care to listen a moment and praise God for His Son; animal crackers to munch and give occasion to express happiness for God's care. But the worship is spontaneous, for who can predict which child will be ready and when?

Worship for fours and fives might be characterized as informal. More able now to engage in cooperative activity, fours and fives can experience simple group worship of short duration. But although much planning goes into the worship, and it may have form, it is still more informal than formal. The leader must be flexible, adept at guiding conversation and sensitive to immediate needs—wonder, perplexity, decision, joy, achievement—turning them into worship experience. The worship attitudes and actions of adults—so easily imitated—and the feeling tone of the group—so easily caught—are especially important. One brief illustration of a worship moment for preschoolers may serve us here:

> "But no one cares," sobbed five-year-old Jane, "and Mittens is gone." "I do," responded Joey. "And I do," said Mary. "And God does, too," added David. There

---

7. Paul H. Vieth, *Worship in Christian Education* (Philadelphia: United Church, 1965), chaps. 8 and 9.
8. Grace W. McGavran, *Learning How Children Worship* (St. Louis: Bethany, 1964), chap. 7.
9. Doris A. Freese, *Children's Church: A Comprehensive How-To* (Chicago: Moody, 1982), chap. 11.

was a hush in the kindergarten room. "Dear God, we are sorry about Mittens. Help grownups to drive more carefully so that we and our pets can cross streets safely. Help Jane to feel better."[10]

Primary and junior worship moves from informal to formal worship. There is more separation now between worship experience and learning experience. Planned group worship increases as students become more capable of attending, participating, and deriving meaning from form. But let us never forget, "Form may express experience and it may induce and intensify experience, but form alone cannot be depended on."[11] Primary worship must be vital to primaries, and junior worship to juniors. The material must be graded to their comprehension; the content related to their experiences; the timing paced to their attentiveness. Leaders must be especially aware of the characteristics, capabilities, and interests of the children. For example, juniors, for all their professed scorn of emotion and clamor for action, are capable of worshiping in considerable depth. Their growing insights, increased vocabulary, favorable response to beauty, order, and a little symbolism make for more fruitful worship in a more formal setting and structure. Nor should we overlook the abilities of elementary school children in planning and leading their own worship under capable adults. The more they are involved actively, the more valuable the worship experience becomes.

TIME FOR CHILDREN'S WORSHIP

When can children best worship? An aware leader or teacher is prepared to use any time of special "God-consciousness" to guide children in approaching God. Since spiritual insight is not likely to occur if children are bored, restless, overexcited, or tired, we do not expect to induce worship during or after periods of dulling inactivity or overstimulating activity. But when learning experiences are structured to lead students into amazing new discoveries about the Lord, it is natural for them to respond by expressing wonder, awe, and joy. We encourage children to worship at any moment they are ready for it.

Should a part of the Sunday school period be set aside for planned graded worship? If children are not worshiping on their own level anywhere else, by all means. If they are worshiping in graded children's churches, then use a larger portion of the Sunday school period for Bible instruction. For the sake of economy in Christian education, avoid duplication of worship experience as well as omission.

If a planned worship program is included in the Sunday school period, should it occur at the beginning of the hour or the end? Those who advocate worship at the end do so on the grounds that Bible instruction prepares the

10. Christine P. Stockley, "Do We Only 'Sit and Wait'?" *Children's Religion* 23 (August 1962):6.
11. Lois E. LeBar, *Children in the Bible School* (Westwood, N.J.: Revell, 1952), p. 298.

heart for worship. Response to God grows out of His revelation and is its consummation. Lois LeBar's suggestions along this line are particularly helpful.[12] Those who would put worship first do so on practical grounds. Students are more alert and attentive at the beginning of the period. They are physically, mentally, and emotionally prepared to enter into a large group program. When the worship service is properly structured to reveal God, they readily respond in worship. Either way, the theme of worship should be closely tied in with the lesson to provide wholeness of experience. Children are easily confused by too many truths in a short span.

Many churches provide time for correlated worship and expression by extending the Sunday school hour or establishing separate church times, departmentally graded, concurrent with adult worship. (For a discussion on children's church, see chap. 16.) Larry Richards strongly favors departmentally graded children's churches, warning that grouping children ages four to eleven into a single worship group produces the same problems as placing them in adult services—too wide a diversity of attention spans, abilities, and comprehension.[13] He suggests that the same groupings used for Sunday school provide the basis for children's church divisions.

A word is in order about children in adult worship services. There are those who contend that children absorb the worship atmosphere from the beauty of adult worship, even though they do not understand the worship language and materials. The quiet atmosphere and reverence of adults produce in children a sense of awe and wonder which is beneficial. It is also suggested that they learn by imitation and thus become proficient in worship skills. But we need to balance this optimistic view by remembering that restless, bored children may become immune to the beauty and may actually be learning habits of inattention—the very thing we deplore. Would it not be wiser to provide each age with its own meaningful training and experience in worship? Periodically, children may join in adult worship in the sanctuary, but they should be prepared for the experience and discuss it afterward in order to heighten understanding and appreciation. Both Mary LeBar[14] and Doris A. Freese[15] answer questions about children in adult worship services.

PLANNING A WORSHIP SERVICE

In preparing a worship service, we determine the needs of the students, define the aim, select the content and materials, decide on the form they will take, and arrange them in sequence to be used.

---

12. Lois E. LeBar, *Focus on People in Church Education* (Westwood, N.J.: Revell, 1968), pp. 39-42, 175-79.
13. Lawrence O. Richards, "The Pastor and Children's Church," Christian Education Monographs, Pastors' Series no. 2 (Glen Ellyn, Ill.: Scripture Press Foundation, 1966).
14. Mary E. LeBar, chap. 5.
15. Freese, chap. 13.

PRINCIPLES FOR BUILDING THE SERVICE

There are a number of fundamental rules for structuring meaningful worship experiences for children. Three rules capsulate the major considerations.

The first is the principle of centrality. A service should center on only one truth or theme. All elements in the service then support this central theme. If there is no unity in the service, thought and feeling are fragments and dispersed, rather than culminating in worship.

The second is the principle of creativity. This is the opposite of anything stereotyped—fixed or routine. Creativity is meaningful, fresh, stimulating. Worship that is creative has three characteristics: (1) It grows out of the needs, interests, and abilities of the group and thus has personal meaning; (2) it is flexible, moving forward on genuine awareness of God's reality and presence; but when these are lacking, it quickly gives place to other spiritual activity; it is not forced; (3) it is varied, recognizing that monotony destroys sensitivity and attention. This does not mean that to be creative each service must have a different format and brand new material. On the contrary, structure must be consistent enough to be comfortable, and the material must be familiar enough to use with ease. There should be just enough newness and variety to promote awareness.

The third is the principle of climax. Worship leads from revelation—insight into our great God—to response of adoration and accompanying praise, confession, thanksgiving, petition, intercession, or dedication. This climax must always be characterized by adoration, but usually is affirmed in some expression of personal commitment.

FORM FOR GROUP WORSHIP

To consummate worship in adoration, submission, and commitment, we must provide a crescendo of experience. The basic structure usually consists of four main divisions.

1. *Preparation.* This may include a quiet prelude to prepare hearts by turning thoughts to the Lord, an opening song which emphasizes the theme, a call to worship to remind us of the need and privilege of worship, and an opening prayer for readiness to worship.
2. *Presentation.* This is the body of the worship experience and may include a variety of content: Scripture, songs, poetry, art appreciation, stories, drama, devotional material, or student projects with inspirational quality.
3. *Response.* The response is the climax or consummation, to which the other divisions lead and therefore is of utmost importance. Unfortunately, many worship services actually skip the very purpose for which they were created. Children may express the climax of worship in song, prayer, affirma-

tions of submission or dedication or aspiration, poetry, gifts to the Lord, or silent adoration.

4. *Closing.* Usually this is a benediction in song, prayer, or poem which invokes the Lord's blessing. It can be any response which signals the end of worship. and provides a satisfying conclusion.

ELEMENTS OF WORSHIP

Scripture. God's Word provides profound, beautiful, and authoritative utterances not found elsewhere. Through His Word, God reveals Himself to man and man responds to God in expressions of faith, wonder, love, adoration, praise, repentance, thanksgiving, petition, and commitment. To serve children's worship, both scriptural revelation and response must be chosen and used wisely. The passage should be appropriate to the purpose of the worship and the age group, understandable, and generally just familiar enough for comfort. It can then be used in a variety of ways. Since newness heightens awareness, and awareness of God is a prerequisite for worship, we need to be open to new ways to use the Word of God. Mary LeBar's chapter "The Use of Scripture in Worship" is filled with creative suggestions.[16] But creative use of Scripture must not preclude ease of use if worship is to be achieved.

McGavran suggests two common misuses of Scripture: (1) group reading of selections responsively when it breaks up the meaning and focuses too much on when to stop and start, and (2) individual reading of difficult passages aloud when it causes embarrassment over mistakes and stumbling, which hinders worship.[17]

Music. Music sets the tone for worship, communicates God's Word, and in particular, provides a special avenue for worship response. The beauty of melody and words permits expression of feeling not always possible otherwise. The following are some important criteria for worship songs: (1) Do the words have valid spiritual content as well as beauty, and do they communicate this well? (2) Do children understand what they are singing so they can truly worship the Lord? (3) Do the words and music fit together to achieve the same message, emphasizing important thoughts? (4) Is the music within the children's range, easy to sing, and of good quality? (5) Do the children know the words and music well enough to use them as a vehicle for worship?

Offering. It is the attitude of heart in the act of giving which makes this such a fine means of expressing worship. Too often, leaders emphasize collecting from children rather than children joyously giving to the Lord whatever they have, whether tangible possessions or intangible abilities and will. We need to teach children that the offering is an act of commitment (Macedonian Christians first gave themselves to the Lord, 2 Cor. 8:5) as well as thanksgiv-

16. Mary E. LeBar, chap. 6.
17. McGavran, pp. 55-56.

ing. The offering will be heightened as a worship experience if it (1) proceeds in a spirit of worship; (2) is tied in to the purpose of the service; (3) is personal, in that the child gives of his own, not someone else's possessions; (4) is sacrificial, in that the child gives what is valuable to him; and (5) is specific, in that the child knows that his offering meets a definite need.

Prayer. Prayer is an absolutely essential part of worship. It may be voiced by the leader in words and ideas of children; it may be the spontaneous and creative expression of children themselves; it may be in the words of Scripture, song, or poem; it may be silent, guided only by music or the leader's comment. Whatever the form, it must be meaningful, vital, direct, and brief.

Devotional features. It is hard to classify the many ways we proclaim God's message to children—roughly equating to the sermon in adult worship. But whether we use stories or materials which are visualized, dramatized, or projected, we must always go beyond instruction. The proclamation must clarify God's revelation, but it must also have an inspirational, uplifting quality that touches the heart as well as the mind and stirs up worshipful response. This is one of the reasons the story form is particularly useful in worship: it allows for an emotional element. (Mary LeBar's *Children Can Worship* includes a chapter on each of the elements of worship with many practical suggestions.[18])

STEPS IN PLANNING WORSHIP

In developing a worship program, the first step is to discover the particular spiritual needs of the children with whom you are concerned. Do they need increased assurance of the faithfulness of the Lord, or a sense of His holiness, or recognition of His power to overcome temptation? If you are planning your own services, be sure to build them to meet these needs. If you are using preplanned programs, check to see that they include the particular needs of your students.

Plan the themes of the programs for a whole year, if at all possible, particularly noting special days and emphases, such as missions and evangelism. Check your themes to be sure that they will meet those particular needs mentioned above. By grouping a number of related services into one unit with an "umbrella" theme, it is possible to meet a more expansive need, each service developing one facet. If possible, correlate the worship themes with the lesson themes.

Detailed planning should be done for at least a month of programs at a time. The trend is toward participation of school-age children in the planning stage. Although leaders will provide most of the ideas, they should help children make them their own. Rather than stating what to do, they may use phrases

18. Mary E. LeBar, chaps. 6-13.

such as "Let's. . . .", "Would you like to . . . ?", "Would it help if we . . . ?"[19]
Freese suggests that in preparation for worship, children work in small groups
on activities related to the worship service. "Whatever the children do in their
small groups becomes their part in the group worship."[20] Children need to
practice beforehand so that they take part effortlessly and smoothly, rather
than causing distraction.

Before the service itself, use the following checklist to be sure everything is
ready:

_____ Room orderly and arranged for worship, with proper temperature, ventilation, lighting.

_____ All materials and equipment prepared and in place, such as
worship center, offering plates, music, and any visuals to be used.

_____ Copies of order of service to pianist and others assisting.

_____ Participants ready and instructed in responsibilities.

_____ Worshipers prepared in attitude and in materials to be used.

THE LEADER'S PART IN WORSHIP

The purpose of the leader is to facilitate worship. To do this adequately, he
must know the Lord personally and be in close communion with Him, enjoying
a genuine deep and growing spiritual life which expresses itself in radiant
Christian personality.

In his role as facilitator, a worship leader has a number of responsibilities.
He needs to understand and value worship experience and know how to
develop it. He does the basic planning, involves the children, supplies materials, oversees the worship setting and preparation, and guides the participants.
He will particularly need to make smooth, thoughtful, and inspiring transitions
between the elements in the worship service. Thus, for his role before the
group, he must have an attractive, warm personality, easy manner, reassuring
confidence, good rapport, ability to speak naturally and clearly. Veith gives
excellent additional helps for the worship leader.[21] Doris A. Freese devotes two
chapters to enlisting and training leaders.[22]

AIDS TO EFFECTIVE WORSHIP

The best laid plans and training cannot *make* children worship. We cannot
command children to commune with the Lord, but we can provide a setting,
materials, and form that are conducive to worship, eliminating anything that
would hinder worship. We attempt to stimulate and encourage worship.

19. Ibid., p. 99.
20. Freese, p. 39.
21. Veith, chap. 5.
22. Freese, chaps. 6 and 7.

PREPARATION FOR WORSHIP

Whereas adults may need only the opening of the worship service itself to prepare them, children need more extensive preparation. Locating and understanding Scripture, finding and learning songs, choosing and preparing participants—all take time and effort. If these preparatory activities are not cared for before the worship time, they interrupt the act of worship. But more significant than any of these is the preparation of the heart for worship. Mary LeBar gives a good example of how one teacher did this.[23] In addition, this period can be used to learn about worship. Veith suggests that ten to fifteen minutes be used for training, and that the transition from preparation to experience be made by a quiet musical prelude.[24]

ORDER AND BEAUTY

Environment affects our emotions, and emotions play a large part in worship. How can we contemplate a God of beauty and order when our eyes are offended by peeling paint, dirty floors, scarred furniture, glaring lights, or clutter? Do we produce a visual for children and then ask them to ignore it? The environment for worship needs to reflect God in cleanliness, orderliness, pleasing color and tasteful accessories in good repair. Beauty is not necessarily found in the ornate or expensive, but in pleasing structure, line, form, and even simplicity. Yet, response must not be only to environment. "For response to become worship, it must be response to God, not just response to beauty, to nature, or anything beside God Himself."[25]

COMFORT

We cannot expect children to contemplate God when they are distracted by bodily discomfort or inability to see and hear. So we try to eliminate overcrowding, keep the temperature comfortable, see that the room is ventilated, use soft but adequate lighting, and make sure that chairs are the right size for the age group.

FOCUS OF ATTENTION

Did you ever try to concentrate in a group when there was nothing to fix your eyes on? You glanced left and right, up and down, and your thoughts roamed with your eyes. In worship, we would rather not fix attention solely on a leader, but our eyes must focus on something. Many leaders plan a visual which directs children's thoughts to God as the center of attention: a Bible, meaningful picture, symbol, or object of God's handiwork. Whatever is dis-

23. Mary E. LeBar, pp. 29-32.
24. Veith, pp. 84-85.
25. McGavran, p. 11.

played should be large enough to make an impression and should be placed in a simple, harmonious, beautiful setting. Drapes of pleasing texture and color may cover the functional chalkboard and hide the common desk. Sometimes a few words in large letters on the backdrop silently guide the children's thoughts (e.g., "Worship the Lord in the beauty of holiness"). Periodically changing the center will heighten awareness.

ATMOSPHERE

Meaningful worship demands an atmosphere of reverence, quietness, orderliness, happiness, and expectancy. Physical environment aids immeasurably, but atmosphere is also produced by participants and activities. The following suggestions will help preserve and enhance the worship atmosphere: (1) encourage adults to exhibit attitudes conducive to worship, bowing hearts as well as heads; (2) have worship leaders prepared, confident, reverent, expectant, pleasant, sensitive to mood; (3) eliminate disturbances and interruptions of latecomers, secretaries, and trespassers; (4) assign activities, such as memorizing, drilling, and explaining, to times other than worship.

APPRECIATION

To appreciate something is to realize the value of it and to be thankful for it. We usually attach value to what we understand, what meets our needs, what we ourselves are personally involved in, what we feel comfortable with, and what is valued by people we esteem.

We can readily transfer these ideas to worship. Children appreciate worship when they understand the form and content of the service; when it taps their interests and is linked to their experiences; when they help prepare and participate; when they know the songs, can handle the Scripture with ease, and are confident of what comes next; and when adults they esteem worship and attach importance to it.

SOLITUDE

Children are not loners, but worship by its very nature is an individual matter and needs a feeling of "aloneness with the Lord" and a "coming apart" from ordinary preoccupations. Simplicity, quietness, beauty, reverence, and quiet music all help promote this deeply personal element in worship. Eliminating any sense of crowding helps children feel alone with God. We can even guide children to planned moments of silence for individual expression of communion with the Lord.[26]

26. Mary E. LeBar, pp. 86-87.

QUIET MUSIC

We have all experienced the power of music to guide wordlessly, to calm anxious or angry hearts, to lift thoughts from mundane matters to delights of the Lord, to turn failure to faith. Music chosen for the purposes of quieting, of producing desire for worship, of bringing to mind spiritual content, and of providing support for moments of communion with God can be one of the most valuable aids to worship.

VISUAL AIDS

Aesthetic beauty expressed in visual form is of special value in worship. The beauty of a picture not only catches attention, it draws forth positive feeling, subduing negative emotion, and opening up the heart for the entrance of God's Word. For example, a picture of a sparrow feeding in the snow helps make God's promise of loving care in Matthew 10:31 come alive. The clarity, vividness, and emotional impact which a picture brings to new spiritual truth, prompts a natural response of worship.

CRITERIA FOR EVALUATING WORSHIP

In order to improve the effectiveness of our worship services, we need to evaluate progress periodically. A checklist is a valuable tool. These items are selected from more extensive checklists.[27]

Was the room in readiness for worship?
Were the people responsible for the worship service on time and prepared?
Was the atmosphere conducive to the worship service?
Did the worship service begin on time?
Was the worship service appropriate for the age level?
Were the needs of the students considered?
Was the objective of the worship service accomplished?
Was the worship service developed and correlated with a theme in mind?
Was there quality in the selection of content?
Did the order of the service build to a climax?
Was there variety in presentation?
Were the elements of worship effectively used (analyze each separately)?
Were transitions smooth from one part of the service to the other?
Did each person participating do his part satisfactorily?
Was there a spirit of expectancy?
Did each individual take an active part in the worship service?

27. Ibid., pp. 115-17.

TEACHING CHILDREN TO PRAY

Prayer is an experience not only akin to worship, but involved in the very heart of worship. What a privilege—God planned, even yearns, for the humans He created to converse with Him! Meditate on such a marvel, and then dare to neglect teaching children to fulfill the desire of God's heart—and theirs.

It is often said of children's learning that as much occurs when "caught" unconsciously, or when "sought" through sense of need, as occurs when "taught" directly. And this is certainly true of prayer. Fortunate is the child who from his earliest years hears sincere prayer in understandable words about meaningful concerns. Prayer is "caught."

Prayer is also "sought," for children need to want to pray before they will express themselves to God. We encourage readiness by talking earnestly about the wonder of prayer, the way to pray, situations which need prayer, and answers to prayer. Appropriate pictures and other visuals can heighten the desire to pray. Pictures of everyday things for which to be thankful, or pictures of people praying, especially help young children. Music and prayer poems can also promote heart attitude for prayer. For example, children may sing these words before prayer time to the hymn tune "Serenity" ("We May Not Climb the Heavenly Steeps"):

> With folded hands and heads that bow
> We come, dear Lord, today;
> Help us to worship only Thee,
> And teach us all to pray.

But prayer, especially group prayer, is also "taught" in a step-by-step process.

The simplest place to begin teaching group prayer is with a "thank You" prayer. One teacher found that a prayer picture such as "The Angelus" by Jean Francois Millet stimulated conversation which easily led into individual thank You's to God. She asked what the children saw in the picture and let them enumerate items. Then she asked them to decide what was happening. They composed a story about the picture: "The church bell, called the Angelus, has rung for evening prayer. The farmer and his wife have been working hard digging up potatoes all day. They cannot get to the church to pray, so they bow right in the field and say thank you to God for the Lord Jesus Christ." Then she continued, "What else do you think these farmers are thankful for?"

The children readily responded, "Potatoes."

This provided a good opportunity to encourage each child to name just one thing he was sincerely thankful for, going around the class in order.

Then the teacher proceeded, "To whom are you thankful for these things?"

"God."

"You have told me that you are thankful, but since God is the One who has given us all good things, He would surely be pleased to have you say thank You to Him. Those who are really thankful may say so to God right now by telling Him what you have just told me."

Children who have never expressed their prayers aloud in a group will need special instruction on how to begin their prayer (by speaking God's name, "Dear God"), what to say ("Dear God, I am thankful for—"), and how to end the prayer ("In Jesus' name, Amen"). You may want to save a full explanation of the closing until you have time to develop the idea of coming to God through Jesus. It is sufficient to say that *Amen* means something like "May it be so." If several students are praying for the first time, name the student who should begin first and the order in which the rest should follow. During the prayer time, you may need to nod to or name each student as his turn arrives. Later, help students to understand that in group prayer, a person prays after the "Amen" of the person praying before him without waiting to be called on by name.

After a number of occasions for "thank You" group prayers, introduce children to the "please help me" petition prayer. You may talk about how King David prayed "Help me, O Lord my God" in Psalm 109:26. Encourage students to talk about situations in which they need God's help—when they are angry, sad, troubled, hurt, in need. Remind them that they have told you and each other, but God is the One who can help them. Then let each one voice his petition to God.

As the group prayer participation becomes more natural, combine "thank You" prayers and "please help me" prayers. Broaden the prayers to "please help someone else" (intercession), possibly illustrating with a prayer of Moses as in Numbers 14:19 or Jesus' prayer for His disciples in John 17. Later, instruct in "forgive me" prayer and add the element of confession. Teach students to include "I love You" (adoration and praise) in all their prayers.

ANSWERING QUESTIONS ABOUT PRAYER

Children need to feel comfortable and secure in participating in the group. Clearing up their questions will help. "Should we say 'Thee' and 'Thou' when we pray?" "Should we close our eyes?" "Can we pray for anything at all and get it?"

Keeping in mind that effective prayer calls for genuineness as opposed to artificiality, it would follow that verbal expression, posture, and content should be natural. Unfamiliar concepts need to be explained carefully. Children who have been exposed to "Thee" and "Thou" all their lives may use them naturally. Children who have not may begin with "You" and "Your." Posture should also reflect honor to God. Students should decide for themselves how they can outwardly show inward attitude. One eight-year-old concluded, "We should close our eyes to shut out the world and shut in God."

Concerning praying for what we want, it is indeed natural for the child to express "wants" to adults and thus to God. And God admonishes us that we have not because we do not ask (James 4:2) and promises to give us the desires of our hearts (Ps. 37:4). Then surely we cannot criticize a child's natural impulse to ask. What we can do is explain that God, like parents, does what is best because He loves us. For this reason, He sometimes does not give us what we want immediately. We can compare our wants to our needs and thus help discourage greed. We can expand answers to include the idea of "wait" and "no" as well as "yes." (McGavran[28] and LeBar[29] both provide fuller treatments on children's expressions of prayer.)

Two further questions often trouble teachers: Should students repeat memorized prayers? Should students who have not made a profession of faith in Christ be called on to pray? Mary LeBar has given excellent answers to both:

> A memorized prayer poem (such as those frequently used for table graces, or with older children, the Lord's Prayer) has a place—*after* spontaneous prayer has first established prayer as vital communion with God. Memorized prayers have both advantages and dangers. Four and five year olds enjoy the unifying effect of praying together. Such a prayer gives them the form, the vocabulary, and the expression which they need help in learning. A timid child gains security in thus hearing his voice aloud. The unchurched child may be helped to remember a rhymed grace or prayer at home. But it is not easy to find rhymed prayers that are simple enough for young children to understand and that also fit their needs. And once the prayer is learned, it all too quickly becomes mechanical. Unlike the spontaneous prayer, the memorized prayer is very limited in application.[30]

> The question as to whether to have unsaved children pray, is a touchier problem. Here the teacher's theology must enter the picture. If he feels a child is definitely not saved because he is sinning against the Light, he should not ask the child to pray—except a prayer for salvation. With young children who love Jesus and wish to please Him, most workers with children will not hesitate to have them pray. Scripture does not say much to guide us at this point.[31]

The practical reasons for this emphasis are to lay a foundation and to build positive attitudes when children are pliable and easily molded. This preparation can pave the way for the child to accept Christ as Savior when he is ready.

PRIVATE WORSHIP

Christian parents and teachers have the added responsibility of teaching children to worship and pray as individuals apart from the group. Such wor-

28. McGavran, pp. 72-74.
29. Lois E. LeBar, *Children in the Bible School,* pp. 355-58.
30. Mary E. LeBar, "Teaching Children to Pray," *Link* 8 (May, 1960):6.
31. Ibid., p. 7.

ship includes both immediate, spontaneous response to God in life's moments, and a regularly scheduled, brief period of private devotions. Private worship is one of the most neglected areas in Christian education of children. One reason may be that children need continual and close adult guidance and supervision to begin and sustain a practice which they must carry on as individuals. They are rarely sufficiently self-motivated or skilled or persevering by themselves. Nor is casual suggestion or a list of Bible references in Sunday school lesson materials sufficient incentive. From inadequate guidance springs unfruitful practice which can soon lead to discouragement. It takes much effort and know-how to teach private worship. It is time that the church wakes up to its responsibility and embarks on an energetic program to communicate the value of private worship, when, where, and how to carry it on, and the materials to use.

In several chapters, McGavran gives particularly helpful illustrations of how to stimulate individual worship.[32] The following summary provides additional pointers.

FOR PARENTS

1. Make worship a part of the family living pattern through sharing both spontaneous worship moments and scheduled family worship.

2. Set aside time for your own private devotions and help children become aware of the joy and strength they supply.

3. Help children establish a time for daily prayer from their earliest years. Bedtime is most common. It is particularly valuable for a father to take a few quiet moments with his children to talk over the day's experiences and then encourage them to talk to the Lord personally.

4. Guide the child in reading devotional literature on his own level as soon as he develops his reading skill to the point of ease and enjoyment. A modern language Bible may encourage a systematic program of Bible reading. There are an increasing number of devotional reading materials available from Christian bookstores.

5. Try to start the evening bedtime rituals soon enough to allow for warm, intimate, companionable guidance in devotions without nagging the child to hurry.

FOR CHURCH LEADERS AND TEACHERS

1. Let children in on some of your personal joys of private worship.

2. Check through opportunities to provide experience in private worship. For example, Christian camping contributes much through its Christian leadership example and coaching, age-mate influence, the setting and stimulus of God's revelation in nature, adequate time in a relaxed, extended, and consecu-

32. McGavran, chaps. 5, 6, and 8.

tive live-in program. Weekday clubs, such as Pioneer Clubs and Christian Service Brigade, also especially emphasize training in daily devotions.

3. Talk frequently with children about their time, place, and means of personal devotions.

4. See that the church library has a good supply of daily devotional readings for children and helps for parents in child training. Show juniors how to use concordances, hymnbooks, and other resources.

5. Include the subject of children's private devotions in parent-teacher meetings and teacher-training sessions.

6. Visit parents to talk about coaching children in private worship. Supply parents with helpful literature.

FAMILY WORSHIP

The family is the vital link in communicating the value of worship. Donald M. Joy cites research studies which point out that strong parental identification is basic to Christian activity.[33] We would expect that the family that sets aside time for family worship is also training for group and individual worship.

The time for family worship has to be adapted to the unique needs of each family. Many find the least pressure and interruption in the moments following the evening meal. Some choose to remain at the table, others to move to the comfort of the living room.

When there are children of varying ages, involve each in some simple way: praying, recalling a memory verse and telling how it helps, singing, reading a contemporary Scripture version, sharing an experience. Look for children's devotional material in your Christian bookstore. One of the best written, best illustrated storybooks for Bible study is V. Gilbert Beers' ten-volume *Family Bible Library.* The questions at the end of each story guide young hearts to think reflectively about God, and older ones too. Mary LeBar gives special insights and helpful suggestions for family worship.[34]

SUMMARY

Worship then, whether group or individual, informal or formal, spontaneous or planned, is the apex of the Christian experience. Evangelism and instruction move toward it; fellowship and service flow from it. Different ages worship in different ways, from spontaneous for two- and three-year-olds, to informal for four- and five-year-olds, to degrees of formal worship for older children. Children need to be taught to worship through careful planning of worship experiences. Older children can be drawn into the planning of worship elements as well as the leading of worship. Although we should be careful to use every

33. Donald M. Joy, *Meaningful Learning in the Church* (Winona Lake, Ind.: Light & Life, 1969), pp. 114-15.
34. Mary E. Lebar, chap. 4.

means to facilitate vital worship, we must recognize that true worship is a personal response to our worthy Lord, not to methods, materials, or environment.

The heart of worship is prayer. Learning to pray needs careful guidance and nurture to become a vital part of the Christian life, whether in a group or private setting. The more leaders experience the reality of God in their own lives, the more effective they will be in the sensitive task of leading children into the presence of the Lord.

FOR FURTHER READING

Allen, Ronald, and Gordon Borror. *Worship: Rediscovering the Missing Jewel.* Portland, Ore.: Multnomah, 1983.

Ban, Arline J. *Children's Time in Worship.* Valley Forge, Pa.: Judson, 1981.

Bess, C. W. *Sparkling Object Sermons for Children.* Grand Rapids: Baker, 1982.

Cully, Iris V. *Christian Worship and Church Education.* Philadelphia: Westminster, 1967.

Dann, Bucky. *Better Children's Sermons: 54 Visual Lessons, Dialogues, and Demonstrations.* Philadelphia: Westminster, 1983.

Fahs, Sophia L. *Worshipping Together with Questioning Minds.* Boston: Beacon, 1965.

Flynn, Leslie B. *Worship: Together We Celebrate.* Wheaton, Ill.: Scripture Press, Victor Books, 1983.

Freese, Doris A. *Children's Church: A Comprehensive How-To.* Chicago: Moody, 1982.

Gobbel, A. Roger, and Philip C. Huber. *Creative Designs with Children at Worship.* Nashville: John Knox, 1981.

Griggs, Donald, and Patricia Griggs. *Teaching and Celebrating Advent.* Nashville: Abingdon, 1980.

———. *Teaching and Celebrating Lent-Easter.* Nashville: Abingdon, 1980.

Herzel, Catherine. *Helping Children Worship.* Philadelphia: Fortress, 1963.

Johnson, Dorothy Grumback, and Kathleen Abbas. *Church Time for Children.* Denver: Accent, 1982.

Johnson, Lois. *Just a Minute, Lord: Prayers for Girls.* Minneapolis: Augsburg, 1973.

Jones, Chris. *Lord, I Want to Tell You Something: Prayers for Boys.* Minneapolis: Augsburg, 1973.

Larson, Jim. *Churchtime for Children.* Glendale Calif.: Gospel Light, Regal Books, 1978.

LeBar, Lois E. *Children in the Bible School.* Old Tappan, N.J.: Revell, 1952.

———. *Focus on People in Church Education.* Rev. ed. Old Tappan, N.J.: Revell, 1968.

LeBar, Mary E. *Children Can Worship.* Wheaton, Ill.: Scripture Press, Victor Books, 1976.

Lee, Florence B., et al. *When Children Worship.* Philadelphia: Judson, 1962.

McGavran, Grace W. *Learning How Children Worship.* St. Louis: Bethany, 1964.

Ng, David, and Virginia Thomas. *Children in the Worshipping Community.* Nashville: John Knox, 1981.

Ortlund, Anne. *Up with Worship.* Ventura, Calif.: Gospel Light, Regal Books, 1975.

Skold, Betty Westrom. *Lord, I Have a Question: Story Devotions for Girls.* Minneapolis: Augsburg, 1979.

Sorenson, Stephen. *Growing Up Isn't Easy, Lord: Story Devotions for Boys.* Minneapolis: Augsburg, 1979.

Sullivan, Jessie D. *Children's Church Handbook.* Grand Rapids: Baker, 1970.

Towner, Vesta. *Guiding Children in Worship.* New York: Abingdon, 1946.

Vieth, Paul H. *Worship in Christian Education.* Philadelphia: United Church, 1965.

Ward, Ruth. *Worship Is for Kids Too!* Kalamazoo, Mich.: Master's, 1976.

25

John F. Wilson

Using Music with Children

- Historical Background
- Values of Music
  SELF-EXPRESSION
  EVANGELISTIC WITNESS
  PERSONAL INVOLVEMENT
- Music in the Church Program
  SUNDAY SCHOOL
  CHILDREN'S CHURCHES
  CHILDREN'S CHOIRS
- Music in Other Activities
- Choosing Music for Children
- Criteria for Selecting Music
- Developing a Hymn Curriculum
- Ways of Teaching Music to Children

Very early in life, children learn to respond to music. The songs their mothers sing to them while rocking them to sleep and the musical games they play with parents and playmates seem to open up unparalleled avenues of self-expression, which they will use and develop the rest of their lives. Soon they become greatly influenced by radio, television, recordings and videotapes, which invade their lives with popular songs and commercial jingles, often filling their minds with anti-Christian values, questionable philosophies, and

JOHN F. WILSON, M. Mus., is executive editor of Hope Publishing Company, Carol Stream, Illinois.

low moral concepts. In his book *Nurtured by Love,* Shinichi Suzuki, the founder of the famous method of teaching music to children, points out the fact that most of what a child learns is the result of what is heard. "It is a frightening fact. By no means only words and music, but everything, good or bad, is absorbed."[1]

There is little question that music is one of the greatest influences upon the shaping of moral behavior among children and youth. Yet, it is also one of the most neglected areas of childhood education in the Christian church today. Although it is true you can find churches of all sizes and denominations, with excellent music programs—graded choirs for children of all ages, well-planned and organized singing in the Sunday school and children's church, "hymn-of-the-month" plans, and other teaching devices—they are the exceptions. Most churches view such programs as "nice, but not necessary."

How tragic that this should be so. How unlike the church to overlook such effective tools for ministering to their children! Several "excuses" are often given for this:

• There are not enough trained music leaders to plan and direct every department of the Sunday school, not to mention youth groups, scouts, and all other clubs and organizations.

• Teachers and superintendents are reluctant to assume leadership in an area that is not their main interest.

• There is not enough time.

• There are not enough pianos, or capable pianists.

• It is too difficult and time-consuming to find appropriate songs to use, especially when so many factors (voice ranges, age levels, musical styles and texts) need to be considered.

In summary, the problems lie mostly in the areas of leadership, materials, facilities, and time. All of these concerns are understandable, but one can be assured that they are not insurmountable. Every church can, and should, have a well-balanced and effective ministry of music within the structures of the Christian education program. Certainly it is most desirable to have expert leaders and trained musicians, but it is not necessary. With the ever-increasing accessability of music and recordings and the availability of modern technological equipment at reasonable costs, a strong music program is well within the grasp of every local church. All that is needed is a vision of what music can do to enhance the church's ministry to children and youth, and of how it can

1. Shinichi Suzuki, *Nurtured by Love: A New Approach to Education,* trans. Suzuki and Waltrand (New York: Exposition, 1969), p. 17.

affect their lives for good. With that vision, even the non-musician can conduct a successful music program.

Historical Background

The use of music to teach children has been successfully practiced throughout history, dating as far back as the time of David and Solomon.

At the time of the establishing of temple worship, David commanded the chief Levites to appoint "singers, with instruments of music . . . to raise the sounds of joy" (1 Chron. 15:16, NASB). He then set aside the sons of his chief musicians, Heman, Asaph, and Jeduthun, to instruct the children in song (1 Chron. 25:1). The educational activities during that period included "the reciting of Scriptures, praying, various types of singing, and discussion and explanation of the Scriptures that had great value in helping the people understand the way of the Lord more perfectly."[2]

In New Testament days, the apostle Paul recognized the teaching potential of music when he charged the Colossian Christians, "Let the word of Christ richly dwell within you, with all wisdom teaching and admonishing one another with psalms and hymns and spiritual songs, singing with thankfulness in your hearts to God" (Col. 3:16, NASB).

In the early Christian church, choir schools were established to teach music and to train children in the worship and doctrines of the church. In some parts of the world and among some denominational groups in America, similar schools are still in existence. During the Protestant Reformation, congregational singing was restored to the possession of the people for the first time since the early years of the Christian church, so that, in the words of Martin Luther, "God might speak directly to them in His Word and . . . they might directly answer Him in their songs."[3]

A new style of gospel song was born during the Sunday school movement of the nineteenth century, to teach the Word of God in simplicity and directness.

Values of Music

Music is valuable to children for at least the following reasons.

IT IS A MEANS OF SELF-EXPRESSION

The fact that music is an enjoyable experience makes it an even more effective teaching tool. When something is fun to do, the learning comes more easily, the retention factors are greater, and the message is more apt to be understood.

2. J. M. Price, James H. Chapman, L. L. Carpenter, and W. Forbes Yarborough, *A Survey of Religious Education* (New York: Ronald, 1940), p. 31.
3. E. S. Lorenz, *Practical Church Music* (Westwood, N.J.: Revell, 1909), p. 191.

IT IS AN EVANGELISTIC WITNESS

Music enhances the ministry of outreach. Children are often attracted to a church by a special interest in participating in the music program, in a choir, in an instrumental group, or in a musical-drama performance. Through this involvement, they are confronted with the message of salvation. On receiving salvation, they are placed into a position of service and discipleship. Perhaps the evangelistic potential of a music program may best be illustrated by the steps in Figure 25.1.

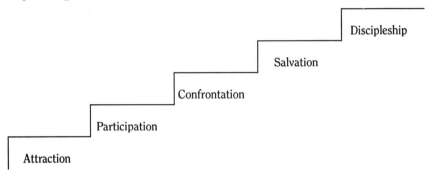

Figure 25.1
Evangelistic Potential of Music

IT IS A MEANS OF PERSONAL INVOLVEMENT

Participation leads to a more direct confrontation with the message. Statistically, one is assured of learning far more through involvement than by mere listening. Since music serves as a means of personal involvement in worship and self-expression, it increases the potential of grasping truths and being changed by them. Involvement also makes one feel more a part of a group.

MUSIC IN THE CHURCH PROGRAM

Music can and should be integrated into each of the following activities.

SUNDAY SCHOOL

The primary purpose of the Sunday school is to teach the Word of God and to help each child both to know Jesus Christ as Savior and Lord and to maintain a growing relationship with Him. A carefully planned program of music, under enthusiastic and competent leadership, can greatly contribute to the fulfillment of this purpose. Each department of the Sunday school should devote some time each week to music activities, or should integrate music into the other activities of the school. Obviously, one person must be responsible for the planning, but others may be enlisted for the conducting and accompanying of the music, especially when several different departments are convening at the same time. Regular workers in each department, members of the adult or youth choirs, or other talented volunteers can help fill these positions.

Smaller churches may find it difficult to maintain consistent music programs in all departments but can solve this problem either by combining two or more departments for a brief portion of the hour each week or by scheduling the music at different times in each department, so that several can share the services of the same music leaders. If necessary, activities can even be conducted biweekly, or once a month, giving an extended time for music on those days.

CHILDREN'S CHURCHES

The purposes of children's churches are to train children in worship, to provide opportunity for worship experience on the level of the children, and to prepare children to enter the regular church services later on. Music in children's churches should include both standard hymnody and contemporary expressions of praise and adoration. Primary and junior children should also learn to sing the Doxology and the Gloria Patri, or any other traditional parts of the service, and should be taught the true function of each of these and other aspects of public worship. (For more on children's churches and worship, see chap. 23, "Teaching Children to Worship and Pray.")

Another distinctive feature of children's churches is the opportunity to participate in leadership roles, such as reading the Scriptures, leading in prayer, and ushering. They should also be taught to lead the singing, to render special musical numbers, or perhaps to sing in a choir or small ensemble. Children who are studying musical instruments should be given opportunity to play in children's churches, perhaps for the prelude or offertory.

Active involvement ought to be encouraged, even if abilities have not been developed fully or the choice of material is not along the usual lines of acceptable church music. This first step may ultimately lead to a lifetime dedication of a child's talents to the Lord.

CHILDREN'S CHOIRS

The choir activities of any church should be structured to meet the needs of children. Some larger churches are able to maintain successfully a choir for every age group, including younger children. Because of size, lack of leadership, or overscheduling of other activities, other churches would find this impractical. Perhaps the most commonly used plans consist of either two or three choirs (in addition to the adult and high school choirs).

Two choirs.
   Junior—grades 3 through 5
   Youth—grades 6 through 8

Three choirs.
Primary—grades 2 and 3 (possibly grade 1 also)
Junior—grades 4 through 6
Youth—grades 7 and 8 (occasionally grade 9 also)

A more expanded system gives opportunity for adjusting the activities to meet varied interests and learning abilities of children. However, it would be better to use two choirs, or even begin with only one choir (grades 4 through 8 is a suggested starter), if there are not enough children available to make the experience a satisfactory one. It is generally agreed that a larger group will result in a better choral sound, especially with very young voices.

Rehearsal times should be planned around local school schedules, scouting, athletics, and other community activities. Also, they need to be coordinated with church activities to avoid transportation problems and conflicts involving the same age groups. If several children's activities are scheduled, have them on the same day or evening, if possible. Many churches find it best to have the primary and junior choirs practice on Saturday mornings. In some churches, the junior choir practices during a portion of the children's church hour or on Sunday evenings before the church service.

Under proper leadership, children's choirs can become effective singing groups that can perform in church services and in special musical programs. Another significant contribution is the effect on the lives of those who participate. The following are the basic functions of the ministry of children's choirs with particular values to the children themselves.

To evangelize. Choirs attract unchurched children who are interested in music. This participation can reach not only the children but also entire unchurched families.

To teach worship. Because of their involvement in the services of the church, children learn to conduct themselves properly in worship, take part in singing, praying, sitting, and standing reverently. In addition, they can realize the value of a true worship experience.

To develop spiritual growth. A carefully chosen choir repertoire includes hymns and anthems based on truths from the Word of God. The constant repetition in rehearsal and the encouragement of the leader to interpret the meaning of the texts open up new areas of understanding and knowledge, whereby children may grow.

To give opportunity for Christian service. Through participation in the church services, children learn to discover the way God uses people to minister His Word to others. They soon realize that they are ministers of the gospel when they sing. Often this helps them develop a lifelong positive attitude toward Christian service.

MUSIC IN OTHER ACTIVITIES

Unlimited possibilities exist for use of children's musical interests and abilities outside the regular services and department activities. Leaders must seek ways of discovering interests and then provide ways in which they can be stimulated and encouraged. This can be done by having talent programs and musical concerts in which children are encouraged to perform, or by awarding scholarships or financial assistance for music camps or schools. Attendance at a local children's symphony concert or a choir program by some visiting children's group (such as the Vienna Boys' Choir or the Korean Orphans' Choir) may be helpful. These activities can generate new interests in musical activities and stimulate the desire to develop talents God has given.

CHOOSING MUSIC FOR CHILDREN

Hymns for children have not always been appropriate theologically or pedagogically. One of the first published books of children's songs in the United States was *Divine and Moral Songs,* published by Isaac Watts in 1720. Although it included some good hymns, it also included many which were moralistic in nature, dealing with bad actions a child must avoid if he wished to please God. Later writers in the eighteenth and nineteenth centuries did not greatly improve the quality of content. Some tended to "talk down" to the children, referring to them as "little lambs." Still others "sugar-coated" the gospel message until it was fairly obscure. Unfortunately the problem still exists today.

In evaluating the words of a song for children, the following questions may be asked:

1. Are the words consistent with the Scriptures?
2. Do the words emphasize important truths?
3. Are the words interesting and clear?
4. Are they on the level of the age group?
5. Do they encourage a spirit of reverence?

Criteria for evaluating the music may include the following:

1. The younger the age, the shorter the phrases should be.
2. The pitch should range from about D to C above middle C, with most of the notes from D to A.
3. The rhythm should be simple, predictable, and consistent with the word accents.
4. The melody and harmony should have distinctive characteristics that make the song easy to learn and remember.
5. All of the above should contribute to the best interpretation of the text.

CRITERIA FOR SELECTING MUSIC

FOR TWOS AND THREES

1. *Rhythm.* This should not be jerky or "catchy" (characterized by dotted notes), but instead, a series of one type of note with little change in rhythm. Choose songs in 2/4 or 4/4 time, because this is easiest to gear to the natural pulsation of their bodies and activities (walking, marching, clapping hands, and so on).

2. *Melody.* This should be simple, pretty, easy to listen to, smooth (no wide leaps), and repetitious.

3. *Harmony.* This should include only basic chords (no discord or close harmony), smooth chord progressions characterized by very few moves of the parts from chord to chord. It should be in major mood (not minor).

4. *Volume.* This should be characterized by one general level, in contrast to use of crescendos or any other startling changes.

5. *Tempo.* This should be a medium pace, but not so slow that they cannot sustain notes if singing or lose interest if listening, nor so fast that they are unable to follow either singing or listening. It should also fit in with the tempo of their activity.

6. *Tone quality.* This should be pleasant and free from harshness, with no wide vibratto, nor such a lack of vibratto that the tone seems thin or sounds almost flat.

7. *Words.* The songs should contain words that will communicate in the realm of their experience. These words should be easy to pronounce, built on vowels, simple, and repetitious.

FOR FOURS AND FIVES

1. *Rhythm.* The teacher may begin to use songs with slightly syncopated rhythm, if it is such that they are able to synchronize their developing rhythmic sensitivity with it.

2. *Melody.* The same rule as for twos and threes applies here.

3. *Harmony.* The teacher may begin to employ music that contains a greater variety of types of chords but still in the major mood.

4. *Volume.* The teacher may begin to use dynamics if they are smooth and used meaningfully for emphasis.

5. *Tempo.* The teacher may begin to brighten the tempo (make it more lively) to fit increased activity, but he should vary it from song to song.

6. *Tone quality.* The same rule for twos and threes applies here.

7. *Words.* The teacher may begin to use songs with new words if they are in a context of known words that bring out the meaning of the new word.

8. *Mediums.* Songs should still be sung in unison. Let the children listen to choral music, if it is simple, well done, and of high quality (hymns, but not

gospel songs or choruses). Begin a rhythm band. Use recorded music related to activities. The children may want to dramatize the songs.

9. *Style.* It is best to use songs with short, repetitious phrases. Keep songs in their range. Associate music with worship by attitudes, using simple but high-quality music (not necessarily choral) to do this. The children may enjoy a special organ concert, or listen to records and the church choir.

FOR PRIMARIES

1. *Rhythm.* The teacher can introduce songs of 3/4 and 6/8 time, and may employ more variety in rhythm.

2. *Melody.* This can have wider leaps if intervals are thirds or fourths.

3. *Harmony.* The same rule for fours and fives applies here.

4. *Volume.* The teacher may emphasize dynamics to increase expression. He may also use more shading of overall level.

5. *Tempo.* The teacher may vary it more from song to song, but still the tempo should not be extreme.

6. *Tone quality.* The teacher may introduce the children to new sounds through instrumental music.

7. *Mediums.* The teacher may introduce two-part harmony in singing. Have them listen to junior choir and instrumental music. Acquaint primaries with names and sounds of instruments.

8. *Style.* The teacher may begin to expand to new areas and types of musical expression. He should continue to associate worship with fine music.

FOR JUNIORS

1. *Rhythm.* Juniors can increase their accuracy of reproduction of syncopation. Use stirring rhythmic patterns, such as 2/4 or 4/4 march time, strongly accented on first beat and third beat of the measure.

2. *Melody.* The teacher may use melodies that stir and awaken new religious experiences, even if they are difficult to reproduce.

3. *Harmony.* The teacher may introduce minor mood, if the song meets other standards (such as "The God of Abraham Praise").

4. *Volume.* The teacher may make full use of dynamics for expression.

5. *Tempo.* The teacher may use wide variety in tempo.

6. *Tone quality.* The teacher should strive for good quality and a blend between voices. He should encourage expression, even if quality is not good.

7. *Mediums.* The teacher may organize musical groups, such as a junior choir or orchestra. The children may enjoy listening to sacred masterpieces.

8. *Style.* The children can expand to four-part harmonies in singing. *Variety* should be a byword. Reach out to new areas, while improving quality.

In our day, more variety in styles of church music is evident than perhaps ever before. Our wonderful heritage of hymnody and our more recent background of gospel songs of personal testimony are now greatly enhanced by the new type of folk songs, with which many children can immediately identify.

DEVELOPING A HYMN CURRICULUM

Clarence H. Benson has suggested, "A graded course in sacred song may be covered just as effectively as a graded curriculum of the Bible."[4] It is important that a carefully planned curriculum of hymns and songs be outlined for each children's department. This kind of planning not only assures a better correlation of songs with study material, but also helps prevent an overbalance of any one style of music which may be favored by either the leaders or the children. Besides standard songs from the hymnal, a new song should be used occasionally. They must be chosen according to meaning of the words and the appropriateness of the music.

After the hymns have been chosen, there are at least two ways in which they can be implemented. One of the most popular ways is through a "hymn-of-the-month" program, in which one new hymn is learned every month. The hymn is taught each week during the month in as many different ways as possible (sung, played, discussed, and memorized). This plan assures the learning of ten to twelve new hymns every year. It can either be carried on departmentally, with each age group learning a different set of hymns, or on a churchwide basis, with all departments learning the same hymns. Another way is to schedule a monthly music class devoted to learning new hymns. If possible, this time should be separate from the Sunday school or church services, and may be part of a social hour or other time during the week.

WAYS OF TEACHING MUSIC TO CHILDREN

Specific approaches in teaching music to different age groups should be considered in the use of music with children. These are general guidelines, and it must be emphasized that specific levels vary considerably within each age group.

TWOS THROUGH FIVES

With children ages two through five, it is not necessary to have a piano for accompaniment of songs. If a piano is used, it should be played softly in an easy, flowing manner rather than with heavy, block chords. The primary purpose in piano playing for young children is to create moods and atmosphere. A record player accomplishes the same purpose and takes far less space.

The tempo should never be fast, the phrases should be short, and the range should be moderate above middle C.

Before teaching a new song, the teacher should learn the song, place it in a

---

4. Clarence C. Benson, *The Sunday School in Action* (Chicago: Moody, 1948), p. 81.

setting, and sing it several times before the children sing it. Also the melody and tempo should be clear. The children should not be encouraged to sing with loud or forced tones. That can be damaging to their undeveloped voices.

Using illustrated slides, pictures, or flannelgraph figures can help children understand the message of the songs. Since younger children usually have very short interest spans, it is better to sing a few songs frequently than to try to teach too many songs at once.

Bernice T. Cory gives several suggestions for teaching a new song to two- and three-year-olds:

> The "play sing" method, in which you sing a song while the children watch your lips and try to say the words silently, helps older Nursery children to learn a song. Letting them supply a simple phrase while you sing most of a song is another effective method to teach new songs. Don't sing too fast. It takes time for a child to say the words, let alone to associate the words with a melody. Be sure to pitch the songs within his range, not too high or too low.
>
> Finger plays, like action songs, invite the children to imitate, and further the teaching process to the extent that the children participate.[5]

Music with four- and five-year-olds should be short and simple, not loud, jazzy tunes that cause confusion. With fours and fives, music can "tell" the children when to put away materials, when to tiptoe to their places, or when to bring an offering. A record player, cassette, or autoharp is as effective as a piano.

A rhythm band, using a few simple instruments, is a good means of musical expression for fours and fives.

Songs for young children should not include words with symbolism such as "Climb, Climb Up Sunshine Mountain" or "This Little Light of Mine."

PRIMARIES

Primary children learn very quickly but also forget easily; therefore, it is important to repeat the same song several weeks in a row until it is remembered. Song phrases should be short and the pitch ranges moderate, but the tempo should be faster than with younger children. The songs should be more rhythmic and bright. Hymns and songs with symbolism, such as "O For a Thousand Tongues," are difficult for primaries to sing with meaning. Published "song charts" are helpful visual aids in teaching songs to primaries. Primaries enjoy illustrating songs and hymns with drawings or pictures.

JUNIORS

Juniors have developed their skills in reading and their ability to memorize. It is important to capitalize on this ability to challenge them to memorize song

5. Bernice T. Cory, *Debby and Dan Go to the Nursery Class* (Wheaton, Ill.: Scripture Press, 1954), p. 18.

texts as well as Scripture verses and passages. Since juniors thrive on competition, contests and awards may be used. One procedure for teaching songs is to write the verses on a chalkboard, and as the children sing them aloud, erase several of the words, perhaps the verbs first, then the nouns, and other parts of speech, until the board is empty. To help children understand the meaning of songs, ask them to rephrase the verses in their own nonpoetic way, or ask them to explain in their own words what the text says. This will not only help them increase their understanding, but will also help them discern between good and bad texts and ultimately will influence their musical tastes and listening habits outside the church.

At the junior level, pitch ranges and lengths of phrases can be more challenging. Styles of music can vary greatly, and should include wholesome entertainment and hymns with great depth and dignity. It is important for the music session to be exciting and enjoyable without cheapening the quality of the literature used or neglecting the worthy hymns.

Songs for juniors should emphasize salvation, service, prayer commitment, stewardship, and missions.

To help juniors learn to choose music on their own, teachers can explain the topical index in the hymnal and ask them to choose songs based on "God's love," "faith," or other subjects. Juniors also need to be encouraged to write their own songs, or at least attempt to express their own thoughts poetically. Self-expression, not academic perfection, is the goal.

As has been previously mentioned, the influence of the media and popular music is greatly felt by all children, especially as they grow older and come closer to the teen years. Therefore, it is imperative that the leaders of these children of junior age become aware of the style and content of the music they are listening to. Although far too many of these songs undermine morals, others are quite acceptable and some even enriching. An acquaintance with current songs could lead to some healthy and meaningful discussions. Some of the better songs could be discussed in light of the Scriptures, to discern between the acceptable and the conflicting philosophies contained in them. In addition, the students will gain a new appreciation for the teacher's interest in, insight about, and concern for their generation. At the same time, it is erroneous to assume that children are attracted only to what is on the "top ten" list. Many children no doubt are participating in school bands, choirs, and community groups. Their Sunday school leaders should show an interest in these activities as well.

SUMMARY

Since the basic goal of Christian education is to develop the whole person, the concern of those who work with children must go beyond the music they teach in the class, club, or rehearsal. This concern should challenge them to seek to improve the quality of the music the children carry out into the world week after week. They must do everything within their power to help children benefit spiritually from music. The effectiveness of music as a tool in Christian education is measured by the results seen in the lives of the children.

Our goal in this chapter has been to lay the groundwork on which a functional and meaningful church music program may be developed with children. It is hoped that leaders will discover their department's strengths and needs for improvement and will build a program that will meet the needs of the children for whom they are responsible.

FOR FURTHER READING

GENERAL STUDIES

Baker, Clara Belle. *Sing and Be Happy: Songs for the Young Child*. Nashville: Abingdon, 1980.

Baker, Susan, Glennella Key, and Talmadge Butler. *Guiding Fours and Fives in Musical Expression*. Nashville: Convention, 1972.

Fortunato, Connie. *Children's Music Ministry*. Elgin, Ill.: David C. Cook, 1981.

———. *Music Is for Children*. Vols. 1-4. Elgin, Ill.: David C. Cook, 1978.

Morsch, Vivian. *The Use of Music in Christian Education*. Philadelphia: Westminster, 1956.

Nash, Grace C. *Creative Approaches to Child Development with Music, Language and Movement*. New York: Alfred, 1974.

Nye, Vernice. *Music for Young Children*. Dubuque, Ia.: Wm. C. Brown, 1975.

Smith, Judy Gattis. *Teaching with Music Through the Church Year*. Nashville: Abingdon, 1980.

Stillwell, Martha, Roy Scroggins, Jr., Ruth Williams, and Kenneth V. Robinson. *Making Music with Younger Children*. Nashville: Convention, 1970.

Wilson, John F. *An Introduction to Church Music*. 1975. Distributed by International Correspondence Institute, c/o Berean College, Springfield, Mo.

SOURCES FOR CURRICULUM MATERIALS AND SONG BOOKS

Alexandria House, Alexandria, IN 46001
Augsburg Publishing House, 426 South 5th Street, Minneapolis, MN 55415
Broadman Press, 127 Ninth Avenue North, Nashville, TN 37203
Choristers Guild, 2834 West Kingsley Road, Garland TX 75041
Concordia Publishing House, 3558 South Jefferson, St. Louis, MO 63118
David C. Cook Publishing Co., 850 North Grove Avenue, Elgin, IL 60120

Fortress Press, 2900 Queen Lane, Philadelphia, PA 19129
Lillenas Publishing Co., Kansas City, MO 64141
Praise Hymn, Inc., PO Box 401,767, Garland, TX 75040
Scripture Press, 1825 College Avenue, Wheaton, IL 60187
Shawnee Press, Delaware Water Gap, PA 18327
Singspiration, Inc., 1415 Lake Drive S.E., Grand Rapids, MI 49506
Word, Inc., Box 1790, Waco, TX 76703

SOURCES FOR RECORDINGS, SONG CHARTS, AND VISUALIZED SONGS FOR CHILDREN

Alexandria House, Alexandria, IN 46001
Broadman Films, 172 Ninth Avenue North, Nashville, TN 37203
Bible Visuals, Box 93, Landisville, PA 17538
Child Evangelism Fellowship, Box 1156, Grand Rapids, MI 49501
Concordia, 3558 South Jefferson, St. Louis, MO 63118
JorDan Communications, 1100 Wheaton Oaks, Wheaton, IL 60187
Praise Book Publications, 110 West Broadway, Glendale, CA 91204
Radiant Productions, 908 South Tower Lane, Mt. Prospect, IL 60056
Scripture Press, 1825 College Avenue, Wheaton, IL 60187
Standard Publishing Co., 8121 Hamilton Avenue, Cincinnati, OH 45231
Word, Inc., Box 1790, Waco, TX 76703
Zondervan Recordings, 1415 Lake Drive S.E., Grand Rapids, MI 49506

HYMNALS FOR CHILDREN

Hymns for the Children of God, Paragon (1981)
Joyful Sounds, Concordia (1977)
Young Voices in Praise, Benson (1979)

26

Joyce L. Gibson

Teaching Missions, Stewardship, and Vocational Education to Children

Joyce L. Gibson is director of junior and Lifeway curriculums, Scripture Press Publications, Inc., Wheaton, Illinois.

"Next week is missionary Sunday, boys and girls. Be sure to ask your parents for extra offering," urged the primary department superintendent. "Now who can remember the names of our missionaries?"

The superintendent pointed to a battered world map with sagging name flags and curled-up photos of missionaries. The primaries wiggled impatiently with a bored "we go through this every month" look on their faces.

Later the superintendent complained to the mother of one of the primary boys. "I can't understand why the children take so little interest in bringing offering money to Sunday school. You'd think they would at least care about our missionaries!"

"What missionaries?" the mother asked blankly.

Contrast this true incident with others, like Jill, who became delighted when her aunt gave her some money. "God answered my prayer!" she confided with a smile. "Now I have something to give Him to say thank You." Jill's conversion just a few weeks before seemed to call for this tangible expression of love. Though her sisters quickly spent their money at the store, Jill saved hers till Sunday, eagerly anticipating the joy of giving all so that others could be reached.

Consider also the experience of a nine-year-old boy who felt so concerned for missionary Lynn Holm in Africa that he woke up his mother at three in the morning, saying urgently, "Mother, I feel we must pray for Mr. Holm right now." Later, when the missionary was home on furlough and the boy's mother checked with him, they learned that at the very time the boy felt his real concern, Mr. Holm had been faced unarmed with a charging elephant![1] Somewhere, missionary education had made a significant impact on that boy.

Giving of life and service, time and talents is woven throughout Scripture, never as a dreary treadmill duty, but as a glad, reasonable response to the one who has shown us mercy (Rom. 12:1). It is well, then, to study carefully the place in Christian education of missionary and stewardship training of children.

MISSIONARY EDUCATION

IMPORTANCE OF INCLUDING MISSIONS IN THE CHILDREN'S PROGRAM

Why are some churches deeply involved in missions? The members give generously, even sacrificially. A significant number of young people volunteer for service at home and overseas. How do we account for this, when many churches of the same denomination give only a token nod to missionary work? One answer is the difference in missionary education. Instead of making mis-

---

1. "Nine-Year-Old Boy Stops Elephant," *Conservative Baptist Impact* 26 (February 1969): 10.

sions an incidental part of the education program, it forms the heartbeat of the church.

Basic to missionary education is the need to recognize that missionary outreach is not optional to the church. It is not a special treat in the form of a film or a guest speaker to be squeezed into the Sunday school hour on the fifth Sunday of a month. Missions is God's imperative. Missions is Christ Himself reaching out in the power of the Holy Spirit through His body, the church, with God's Word to the world.

Missionary education, then, is a program of learning through which children discover God's view of the world and are thereby led to respond to Him by doing their part in taking the gospel to that world, whether nearby or far away. Missionary education, to be effective, must be saturated with prayer (Matt. 9:37-38), woven throughout by thoughtful planning, and sustained by the love of Christ, which compels true believers to consider themselves debtors to all mankind.

INGREDIENTS OF EFFECTIVE MISSIONS EDUCATION

Inspiration. Some would name as motives for missions the plight of the unfortunate, the strangeness of foreign cultures, or the prospective missionary's appetite for adventure. The biblical motive for missions, however, is not pity, or duty, or even desire for heavenly reward. The inspiration of missions is glad obedience prompted by the love of Christ. A lesser motive is unworthy of the One who died in our place. The church that is faithful in missionary education will teach clearly and compellingly Christ's command, "Go ye." Evangelism is the heartbeat of God. Our appropriate response is availability to His leading and prompt obedience when He indicates His will.

Information. Children should be given the facts of missions and not a vague stereotype of missionary work.

Missions, according to the New Testament pattern, grows out of a local body of believers who represent Christ and is seeking to win the lost in its community. From this body, the Holy Spirit calls some believers to represent Christ away from the local church. These witnesses-away-from-home are called missionaries. They may serve only a few miles from the home church, involved in what we call home missions; or they may be halfway around the world in what we call foreign missions. They usually work under the direction of a mission or a sending agency. Wherever they are and in whatever capacity they serve, these sent ones cooperate with the local body of believers in their new area.

Michael Griffiths, general director of the Overseas Missionary Fellowship, wrote, "Today missionaries are comrades in arms, international reinforcements to work alongside national brethren in small, struggling emerging churches. We need a truly international and interracial missionary force. The modern missionary may be an Asian, an African, or a South American just as much as a North American or a European."[2]

In informing children about missionary work today, we can no longer leave the impression that a missionary will necessarily sign up with one mission board for a lifetime of service in one country, doing one kind of work. Christians are needed who are available for specialized service for a specific period of time.

Short-term missions is a popular and challenging ministry at home and abroad currently. Some workers give a one-year term for a specific assignment. Others stay for only a few weeks, or may stay on for two years and more. Some individuals become career missionaries as a result of short-term missions.

In giving children factual information about missions, church workers should avoid undue emphasis on strange customs, costumes, culture, or language. They should not expose children only to the scenic tourist attractions of the country. Neither should they picture only the rural areas, ignoring the modern cities teeming with well-educated people.

Involvement. At each level, the church will seek to involve children in appropriate learning activities and practical projects that are within the understanding of the age group. These activities will include remembering specific prayer requests, giving personal spending money for both home and foreign needs, participating in teamwork, and personal experience in reaching out to the world near at hand.

Since outreach is basic to the local church program, it will be perfectly natural to integrate a planned curriculum of missionary education in many different situations within the varied church educational agencies. Each department should have a specifically designed program with goals, content, and methods fitted to its age group. The projects should be tangible: raising money for famine relief or targeting prayer for a group of "hidden people." The methods should involve all the senses.

Illustration. Elton Trueblood defines a missionary as "anyone who serves as a consequence of being profoundly touched by the love of Christ. The validity of the conception has little to do with geography."[3]

For missionary education to do its job, the local church at home must embody the same compassion for the lost here that it expects its missionaries to have overseas.

Ralph R. Covell wrote about this desperate need:

> Many churches continue to operate on a "come-to-me" philosophy which is the very opposite of missions. We profess a great concern for people if only they will come to us and receive from our generosity. Missions by proxy is easy because we need not be involved. And where we might become involved, we have quickly

2. Michael Griffiths, "The Lord's Guerilleros," *East Asia Millions* 81 (February-March 1973): 9.
3. Elton Trueblood, *Validity of the Christian Mission* (New York: Harper, 1972), p. x.

tucked our robes about us and gone by on the other side as we seek a comfortable haven in the safe suburbs.

In doing this we have forsaken multitudes who need the Saviour whom we proclaim. Some are black; some are white; some are rich; some are poor. Are we as concerned about these at home as we are about those abroad? Only as we are, will there be integrity and authenticity to our work overseas. Only then will we continue to attract committed young people. Only then will we be willing to give in the increasing measure that is necessary. Only then will our missionaries have that deeply-rooted concern—rooted in the community of concern at home—to convey Christ's love adequately to the distant lost sheep.[4]

Since missions is Christ reaching out through a believer, all Christian education workers in the local church at home should be vitally concerned with missions. They should be working out in their daily lives the same quality of concern that they picture in foreign missionaries. We cannot allow our children to think of missionaries as the only Christians who live sacrificial lives, giving themselves in tireless service for the lost. Hudson Taylor, founder of the China Inland Mission (now Overseas Missionary Fellowship), wrote, "There are not two Christs—an easy-going one for easy-going Christians, and a suffering, toiling one for exceptional believers. There is only one Christ. Are you willing to abide in him, and thus to bear much fruit?"[5] This searching question should be in the forefront of each teacher's thinking.

Findley B. Edge said this about the Christians' attitude:

The desperate need of the world is for people who care. This is what the Gospel is all about. God cares and cares deeply. He calls us to be a people who care and care deeply. No greater opportunity for evangelism is open to us. The world can be won by a people who are willing to care and to care deeply—who are willing to love and to love unconditionally. To be an expression of this caring love is the general mission to which all Christians are called *all of the time*. It must be repeated here . . . we do not have the motivation to give ourselves in this type of unconditional caring unless we are so committed to God that to give a witness of Him is the deepest desire and basic purpose of our existence. This kind of caring goes back to the depth and quality of a person's experience with God.[6]

This kind of caring and willingness to become personally involved must be illustrated to our children. We will show it as we welcome newcomers, follow up absentees, or reach out into the community through weekday clubs or vacation Bible school. We will show it as we pray daily, make personal contacts,

4. Ralph R. Covell, "Urban Crisis: Test of Our Missionary Concern," *World Vision Magazine* 13 (October 1969): 12.
5. Dr. and Mrs. Howard Taylor, *Hudson Taylor and the China Inland Mission* (London: CIM, 1918), p. 626.
6. Findley B. Edge, *The Greening of the Church* (Waco, Tex.: Word, 1971), p. 148.

and pay whatever price is necessary to open clear channels of communication with even the most difficult students.

HOW TO TEACH MISSIONS

Like other aspects of Christian instruction, the content and method of missionary education should be regulated by the needs and capacities of the students. A total church program should be drawn up, correlating the scope of missionary education for each age group and for each agency working with that age group. A committee should review this periodically to be sure there is no overlapping or overlooking in the program. If copies of the program are distributed to all Christian education workers and parents of the children, the whole church can cooperate in making missionary education balanced and effective.

Lois LeBar wrote,

> In a worthy attempt to give missions the place it should have in Sunday School, some schools set aside their regular lessons once each month or quarter in favor of a missions emphasis. This seriously disrupts the continuity of a curriculum unit that is progressively developed. Another idea is to feature one country in each year of the school, such as Japan in first grade, Guatemala in second grade, Germany in third, etc. Each room or department then keeps its own mission museum of pictures, curios, and costumes. These collections are valuable, but this system is not adaptable to the special interests of local churches. If a church is especially interested in missionaries who have recently gone from their midst to Taiwan, Peru and France, pupils in three grades would be concentrating on these countries, but all the other grades would be studying other countries. Because mission emphasis is woven into the warp and woof of Scripture, it becomes an integral part of all Bible study. If each teacher stresses missions whenever Scripture stresses it, it will have a constant emphasis. Once or twice a year the whole church can have a special missions week in which missionaries speak, classes make exhibits, current needs are presented, and calls to prayer, giving and enlistment are given.[7]

When should missionary education begin? In the nursery! If we lay a firm foundation in the preschool years, we will not have to tear down faulty concepts later and rebuild according to God's Word.

TWOS AND THREES

Biblical concepts. God loves everyone. God wants everyone to love Him.

Methods and materials. Two- and three-year-olds are naturally curious. They enjoy handling a new object—looking at it, feeling it, even smelling it! Take advantage of this natural curiosity when giving a missions presentation, and have several objects available that they can see and touch. Such items as

7. Louis E. LeBar, *Focus on People in Church Education* (Westwood, N.J.: Revell, 1968), p. 173.

eating utensils, models of homes, and articles of clothing will help nursery-age children realize that life is different for the missionaries who live "far away."

A discussion of pictures depicting foreign families eating, playing, and working, can also be used to help the children become aware that there are people in the world whose skin color and way of life is different from theirs.

Two- and three-year-olds enjoy playacting. Let them act out situations that demonstrate giving and expressing love to others, such as the following: lending toys to a friend, helping Mother with a simple task, and giving a small gift to an elderly neighbor or relative.

Other possible approaches include telling true missionary stories, visualizing stories with puppets, inviting a missionary to visit the department, and providing handwork for the children to do which emphasizes God's love in action.

FOURS AND FIVES

Biblical concepts. Sin is disobeying God. Jesus died for everyone's sin. Jesus is our Savior. Jesus will save everyone who comes to Him.

Methods and materials. Emphasize needs nearby (home missions), being sure that we do not talk simply about physical needs and arouse only sympathy. Stress that these boys and girls have not heard about Jesus.

However, do not ignore foreign missions. Recognize the fact that four- and five-year-olds have a broadening world awareness because of television, books, magazines, and travel.

Introduce missionary families of the church who have small children. Point out, "These children are going to help their parents tell boys and girls in the land of _____ about Jesus."

Work with missionary speakers to help them present information on a level that preschoolers can understand.

What four- and five-year-olds can do. They can understand simple, concrete needs of a particular missionary and his children and pray for them; give money; share what they are learning with visitors and newcomers; listen to and act out missionary stories,[8] enjoy missionary visits; view slides and handle curios; view missionary pictures and picture books;[9] learn missionary songs that have been carefully visualized; play games of the country being studied;[10] color missionary coloring books (available in Christian bookstores); and play with missionary paper dolls and stand-up figures.[11]

8. See the list of books with missionary stories for children at the end of this chapter. Also see chap. 31, "Story Playing with Children."
9. For example, see Dana Eynon, *World Full of Children* (Cincinnati: Standard); *'Round the World Storybook* (Cincinnati: Standard); and Margaret C. Hayes, *Children in God's World* (Cincinnati: Standard). See also the list of picture sets at the end of this chapter.
10. See the list of books with missionary games, programs, and activities at the end of this chapter.
11. See, for example, *Children of God's World Paper Dolls* (Cincinnati: Standard); and *World's Children Cutouts* (Warrenton, Mo.: Child Evangelism Fellowship).

These children can understand the need for giving money for missions if they are presented with a specific missionary project to which their money will go. In selecting a project, choose one that will be meaningful to their age, a project that fits into the overall church program, and one that reminds children of a missionary's ministry.

In one church, the children in the fours and fives department were asked over a period of several weeks to bring boxes of Jello for their missionary to take back to the field with her. (She served in Korea, where Jello was not available.) On the last Sunday, the missionary visited the department to receive the supply of the product. In introducing the missionary, the superintendent asked the boys and girls what the missionary did in the country far across the ocean. It is not surprising that one bright boy answered, "Eat Jello!" How unfortunate that these youngsters had not heard anything about their missionary's work in Christian radio through which she was reaching many children with the love of Christ!

PRIMARY

Biblical concepts. Everyone has sinned. Sinners need the Savior. Jesus died to take the punishment for everyone's sins. Jesus wants me to tell others about Him. Jesus wants me to give money and pray for missionaries and nationals.

Methods and materials. Expand missionary information as the group is ready for it. Use books, prayer reminders, letters from missionaries, pictures, filmstrips, slides, murals, posters, missionary stories on flannelgraph or flash cards. Teach the children missionary songs, explaining the meaning of the words to them. Primaries enjoy playing games from foreign countries, dressing in the costumes of foreign lands, eating foods and singing songs from other nations.

What children this age can do. Primaries can assume personal responsibility for inviting friends to Sunday school and can understand that this is an important part of the church's missionary program. They can tell others about Jesus, and they can show unselfish love to their families and friends. They can give their money, and they can remember prayer requests both at church and at home. Primaries can write letters or tape-record messages to missionary children and/or national children, collect clothing or food for missionaries, take handmade gifts to shut-ins, collect and send used Christmas cards to missionaries, and do many other things. They can also make murals or tabletop scenes of missionary villages.

JUNIOR

Biblical concepts. Juniors can comprehend deeper understanding of Bible truths already taught. Children are lost not because they live in a different country and have different customs, but because they have not received Christ as Savior. We must choose daily what is important to us—the self-centered values of society around us or the values of following Christ and expanding His work here on earth.

Methods and materials. Many of the ideas suggested for primaries can also be used with juniors. Teach juniors the plan of salvation. Encourage them to share Christ with others. Juniors enjoy relating current events to missionary work. Relate geographical knowledge gained in school to missions. Use maps, population charts, factual studies of people, and photos. Acquaint students with basic facts about mission fields and mission boards. Present the lives of well-known missionaries, from the past as well as the present. Encourage individual and group study about national Christians and the church overseas. Stimulate personal research and reading of missionary stories and biographies. Field trips can be profitable if juniors see firsthand how Christians are reaching out to the lost with Christ's love.

An occasional social can have the flair and flavor of a foreign country—with food, games, songs, or visit in a home or church of another nation.[12]

One group of junior boys consulted a file of correspondence from a mission school in India to make puppets, write a factual script, and present a puppet playlet for the whole church, making the work of the mission school come alive for children and parents. With a little encouragement, juniors can illustrate missionary passages from Scripture and missionary songs, make posters for a missionary conference, and provide tours through a curio display.

What youngsters this age can do. Juniors can express genuine concern for people they know who have not received the Savior. They can pray with a deeper understanding regarding their personal contribution to the Lord's work in another country.

Most juniors have more spending money to give than primary children. They want practical projects for both foreign and home missions. They prefer giving money for a specific piece of equipment rather than for a general fund. They may wish to support an orphan out of their missions fund. Juniors like a slice of the action at home too, and enjoy distributing flyers for the church, going with adults to call on prospect families, and planning picnics and socials that are aimed at an evangelistic thrust for their unchurched peers.

Juniors can plan and produce missions-oriented bulletin boards, posters, and charts. They can build model villages, representing the "fields" of specific missionaries. Girls enjoy dressing dolls in national costumes. Some juniors may be interested in starting a pen-pal club, each writing regularly to a missionary child.

Today, many teens are involved in outreach through service and musical

12. See the list of books with missionary games, programs, and activities at the end of this chapter. Decorations, placemats, party favors, and visuals on missionary themes are available from Wright Studios, 5264 Brookville Road, Indianapolis, Ind. 46219.

groups working in their own communities and through summer programs in which they teach Bible school in urban or rural areas or go abroad to serve on a mission station. Many of these teens can have a dynamic influence on hero-worshiping preteens. Since today's juniors are tuned in to the teen world, church young people returning with glowing testimonies can communicate with an authenticity that a secondhand missionary story can never do! Let juniors become as deeply involved in this type of ministry as possible.

WHERE TO TEACH MISSIONS

Each church agency offers a unique opportunity for missionary education.

Sunday school. Wherever natural, missionary emphasis should be woven into the Bible instruction. For example, a lesson on prayer could include references to answered prayer for missionaries; a lesson on God's will could include, perhaps, the testimony of a missionary supported by the church. In addition, each department should have a bulletin board which should feature up-to-date information on various aspects of the church's missionary outreach. Most Sunday schools encourage missionary giving on a weekly or monthly basis.

Children's church. In worship, where the focus is on God and the service is designed for response to Him, leaders have a prime privilege of opening lives to missionary commitment. Through careful choice of Scripture, music, and Bible talks, boys and girls can be challenged to set their lives according to God's values.

Sunday evening groups, or family-night groups. These agencies, with their more informal programming, are ideal for indepth studies of missions. Here, youngsters can listen to true accounts, become involved in research, and express creatively what they are learning of needs around the world, as well as in their own community.

Weekday clubs. Here, missionary education has practical application as children work for badges and seek to bring in their nonchurched friends. Counselors, when working on an individual basis with the children, can keep children alert to God's call to service.

Choir. In selecting choir numbers, a director asks, Does this music glorify God and bring us to a clearer understanding of Him and His purposes for man? Much of our fine Christian music is on the theme of God reaching out to man. If the director is sensitive to the message of the song, he can enrich the choir's appreciation of it. Where music is linked with meaning, children's attitudes can be deeply influenced.

Summer ministries. This ministry offers tremendous opportunity for children to reach out into the community, thus giving them practical experience in missions at home. In addition, through the concentrated instruction, greater concern for missions is generated. Many summer ministry programs have a missionary offering project, and through brief talks each session, teachers draw a clear picture of at least one aspect of missionary work.

STEWARDSHIP EDUCATION

WHAT STEWARDSHIP EDUCATION INCLUDES

Missionary education touches on another aspect of Christian training—stewardship, or total life commitment. It is natural to think of money when we consider stewardship, but the Bible reflects no such narrow view. It teaches, rather, that every area of a Christian's life is a trust from God. It involves holding time, talents, and treasures in an open hand to be invested for eternity, under God's direction.

Giving of life or money, time or talents is woven throughout Scripture, never as a dreary duty, but as an aspect of Christian life that is joyous, victorious, freely expressed. This wholehearted investment of self is contrary to the attitudes of children who are growing up in a pleasure-oriented society. "Boredom, underachievement (failure), hostility, negative work values are common circumstances prevalent among too many youths in our schools today,"[13] wrote a public school educator. But this is not so for the Christian child who views all of life's opportunities as possible calls to stewardship under God's direction. Children find purpose as they make the most of opportunities to invest in heaven's treasures.

Stewardship education is a program of learning through which children are led to discover God's claim on all resources, including time, talents, and money.

CONTRIBUTION OF STEWARDSHIP EDUCATION TO THE TOTAL PROGRAM

Education for total life commitment gives a perspective and relevance to Bible instruction for which there is no substitute. Imagine the congregation in which each believer is actively offering time, talents, and treasures to his Lord. The local church program would flourish as Christians invest their time, creativity, and skills in the Lord's work, both in the local church and the community and beyond to the ends of the earth.

A group of Sunday school teachers were sharing insights in a teacher training class. As the discussion progressed, enthusiasm mounted. How much they could do if only the budget were not so limited, if the supply cupboard were not so bare, if the facilities and furnishings were not so inadequate!

Then the teachers had an idea. Going over the church directory, they listed each person high school age and older, jotting down the known interests, hobbies, and profession of each. Within a few minutes, an amazing picture

13. Joyce Fern Glasser, *The Elementary School Learning Center for Independent Study* (West Nyack, N.Y.: Parker, 1971), p. 189.

began to form. If each person on the list gave the Lord only a few hours doing what he enjoyed most, the learning resources would be stockpiled!

Attractive furnishings for the nursery department, for example, could be made by teen boys, led by a young father who had recently designed creative items for his child's room. In the primary department, photos to illustrate hymns and Scripture could be flashed on a screen. God-honoring nature and science displays would decorate the junior department. Walls in the teen area would be covered with meaningful banners and posters. For problem readers, the library would offer true stories from missionary literature and take-home papers recorded on cassettes. The supply closet would bulge with Bibletime and foreign costumes, models, and curios. Talented church members could write missionary and seasonal worship programs, geared to the needs of the congregation. Creative forms of outreach into the community would capture interest through art, puppets, music, and testimony. These and many other resources could be made available if only people would tithe their *time* for a month or two. Surrounded by such evidences of the joy of giving, children would clearly see the benefits of stewardship.

But who would start the ball rolling? Where does this type of stewardship begin? Again, in the Christian education program in the children's division.

HOW TO TEACH STEWARDSHIP EDUCATION

By God's Word. Almost any Bible lesson leads to a practical discussion of giving God first place. Whenever teachers take time to probe behind the factual content of the Bible stories, they find concepts which enable them to view some aspect of life and its values from God's point of view. *My Utmost for His Highest,* wrote Oswald Chambers to adults. We translate this for your youngsters as "My best for Jesus," whether it is memorizing songs or Scripture for a special program, working on a poster or bulletin board display, giving part of their spending money, or developing skills of reading and writing.

By personal example. Children quickly sense the value system of their instructors. Though they are not able to articulate their discoveries, children discern the difference in Christians whose choices are governed by time and whose choices are governed by eternity. Do they sense in us a glad abandonment to Christ's claims in the everyday decisions we make?

By personal testimonies. Christians who are being good stewards can give brief testimonies to boys and girls. The church library can make available the stories of Christians who are gladly investing time and talents for Christ and His church. We will not limit these testimonies to those who have spectacular stories, but will include the housewife who decorates the church so tastefully for special days, the high school student who leads singing in vacation Bible school, the mechanic who keeps things in order around the church, or the businessman who is letting God run his factory.

By personal experience. Many teachers who are faithful with exhortation, personal example, and true life stories, hope that instruction will automatically become a part of life. However, in stewardship education, the old adage holds true: experience is the best teacher. Lois LeBar described the way to teach one principle through experience.

> Although children in the Bible school often repeat the Scripture verse, "It is more blessed to give than to receive," they seldom really believe those words until they have personally enjoyed a practical experience in giving. If we are to change the natural tendency of *getting* to the transcendent attitude of *giving,* we must so arrange circumstances that the child receives more satisfaction from giving than from getting. During the early formative years most children have never been privileged to have this experience, they see very few examples of sacrificial giving in the people they know, and thus they grow up secretly questioning God's high standards of stewardship.[14]

In the nursery department, children can enjoy a book with colorful pictures that show specific ways their money is used when they give because they love Jesus.

Four- and five-year-olds respond to specific needs. They can learn to give so that someone else can hear about Jesus and so that the home base can meet its practical needs for Sunday school supplies, heat, electricity, and so forth.

Primaries and juniors usually have a little money of their own. They can give because they want to offer a part of themselves in this way. The act of giving can be made especially significant when the leader uses Scripture, a brief responsive reading, poem, prayer, or song to involve the children in genuine worship.

Primaries and juniors should understand that giving is broader than the definition of "Contributions" provided by the Internal Revenue Service!

> There are the intangible gifts of love and trust and devotion and prayer which we can give personally to Christ, but material things go to others in His name, for He said, "Inasmuch as ye have done it unto one of the least of these My brethren, ye have done it unto Me.[15]

Children who are taught the joy of full life commitment can grow up forming the habits of simple living and regular, liberal giving. They will not speak of making great sacrifices, for they will be investing time and talents in what their hearts love best.

14. Lois E. LeBar, *Children in the Bible School* (Westwood, N.J.: Revell, 1952), p. 315.
15. Ibid., p. 318.

VOCATIONAL GUIDANCE

WHAT VOCATIONAL GUIDANCE IS

Several years ago, when an adult asked a child, "What do you want to be when you grow up?" he would have received a specific reply, such as "Airplane pilot," "Nurse," or "Mechanic."

Today's child is apt to answer such a question with a shrug, "How do I know what jobs will be needed when I'm grown up?"

And he's right! Some of today's current fields of work—in lunar geology and microcomputers, for example—were almost unheard of a few years ago. In the technological explosion, vocational guidance is even more necessary for young people than previously. They need assistance in discovering their aptitudes and developing skills needed for general categories of work.

WHY VOCATIONAL GUIDANCE AT EARLIER LEVELS

A goal in public school education is to see all children starting at an early age to study job clusters, gradually narrowing career choices with guidance and counseling, and then developing a skill in the chosen job cluster.

Even in primary grades, children are having some firsthand experience with jobs. They are studying the skills required in various occupations and are beginning to get the big picture of job choices. Today's vocational guidance at school is eliminating the emphasis on sex-based work. For example, equal opportunity will expose girls to such training as welding.

Research reveals that career decisions are rooted back in early childhood when the "career image" starts to form. By sixth grade, most children have at least tentatively outlined the courses of study they will select in junior high school, based on vocational potential.

HOW TO TEACH VOCATIONAL GUIDANCE

The church, keeping in mind its goal of life commitment, can make career exploration a valid part of Christian education. Future work should be considered from the viewpoint of God's will, opportunities it presents for Christian witness, and opportunities for investing talents and skills in serving Christ, whether in so-called secular work or full-time Christian service. Whatever career a person chooses, he needs to be a full-time Christian. God has given special abilities and gifts to do specialized work. The child needs to be aware of this.

Christian educators need to recognize that they do not know now what is best for children when they grow up. The future is in God's hands. Adults' ignorance of future opportunities, plus their tendency to impose their own hopes on young people may account for some of the restlessness and defeats experienced by youth. How much stability and assurance young people have when they sense they are being directed by the Lord in their career preparation!

In counseling children, we will want to stimulate them to think big, to anticipate new ways of serving the Lord, new mediums for communicating the gospel, and new God-honoring channels to express creativity and learning. The possibilities are almost endless! The minds of children should be closed only to those career possibilities that are not in harmony with the Word of God.

Lois LeBar wrote,

> Should Christians be more or less colorful and productive than other people? Does the dull, drab personality reflect the Christian life? Where are the Christian scholars who are forging new frontiers of knowledge based on scriptural foundations? Where are the writers who give vision of the Christian pathway from the realistic existential situation to exalted heights in Christ? Who will conduct the scientific experiments? Where are the educators who are working out on the growing edge of the field?[16]

Intercristo—career and human resources specialists in Seattle, Washington—is prepared to handle inquiries from more than 100,000 individuals a year concerning Christian service placement opportunities. Intercristo's Career Placement Network has listings of over 35,000 job openings in hundreds of Christian organizations around the world in the following occupational fields:

administration and office
agriculture
camping and recreation
communications and the arts
construction and trades
data processing
education
food service and hospitality
health care and medicine
liberal arts
maintenance and repair
marketing and public relations
ministry
science and technology
social sciences and service
translation and linguistics
transportation

16. Lois E. LeBar, *Education That Is Christian* (Westwood, N.J.: Revell, 1958), p. 174.

While stimulating children to explore vocational possibilities, we must also stress that building Christian character and developing spiritual gifts are key ways to prepare for any vocation. Such biblical virtues as diligence, cooperation, and self-control are desirable in all professions.

RESOURCES AND ACTIVITIES IN VOCATIONAL GUIDANCE

Personal testimonies, library materials, and field trips all provide learning opportunities for children. Adults who are alive to the potential in their chosen vocation can share insights with children and arouse appreciation for the avenues of serving God in various kinds of work.

Although not *every* Christian can be employed as a pastor, Christian education director, missionary, or teacher in a Bible college, it is important that all young people in the church be made aware of all the possibilities in "specialized Christian ministries." Preparing youth to consider such careers can be provided in the church, using methods similar to these: provide instruction for the various kinds of ministry as part of the total curriculum in the church and the home; encourage children to serve the Lord *now* in specific ways, telling others about Christ, Christian literature, visiting the sick and aged, and doing projects in the church and at home; invite resource people into the department to present their ministry; conduct field trips of Christian organizations, publishing houses, mission board offices, other churches; have personal or taped interviews with people working in a variety of ministries, encouraging the children to ask their own questions, and possibly do part of the interviewing themselves, reporting their findings; encourage parents to invite guests home for dinner or overnight to get acquainted on a more informal basis; show slides or filmstrips; provide literature about different kinds of ministries; have children write for materials, study what they receive, and make a scrapbook of the materials; provide books, magazines, and pamphlets which relate to Christian ministries; train parents in specialized ministries so they can teach their children at home.

SUMMARY

Missionary, stewardship, and vocational education are essential in the spiritual training of children. Probably at no other time in life will foundational teachings in these areas be so significant! We can challenge children to give their best in each of these areas.

Children can grasp instruction in these topics by leaders and teachers who present the concepts on their levels intellectually and spiritually. Since we are building foundations, much of the teaching will involve giving basic information, creating awareness, and building positive attitudes.

Children can also become involved personally in meeting missionaries and others in specialized Christian ministries, giving toward practical projects related to everyday life, and discovering more about various kinds of careers and vocations.

One of the most important questions children can ask is, "What does God want me to be when I grow up?" We realize this question not only includes what we do, but more importantly what we are!

FOR FURTHER READING

GENERAL STUDIES

Anderson, Virginia. *Making Missions Meaningful.* Wheaton, Ill.: Pioneer Girls, 1966.

Cook, Harold R. *Highlights of Christian Missions.* Chicago: Moody, 1967.

———. *Introduction to a Study of Christian Missions.* Chicago: Moody, 1979.

Gerber, Vergil, ed. *Missions in Creative Tension.* South Pasadena, Calif.: William Carey Library, 1971.

Gilleo, Alma. *How to Teach Missions.* Elgin, Ill.: David C. Cook, 1964.

Glover, Robert H. *Bible Basis of Missions.* Chicago: Moody, 1979.

Griffiths, Michael C. *Give Up Your Small Ambitions.* Chicago: Moody, 1971.

Haskin, Dorothy C. "How You Can Teach Missions to Children." *World Vision* 16 February 1972): 12-13.

Howard, David M. *Student Power in World Evangelism.* Downers Grove, Ill.: InterVarsity, 1970.

———. *Why World Evangelism?* Downers Grove, Ill.: InterVarsity, 1971.

Hulbert, Terry C. *World Missions Today.* Wheaton, Ill.: Evangelical Teacher Training Assn., 1979. (Teacher's guide also available.)

Kane, J. Herbert. *Christian Missions in Biblical Perspective.* Grand Rapids: Baker, 1976.

———. *Life and Work on the Mission Field.* Grand Rapids: Baker, 1980.

Lovering, Kerry. *Missions Idea Notebook.* New York: SIM, 1967.

McGavran, Donald, ed. *Crucial Issues in Missions Tomorrow.* Chicago: Moody, 1972.

Morningstar, Mildred. *Teaching Johnny to Give.* Chicago: Moody, 1972.

Pearson, Dick. *Missionary Education Helps for the Local Church.* Palo Alto, Calif.: Overseas Crusades, 1966.

Peters, George W. *A Biblical Theology of Missions.* Chicago: Moody, 1972.

Olford, Stephen. *The Grace of Giving.* Grand Rapids: Zondervan, 1972.

Troutman, Charles. *Everything You Want to Know About the Mission Field, But Are Afraid You Won't Learn Until You Get There.* Downers Grove, Ill.: InterVarsity, 1976.

Vinkemulder, Yvonne. *Enrich Your Life.* Downers Grove, Ill.: InterVarsity, 1972.

Wagner, C. Peter, ed. *Church/Mission Tensions Today.* Chicago: Moody, 1972.
Zuck, Roy B. *The Pastor and Missionary Education.* Christian Education Monographs, Pastors' Series, No. 22. Glen Ellyn, Ill.: Scripture Press Foundation, 1967.

OTHER SOURCES

MATERIALS WITH MISSIONARY GAMES, PROGRAMS, AND ACTIVITIES

Keiser, Armilda B. *Here's How and When.* New York: Friendship, 1952.
Millen, Nina. *Children's Games from Many Lands.* New York: Friendship, 1964.

BOOKS WITH MISSIONARY STORIES FOR CHILDREN

Arnold, Charlotte E. *Missionary Stories and Illustrations.* Grand Rapids: Baker, 1970.
Doan, Eleanor L., and Gladys McElroy. *Missionary Stories for Preschoolers.* Glendale, Calif.: Gospel Light, 1963.
———. *Missionary Stories for Primaries.* Glendale, Calif.: Gospel Light, 1963.
———. *Missionary Stories for Juniors.* Glendale, Calif.: Gospel Light, 1963.
Haskin, Dorothy C. *Tell Every Man.* Grand Rapids: Baker, 1968.
Millen, Nina. *Missionary Stories to Play and Tell.* New York: Fellowship, 1958.
Worman, Theresa. *Missionary Stories and More Missionary Stories.* Chicago: Moody, 1974.

MISSIONARY SONGBOOKS FOR CHILDREN

Holcomb, Louanah. *Missionary Melodies.* Nashville: Broadman, n.d.
Thomas, Edith. *The Whole World Singing.* New York: Friendship, 1950.

MISSIONARY CANTATAS

M-I-S-S-I-O-N-A-R-Y — That's Us. Camphill, Pa.: Christian Publications, 1985.

SOURCES OF MISSIONARY FLANNELGRAPH AND/OR FLASH CARD STORIES

Accent B/P Publications, Box 15337, Denver, CO 80205.
Bible Visuals, Inc., Box 4842, Lancaster, PA 17604.
BCM International, 237 Fairfield Avenue, Upper Darby, PA 19082.
Child Evangelism Fellowship, Warrenton, MO 63383.
Regular Baptist Press, Box 95500, Schaumburg, IL 60195.
Scripture Press Publications, Inc., 1825 College Avenue, Wheaton, IL 60187.

Standard Publishing Company, 8121 Hamilton Avenue, Cincinnati, OH 45231. Mission Pak, *Jesus Makes the Difference.* Ten exciting, true missionary stories, each illustrated with a classroom-size picture.

RESOURCES FOR MISSIONARY EDUCATION

Association of Church Missions Committees, Box ACMC, Wheaton, IL 60189-8000

Has an excellent *Missions Education Handbook* which contains many sources for missions education programs. The handbook has listings of films, maps, overhead transparencies, videotapes, cassettes, multi-media learning kits, missionary Bible studies, vacation Bible school packets and other sources.

Back to the Bible Broadcast, Box 82808, Lincoln, NE 68501

Has booklets and tracts on missions.

CAM International, 8625 La Prada Drive, Dallas, TX 75228

Has literature, "how-to" articles, and slide-tape presentations on various aspects of missions.

Conservative Baptist Mission Societies, Box 5, 25 W 560 Geneva Road, Wheaton, IL 60187

Has a Missionary Idea Kit containing ideas on how to have a missions emphasis in the church and the home.

Far Eastern Gospel Crusade, P.O. Box 513, Farmingham, MI 48024

Has a packet of stories, songs, and other program suggestions for all age groups about missions.

Friendship Press, Service Center, 7820 Reading Road, Cincinnati, OH 45237

Has literature for missions education.

Greater Europe Mission, Box 668, Wheaton, IL 60187

Has ideas for missions education.

IFCA, Box 7250, Mannheim Road, Westchester, IL 60153

Has ideas for missions education.

Intercristo, 19303 Fremont Avenue North, Seattle WA 98133

Has a career placement network and literature on opportunities in Christian service internationally.

Neibauer Press, Inc., 20 Industrial Drive, Ivyland, PA

Has missions education ideas and literature.

Overseas Missionary Fellowship, 404 S. Church Street, Robesonia, PA 19551-0404

Has literature for missions education.

PS Production, Box 391, Glen Ellyn, IL 60138

Has resources for missions education.

SIM, 10 Huntingdale Boulevard, Scarborough, Ontario, Canada MIW 2S5

Has missions education ideas and literature.

Slavic Gospel Association, Box 1122, Wheaton, IL 60189
   Has resources for missions education.
The Evangelical Alliance Mission, Box 969, Wheaton, IL 60189
   Has literature and films for missions education.
Wycliffe Bible Translators, Huntington Beach, CA 92647
   Has a list of positions open for career and short-term missionaries and job
   descriptions for several positions.
World Christian, P.O. Box 40020, Pasadena, CA 91104
   Has literature on missions education.

Part 6

Utilizing Methods and Resources

27

Joanne Brubaker

Methods and Materials for Children

- How Important Are Methods and Materials?
- Variety in Teaching
  JESUS USED VARIETY
  THE NEEDS OF CHILDREN DEMAND VARIETY
- Factors to Consider in Selection
- Some Key Methods and Materials
- Interest and Learning Centers
- Appropriate Methods and Materials to Use
- The Resource Center
- The Use of Books
- Setting Up Book Centers
- Beginning a Church Reading Program
- Recommended Reading for Children

The task of teaching has been compared to "opening the shutters on the windows of a house. Using one method will let the light stream through one

JOANNE BRUBAKER, co-editor of *Childhood Education in the Church,* is the former director of Circle Center for Child Development, Zion, Illinois, a Christian education consultant, a free-lance writer, and an illustrator.

window. But it is only when many windows are opened that the house comes alive and is enjoyable as a home."[1]

A group of primary children were engaged in a hymn memorization program that lasted for several weeks. Lines from the hymn read,

> There is a green hill far away,
> Without a city wall,
> Where the dear Lord was crucified,
> Who died to save us all.

While learning the words, the group read related Scripture passages and were shown slides of Jerusalem centering on the final events of Jesus' life. They talked about the meaning of the words, "without a city wall," and decided this could best be illustrated by setting up a diorama. Three groups were designated: one to make a city wall of sugar cubes and glue, another to construct a Palestinian village using the cubes and styrofoam balls, and a third to fashion a cross of small pieces of rough wood set in clay.

Throughout the project there was much discussion on the meaning of sin and the necessity of Jesus' death. The series was culminated by an appeal to receive Him as Savior from sin. Jimmy, a first grader, responded and was later asked to tell the group about his conversion. So sincere was his testimony that a junior-age helper later observed, "When Jimmy was telling about accepting Jesus as his Savior, I was so happy, I felt like crying. It seemed like God was looking down and smiling." Truly a house had "come alive" as the light of God's love beamed through the windows of a small boy's heart.

How Important Are Methods and Materials?

Isn't it enough to just "teach the Bible?" Hasn't God promised to bless His Word as it goes forth? (Isa. 55:10-11). Are methods and materials really that essential?

Through the years, the church has had to rely almost entirely on volunteer help in its educational program. Often that help has been lacking both in training and in understanding of educational methods. In the early days of the Sunday school, little thought was given to grading by age groups; it was enough that a Bible lesson was "taught." But church educators began to realize how children learn and what they can learn at different ages. Materials were adjusted to the learning level of children, and methods were adapted to meet their learning needs. Nevertheless, while teaching methods have improved and materials become more readily available, we are reminded that "no statistics can record the influence for God on thousands of children who have

---

1. Eleanor Shelton Morrison and Virgil E. Foster, *Creative Teaching in the Church* (Englewood Cliffs, N.J.: Prentice-Hall, 1963), p. 101.

been with consecrated teachers who loved God and the children. No matter how little these teachers knew of the 'best methods' they came nearer to substituting for the missing Christian influence of the home than any other phase of church life could do."[2]

It seems evident, then, that the availability of curriculum materials and knowledge of the best teaching techniques do not in themselves assure a successful teaching experience. Neither can they serve as a substitute for teachers who would shortcut their own personal involvement with the Word of God. Jesus said, "It is the spirit that quickeneth; the flesh profiteth nothing: the words that I speak unto you, they are spirit, and they are life" (John 6:63). Preparation of mind and heart is a process which takes time. The Word must indeed grasp us before it can grasp anyone else. "Thus spake Jehovah like a firm grasp of the hand" (Isa. 8:11, Rotherham).

In a real sense, teachers come before methods or materials, because they are the vessels through whom the truth comes. The degree of their submission to the Holy Spirit in their teaching and the way in which they relate to their students can help or hinder the receiving of that truth. Perhaps what may count most is a hand on the shoulder and a smiling face that says, "I really like you." A classroom that projects an atmosphere of warmth, of anticipation and eagerness to learn is not dependent on materials and well-chosen teaching methods alone.

However, really good teachers are aware of certain basic elements of effective teaching, and they will want to sharpen their skills even more toward becoming truly creative teachers. Observing creative teachers who use good teaching techniques is probably the best (and most painless) way to accomplish this. Well-written teacher's manuals will include many good ideas for enrichment of teaching, and there are many books devoted to effective teaching methods. Filmstrips and videotapes are available from Sunday school publishers. Some courses are complete with leader's guide, student workbooks, cassettes, duplicating masters, and overhead transparencies. Skill in teaching comes through observation, experience, practice, and self-evaluation.

VARIETY IN TEACHING METHODS AND MATERIALS

Most teachers have found at least one teaching procedure that works well for them. The challenge facing the Christian teacher is to refuse to settle for one or two comfortable approaches, but to seek out new ways of making learning a living experience. Variety in teaching does not mean a hodgepodge of unusual approaches just to gain attention. It is not controlling a class by the use of novel techniques to "keep them quiet so they will listen." It does involve a "many-faceted, imaginative approach with an inner consistency. The proce-

2. Anna B. Mow, *Your Child* (Grand Rapids: Zondervan 1966), p. 41.

dures support one another, the parts complementing each other to make a whole experience. They are integrally related to each other, flowing out of what has gone before, anticipating what is to come."[3]

Effective instruction is creative. It includes using many different techniques and teaching styles. It happens in different settings; in large groups or small groups, or with an individual. It can be through discussions, role play, reports, or projects. It is not one technique above another. It requires teachers who realize their responsibility is "not simply to transmit information"; their "responsibility continues until the child has learned." Truly, "when the learner learns, and wants to learn more, good teaching has taken place."[4]

JESUS USED VARIETY

Jesus, the Master Teacher, had all nature at His disposal to interpret God's message—to illustrate His love and power. Yet He chose many times to use methods which were well within the range of the Christian teacher's human abilities and limitations. He asked questions, used illustrations and told stories. He used objects that were at hand and involved His students in projects and assignments. He stretched their imagination by painting visual pictures. His methods varied widely, but were always suitable to the occasion, and drew from His listeners the response He desired, or anticipated.

THE NEEDS OF CHILDREN DEMAND VARIETY

Today the teacher's workshop is well-stocked. Never before has there been such a huge collection of "proven ideas" for the Christian educator, ready for immediate use whenever needed. Activities, Bible games, teaching hints—more and still more materials abound, all geared to helping the teacher "creatively challenge the students' educational experience." And all this is supposed to make the teacher's day a richly rewarding experience in teaching and learning! But it does not always turn out that way. Materials are meant to be a guide, but if followed too rigidly, with little thought for the differences in students, the lesson may fall flat. There are principles for using both methods (ways of doing) and materials (tools in doing) effectively, for materials without meaning are of little value, and inappropriate methods can muddy the message. (For a discussion of *curriculum* for children's ministries see chap. 15.)

Children have different needs. Effective teachers know how to individualize teaching to meet the unique needs of each child. They know what methods work best with their particular age group. Standing on a chair to illustrate a point might work with preschoolers, but older children would probably be

3. Morrison and Foster, p. 70.
4. June Crabtree, *Basic Principles of Effective Teaching* (Cincinnati, Ohio: Standard, 1982), Foreword.

embarrassed and find the teacher rather silly. Some students may have a wealth of Bible background, and others have nothing to draw on so their response is limited. Materials may need to be adjusted, or even substituted to make the lesson fit; methods may need to be changed. The important ingredient for the teacher is flexibility.

Children come in different ages, colors, sizes, personalities, and backgrounds. But all are creatures with unlimited imagination, though with limited attention spans. Capturing the child's imagination requires a creative teacher who is able to make learning an exciting adventure.

Though differing in needs, all children come into the world "equipped by God for response."[5] Effective, creative teaching can help chart the direction that response takes.

FACTORS TO CONSIDER IN THE SELECTION OF METHODS AND MATERIALS

1. What is the purpose of the lesson? We must not overlook the meaning of the lesson in our enthusiasm for the method.
2. What specific aims do we want to accomplish? Methods and materials are aids to effective teaching and should be carefully chosen. They are not ends in themselves, but means to reaching desired goals.
3. Does the method enhance the message? The method should not overshadow the truth nor detract from it. Children should remember the message, not the method.
4. Is the method and material appropriate for the occasion? The size of the group will help determine this, as well as the background and experience of the students.
5. Has the time element been considered? Is there adequate time to use the method and material effectively?
6. Has the guidance of the Holy Spirit been sought as to the individual needs of the students and the most effective method and material to use in meeting those needs?[6]
7. Is the method or material appropriate for the age level? We need to consider the students' level of understanding and ability to participate. (See part 2 on the developmental stages of children.)
8. Does the method involve the students? Methods which make children "think and do," which allow freedom to discover, to explore, and "try on" are best.
9. Do the children know how to participate effectively? The method may not work if they do not understand the mechanics of it.

5. Mow, p. 15.
6. For a discussion of the relationship of the Holy Spirit to the selection of methods and materials and other aspects of teaching and learning, see Roy B. Zuck, *The Holy Spirit in Your Teaching,* rev. and enlarged ed. (Wheaton, Ill.: Scripture Press, Victor Books, 1985).

10. Can the method be used with ease and familiarity so that the message can receive key attention? This means practice ahead of time, as the effective use of the method is dependent to a great degree on our skill as teachers and leaders.
11. Are materials ready and in order? We need to be relaxed and not preoccupied with preparation when students are there so we can give them wholehearted attention.
12. Is variety used in teaching methods? No one method is best, and the worst method is the one that is used all the time.

SOME KEY METHODS AND MATERIALS TO USE WITH CHILDREN

"Without any aids, she talked me up the long road to Calvary and made me participate in the pain and dust and flies and smells of that awful Jerusalem day."[7] Such was the experience a writer recalled of her adolescent days in a class where the teacher had used perhaps the oldest *impressional method* of teaching—the well-told story.

Impression is one of the ways individuals learn. Through the use of the senses, especially seeing and hearing, the teacher gains attention and interest, creates desire, and inspires learners to action. Some other methods and materials which could be thought of as impressional are filmstrips and slides, overhead transparencies, object lessons, flannelgraph, puppets, bulletin board, chart, chalkboard, record player, tape recordings, and pictures.

Another way individuals learn is through the *expressional method* of teaching. Students learn by participating, or direct involvement. Younger children, especially, have bodies built for activity, and generally if they are participating they are moving. Older children become involved as their thinking is put into words and action. An older group of children might write a paraphrase of Psalm 23 to reinforce the theme of a picture study of Plockhorst's, "The Good Shepherd."[8] Or they might make a diorama of a Palestinian countryside. Younger children could create a mural of a pastoral scene. Methods and materials which are expressional include discussion, guided conversation, buzz session, drama, role play, mime, fingerplays, handwork, creative crafts, creative writing, choral reading, questions, review, workbooks, problem solving, interview, direct Bible study, memorization, prayer, testimonies, and field trips. Usually students learn best by a combination of both the *impressional* and *expressional* method of teaching.

The following is a brief discussion of some of the key methods and materials to use in ministries to children.

7. Marlene D. LeFever, *Creative Teaching Methods* (Elgin, Ill.: David C. Cook, 1985), p. 190.
8. Cynthia Pearl Maus, *Christ and the Fine Arts* (New York: Harper & Row), pp. 539-41.

STORYTELLING

No matter what form the story takes—illustration, a "slice of life" experience, a parable, an anecdote, a narrative in prose or verse, or a section lifted out of a book—no other teaching tool has quite the universal appeal or impact. Age is no barrier. (See chap. 30 for more on this valuable teaching method.)

DRAMATICS

Story playing, drama, skits, role play, mime, fingerplays and action rhymes, the use of puppets, posing "living" pictures, all have tremendous value in helping children apply what they have learned, and in leading them away from teacher-centered learning situations. (See chap. 31.)

QUESTIONS

Questions are verbal inquiries by teachers or students with an anticipated response, one from the other. When used by teachers, they are a means of stimulating interest, testing knowledge, helping students express thoughts, reviewing past learning, and guiding present learning experiences. There are *factual* questions which help teachers discover what facts or information the students have. And there are *thought* questions, designed to stimulate thought and deepen understanding. Questions should be written out in advance by the teacher and should be brief and clear. The value of using a catechism is that questions and accurate answers are memorized, thus building a foundation of Bible truths.

DISCUSSION

Effective teachers will use this method often in their teaching as it encourages each student to contribute in personal, unique ways. Good discussions can liven up a dull class, bringing meaning to the learning experience as group members search for truth. Skillful guidance is needed by the teacher so that discussions do not end up in debates or wander off course. With younger children, discussions will take the form of guided conversation.

PROJECTS

A project is a learning activity that takes place during or outside of class time. They are sometimes called "do projects" because they help students to be "doers" of God's Word, thus putting into practice the lesson aims. Teachers should direct the group in planning the procedure and, after completion of the project, lead in a discussion and evaluation. A project outside of class might be a field trip to a museum, a visit to a nursing home, or collection of money for someone in need. Students should understand that the project is a result of the Bible teaching.

AUDIO AND VISUAL MEDIA

Audio methods *tell* students the truths of the Bible while visual methods and materials *show* the truth. They are usually thought of as teaching aids rather than teaching techniques. However, skill is required to use them effectively, and teachers must learn to "think visually." (For a discussion of media materials, including visuals, audio materials, manipulative media, and real objects, see chap. 28).

CREATIVE ACTIVITIES

The possibilities of creative activities are endless. They can be done in presession, during the class period as part of the lesson, or at home. Results should be displayed or used in class to add meaning to the lesson. (Creative writing and constructive arts and crafts are discussed in chap. 32.)

INTEREST AND LEARNING CENTERS

INTEREST CENTERS

Each department of the children's division should have interest centers for the children. Interest centers may be located in a corner of the room or on a table. These are particularly helpful for younger children, and arouse curiosity in objects, acquaint children with new ideas or materials, or provide activities that children enjoy doing or in which they have special interest. A display of sea shells, missionary curios, dioramas, book tables, grocery store, games to play, pretend activity, or a table depicting the theme of a learning unit, a worship service, or season of the year are some suggestions for interest centers. Kinds of interest centers will vary according to the interests and needs of the group.

Since younger children depend on the five senses for much of their learning, they need to be able to touch and handle objects. Unbreakable and durable materials should be used, especially with younger ages. Pictures can be sprayed with clear plastic so that the children can handle, touch, and feel them without damaging them. Cloth objects and three-dimensional material with varied kinds of surfaces can be used in displays. Personal involvement in activities will provide opportunities for self-discovery, securing attention, creating interest, emotional release, self-expression, and manipulation of objects.

Interest centers can be used during presession, group participation, show-and-tell, teaching of new and unfamiliar ideas, free play, and guided activities. They can also be used as springboards for informal discussion with younger children and in lesson approaches and applications. Students can help in constructing interest centers, depending on the age and type. Perhaps the greatest asset to effective use of interest centers is the creativity and ingenuity of the teaching staff!

LEARNING CENTERS

What a learning center is. "Come and see!" "Come and learn!" "Come and do!" And the children come—individually or in small groups, to become involved at learning centers. In a more structured grouping, an invitation to such learning activities would not be possible. But here a shy child can choose a quiet corner and pursue learning in an individual way. Or another child who needs companionship can join a small group.

Learning centers, or activity areas, can be thought of as expanded interest centers, and usually work best with school age children who are able to read. They are more than fun areas to spark interest and enthusiasm. They can be some of the most effective tools the teacher uses to involve students and individualize teaching.

A tabletop or corner of the room that can accommodate one or more children can be set aside as a learning center. Materials are attractively displayed with instructions and procedures carefully outlined for student involvement. The room arrangement, materials and equipment, staff, age level of the children, and concepts to be learned are all factors to consider in the organization of learning centers. Most centers will have not just one, but a combination of learning activities where children participate by hearing, seeing, touching, and doing.

Some themes for developing learning centers are Bible geography, Bible history or Bible background, Bible memory, missions, science, seasonal, Bible search, record a message, exploring feelings, listening to cassettes and records, books, creative art and writing, Bible games, and music. As an example, a memory verse center might include a Bible, chalkboard, word cards, a puzzle, pictures related to the verse, and art materials to illustrate the verse. All centers should be designed to define a specific focus. (For excellent ideas for learning centers see *Basic Principles of Effective Teaching,* by June Crabtree, pp. 41-54).

Staff are needed who are alert to their responsibility to invite and encourage children to explore all the centers and ultimately learn in several. The role of teachers is to supervise and guide as they interact with students. They should introduce centers and give step-by-step instructions as to their use. They suggest rather than command, praise accomplishments, show understanding and help when needed. They are consistent in their expectations and redirect energies into more productive channels when necessary.

Learning centers give teachers opportunities to observe students in an informal setting. They can discover the needs, interests, and abilities of children and take advantage of moments of readiness, keen interest, and desire.

They help teachers to plan instruction with each individual child in mind. Situations are created where teachers can guide children in their thinking about God and their relationship to Him.

Values to children of a learning center

• Children learn to make their own choices through a variety of learning activities.

• They learn through direct personal experiences and discoveries.

• Energies are directed in constructive ways.

• Self-confidence and competence are built as new skills are learned and tasks completed.

• Children enlarge their vocabulary and improve their communication skills through creative use of language and a variety of materials and equipment.

• Opportunities are given for children to improve thinking skills, solve problems, and grow in areas of need.

• More opportunities are given to memorize Scripture and develop understanding of Bible truths.

• Children can develop physical coordination and motor skills as they move about in different areas of the room and try out new materials and equipment.

• Social opportunities are afforded children as they learn to relate to others, show respect, be responsible as members of a group, and plan projects together.

• Children learn to use and care for materials and equipment.

• Activities are enjoyable as well as meaningful, as children are invited to learn in the least coercive way.

APPROPRIATE METHODS AND MATERIALS TO USE WITH CHILDREN

INFANTS AND TODDLERS

Impressional method

Bible-in-hand	God's wonders	Pictures
Books	(flower, gold fish, small	Puppets
"Farmer Says" talking	animal in cage)	Record player
toy	Mirror	Simple stories
Felt peek-board	Mobiles	Touch and feel book
(baby looks for hidden	Peek-a-boo box	Wind up toys
animal, person, item)		(animals, baby)

Expressional methods

Action songs (to nursery rhymes, familiar tunes, clapping, pat-the-Bible)	Dolls	Rhythm games
	Hide and seek games	Toys (balls, blocks, pull toys, stacking and nesting toys)
	Prayer experiences	
Cradle gym	Puzzles	

TWOS AND THREES

Impressional methods

Bible-in-hand	Field trip	Picture walk
Books	Filmstrip, slides	Puppets
Bulletin board	Flannelgraph	Record player
Chalk drawing	Interest centers	Storytelling
Demonstration	Lapboard	Touch and feel book or box
Diorama	Models	
Discovery table (prism, magnets, tasting tray, magnifying glass)	Nature walk	
	Peepbox	
	Pictures	

Expressional methods

Activity music	Finger plays, action rhymes	Memorization
Art activities (finger/pudding paints, crayon rubbings, felt pens, wetting chalk, pasting, collage, crafts, murals, scrapbook, stickers)	Games	Playtime
	Guided conversation	Prayer experience
	Handbook	Pretend play
	Home-living center (housekeeping, dolls)	Rhythm instruments
	Manipulatives (puzzles, clay, play dough, sand play, water play, sorting, stringing)	Sharing time
Cooking		Show-and-tell
Dress-up		Story play (with narration)

FOURS AND FIVES

Impressional methods

Bible-in-hand	Flash cards	Picture walk
Books	Hook-n-Loop board	Pocket chart
Bulletin board	Interest centers	Posters
Chalkboard	Magnetic board	Puppets
Demonstration	Models	Record player
Diorama	Montage	Storytelling
Discovery table	Motion picture	Tape recorder

Exhibit
Field trips
Filmstrip, slides
Flannelgraph

Nature walk
Opaque projector
Overhead projector
Peg board

Television
Three D Viewer
Feelie bag, box

Expressional methods

Activity music
Art activities
(crayons, scissors,
chalk, collage,
finger paints, spatter
painting, stencils,
spool painting, crafts,
felt pens, collage,
murals)
Cooking
Dress-up

Finger plays, action
rhymes
Games
Guided conversation
Handbook
Handwork
Home-living centers
Manipulatives (puzzles,
clay, play dough,
sewing cards, sand
table, water play, hand
puppets)

Memorization
Music
Prayer experience
Pretend play
Rhythm instruments
Sharing time
Show-and-tell
Story play
Table games

PRIMARIES AND MIDDLERS

Impressional methods

Banners
Bible-in-hand
Books
Bulletin board
Cartoons
Chalkboard
Charts
Comics
Display
Field trip

Filmstrip and slides
Flannelgraph
Flash cards
Map and globe
Models
Motion picture
Object lesson
Overhead projector
Pictures
Picture folders

Picture study
Picture walk
Pocket chart
Posters
Puppets, muppets
Record player
Stickarama board
Storytelling
Tape recorder

Expressional methods

Art activities (drawing,
pasting, coloring,
crafts, collage,
diorama, murals)
Choral reading
Creative writing
(poetry, stories, songs,
Scripture paraphrase)
Discussion (buzz groups,
committee work,

Drama (pantomime, role
play, living pictures,
simple dramatization,
skit, story play)
Games
Informal conversation
Interest/learning centers
Jobs-to-do board
Memorization
Music

Puppets
Puzzles
Question and answer
Rhythm instruments
Sharing time
Show-and-tell
Spontaneous speaking
Tape recordings

interest groups, guided discussion, interview, circle conversation, "What would you do?")

Project (apprenticeship, assignment, group work, notebook, problem solving, scrapbook, workbook or student manual)

MIDDLERS AND JUNIORS

Impressional methods

Bible-in-hand
Bulletin board
Chalkboard
Chart
Comics
Demonstration
Exhibit
Field trip
Filmstrip, slides

Flannelgraph
Flash cards
Hook-n-loop board
Map and globe
Models
Motion picture
Object lesson
Overhead projector
Pictures

Picture study
Picture walk
Pocket chart
Posters
Puppets
Record player
Storytelling, illustration
Tape recorder
Videotape

Expressional methods

Act activities (diorama, collage/montage, crafts)
Bulletin boards
Catechism
Choral reading
Creative writing
Direct Bible study
Discussion (brainstorm, buzz groups, guided discussion, committee work, simplified panel and debate)

Displays
Drill
Games
Informal sharing
Interest/learning centers
Memorization
Music
Prayer experience
Project (assignment, group work, research and report, interview, recitation)
Puppets/muppets

Puzzles
Question/answer
Reading
Review
Scripture search
Show-and-tell
Spontaneous speaking
Student manual
Tape recordings
Testing

THE RESOURCE CENTER

Most materials will be stored in individual department and class areas. Items that are used infrequently or can be shared by other workers in the children's ministries should be kept in a central location. This could be a corner of a Sunday school office or another area where there is room for a file cabinet and shelves for audiovisual materials. Or it could be incorporated into the existing church library. But it should be a place that is easily accessible to workers. Materials might include filmstrips, transparencies, tapes, records, maps, large pictures and posters, and games. Neatness and order are essential!

Some churches seem to get this far but no farther. As a result, many materials are left to collect dust because teachers and leaders are not aware of their availability. A Resource Center chairman or committee should be appointed to collect and list all materials. A listing by categories (such as filmstrips, tapes, etc.), a brief description of each item, and the suggested age level should be given to the leaders and teachers of all agencies of the church ministering to children. This will need to be given out at least once a year because of personnel changes. A check-out system should be set up and carefully maintained by the Resource Center chairman. The center should be kept open at times convenient for most of the workers.

THE USE OF BOOKS WITH CHILDREN

One of the greatest legacies parents can pass on to their children is a love of good books—all kinds of books. This regard for books and the written word must begin early. As young children observe that books occupy a prominent place in their parents' lives and are read to regularly, they will develop an interest in books as well. This can be demonstrated by the preschooler who gathered his story papers up in his arms and exclaimed, "I'm rich!"

There is a special sort of homey atmosphere, a sense of quiet peace and security when parents gather their children around them for a journey into the land of wonder and imagination. The humdrum of daily life, anxieties, and differing opinions melt away as hearts are renewed, cares lifted, and family relationships strengthened. Every child deserves the heritage of such a home, where books are thought of as indispensible, beginning with the Bible, and where the best that literature has to offer is made available to them. It is their passport to a richer, fuller life, a life lived worthily, in accordance with the will of God.

Good literature can be a great aid, inspiring children to be their best. The classics, great novels, biographies, books of history, and great poems all contribute to the child's search for truth. It is out of the Bible that have grown the great "companions of the heart," such as *Pilgrim's Progress*. The treasuries of this great allegory have been unlocked to children in the version, *Little Pilgrim's Progress*, by Helen Taylor (Moody).

Children will also enjoy excursions into the magical lands of Narnia in C. S. Lewis' seven-volume series, *The Chronicles of Narnia* (Collier Books). The more recently published Chariot Family Reading Series (David C. Cook) combines the talents of that 19th century "mythmaker," George McDonald *(The Christmas Stories* and *The Princess and the Goblin),* with David and Karen Mains *(Tales of the Kingdom).* Hero, the main character of the Kingdom tales symbolizes every child and the plight of often being pulled in opposite directions by good and evil. Imaginative illustrations enhance the creative fantasy of this series. These are good read-aloud books or can be read separately, providing good material for sharing insights.

Because children are so vulnerable to life's impressions, the quality of the books they read is especially important. They must not only say something of value, but be carefully written with the same skill as books for adults. C. S. Lewis stressed that a book worth reading only in childhood is not worth reading then. Descriptive words, good sentence structure, and effective writing style should whet the appetite for more, as in Kenneth Grahame's *The Wind in the Willows*. Who would not smile at Rat's bothersome behavior toward "his friends the ducks"!

> And when the ducks stood on their heads suddenly, as ducks will, he would dive down and tickle their necks just under where their chins would be if ducks had chins, till they were forced to come to the surface again in a hurry, spluttering and angry and shaking their feathers at him, for it is impossible to say quite all you feel when your head is under water.[9]

People of all ages have a special affection for stories in which animals talk and act like humans. It is not difficult to see then, why children are so entranced by the whimsical antics of *Winnie-the-Pooh,* by A. A. Milne. Christopher Robin, Piglet, and James James Morrison Morrison are only a few of the other characters made famous by Milne.

Other guidelines for choosing good books are these:

• The books should be within the experience of childhood.

• If the experience is to be relived vicariously, such as through young Hamid and his sister Rahma in *Star of Light,* by Patricia St. John (Moody), it must be understood and appreciated by the child.

• The book should expand the child's vocabulary and help him to develop reading skills. If read aloud, such a book will help to develop the child's listening skills.

• Children should be able to find answers to life's problems, such as the issue of racial intolerance.

• The book should stimulate imagination, arouse sympathy, and develop courage. It should inspire selflessness, as in *The Giving Tree,* by Shel Silverstein (Harper and Row).

• Emotionally charged issues, such as child abuse, should be treated honestly, with sensitivity, and with consideration of the child's developmental stage.

9. Kenneth Grahame, *The Wind in the Willows* (New York: Airmont, 1966), p. 26.

- The writing should be authentic both historically and factually.

- The book should meet basic literary requirements as to story structure. (See chap. 30.) Charles Dickens once said, "There are books of which the backs and covers are by far the best parts."

- The format of the book, including type and binding, should be of high quality, easy to read, and sturdily bound.

- The illustrations should be attractive and appropriate to the content. A good example is Ella K. Lindvall's "People of the Bible" series (Moody). These Bible stories (retold) about people of the Bible and the God they followed are beautifully illustrated.

SETTING UP BOOK CENTERS FOR CHILDREN'S MINISTRIES

A quiet corner away from the mainstream of activity, with a table and chairs, and a bulletin board with informational pictures relating to special books on display is ideal for a book center. Books should be chosen that reinforce the lesson theme. In more informal settings, bean bag chairs are favorites with children, as is a "rainbow barrel" (a large cardboard storage barrel with a child-size opening cut out of the side and a rainbow painted around the opening). A soft pillow invites one or two younger children to cozy up with a book.

BEGINNING A CHURCH READING PROGRAM FOR CHILDREN

1. Invite Sunday school children to the library as part of a regular class period to get acquainted with the librarian and find out what books are for children. Allow children to check out books on the spot.
2. Sponsor reading contests on a graded basis. Have a "Treasure Chest Reading Club" chart for each child, denoting gems earned with each book read.
3. Have the librarian visit each department with a "traveling bookshelf" (push cart).
4. Publicize new books via department memos. Limit to three or four selections with a description of each.
5. Have a book bulletin board where book jackets are displayed with one-line descriptions and suggested age level.

RECOMMENDED READING FOR CHILDREN

EARLY AND MIDDLE CHILDHOOD

Bible and Bible-related

The Bible in Pictures for Little Eyes, Kenneth N. Taylor (Moody). A children's classic.

Pattibooks, Mary E. LeBar (Scripture Press).

Tiny Question Books, Faith McNaughton Hinds, Faith McNaughton Lowell (Scripture Press).

First Steps in the Bible, Ruth Graham Dienart (Word). A devotional Bible story book of ninety-one stories.

Frances Hook Picture Books (Standard). *My Book of Friends* and five others. Also *Books of the Seasons* and *Books of Understanding* (on feelings).

Prayer for a Child, Rachel Field (Macmillan). A Caldecott Medal book beautifully illustrated by Elizabeth Orton Jones. A gentle prayer for familiar things.

Tiny Thoughts for Little People, Kenneth N. Taylor (Tyndale House). ABC book with charming illustrations by Katheryn E. Shoemaker.

See and Share series, V. Gilbert Beers (Moody). *My Favorite Things to See and Share,* and others.

Little-Big Books, Gordon Stowell (Word). *The Boy Who Shared,* and several other Bible stories. Loved by tiny tots.

Palm Tree Bible Stories (Concordia). *Noah's Big Boat, Becky Gets Up,* and many others, retold with skillful imagination.

Noah's Ark, illustrated by Peter Spier (Doubleday). Translation of a seventeenth century Dutch poem on one page. The rest of the book is humorous illustrations of life with animals on the ark. A Caldecott Medal book.

The Bible-Time Nursery Rhyme Book, Emily Hunter (Manna).

Discovering in God's World series (Regal): *Discovering Little Things, Discovering Colors, Discovering at the Zoo, Discovering Out of Doors.* Lovely photographs.

"Let's Talk About" series, Joy Wilt Berry (Word). *Whining, Teasing, Being Selfish,* and others.

Stories to Grow on, Ethel Barrett (Gospel Light). *Gregory Grub, Buzz Bee, Blister Lamb, Quacky and Wacky.* Excellent for developing listening and reading skills. Tapes included.

Especially for Children series, Bill and Gloria Gaither (Impact Books). Titles include *Jesus, I Heard You Had a Big House.* With records.

Creek Bank Kids. (Impact Books). Eight volumes with records.

Living in God's Family, Mary E. LeBar (Scripture Press). For boys and girls who know the Savior.

Children's Bible Basics, Carolyn Nystrom (Moody). Eight books which answer children's basic questions about the faith.

God's Word in My Heart series, Elspeth Campbell Murphy (David C. Cook). *God Cares When I'm Disappointed* and others. Children easily identify and learn to turn to God for help.

David and I Talk to God series. Elspeth Campbell Murphy (David C. Cook). Psalms beautifully paraphrased for children.

Alerting Kids to the Danger Zones, Joy Wilt Berry (Word). Covers problems of abuse and neglect, kidnapping, and sexual abuse.

Ready-Set-Grow series, Joy Wilt Berry (Word). Topics cover self-concept, sibling rivalry, communication skills, and others.

Secular

The Day the Sun Came Up, Alice Gouday (Charles Scribner's Sons).

Treasury of Animal Stories, Beatrix Potter (Warner). More than twenty volumes including *The Tale of Peter Rabbit.* Children's favorites.

Goodnight Moon, Margaret Wise Brown (Harper).

Make Way for Ducklings, Robert McCloskey (Viking).

Blueberries for Sal, Robert McCloskey (Viking).

Owliver, Robert Kraus (Windmill Books and E. P. Dutton).

Peter's Chair, Ezra Jack Keats (Viking). On accepting a new baby. Keats has written a number of good books for young children.

Five Senses, Tasha Tudor (Grosset). Lovely pastel illustrations by a famous artist.

Rhythms to Reading series, Lucille Wood, illustrated by Paul Taylor (Bomar). Excellent seasonal and other books with activity records. Very useful for listening and expressional activities for preschoolers.

Bread and Jam for Frances, Russel Hoban, illustrated by Lillian Hoban (Harper & Row). Hoban has written several charming, amusing stories about a little badger in typical "childlike" situations.

Curious George books, H. A. Rey. (Houghton Mifflin). Every child's favorite monkey.

Be Nice to Spiders, Margaret Bloy Graham (Harper & Sons).

The Little House, Virginia Lee Burton (Houghton Mifflin). A little house is enveloped as a city builds around it.

Are You My Mother? P. D. Eastman (Random House).

Book of Nursery and Mother Goose Rhymes, Marguerite deAngelis (Doubleday). Beautifully illustrated.

LATER CHILDHOOD

Bible and Bible-related

The Survival Series for Kids, Joy Wilt Berry (Word), 24 volumes. Titles include, *What to Do When Your Mom or Dad Says . . . Clean Your Room! Get Good Grades! Do Something Besides Watching TV!*

The Bradford Family Adventure series, Jerry Jenkins (Moody). *The Kidnapping, Two Runaways,* and two others.

Jungle Doctor Series, Paul White (Moody). Picture fables about jungle animals. Filmstrips available.

Biblearn series, Elsie Rives (Broadman). Thinkback questions at end of each chapter. Outstanding illustrations.

Sugar Creek Gang series, Paul Hutchens (Moody). Adventure stories filled with laughter, suspense, mystery.

Who What When Where Book About the Bible, William L. Coleman (D. C. Cook).

Prairie Adventure series, Margaret Epp (Scripture Press). *Sarah and the Lost Friendship* and others.

Secular

Animals Can Be Almost Human, selected authors (Reader's Digest).

Charlotte's Web, E. B. White (Harper). Story of a pig and a spider.

The Borrowers, Mary Norton (Harcourt). A fascinating world of little people.

The Incredible Journey, Sheila Burnford (Little). A trio of household pets travel across vast stretches of country to return home.

Rascal, Sterling North (Dutton).

The Witch of Blackbird Pond, Elizabeth George Speare (Houghton). Historical setting is Puritan Connecticut.

Soup, Robert Newton Peck (Knopf).

Soup for President, Robert N. Peck (Knopf). Fictionalized biography.

The Best Christmas Pageant Ever, Barbara Robinson (Avon, Camelot and Flare imprints; Harper & Row; Tyndale).

Bridge to Teribethia, Katherine Patterson (Avon, Camelot; Harper & Row). On friendship and dying.

Ben and Me, Robert Lawson (Little). Ben Franklin from a mouse's viewpoint.

Cricket in Times Square, George Selden (Ariel).

BOOKS OF POETRY

Favorite Poems Old and New, Helen Ferris (Doubleday).

Hello Day, Dorothy Aldis (G. P. Putmam's Sons).

A Child's Garden of Verses, Robert L. Stevenson (Scribner).

Where the Sidewalk Ends, Shel Silverstein (Harper & Row).

For other book suggestions see chapter 22 (devotional and Bible storybooks) and chap. 30 (Bible-related and secular books). Also see *Honey for a Child's Heart* by Gladys M. Hunt (Zondervan).

SUMMARY

Effective teaching does not always *just happen.* Good teachers are aware of the importance of using a variety of good teaching techniques. They know that the *way* a lesson is taught determines, in part, *what* is learned or accomplished. They realize that effective instruction takes place when the developmental needs of children and their differences form the basis of all that they want to accomplish in their curriculum goals. When teachers hold to these beliefs about teaching, then the selection of appropriate methods and materials becomes a major task. For they are the means of helping to accomplish those goals. Time is limited; souls are at stake.

Lives are not changed through teachers, through methods, or through materials alone. But effective teachers using creative methods of teaching are co-workers with God, and materials are tools through which the Holy Spirit can work to bring about life-changing insights to learners.

FOR FURTHER READING

BOOKS, JOURNALS, AND OTHER SOURCES

Alessi, Vincie, ed. *Programs for Advent and Christmas*. Vols. 1 and 2. Valley Forge, Pa.: Judson, 1978.

Bolton, Barbara J., and Charles T. Smith. *Creative Bible Learning for Children*. Ventura, Calif.: Gospel Light, Regal Books, 1977.

Crabtree, June. *Basic Principles of Effective Teaching*. Cincinnati: Standard, 1982.

Daniel, Eleanor. *Teach with Success*. Rev. ed. Cincinnati: Standard, 1980.

Fullbright, Robert. *New Dimensions in Teaching Children*. Nashville: Broadman, 1971.

Gangel, Kenneth O. *24 Ways to Improve Your Teaching*. Wheaton, Ill.: Scripture Press, Victor Books, 1974.

Griffin, Dale E. "Interest Centers That Attract." *Interaction* 10 (September 1970): 15-17.

Hammack, Mary L. "Organize an Instructional Materials Center." *Success* 23 (Fall 1971): 6-7.

———. *How to Organize Your Church Library and Resource Center*. Valley Forge, Pa.: Judson, 1985.

Harrell, Donna, and Wesley Haystead. *Creative Bible Learning for Early Childhood*. Ventura, Calif.: Gospel Light, Regal Books, 1977.

Huber, Evelyn. *Doing Christian Education in New Ways*. Valley Forge, Pa.: Judson, 1978.

Hunt, Gladys M. *Honey for a Child's Heart*. Grand Rapids: Zondervan, 1974.

Lee, Rachel. *Learning Centers for Better Christian Education*. Valley Forge, Pa.: Judson, 1982.

LeBar, Lois E. *Children in the Bible School*. Westwood, N.J.: Revell, 1952.

LeFever, Marlene D. *Creative Teaching Methods*. Elgin, Ill.: David C. Cook, 1985.

McDaniel, Elsiebeth, and Lawrence O. Richards. *You and Children.* Chicago: Moody, 1973.

Pigrem, Sheila. *Help, I Can't Draw!* Minneapolis: Augsburg, 1978.

Rives, Elsie, and Ann Tonks. *Bible Teaching for Children Through the Sunday School.* Nashville: Convention, 1984.

"Seven Ways Unit Planning Can Make You a Better Teacher," *Teach* 14 (Winter 1973): 52-53.

Show Me the Story. Flannelgraph kit. Minneapolis: Augsburg, 1981.

Tell Me a Story. Cassette. Minneapolis: Augsburg, 1973.

Tobey, Kathrene. *Learning and Teaching through the Senses.* Philadelphia: Westminster, 1970.

Towns, Elmer. *The Successful Sunday School and Teachers Guidebook.* Carol Stream, Ill.: Creation House, 1976.

Zuck, Roy B. *The Holy Spirit in Your Teaching.* Rev. and enlarged ed. Wheaton, Ill.: Scripture Press, Victor Books, 1985.

SELECTED PUBLISHERS AND SERVICE ORGANIZATIONS

Accent B/P Publications, Box 15337, Denver, CO 80215

Awana Youth Association, 3201 Tollview Drive, Rolling Meadows, IL 60008

BCM International, 237 Fairfield Avenue, Upper Darby, PA 19082

Child Evangelism Fellowship, Warrenton, MO 63383

Christian Service Brigade, Box 150, Wheaton, IL 60187

David C. Cook Publishing House, 850 North Grove, Elgin, IL 60120

Evangelical Teacher Training Association, Box 327, Wheaton, IL 60187

Gospel Light Publications, 2300 Knoll Drive, Box 3875, Ventura, CA 93003

Pioneer Clubs, Box 788, Wheaton, IL 60187

Regular Baptist Press, 1300 North Meacham Rd., Box 95500, Schaumburg, IL 60195

Scripture Press Publications, Inc., 1825 College Avenue, Wheaton, IL 60187

Standard Publishing, 4121 Hamilton Avenue, Cincinnati, OH 45231

Success With Youth, Inc., Box 27028, Tempe, AZ 85282

28

Ruth C. Haycock

Using Visual and Audio Media with Children

- Necessity of
- Selection of
- Variety of
  VISUAL MATERIALS
  AUDIO MATERIALS
  MANIPULATIVE MEDIA
  REAL OBJECTS

Audio and visual media for teaching children are designed to produce meaningful involvement of children with the truth, which will enable them to learn and to change in the direction of conformity to the will of God. This is our objective as Christian educators.

THE NECESSITY OF AUDIOVISUAL MEDIA

Several facts indicate forcibly and clearly that audio and visual materials must be a part of our teaching equipment.

First is the fact that in the years since World War II, their value has been

RUTH C. HAYCOCK, Ed.D., was part-time professor of Christian school courses at Piedmont Bible College, Winston-Salem, N.C., and served as a Christian education consultant and workshop leader. She is now deceased.

proven over and over again. Hundreds of studies done in the armed services and in schools have pointed up the effectiveness of audiovisual media in speeding up learning, lengthening retention, clarifying concepts, and promoting action. There is overwhelming proof that the careful use of well-chosen materials improves learning.

Second, if we actually believe that God's Word is all important and that no occupation is more crucial than helping students to understand it, we are compelled to use every means for effective teaching. Failure to capitalize on available media indicates ignorance, laziness, or lack of concern.

Third, when we consider how much the life and future of each student depends on his understanding of God's plan, we sense also the brevity of time. Time is short in view of the prospect of the Lord's soon return. In addition, in the local church, we have only a short part of each week in which to teach eternal truth. We must, therefore, use every available means.

Fourth, what about the other activities of our students each week? Consider television, with its realistic sight and sound, for several hours a day. Consider the public school room, with its well-trained teachers propagating, for the most part, a humanistic, nonbiblical viewpoint. Consider the children's secular organizations and their success in inculcating their philosophies. Consider the attractive literature for children, well illustrated and well written, each piece teaching some secular viewpoint. These competitors know that if they can mold the thinking of today's children, they will have tomorrow's adults.

Fifth, American boys and girls are 2,000 years removed from the time of Christ and several thousand more years from the earlier events of the Bible. They are growing up in a modern culture, far from the rural and Middle Eastern setting of David or Abraham. Even rural children, through mass communication media, know the modern world, but not the Bible times world. This limited Bible background necessitates our being sure that children get the message we are giving them.

Sixth, believers, as those who trust the Bible both for its content and for the methods it reveals, have a reason beyond all of the above for using such instructional media. It has been said, "If we would teach scripturally, we must teach visually." On many occasions, God Himself used some visual object to emphasize a truth to Israel. Think of the burning bush, Moses' leprous hand, the rainbow, and Gideon's fleece. When Christ came and was known as the master Teacher, He too used things and events to portray truth. For example, He used a child to talk about the simplicity of faith and the folly of pride (Matt. 18); and He used a coin to show man's responsibility to government as well as to God (Mark 12:17).

God knows the nature of man; God knows how we learn and understand. Jesus was an unusual teacher not only because He knew all the truth and was Himself the truth, but also because He knew people. He used visual teaching methods with adults; how much greater is our need, as we teach children, with their greater limitations of background and experience, to use audiovisuals?

THE SELECTION OF AUDIOVISUAL MEDIA

The mere recognition of the values of supplementary materials, or even the use of an abundance of them in our teaching, does not guarantee that a child will understand the truth. Several criteria can help determine which materials to select: (1) our purpose in the particular lesson or part of the lesson; (2) our knowledge of our students; (3) the particular materials at our disposal, including their quality, accuracy, legibility; (4) their possible relationship to other materials and experience.

For example, in the story of Zacchaeus, unless we are concerned with the geography of the situation, it is not necessary to use a map. Do we want youngsters to realize how urgently Zacchaeus wanted to see Jesus, even to the extent of putting aside his dignity? Perhaps, then, a picture or flannelboard presentation will help. These could also emphasize the crowd and the elegance of Zacchaeus' home, if desired; a filmstrip or standup figures could do likewise. If we wish to show the restitution which Zacchaeus made, we may use actual coins or dollar bills, or a chalkboard sketch of them. With a group of juniors who have heard the story before, we may merely write the name Zacchaeus on the chalkboard to fix the name and the spelling. Or a thought question may capture attention or relate the lesson to contemporary life.

We teachers must think carefully about our purposes as we choose materials, but we must think of our students too. Writers in chapters 3 through 10 have portrayed the student and his needs at each level. These stages of development must be kept in mind as we choose illustrative material.

The question is often asked, Which is a better visual medium for a particular lesson: a filmstrip, a flannelboard story, or something else? The answer depends, as we have just seen, on the purpose and the students, but the answer also depends on which *specific* filmstrip and other *specific* presentations we are comparing. How accurate is each? Is it biblical? How does the artwork affect the students? Are the words legible? Are the concepts simply and directly expressed or illustrated? A good teacher will consider these and other qualities when selecting a visual.

Another consideration in the selection of materials relates to other activities and experiences being provided within a lesson or unit. For example, it is often helpful to show a film or filmstrip in the departmental session; however, for this presentation to be valuable, teachers must plan together with their superintendent so that they can relate other learning to it in the smaller groups. In a shepherd series, a filmstrip or picture series might be part of the preparation for a trip to a sheep farm, with other material as follow-up. Each separate item should fit into the total experience of the group.

THE VARIETY OF AUDIOVISUAL MEDIA

In an attempt to present briefly some of the possibilites, materials will be considered under four major headings: visual, audio, manipulative, and real.

These categories overlap, but no classification can be clear-cut since many materials combine more than one classification. Also, many may be used in several ways.

VISUAL MATERIALS

Visual boards. Visual boards have been useful at all levels for many years. Almost every classroom has had chalkboard and bulletin boards. More recently have come newer boards: flannel, felt, hook and loop, pocket, magnetic, electric, plastic—and perhaps some others!

With all except electric boards, the basic idea is to devise some way to make pictures, words, or objects adhere to a board. Prepared figures can be of better quality than those produced on the spot; many are commercially produced.

Chalkboards suitable for personal or classroom use can be made by coating the smooth side of a sheet of Masonite with two coats of shellac and two coats of chalkboard paint. Most new chalkboards should be coated with chalk dust by rubbing the surface with the side of a stick of chalk, and then erasing it. This process prevents lines drawn on it from being so bold that they can never be erased.

The most popular flannelboards are twenty-four by thirty-six inches, since commercially made scenery and figures are usually designed for this size. Boards may be flat or hinged. If the board is made of double strength (or double thickness) corrugated cardboard, or light wallboard, the hinging may be made with twenty-four-inch strips of adhesive tape two inches wide. The board should be taped while in a closed position so it will open and close easily. For home Bible classes, chalkboard paint on the back is useful.

In recent years, pocketboards are no longer used exclusively by teachers of young children but are also being used with all age levels. Pocket-boards are useful for getting words before a group—key words, Bible verses, an outline, a scrambled list. The word strips require no backing and easily go on the board straight. Children can arrange words for drill and reviews.

An electric board is a tool used for drill and review. The child matches questions and answers, Bible references and verses, people and events, writers and quotations, places and people or events, cities and map locations, or any information suitable for a matching question in a test. When he connects the correct items he receives immediate reinforcement by the sound of a bell or the flashing of a light. Children think of the board as fun, and use it best individually or in small groups.

Flat pictures and graphics. In this section are included pictures, murals, posters, charts, flash cards, and maps—that is, nonprojected materials produced by photography or by drawing and lettering in various combinations. They may vary in size from a single new word on a flash card to a wall-size mural.

We may divide pictures and graphics on the basis of their producers: those commercially produced, those prepared by the teacher or assistant, and those made by children as part of the learning experience.

Teachers of preschool and primary grade children have long used Bible pictures to accompany storytelling. Many are available with correlated story papers for children to take home. For use with children between the ages of two and five, these flat pictures are often preferred to flannelgraphs since they have no loose pieces to get lost. Young children need to see the same picture a number of times; flat pictures are easily stored and handled, even by children. Laminating kits are available from school supply houses to preserve and protect pictures. Some art supply stores will also laminate pictures. A study of church supply catalogs shows also that an increasing number of pictures for background and application are being published. A teacher of juniors may, on occasion, use a print from a famous or contemporary artist in discussing a Bible event. Every church should develop a classified picture file in order to conserve purchased pictures and collect useful free ones.

Flash cards have grown in popularity and availability in the last fifteen years. Whereas they were once used only in day school for drilling children on words or arithmetic tables, now they are storytelling favorites as well. Usually a flash-card story is made up of several pictures showing consecutive scenes. The teacher displays them on an easel or holds them as he tells the story. They are convenient to handle and are especially valuable for outdoor work or situations where a teacher must move quickly from one class to another. Drill-type flash cards, usually made by the teacher, are as helpful in teaching Bible facts, verses, references, and books of the Bible as in fixing arithmetic combinations.

Fourth graders begin the serious study of maps in social studies. So in their Sunday school lesson, they should be introduced to maps of Bible lands. Particular care should be taken to relate the Bible history areas of the world to broader areas studied in school.

Many publishers today are providing correlated packets of teaching materials for church agencies and a host of supplementary materials from which a teacher may choose. In addition, most teachers will at times want to prepare their own illustrative material. With a little practice, life can be added to lessons by the use of simple sketches and stick figures. These can be done in advance or during the story or lesson presentation on the chalkboard. Colored chalk will stimulate added interest, even with the simplest chalkboard art.

Figure 28.1, dealing with Psalm 1, is an example of illustrating a Scripture portion with chalk. It is helpful to remember that children do not expect perfection, though this fact does not permit sloppiness; what we do should be done as unto the Lord.

Often when children are asked to review a unit of study and tell what they liked best, they will mention a project in which they themselves were involved,

PSALM 1

GODLY   UNGODLY

Figure 28.1

such as, "when we made the big mural of the life of Abraham," or "when we made the tabernacle model." These kinds of activities do not fit every agency because of their unusual demands in time and space, but in vacation Bible school or day camp, there can be opportunity for such student projects that visualize truth.

Projected materials. Projected materials include all those that require a projector: motion pictures, filmstrips, slides, overhead transparencies.

The term *film* is most often used for a 16-mm motion picture. The term distinguishes it from a series of still pictures printed on film known as a filmstrip and from a "movie" produced on 35-mm film and shown in the local theater.

Sound films provide both visual and audio presentations for maximum impact. They are therefore particularly valuable in making a story live, in producing an emotional response which leads to action or discussion, and in providing the explanation of a process. Because of the increasing cost of film rental, their use is often limited to special occasions and large group assemblies. For smaller groups in schools, 8-mm film loops, often called single concept films, are available on many topics; so far none have appeared on suitable subjects for children in the church.

In some schools, children have produced exciting 8-mm films to culminate study units in art, social studies, and science. This kind of creative project might also be produced by a church group in situations where time and finances are sufficient. Simple movie cameras requiring little knowledge of lighting or other photographic techniques are on the market.

Filmstrips, the most common of the projected materials, have several advantages: compactness, low-cost projectors, relatively low purchase price, availability in great variety. They are strips of still pictures, many with accompanying sound on records or cassette tapes. This means that a sound filmstrip does not require a sound filmstrip projector, but may use an easily available record player or cassette player for the narration.

At least two filmstrip adaptations have appeared, each with Bible materials and designed to provide suitable yet inexpensive visuals for use with individual classes of children. One, for use with a "Phonoviewer," uses a mounted strip of film, along with a record or cassette tape, to present a TV-like picture. Another, called "split-35," is a half-width filmstrip, usually packaged with narration for the teacher, or with a record for phonograph accompaniment. Either a special small projector or an adapter is used to project the pictures.

Slides, usually in two-by-two inch mounts, are the simplest of the photographically produced media. Most cameras can use color slide film; many have automatic exposure control and simple focusing devices which enable even an amateur to get good slides. For children, some of the best uses of slides are for showing what has been done, presenting the work of "our missionary," promoting camp or VBS or other special programs, leading into worship through a portrayal of God's handiwork.

Overhead projectors have become popular at all levels in schools and colleges. They project large transparencies which may be purchased, hand-drawn on acetate or clear plastic, or reproduced from paper copy by use of a copy machine and special film. As with most other projectors, these can best be used in a department session. Here is an excellent way of getting before a group the words of a song, directions for a presession activity, a Bible verse to be discussed, or the contributions of students. During presession, each junior can be given a sheet of film and a marker, along with instructions for preparing a chart, paragraph, or outline. Some of their work may then be projected and discussed.

Television and videotape. Closely related to projected materials are television and videotape, though these media operate electronically rather than photographically. By using a television camera and microphone in one room connected by cable to a monitor (or a home TV receiver plus an adapter) in another room, it is possible to show a class what is going on before the camera. This is known as closed-circuit television. The program is not broadcast but merely cabled to the monitor being viewed by the class.

Closed-circuit television makes it possible for a teacher training class to observe a group of children unobtrusively, or to observe a teacher without the students' being conscious of visitors. It enables a group of children to role play without an obvious audience.

The next step beyond this use of television is recording on videotape in order to have playback later. The camera and microphone feed into the videotape recorder, which records both sound and picture signals. When playback is desired, the recorder is connected with the monitor and the program is produced on the TV screen.

The videotape program may be played again and again, or the tape may be reused. The initial cost of tape is likely to deter a church from saving many taped programs, but a church which telecasts its services can make many inexpensive uses of the same equipment and tape.

Videocassettes are perhaps the newest format in which to provide realistic portrayals of the application of Bible truth. Though the variety for children is now limited, more is sure to come as equipment becomes more common in churches.

AUDIO MATERIALS

With listening materials becoming more plentiful each year, a Sunday school teacher has less excuse than ever for requiring children to listen to his rendition of the lesson fifty-two weeks of the year. Consider, for example, what can be done with phonograph records: they can set the mood as children enter the room, or as they rest in vacation Bible school or camp; they can introduce a new song, or provide accompaniment for singing; they can tell a story; they can give variety to Scripture reading; they can provide activity music for preschoolers; they can be a source of short selections with which students may react.

Phonograph records are reasonably priced and do not require costly equipment. For use in children's work, a player for single records is often preferable to one with an automatic changer. The same player may be used for the narration of filmstrips.

A tape recorder may be used for all of the above purposes, with prerecorded material for children's work becoming increasingly abundant. Some publishers are providing either records or a cassette to accompany each quarter's Sunday school material. In most cases, these recordings, more available for older than for younger children, are made up of several sections, each for a different lesson.

A teacher may record material for use as a listening experience and for discussion. The recording may be a dramatization or telling of the Bible story or of a modern story similar to it, or a dialogue of children's voices applying the truth to be taught, or showing the need of such application. The taping may be done by adults, by primaries or juniors, or as a special project by teenagers. Over a period of time, creative teachers can accumulate a small library of short recordings suitable for use in teaching situations.

In today's schoolrooms, many programs of individualized instruction depend heavily on the use of *cassette recorders*. Whole series of materials are prepared, using a combination of tapes, filmstrips, activity cards, and worksheets. Students progress at their own rate either within set limits or without limits.

The concept of individual study and progress is in keeping with the Bible's emphasis on the individual and his worth. Some vacation Bible schools have partially used this idea, with a number of activity centers in each department and each student making some choices. As Christian teachers give more attention to nonclass methods of instruction, they will undoubtedly use more recorded material, mostly on cassette tapes and used with headphones.

Tape recorders are of several types: reel-to-reel and cassette, monaural and stereo, two-track and four- or eight-track, battery and AC operated. For many noncritical purposes, a monaural cassette recorder is practical and portable. Preferably, it should operate on either battery or alternating current.

MANIPULATIVE MEDIA

In various ways throughout this book and in this chapter, the message has been reiterated: students must become involved with the truths of a lesson if they are to learn and change. When children use and react to media presentations, they are involved in learning; when, in some cases, they actually produce the materials, they are surely involved. Three-dimensional projects which children can manipulate give opportunity for further participation.

A fifth grade class, wanting to present the Christmas story to their parents, prepared a *shadow box*. They used a suit-box cover, cutting a large window and covering the window with blue tissue paper. They then stood the box on edge on a table, placed a light behind it and used silhouette figures, which they changed as a narrator read the story.

There is something secretive about a *peep box*. Perhaps it is the fact that only one person can see at a time and the rest must wait. Third graders can use a shoe box as a base, cut a viewing window on one end and a skylight in the top. They can use small, stand-up figures or pictures from take-home papers to portray their favorite story out of their current series.

Preschool children are often intrigued by *stand-up figures or figurines*, which they can move about in portraying a Bible story after they have seen their teacher do it. Primary children can prepare a sandbox or stand-up presentation themselves and then enjoy explaining their production. (Also see chap. 31.)

A model or replica of some real thing can solve several problems: the real thing may be too small or too large to see advantageously, such as a Palestinian village; it may not be available, or may no longer exist, such as the tabernacle in the wilderness or Noah's ark; it may be too fragile or too expensive to handle.

Models may be made of many materials: paper, papier-mâché, clay, soap, wood. Instructions for the use of a variety of materials may be found in craft books; also, project kits are listed in Christian education supply catalogs. The production of a collection of models could be an exciting VBS project for a junior or older group.

A world globe is actually a model of the earth and should be used to help juniors visualize the location of Bible events, the placement of their missionaries, the time-zone differences where these missionaries serve, climate differences as shown by proximity to the equator.

A *diorama* is a model of a whole scene, rather than of one object. It may be small, made by children from a carton, or it may be life-size, in a museum. For students, the more valuable dioramas are usually those they make, depicting a Bible story, the camp of Israel, or a mission station.

Puppets too may be used in a variety of ways with children of all ages. One or two puppets may be involved in a "dialogue" with the teacher, or between two Bible characters. More elaborate puppet plays may portray either a Bible story or a modern application of scriptural truth. Many puppet scripts are available, or junior age children may write their own. In the process, they may scrutinize a Bible passage much more carefully than usual. (For more on puppets, see chap. 31.)

Programmed learning is a form of teaching in which a learning task is divided into many small steps arranged so that the students must understand or complete one before going on to the next. Programmed learning may use only words and be prepared in book form, or it may involve the use of various audio, visual, or manipulative materials.

REAL OBJECTS

Almost all the visual and audio media which have been discussed thus far are in some way representations of real objects, but not real in themselves. Real things have been represented by words, lines, diagrams, maps, photographic reproductions, drawings, models, or combinations of these. Perhaps the infrequency with which we show children the real thing in church education grows out of the fact that we are teaching the Bible, theology, and interpersonal relationships. We are dealing with events of the past, with abstract matters, with applications to life that involve people with their viewpoints and emotional responses. These cannot be brought into the classroom for study as tangible objects can. The result is that the teacher of scriptural truth must look to the Lord for other ways to make the instruction clear and relevant.

Real objects, nevertheless, do have a place in Christian teaching. Missionaries have used curios to help people understand life in the countries where they work. One missionary, a children's worker in Africa, met the need of primary children by wearing an African dress and visiting with six children at a time at a children's party. The small groups permitted questions, explanations, and handling of items of special interest to the children.

A visit to certain museums can open the eyes of children to the high-quality workmanship exhibited by people who, in other ways, seem primitive. Such an experience can give children a respect for the people to whom their missionaries go. A trip to a children's home can lead juniors to a new appreciation of their own parents, as well as a desire to remember these needy children ·on special occasions.

Teachers have not only used objects for their own value, but have often used them to represent something else in object lessons. Such use can be valuable if the relationships are clear to the children. Teachers should ask these two questions regarding object lessons: First, does this object actually make the truth more clear, or are the relationships so symbolic that they make learning the real truth more difficult? Second, is the child so mystified by the object or action related to it that he remembers only the action and loses the meaning entirely, as is sometimes true of gospel magic? Real objects, like all other visual and audio materials, are of value whenever they *help* children to understand and learn.

SUMMARY

The Christian teacher's use of audio and visual media is in keeping with the best we know of effective teaching methods. More than that, it is one application of the scriptural principle illustrated in both Testaments—the importance of variety if real teaching and learning are to take place.

Many of the media available today are more complex than those used in biblical times; some confuse children rather than help them understand; some are produced by persons without a high regard for the authority and accuracy of the Bible. For all these reasons, whatever is used must be chosen carefully in view of the teacher's objective. The Holy Spirit can direct the teacher who is familiar with many possibilities.

FOR FURTHER READING

Anderson, Paul, and Irene Francis. *Storytelling with the Flannelboard, Book One.* Minneapolis: Denison, 1961.
———. *Storytelling with the Flannelboard, Book Two.* Minneapolis: Denison, 1961.
Arnold, Glenn F. "How to Produce a Children's Film Without Actually Crying." *Moody Monthly,* 71 (April 1971): 37-39.
Ballard, Mona, and Joyce Hicks. *Bridges: Bulletin Boards for Mainstreaming.* Vol. 1. Minneapolis: T. S. Denison, 1981.

Barnhouse, Donald Grey. *Teaching the Word of Truth.* Grand Rapids: Eerdmans, 1958. Excellent chalkboard lessons on Bible doctrines.

Bolton, Barbara J., and Charles T. Smith. *Bible Learning Activities for Children, Grades 1-6.* Glendale, Calif.: Gospel Light, Regal Books, 1977.

Darkes, Anna Sue. *How to Make and Use Overhead Transparencies.* Chicago: Moody, 1977.

Getz, Gene A. *Audio-Visual Media in Christian Education.* Chicago: Moody, 1972.

Green, Lee. *Teaching Tools You Can Make.* Wheaton, Ill.: Scripture Press, Victor Books, 1978.

Green Lee, and Don Dengerink. *Five Hundred and One Ways to Use the Overhead Projector.* Littleton, Colo.: Libraries Unlimited.

Griggs, Patricia. *Creative Activities in Church Education.* Nashville: Abingdon, 1980.

Harp, Grace. *Handbook of Christian Puppetry.* Denver: Accent, 1984.

Jensen, Mary and Andrew Jensen. *Audiovisual Idea Book for Churches.* Minneapolis: Augsburg, 1974.

Kemp, Jerrold E. *Planning and Producing Audiovisual Materials.* 4th ed. New York: Harper & Row, 1980.

Lindgren, Carl. *Teaching Bible Truths with Simple Objects.* Wheaton, Ill. Scripture Press, Victor Books, 1979.

Liu, Sarah, and Mary Lou Vittitow. *Creative Bible Activities for Children.* Wheaton, Ill.: Scripture Press, Victor Books, 1977.

Mathre, T. H. *Creative Bulletin Boards.* Minneapolis: Denison, 1962.

Minor, Ed. *Handbook for Preparing Visual Media.* 2d ed. New York: McGraw Hill, 1978.

Minor, Ed, and Harvey R. Frye. *Techniques for Producing Visual Instructional Media.* 2d ed. New York: McGraw Hill, 1977.

Nardini, Mary Lois, and Patricia Quinette. *Fundamentals of Bulletin Board Design.* Minneapolis: T. S. Denison, 1979.

Rodin, Shelly. *When Puppets Talk.* Wheaton, Ill.: Scripture Press.

Rynew, Arden. *Filmmaking for Children.* Dayton, Ohio: Pflaum/Standard, 1971.

Satterthwaite, Les. *Graphics: Skills, Media, and Materials.* Dubuque, Iowa: Kendall/Hunt, 1972.

Three Easy Steps—Flannelgraph "How to" from the Experts. Warrenton, Mo.: Child Evangelism.

Vonk, Idalee. *Storytelling with the Flannelboard, Book Three.* Minneapolis: Denison, 1983.

Warner, Diane, *Puppets Help Teach.* Denver: Accent, 1975.

———. *Bible Puppet Scripts for Busy Teachers.* Denver: Accent, 1983.

Wright, Lewis, and Deone Beasley. *How to Construct Colorful Bulletin Boards.* Minneapolis: Denison, 1970.

SELECTED SOURCES

Note: All publishers of Sunday school lesson materials produce and distribute a variety of audio and visual aids. Those listed here are sources of somewhat specialized products.

BCM International, 237 Fairfield Avenue, Upper Darby, PA 19082 (formerly Bible Club Movement). Flannelboard equipment and materials, flash card stories, illustrated songs.

Bible Visuals, Inc., P. O. Box 93, Landisville, PA 17538. Flash card stories for much of the Bible.

Child Evangelism Press, Warrenton, MO 63383. Flannelboard Bible lessons and related materials, illustrated songs and Bible verses; flash card stories.

Faith Venture Visuals, P. O. Box 423 (510 East Main Street), Lititz, PA 17543. Most complete source for overhead projector supplies, seminars, biblically-based teaching materials.

29

Chris Templar

Using Computers with Children

- **Why Use Computers with Children?**
- **Ways to Use the Computer in Christian Education**
  DRILL AND PRACTICE
  TUTORIAL
  SIMULATION
  COMPUTER PROGRAMMING
  AS A TOOL
- **How and Where to Start**
- **Selecting a Computer**
- **Using the Computer in the Christian Home**
- **Creative Bible Learning Activities**
  ACTIVITIES USING LOGO
  ACTIVITIES USING COMMERCIAL SOFTWARE
- **Potential Problems in the Use of Computers**
- **Trends in Tools for the Information Age**

The computer revolution has already reached into the realm of elementary and middle school education. For several years computers have been transforming the work place. Word processors began to replace the typewriter in the office. Sophisticated computers were developed which could aid in the design of new

Chris Templar, Ed.D., is professor of Christian education and computer education at Johnson Bible College, Knoxville, Tennessee.

buildings, cities, and machinery. The needs of the space program led to an increased emphasis on the development of necessary computer applications. This research opened the way for further applications of computers in industry, medicine, and in other fields. But when computers were large, expensive, and fairly sensitive to the atmosphere in which they operated, use in education was minimal.

The possibility for significant change did not arise until the introduction of personal computers in the late 1970s. In the beginning, the hardware was available before suitable software was written, thus slowing down the rate of implementation. In many places the early introduction of computers into schools depended on either an interested teacher or the interest of a group of concerned parents. At first parents often financed the purchase of the school's only computer.

However, between 1982 and 1985 the situation changed radically. In 1982 it was estimated that about 30 percent of elementary and secondary schools owned computers. By the beginning of 1984 this had grown to about 68 percent, and in early 1985 between 75 and 80 percent of all schools in America had at least one computer. In Arizona, the state with the highest ratio, there was one computer for every 18.3 students. Not only did the ratio of computers per student increase but the decision-making locus changed. Increasingly, computer education was being planned at a county-wide or even state-wide level, and buying decisions were removed from the individual schools. By 1985 computer education in many states ranked, in priority, second only to basic skills development.[1]

This phenomenal growth rate during years in which educators were faced with the problem of declining school budgets, rising costs, and declining enrollment, reflected the high priority being placed on the development of computer education. Why was so much emphasis being placed on the development of computer education and why were computers being used so extensively in the education of children?

WHY USE COMPUTERS WITH CHILDREN?

Although some still raise questions regarding the validity of the computer in the educational process, a consensus is beginning to develop concerning some of the ways computers can help those who work with children and the children themselves. Among these are the following:

The use of computers in education helps to:

1. Individualize teaching and learning
2. Develop creativity

1. Janice L. Flake, E. Edwin McClintock, and Sandra V. Turner, *Fundamentals of Computer Education* (Belmont, Calif.: Wadsworth, 1985).

3. Reinforce previous learning
4. Provide extensive drill on factual knowledge
5. Recreate unfamiliar situations and allow learners to participate in them
6. Motivate learning
7. Develop structured logical thinking
8. Allow for access to extended data bases
9. Improve self-confidence
10. Introduce necessary skills for careers

A careful examination of this list of outcomes by the Christian educator demonstrates how many of them, with some rephrasing, are also applicable to Christian education.

At the present time the use of the computer in Christian education has frequently been restricted to its use in administration. Since this reflects only a small part of the role the computer plays in education as a whole, the Christian educator must ask what other roles the computer can play in the church's education of its children.

WAYS TO USE THE COMPUTER IN CHRISTIAN EDUCATION

Computer use in education has frequently been divided into five areas: drill and practice, tutorial, simulation, programming, and the use of the computer as a tool. To help determine meaningful ways to use the computer with children, both in the church and in the Christian home, these five ways of using the computer need to be examined together with their relationship to the ten outcomes listed above.

DRILL AND PRACTICE

Drill and practice programs focus either on the development of skills or on the acquisition of factual knowledge. When the development of skills is the primary goal, the program will usually also focus on the development of speed and accuracy. A well-designed program will provide most or all the following:

1. The opportunity for a limited number of tries at any one question or problem.
2. The ability to keep track of the number of correct and incorrect responses.
3. The answer to a question to which an incorrect response was given.
4. Subsequent repetition of questions missed.
5. Praise and encouragement or some other form of motivation, such as points or runs in a game.
6. The ability for the learners to control the pace at which they proceed. This insures that the slower reader is not discouraged by never being

able to complete the reading of the instructions or questions. When the aim of the program is to develop speed in a particular skill, the speed at which the instructions are displayed should still be controllable.

7. The ability to tailor the material to the needs of the individual student either through choosing different difficulty levels or different subjects, or through using a bank of material supplied by the teacher.
8. An attractive format consisting of either meaningful graphics, or intriguing methods of use, such as a game played against the computer or against another player.

Well-developed drill and practice programs can be highly effective in helping students acquire skills and factual knowledge. The computer is more patient than the human teacher and will continue to offer questions for as long as the student continues to play the game or use the program. On the other hand, students become rapidly bored with poorly designed or non-motivating programs. There is danger that a student will associate the material taught with the poorly designed program and become "turned-off" to both. It is therefore incumbent on Christian educators to evaluate biblical drill and practice programs carefully and encourage high standards in all materials produced to help children learn Bible truths and biblical content.

At present the majority of Bible software are poorly written drill and practice programs. They tend to employ techniques that are dated or are inferior to those being produced to teach facts in other subjects. There is a need for skilled Christian programmers to develop quality drill and practice and other types of programs as a part of their Christian ministry. Only the highest quality and most effective use of the machine should be acceptable in biblical computer materials.

TUTORIAL

Typically teachers in various educational ministries have a wide variety of students in their classes. Often more than one school grade is represented. Some are from a Christian background, whereas others have had little or no Christian teaching. They represent a wide variety of educational needs and teaching levels. In a conventional learning situation, it is often impossible to meet all those needs. Using well-designed computer tutorial programs is one solution to the problem.

The distinguishing characteristic of a tutorial program is that it instructs the learner in a body of material. That is, it teaches new material or ideas. This is in contrast to the drill and practice type of program, which normally drills on material that has already been presented.

In its simplest form, the tutorial program differs little from a programmed learning text. The learner is presented with some concepts, ideas, or facts and is then asked a question about the material. On the basis of the answer, the program may give more reinforcement in the particular area being studied, or it may take the learner on to new material.

Another type of tutorial currently being explored includes a data base. "Expert systems" are generated from the data base.[2] Through the use of this dynamic data base, students become actively involved in the learning process. This type of learning is called either "Intelligent Computer-Assisted Instruction (ICAI)" or "Expert Systems." These programs can become much more sophisticated than anything found in a program based on a textbook. Although this type of tutorial program is currently in its infancy, it offers the potential for teachers to obtain individualized instructional material for their students that will help meet some of the diverse needs described above.

With these more recent developments in the types of tutorial programs being written, it is possible to apply principles from different learning theories and also to take advantage of individual discovery and control of the learning process. In harmony with the new emphasis on teaching that uses both hemispheres of the brain, tutorial programs that use problem-solving techniques, graphic representation, and principles of task analysis are also using right-hemispheric—and therefore nonlinear—processes. The effective development of this type of program takes a large investment of time.

Generally speaking, the computer tutorial will only be one element in the curriculum design. Opportunity should be given for the student to interact with the material at different levels and in different ways. The excitement that ICAI can generate should not allow the teacher to neglect a multi-sensory approach to the material. Christian truths need to be experienced within a community and in social interaction and not exclusively through interaction with a machine.

While some simple tutorial material is available on biblical topics, the potential of biblical ICAI has yet to be fully explored and developed.

SIMULATION

Simulation is probably one of the most underdeveloped types of educational computer programs. A simulation offers students the opportunity to interact with a situation without the risks of real-life involvement, or it allows them the opportunity to experience something that they could not experience in real life. A popular simulation in the elementary school, for example, allows students to imagine themselves as pioneers on the Oregon Trail.[3] Similar simula-

2. See Maryse Quere, "Expert Systems: Towards CAI of the Future," in *Proceedings WCCE85 of the 4th World Conference on Computers in Education* (Amsterdam: Elsevier Science Publishers B.V., 1985), p. 159.
3. Copies of this program are available both in the public domain and from the Minnesota Educational Computing Consortium.

tions could be developed that would allow students to become Israelites wandering in the wilderness, a Jewish family at the time of Christ, or a member of the early church facing the daily threat of imprisonment and persecution.

Certain features distinguish simulations from games and other types of computer programs. A simulation should meet the following criteria:

1. It is a working analogy of a real-world situation.
2. The learner must actively participate in the simulation and in the decision-making process.
3. The simulation is usually developed to teach specific information or to demonstrate a particular process.
4. Usually a simulation does not involve competition with other players, although those playing may be able to fail to achieve a goal in various ways. It is even true that in a simulation on the early church, for example, a player's failure to avoid persecution or even death for his faith is an integral part of the simulation.
5. There are specific rules for interacting within the simulation.
6. Meaningful feedback is essential if the simulation is to be both motivating and realistic.

Another strength of simulations is that often they can be played by individuals, small groups, or a whole class, even when only one computer is available.

COMPUTER PROGRAMMING

Learning a computer language allows the user to have control over the machine rather than being controlled by the machine, as is the case in the various types of programs discussed above. Although there may be little room for the teaching of computer languages within the time constraints of the Christian education program, the Christian educator should not neglect the application of this skill to biblical material when it has been learned elsewhere.

At first, the predominate computer language in education was BASIC. However, the thought processes that are necessary for effective use of this language are too difficult for most elementary school children. This problem has led to research and development of languages that allow children to control the computer. The first to be developed and extensively used was LOGO, which by 1985 had become the most popular language to be taught to both preschool and elementary aged children.[4] As studies about artificial intelligence and natural language on computers develop, other languages will likely become popular. Two such languages which are currently under development are Blocks and Prolog.

4. For help in learning the LOGO language, see the books listed at the end of this chapter.

Since LOGO offers almost limitless possibilities for the teaching of biblical material, some of these will be explored in a separate section later in this chapter. For more details on the use of LOGO in biblical settings, see the forthcoming book by the author and Richard Beam tentatively titled *Biblical Explorations Using LOGO.*

USING THE COMPUTER AS A TOOL

There are a variety of ways in which the computer can be used as an instructional tool. Among these are word processors, electronic spreadsheets, graphics packages and tablets, story development software, data base management systems, authoring languages and voice and music synthesizers. Child level software is available for most of these applications.

One strength of using the computer as a tool is that it allows children to explore and extend the gifts they have. For example, word processing allows children to learn to be more effective writers because of the ease with which they can edit; graphics tablets allow children to explore drawing and art ideas in ways not possible with conventional materials. In Christian education these tools become especially significant as they allow for creative expression of the material learned and also for the development of the God-given gifts the children possess.

In addition, the community nature of Christianity can be emphasized as one group of children uses a story-development program to write Bible stories that can then be read and enjoyed by another class, or uses a word processing program to develop electronic Bible stories that have been illustrated using a Koala pad or similar graphics tablet.

Simple data base management programs can be used to allow children to build reference files of Bible characters or events and then to generate quizzes with which to test their friends.

The applications of the computer as a tool in Christian education are limited only by the creativity of the teacher or the students.

How and Where to Start

In many schools, computers can be effectively used where only one machine is available for a whole class. In a church educational setting, it is not necessary that there be multiple machines in order for serious use to be made of the computer. At the present time a more important limiting factor is the lack of quality software. For this reason, it is suggested that the computer be introduced and used either as a tool or that the students' knowledge of LOGO be harnessed.

Although those using the computers do not have to be experts in computer education, as with any other instructional aid, teachers should have specific objectives in and reasons for using the computer as an aid in a specific teaching-learning situation.

The following are some of the ways in which a computer can be introduced and used in a church setting.

1. Place the computer on a rolling cart and allow a teacher to check it out as with other audiovisual materials for a limited time. Children can rotate through the activity during a specified time. If children work in pairs at the computer, in one or two weeks all children will have had an opportunity to use it meaningfully.
2. Place the computer in the church library or some other central location and allow designated children to work on it each week.
3. Work as a class in preparing and designing a group computer project and then have the machine available for specified times after school to encourage students to implement their parts of the project.
4. Use the computer as a part of a Sunday night or midweek group Bible learning activity.
5. Organize a computer club where teenagers help children to develop creative Bible materials that can be used in other learning situations.
6. Set up a small computer lab for use in different teaching situations.

Since computers are now used so extensively in education, it may no longer be necessary in most situations for the teacher to teach students either how to use a computer or how to take care of the equipment. It would be helpful, however, for the person who is introducing computers in a church to visit the local schools and become aware of the principles taught for computer use and care. Basic ground rules need to be established in this area, but care should be taken so that the frequent fear adults have of the machine is not reflected in unnecessarily protective behavior toward it. Do not lock up your computer in a church office or audiovisual closet; use it!!

SELECTING A COMPUTER

There is a basic difference between the type of computer needed for use in the church office and for use in biblical education. Consequently, although with care it might be possible for one machine to perform both functions, it is usually better to consider a separate and different machine for use with children. The following are some features to consider.

1. *Software.* Make sure that a child-related word processor, a good graphics program, music development programs, story writing programs, a simple data base, and a good version of LOGO are available for the machine, together with any biblical software you wish to use. However

good the machine, if suitable software is not available, its use will be severely restricted.

2. *Service.* The computer needs to be able to be repaired locally rather than having to be returned to the manufacturer.

3. *Reliability.* The machine needs to have been around long enough (several months) for initial problems to have been corrected and for the manufacturer to have developed a strong commitment to maintaining support for the machine.

4. *Capacity.* The machine should have an adequate memory (at least 64K) to do what is needed.

5. *Peripherals.* For most work with children, a dot matrix or color printer, at least one disk drive, and a simple graphics tablet such as a Koala pad will be helpful if not essential.

6. *Color.* With children it is important to select a computer that uses either a color television or a color monitor.

USING THE COMPUTER IN THE CHRISTIAN HOME

Because a larger percentage of families are now buying personal computers, it is important for the church to consider ways to help parents use computers in the Christian education of their children. Many families assume that they will purchase programs that will help children with subjects studied at school. The personal computer can also be effectively used within the home as a tool in developing Bible knowledge.

It is important, however, that the computer not be used to supplant the television as a babysitter. Computers in the home give parents and children the opportunity to work together in solving problems and in learning new material.

The following are some ways the church can help Christian families use their computers in biblical education:

1. Schedule a parents' evening and share with families ways the computer is being used in the church's educational program.

2. Provide an information or idea sheet of joint projects and related projects parents might wish to work on with children at home.

3. Build up a collection of software in the church library that families can check out. The collection should include locally developed programs and public domain and commercial software. Note: Take care to protect the copyright and licenses of the commercial software.

4. Encourage parents who use the computer at home for work-related activities to involve their children in some of those experiences where possible.

5. Give parents guidance regarding types of software to purchase and moral and ethical issues to consider (excessive violence and emphasis on symbols or material from the occult would be two examples).

The computer can be useful in family Christian education. It can enrich the process but must never be allowed to usurp the role of the parents in the Christian education of their children.

CREATIVE BIBLE LEARNING ACTIVITIES

The following are suggestions of some creative ways in which the computer can be used in Christian education. In most cases the emphasis is on the child's being an active participant in the development of the activity rather than passively playing a game or working through a pre-prepared drill and practice program. This is not to suggest that there is no place for the latter in Christian education but rather to encourage teachers to work toward the creative involvement of their students with the computer.

The material has been divided into two sections. The first gives ways in which LOGO can be used to develop creative activities. The second offers ways in which commercial software can be used. Unless the church has a large budget for software, it is probable that the most realistic approach for most churches is to purchase a LOGO program and develop creative activities in that language. Because LOGO is being taught so widely and is discovery oriented, the teacher who has only a very limited knowledge will find that many children can take the ideas and work with them. Examples of most of these LOGO activities can be found in the Radio Shack public domain collection.

ACTIVITIES USING *LOGO*

1. *Adventure stories.* In these, a Bible story is written in sections. At the end of each section the person reading the story is forced to make a choice regarding the next event. A choice not in line with the biblical account would lead to the end of the story and the option to start again. With the use of five or six utility procedures, children can very easily develop this kind of story. Story development involves them in the biblical story and also gives them the opportunity to invent realistic alternatives.
2. *Adventure games.* In these, characters usually must find their way through a grid-like maze, collecting objects as they go and avoiding various hazards and pitfalls in order to get safely to a predetermined goal. Extensive games could be developed on topics like the journey of the Israelites through the wilderness or one of Paul's missionary journeys. Smaller games can be built around individual Bible stories. Many children will spend hours seeking to solve these games. After one group has developed a good adventure, it should be made available for others to play.
3. *Generating poetry.* In this activity, students could either write original

poetry based on Bible themes or rewrite Bible poems in their own words.

4. *Memory work.* These consist of activities to help students learn a single memory verse or a whole passage of Scripture. A variety of techniques can be employed here: substitution of synonyms to aid in comprehension, fill-in-the-gaps, mixed words, finish-the-sentence, or even allowing the program to check if the verse has been typed in correctly.

5. *Map work.* In these, the students use the graphics capability to draw and label maps showing biblical events or places.

6. *Bible pictures.* Here "instant" versions of the language are used to produce Bible pictures or pictures of background material related to the material being studied. These activities would be especially relevant for younger children. A super-procedure can be used to combine the pictures into an electronic storybook.

7. *Animated video stories.* Animated sequences can be developed and then recorded on a video cassette recorder. A script can be added and a video movie of a Bible story produced.

8. *Illustrated stories.* The graphics and list-processing features of LOGO can be used to develop illustrated Bible stories for younger children to read and enjoy.

9. *Bible quizzes.* Quizzes for others in the class to take on the material being studied can be developed. Again, utility frames can be used so that the emphasis is on the content of the questions rather than on the ability to program.

10. *Bible microworlds.* Older children or teenagers can produce an extensive series of on-and-off-the-computer explorations around a larger section of material, such as one of the epistles, that can then be used to help others explore and discover the meaning of this material. Here the material may include examples of all the activities given above and more within the one simulated environment. One example of Bible microworld is one on Philippians prepared for elementary children. It can be found in the Radio Shack public domain collection. A microworld is a larger, more time-consuming project than the others mentioned above and should not be attempted until a teacher has a well-developed experience with the language.

11. *Music.* Most versions of LOGO allow for at least one voice music to be written. Students could write both the words and music for poems or hymns based on concepts that have been studied.

12. *Simulations.* In these, the students could develop simulations of biblical events or of the background to those events.

13. *Information files.* A data base of biblical people or events could be developed. But note that this should be attempted only if at least 128K of memory is available.

ACTIVITIES USING COMMERCIAL SOFTWARE

In this section, where reference has been made to specific programs it is only to give the reader an idea of the type of program being referred to and not to suggest that this is the only program that can be used for the activity. In most instances many different but similar programs are available and many new ones are in the process of being developed.

1. Adventure game creators can be used generally for developing games, although they allow for less flexibility than if LOGO is used for developing stories, as in number 2 above.
2. Story programs such as *Kidwriter* or *Story Tree* allow students to write their own illustrated Bible stories and then share them with their friends.
3. Simple word processors such as *Bank Street Writer* can be used for any creative writing project.
4. *Micro Illustrator* and a Koala pad or a similar graphics tablet can be used to draw pictures on the screen. With the addition of a color graphics printer, these pictures can be printed out for book covers, bulletins, displays, and so on.
5. Biblical data bases can be created with programs such as *Phi Beta Filer.*
6. An illustrated news sheet on the material being studied can be produced with *The Newsroom.*
7. Word search generators can be used to develop word searches.
8. A music program such as *Songwriter* could be used by a class or choir to write original music compositions based on material studied to be performed at a parents' evening.
9. *Print Shop* can be used to produce banners, signs, and other similar materials highlighting the material being studied.

These activity suggestions should be regarded as ideas to help the teacher get started.

POTENTIAL PROBLEMS IN THE USE OF COMPUTERS

Probably the most important potential problem which the church must face in using computers is that of time. Whenever educators use discovery learning or creative activity methods, more time is needed for the activity to be completed. Many of the above activities cannot be completed within one Sunday school lesson period. Since computers tend to motivate students highly and many will have computers at home, one partial solution is to encourage students to complete sections of the project at home. Another answer might be to use both the Sunday school hour and the extended session or children's church time for several weeks to complete a meaningful project.

The increased enthusiasm and higher degree of learning that takes place through the execution of many of these projects must challenge us to find creative solutions to this problem.

Other potential problems are these:

1. Adults' fear of machines. This will become increasingly less significant as children in the computer generation become tomorrow's Christian educators.
2. Little available software. Most of the suggestions given above do not require specially designed software for the church. In fact, the more creative projects can be developed using regular multipurpose commercial software.
3. Broken hardware. Most hardware problems occur within the first three months of the life of the computer. As with any piece of sophisticated equipment, there is always the possibility it will break down and alternate plans may need to be made.
4. Available hardware. As workers in the educational program begin to see the possibilities, a scheduling problem may arise. The use of the computer should be scheduled in advance in a similar manner to projectors and other teaching aids.
5. Teachers who are not skilled to use the computer. Sometimes the church may need to examine others in the congregation who have computer skills and recruit them to be active in the computer part of the educational program. Those who are interested and excited about computers will be the most effective teachers in this area, provided they also meet normal standards regarding Christian commitment.

TRENDS IN TOOLS FOR THE INFORMATION AGE

Although it is impossible to predict all the changes and developments that will occur during the next decade, the following are some developments that are already on the horizon.

1. Significant development will occur in the area of artificial intelligence and fifth-generation computers leading to the use of more "natural" language machines.
2. Hardware developments will include more and cheaper memory, faster and more powerful machines, greater storage capabilities, higher graphics resolution.
3. Interactive video will allow for exciting new types of software and Bible teaching materials.
4. More software will become available for church use. This will mean that

individuals and Christian education committees will need to develop good standards of evaluation to make sure that only quality materials are used in their educational programs.

SUMMARY

The computer is a tool already being used extensively in both business and education. The church needs to expand its vision for the use of the computer in Christian education. Although many types of programs can be used to further differing educational goals, one of the most effective ways the computer can be used for Christian education is as an aid in creative Bible learning activities.

Churches should be encouraged to discover the interests and abilities which already exist among their members in both the use of personal computers and in computer programming, and they should harness these abilities in their educational programs. Computers are strong motivators. Children today love to learn about using computers; their effective use should therefore be encouraged.

FOR FURTHER READING

Bearden, Donna. *1, 2, 3 My Computer and Me*. Reston, Va.: Reston, 1983.
————. *A Bit of LOGO Magic*. Reston, Va.: Reston, 1984.
Bearden, Donna, and Kathleen Martin. *Mathematics and LOGO*. Reston, Va.: Reston, 1985.
————. *Primarily LOGO*. Reston, Va.: Reston, 1984.
Bearden, D., K. Martin, and J. Muller. *The Turtle's Sourcebook*. Reston, Va.: Reston, 1983.
Becker, Henry Jay. *Microcomputers in the Classroom, Dreams and Realities*. Eugene, Ore.: International Council for Computers in Education, n.d.
Bedell, Kenneth, and Parker Rossman. *Computers: New Opportunities for Personalized Ministry*. Valley Forge, Pa.: Judson, 1984.
Bitter, G., R. Camuse, and Arizona State University. *Using a Microcomputer in the Classroom*. Reston, Va.: Reston, 1984.
Coburn, P., P. Kelman, N. Roberts, T. Snyder, D. Watt, and C. Weiner. *Practical Guide to Computers in Education*. Reading, Mass.: Addison-Wesley, 1982.
Cuban, Larry. *Teacher and Machines: The Classroom Use of Technology*. New York: Columbia U., Teachers College Press, 1985.
Davis, Dennis M., and Steve Clapp. *The Third Wave and the Local Church*. Champaign, Ill.: C-Four Resources, 1983.
Dilday, Russell H., Jr. *Personal Computer: A New Tool for Ministers*. Nashville: Broadman, 1985.
Feigenbaum, E. A., and P. McCorduck. *The Fifth Generation: Artificial Intelligence and Japan's Computer Challenge to the World*. Reading, Mass.: Addison-Wesley, 1983.

Flake, Janice L., C. Edwin McClintock, and Sandra V. Turner. *Fundamentals of Computer Education.* Belmont, Calif.: Wadsworth, 1985.

Geoffrion, Leo, and Olga Geoffrion. *Computers and Reading Instruction.* Reading, Mass.: Addison-Wesley, 1983.

Goldberg, Kenneth P., and Robert D. Sherwood. *Microcomputers: A Parents' Guide.* New York: John Wiley & Sons, 1983.

Graham, Neill. *The Mind Tool Computers and Their Impact on Society.* Saint Paul, Minn.: West, 1983.

Graves, D. H. *Writing: Teachers and Children at Work.* Exeter, N.H.: Heinemann, 1982.

Hunter, Beverly. *My Students Use Computers.* Reston, Va.: Reston, 1983.

Iles, Robert H., and William L. Callison. *Selecting Computers for Ministry.* Pasadena, Calif.: New Beginnings, 1985.

Libeskind, S., R. Billstein, and J. Lott. *LOGO Activities in Elementary Geometry.* Missoula, Mont.: University of Montana, 1983.

Naisbett, John. *Megatrends.* New York: Warner, 1983.

Papert, S. *Mindstorms: Children, Computers, and Powerful Ideas.* New York: Basic, 1980.

Roberts, N., D. F. Anderson, R. M. Deal, M. S. Garet, and W. A. Shaffer. *Introductions to Computer Simulation: The System Dynamics Approach.* Reading, Mass.: Addison-Wesley, 1983.

Shoshak, Robert, ed. *Computers in Composition Instruction.* Eugene, Ore.: International Council for Computers in Education, 1984.

Sloan, Douglas, ed. *The Computer In Education: A Critical Perspective.* New York: Columbia U., Teachers College Press, 1985.

Tatchell, Judy, and Bill Bennett. *Osborne Guide to Understanding the Micro.* Tulsa, Okla.: Hayes, 1982.

Taylor, Robert P., ed. *The Computer in the School: Tutor, Tool, Tutee.* New York: Columbia U., Teachers College Press, 1980.

Templar, Chris, and Richard Beam. *Biblical Explorations Using LOGO.* Forthcoming.

Terry, Colin, ed. *Using Microcomputers in School.* New York: Nichols, 1984.

Thornburg, David. *Discovering Apple LOGO: An Invitation to the Art and Pattern of Nature.* Reading, Mass.: Addison-Wesley, 1983.

Walker, Decker, and Robert Hess. *Instructional Software, Principles and Perspectives for Design and Use.* Belmont, Calif.: Wadsworth, 1984.

OTHER SOURCES

CHRISTIAN EDUCATION

Christian Computer Users Assoc. Inc.
1145 Alexander, S.E.
Grand Rapids, MI 49507

Church Computer Users Network
P. O. Box 1392
Dallas, TX 75221

Church Computer Users Group
Johnson Bible College
Knoxville, TN 37998

LOGO

The National LOGO Exchange
Box 5341
Charlottesville, VA 22905

Turtle News
Young People's LOGO Association
P. O. Box 855067
Richardson, TX 75085

30

Ruth Beam

Storytelling for Children

- Stories and Storytellers
- Preparing to Be a Storyteller
- Overcoming Fear of the Audience
- Preparing the Story
- Presenting the Story
- Choosing Stories
- Story Interest Guide for Each Age Group
- Adapting the Story
- Structuring Stories
- How to Structure Stories If You Are the Author
- Checklist for Storytelling
- Mining the Bookshelves
  FROM THE BIBLE
  FROM BIBLE-RELATED STORY COLLECTIONS
  FROM SECULAR SOURCES

Children are imaginative. If you ask them, they will tell you what they think is at the end of God's rainbow. Bible stories, your stories, classical tales, role plays, and pantomime will capture their attention and stimulate their insight.

Tomorrow's young citizens are starved for the sound of a grown-up voice

RUTH BEAM, M.A., professor of communications, teaches oral interpretation and English composition at Moody Bible Institute, Chicago, Illinois.

that speaks without tension or haste. Electronic programming and the busy-ness of our life-style are making us terse. Wise is the person who takes time for stories; he or she will bring a sure sense of pleasure and relaxation. Stories have the power to enrich for a lifetime; yet they prepare a child for the ups and downs of reality.

STORIES AND STORYTELLERS

Through Bible stories children learn about the joys *and* faults bundled up in human relationships. Knowledge of God's Word can lead them to increase in the favor of God, man, and even their enemies. The Holy Spirit can activate the Scriptures to accomplish His purposes if we nurture rather than lecture. If we, as concerned adults, communicate these truths, then they, as receptive listen-ers, have a chance of emulating and developing attitudes of kindness and right living. Salvation, honesty, generosity, understanding and the acceptance of others can become a part of all children.

Throughout the Scriptures God used tellers of His story. He inspired Moses to recapture and *write* the events that occurred from Creation to Joshua. He moved a less well-known man—Nathan the prophet—to *tell* David a much shorter narrative. Nathan's well-chosen parable of the rich man who stole the poor man's ewe lamb initiated a delicate yet masterful confrontation. The lowly prophet faced a multi-talented king with a story. David was caught short; his emotional, self-condemning response indicated his conviction of sin—a direct result of God's use of a story.

During Christ's lifetime, crusty Hebrews, Greeks, and Romans were con-fronted with the explosive gentleness of Jesus' philosophy of the turned cheek, the helping hand, and the forgiving word. His probing use of parables, rein-forced by His love, motivated the children, the masses, His disciples, apostles, and all other followers of the Way.

These lives born anew through the living and the written Word were des-tined to transform the history of all succeeding generations. The world has profited from stories of God-motivated heroes ever since.

PREPARING TO BE A STORYTELLER

Storytelling, like any art or sport, requires utmost dedication if the partici-pators or spectators are to be kept interested. However, as Gladys Mary Talbot once observed, "Unlike other arts, all of you may participate in this one, provided you are willing to pay the price—study, work and practice."[1]

Frequently a student of mine will remark that he or she has no special speaking or musical gift. Early in our Christian lives a feeling of hopelessness often develops over not having a "ministry." Yet it astonishes a student or any

1. Gladys Mary Talbot, ed., *Stories I Love to Tell* (Chicago: Moody, 1949), p. 9.

one of us to find that we can speak and repeatedly hold the attention of an audience—not while preaching or making a speech, but while sharing a story!

To become a storyteller, no expensive equipment is necessary. God has built it all in. He has given us a *voice,* and by using our own best voice we may take on the role of narrator. Then we have the option of varying our voice to suggest the dialogue spoken by the characters. We have *facial flexibility* for showing our interpretation of key words. And not the least, God has given us a *body* whereby we may *gesture* and assume various stances which demonstrate to the audience the mood, age, sex and state of health of our characters.

We can bring a story to life without anything in our hands. No construction paper, objects, or figures are needed, just ourselves as God made us, speaking the truth in love. (See 1 Corinthians 13:1, NASB.)

OVERCOMING FEAR OF THE AUDIENCE

My personal formula for feeling at one with the audience came from our pastor, Rev. Christopher Lyons. During a Sunday morning worship service he said, *"It is my hope that each person who comes to our services will leave feeling more enriched than when he walked in."* I thought, "What a worthy aim for a teacher, regardless of the age of the students." His desire for the members of the audience eliminates fear and puts the emphasis where it should be—on the needs of the persons listening.

Present your story as a carefully selected gift to be given away with an outstretched arm. Do not be afraid. Move toward your audience. Eliminate the barrier of your self-consciousness, which is, as Ethel Barrett says, a subtle form of pride.

If discouragement and doubt come, as they surely will, put to use what Lois LeBar said to encourage me as a young graduate student: "Remember, you are the authority on this material. No one to whom you will be speaking will have worked on it as thoroughly as you have." If that does not help as you face your audience, remember the words of the apostle John: "There is no fear in love; but perfect love casts out fear" (1 John 4:18, NASB).

PREPARING THE STORY FOR TELLING

As any performer or musician will acknowledge, much preparation goes into a presentation that looks easy. The same is true of storytelling, but children are the best beginning audience. If you have a date to tell a story, you will appreciate a recipe for learning it—one that has been used often with success, and one for which you have all the ingredients. Let us think of story preparation as seven steps to success.

1. Choose a story you *want* to tell. Read the story to capture the central plot and to meet the main characters.

2. Reread and, if necessary, adapt as you go along. (See Adapting the Story, which follows later in this chapter.) If it is possible, type out the story, double-spaced. If you are the typist, this exercise will acquaint you with the exact words of the story better than anything else.

3. Relax and close your eyes. Visualize the action of the story as though you are seeing a film.

4. Mark the paragraphs which form the introduction, the main events, the climax, and the conclusion. Work toward giving each of these a differing mood and pace.

5. At least *three weeks* before telling the story in public, begin reading it through, *aloud,* each night. Use your own best voice for the narrator's lines; and for the characters, seek to give a hint of their personality, age, and sex by the manner in which you speak. Go through the entire story *without backtracking,* no matter how bad you think you sound.

6. Practice telling the story aloud to an empty room, a tape recorder, a mirror, and a supportive friend. If you can include a number of gestures suitable to the characters and their actions, these will put you and your audience at ease. Move around. Refer to your story script only when you cannot go on.

7. The essence of the story may be learned by sketching each scene in cartoon or stick figure form. In spare moments or while riding in a car or bus, verbalize the sequence of events from the picture script. Look away from the sketches and be able to recall these in order. This is a fail-safe method that will keep you speaking naturally in case you do not remember some of the exact words you intended to say.

Presenting the Story

Whether standing near a center of interest, such as a glistening Christmas tree, or in front of a story coordinated background before a large audience, or sitting in the midst of a discussion group, or while riding on a long trip, or sitting on a bed alongside a child when the lights are low, the well-chosen story will charm its way into the heart of a listener.

In an informal, impromptu, one-to-one situation, you will speak with ease if you visualize mentally the entire story movement as you present it. Make the language your own as each person, place, event, important conversation, and truth comes before your mental vision.

Stories for use in the church should be presented in a more structured manner. Prepare for Sunday school worship services, vacation Bible school, children's church, camp programs, missionary meetings, and open-ended story discussions as outlined in Preparing the Story for Telling.

For little children, use short sentences and simple words. If they are sitting on a story rug, be seated among them so as to maintain eye contact with all.

Whatever the setting or situation, the storyteller needs to be seated one level higher than his audience. Strong, resonant tones emerge with greater ease if the teller stands.

Use dramatic language. Speak loudly enough to be heard easily. Choose words and phrases to add atmosphere to the message. Observe light and shadow; make contrasts evident by raising and lowering your voice. Use the pause to create suspense and surprise, to show the passage of time, and, if need be, to gain or regain attention.

When you are invited to tell stories outside your home and church, seek to use material you have told elsewhere, some time before. You will be able to anticipate the outcome of your story if you give previously prepared and tested material. Also, your poise will be increased. Nothing is worse than fighting first-time fears in front of a large banquet, conference, rally, or retreat audience.

The larger the audience, the larger the gestures needed. Most important, though, the same earnest heart preparation before the Lord is required whether the story is given to one or many. Then when you walk into view, when you look into the faces of your audience, and open your mouth to speak, your inner self shines through; your whole person will speak.

CHOOSING STORIES

Have confidence if you choose a story from a reputable and spirited printed source—it indicates that a compiler, editor, or publication board has assessed its worth. Some stories, however, are *unforgettable* because the author weaves two or more layers of interest-catching emotions into a situation dilemma we recognize. Such is true of Barbara Robinson's *The Best Christmas Pageant Ever*,[2] which introduces six unchurched Herdman children who volunteer for all the major roles in the Christmas program. Heart-warming unorthodoxy and humor begins with line one. Liking such a story puts joy into learning the lines.

If you feel comfortable answering the following questions, the problem of story choice will be solved.

Regarding the story
    Do you *like* the story and have a strong desire to communicate it?
    Do you agree with its content?
    Do you appreciate the style of writing?
    Is it within your scope of ability to tell?
Regarding the audience
    Will the story develop a companionship between you and your audience?
    Will it interest the age group present?

2. Barbara Robinson, *The Best Christmas Pageant Ever* (Wheaton, Ill.: Tyndale, 1982).

Is it suitable for the sex or sexes present? (A rule of thumb: If the boys like it, the girls will also.)

Does it move with enough action, dialogue, and suspense to maintain interest?

Does it tell its own message?

Will it leave a lingering impact?

Regarding the occasion

Does the story fit the season of the year, or can it be adapted to do so?

Does it lend itself to the environment of the occasion?

Can the length be adjusted to meet your needs?

Does it fulfill your aim: to inform? to enrich? to stimulate emotions, imagination? to motivate? to comfort? to admonish? to entertain?

Can it be given to the glory of God?

As the storyteller becomes more adept at presenting stories, he becomes aware that certain subjects capture the attention and blend with the personalities of certain age groups.

The route to gaining this knowledge cannot come alone from words on a page. Table 30.1 and the material in part 2 of this book will help, but the surer way of knowing what children like is to *know children.*

Talk with them. Learn what makes them laugh and cry. Invite them on fun outings; take them to museums, zoos, forest preserves, on bicycle trips—places that interest *them.* Invite the youngsters to eat at your house; find out what their favorite foods are. Help them to make crafts and gifts for others. Visit them in their homes. Listen to their joys and troubles—relationships at school, home, and church. Study Scripture together—verses that shed light on these interests, needs, and problems. Pray with them. Somewhere in the midst of knowing and loving them, there will be opportunities to tell these boys and girls stories that fit!

TABLE 30.1

STORY INTEREST GUIDE FOR EACH AGE GROUP

AGE GROUP	STORY CHARACTERISTICS	SUGGESTED	
		BIBLE STORIES OR BOOKS	SECULAR STORIES OR BOOKS
NURSERY 0-3 years	(Years) 0 (Story readiness) singing, fingerplays, sentence-length conversational stories	Jesus blessing the children	Finger and toe plays

	1 Pictures of the familiar; "running" narratives by mother	Baby Jesus Baby Moses	Nursery rhymes
	2 Conversations about experiences: stars, thunder, dark, flowers	Infant Samuel	"Three Bears"
	3 Answering questions with verbal and written stories; some repetition in vocabulary	Little Lost Lamb	"Three Pigs" "Three Billy Goats Gruff"
KINDERGARTEN 4-5 years	Rhythm, rhyme, and repetition Familiar things and places: pets, toys, concrete objects; mechanized hero Concrete language; simple plot; few characters Animals—their names and calls	Creation Noah's ark Boy Samuel Boy Jesus Good Shepherd Jesus blessing the children *The Bible in Pictures for Little Eyes*	"Gingerbread Boy" "Little Engine That Could" "Peter Rabbit" "Make Way for Ducklings"
PRIMARY 6-8 years	Fact, fairy tales, folk, and fantasy Bible miracles; "helping" situations One child in one foreign country Animals—their homes and habits	Crossing Red Sea Healing of Naaman Wedding of Cana Feeding of 5,000 Rescue of Peter	"Jack and the Beanstalk" "Rumpelstiltskin" "Sleeping Beauty" "Little Match Girl" *The Lion, the Witch, and the Wardrobe* Winnie-the-Pooh stories
JUNIOR 9-11 years	Heroism: action, adventure, danger, daring Real people in physical conquest Chronology, biography, geography Animals—care and breeding	Wilderness wanderings Tabernacle Life of David, Daniel, Samson Paul's journeys	*Tom Sawyer* *Robinson Crusoe* *Heidi* *Little Women* *Misty of Chincoteague* *Rascal*

ADAPTING THE STORY

Oh, the disappointment of finding a story one likes, only to discover that some parts within it will not fit the storyteller's purpose!

Since most stories are written to be read, stories frequently need adapting and can be changed without harming the original narrative. Some descriptive details, important to the silent reader, may be portrayed by the storyteller's tone of voice, facial expression, or gestures. Therefore, these actual words may be eliminated.

Adaptation may also include some *additions* to the story. Care should be taken to preserve the total effect desired by the author, and in no case should the original or adapted story be reproduced in printed form without permission in writing from the publisher or author.

PARTS OF A STORY THAT FREQUENTLY NEED ADAPTING

Title. If it conveys ambiguous meaning, such as "United Nation," then it may need to be revised as well as shifted from the past tense. Try "Uniting a Nation."

Length. Tales written to be read frequently need to be shortened.

Word choice. Obscure words such as *damsel, laconic,* and *atmospheric filament* should be changed and suitable synonyms put in their place.

Phrasing. If it is old-fashioned or involved, update and simplify it. "Lay this to his offence" should be changed to, "Blame him." Tedious sentences that run on for six lines need to be shortened.

Names. Some stories, especially the old folktales, include characters who have no names. If more than one character is involved and names would enliven the story as well as clarify who is speaking, add appropriate names.

Number of characters. In "The Gingerbread Boy," a farmer and a thresher appear. Since few children today understand the work of a thresher, this character can be eliminated without damaging the plot.

Number of events. In a retelling of *Pilgrim's Progress* some happenings in Interpreter's house would be beyond the knowledge of young children because they are highly symbolic. Rather than trying at great length to explain these, eliminate them.

Sequence of events. For young children, flashbacks should be eliminated and the story told in simple, chronological order.

Amounts of narration. Usually there is too much in any given story. Eliminate lengthy descriptions, remove dialogue tags ("he said"), and delete references to minor incidents which do not advance the plot.

Amount of dialogue. In most cases, increase this. An author may write, "The woman screamed," but as Charles Dickens advised, "Don't say the woman screamed; bring her in and let her scream."

Person in which the story is told. If a long story is told in the first person, consider your ability to maintain the voice characterization of the speaker, since it is difficult to interpret paragraph after paragraph in a voice different from your own.

Placement of the moral. Weave in the truth being taught throughout the story. Make the truth come out of the characters' mouths.

Age level of the story. To raise it, remove the words such as *little, Daddy, Mommie,* and so on. To lower it, simplify the vocabulary and sentence structure, providing, of course, the subject matter is suitable.

Pace. Enliven the movement of the story by exchanging tired nouns, adjectives, and verbs which have little or no action in them. Use kinetic words which *run* and *jump,* and *march* and *fight.* The moods are intensified by kinesthetic words which demonstrate reactions and attitudes. Add such words as *breathless, nervously, casually,* and *noisily.*

Spiritual truth. Often a secular book contains a gripping story of a character, such as Florence Nightingale or Madame Chiang Kai-shek. Since both of these women were called of God and used by Him, add specific information to portray this.

Season. When a long story, such as "Dopshun in Search of a Mother," is prepared, seek to change its seasonal emphasis by changing the Sunday school promotion program in the story to the type of program that fits the current event or season. Thereby the story may be used (with a new audience) more than once a year.

STRUCTURING STORIES

Whether you are *writing* your own story, *retelling* a Bible story, *preparing* a story already written, or *condensing* a booklength story, it is of considerable value to observe its four major parts, namely, the introduction, body, climax, and conclusion.

In the *introduction,* the teller should set the stage and plunge into the action immediately. He should tell who is there, establish where and when the action is taking place, and give a *hint* of what is about to happen. He should reveal a seed of the conflict or suspense to come. As Laura Emerson advises, *"Begin at the latest possible moment* as close to the conclusion as possible, rather then leisurely tuning up as an orchestra before a concert."[3] Arouse an emotion quickly. The two introductions which follow are contrasts in the extreme, but Emerson makes a point when she contrasts them side by side.

> Once we decided to have a picnic so Uncle Jack and Aunt Sue got out the old Ford. I like a Chevrolet much better. Then they found they had a flat tire. I wanted to tell you

---

3. Laura S. Emerson, *Storytelling* (Grand Rapids: Zondervan, 1959), p. 47.

about the lunch. I like hamburgers, but they all wanted wieners. Well, after we were all ready to start, et cetera.

I was eating a sandwich by the lake when I heard Jim call, "Help, help!"[4]

The *body* develops the "what" of the story; it relates the ups and downs of the hero. The hero generally starts out on top, but before long, an antagonist muddles the tempo of his life. Or in some cases, the conflict may be in the form of a disaster, a tedious trial, or temptation to violate right. The hero struggles against the conflict; suspense should build up and increase until the final clash or choice of action occurs. Mounting action forces opposition between good and evil. The dialogue, actions, and reactions of the characters should demonstrate the truths to be learned. The appeal and winsomeness of the love of God should operate powerfully in circumstances and lives.

The *climax* marks the pinnacle of action and suddenly reveals the "why" of the story, that is, its reason for existing. The plot generally turns in an unexpected manner; the true character of the hero and antagonist should emerge in the final outcome. To be of positive benefit in teaching biblical truth, the hero needs to *struggle* with right and wrong. His final choice should reveal what is exemplary. His life should be a challenge, not a truce.

The *conclusion* of the story should be short, account for all major characters, tie all ends together. No moralizing should need to be included. In young children's stories, the ending should be satisfying; the truth should be palatable, understandable. Good should win out and evil be punished, and God should have His rightful place of glory.

The following study tells how to construct an effective story.

How to Structure Stories If You Are the Author

INTRODUCTION

Introduce place, characters, time, mood, and pace.

Tell who, when, where, and give a hint of what or a promise of future action or problem.

Get attention and arouse emotion and suspense as soon as possible—e.g., love, compassion, dislike.

Get the story off the ground and moving.

Set the scene by introducing hero and antagonist with a *seed* of trouble to follow.

4. Ibid.

BODY

Develop the "what."

Hold attention with action and suspense.

Relate a series of incidents revealing project or difficulty, seeming fulfillment, touch of humor, the upset, near tragedy—clash on clash—leading to final clash between hero and problem (antagonist, adverse conditions in nature, conflict or handicap, error in judgment).

Weave in true teaching throughout body, especially through dialogue.

Include hazards to be overcome, choices to be made.

CLIMAX

Reach highest point of interest and suspense in story.

Require final choice to be made.

Show turn of plot.

Reveal characters' true selves by their conversations, actions, and reactions.

Determine the way the story will go.

Explain mystery.

Reveal kernel of truth, purpose for which story was written.

CONCLUSION

Account for all major characters.

Tie up all ends.

Fulfill all promises.

Be brief, and for young children, make it satisfying.

If possible, reiterate truth, but do not add a moral.

Depending on the story and audience, either fully answer question raised in the beginning or leave it open-ended as a stimulus for discussion.

CHECKLIST FOR EFFECTIVE STORYTELLING

The storyteller succeeds best when the audience focuses its attention on the message, not on the messenger. The audience should not see the proverbial wheels go round; the mechanics should be hidden, but the vehicle should proceed smoothly.

Once the storyteller experiences the feeling of having presented a story as a carefully prepared gift, tied up with trimmings and given with love, no other approach to an audience will seem adequate. To glorify God and have an outward expression of ease that comes from within, consider the following guidelines:

1. Ask God to give you natural poise; be at one with Him.
2. *Know* your story; *live* your story.

3. Know and *love* your audience.
4. Stand erect before your audience in comfortable shoes. Avoid bending forward, leaning into the audience: it conveys a "talking down" impression.
5. *See* the scene you are setting. Do not allow your voice to say one thing and your body and face to say another.
6. Vary voice level, rate of speech, age level, personality, and sex of each character being interpreted.
7. Cultivate a pleasing, resonant voice.
8. Speak loudly enough to be heard by all, including the hard-of-hearing.
9. Avoid slang, grammatical errors, and mispronunciations.
10. Maintain gracious eye contact with all in your audience.
11. Use cultured, yet vivacious gestures.
12. Avoid nervous gestures, clasped hands, rocking backward and forward, and scraping feet.
13. Know how and when to vary narration speed, and introduce dialogue with a fast attack.
14. Know attention span of various age groups and audience types.
15. Know when to quit.
16. Take training in speech and gestures in an oral interpretation or storytelling class.
17. *Pray* over your stories. Let words live on your tongue for God's glory.

MINING THE BOOKSHELVES

When a storyteller goes prospecting for tales, he will find no shortage. He may select Bible, Bible-related, and secular stories from the bookshelves of the past and present. The following is a representative list of literary nuggets.

FROM THE BIBLE

Allegory: The trees look for a king, Judges 9:8-15
Animal: Creation; Noah, his ark and animals
Biography: Patriarchs, Samuel, Saul, David, Jesus, Paul
Character building: Joseph, Ruth, Daniel, Esther, Peter, Paul, and Timothy
Chronology, geography, history: Abraham's journeys; wilderness wanderings; Christ's birth, life, death, and resurrection; Paul's missionary journeys
Miracles: Creation; Elijah on Mount Carmel; Jonah and the big fish; birth of Jesus; water into wine; raising of Lazarus
Missionary: Jonah; Christ's earthly ministry to men; Paul's journeys
Parables: The sower; the prodigal son; the lost coin; the good Samaritan
Psalmists' songs: The shepherd, Psalm 23; the King of glory, Psalm 24; missionary song, Psalm 67; David's battle song, Psalm 144; David's hymn of praise, Psalm 145. (These are suitable for verse choirs, role playing, and pantomime.)

Salvation: Zacchaeus; woman at the well; Philippian jailer; Ethiopian eunuch
Symbolism: Tabernacle; Levitical offerings

FROM BIBLE-RELATED STORY COLLECTIONS

Allegory:
  Pilgrim's Progress, John Bunyan
  The Chronicles of Narnia, C. S. Lewis
Biography:
  "Handel's Messiah"*5
  "Honest Abe"†
Doctrine:
  "How Shall We Know Him?"†
  "Thirty Pieces of Silver"*
Life choices:
  "All This I Did for Thee"†
  "The Seventeen Beggars"†
Missionary:
  "A Live-the-Jesus-Book Girl"*
  "Now's Your Chance, Lord"*
Salvation:
  "All This I Did for Thee"†
  "How Shall We Know Him?"†
  "The Storm"†
  "Tears of the Sea"†
Special Days:
  "The Maid of Emmaus" (Easter)†
  "Dopshun in Search of a Mother" (Mother's Day)†
  "Thanksgivin' Ann" (Thanksgiving)†
  "Be Thou Faithful" (Christmas)†
  "The Browns' Christmas" (Christmas)‡
Steadfastness:
  "Lions in the Way"*
Witnessing:
  "Catarina's Ten Fingers"*

FROM SECULAR SOURCES

Animal:
  Winnie-the-Pooh, A. A. Milne

5. This story and the stories below that are marked with an asterisk(*) can be found in *40 Stories for You to Tell,* compiled by Gladys Mary Talbot. The stories marked with a single dagger(†) can be found in *Stories I Love to Tell,* compiled by Gladys Mary Talbot; the story marked with a double dagger(‡) can be found in *My Favorite Christmas Stories,* by Theresa Worman.

The Wind in the Willows, Kenneth Grahame
Charlotte's Web, E. B. White
Misty of Chincoteague, Marguerite Henry
Rascal, Sterling North
Biography:
   Abraham Lincoln, Ingri and Edgar Parin d'Aulaire
   The Story of George Washington Carver, Arna Bontemps
Character building:
   The Adventures of Pinocchio, C. Collodi (pseudonym for Carlo Lorenzini)
   The Plain Princess, Phyllis McGinley
   The Door in the Wall, Marguerite de Angeli
Epic:
   The Iliad and the Odyssey of Homer, retold, Alfred John Church
Fable:
   Aesop's Fables, retold by Anne Terry White; illustrated by Helen Siegl
Fairy tale:
   The Little Match Girl and *The Ugly Duckling,* Hans Christian Andersen
Fantasy:
   The Secret Garden, Frances Hodgson Burnett
   The Chronicles of Narnia, C. S. Lewis
Fiction:
   Heidi, Johanna Spyri
Folk:
   Uncle Remus Tales, Joel Chandler Harris
Historical fiction:
   Caddie Woodlawn, Carol Ryrie Brink
   The Courage of Sarah Noble, Alice Dalgliesh
   The Long Winter, Laura Ingalls Wilder
Humor:
   Madeline's Rescue, Ludwig Bemelmans
   Alexander and the Terrible, Horrible, No Good Very Bad Day, Judith
      Viorst
Mechanized Hero:
   The Little Engine That Could, Watty Piper (retold from *The Pony
      Engine,* Mabel C. Bragg)
   Mike Mulligan and His Steam Shovel, Virginia Burton
Nature:
   Time of Wonder, Robert McCloskey
   The Snowy Day, Ezra Jack Keats
Social:
   Blue Willow, Doris Gates
   The Hundred Dresses, Eleanor Estes
   . . . And Now Miguel, Joseph Krumgold

Space:
   Miss Pickerell Goes to Mars, Ellen MacGregor
   A Wrinkle in Time, Madeleine L'Engle

For additional titles see *Honey for a Child's Heart* by Gladys M. Hunt, and Berta Parrish's article, "Escape from the Summer Blahs."[6] Hunt's book is written from the evangelical Christian perspective and gives helpful insights concerning the use of valuable books with children. Her book contains fifty-eight pages of bibliography, including a section on "Helping Pre-schoolers Through Third Graders Grow as Christians," and "Helping Third Through Sixth Graders Grow as Christians" (pp. 171-76).

Also, I have found it helpful to write for current catalogs from the evangelical press. A description of their latest publications will help you to purchase new stories and books which may not be stocked by the bookstores you use. A short, representative list follows.

Abingdon Press, 201 Eighth Avenue South, Box 801, Nashville, TN 37202.
Broadman Press, 127 Ninth Avenue North, Nashville, TN 37234
David C. Cook Publishing Company, 850 North Grove, Elgin, IL 60120
Moody Press, 2101 West Howard Street, Chicago, IL 60645
Gospel Light, 2300 Knoll Drive, Ventura, CA 93003
Scripture Press, Box 1825, Wheaton, IL 60187

SUMMARY

Concerning you. Are you frightened? Suggestion: In the moments before beginning your story, take a deep breath, then swallow four times before taking a new breath. The counter tension created in your throat and breathing apparatus acts to dissipate nervousness.

Concerning your story. We are becoming bored with the plastic, packaged, and the processed. Formula stories from educational packets seem bland—like ready-to-eat dinners. We welcome the return of the green grocer, Laura Ashley prints, and country kitchens; let us also invite back stories which bear the mark of our own preparation and wear our own voiceprint.

Concerning the children. We want *to be there* to satisfy hunger as the Lord Jesus did when he offered the bread of life in John 6. We want the children to *taste and see, seek and find* the LORD whose Word is life-changing and memorable.

FOR FURTHER READING

Allstrom, Elizabeth. *Let's Play a Story.* New York: Friendship, 1957.
———. *You Can Teach Creatively.* Nashville: Abingdon, 1970.

6. Berta Parrish, "Escape from the Summer Blahs." *Moody Monthly,* July-August 1985, pp. 18-20.

Arbuthnot, May Hill. *Children and Books.* 3d ed. Glenview, Ill.: Scott, Foresman, 1964.

———. *Children's Reading in the Home.* Glenview, Ill.: Scott, Foresman, 1969.

Barrett. Ethel. *Storytelling, It's Easy.* Grand Rapids: Zondervan, 1960.

Doyle, Brian, ed. *The Who's Who of Children's Literature.* New York: Schocken, 1971.

Duff, Annis. *Bequest of Wings.* New York: Viking, 1944.

Griggs, Patricia. *Using Storytelling in Christian Education.* Nashville: Abingdon, 1981.

Hunt, Gladys M. *Honey for a Child's Heart.* Grand Rapids: Zondervan, 1978.

Larrick, Nancy. *A Parent's Guide to Children's Reading.* Garden City, N.Y.: Doubleday, 1975.

Lee, Charlotte I., and Timothy Gura. *Oral Interpretation.* 6th ed. Boston: Houghton Mifflin, 1982.

Sawyer, Ruth. *The Way of the Storyteller.* New York: Penguin, 1977.

Tooze, Ruth. *Storytelling.* Englewood Cliffs, N.J.: Prentice-Hall, 1959.

Trent, Robbie. *Your Child and God.* Rev. ed. New York: Harper & Row, 1952.

Ward, Winifred. *Stories* to *Dramatize.* Anchorage, Ky.: Children's Theater, 1952.

White, William. *Speaking in Stories.* Minneapolis: Augsburg, 1982.

Worman, Theresa, *My Favorite Christmas Stories.* Chicago: Moody, 1965.

31

Elsiebeth McDaniel

Story Playing with Children

- Why Story Play Is Effective
- What Is Achieved Through Story Play?
- Finger Plays and Action Rhymes
- Role Play
- Creative Drama
- Puppetry

Story playing is a method of teaching frequently overlooked. There is little argument about the use of visuals, questions, discussion, and projects, but many teachers find it difficult to see values in relating "let's pretend" to Christian education. However, pretending is part of child growth. The young child pretends about many things: he is a policeman, daddy, mother, truck driver, nurse, doctor, astronaut, and many other roles.

Young children do not have to be taught to pretend. They engage in it spontaneously as a way to learn. If pretending, or "playing out," situations and relationships is a natural and effective way to learn, why eliminate this method in our teaching? "Let's pretend" can be refined and adapted to meet the needs of various age groups, including adults.

ELSIEBETH McDANIEL, M.A., is director, early childhood publications, at Scripture Press Publications, Inc., Wheaton, Illinois.

WHY STORY PLAY IS EFFECTIVE

When has learning really taken place? "The process of learning, it is held, does not reach its consummation until reasoning has issued forth in creative expression."[1] Surely playing out the story may often be the creative expression necessary to complete the process of learning. This is especially true if the story play originates with the students' request. When children can dramatize a story in simple form, they more readily learn the story. If fifth graders can develop a skit to show application of Bible truth, they have understood the principles the teacher hoped to communicate.

Story playing may take one of several forms—skits, puppet plays, role playing, fingerplays, or simple dramatization. In this chapter, we are not dealing with practiced dramatization. Practiced plays, even though they may be written by children, are not a spontaneous form of "let's pretend." They are usually performed to entertain. Some students will enjoy being in a play, but the work of memorization, details of costuming, and the continuing rehearsals deprive children of the joy found in simple drama. This chapter is concerned with the story playing that is enjoyed as a more or less spontaneous response by the learners themselves—not a public production.

The main purpose of story play is to help a child "get inside the skin" of another person. Through taking a part—becoming another person—a child learns how a particular person felt in a specific situation and why he reacted in a certain way. Story playing is more valuable for its activation of emotion than its influence on factual recall.

Helping children empathize seems more important than ever before. Currently, there are desensitizing factors in every child's experience. Along with the advantages of TV come disadvantages. Television seems to provide an "instant mix" of emotions—violence, death, and individual accomplishment. Many scenes lack reality, but they are presented as reality. Constant exposure to this type of program can endanger the emotional health of a child: he learns not to feel.

A second factor dulling emotional reaction is the element of change. In the last few decades, change has occurred so frequently, rapidly, and universally that people seem to have learned to react unemotionally. Our present culture seems to downplay emotional response.

However, the Bible makes it clear that man is an emotional creature. Any concordance lists many references for such emotions as anger, love, joy, covetousness, envy, fear, sadness, and jealousy. People respond emotionally in varying degrees. Educators recognize that affective learning occurs when emotions are stirred. The whole subject of story play is associated with emotions—feeling and responding.

1. Cornelius Jaarsma, *Human Development, Learning and Teaching* (Grand Rapids: Eerdmans, 1961), p. 212.

Why do some teachers hesitate to use story play in any form? Some teachers think story play is entertainment only. Still others believe that telling is teaching and story play is a waste of time. And then there are some authoritarian teachers who feel insecure in a situation where children take the lead. This type of teacher finds it difficult to establish a free, open relationship with students to help them dramatize a story or event in a simple way. The authoritarian teacher is afraid of losing control of his class. At the bottom of his fear is a lack of trust in his students and in himself. A teacher who lives with and relates to children easily needs have no fear about introducing some form of story play. True, if students are not accustomed to this teaching method, it may take more than one attempt to provide a satisfactory learning experience. In time, however, the children will participate freely and prove to a doubting teacher that learning is taking place.

Books are available on creative drama, puppetry, role playing, fingerplays, and action rhymes, but they will be useless unless a teacher understands the value of this teaching method. It is more important for a teacher to "want-to" than to know all details of the "how-to."

> Few teachers believe that creativity has no place in the Sunday school, but many teachers hesitate to put it to work for them. Some Christians think that creativity is a gift God has given only to the few. God has given some measure of creativity to every individual. However, if the gift is neglected, it withers and may disappear. Creativity is combining something old with something new to produce something different. It is thinking and learning in fresh, new ways.[2]

Story play may be a fresh, new way—an open door to many teachers.

The forms of story play discussed in this chapter include fingerplays and action rhymes, role playing, simple dramatizations, and puppetry. Successful use of these types of story play demands enthusiasm—belief in what you are doing, some know-how, and a respect and love for the students.

WHAT IS ACHIEVED THROUGH STORY PLAY?

There are several advantages to this method of teaching. Remember, a teacher must see the advantages of a method and have the "want-to" before he is interested in the "how-to."

1. Story play makes an event seem more real. Each involved child thinks and feels as someone in the story. He may become a person who formerly existed only as a name on a page.

2. Children may be more honest when they are not revealing themselves.

2. Elsiebeth McDaniel and Lawrence O. Richards, *You and Children* (Chicago: Moody, 1973), p. 88.

When children are acting out endings to a problem situation, for example, they will probably suggest real action, not merely answers acceptable to a teacher.

3. Teachers benefit because they have an opportunity to know the children in a new way. They see the students' strengths and weaknesses as they show how they feel about situations. There are other factors, of course. A child may reveal selfishness and be insensitive to others. Perhaps another child, usually shy and self-conscious, will develop self-confidence through pretending to be someone else.

4. Ideas, feelings, and concepts of the story become a part of the child. It is good to talk about being kind, for example, but for a student to feel the part of a child who is excluded from the group helps him understand loneliness. Then he values being part of the group and may be interested in helping other children enjoy a sense of belonging.

5. Bible stories become real: they come alive. Children get a feel for characters of long ago.

6. Playing a story helps children think of others, reach out to other people, and turn away from their self-centeredness.

7. Story play, role play particularly, gives the learner an inside view of another person. This experience helps a child respect others and teaches him sensitivity in personal relationships. It helps students by providing insights few other methods can offer.

Perhaps this quotation best sums up the value of story play:

> The story the child plays, like the picture he paints, the figure he fashions from clay, the story he writes, is a way of enjoying again and of sharing with another something that is important to him. In it he is forever adding more to himself, finding out more about himself, entering into new sets of relationships with others and learning from them. The story lived by acting stays long in his life. No one knows the limit of its teaching.[3]

FINGERPLAYS AND ACTION RHYMES

Fingerplays and action rhymes are not a new method of teaching, but an old and effective technique. Often, parents use this type of teaching in "Pat-a-cake, pat-a-cake," or "How big is baby?" Even a young baby responds happily to these words and rhythms. Public school teachers and Christian educators can also utilize this successful method to help young children pretend both actions and characterizations through fingerplay.

Fingerplays are used to relax children, to impress a story, to introduce a story, to teach rhythm, and sometimes to quiet children after an exciting activity. Both action rhymes and fingerplays may be used with children from babyhood through the age of six or seven. Of course, the older children may be

3. Elizabeth Allstrom, *You Can Teach Creatively* (Nashville: Abingdon, 1970), p. 63.

freer to suggest their own actions or even music for the words. Preschoolers, on the other hand, will enjoy doing the actions, but may not memorize the words. Some children, after hearing the rhyme a number of times, may enjoy repeating parts of it with the teacher.

The teacher is most concerned, however, with the children's participation in the actions. Even a shy or self-conscious child may lose himself in this type of group activity. And when a child is doing, he is learning! Fingerplays and action rhymes become familiar friends as children act out the same ones again and again.

Young children's muscles need action! Often the joy of moving head, arms, trunk, legs, and fingers is more important than the words. Because feeling the words and moving with them is important, it is not necessary for all children to make the same motions. Some children may demonstrate the round sun by holding their arms over their heads to make a circle. But other children will be happy making a small sun with fingers held in front of them. Encourage large muscle movements, but give each child an opportunity to gain satisfaction through participation.

Here is a typical action rhyme used with preschoolers.[4]

The city wall was very high.
(Show great height by standing on tiptoe, arms reaching high.)
The gates were shut up tight.
(Interlace fingers of hands to form a tight gate.)
But God would take His people in.
They would not need to fight.
March, march, march, march,
(March around room or in place.)
Their feet went tramping round.
The trumpets blew.
(Blow on pretend trumpet.)
The people marched.
(March around the room or in place.)
There was no other sound.
Obeying God, they marched and marched.
(March around the room or in place.)
For seven days, around the wall.
Then they shouted loud.
(Pause and let children shout.)
Oh, what a shout!
Crash! Bang!
(Clap hands.)
The walls did fall!
(Quickly stoop to floor.)

4. © 1973, Scripture Press Publications, Inc. World rights reserved. Used by permission.

To use fingerplays, the teacher must tell the story, sing the song, or repeat the rhyme—whatever form the story play takes, demonstrating the appropriate gestures and facial expressions. The teacher should thoroughly learn the words and actions, because this teaching method cannot be effective if he is tied to a book. A teacher must make the fingerplay so much a part of him that he can use it spontaneously. Then fingerplay becomes a vehicle for new ideas, attitudes, and appreciations.

Some teachers may wish to use finger puppets to introduce or review a fingerplay, adding a new aspect. This is an interesting approach, but should be used sparingly. A teacher will soon discover that long fingerplays are for him to recite or tell, but they are too long for the children to learn. He must also remember that young children cannot imitate him perfectly, and he must be willing to accept their performance.

In using fingerplays, choose plays and rhythms for one unit of study. A fingerplay may tell the story of a character in an individual lesson, but its use is limited. A fingerplay about a Bible character, for example, can best be used in teaching the lesson. Or it may be used for review. However, fingerplays that fit the theme and purpose of the unit can be used again and again.

Many books of fingerplays and action rhymes are available. However, do not overlook the opportunity to use recorded action rhymes—also available from some publishers. Records and commercial or homemade cassettes add other dimensions to teaching—learning through music.

Role Play

In role playing, children assume the parts of other persons: they play a role. However, the play is not rehearsed, and it is not meant to entertain. Role play usually presents a problem situation before it has been developed to the point of solution. The children who assume the roles in the situation show what they would have done—how they would have reacted to an incident or situation. Because Christianity deals with personal relationships, role play serves effectively in teaching biblical principles about attitudes.

Unlike some teaching methods, a novice should not decide, "Today we'll try role play." The teacher using this method should understand the method and how to use it before trying it in a class situation. Role playing is used by some psychologists and psychiatrists, but no teacher should attempt to use role playing to solve psychological problems! Role playing in the classroom must be limited to typical everyday experiences of the boys and girls involved.

Before using role play, a teacher should try to learn as much about it as possible. He should read; observe role playing in a classroom; and, if possible, see a film about it and discuss the method with other teachers. Then he may be ready to try it. As a teacher works with role playing, he will develop insight into the possibilities of this method.

The teacher of second graders has decided to try role playing. She has also decided to use it to solve home problems. She says, "There is trouble in the Smith home. Bobby and Betty want different TV programs. What do you think happens?" Then after a few volunteers have suggested what might take place, the teacher may say, "Would you like to show us what you think happened?" The teacher should choose children who have been quick to volunteer, because these children have sensed some identification with Bobby and Betty. The teacher repeats the situation so that all will understand.

"Now Ronnie and Janet, show us what you think took place. How did Bobby and Betty solve their problem?" After these children demonstrate their solution, the teacher may call on other volunteers. Perhaps some child will want to add a mother or father to the scene. The enactment may be repeated several times with different volunteers. The teacher will stop the action whenever players have developed a solution, have reached the end of their idea, or the teacher wants to add more information to the problem.

At the end of the role play, or after each enactment, the teacher should lead discussion about the solution. However, the teacher is always very careful never to suggest that there is only one solution. If this happens, the children will slant any future role playing toward seeking the teacher's approval. The teacher must guide through evaluation toward the right solution. Or he may file various solutions for future reference, attempting to explain how they do or do not line up with Bible principles. If Ronnie suggests that Bobby gets his choice of TV because a parent intervenes after Betty hits him, this is not a Christian solution. However, the teacher must help the children reach this decision. He must not tell them what they should feel or think.

A beginning teacher may wish to use pantomime as an easy way to lead up to role play. Pantomime, acting out without words, can be introduced as a game. Play out situations that the children experience, asking, "What do you do before coming to Sunday school? before school? at bedtime? Sunday afternoon?" Even young children can enter into this type of role playing. However, problem solving or using several roles may be more effective with children in third grade and beyond. Role playing rewards the teacher with an opportunity to see problem-solving in action. As a result, children usually become more considerate of one another.

A teacher who wants to study this method can find a chapter on role play in many texts. The material in this chapter explains the method and lists some advantages. More information will be needed to use the method successfully. However, a sequence is given here to explain what may be necessary in a good role-playing of an unfinished story.[5]

5. Hildred Nichols and Lois Williams, *Learning About Role-Playing for Children and Teachers* (Washington, D.C.: Association for Christian Education, 1960), pp. 22-23.

1. Explain the purpose: to get ideas for endings to a story.
2. Read structured, open-end story, dramatically.
3. Define roles.
4. Choose "characters" from those who have identified with roles.
5. Set the stage: "This is the living room," etc.
6. Sensitize the audience and prepare them for intelligent and related observation.
7. Begin the enactment.
8. "Cut" at the proper time.
9. Repeat the enactments as interest and time permit.
10. Lead discussion and evaluation by the group.

CREATIVE DRAMA

Dramatization may take several forms. Each form becomes more refined as the age of the group increases.

Pantomime is a demonstration, or acting, without words. All children enjoy it. They may pantomime an action, the end of a story, a Bible verse, or a song. Sometimes pantomime is used to show how a person feels as a reaction to music, Bible truth, or a story. Simple pantomiming can be done by fours and fives, but older children will want more involved pantomimes. Perhaps they will want more characters, a longer episode, or more practice before presenting the pantomime.

Posing pictures is a favorite activity with young children. The teacher may display a biblical or modern picture and then suggest that volunteers take the same positions as the pictured characters. This is an easy way to help young children feel the part of another person. When older children pose pictures, they will want costumes and suitable scenery. Picture-posing is a spontaneous activity with young children, and they will learn from it. Older children, too intent on details, may develop skills only and lose the learning value of acting out an event or situation. They will see the performance, not sense the feelings.

Tableaux are very similar to picture posing except that the teacher uses the children's original ideas of how to demonstrate a scene, event, or situation. The children are not trying to imitate or duplicate an illustration, they are showing how they think it might have been. Because a tableau is a "still" picture, older children may perform better than younger children. Children in grades three through six will want scenery, costumes, and possibly even music. When this form of dramatization concentrates on performance instead of feeling, some of the learning value may become secondary to development of skills and poise. The children may have learned how to perform without realizing how they felt.

Simple dramatization is a favorite activity with children of all ages because they are involved. The purpose of dramatizing or playing out a story is not to present a finished play, but to help children feel the parts they take.

Very young children, under school age, enjoy dramatizing events in which all children can play the main character. A group of children may all be Jacob taking his long journey, lying down to sleep, seeing the angel vision, and awaking to set up a memorial stone. They will all enjoy placing the baby Moses in his basket and then being Miriam, standing guard. However, there are some stories that require more than the main character. When playing crossing the Red Sea, one child may be Moses and the others the group of people following him. The story may be replayed with a new Moses. The crowning of Josiah is another story requiring a main character and a crowd of people. The teacher should follow the children's desires in deciding to assign parts or ask all children to be the main character.

No child should ever be allowed to play the part of the Lord Jesus. By asking an adult to read or speak Christ's words, we maintain the attitude that Jesus, the Son of God, was not a mere man. Since no one can adequately take His part, the teacher will say His words and be sure the children understand the teacher is not assuming His role.

Not all stories can or should be dramatized. Often the children are the best judges of the dramatic possibilities of a story. They seem to sense that good dramatization requires action and vivid dialogue. The characters must be real people. The story to be dramatized should have an emotional appeal and a climax. Children of school age can do good characterizations, and they will be interested in choosing parts. They may want to improvise scenery and costumes. However, the teacher must guide so that the spontaneity of original drama is not lost through a struggle to present a finished play. The important factor is the children's involvement in pretending to be another person. The children should have freedom in becoming those other persons; their speech and actions should be their own. A teacher may be tempted to write dialogue or define action, but this does not help children become the characters they have chosen to represent.

> Today's way—learning through informal dramatics—begins *not* when the teacher expresses preconceived notions about what the children are to do, but when the children themselves have an experience which so captures their attention, so sparks their imaginations, that they want, by means of words and actions, to relive the experience themselves.[6]

Children will not reproduce the event exactly as it happened. A teacher should not expect them to because the children are imagining, pretending, and feeling the event as they understand it. Perhaps no two groups of children would present the same enactment. However, the purpose of the acting is to give children the feeling of being another character and acting as they believe he would have acted.

6. Allstrom, p. 48.

What steps should be taken in dramatizing a story? First, the children should not enter into dramatization at the command of a teacher. They should follow the teacher's lead enthusiastically, if they are interested. If they have had previous good experiences with drama, the children may suggest dramatization after hearing a story. If the children seem ready to dramatize a story, the story should be reviewed. In reviewing the story, the children should notice the sequence of events, the people involved, what they did and said, and how they felt. Next, the group must decide who will play each part. If more than one child wants the same part, the teacher may suggest acting out the story more than once, allowing all interested students an opportunity to play the part.

The story should be played out without tedious rehearsals. And then the dramatization should be evaluated. Sometimes the evaluation will be on the performance itself, but at other times, depending on the teacher's reason for using the method, questions may center on how the characters felt, why they acted as they did, and the results of their actions. Questions to guide the evaluation are more helpful than a teacher's critique.

PUPPETRY

Children of all ages enjoy puppets! Puppets help children become familiar with the Bible stories and their application to modern life. Timid children are encouraged to participate because they may remain hidden behind a puppet screen, or they forget themselves in the fun of working a puppet. Aggressive children learn to share and participate as they join in presenting a puppet play. All puppeteers can release their feelings through the action of the puppets. Preschoolers are easily satisfied with finger or glove puppets, children in primary grades enjoy hand puppets, and older children will want to make their own puppets and write scripts.

There are several types of puppets. This chapter describes them briefly, but books on the subject, listed at the end of the chapter, give details of construction and manipulation. The size of puppet must be related to the size of the audience. Finger puppets, for example, should be used with no more than ten or twelve children—a small enough group so everyone can see the puppets. The type of puppet should usually be determined by the teacher. Certainly he is the one to decide whether making puppets is a justifiable activity to include in the curriculum. Making puppets, designing scenery, and writing scripts may need to be done outside of class.

Puppets need not always represent people. They may be talking animals or talking trees, articles of clothing or even furniture that speaks. The children's sense of "let's pretend" may lead to the creation of almost any character.

The puppet production may be done very simply. Finger, glove, hand puppets, paper-bag, and sock puppets may all be used with or without a screen. (See Figure 31:1, Types of Puppets, for drawings of various kinds of puppets.)

Figure 31.1

Types of Puppets

Paper-bag mask

Paper-bag puppets

Hand puppet

Finger puppet

Stick puppets

Body puppet

Younger children will be satisfied with a simple production, merely holding the puppets in front of them. Older children will enjoy manipulating the puppets along a table edge, kneeling behind it to be out of sight. The top of an upright piano makes a good puppet stage. However, older children may be able to work with adults in designing a puppet stage from cardboard or plywood. This is a good project for junior high or high school woodworking students.

Finger puppets may be made of paper or cloth, or constructed from a short cardboard tube and a molded head made from a mixture of sawdust and wheat paste. The puppet or puppets are slipped over the tips of the fingers. This novel puppet has a limited use.

Paper-bag puppets are, as the name implies, constructed from paper bags. Bags may be of various sizes, and colors. However, children do best with a size 4 or 5 bag. A larger bag is too hard for them to control. The bag puppets may be made by using the flat surface of the folded bag for the head of the character. Then the mouth and bottom part of the face are placed under the bottom fold. The puppet can open its mouth to "speak." Another type of bag puppet is made by stuffing the bottom half of the bag with paper or cloth. Tie the bag in the center to form a head and use paint, crayon, or colored tape to make the face. Yarn may be added for hair. Bag puppets are worked by slipping the entire hand into the bag.

Molded puppets may be made from papier-mâché or Styrofoam balls. Puppet-making takes time! A teacher must consider how valuable this experience will be to his students. Because of the time involved, it is better to include this activity in weekday clubs or vacation Bible school. Puppet books give detailed directions on making papier-mâché from a commercial mix or by tearing newsprint and mixing it with a wheat paste or similar mixture. Styrofoam balls may be covered with masking tape, and decorated. However, the ball cannot be shaped as can papier-mâché. A cardboard tube must be used for the base of the Styrofoam papier-mâché head. The tube provides an opening to move the head or to attach a rod, as needed for some puppets.

Box puppets are similar to paper-bag puppets. Boxes of various sizes can be used. The box must be covered with paper and two ends or sides left open to insert the fingers and work the puppet. Round boxes can also be used, but the bottom must be left open for the puppeteer to insert his hand.

Stick puppets are cutouts attached to a ruler, piece of cardboard, or other substitute for a stick. The characters, usually of paper, may be purchased, cut from magazines, or designed by the puppeteer. Stick puppets can be manipulated as other puppets or they may be used as shadow puppets. Anyone who knows how to make shadow pictures can use stick puppets in the same way. A sheet is suspended and a bright light placed behind it. The stick puppets must appear between the light and the sheet, thus casting a shadow on the sheet. However, only limited action can be shown, and the puppeteers must practice before presenting the play.

Glove puppets are made by gluing a puppet head to the fingers of a glove. The puppet heads may be made of paper or from matchboxes or small medicine bottles. Heads may be fastened to all fingers or only one finger, or the glove finger itself may be decorated to represent a head.

Hand puppets are available commercially. The audiovisual library of every church should have a collection of them. Hand puppets are available to represent Bible characters, modern people of many foreign lands, and a variety of animals. These puppets require no preparation on the part of the teacher or student and are simple to manipulate. The usual hand puppet consists of a head and a small garment which fits over the puppeteer's hand. The puppet is worked with two fingers and the thumb. The index finger is inserted into the hollow head.

Sock puppets are easily made and some are available commercially. The toe of the sock becomes the puppet's head. Buttons, yarn, or felt are attached to make the face. Animal puppets are often the sock type, because the foot of the sock lends itself to a variety of heads and the leg becomes the animal's neck.

The puppets listed thus far are usually manipulated with hands. However, there are also masks that can be fitted over the head. Then there is also the whole body puppet in which the performer sticks his head and hands through openings in an immobile costume. Draw a figure without face or arms on 2 ft x 3 ft. posterboard. Paint it. Cut a hole for the face and arm holes. Preschoolers especially enjoy this type of puppet because they really feel that they are the character.

Puppets must act! The action must have meaning, and the dialogue should relate to the action. Children will need practice to link action and conversation. It is easy for the puppeteer to become so engrossed with moving a puppet that he forgets to speak for the character. Here, as in any form of story play, if the teacher strives for perfection, the fun of "let's pretend" is lost. As children work with puppets, they will learn to "walk" the puppets or move them in other characteristic actions. Practically any story with action can be adapted to a puppet play. A teacher should follow the same steps in developing a puppet play as he does in creating a simple play.

SUMMARY

Playing out the story may often be the creative expression necessary to complete the learning process. Children love to pretend. Preschoolers may all pretend to be the main character, but fifth and sixth graders will want more sophistication in their role playing or dramatization of Bible truth.

Story play helps a child "get inside the skin" of another person and is more valuable for its activation of emotion than its influence on factual recall. Creative drama, puppetry, role playing, finger plays, and action rhymes are all part of story play.

This method—story play—in any form requires some teacher preparation and much student participation. When used successfully, it helps children *feel* what is taught and helps a teacher evaluate what he thinks he has taught.

FOR FURTHER READING

Allstrom, Elizabeth. *You Can Teach Creatively.* Nashville: Abingdon, 1970.
Autry, Ewart A., and Lola M. Autry. *Bible Puppet Plays.* Grand Rapids: Baker, 1975.

Bauer, Caroline Feller. *Handbook for Storytellers*. Chicago: American Library Assn., 1977.

Beegle, Shirley. *Bible Story Finger Plays and Action Rhymes*. Cincinnati: Standard, 1964.

Edwards, Mildred S., and Joy Latham. *We Sing and Play*. Kansas City, Mo.: Lillenas, 1966.

Faust, David, and Candy Faust. Rev. ed. *Puppet Plays with a Point*. Cincinnati: Standard, 1979.

Griffith, Bonnie. *The Treehouse Gang: Puppet Plays for Children*. Cincinnati: Standard, 1982.

Hodson, Violet. *Puppet Plays: Adventures of Charlie and His Friends*. Cincinnati: Standard.

Horton, Jan. *Using Puppets to Teach Biblical Truths*. Videos. Nashville: Cokesbury.

Jarrell, Ruth. *Using Puppets for God*. Franklin Springs, Ga.: Advocate, 1975.

Le Hays, Barbara. *Musical Bible Plays for Children*. Cincinnati: Standard.

London, Carolyn. *You Can Be a Puppeteer*. Chicago: Moody, 1972.

———. *Puppet Plays for Special Days*. Chicago: Moody, 1977.

Morrison, Eleanor J., and Virgil E. Foster. *Creative Teaching in the Church*. Englewood Cliffs, N.J.: Prentice-Hall, 1963.

Nichols, Hildred, and Lois Williams. *Learning About Role-Playing for Children and Teachers*. Washington, D.C.: Association for Childhood Education, 1960.

Play Me the Story Puppet Kit. Minneapolis: Augsburg. 1983.

Renfro, Nancy, and Lynn Irving. *Pocketful of Puppets: Poems for Church School*. Nashville: Cokesbury Renfro Studios, 1982.

Rives, Elsie, and Margaret Sharp. *Guiding Children*. Nashville: Convention, 1969.

Robertson, Everett. *Using Puppetry in the Church*. Nashville: Broadman, 1976.

Roderick, Bruce. *Teaching with Puppets*. Cincinnati: Standard, 1975.

Rottman, Fran. *Easy-to-Make Puppets and How to Use Them*. Vols. 1 and 2. Glendale, Calif.: Gospel Light, Regal Books, 1978.

Sapp, Phyllis Woodruff. *Creative Teaching in the Church School*. Nashville: Broadman, 1967.

Segal, Marilyn, and Don Adcock. *Just Pretending: Ways to Help Children Grow Through Imaginative Play*. Englewood Cliffs, N.J.: Prentice-Hall, 1981.

Sylwester, Roland. *Teaching Bible Stories More Effectively with Puppets*. St. Louis: Concordia, 1976.

———. *The Puppet and the Word*. St. Louis: Concordia, 1982.

Whittaker, Violet. *Give Puppets Another Hand*. Grand Rapids: Baker, 1978.

32

**Eleanor L. Doan and
Joanne Brubaker**

Creative Activities for Children

- Children and Creativity
- The Purpose of Creative Activities
- How to Encourage Children to Be Creative
- How to Lead Children in Various Kinds of Creative Activities
  CREATIVE WRITING
  CONSTRUCTIVE CRAFTS AND ART
  CONTAINER CRAFTS AND COLLAGES
  PAPER SACKS
  OTHER "SCRAP" ART
  FAVORITE TACTILE ART EXPERIENCES
  MOSAICS
  DECOUPAGE
  CRAYON ART
  PRINTING
  WIRE CRAFT
  MACRAME
  JEWELRY MAKING
  STYROFOAM ART
- Creative Activities in Church Agencies

ELEANOR L. DOAN was manager of special projects and information services, Gospel Light Publications, Ventura, California, and is now retired.

JOANNE BRUBAKER, co-editor of *Childhood Education in the Church,* is the former director of Circle Center for Child Development, Zion, Illinois, an early childhood consultant, a free-lance writer, and an illustrator of children's books.

Creativity. A magical, illusive quality bestowed by God on a favored few and wistfully desired by others. So it may seem. In reality, the potential for creativity lies within each of us.

The creative process has been traced by one author through three stages—desire, discovery, and action. Beginning with a need or desire, it continues when the desire produces discovery, which is largely "determined by one's inner resources—natural abilities [and] acquired skills, and by one's exterior resources—available materials." Finally, the discovery is translated into action, "which may involve research, experimentation, development of techniques and skills." Creativity is not viewed as a quality belonging only to the artist. "The same process that produces a sculpture or a concerto or a poem is continually at work in each individual who remains responsive to the needs of life and is willing to mobilize both inner and outer resources to meet them."[1]

Creativity is "an attitude, an approach, a way of seeing." The first recorded act of God stemmed from His creative nature. The creative thought was in the heart of God as His Spirit was "moving (hovering, brooding)" over the formless mass of earth (Gen. 1:2, Amp.). Then He spoke and His creative power was let loose, fashioning a world and its heavenly host.

God is creative. "All things were made by Him" (John 1:3), and "all things were created by him" (Col. 1:16). Man is the crowning achievement of His creation. Kate Douglas Wiggin declares that "every child born into the world is a new thought of God, an ever fresh and radiant possibility." Each is endowed with an individual personality and set of abilities, with individual needs and responses. Although all children are born with their own creative capacity, research tells us that part of their creativity is lost by the time they are five.[2] The responsibility then lies with the adults around them to keep and expand the creativity of the early years. Children need to be taught to "use what they already have." "When we expose our students to our creative attempts in the classroom and in our lives, we encourage them to polish in themselves the reflection of the Creator."[3]

CHILDREN AND CREATIVITY

To be creative, according to Webster, is to be productive. And an activity is an educational procedure designed to stimulate learning by firsthand experience. Therefore, a creative activity is a productive, first-hand, learning experience.

Creative activities have an important place in the total learning situation, bringing a new dimension into learning experiences. They enable children to

---

1. Miriam H. Rockness, *A Time to Play* (Grand Rapids: Zondervan, 1983), pp. 124-25.
2. Willard Abraham, *Living with Preschoolers* (Phoenix, Ariz.: O'Sullivan Woodside, 1976), p. 35.
3. Marlene D. LeFever, *Creative Teaching Methods* (Elgin, Ill.: David C. Cook, 1985), p. 20.

add doing to seeing and listening. Children are shifted from a passive to an active role where they can put themselves totally into the learning experience. Their participation gives them opportunity for self-expression. When they are involved, they learn by doing—a firsthand learning experience which can be meaningful and lasting. Creative activities help children to discover for themselves whether they can do what they think they can or what they want to do. They present new opportunities to apply Bible truths to daily life.

Children enjoy creative activities. They naturally like to use their entire bodies in movements which are all their own. They like to play "make believe," to experiment with rhyming sounds and words, to use art materials, to explore the feel of different textures—a squishy piece of clay, rough bark from a tree. An exciting world comes alive as all their senses are employed to discover and explore its wonders. As children learn of the world and people about them, there is a growing awareness of God, His creation, and His Word.

With the involvement of various learning experiences comes the related teaching of such Bible truths as helping (2 Cor. 1:11), sharing (Heb. 13:16, TCNT), consideration for others (Matt. 7:12), and being doers of the Word and not hearers only (James 1:22).

God established the basic growth pattern of children, which was exemplified by the Lord Jesus Himself when He became God-man. "And Jesus increased in wisdom and stature, and in favour with God and man" (Luke 2:52). Jesus grew as a little child, went to school, played with other children, lived in a family, obeyed His parents, went to the synagogue, and learned about God. The fact that He lived and grew as other children is evidence that He experienced productive, firsthand learning experiences (creative activities).

THE PURPOSE OF CREATIVE ACTIVITIES

Creative activity is a method of teaching which can be used profitably to foster learning. These activities provide enjoyable ways for children to become more completely integrated personalities, opportunities to show loving concern and respect for others, and motivations to express their relationship to God and His Word in daily living.

Some of the purposes and values in the use of creative activities are as follows:

1. It makes learning more enjoyable, lasting, and meaningful.
2. It provides opportunity for self-expression and development of creativity.
3. It instills pride in accomplishment and builds self-confidence.
4. It contributes to the development of proper self-concepts.
5. It provides for participation in group situations and reaction to established group approval and behavior.
6. It deepens the child's sensitivity toward others and provides opportunity for him to demonstrate loving concern in words and action.

7. It is therapeutic for the child's need for individual expression.

8. It relieves periods of physical restlessness with meaningful activity, coordinating mind and muscle.

9. It prompts respect for both adult and peer leadership.

10. It develops leadership abilities and a sensitivity to carrying out responsibilities.

11. It affords opportunity for the practice of the principles of Christian living.

12. It helps the child respect the property of others.

13. It teaches cooperation, sharing, and taking turns.

14. It can emphasize a Bible concept or illustrate a truth.

15. It provides opportunities for the child to express his relationship to God and his response to Bible teaching.

Keeping these purposes and values in mind, teachers and leaders will have opportunity to observe the children's developing theological concepts and behavioral responses. This will help guide the leaders in their teaching and in their relationships with the children and in the selection of creative activities to effect successful learning experiences.

HOW TO ENCOURAGE CHILDREN TO BE CREATIVE

All children can be productive, or creative. But the extent to which they express their creativity depends, to a large degree, on the teacher. The following are some ways in which to encourage and foster creativity among children.

1. Discover each child's level of understanding—what the child knows (or doesn't know)—about Bible teaching. This can come from observing children in self-expression through music, role playing, rhymes, games, verbalizing, and handcrafts, which are selected to retell and/or apply the Bible truths.

2. Be personally interested in each child. Commend him for work well done. Visit in the child's home and get acquainted with the family. Take time with each child individually on Sunday. Comment on new clothing, birth of a sibling, and so on. Remember birthdays by sending a card. Listen; be sensitive to feelings; encourage efforts.

3. Choose purposeful activities that will meet children's needs. Evaluate the way(s) each activity considered will meet the needs of the children in your group: Will it help them relate to each other? cooperate? develop physical skills by using excess energy? express creativity and originality? share? gain self-confidence? apply a Bible truth? communicate?

4. Provide a variety of activities and materials. Evaluate choices in view of children's ages, environment for activities, abilities and interests, physical needs, seasons, and learning goals. Consider activities for *listening* (records,

cassette tapes); for *thinking* (writing stories and poems, riddles, rebuses, slogans, letters); for *doing* (games, role play, drama, arts and crafts, motion songs, fingerplays).

Consider media: for *creating* (clay, newspapers and cardboard, seeds, household discards, string and yarn, shells, pictures); for *decorating* (paints, crayons, glitter, stickers); for *expressing a role* (costumes, yardage, wigs, paper sacks for puppets, hats, etc.).

5. Encourage children to do their best, to be original. Communicate your confidence in their ability to achieve by commending their efforts. Give suggestions to the less creative child and allow extra time for the child slower at manipulation. Stimulate originality through conversation. "Close your eyes and think about (name story or incident discussed or to be visualized). Now draw the picture you see." "What ideas do you have for a song? Can you think of a first line?" Also encourage originality by providing a variety of media and letting children choose what to use to illustrate a Bible verse, story, song, rebus, etc.

6. When children seem overly sure of their abilities, do not dispute their claims. Redirect their interests and guide them into activities compatible with their abilities. To redirect the child's interest, you might comment, "I'm sure you could (name the activity), but here's something which really requires the talent you have"; or, "Have you ever tried (name activity)? It just suits what you can do."

7. Guide the overactive child into activity which will hold interest and work off energy. Encourage participation in games, music, field trips, and finger fun. Let the child be your supply assistant, errand runner, prop man, and performer of other energy-consuming jobs.

8. Provide challenging projects for the precocious child. Let him make patterns or prepare materials for the class, a second craft item to use as a gift, gather props for plays, write a TV play for using puppets children make, tape a story which the children can pantomime, do a research project.

9. Be firm and fair. Do not expect perfection. Do not do anything for a child that he can do for himself. Have some basic rules for all activities: completing one project before another is started, putting away materials and objects used, and sharing. Endeavor to keep a capable child from doing slipshod work. Do not let the less capable get discouraged from seeming failure or by comparing accomplishments with those of another.

10. Let the children select their activities occasionally. Periodically have "Choice Day" for activities. Encourage each child to tell why the activity he has chosen is his favorite. Have first, second, and third choices if a particular activity precludes many participants.

11. Display projects the children make. Provide bulletin boards and tables inside (at child's eye level) and outside the classroom for mounting and displaying projects. Occasionally let each child select what he feels is his best project

for display. Sometimes have a committee (composed of children) choose the best projects from each child's contributions. Guide the children in arranging the display.

How to Lead Children in Various Kinds of Creative Activities

Here are some activities which children enjoy, with suggestions for leading them to participate.

CREATIVE WRITING

The learning tool of creative writing can help children crystallize their thoughts and reduce generalities to specifics. It can help them express random thoughts succinctly, and it can encourage originality.

Creative writing forms can include stories, poems, rebuses, riddles, songs, plays, fingerplays, poster slogans, cartoon quips, letters, and Scripture paraphrases.

When encouraging children to write stories, motivate their thinking by asking questions. "What happened (this past week, during vacation, at school) that reminded you of something Jesus told us we should do?" Or prompt their thinking by starting a story and letting the children build on it (e.g., "On the way home from school, Steve saw a boy, much bigger than he was, breaking open a gum ball machine. And then, what happened?").

Ask children to choose subjects for a poem. Write these on the board. Ask the children to think of words that rhyme and write them on the board. If further help is needed, suggest a first line, such as "When I look around, I see—."

Have the children cut out magazine pictures and use them to write rebuses and riddles. (A rebus is a story which occasionally substitutes pictures for words.) Children can use the pictures literally for the words they want to use (e.g., the picture of a house to "read" *house*) or as the symbol of a word they want read (e.g., the picture of a tire plus the letter *D* for the word *tired*).

Songs (lyrics) can be written in somewhat the same way as poems, rebuses, and riddles. Select a familiar tune and let the children compose different verses. For younger children, "Mulberry Bush" is always a good tune. For older children, you might use "Brighten the Corner." Motion songs are fun for them to write. Discuss what they want to express and decide on words and motions that fit together.

Whereas it would be difficult for most children to write a play by themselves, they can enjoy composing a play together. Help the children think of a story they want to dramatize. "Shall we write a Bible-story play? a play that illustrates a Bible truth? a missionary story? an adventure story?" After the subject is selected, outline the story on the chalkboard as the children tell it. Questions, such as, "What happened first in the story play?" "What happened next?" might stimulate ideas. Follow the same procedure in listing the characters. Sometimes it helps to have the children stage the play impromptu before writing it.

Fingerplays can be an individual or group activity. Explain that fingerplays are messages or stories told by the hands. Ask some of the children to let their fingers "say something." Have others guess what they are "saying." Then reverse the procedure. Let the children then choose the most obvious "finger talk" and write words to go with it.

Writing poster slogans and cartoon quips is a fun activity for children. Mount magazine pictures on poster paper and let the children discuss "what the picture says." From the discussion, children come up with appropriate slogans and quips.

Letter writing is a good group activity for younger children and a good individual project for juniors. Guide the children in deciding who should receive the letter(s): a shut-in, class member who is sick, missionary friend, or pen-pal. Teachers will write the letter for preschoolers, incorporating their thoughts. The letter dictated by primaries can be written on the chalkboard by the teacher and then copied by the children. Juniors can compose or write their own letters. Sometimes rebus letters are fun for both juniors and primaries.

CONSTRUCTIVE CRAFTS AND ART

The possibilities of craft and art projects which can be made by children—and the materials from which they can be made—are almost endless. This is significant, in that the variety of opportunities afforded the child to express himself opens the door to new learning experiences.

The teacher-child relationship is an important key to the child's becoming more self-confident and sure of his worth as an individual. This helps the child more readily to accept and respond to God's love, and show love for others. The primary concern of the teacher should not be how well the child made the craft, but rather what the child learned.

In the development of artistic expression, each child passes through various stages of development and progresses at his own rate, just as the child does in other areas of growth. Individuality is obvious: the child makes a project "just the way I want it." A first experience in creative arts may not result in anything recognizable to anyone but himself. Ask the child to tell you about the painting (picture, modeling, or whatever type of project he is working on). Never ask, "What is that?" An understanding, positive attitude encourages a child to respond with eagerness, confidence, and pride. Response communicates what the child thinks and feels.

Usually a child's first creative art experience is manipulating materials such as clay, soft paint (finger paints or chocolate-pudding "paint"), and crayons. He squeezes and scribbles, making nothing specific. He discovers how these materials feel and smell and look (and sometimes how they taste!). As muscle coordination improves, the child begins to control the materials. While the finished project is more readily identified, this is not as important as the teacher's showing acceptance of the work. "You chose nice bright colors for your picture." "Your painting shows you worked hard." "Your animal is very good. I like the way you made the bear's ears."

As children grow, they become more adept in handling materials, and thus they put more effort into expressing what they think and feel. The teacher's role continues to be one of encouraging children, making them feel important and needed, and accepting their efforts. Children should not be made to feel there is only one right way to do it.

In leading children into art activities, keep in mind that you are teaching the children—not arts and crafts.

Involve the children as helpers. Ask them to help you gather and sort the supplies needed. After they have completed an activity, ask them to help you put the supplies away.

When you introduce a new project, demonstrate the use of materials, and show several made-up crafts as ideas. Ask the children, What else can be made from—?"

Encourage individual creativity in thinking and doing. Do not give the impression that every child's project should be "just like teacher's."

Think of each art activity in relationship to Bible learning, directing the child's thoughts, conversation, and action to this end.

Allow the children freedom to experiment with materials. Be positive while observing their efforts and when making suggestions.

Be alert to the children's physical safety. Provide adequate supervision, especially when using tools.

With all this in mind, here are starter ideas for various materials to use in craft and art activities. Included are some "lead in" suggestions to use with the children.

CONTAINER CRAFTS AND COLLAGES

Cardboard containers (all sizes and shapes). "Jerry, look at all these boxes. What do you think we could make out of them?" "Houses? Fine. How do you think we should go about making them?" "Nancy, what ideas do you have for using that box you are holding?" "Doll furniture is a good idea, and that box would make a nice table."

Here are some other ideas for cardboard containers. Cover graduated sizes of square boxes with bright shelf paper for building blocks. Cut milk and cream cartons to appropriate height, cover with contact paper and use for planters or crayon holders. Use boxes to make dioramas. Small cereal boxes with perforations on one side make good puppet heads when folded on the side opposite the opened perforation. (To manipulate, place fingers in upper portion and thumb in lower portion).

Plastic containers (all sizes, shapes, colors, thoroughly washed and labels removed). "Do you know what we are going to do with these bottles, baskets, and plastic trays? Terri, you look eager to tell us." "You saw a sand scoop your cousin made from a big bottle? I think that's a good idea." "Lorrie, how do you think we could use this small bottle?" "Yes. You could paste a picture on it or wrap it with yarn, and it will be a beautiful vase."

Here are some other ideas for plastic containers. Make shadow pictures from meat trays by gluing on several plastic flowers. Trinket trays can be made by covering the container with contact paper. Surprise baskets can be made by attaching a long chenille wire to opposite sides of plastic berry or tomato baskets, lining them with a paper doily or napkin, and filling with cookies. Cut off the bottom of a large bottle so that it will be about two inches deep, line it with felt, and use it for an offering plate in Sunday school or children's church. Make a food dish for pets by cutting off the bottom of a large plastic bottle, about four inches deep. Cut off the bottoms of small bottles (all colors), one-half inch deep, glue Christmas-card pictures in the bottom, attach a hanger by gluing string to the back or putting it through a hole punched in the tip, and you have attractive Christmas tree ornaments.

Cloth (assorted prints, colors, fabrics). "How do you think we can use this cloth to illustrate a Bible story?" "That green will make a nice tree, Steve. What story did you have in mind?" "The creation story in a collage picture is a very good idea." (A collage is a picture constructed out of commonplace scrap materials and glued to a flat surface). The cloth can be cut in the shapes desired, to represent days of creation, then pasted on cardboard.

Seeds (assorted). "Yes, Susan, seeds can be used to make a collage picture. And a bird would be nice to make." Or, a child could make a show box of some of the seeds God made by gluing some of each kind of seed on a square of cardboard, gluing them in a box, and labeling the seed. Or, sprinkle some lettuce seeds on a damp sponge and place this in a shallow container, keeping the sponge moist so the seeds will sprout.

Shells. Children never cease to be thrilled with God's wonders, and shells are one of His wonderful creations. Discuss what shells are, what lived in them, what day of creation they represent. Listen to the sounds inside big shells. If given an assortment of shells, children may glue them in a box and label them for a show box. Or a collage picture may be made of shells glued to posterboard.

PAPER SACKS

Use paper sacks in assorted sizes and colors. "I am thinking of something we can all make from paper sacks and use to tell Bible stories. Who can guess what it is?" "Good, most of you said 'Puppets.' Think of the Bible character you want to make, and choose the materials you need." "Yes, I think a sheep would be a good 'character,' Ted. And I like your idea of covering the paper bag with bits of cotton too. With Tom's idea of using his David puppet, you and Tom can tell a story together."

There are many other uses for paper sacks. Choose a paper sack which will fit over the head, cut out one of the wide sides (one inch from all the creases) and use for a wig to represent a Bible character. From another paper bag the same size, cut a four-inch crown and glue it on to the "wig" to represent a king or queen. With paint, cloth, or crayons, draw a clown's face on the wide side of a large paper sack, then stuff it with shredded newspaper and tie it at the top with yarn to make a clown's head pillow. Cut an opening on one wide side of a paper sack, and cut a slit on each of the narrow sides (close to the crease) half-an-inch longer on each end, so you can use the sack as a TV "screen."

OTHER "SCRAP" ART

Magazine pictures. "How many things can you think of that we can make from these pictures, to tell of God's love?" Here are some ideas the children may think of. Murals can be made to illustrate Bible stories, such as "The Good Shepherd" or "God's Creation," by cutting out and pasting pictures on strips of shelf paper. Make a book from wrapping paper and have children find pictures to illustrate a favorite song. Find suitable pictures to paste onto construction paper to make greeting cards. Paste pictures on large cards to illustrate Bible verses. Make scrapbooks for children in hospitals. Magazine pictures can be pasted on cardboard, then cut in pieces as a puzzle, and placed in an envelope for a gift.

Straws (both plastic and paper). Cut straws in various lengths and glue them on construction paper to make pictures of flowers, birds, trees, or people. Cut several straws in varied lengths and string them on yarn to make necklaces. Squeeze little blobs of paint on construction paper, then point one end of a straw in the paint and blow to move the paint and "paint" a picture. Combine pieces of straws and gummed reinforcements to make figures of animals and people and illustrate the story of Noah and the ark.

Yarn and string. A yarn picture of Abraham's home can be made by arranging brown yarn in the shape of a tent and green and brown yarn to form trees on the sides of the "home." Talk about other Bible scenes that can be "drawn" with yarn. Suggest how children can make scenes on the flannelboard by using white yarn for clouds, brown and green for mountains and trees, blue for water, yellow for sun. (Flannelboard figures to represent Bible stories can be made from chenille wire.) Both yarn and string can be used on the flannelboard or glued on cardboard to make faces illustrating being happy, sad, mad, or whatever emotion you want.

There are many other ideas for making things of yarn and string. Paint with string by dipping the string in paint, arranging it inside a piece of folded paper, closing the paper, and pressing it under a book until dry. Glue a yarn or string border all around a piece of cardboard, and then "print" words, in yarn, from a Bible verse (e.g., "Be Ye Kind") to make a motto.

Cotton. Talk about where we get cotton. "Cotton represents which day of creation? How many things do we use every day that are made of cotton?" "Let us thank God for His gift of cotton." Have the class make a poster or mural showing all the things they named which are made from cotton.

Here are some other suggestions for ways to use cotton. Spread a thin layer of cotton on a plastic meat tray, saturate it with water, and sprinkle with a fast-growing seed (grass or radish) to observe how God makes seeds grow. Make a picture by gluing strips of brown yarn on a piece of construction paper, and then adding small, oblong cotton balls for pussy willows. Another use for cotton balls is to dip them in tempera paint and "paint" a design or picture on white construction paper.

Spools (assorted sizes and colors). Use spools for design printing. Make designs by gluing to one end of a spool a piece of sponge, layer of cotton, piece of burlap, or strips of string. Dip designs in paint and stamp out pattern on construction paper or poster board. Fasten piece(s) of sponge (dipped in green paint) on tree twigs and stand up the twigs in spools. Cut out the front and back of animals, glue them on opposite ends of a spool, then cover the spool with cotton or material appropriate for the animal. Small children can string spools on long shoelaces. Make spool dolls by stringing spools on shoestrings for the arms, legs, body, and head.

FAVORITE TACTILE ART EXPERIENCES

Clay. Encourage the children to make something out of the clay that will help recall a Bible story or a Bible truth. They might make animals, waterpots, oil lamps, scrolls, or tablets of stone.

Play dough. A recipe for inexpensive play dough is to combine 2 cups flour (not self rising), 1 cup salt and 1 tbsp. alum. Gradually stir in 2 cups boiling water. Mix well and add 2 tbsp. baby oil and food coloring. Knead until smooth. This has a nice smooth texture and will keep several weeks if stored in a tight container.

Finger paint. A quick finger paint can be made by adding a nondetergent liquid soap to liquid starch. Tempera is sprinkled on top of the starch as used. Provide plenty of time and elbow room!

MOSAICS

Mosaics are ancient decorative art media (dating back as far as 4000 B.C. in Mesopotamia) which have been used through the centuries to decorate, to communicate ideas, and to chronicle events. Today, mosaics offer scores of teaching-learning opportunities for children. Discuss with students various materials that can be used in making mosaics (list on chalkboard for older children): seeds of all kinds; small, colored rocks; eggshells; seashells; fungi; leaves; pine cones; ceramic tiles; fruit stones; dried vegetables, such as beans and peas; colored glass; beads; or pieces of colored paper.

Encourage discussion of how Bible stories or truths can be visualized in mosaics. "What story would mosaics of fish tell? ravens? doves? donkey? animals? basket? boat?" Yes, you could make a very interesting map from mosaics. And a Bible verse. And people—."

Mosaics can be made on boards, plywood, cardboard, dishes, paper plates, boxes, cork, plastic, or floor tiles.

While older children are making mosaics, tell about some of the mosaics which have been found and preserved in churches and buildings dating back to the time of Christ and the first century.

DECOUPAGE

Decoupage (the art of decorating surfaces—usually wood—with paper cut-outs) is an excellent activity for combining muscular dexterity, imagination, and learning recall. Children may cut pictures, Bible verses, mottoes, decorative designs from Sunday school papers, greeting cards, periodicals, calendars, or posters. The selection of materials and arrangement on the wood allow opportunity for discussion. Encourage the children to tell the meaning of their design, what the motto means to them, or the reason for the Bible verse or picture selected. Observe the originality shown in design and compliment the child's effort. The time spent distressing the wood and finishing the surface is enjoyable to children and provides muscle activity and dexterity. This activity also affords opportunity for cooperation and sharing.

CRAYON ART

Crayon techniques can open the door to a variety of meaningful, creative, craft projects. Since children feel at home using crayons, they can be challenged to try new crayon techniques. For example, "stained glass" can be made for classroom windows. Designs can be drawn with wax crayons on heavy paper, cut to fit the windows. The "window" design is completed when the entire surface has been colored. To add the stained-glass effect, children may dip cotton into baby oil (or cooking oil) and rub completely over the reverse side. Talk about the colors, the design, and why stained glass is used in churches.

Interesting wall hangings (e.g., a class motto or Bible verse) can be made by using wax crayons on muslin. Coloring is made easier if the cloth is stapled to a large piece of cardboard, held in embroidery hoops, or taped to the floor.

Small children may use stencils. When completed, press the hangings on the "wrong" side with a warm iron.

Interesting crayon pictures can be drawn on sandpaper, cheesecloth glued over cardboard, or muslin glued to wood.

PRINTING

Relief printing (the application of ink to a raised surface) is a versatile artcraft project which can be used by children of almost all ages for making words or designs. It is an excellent medium to challenge students to explore new ideas and thus bring about new learning experiences.

Encourage children to talk about what they want to print—and *why*. Listening to the "what" and "why" of a project will prompt guidance in the conversation and activity for learning.

The most commonly used materials for carving raised designs are linoleum squares mounted on wood, balsa wood, potatoes, and spools. Raised surfaces can be made in numerous other ways. Toothpicks and string can be glued to a cork surface (or rough side of linoleum blocks), and rubber bands, paper clips, yarn, string, or spaghetti can be arranged at random and glued to bottles. A continuous design can be made on shelf paper by rolling the bottle over ink and pressing it on the paper. Words can be made from alphabet macaroni and glued (backwards and in reverse) on wood for printing Bible verses and mottoes.

A profitable project would be for the children to select and illustrate a favorite proverb or other Bible verse to illustrate and/or print.

WIRE CRAFT

Wire craft challenges the child's imagination and provides exercises in muscle coordination. Children in the middle grades can handle a wide range of wire—from chenille wire to coat hangers—while young children should be limited to using chenille wire.

What the child chooses to make will reflect past learning experiences and open vistas to new learning experiences. Asking the children to "Tell me about—" opens the door for the child to share his thinking. If the young child makes chenille wire figures, suggest that he place them on a flannelboard and tell the story he has in mind.

Older children may sculpture with copper wire, lightweight wire, or even coat hangers. Faces, butterflies, figures, and abstract forms can be fashioned from coat hangers. Dimensional forms are attractively shaped by winding string around the wire to fill out figures or designs, or to enclose a form.

Mobiles can tell a story, represent a season or illustrate a truth or Scripture portion, and thus provide learning experiences. Chenille wire, buttons, paper objects, bits of plastic, and scores of other materials can be used in mobile making.

MACRAME

Macrame (creative knotting, braiding, and twisting) is a challenging and interesting craft for children. Suggest that they find twine, heavy cord, or rug yarn to make belts, necklaces, bookmarks, and wall hangings. Originality and imagination will be refreshing as each child expresses his ideas in knotting, braiding, and twisting the twine.

Psalm 139:14 (TLB) is a good Bible verse to discuss while children are engaged in this project: "Thank you for making me so wonderfully complex! It is amazing to think about. Your workmanship is marvelous—and how well I know it." Then the teacher could add this comment: "Our minds tell our hands what to do, and our eyes are guides to help our hands. God's workmanship is marvelous!" Or, "Everything God made is good. He made the plants from which we get cotton, jute, linen, and sisal, which is made into rope and twine."

JEWELRY-MAKING

Jewelry-making is an excellent craft to stimulate creativity and motivate children to think of others. Many of the materials for jewelry-making can be found in items usually considered junk. "Beads" can be made by rolling and gluing small triangles cut from colored magazine pictures, over a thin knitting needle. Remove from needle and spray with clear plastic. Children may roll small balls of patching plaster (tinted with vegetable coloring), then pierce with knitting needle for stringing. Colored plastic straws may be cut in varying lengths. Assorted sizes and colors of seeds may be gathered and pierced for stringing. Circles, triangles, and squares of cork and plastic (from bottles) can be cut out and punched.

Bracelets and necklaces may be made from stringing (use plastic thread for bracelets) seeds, magazine picture beads, cut-up plastic straws, assorted beads, buttons, small plastic foam shapes used for packing, and beads made from plaster. Pendants can be made by gluing seeds in a mosaic design on cork and fastening the design to a ribbon or shoelace. Cork covered with foil and "engraved" and wire fashioned in a design also make interesting pendants. Pins may be made from copper wire shaped to spell a name. Or use varied shapes of wood, cork, or plastic and make names from macaroni letters or designs from seeds, colored string, or buttons. Glue safety pins to back of pins. Headbands, wristbands, and belts can be made by sewing assorted buttons or beads on ribbon or burlap. Cut circles, squares, or triangles from plastic bottles or cork, punch holes so that they can be fastened together with yarn, twine, ribbon, or shoelaces. Key chains can be made by fastening tumbled colored stones to copper wire, cutting various shapes from plastic, and attaching braided, plastic-coated wire.

STYROFOAM ART

Plastic foam comes in many shapes: sheets, balls, cones, cubes, circles, letters, and in assorted twists and macaroni shapes for packing. To cut plastic foam, use a sharp kitchen knife. If you wish to paint the foam, use a water-base paint.

"What shall we cut from the plastic foam to decorate our room? A fish? Good. What will a fish represent? Our class motto 'Fishers of Men.' That's a good idea, Gary." "A sword and shield for Ephesians 6 is a good idea too."

Guide children to think of things they can help make to visualize Bible stories, lesson applications, or mottoes. Puppet heads can be made from the balls, and figures can be made from cones and balls. Birds and animals can be cut from sheets for bulletin boards, murals, and posters. Small figures and letters can be used on the flannelboard. Houses can be made from pieces of thin sheet foam put together with toothpicks. The plastic foam used for packing can be tinted with vegetable coloring and glued on cardboard to make mosaics, or strung to make necklaces.

Other materials useful for crafts are chenille wire, crepe paper, egg cartons, felt, gimp, ice cream sticks, leather, and rope. Other ideas for crafts can be gained by visiting public schools, Christian schools, Christian bookstores, craft and hobby shops, and by reading craft magazines. (See the list of craft magazines at the end of this chapter.)

CREATIVE ACTIVITIES IN VARIOUS CHURCH AGENCIES

SUNDAY SCHOOL

In all children's departments (except babies, toddlers, and nursery), creative activities can be used during the presession moments (before Sunday school formally begins), during the class time (depending on available time), and during the extended sessions or children's church. For nursery age children (twos and threes), creative activities are very desirable during church time.

SUNDAY EVENING

Sunday evening expressional programs for fours and fives, primaries, and juniors, offer excellent opportunities for creative activities.

CHURCH-RELATED PROGRAMS

Church-related programs may include nursery schools, day-care programs, child care programs (in operation whenever parents of young children attend church activities), the home, and released time. Creative activities for preschoolers—and sometimes primaries—are desirable in all these programs, except the last, which should be for juniors.

WEEKDAY ACTIVITIES

Several weekday activities provide excellent opportunities for using creative activities: weekday clubs, weekly Bible classes (for primaries and juniors), recreational programs (for juniors), and missionary organizations (for primaries and juniors).

SUMMER AND VACATION MINISTRIES

Camping, vacation Bible school, and recreational activities are opportunities in summer when creative activities can be used for children ages two through eleven.

SUMMARY

Creative activities for children can be a significant plus factor in the total learning situation. What is needed are teachers and parents who see the importance of firsthand experiences in applying Bible truths to daily life. Children need teachers who are open to the creativity in the world around them, who see the possibility of creativity in their students, and who can guide children into activities compatible with their abilities.

FOR FURTHER READING

BOOKS

Allstrom, Elizabeth. *You Can Teach Creatively.* Nashville: Abingdon, 1970.

Arvois, Edmond. *Making Mosaics.* New York: Sterling, 1964.

Benson, Kenneth R. *Creative Crafts for Children.* Englewood Cliffs, N.J.: Prentice-Hall, 1958.

Bolton, Barbara J., and Charles T. Smith. *Creative Bible Learning for Early Childhood.* Ventura, Calif.: Gospel Light, Regal Books, 1977.

Crane, John, and Diane Crane. *Scrap Craft.* Dansville, N.Y.: Owen, 1963.

Doan, Eleanor L. *Handcraft Encyclopedia.* Glendale, Calif.: Gospel Light, 1961.

———. *Creative Handcrafts for Early Childhood, Ages 3, 4, 5.* Glendale, Calif.: Gospel Light, 1973.

———. *Creative Handcrafts for Children, Grades 1, 2, 3.* Glendale, Calif.: Gospel Light, 1973.

———. *Creative Handcrafts for Children, Grades 4, 5, 6.* Glendale, Calif.: Gospel Light, 1973.

———. *Creative Handcrafts for Youth.* Glendale, Calif.: Gospel Light, 1973.

———. *261 Handcrafts and Fun for Little Ones.* Grand Rapids: Zondervan, 1963.

———. *145 Fun-to-Do Handcrafts.* Grand Rapids: Zondervan, 1972.

————. *157 More Fun-to-Do Handcrafts.* Grand Rapids: Zondervan, 1972.

Dotts, M. Franklin, and Maryann J. Dotts. *Clues to Creativity.* 3 vols. Boston: Friendship, 1974.

Edge, Findley B. *Helping the Teacher.* Nashville: Broadman, 1959.

Eitzen, Ruth. *Fun to Do All Year Through.* Valley Forge, Pa.: Judson, 1982.

52 Year-Round Crafts series. Cincinnati, Ohio: Standard, 1980-1984. (For preschool, primary, and middler-junior.)

Flemming, Bonnie M., Darlene S. Hamilton, and JoAnne D. Hicks. *Resources for Creative Teaching in Early Childhood Education.* New York: Harcourt Brace Jovanovich, 1977.

Gale, Elizabeth Wright. *Have You Tried This?* Valley Forge, Pa.: Judson, 1960.

Griggs, Patricia. *Creative Activities in Church Education.* Nashville: Abingdon, 1974.

Hammond, Phyllis E. *What to Do and Why.* Valley Forge, Pa.: Judson, 1963.

Harrell, Donna, and Wesley Haystead. *Creative Bible Learning for Children.* Ventura, Calif.: Gospel Light, Regal Books, 1977.

Hull, Opal. *Creative Crafts for Churches.* Anderson, Ind.: Warner, 1958.

Jackson, Sheila. *Simple Stage Costumes and How to Make Them.* New York: Watson-Guptill, 1969.

LeFever, Marlene D. *Growing Creative Children.* Carol Stream, Ill.: Tyndale, 1981.

Leighton, Audrey. *Fingerplay Friends.* Valley Forge, Pa.: Judson, 1984.

Liu, Sarah, and Mary Lou Vittitow. *Creative Bible Activities for Children.* Wheaton, Ill.: Scripture Press, 1977.

Morrison, Eleanor J., and Virgil E. Foster. *Creative Teaching in the Church.* Englewood Cliffs, N.J.: Prentice-Hall, 1963.

Pesch, Imelda Manalo. *Macramé.* New York: Sterling, 1970.

Pitcher, Evelyn, et al. *Helping Young Children Learn.* Columbus, Ohio: Merril, 1966.

Quick Crafts for Sunday School Teachers. Nashville: Cokesbury.

Revoir, Trudy W. *Christmas Worship for the Church Family.* Valley Forge, Pa.: Judson, 1982.

Richards, Lawrence O. *Creative Bible Teaching.* Chicago, Moody, 1970.

Sapp, Phyllis. *Creative Teaching in the Church School.* Nashville: Broadman, 1967.

Schaupp, Jack. *Creating and Playing Games with Students.* Nashville: Abingdon, 1981.

Self, Margaret M. *158 Things to Make.* Glendale, Calif.: Gospel Light, 1971.

————. *202 Things to Do.* Glendale, Calif.: Gospel Light, 1971.

Simms, Caryl, and Gordon Simms. *Introducing Seed Collage.* New York: Watson-Guptill, 1971.

Squires, John L. *Fun Crafts for Children.* Englewood Cliffs, N.J.: Prentice-Hall, 1964.

Sunderlin, Sylvia, ed. *Bits and Pieces,* Washington, D.C.: Association for Childhood Education, 1967.

Taylor, Barbara. *When I Do, I Learn.* Provo, Utah: Brigham Young, n.d.

36 Creative Ideas for Children in the Church School. Nashville, Cokesbury.

Turner, G. Alan. *Creative Crafts for Everyone.* New York: Viking, 1959.

Vermeer, Jackie, and Marian Lariviere. *The Little Kids Craft Book.* New York: Taplinger, 1973.

Watson, Ernest W., and Norman Kent. *The Relief Print.* New York: Watson-Guptill, 1955.

Weiss, Harvey. *Clay, Wood and Wire.* New York: Scott, 1956.

Wing, Frances S. *The Complete Book of Decoupage.* New York: Coward-McConn, 1965.

Wylie, Joanne, ed. *A Creative Guide for Preschool Teachers.* Racine, Wis.: Western, 1965.

Yates, Brock. *Plastic Foam for Arts and Crafts.* New York: Sterling, 1965.

Year-Round Preschool Activity Patterns. Nashville: Cokesbury.

Yemm, Marta. *Years to Grow: A Pre-primary Curriculum Resource Book.* Minneapolis: Dennison.

Yoder, Glen. *Take It from Here.* Valley Forge, Pa.: Judson, 1973.

MAGAZINES WITH CRAFT IDEAS

Arts and Activities. 8150 North Central Park Avenue, Skokie, IL 60076.

Church Recreation. 127 Ninth Avenue North, Nashville, TN 37203.

Crafts 'n Things. 14 Main Street, Park Ridge, IL 60068.

Instructor. P.O. Box 6099, Duluth, MN 55806.

Pack-O-Fun. 14 Main Street, Park Ridge, IL 60068.

School Arts. 50 Portland Street, Worcester, ME 01608.

Shining Star. Box 299, Carthage, IL 62321-0299.

Teacher. 22 West Putnam Avenue, Greenwich, CT 06830.

Teachers' Arts and Crafts Workshops. Brookhill Drive, West Nyack, NY 10994.

OTHER SOURCES

Kenworthy Educational Service, Inc., P.O. Box 3031, Buffalo, NY 14205.

S & S Arts and Crafts, Colchester, CT 06415.

Part 7

Ministering to Children Beyond the Church

33

Gene A. Getz and
Wallace Getz

The Role of the Family in Childhood Education

- **The Home in Childhood Education**
  NATURAL AND SPONTANEOUS ENVIRONMENT
  OPPORTUNITY FOR POSITIVE PARENTAL EXAMPLES
- **The Early Years Are Crucial**
- **Ages One Through Three**
- **Ages Four Through Seven**
- **Ages Eight To Twelve**
- **The Church Working with the Home**
- **The Home Working with the Church**

THE HOME IS BASIC IN CHILDHOOD EDUCATION

The Scriptures reveal that the home is basic in childhood education. However, it is important to emphasize that this does not mean that the church or Christian school is unnecessary. Parents in today's world would be naive indeed to say that they can do the job alone. The demands, pressures, and influences in our twentieth-century culture prohibit parents from drawing that conclu-

GENE A. GETZ, PH.D., is an adjunct teacher in pastoral ministries at Dallas Theological Seminary, Dallas, Texas; he is also pastor of the Fellowship Bible Church North and the director of the Center for Church Renewal, both in Plano, Texas.
WALLACE GETZ, M.A., is on the staff of the Fellowship Bible Church North and the Center for Church Renewal, Plano, Texas.

sion. Parents need support and help in the Christian nurture of their children as perhaps never before.

Why does the Bible place a strong emphasis on the home in the Christian nurture of children? Generally speaking, the answer lies in the fact that there are certain learning experiences that children can have at home which are almost impossible to get in any other setting—church or school.

THE HOME PROVIDES A NATURAL AND SPONTANEOUS ENVIRONMENT

It is almost impossible to reconstruct the home environment in any other setting. The home provides "wall-to-wall," twenty-four-hours-a-day experiences. The family is normally a small unit of people (which varies from culture to culture), including all age levels, who eat together, play together, travel together, and sleep under the same roof. Even communal structures are difficult to maintain on a long-term basis when more than one family unit lives together. And in our Western culture, in-laws in the same house often create serious problems.

The naturalness of the home environment is well illustrated in Deuteronomy 6, in which Moses prepared the Israelites for entering the promised land. After wandering for forty years in the wilderness because of their sin, they were then ready to settle down in Canaan.

Moses warned parents in Israel regarding their own relationship to God: "And you shall love the LORD your God with all your heart and with all your soul and with all your might. And these words, which I am commanding you today, shall be on your heart" (Deut. 6:5-6, NASB). Then Moses instructed parents to teach the Word of God to their children. He indicated *when* and *where* and *how* this is to take place: "When you sit in your house and when you walk by the way and when you lie down and when you rise up" (Deut. 6:7, NASB).

At least three things become obvious from this passage.

1. Parents need *more than head knowledge* about the Bible. In order for them to impart the Word of God effectively to their children, the truths of the Bible must first permeate the parents' lives. An ability to quote Scripture and to teach doctrine to our children is not enough! More important than what we say about God to our children is what we are in their presence. Parents who love God with their whole heart, soul and energy will become obvious examples of Christian truth and virtue.

2. Effective teaching in the home must also involve *more than a period of instruction*. It must *happen* naturally and spontaneously—when we are seated at the table eating or in the family room watching television. It may occur when we are walking through the woods or even around the block. It may happen when we tuck the children into bed at night or when we awaken them in the morning.

3. The Word of God *must permeate the total atmosphere of the home.*

Christ must be the center of every activity—whether we are in serious discussion or enjoying happy moments together building block houses, wrestling, biking, swimming, or eating out. Some of the most natural opportunities for teaching biblical truths happen in the regular activities of daily living, and if we pass them by, they may never occur again. What's more, these parent-child opportunities happen *only* in the home—not at school or in church. In the home, the realities of life are obvious—where we *are* what we *really* are—both as parents and children.

THE HOME PROVIDES AN OPPORTUNITY FOR POSITIVE PARENTAL EXAMPLES

Marshall McLuhan's theme, "the medium is the message," is more than a twentieth-century truism. It is doubtful that McLuhan himself understood the profound biblical implications of this observation—a conclusion which he built on communication phenomena in our contemporary culture.

From Old Testament days until now, God designed the home to be one of the more significant illustrations of this concept. *A godly home becomes a message in itself.* This is the thrust of Deuteronomy 6.

How were men to recognize Christians and who they were? Jesus explained it: "By this all men will know that you are My disciples, if you have love for one another" (John 13:35, NASB).

How were men to know that Jesus Christ is the Son of God? Again Jesus said it clearly when He prayed that we "may all be one; even as Thou, Father, art in Me, and I in Thee . . . that they may be perfected in unity, that the world may know that Thou didst send Me" (John 17:21, 23).

The very love and unity in the body of Christ itself becomes the message of Christ. The medium (the functioning body) was to *become* the message to the world.

God designed the home so that children could learn by example. Their value system is to emerge in the context of dynamic Christian living, where father and mother demonstrate biblical realities. As children observe their father loving their mother as "Christ loved the church" and as children see their mother submitting to their father as "the church is to be subject to Christ," they are learning biblical truth by direct experience. This is far more meaningful than mere verbalization.

The lesson is clear. If we want our children to "love as Christ loved," we must not just *tell* them to "love as Christ loved." Rather we must "love as Christ loved." If we want them to pray, *we* must pray. If we want them to be kind to others, *we* must be kind to others. If we want them to share their faith, *we* must share *our* faith. If we want them to read their Bibles, *we* must read *our* Bibles.

As will be shown in more detail later, God made children with a natural tendency to become what their parents are. J. A. Hadfield, a psychologist who has spent much of his life studying the development and growth patterns of children, has made a rather stunning statement. "We see," he says, "that it is by a perfectly natural process that the child develops standards of behavior and a moral sense. So that *if you never taught a child one single moral maxim, he would nevertheless develop moral—or immoral—standards of right and wrong by the process of identification."* [1]

This is a profound statement indeed. But it is not so surprising when we look at what Scripture says about the home. Students of human behavior—secular though they may be—have discovered through the process of observation many notions that correlate either partially or totally with biblical truth.

Take the observations of psychologists and psychiatrists regarding the father image. Unknowingly they have confirmed to a great extent the importance of reflecting Christ in our parental life-style. For whether we recognize it or not, a child's view of God is very often his view of his parents—especially of his father.

The father image, of course, is of particular significance in Scripture, and this is not without design. God the Father is desirous that children grow up with a correct view of who He really is and what He is really like. Thus Paul instructs fathers, "Do not provoke your children to anger; but bring them up in the discipline and instruction of the Lord" (Eph. 6:4, NASB). And again, "Fathers, do not exasperate your children, that they may not lose heart" (Col. 3:21, NASB). Bruce Narramore states the following:

> My experience in counseling neurotic adults has invariably shown that their image of God has been colored by negative experiences with parents, God's representatives on earth. This is not to say that biblical teachings on God's character failed to influence our spiritual relationships, they certainly do. *But negative emotional reactions stemming from childhood interfere with our ability to apply biblical knowledge.* Think of your own Christian experience. Haven't you sometimes feared a vengeful God or felt He didn't understand? Have you had difficulty believing God's will was best for you? Have you resented God's direction or discipline? Most of these feelings are emotional hangovers from childhood experiences.
>
> In a real sense God has given us a divine opportunity to shape our children's lives for time and for eternity. It is beautiful to realize we can actually teach our children the love and character of God. It is awesome to know that our own hangups can drive wedges between our precious children and God, the Creator of the universe. [2]

The Early Years Are the Crucial Years

James R. Dolby, a Christian psychologist, states: "I concur with those who say that the first year of life is the most important year in a person's existence.

---

1. J. A. Hadfield, *Childhood and Adolescence* (Baltimore: Penguin, 1962), p. 134. Hadfield's italics.
2. Bruce Narramore, *Help! I'm a Parent* (Grand Rapids: Zondervan, 1972), pp. 13-14. Narramore's italics.

During this year he learns whether the world is cruel or comfortable; he learns that he is a separate entity apart from the world of stimuli outside him. This year is the foundation on which all personality rests."[3]

Unfortunately some Christians have interpreted a statement of this nature to mean that man cannot change nor can he be a responsible human being. Man *can* change, and man *can* become a responsible individual through the power of the indwelling Christ. And man can change without remembering and understanding all that has happened in his past life. He can forget the past and move on.

But a person can never be made over completely in his emotional and physical life. In fact, the Bible teaches that the effects of the sins of the fathers is sometimes seen in the third and fourth generation of children (Num. 14:18). Though this may have specific reference to Israel and God's judgment on them, the principle inherent in these words of Scripture is verified again and again in today's world. An immature and carnal parent produces immature and carnal offspring, who in turn produce immature and carnal offspring.

The early years, then, are the crucial years, and, of course, the home provides the context for the early years. Pine underscores this fact in this striking statement: "If a child's educational achievements depend so heavily on what he learned before the age of six, the home—not the school—emerges as the major educational institution in the land."[4]

Mature psychological development in a child provides the foundation on which mature spiritual development takes place. For example, the greatest psychological need of a child during his first year of life is for security and love. An environment that is filled with uncertainties, adult disagreements, and impatience, creates insecurity for a child. Children in the first year of life need exposure to parents who are truly manifesting the fruit of the Spirit—"love, joy, peace, patience, kindness, goodness, faithfulness, gentleness, self-control" (Gal. 5:22-23). The human being who manifests these characteristics makes the child's environment a *secure* place for him to grow in and to develop. In turn, a secure environment enables a child to develop those personality traits that prepare the way for biblical teaching and learning.

Children begin to learn biblical truth the moment they are born, but mainly at the nonverbal and emotional (affective) level. Here is an excellent example of McLuhan's statement that "the medium is the message." The environment in which a child lives *is* the Christian message itself. And if the environment radiates love and security, he immediately picks up these "signals"—though mainly at the subconscious level. His personality is being formed. The foundations are being laid for an acceptance of the biblical message at the conscious level. Conversely, if the environment reflects hostility, uncertainty, and insecur-

---

3. James R. Dolby, *I, Too, Am Man* (Waco, Tex.: Word, 1969), p. 78.
4. Maya Pines, *Revolution in Learning: The Years from Birth to Six* (New York: Harper & Row, 1967), p. 52.

ity, the foundations are being laid for a rejection of the biblical message at the conscious level.

GUIDING CHILDREN
AGES ONE THROUGH THREE

There are various approaches to describing the phases of early child development from ages one through three or four. The following, adapted from Hadfield, are graphic and realistic. Though they originate in the psychological literature, they seem to correlate very significantly with biblical concepts.[5]

SELF-DISPLAY

A two-year-old child who calls attention to himself is naturally moving from the security of the first year to the exploration of the second year. Self-display appears naturally and innately.

However, if the child becomes extensive in his "showing off," he is doing so because of insecurity and lack of attention. To snub him or to punish him only aggravates his problem. A "limelight" child at the age of two needs attention— not negative and disciplinary—but personal and positive attention.

CURIOSITY AND EXPLORATION

Children of two are also naturally curious. They have an innate desire to explore. Consequently, they need an environment that is conducive to this need.

Parents who overly restrict them and force them into an unnatural role are working against their natural God-created tendencies. This is the way they learn, and this is the way they develop healthy personalities. Unfortunately our present culture has created an environment in many homes that works against children rather than with them. Our living rooms are filled with "thou-shalt-not-touch" items which create frustration for two-year-olds. As much as possible, they need an environment that allows them freedom to move about, to play, to touch. All of this is forming a foundation for continued and future exploration and interest in biblical truth at the cognitive level. Research shows that healthy interest and motivation to learn in later life is very much related to the full expression of this need during these years.

IMITATION

The natural capacity to imitate comes into full force between one and two years of age. *What* children imitate comes from their environment. It is a

5. J. A. Hadfield has outlined various places in his book *Childhood and Adolescence,* which, in my opinion, correlate significantly with biblical precepts.

subconscious process, unrelated to their power to reason, and *is far more effective than verbal teaching.*

Parents must be living models of Jesus Christ with this age. Children naturally and spontaneously imitate another person's behavior. They reflect either our bad habits or our good habits. If we act in impatient ways, they reflect impatience. If we are selfish, they reflect selfishness. If we are insecure, they reflect insecurity. If we constantly strike out, they learn to strike back.

Fortunately and unfortunately, they also imitate other children. This means that parents should attempt to create an environment where older children do not take advantage of younger children and set bad examples. For instance, a four-year-old who constantly hits a two-year-old teaches him to strike at others.

When teaching two-year-olds, then, it is important to teach biblical truth by example as well as by formal teaching. Children who are growing and developing in an environment that reflects the fruit of the Spirit learn to reflect these personality traits, even though they are too young to understand and comprehend biblical doctrine didactically.

SELF-WILL

The most misunderstood phase in child development is the self-will phase. It is a particularly difficult phase for Christians because of their view of the biblical doctrine regarding the "old nature."

There is no doubt that every child is born into this world with a sin nature. This sin nature is the capacity to serve sin and self. As children mature and develop, this capacity is greatly affected by environmental conditions. If children are in an environment that is characterized by Christian attributes, they tend to take on the same characteristics, even apart from conversion. If they are in an atmosphere that is characterized by non-Christian attributes, they tend to take on these characteristics.

Christians frequently make the mistake of classifying the old nature as a full-blown manifestation of sin. We do this because we see the child through adult eyes (our own adult perspective and what is true in our own adult lives). We often interpret the biblical reference to the degenerative manifestation of the sin nature in adult people as being applicable to small children from birth. We tend to classify every manifestation of anger in a child in the same category as if an adult lost his temper. Every manifestation of self-centeredness is classified as the same type of manifestation as it also appears in our adult lives. Every evidence of interest and curiosity in his sexual nature is sometimes classified as a manifestation of the same thing we see in mature sinning adults. To many Christians, these characteristics in a child are proof positive that man is a sinner by nature.

Actually this is an inaccurate interpretation of child behavior—physically, psychologically, and spiritually. The sin nature in a child is not synonymous with being a "practicing and mature sinner." Rather it is a capacity that causes an individual to become a "practicing sinner." How we as parents and teachers handle these natural characteristics just described has a great deal to do with how quickly a child develops spiritual problems.

The self-will phase is a natural phase in children of two. It is biological as well as psychological. They are learning to cope with their world—including people. It is important for Christian parents to distinguish this phase from what the Bible classifies as the "old nature." Functionally speaking, it helps to preserve this biblical concept until the child's personality is organized, coordinated, and harmonized at about age four. This capacity seems to come into full fruition at this time, that is, unless we misunderstand the self-will period and begin to work against it. If we do, the imitation capacity takes over, and the natural process of anxiety, anger, aggression, fear, and insecurity begins a premature manifestation of sin problems.

Christian parents then must understand the self-will period in two-year-olds. It must be channeled and directed—not broken. Children need to learn to cope with their world but in appropriate ways. If they have the right behavioral models, combined with understanding adults, they will move naturally into the suggestibility phase around age two-and-a-half or three—a phase where they *naturally* desire to be like their parents.

SUGGESTIBILITY

If a child does not naturally begin to develop traits that are more cooperative around two-and-a-half to three years, then his self-will phase may be extending into the suggestibility phase. This means that the child's parents have probably "worked against" the self-will phase rather than "with it."

Parents need to understand what has happened. To continue to force and repress the child who is engaged in this struggle will only cause the self-will phase to continue to extend itself into later years, producing an anxious and perhaps aggressive and angry personality. Herein lie the roots to some very significant spiritual and psychological problems which may appear in later life.

How do you teach children from two-and-a-half to three? How do you get them to respond? Remember that normal children of this age will usually *imitate* what you do but tend *not* to do something *if you tell them to*. In other words, the best way to teach kindness, cooperation, respect, and reverence toward God and the Bible is to demonstrate these characteristics in our own lives as parents.

Remember too that children of two-and-half to three detect "verbal" and "life" contradictions very quickly. They will reject "words" and "do what you do" if the two are not in harmony. You do not have to tell children of this age to "do what you do" and "not as you say." They will follow your examples automatically.

IDENTIFICATION

The next phase in the child's development is identification—the tendency to "take over" the personality of a parent. The three-year-old may say, "I'm Daddy mowing the lawn," or, "I'm Mommy washing the dishes," or, "I'm Teacher telling a story."

Since children normally identify with those they love and admire, it is important for parents to establish a relationship with them that reflects security and a feeling of comfortableness. The more a child is attracted to a parent or a teacher, the more he will want to be like him.

Again, this underscores the importance of adults being the right behavioral model. The more the adult exemplifies Jesus Christ, the more the child will reflect these same traits, even though he may not be able to understand fully Christian truths.

This process can also be dangerous. All adults have weaknesses. We all have strengths which may not suit the temperament and innate capacities of the child. Therefore, it is important to expose children to a variety of behavioral models—both adults and children—who also exemplify Christian virtues. Significantly, God designed a natural context in which this can happen—the family. It takes two persons to bring a child into the world. Thus the child has two personalities with which he identifies from birth. Also, it seems logical that the more children there are in a family, the more opportunity an individual child has to mix with a variety of personalities in close range and to incorporate into himself those characteristics and interests most suited to his or her temperament. This is why it is sometimes true that an only child or the first child has difficulties.[6]

Fortunately, a child is not locked in to bad identifications, and he can change rather quickly if he is exposed on a regular basis to people who exhibit positive characteristics. The key term here is *regular basis,* and it is the home that provides the context for this exposure at close range on a consistent basis.

EGO IDEAL

Between the ages of three and four, a child begins to move toward developing a well-organized personality. Adults begin to see duality in his personality, self-consciousness, self-criticism, self-control, and the development of the will.

From a biblical perspective, this is an extremely important age. It is at this

---

6. A first child often has difficulties also because of the insecurity faced by parents with their first child. Parents also tend to try too hard with the first. They want to produce the perfect child. The more relaxed the parents are with their child, the more the child is relaxed.

time that the biblical doctrine regarding the "old nature" becomes very significant. The Adamic nature begins to become a force in the child's life, a force which a child does not understand but one which Christian parents *must* understand. The child naturally and normally begins to be pulled internally in two directions—to imitate what is good and to imitate what is bad.

If a child has felt the necessary security of the first year and has had good behavioral models in the second, and if we have handled the self-will phase with understanding and discretion, the child will find it rather easy to continue to conform to positive examples in his life.

Conversely, if we have violated the natural bent of the child in his early years, the child will have a much more difficult time responding to certain norms. He is now at an age when he begins to scrap the personality of the parent and keep the character of the child. He is now becoming his own person. He is shedding the aspects of identification and is establishing within himself guiding principles. Put another way, he no longer says, "I am a kind, gentle, and unselfish man like Daddy"; rather, he says, "I am a kind, gentle, and unselfish boy."

Since children between three and four have a capacity for self-consciousness, they also have a capacity for self-criticism. They can now develop very strong feelings of shamefulness. They can also feel stupid, selfish, and clumsy.

This has significant implications for Christian parents. Very quickly, we can develop a morbid self-consciousness in a child by confronting him with adult concepts of sin and degeneration. He feels guilt naturally, especially if an adult whom he admires often "says so." When a relatively good child from a Christian home becomes obsessed with feelings of shame and unworthiness, he has, no doubt, been inappropriately exposed to the concept of sin. He has developed an overly sensitive conscience.

This type of problem in a child is often reflected by unusual criticism of others—both children and adults. The child may try to pull others down to his own level. He may also project his own self-criticism on others and feel they are perpetually criticizing him. When in a group, he may also develop ideas of reference, that is, he may feel that the scolding of a group of children by a teacher is a direct reference to himself.

This is not to say that we should not deal with the concept of sin. But it does mean that we must deal with it at a child's level, not an adult level. In fact, children of four are very cognizant of tendencies to do wrong things, even without being verbally reminded. They are very much aware of the natural inner struggle that begins to emerge in their personalities. If they have developed normal personality patterns, they are ready to understand clearly the positive aspects of the gospel—that Jesus Christ desires to be their Savior from sin.

As children grow through the school years, patterns of acceptable or unacceptable behavior continue to develop more fully. If a positive foundation has been laid carefully in his earlier years, the child may be more inclined toward positive attitudes and behavior in accord with the Word of God through parental example.

GUIDING CHILDREN AGES FOUR THROUGH SEVEN

Children between ages four and seven need adults who understand their *individuality*. They have all the "ingredients" of grownups. Their personalities are organized, and they can make judgments. They feel independent and have a new sense of power and self-assurance. They now have a will in the *true* sense of the word. They respond naturally to rivalry. Their imagination is very keen—so much so that they confuse fact and fiction.

If a child's environment has been proper, as described in the previous sections, he may now be ready for conversion. A child of four or five can, with clear understanding, invite Jesus Christ to be his Savior. Since he is aware of sin, he can make his decision in the light of his *need* for a Savior. (For more on this subject, see chap. 23, "Evangelism of Children.") True, his understanding is limited and immature, but one who works closely with children can testify to their ability to grasp their need for salvation. The gospel need not be presented with great force and condemnation; rather, a simple story of another child inviting Christ to be his Savior can ignite in the heart of a child his need to do so himself.

A child from four to seven is capable of understanding biblical truth. Parents can encourage children in this age group to memorize Scripture, listen to appropriate biblical stories, and learn basic doctrine. These biblical truths must be taught at their level of understanding, must be visualized whenever possible, and must be integrated into activities that are normal and natural to him.

GUIDING CHILDREN EIGHT TO TWELVE

Normally, children in this age group move from *individuality* and self-centeredness to *socialization* and group interest. They are generally healthy, have keen minds, are more goal-oriented than before, like to collect things, and are extroverted. They do not outwardly show too much concern for adults, but they are concerned about their peers and about being a part of the group. They will respond to authority but do so more quickly when they choose to do so. Their interest in play, hobbies, and games is at an all-time high.

Since children from eight to twelve tend to put adults in a secondary place in their thinking, it is wise to avoid authoritarian attitudes in discipline and control. They want to be treated more as adults than children. Understand, of course, they *are* children—and down deep they know this too—but they are struggling toward maturity. If they are involved in setting boundaries for themselves, they will more willingly abide by the rules. In fact, they may be harder on themselves than an adult may be.

Children of this age are capable of learning significant portions of Bible doctrine, of memorizing Scripture easily. And they respond enthusiastically to well-presented biblical accounts reflecting heroism, bravery, and courage.

Children in this age level are capable of assimilating many facts without regard to application. Therefore parents must help their children relate Scripture to life. Parents must be careful however, that they do not cause a child to expect more from his life than he can give—causing excessive guilt. But he must be taught to integrate truth into his life.

Again this can best be done in the activities he likes best. Natural sports provide unlimited opportunities for biblical *input* as well as application. Since games are organized and have rules, they reflect essential elements of balanced living. Consequently, they provide unique opportunities for life-related learning. Also, their behavior at play reflects their homelife and their deepest needs. For example, a child who is unusually hostile while at play (beyond normal aggressiveness) may be repressed at home, or he may be insecure and unsure of himself because of lack of direction and control at home.

Though children during this age level have keen minds, they must still be motivated to learn. Old methods and approaches in biblical teaching may not hold interest too long for the "Sesame Street" generation. Much biblical truth is not naturally exciting to an eight- through eleven-year-old. But there is nothing more important. The god of this world is bent on crowding out the most essential things from children's lives. Christian leaders and educators in the twentieth century must decide which one to follow and lead children to follow. In many cases, complacency already reflects that decision.

The Church Working with the Home

Parents have a significant, irreplaceable role in nurturing their children in the things of God. Fortunately, however, this monumental task need not be carried on without assistance. The alert local church can do much to support and aid parents in their role of child training by following these three suggestions:

First, the church should *provide training for parents on how to understand and rear their children.* Many fathers and mothers are not as aware as they should be of the concepts discussed in the preceding pages of this chapter. For example, they are not sufficiently sensitive to the power of nonverbal communication in the life of a small child. Furthermore they do not see the significant correlation between proper psychological development and spiritual development. Also many do not understand the natural phases through which all children develop—their natural bent.

Second, the church must *provide the home with a program of Christian education that supplements and supports parents in their task of child nurture.* Today there is a strong movement to place Christian education back in the home, "where," they say, "it belongs." Though this emphasis is good in some respects, it is also dangerous, for it tends to overlook or unduly minimize the role of the local church.

On the one hand, we *do* need to put Christian education back in the home. There are some aspects of Christian education—some basic aspects—that only the home can implement.

But there are also aspects of Christian education of children that most parents cannot handle alone. Our culture has created so many competitive forces and demands on the home that it is almost impossible for the average parent to provide all that a child needs in the way of Christian nurture.

Unfortunately, in our zeal to provide this Christian nurture in the church, we have gone to the other extreme—developing curriculum, multiplying agencies, and giving parents the impression that the church has the answer for the Christian education of their children. Many parents—already overly pressured with demands on their time—have gladly relinquished their child nurture responsibility to the church.

The answer, of course, is that we need *both* child nurture in the home and child nurture in the church. There are certain objectives the church cannot achieve. The home, with its natural and spontaneous environment, its father and mother figures, its wall-to-wall experience, is basic to effective Christian education.

But there are also certain objectives that parents have difficulty achieving alone. For example, a well-trained staff of teachers in a well-equipped classroom can provide a quality experience in learning and applying Bible content that would be very difficult for parents to duplicate.

The home, then, needs the church in the nurture of its children. But it needs a supplementary and supportive program—not one that competes or encourages parents to relinquish their own responsibilities.

Third, the church needs to *provide a program of Christian education that incorporates biblical principles of child nurture.* In the Bible, child nurture is described in the context of an informal, warm, and accepting atmosphere. Also in Bible times, parents were the primary teachers. Learning was individualized within the context of small, closely knit family units. And learning took place in a variety of ways.

These biblical realities translated into principles provide us with some significant guidelines for carrying out Christian education of children in the local church. Teachers and others who work with the young should carefully consider the following questions regarding the use of biblical principles:

1. Is the learning environment in our Sunday schools and other agencies warm and accepting, creating an informal climate for learning? Or is the atmosphere formal, cold, and academic?
2. Are our children exposed to husband-and-wife teams who can function not only as teachers but also as parental substitutes—demonstrating the same qualities of exemplary life as dedicated Christian parents?

3. Is learning individualized, and does it take place in small, closely knit groups that simulate family units? Or is it a larger group process, where individual children are lost in the mass?
4. Does learning happen in a variety of ways—visually, verbally, and through active involvement—using a variety of media and techniques? Or is it a process that consists of one basic approach—"listening" to a teacher "talk"?

There is much, then, that the church can do to assist parents in Christian education. The challenge, however, is to help parents truly function as parents, to supplement but not to replace the home, and to utilize biblical teaching-learning principles with children.

THE HOME WORKING WITH THE CHURCH

Christian education is a two-way street. The home needs the church, but also it is true that the church needs the home.

A local church cannot adequately meet its objectives with children without *specific* support from Christian homes. What are some ways by which the home can help the church in the Christian education of children?

First, parents should not expect the church to solve problems that can only be effectively solved at home. For example, a discipline problem at home must be solved at home. The church should not be expected to do it.

Second, parents can cooperate with teachers and workers in solving discipline problems, in doing homework, and in applying Christian truths.

Third, parents can encourage their children to become involved in the Christian education program. They can get them to church on time. They can talk about the importance of Sunday school and church. They can pray together for their teachers and pastor. They can encourage their children to prepare their lessons. They can encourage Bible reading and memorization of verses.

Fourth, parents can encourage the workers in their church who minister to their children. Parents can invite them to dinner, pray for them, talk with them about their children, and express appreciation to them.

SUMMARY

In summary, then, it must be restated that the Bible clearly focuses on the home as basic to childhood education. It provides a natural and spontaneous environment for Christian learning. God has created the family structure to provide parental behavioral models for children to emulate, models that in themselves provide basic doctrinal input regarding God and what He is like.

How important for parents to become more and more like Jesus Christ—in their relationship as husband and wife, in their relationships with their children, as well as in their relationships with other people—both Christians and non-Christians.

How important, too, for parents to understand the natural phases of child development, so that they can work with the natural way of the child rather than against it.

As parents and teachers work cooperatively, as church and home complement each other in their roles, the task of educating children in spiritual living will become far more effective than is otherwise possible.

FOR FURTHER READING

Adams, Jay E. *Christian Living in the Home.* Nutley, N.J.: Presbyterian and Reformed, 1972.

Adelsperger, Charlotte. *When Your Child Hurts.* Chappaqua, N.Y.: Christian Herald, 1981.

Anderson, Robert H., and Harold Shane. *As the Twig Is Bent: Readings in Early Childhood Education.* Boston: Houghton Mifflin, 1971.

Brandt, Henry R. *Keys to Better Living for Parents.* Chicago: Moody, 1962.

Brandt, Henry R., and Homer E. Dowdy. *Building a Christian Home.* Wheaton, Ill.: Scripture Press, 1960.

Bye, Beryl. *Teaching Our Children the Christian Faith.* London: Hodder & Stoughton, 1965.

Campbell, D. Ross. *How to Really Love Your Child.* Wheaton, Ill.: Scripture Press, Victor Books, 1977.

Carlson, Lee, ed. *Christian Parenting.* Valley Forge, Pa.: Judson, 1985.

Christopherson, Victor A. *Child Rearing in Today's Family.* Valley Forge, Pa.: Judson, 1985.

Deal, William S. *Counseling Christian Parents.* Grand Rapids: Zondervan, 1970.

Dobson, James. *Dare to Discipline.* Wheaton, Ill.: Tyndale, 1970.

———. *Hide or Seek.* Old Tappan, N.J.: Revell, 1974.

———. *The Strong-Willed Child.* Wheaton, Ill.: Tyndale, 1978.

Dodson, Fitzhugh. *How to Father.* Los Angeles: Nash, 1973.

———. *How to Parent.* Los Angeles: Nash, 1970.

Dolby, James R. *I, Too, Am Man.* Waco, Tex.: Word, 1969.

Drakeford, John W. *The Home: Laboratory of Life.* Nashville: Broadman, 1965.

Edens, David, and Virginia Edens. *Why God Gave Children Parents.* Nashville: Broadman, 1966.

Evans, Laura Margaret. *Hand in Hand: Mother, Child and God.* Westwood, N.J.: Revell, 1960.

Feucht, Oscar E., ed. *Family Relationships and the Church.* St. Louis: Concordia, 1970.

———. *Helping Families Through the Church*. Rev. ed. St. Louis: Concordia, 1971.

Gangel, Kenneth O. *The Family First*. Minneapolis: HIS International, 1972.

Gangel, Kenneth O., and Elizabeth Gangel. *Between Christian Parent and Child*. Grand Rapids: Baker, 1974.

Getz, Gene A. *The Christian Home in a Changing World*. Chicago: Moody, 1972.

———. *The Measure of a Family*. Ventura, Calif.: Gospel Light, Regal Books, 1976.

Ginott, Haim G. *Between Parent and Child*. New York: MacMillan, 1965.

Hadfield, J. A. *Childhood and Adolescence*. Baltimore: Penguin, 1962.

Hazelip, Harold. *Happiness in the Home: Guidelines for Spouses and Parents*. Grand Rapids: Baker, 1985.

Hendricks, Howard, *Heaven Help the Home*. Wheaton, Ill.: Scripture Press, 1973.

Henrichsen, Walter A. *How to Discipline Your Children*. Wheaton, Ill.: Scripture Press, Victor Books, 1981.

Heynen, Ralph. *The Secret of Christian Family Living*. Grand Rapids: Baker, 1965.

Kesler, Jay. *The Family Forum*. Wheaton, Ill.: Scripture Press, Victor Books, 1984.

Krumboltz, John D., and Helen B. Krumboltz. *Changing Children's Behavior*. Englewood Cliffs, N.J.: Prentice-Hall, 1972.

LeBar, Lois E. *Family Devotions with School-Age Children*. Westwood, N.J.: Revell, 1973.

Lee, Mark W. *Our Children Are Our Best Friends*. Grand Rapids: Zondervan, 1970.

Leman, Kevin. *The Birth Order Book*. Old Tappan, N.J.: Revell, 1984.

Matthews, Charles A. *The Christian Home*. Cincinnati: Standard, n.d.

Meier, Paul D. *Christian Child-Rearing and Personality Development*. Grand Rapids: Baker, 1977.

Narramore, Bruce. *A Guide to Child Rearing*. Grand Rapids: Zondervan, 1972.

———. *Help! I'm a Parent*. Grand Rapids: Zondervan, 1972.

Narramore, Clyde M. *How to Succeed in Family Living*. Glendale, Calif.: Regal, 1968.

———. *How to Understand and Influence Children*. Grand Rapids: Zondervan, 1957.

Reed, Bobbie. *Christian Family Activities: Families with Preschoolers, Families with Children, One Parent Families*. Cincinnati: Standard, 1982.

Scudder, C. W. *The Family in Christian Perspective*. Nashville: Broadman, 1962.

Small, Dwight H. *Design for Christian Marriage*. Westwood, N.J.: Revell, 1959.

Strauss, Richard L. *How to Raise Confident Children.* Grand Rapids: Baker, 1984.

Tournier, Paul. *To Understand Each Other.* Richmond, Va.: Knox, 1962.

Wagemaker, Herbert. *Why Can't I Understand My Kids?* Grand Rapids: Zondervan, 1973.

Webb, Barbara Owen. *Devotions for Families with Young Readers.* Valley Forge, Pa.: Judson, 1985.

Zuck, Roy B., and Gene A. Getz, eds. *Ventures in Family Living.* Chicago: Moody, 1971.

34

Michael Beidel

The Role of Home Schooling in Childhood Education

- • **Historical Background**
- • **Questionable Motives for Considering**
- • **Positive Reasons for Considering**
- • **Important Considerations**
  COMMITMENT OF PARENTS
  PARENTAL ABILITY TO TEACH
  POSSIBLE TRANSITION TO PUBLIC SCHOOL
  COUNSEL FROM SCHOOL OFFICIALS
  "UMBRELLA ARRANGEMENT" WITH A CHRISTIAN SCHOOL
- • **Selection of Materials**

Home schooling—that is, the choice of parents to educate their own children at home rather than sending them to a school—is not a new phenomenon. The increased secularization of public education and the predominant influence of secular humanism in textbook selection and in teacher training in the education departments of most colleges and universities have provided an impetus for a phenomenal growth in the home school movement. Raymond Moore,

Michael Beidel is headmaster of Trinity Christian Academy, Addison, Texas.

whose academic credentials, books and publications, and persuasiveness give him credibility, has been the leading spokesman and proponent for home schools. Recently, Bill Gothard and James Dobson have become supporters of that educational alternative. Home schooling, as the term is used in this chapter, refers to the activity of parents educating their own children in their home. That means of education precludes the child's attendance and involvement in a more traditional public or private school. It presumes also that the parents are primarily responsible for selecting and teaching the curriculum to the child.

HISTORICAL BACKGROUND

Historically, "home schools" preceded both private and public schools as we traditionally know them. Biblically, both Moses and Daniel attended "schools" in Egypt and Babylon, respectively. But in ancient Israel, normally Jewish parents provided both academic and religious education for their own children. During Jesus' life on earth, most Jewish towns provided a school for their school-aged children beginning at six years of age.[1] In fact, those towns and villages which refused to provide a school were viewed with disdain by the rest of the Jewish community. In primitive America, especially on the frontier, children were often taught at home by one or more parents. Larger communities and more developed settlements, however, provided schools in the traditional sense for their inhabitants. Both the Pilgrims and the Puritans had mandatory schooling for their children, which began when the children were six.

QUESTIONABLE MOTIVES FOR CONSIDERING HOME SCHOOLING

In the same way that Christian schools are not for every Christian family, home schooling is likewise not the educational solution for every Christian family.

Inordinate fear of humanistic and/or evolutionary viewpoints propagated in most public school curricula is, by itself, not a legitimate reason for considering home schooling. One group conducts seminars which border on the pornographic to scare "unknowing" parents about the dangers of public school education, while using their own distortions and exaggerations. Although it is true that humanism and evolution are antibiblical, great numbers of parents have done well with their children by openly discussing those viewpoints and countering them with wisdom and intellectual integrity. There is great benefit in allowing older elementary, junior high, and high school students freedom to question their own values and to examine other values in the context of their

1. Alfred Edersheim, *Life and Times of Jesus the Messiah* (Grand Rapids: Eerdmans, 1974), pp. 230-32.

own homes, and with the resource of their own parents and churches. "For God has not given us a spirit of fear, but of power and love and a sound mind" (2 Tim. 1:7).

Another questionable motive is a desire to escape the obvious conflicts that exist between a Christian family and the teaching their children are receiving in a public or private school. Again, a healthy tension between home and school is not entirely bad. One of God's primary means of bringing believers into greater maturity in their relationship with Him is through tension and disagreement that is worked through and resolved in wisdom and in submission to the Lord. One of the most powerful confidence-builders in believers is the realization that the truth to which they are strongly committed will stand the test of the most adamant skeptic or critic.

A third motive which warrants scrutiny is the problem of guilt because of the misperception that "good parents are home schooling," or that home schooling makes parents more spiritual and responsive to their children's needs than if they had placed them in a public or private school. Related to this, there tends to be terrific pressure from home schooling disciples which promotes a feeling of guilt among parents who are not teaching their children at home. Paul's admonition in Romans 12 to "not be conformed to the world" includes an encouragement to resist unthinking or unwitting conformity to a segment of the Christian world.

Fourth, the bandwagon mentality, which tends to respond to fads and fashions, is another questionable motive. Families involved in home schooling tend to be overly enthusiastic about its merits; that, combined with the support of nationally recognized Christian leaders, provides a strong persuasion factor that is difficult for some to resist.

POSITIVE REASONS FOR CONSIDERING HOME SCHOOLING

There are a number of very good reasons why a family might want to consider home schooling as an educational alternative for its children. Perhaps the soundest reason is the recognition that development of a healthy self-concept in a child is primarily the result of healthy interpersonal relationships with adults. A home schooling environment would obviously provide opportunity to meet those kinds of needs, particularly at the early elementary age.[2]

Another good reason for considering home schooling at the early elementary level is that children's formal schooling ought not to be rushed at those early ages. The emphasis in public schools and even in the curriculum of some private and Christian schools is counter to that philosophy. Research indicates that, considering a child with a given intellect, whether he is taught reading early or later in those early elementary years, his reading skills will eventually

---

2. Raymond Moore and Dorothy Moore, *Home Grown Kids* (Waco, Tex.: Word, 1981), pp. 32-33.

stabilize.[3] It is true, also, that when one considers the developmental variables which together contribute to a child's ability to learn, the level of maturation for the collection of those variables is somewhere between eight and ten years of age.[4] That, coupled with the fact that boys tend to lag behind girls in their maturational development by one or two years, suggests that early elementary education at home could be a viable alternative for a family. It provides a one-on-one or two-on-one setting that allows for adjustment for individual learning differences and encourages opportunities for the sensitive parent to integrate truth and character development into the curriculum.

A commitment to developing emotional stability in one's child is another good reason to consider home schooling at the early elementary level. Healthy child-adult relationships, particularly with the child's parents, are important in nurturing a healthy emotional life. Home schooling provides an environment promoting security, respect, self-worth, and a sense of importance, when the parents recognize and are committed to developing those qualities as they interact with their child. As was mentioned earlier, a child at the early elementary age is usually quite eager to please his parents and is, therefore, especially receptive to attempts to develop his sense of self-worth and emotional well-being.

Related to that, an older child who is seriously learning disabled, lacks motivation, or is otherwise similarly handicapped academically can benefit from a home school environment if the parents are adequately equipped to meet that special need. Contrary to some opinions, the parent must possess not only special skill and sensitivity in dealing with the child's spiritual and emotional needs, but must also possess some degree of academic expertise to handle the curriculum, especially as it increases in complexity during the upper elementary, junior high, and high school ages. Again, the tutorial potential which a parent has in dealing with his child one-on-one gives him great advantage in meeting that child's special needs, especially in nurturing his self-concept with a healthy biblical perspective.

Geographical location and/or the quality of the other educational alternatives provide another good reason for home schooling. I know of two families for whom home schooling would be the most reasonable alternative because of where they live. The one family manages and lives on the premises of a Christian camp; the other lives in a rural area. Similarly, a missionary family whose alternatives for education are limited might well meet their childrens' educational needs best by teaching them at home.

Financial feasibility provides another pure motive for considering home

---

3. David Elkind, *The Hurried Child* (Reading, Mass.: Addison-Wesley, 1981), p. 33.
4. Raymond Moore and Dorothy Moore, *Better Late Than Early* (New York: Reader's Digest, 1975), pp. 34-35; Joseph M. Wepman, "The Modality Concept—Including a Statement of the Perceptual and Conceptual Levels of Learning." *Perception and Reading* (Proceedings of the Twelfth Annual Convention, International Reading Association, Newark, Del., 1968), pp. 1-6.

schooling for one's children. Some families who are very much committed to educating their children Christianly can simply not afford to send them to a Christian school. A viable alternative is teaching the children at home, where the primary cost—which involves large amounts of *time* spent in teaching the children—is affordable and in agreement with their philosophical commitment regarding the importance of Christian education. Time, then, is the significant factor.

IMPORTANT CONSIDERATIONS REGARDING HOME SCHOOLING

COMMITMENT OF PARENTS TO THE TASK

Even with what one would consider to be pure motives, a number of other cautions must be considered in "testing the waters." Any one of these could well be the Lord's means of discouraging home schooling. First, both parents must have a high level of commitment to teaching their children at home. Although the mother is usually the primary teacher, because of inordinate demands which proper home schooling makes on the family, the father must be enormously supportive and actively involved in the teaching process and in sharing some of the other normal household responsibilities with his wife. Biblically, the father is given primary responsibility for educating and disciplining his children (Eph. 6:1-4). Although some of the educating responsibility is often delegated to the wife and/or the school, wisdom dictates that he be more than nominally involved in the learning process.[5]

PARENTAL ABILITY TO TEACH

Although it is certainly not a necessary prerequisite that a parent be a trained teacher to teach his children effectively at home, it is certainly best that the parent primarily involved in educating his child have the gift to teach. In addition, as the curriculum becomes increasingly sophisticated, it is essential that a parent have some background and training in each discipline he teaches. That is particularly true in mathematics and science, which are constantly in a state of change and update. The kind of nonsuperficial, nontrivial teaching and learning which stimulates and challenges the student with the joy of learning usually comes out of the reservoir and background which a gifted teacher brings to the classroom, particularly as the older child is able to master more complex levels of thinking and learning. In contrast, children are academically demotivated and frustrated by continued superficial treatment of subject matter which provides little or no intellectual challenge, or, worse yet, gives them the illusion of understanding a discipline well—when, in fact, they understand only in a shallow way.

5. Nancy Troupos, "Home Schooling: Is It for You?" *Baptist Bulletin* (February 1985).

POSSIBLE TRANSITION TO PUBLIC SCHOOL

Another very real problem is the difficulty in finding a school that will acknowledge the work done in teaching a child at home when the parents decide to put the child into a "regular" school. The older a child is when he is placed in school, the more difficult it becomes for the school accepting him to evaluate his work and to place him wisely. The best recourse for a family considering home schooling is to identify a school or schools which would accept the child, should the family so decide. The subject of an "umbrella school" and the possibility of a coordination between home and school with curriculum while the child is taught at home will be discussed later in this chapter. State and regionally accredited schools are sometimes hesitant to jeopardize their accreditation status by indiscriminately accepting home-schooled students, even when those children have been well educated. More significantly, the predominance of colleges and universities will admit only students who have graduated from an accredited high school. That suggests that a family consider very carefully a decision to home school their child for the entirety of his elementary and secondary education.

COUNSEL FROM SCHOOL OFFICIALS

The possibility of encountering opposition by either local or state public school educators or agencies is another consideration. Either of those entities provides a formidable foe. Paul's statement in Romans 13 that government is established by God for our protection suggests that we be wise and above reproach in dealing with either group. Seeking counsel and suggestions from the local public school officials about the implication of teaching one's children at home is wise. Additionally, it is wise also to attempt to place one's home school activities under the umbrella of a Christian school.[6]

Biblically, the home was the first institution established by God. In the garden, God said, "for this reason a man shall leave his father and mother and cleave to his wife, and the two of them shall become one flesh." In God's economy, then, the family is the most basic unit. The church, which is God's other divinely ordained institution, was "born" on the Day of Pentecost (Acts 2). The church, which is the body of Christ, is made up of families. The school, which has no divine origin as do the family and the church, is in a sense subject to both of those organisms. As such, it ought to function in interdependence with both church and family. In respect to home schooling, the implication seems to be obvious. The school should make itself available to a family wishing to home school its children, as long as the relationship does not infringe on its primary commitment to those families who are a part of its

6. Moore and Moore, *Home Grown Kids.*

constituency. Obviously, its board and administration must make that judgment.

"UMBRELLA ARRANGEMENT" WITH A CHRISTIAN SCHOOL

Increasingly, Christian schools, particularly those associated with the Association of Christian Schools International, are providing an umbrella arrangement for families desiring to teach their children at home. The most prominent of these is the Dayton Christian School System in Dayton, Ohio. Generally, the Christian school provides its own authority and validation of the education which children under its umbrella auspices are receiving at home. These include: (1) a permanent file in its official school records; (2) provision of a transcript or other record should the family need it for some reason; (3) a means of testing the home-schooled child periodically with standardized and sometimes locally constructed tests which contain national norms; (4) a prescribed curriculum for each grade level, which includes textbooks and supplemental alternatives; and (5) a suggested timetable for covering individual topics and disciplines. The school, in exchange for providing an umbrella of protection, will usually impose requirements on the families under its umbrella. These should include a nominal tuition charge to cover record-keeping and curriculum costs, a written statement of commitment from both father and mother to the home schooling program, the requirement that both parents be actively involved in a local church that provides good biblical teaching and nurturing, and that the parents agree to follow the curricular and testing guidelines established by the school. In fact, if a Christian school offering an umbrella relationship does not require these criteria, a family should be very cautious about affiliating with it.

SELECTION OF MATERIALS IN HOME SCHOOLING

Selecting textbooks and curriculum is one of the most difficult aspects of the home schooling process because of the conflicting opinions about options. Christian publishers would obviously provide "safer" materials than would secular publishers in the sense that they would contain fewer humanistic, secular emphases. Fortunately, in a home schooling setting, the parent is able to discern those subtle emphases in teaching the children. The criteria, then, for selecting textbooks should include: (1) its integrity in treating the subject matter; (2) its conformity with the choice of textbooks of schools recognized to be academically good (one need not restrict his textbook selections to those books a particular Christian school recommends; the exception, of course, would be in an arrangement where a Christian school provided an umbrella of protection for a family); (3) the inclusion in the textbook of selections that allow for creativity, flexibility, and a development of thinking processes, particularly those used at the upper elementary level or above; (4) materials that allow for the integration of truth.

The primary requisite for teaching a biblical perspective to a child is a teacher who lives and thinks biblically. It is fallacious to suppose that curriculum written from a distinctively Christian viewpoint will guarantee the transfer of that perspective from teacher to student. Jesus Himself enforces that principle in Luke 6:40 when He says, "And every student, when he is fully trained, will be like his teacher." A combination of competent teaching skills and godly discernment are essential to the effectiveness of teaching Christian truths; a doctrinally pure textbook is not.

Because the state education agencies are for the most part still uncertain about how to deal with the issue of home schooling and the concept of what a school actually is by definition, some are more amenable to the home schooling movement than are others. For that reason as well as to obtain the benefit of the counsel and experience of those involved in Christian education, an umbrella arrangement with a reputable Christian school is the wisest recourse when that is feasible.[7] The cost of the arrangement is usually nominal (approximately $300 per year) and the advantage is well worth that expense. As mentioned before, the school will maintain permanent records for the child, will prescribe curriculum and textbook options and even help the family in the acquisition of them. They will also provide periodic testing of the child to substantiate the effectiveness of the teaching-learning process at home. Good resources and counsel for parents will be provided as questions arise about teaching and curriculum and strategies are needed to stimulate, challenge, and meet the special needs and frustrations of the child. In addition, home schooling parents have an opportunity to examine the quality of the Christian school, should they later want to enroll their child.

SUMMARY

In summary, home schooling is not a new phenomenon. Biblically, because the home was the first institution ordained by God, children were educated at home before there were schools to attend. Home schooling is an enormous undertaking with a number of advantages, including the opportunity to solidify the family, to meet special educational and emotional needs of the children individually, to be flexible in a way not possible in the more regimented traditional school, and to benefit from the stimulus of parent and child growing and learning together.

Deterrents and potential problem areas include wrong motives in choosing to educate the children at home, a lack of wisdom or discretion in selecting textbook and other curricular materials, a lack of teaching and motivational

---

7. Troupos, "Home Schooling: Is It For You?"

skills necessary in the educational process, an unwillingness to conform to the high level of commitment and daily discipline necessary to educate effectively at home, and the possibility of state or local government interference or intervention.

Home schooling is most effective in meeting the educational needs of lower elementary children. The increased complexity of the curriculum and the advantage of extracurricular opportunities make the Christian school an attractive alternative for families with children in upper elementary years or older.

Although home schooling is attractive because of the stature of some of its proponents in the Christian community, it is not for every family. God in His grace deals with each family individually and gives each parent wisdom to know how his child's educational and emotional needs can best be met.

FOR FURTHER STUDY

Ikenberry, Kevin. *The Home Education Reporter.* Manessas, Va.: Rutherford Institute, 1985.

Moore, Raymond, and Dorothy Moore. *Better Late Than Early.* Washougal, Wash.: The Hewitt Foundation, 1975.

———. *Home Grown Kids.* Waco, Tex.: Word, 1981.

———. *Home Spun Schools.* Waco, Tex.: Word, 1982.

———. *School Can Wait.* Washougal, Wash.: The Hewitt Foundation, 1979.

Whitehead, John, and Wendell R. Bird. *Home Education and Constitutional Liberties.* Westchester, Ill.: Good News, 1984.

35

Roy W. Lowrie, Jr.,
and David L. Roth

The Role of the
Christian School

- Educational Philosophy and Purpose
- Specific Objectives
- Pros and Cons
- Statistical Data
- Patterns of Organization
  THE PARENT-SOCIETY SCHOOL
  THE CHURCH-RELATED SCHOOL
  THE PRIVATELY-OWNED SCHOOL
- Essentials for Quality Christian Education
- Qualifications for Teachers and Administrators
- Curriculum
- Buildings and Equipment
- Role of the Church
- An Evaluation

Roy W. Lowrie, Jr., Ed.D., is headmaster emeritus of the Delaware County Christian School, Newton Square, Pennsylvania, and president of the Association of Christian Schools, International.

David L. Roth, Ed.D., is principal of Wheaton Christian Grammar School, Wheaton, Illinois. He also serves as visiting professor at Grace Theological Seminary and Trinity Evangelical Divinity School.

In the broad spectrum of Christian education, the vigorous growth of Christian schools is among the more significant developments during recent years. Many new schools are starting, and many existing schools are growing.

The Christian school is not designed to replace the church or the home. Instead it seeks to supplement the responsibility of the church and the home. Because the Christian school and the evangelical church each adheres to a biblical philosophy of life, they seek to teach in harmony. By contrast, the non-Christian school and the evangelical church do not believe the same philosophy of life. The church teaches a philosophy of life based on revelation from God, whereas the non-Christian school rejects revelation and teaches a philosophy based on man's reason. The result is confusion for students, as they hear widely divergent teachings at church and in school.

The Christian school also seeks to work cooperatively with the Christian home. The school reinforces the home as the biblical directives and admonitions to parents are exercised by the teachers. During the school day, teachers stand in the place of parents.

Educational Philosophy and Purpose

To comprehend the Christian school, its biblical basis must be examined, for the school justifies its existence from the Bible. The reasoning is this: if the Bible is true, education—to be true—must be based on the Bible. To put it another way, since there is a revelation from God, a school should be based on that revelation and not on the reason of natural man. To exclude the Bible from the philosophical foundation of a school is to present a false, distorted, and invalid education. The fear of the Lord is the beginning of wisdom and of knowledge.

The following statements of educational philosophy, purpose, and objectives are typical of Christian schools:

1. God is the Creator and Sustainer of all things and the Source of all truth.
2. God maintains control over His entire universe.
3. Because of sin, man tends to omit God and thus fails to relate himself and his knowledge to God, the Source of all wisdom.
4. Regeneration is by faith in Jesus Christ. True meanings and values can be ascertained only in the light of His person, purpose, and work.
5. God has revealed Himself in a general way in His created universe and in a specific way in the Bible.
6. The home, the church, and the school should complement each other, promoting the student's spiritual, academic, social, and physical growth.
7. The teacher stands in the place of the parents, the place of authority and responsibility.
8. God has given differing abilities to each student. It is the teacher's respon-

sibility to challenge each child according to his ability and to seek to teach him at his academic level.

9. The Christian is not to be conformed to the world, but must accept his responsibility and his role in our democratic society.
10. The student's home, church, and school experience should be a preparation for a life of fellowship with God and of service to man.
11. The prayer of a righteous man has a powerful effect in the education of a child.

The purpose of Christian schools is to provide a sound academic education integrated with an evangelical Christian view of God and the world. The Bible is specific in stating the principles which underlie Christian education. Paul presented a comprehensive principle when he wrote of Christ, "For by him were all things created, that are in heaven, and that are in earth. . . . And he is before all things, and by him all things consist" (Col. 1:16-17). And the writer of the fourth gospel said, "All things were made by him; and without him was not any thing made that was made" (John 1:3).

There is an important difference between the Christian and the non-Christian viewpoints on a given subject. Even though knowledge is factually the same for both, no subject can be taught in the totality of its truth if the Creator is ignored or denied. Knowledge is purified by the recognition of God's place in it. No other approach to education can be entirely God-honoring, for parents and children.

Christian parents are responsible for the education of their children; and that education includes the counsels of God revealed in His world as well as those revealed in His Word. These parents want their children to be educated at home *and* at school with the consciousness that all truth is God's truth, including history and geography, science, music, and the arts, and that Jesus Christ is to be central in all learning and living.

SPECIFIC OBJECTIVES

The Christian school has numerous objectives in common with public schools and with other independent schools, although the Christian school sees these common objectives from the biblical perspective. It should be noted, however, that the Christian school has distinctive objectives which cannot be reached in the public schools, and which are not accepted by other independent schools. To illustrate, the first ten objectives in the following list are distinctive to the Christian school, while the last ten objectives would also be accepted by public and other independent schools:

1. To teach that the Lord Jesus Christ is the Son of God who came to earth to die for our sins

2. To teach the necessity of being born again by the Spirit of God by receiving the Lord Jesus Christ
3. To teach that growth in the Christian life depends on fellowship with God through reading the Bible, prayer, and service
4. To teach that the Bible is the Word of God and that it is practical and important
5. To teach the application of biblical ethics and standards of morality to every part of life
6. To teach students to manifest fairness, courtesy, kindness, and other Christian graces
7. To stress the urgency of world missions
8. To teach students to get along with non-Christians and with Christians who hold differing views
9. To relate the various subject matter areas with the truth of the Bible
10. To teach that God is the Creator and Sustainer of the universe and of man
11. To teach students to apply themselves to their work and to fulfill their responsibilities
12. To teach students to work independently and cooperatively
13. To teach students to think for themselves and to stand up for their personal convictions in the face of pressure
14. To develop the students' creative skills
15. To help develop the students' appreciation of the fine arts
16. To help the students develop effective communication skills
17. To teach the knowledge and skills required for future study or for occupational competence
18. To help students develop discretion in physical and mental recreation
19. To help students appreciate their national heritage and the current problems facing their country and the world
20. To show students their present civic responsibility and to prepare them for adult responsibility as citizens of their nation.

Pros and Cons of the Christian School

Arguments favoring Christian schools include the following: (1) teachers are born again, dedicated, not merely holding a job; (2) parents have high interest in the education of their children; (3) exceptionally good relationships exist between the school and the home; (4) it provides a good student-teacher ratio for instruction; (5) in general, students do not have serious learning or behavior problems; (6) unity is felt within the faculty; (7) good relationships exist between the faculty and the administration; (8) enough problems arise that God must be sought and trusted daily; (9) the opportunity is given to learn from the Bible daily; and (10) academic work is integrated with the Bible.

Arguments against Christian schools include the following: (1) facilities are inadequate or inferior; (2) programs are restricted, especially in music and athletics; (3) students are too sheltered; (4) students and teachers should be in other schools as witnesses; (5) the school is for students who cannot do well in other schools; (6) teachers are not highly qualified; (7) finances are too meager to provide quality education; (8) principals are not highly trained; (9) faculty and administrative turnover is excessive; (10) money spent on the school should go to foreign missions; and (11) the tuition costs are too high.

Since each Christian school is independent, apart from a few which are a system, each must be considered on its own merits and limitations determined. Sweeping generalizations about the schools should be heard with caution.

STATISTICAL DATA

The United States Department of Education's National Center for Education Statistics (NCES) generates the most comprehensive and authoritative data on nonpublic schools. NCES surveys over the past few years indicate a period of growth for private elementary and secondary education. As indicated by Table 35.1, "Private education is assuming an increasing share of the American educational effort at the elementary and secondary levels."[1]

TABLE 35.1
PRIVATE AND PUBLIC SCHOOLS AND ENROLLMENTS
ELEMENTARY AND SECONDARY LEVELS
U.S. TOTALS, FALL 1980 AND 1983

CATEGORY	TOTAL	PUBLIC	PRIVATE	PERCENTAGE PRIVATE
Schools				
Revised 1980	110,400	85,900	24,500	22.2
Current 1983	112,700	85,000	27,700	24.6
Enrollment (In millions)				
Revised 1980	46.2	40.9	5.3	11.5
Current 1983	45.2	39.5	5.7	12.6

SOURCES: U.S. Department of Education, National Center for Education Statistics, surveys of private and elementary schools; *Digest of Education Statistics, 1983-84* (Washington, D.C.: Government Printing Office, 1984); and *The Condition of Education, 1984* (Washington, D.C.: U.S. Government Printing Office, 1984).

Table 35.2 gives a further breakdown of the number of private schools, students, and teachers. Catholic private education accounts for the largest portion of American private education activity. However, "other affiliated" and "nonaffiliated" segments are increasing, whereas the Catholic share is decreasing.

1. U.S. Department of Education, National Center for Educational Statistics, Bulletin, *Private Elementary and Secondary Education, 1983 Enrollment, Teachers and Schools,* December 1984.

TABLE 35.2
1983 NCES PRIVATE SCHOOLS SURVEY

CATEGORY	NUMBER
Total schools	27,700
Not religiously affiliated	8,000
Affiliated-Catholic schools	9,700
Affiliated-other schools	10,000
Total enrollment	5,715,000
Total FTE teachers	337,200

SOURCES: U.S. Department of Education, National Center for Education Statistics, surveys of private and elementary and secondary schools; *Digest of Education Statistics, 1983-84* (Washington, D.C.: Government Printing Office, 1984); and *The Condition of Education, 1984* (Washington, D.C.: U.S. Government Printing Office, 1984).

PATTERNS OF ORGANIZATION

The three main organizational patterns for Christian schools are listed and described as follows:

THE PARENT-SOCIETY SCHOOL

This school is started by a group of parents, perhaps with interested friends or relatives, who form a legal corporation for the purpose of operating the school. To be eligible for membership in the society of corporation, a person must subscribe to the school's doctrinal platform and make a minimum financial contribution annually. The corporation, frequently called the school society, elects a board of trustees from among the society members. Since society members must agree to the school's doctrinal platform, dissidents do not get on the board. The board is responsible for operating the school.

The school property belongs to the society. Typically, the great majority of corporation members are parents; thus this organization is often called a parent-controlled school. Only parents who fulfill the requirements for membership, however, belong to the corporation. It is possible, then, to be a school parent and not a corporation member. Only corporation members vote on school matters.

THE CHURCH-RELATED SCHOOL

This school is owned and operated by a local church. It is governed by one of the existing church boards, or, more likely, a new board—with some representation from present boards—is established to operate the school. Facilities are used jointly by the church and by the school and are owned by the church.

This type is also called a parochial school. Most Christian schools established recently are in this group. There are fewer state regulations on this type because of the favored position which the church has with the state. In recent years, some parent-controlled schools have had court cases with the state, while similar schools owned by local churches were not involved in litigation.

THE PRIVATELY-OWNED SCHOOL

This school is owned and operated by an individual, by a family, or by a group of people. It may or may not have a board. If it has a board, that board is usually advisory only, for the school is really run by the owner or owners. Unlike the first two types, this school may be a proprietary school. Property belongs to the owner. Policies, procedures, and standards are established by the owner.

Each organizational pattern has advantages and disadvantages. Since organizational structure has lasting consequences, it is important for steering committees of proposed schools to investigate organizational patterns carefully. Whatever the organizational pattern, the essentials for quality education are the same for any Christian school.

ESSENTIALS FOR QUALITY CHRISTIAN EDUCATION

Christian school administrators accept the responsibility to operate sound academic schools. To put it simply, no child should have to take an academic penalty to get a Christian school education. A second-rate education, though based on the true philosophy of life, is unacceptable.

The following essentials for quality education are each important; thus no attempt has been made to rank them in order of importance: (1) a primary desire to see God honored through the education offered to children and young people; (2) a clear understanding of the philosophy, purposes, and objectives of the Christian school; (3) a principal or headmaster with leadership ability who is qualified spiritually, academically, biblically, and administratively to be the chief administrator; (4) a school board which works vigorously within clearly defined responsibilities; (5) a qualified faculty, born again, trained in the academic field for which each is hired, trained in Bible; (6) a low turnover rate in the faculty and in the administration; (7) a program of prayer by faculty, students, teachers, parents, and board which permeates the entire school program; (8) a financial stability which provides operational and capital improvement funds; (9) a selected student body whose educational needs can be met by the school; (10) a large enough enrollment to keep teachers from being spread too thin, for too many lesson preparations are required when several grades are combined in the same classroom; (11) adequate salaries to allow teachers and administrators to work without constant worry about the financial status of their families; (12) complete trust that God will do everything that He has promised in His Word, and the willingness to take steps by faith by individuals and by the corporate school body.

The main essential for quality education is the teacher. Buildings and equipment are necessary, but are secondary. Some of the qualifications for teachers and for administrators will now be considered.

QUALIFICATIONS FOR TEACHERS AND ADMINISTRATORS

Christian schools need teachers who are spiritually qualified. Teachers must be born again persons to whom God has given the gift of teaching, who find their natural place in the classroom with children. They must have preparation in Bible and a continuous desire to study God's Word.

Teachers must be able to lead students to Christ, be sensitive to the leading of the Holy Spirit, and be wholesome, exemplary Christians. Their own faith must be lively and growing as they experience God in their personal lives. They must know how to pray and how to ask in faith for the wisdom that is from above.

Other qualifications include these: self-disciplined, conscientious, hardworking, respectful of authority, able to function as a team worker, healthy, possessing a sense of humor, patient, enduring, happy, not a murmurer, evidencing the fruit of the Spirit, and walking in the Spirit.

Christian schools need teachers who are academically qualified, well trained and competent in the content of the subjects they teach and in varied methods of instruction. Teachers also need an understanding of child growth and development. They must be willing to continue their education, earning at least the master's degree. Academic qualifications are essential because the quality of instruction will affect about sixty years of the child's subsequent life, if the Lord tarries. A Christian school should never offer a contract to a teacher to work in an area for which he is not trained.

To be properly prepared for teaching, Bible college graduates need training in academic subject areas, while graduates of other colleges need training in Bible. Since the school purposes to integrate a sound academic education with the Christian view of God in the world, both academic and Bible training are essential. There are no shortcuts. This preparation takes time, usually more than four years.

Christian school principals should meet all the spiritual and academic qualifications for teachers plus at least three years of teaching experience before becoming principals. Additional qualifications for principals include the following: (1) the spiritual gift of administration; (2) leadership ability; (3) graduate study in school administration, preferably in Christian school administration; (4) courage; (5) vision; (6) endurance; (7) the ability to work with adults as well as with children; (8) fiscal responsibility; and (9) the qualifications of 1 Timothy 3:2-6, even though the school is not a church.

The greatest need in the Christian school movement today is qualified principals. Men and women are needed to train for administration to lead these schools to become strong institutions, spiritually and academically.

Schools need teachers and principals for whom the Christian school is their life ministry and not a stepping stone to another job, nor simply one of two jobs. God is raising up teachers and principals who are planting their lives in this field of Christian service. Some are beginning teachers; others are experienced teachers and principals who are being called out of other school systems into God's school system, where Jesus Christ and the Bible are central in every aspect.

CURRICULUM

Christian schools give serious attention to curriculum development, for they are academic schools, not "vacation Bible schools" operating for nine or ten months. Students take the same standardized achievement tests that are given to students from other schools. Christian school graduates compete for college entrance just like anyone else and are accepted on the basis of their educational preparation.

Bible instruction has a central place in the curriculum. Most other subjects are taught at the same grade level as the other schools in the community to facilitate the transferring of students in and out of the school. The Christian school has complete control, however, in the choice of books and materials for each subject. This is an important factor in curriculum development.

The difference in Christian schools is not so much in the subjects offered, but in the way in which these subjects are taught from the Christian perspective. The late Frank Gaebelein, headmaster emeritus of the Stony Brook School, Stony Brook, New York, expressed it in this way, "All truth is God's truth." This refers not only to the Bible but to all academic truth. All truth is ultimately from God.

A current trend in Christian schools is to develop a curriculum which is Christian in actual content. It appears that this trend may grow. New materials are being developed, although slowly. The development of these materials is difficult because the Christian schools are independent and do not agree on what constitutes a Christian curriculum. This is analogous to evangelical churches which do not agree on what constitutes the proper Sunday school curriculum.

The schools are careful to fulfill any curriculum requirements of the department of education in the state in which the school is located.

BUILDINGS AND EQUIPMENT

The days of Mark Hopkins sitting on a log with his student are gone. Christian school buildings do not have to be luxurious, but they should meet recognized standards for good school buildings from the standpoint of room sizes, health, safety, and sanitation. Outdoor play space should also meet recognized standards for that size school. Schools must obtain whatever legal permits are required in that community for use of the buildings as a school.

Schools held in existing buildings which were not designed for school use have problems. Some of these problems can be resolved, others cannot. It is often difficult to operate a school in facilities not designed for children's use.

Some churches are building their Christian education facilities according to school specifications. Facilities are shared by the school and by the church, thus gaining efficient use of the property. This is an encouraging trend. In this approach, care must be taken to provide proper outdoor play areas.

When schools build new facilities, the recognized planning principle is this: determine the school's program, then design the plant for that program.

Equipment for Christian schools should be sufficient in variety, quantity, and quality for the school to accomplish its stated objectives. Schools must achieve the financial stability required for the annual purchase of equipment and supplies. Because a school is Christian does not mean that it can get by with inadequate buildings, insufficient equipment, or sparse supplies. There is a relationship between facilities, equipment, and the quality of education offered by a school, whether or not that school is Christian.

ROLE OF THE CHURCH

The school sees its work as supplemental to the evangelical church, but the church does not often feel that way about the school. This is unfortunate and may be due to the following reasons: (1) the school may attract money away from the church; (2) division may occur in the church because of the school; (3) there may be misunderstanding of the philosophy and objectives of the school.

The role of the church in a church-related school is clearly illustrated in the Norfolk (Va.) Christian School, which is sponsored by the Tabernacle Church. Church membership and fellowship depend on relationship and fellowship with Christ, not on enrollment in that church's school. The Tabernacle Church teaches the sovereignty of God over every aspect of life, including education, and teaches Christian family living, with the result that many parents send their children to the school. The church and the school work harmoniously in their programs for the growth of the students and of the parents.

The role of the church to the other kinds of Christian schools includes the following: (1) prayer; (2) financial help; (3) student enrollment; (4) encouragement and understanding.

Regardless of organizational structure, all Christian schools are serving within the Body of Christ, His church. It should be recognized that the whole Body of Christ profits when any child or young person receives an education in which Jesus Christ is central. Believers do not choose a church home on the basis of the preacher's degree, the architecture, or the equipment of the building, but on the truth that is taught and preached in the church. Similarly, churches should recognize that a school should be chosen in the same way, and should help support Christian schools exhibiting high standards. Many churches are indifferent and some are even negative toward these schools. But these attitudes appear to be changing as the times become more evil.

The schools must do a better job of interpreting themselves to the churches and not become defensive or uncommunicative. Strong bonds need to be built between the churches and the schools. They are not to be competitors.

AN EVALUATION

The Christian school is a testimony to God's name in elementary and secondary education. Every major court decision in the past decade has gone against allowing Bible reading and prayer as religious exercises in tax-supported schools. Even with electives in philosophy of religion and the Bible as literature, public schools are far from being Christianized. Christian schools are the answer to the dilemma of education.

New schools need time to become established, to purchase property, to develop a strong faculty, to become accredited. This often takes years, during which the school is open to criticism. There is much hope, however, because the schools are based on the true foundation, the Bible, which foundation is lacking in other schools, regardless of their buildings or reputations.

The need for Christian schools will undoubtedly increase noticeably in this decade. It is apparent that the enemy is coming into education like a flood, and it is equally obvious that the Lord will raise up His standard in education too. As older teachers retire from public schools during this decade and are replaced by beginning teachers who do not accept the life values and standards of their predecessors, public schools will change radically and quickly. This trend has already started.

To serve God as a Christian school teacher or principal is a worthy use of one's life. There are many positions open now, and there will be in the future. These schools offer an unusual opportunity to affect children and young people for God.

SUMMARY

The rapid growth in the Christian school movement is among the more significant developments within the body of Christ today. The presupposition on which the Christian school educational philosophy is built is that "if Christ is to be preeminent in all things, that must include a child's education." Christian school educators are convinced that the Christian school, the evangelical church and the Christian home should work together. The ultimate goal of all three institutions is to help the student develop a Christ-centered world and life view.

FOR FURTHER READING

Baker, A. A. *The Successful Christian School.* Pensacola, Fla.: A Beka Book, 1979.

Billings, Robert J. *A Guide to the Christian School.* Hammond, Ind.: Hyles-Anderson, 1971.

Byrne, Herbert W. *A Christian Approach to Education.* Milford, Mich.: Mott Media, 1977.

Cummings, David B., ed. *The Basis for a Christian School.* Phillipsburg, N.J.: Presb. & Ref., 1982.

Fakkema, Mark. *Christian Philosophy: Its Educational Implications.* Chicago: National Union of Christian Schools, 1952.

Gaebelein, Frank E. *Christian Education in a Democracy.* New York: Oxford U., 1951.

————. *The Pattern of God's Truth.* Chicago: Moody, 1973.

Kelly, Bill. *A Guide for Principals and Board Members on Christian School Growth.* Whittier, Calif.: Western Association of Christian Schools, n.d.

Kienel, Paul. *The Christian School: Why It Is Right for Your Child.* Wheaton, Ill.: Scripture Press, Victor Books, 1974.

————. *Reasons for Sending Your Child to a Christian School.* LaHabra, Calif.: P.K. Books, 1978.

————. *What This Country Needs.* San Diego: Beta Books, 1976.

Kienel, Paul A., ed. *The Philosophy of Christian School Education.* Whittier, Calif.: Western Association of Christian Schools, 1978.

Kraushaar, Otto. *American Nonpublic Schools.* Baltimore: John Hopkins U., 1972.

Lockerbie, Bruce D. *The Way They Should Go.* New York: Oxford U., 1972.

Lowrie, Roy W. *Administration of the Christian School.* Whittier, Calif.: Association of Christian Schools, International, 1984.

————. *To Those Who Teach in Christian Schools.* Whittier, Calif.: Association of Christian Schools, International, 1978.

————. *Serving God on the Christian School Board.* Whittier, Calif.: Association of Christian Schools, International, 1976.

————. *Your Child and the Christian School.* Wheaton, Ill.: National Association of Christian Schools, 1967.

May, Philip. *Which Way to Educate?* Chicago: Moody, 1975.

Morris, Henry M. *Education for the Real World.* San Diego: Christian Life, 1977.

Rafferty, Max. *Suffer Little Children.* New York: Devin-Adian, 1962.

MANUALS AND KITS FOR CHRISTIAN SCHOOLS

The following can be ordered from Association of Christian Schools, International, Box 4097, Whittier, CA 90607:

Manual of Administration for Christian Pre-Schools
Manual for New and Young Christian Schools
Manual of Administration for Established Christian Schools
Christian Teacher's Manual
Christian School Parent Ministry Handbook
How to Start and Run a Tutoring Program

The following can be ordered from A Beka Books, Box 18000, Pensacola, FL 32523:

Bible Curriculum Materials Kits (nursery through sixth grade)
Day-by-Day Bible Curriculums (nursery through sixth grade)

SELECTED CHRISTIAN SCHOOL ORGANIZATIONS

American Association of Christian Schools, 1017 N. School Street, Normal, IL 61761.

Association of Christian Schools, International, P.O. Box 4097, Whittier, CA 90607.

National Christian School Education Association, 464 Malin Road, Newtown Square, PA 19073.

National Union of Christian Schools, P.O. Box 8709, 3350 East Paris Avenue, Grand Rapids, MI 49508.

Ohio Association of Christian Schools, 1960 Fay Meadow Avenue, Columbus, OH 43229.

Western Association of Christian Schools, P.O. Box 4097, Whittier, CA 90607.

SELECTED CHRISTIAN SCHOOL CURRICULUM PUBLISHERS

A Beka Book Publications, 125 East St. John Street, Pensacola, FL 23503.

Accelerated Christian Education, Box 1438, Lewisville, TX 75067.

Alpha Omega Publications, P.O. Box 3153, Tempe, AZ 85281.

Association for Bible Curriculum Development, 1515 North Los Robles, Pasadena, CA 91104; being published by Lifeway Bible Curriculum, 1825 College Avenue, Wheaton, IL 60187.

Baptist Day School Association, 9845 Woodley Avenue, Sepulveda, CA 91343.

Bob Jones University Press, Greenville, SC 29614.

Concordia Publishing House, 3558 S. Jefferson Avenue, St. Louis, MO 63118.

Index

Moody Press, a ministry of the Moody Bible Institute, is
designed for education, evangelization and edification. If
we may assist you in knowing more about Christ and the
Christian life, please write us without obligation to:
Moody Press, c/o MLM, Chicago, Illinois 60610.